ARGUING ABOUT METAETHICS

'In recent years, metaethics has been one of the most exciting growth areas in philosophy. This volume contains the most comprehensive and up-to-date set of readings currently available, and will be valued by advanced undergraduates, postgraduates, and professionals with interests in recent and contemporary metaethics.'

Alex Miller, *University of Birmingham*

Arguing about Metaethics collects together some of the most exciting contemporary work in metaethics in one handy volume. In it, many of the most influential philosophers in the field discuss key questions in metaethics:

- Do moral properties exist?
- If they do, how do they fit into the world as science conceives it?
- If they don't exist, then how should we understand moral thought and language?
- What is the relation between moral judgement and motivation?

As well as these questions, this volume discusses a wide range of issues including moral objectivity, truth and moral judgements, moral psychology, thick evaluative concepts and moral relativism.

The editors provide lucid introductions to each of the eleven themed sections in which they show how the debate lies and outline the arguments of the papers. *Arguing about Metaethics* is an ideal resource text for students at upper undergraduate or postgraduate level.

Andrew Fisher is a teaching fellow in philosophy at the University of Nottingham, UK.
Simon Kirchin is a lecturer in philosophy at the University of Kent, UK.

ARGUING ABOUT METAETHICS

Edited by
Andrew Fisher and Simon Kirchin

Routledge
Taylor & Francis Group

LONDON AND NEW YORK

First published 2006
by Routledge
2 Park Square, Milton Park, Abingdon, Oxon OX14 4RN

Simultaneously published in the USA and Canada
by Routledge
270 Madison Ave, New York, NY 10016

Routledge is an imprint of the Taylor & Francis Group, an informa business

Typeset in Sabon and Frutiger by
Book Now Ltd
Printed and bound in Great Britain by
TJ International Ltd, Padstow, Cornwall

British Library Cataloguing in Publication Data
A catalogue record for this book is available from the British Library

Library of Congress Cataloging in Publication Data
Fisher, Andrew.
Arguing about metaethics/Andrew Fisher and Simon Kirchin
p. cm.
Includes bibliographical references and index.
1. Ethics–Textbooks. I. Kirchin, Simon. II. Title.

BJ1012.F537 2006
170'.42 2006043931–dc22   2006043950

ISBN 10: 0–415–38028–6 (hbk)
ISBN 10: 0–415–38027–8 (pbk)

ISBN 13: 978–0–415–38028–7 (hbk)
ISBN 13: 978–0–415–38027–0 (pbk)

CONTENTS

CONTENTS

CONTENTS

CONTENTS

ACKNOWLEDGEMENTS

William Frankena, 'The Naturalistic Fallacy', in *Mind* 48, 1939, 464–77, Oxford University Press. Reprinted by permission of Oxford University Press.

Frank Snare, 'The Open Question as a Linguistic Test', in *Ratio* 17, Blackwell. Reprinted by permission of Blackwell Publishing.

John Mackie, 'The Arguments from Relativity and Queerness', in *Ethics: Inventing Right and Wrong*, 1977, 36–42, Penguin. Reproduced by permission of Penguin Books Ltd.

David Brink, 'Moral Realism and the Sceptical Arguments from Disagreement and Queerness', in *Australasian Journal of Philosophy* 62, 2, 1984, 112–25, Routledge. Reprinted by permission of Taylor & Francis Ltd. www.tandf.co.uk

Richard T. Garner, 'On the Genuine Queerness of Moral Properties and Facts', in *Australasian Journal of Philosophy* 68, 2, 1990, 137–46, Routledge. Reprinted by permission of Taylor & Francis Ltd. www.tandf.co.uk

Nicholas L. Sturgeon, 'Moral Explanations', in *Morality, Reason and Truth* (eds) David Copp and David Zimmerman, 1985, 49–78, Rowman & Littlefield. Reproduced by permission of Rowman & Littlefield Publishers, Inc.

Peter Railton, 'Moral Realism', in *Philosophical Review* 95, 1986, 163–207. Copyright 1986 Cornell University. Reprinted by permission of the publisher and the author.

Terence Horgan and Mark Timmons, 'Troubles for New Wave Moral Semantics: The Open Question Argument Revived', in *Philosophical Papers* 21, 1992, 153–75. Reprinted by permission of the journal and the authors.

Frank Jackson, 'Critical Notice of Hurley', in *Australasian Journal of Philosophy* 70, 1992, 475–88, Routledge. Reprinted by permission of Taylor & Francis Ltd. www.tandf.co.uk

John McDowell, 'Values and Secondary Qualities', in *Morality and Objectivity* (ed.) Ted Honderich, 1985, 110–29, Routledge. Reprinted by permission of Taylor & Francis Books Ltd.

David Sosa, 'Pathetic Ethics', in *Objectivity in Law and Morals* (ed.) Brian Leiter, 2001, 287–329, © Cambridge University Press. Reprinted by permission of the publisher and the author.

Simon Blackburn, 'Realism and Variations', in *Spreading the Word*, 1984, Oxford University Press. Reprinted by permission of Oxford University Press.

Frank Jackson and Philip Pettit, 'A Problem for Expressivism', in *Analysis* 58, 1998, 239–51. Reprinted by permission of the authors.

Michael Smith and Daniel Stoljar, 'Is There a Lockean Argument against Expressivism?', in *Analysis* 63, 76–86. Reprinted by permission of the authors.

Simon Blackburn, 'The Frege–Geach Problem', in *Spreading the Word*, 1984, Oxford University Press. Reprinted by permission of Oxford University Press.

G. F. Schueler, 'Moral *Modus Ponens* and Moral Realism', in *Ethics* 98, 1998, 492–500, University of Chicago Press. Reprinted by permission of The University of Chicago Press and the author.

Simon Blackburn, 'Attitudes and Contents', in *Ethics* 98, 1998, 501–17, University of Chicago Press. Reprinted by permission of The University of Chicago Press and the author.

Bob Hale, 'Can There Be a Logic of Attitudes?', in *Reality, Representation and Projection* (eds) John Haldane and Crispin Wright, 1993, 335–63, © 1993 by The Mind Association. Used by permission of Oxford University Press.

Michael Smith, 'Why Expressivists about Value should Love Minimalism about Truth', in *Analysis* 54, 1994, 1–11. Reprinted by permission of the author.

John Divers and Alex Miller, 'Why Expressivists about Value should Not Love Minimalism about Truth', in *Analysis* 54, 1994, 12–19. Reprinted by permission of the authors.

John McDowell, 'Non-cognitivism and Rule-following', in *Wittgenstein: To Follow a Rule* (eds) Stephen Holtzman and Christopher Leich, 1981, 141–62, Routledge. Reprinted by permission of Taylor and Francis Books Ltd.

Simon Blackburn, 'Reply: Rule-following and Moral Realism', in *Wittgenstein: To Follow a Rule* (eds) Stephen Holtzman and Christopher Leich, 1981, 163–87, Routledge. Reprinted by permission of Taylor and Francis Books Ltd.

John McDowell, 'Projection and Truth in Ethics', in Lindley Lecture, 1987, University of Kansas Press. Reprinted by permission of The University of Kansas.

Stephan Burton, '"Thick" Concepts Revised', in *Analysis* 52, 1992, 28–32.

Eve Garrard and David McNaughton, 'Thick Concepts Revisited: A Reply to Burton', in *Analysis* 53, 1993, 57–8. Reprinted by permission of the authors.

Stephan Burton, 'Reply to Garrard and McNaughton', in *Analysis* 53, 1993, 59–61.

Michael Smith, 'The Externalist Challenge', in *The Moral Problem*, 1994, 60–76, Blackwell. Reprinted by permission of Blackwell Publishing.

James Dreier, 'Dispositions and Fetishes: Externalist Models of Moral Motivation', in *Philosophy and Phenomenological Research* 61, 2000, 619–38. Reprinted by permission of the journal and the author.

Michael Smith, 'The Humean Theory of Motivation', in *Mind* 96, 1987, 36–61, Oxford. Reprinted by permission of Oxford University Press.

ACKNOWLEDGEMENTS

Philip Pettit, 'Humeans, Anti-Humeans, and Motivation', *Mind* 96, 1987, 530–3, Oxford. Reprinted by Oxford University Press.

Michael Smith, 'On Humeans, Anti-Humeans, and Motivation: A Reply to Pettit', *Mind* 96, 1987, 589–95, Oxford. Reprinted by permission of Oxford University Press.

Every effort has been made to trace and contact copyright holders. The publishers would be pleased to hear from any copyright holder not acknowledged here so that this section may be amended at the earliest opportunity.

We are grateful to Tony Bruce, Richard Cook, Priyanka Pathak, and all at Routledge for their support as we edited this book. We are also grateful to anonymous referees for their comments on the project and our introductions, and particularly to Alex Miller for discussion. We are also most grateful to Rosie, Freya and Elizabeth, and Penny and Freddie, for their love and patience.

1

INTRODUCTION

STARTING THOUGHTS

1

Imagine we are debating whether it is right to torture people who are suspected of being terrorists. And, moreover, these people are suspected of hiding a bomb that is soon to detonate. As we are debating we might raise a number of considerations such as 'torture is always wrong, no matter what the consequences', 'we have a duty to protect innocent people in our society' and 'the possible consequences of inaction here outweigh any pain caused to the suspects'. As the conversation develops (the bomb has a long fuse), perhaps our various views crystallize, with some people being in favour, and some not, of torturing the terrorists. At this stage, other types of question might be raised and points made. We might wonder – given the polarized views – whether there is a fact of the matter about whether the torture is right or wrong. After all, why assume that someone has to be right and someone has to be wrong?

After reflecting we might form an opposite view. Torture – along with female genital mutilation, chemical dumping, genocide and the like – are such important moral matters that we cannot say that someone or some state is justified in carrying out such things just because they feel like it and they think they are justified. We might come to believe that there are moral standards that apply to everyone irrespective of what they feel like doing; there is a difference between what seems right (or wrong) to people and what is, in fact, right (or wrong). Even if we disagree about whether the torture is right or wrong, we think that there is a correct answer to the question. What we are doing when we debate such moral questions is trying to find this answer, an answer that does not depend simply on our opinions and reasoning about the issue. We are helping each other develop the correct perspective on the issue. From this we might generalize and conclude that there are correct and incorrect answers to many, if not all, moral

1

questions, from the significant, such as torture, to the relatively trivial, such as whether you should keep an appointment with a friend or whether you should recycle that drinks can you've just finished.

These latter questions and points serve to introduce much of the area of philosophy known as *metaethics*. Metaethics is not concerned with which actions are right or wrong, or good or bad, nor is it concerned with which type of feature – consequences, say – we should concentrate on when trying to justify our actions. Rather it is concerned with whether actions, institutions, people, situations and many more things are right and wrong, good and bad, in the first place. The world is full of many things, from trees and tables, to colours and sounds, corporations and states, electrons and elephants. One of the key questions of metaethics is whether it makes sense to add moral values to this list. Just as we might think of an action, such as a stabbing, as having the properties of being swift and being surprising, we might ask whether it has any moral properties such as wrongness or cruelty. Relatedly, just as we might say that there is something about the world that makes it true, and not just a matter of personal opinion, that someone's hair is brown (namely, her brown hair), we might say that there is something about the world that makes it true that someone is wicked (namely, the wickedness of her character).

2

This central question is a question of metaphysics as it concerns whether something exists. This gives metaethics its name: we are concerned with the metaphysics of moral reality. From this central question arise a number of other questions that interest metaethicists. Many of these questions are metaphysical in nature also, but we shall see that issues in the philosophy of language and in moral psychology are key ingredients in current metaethics as well. In this introduction we will lay out a few of these questions. §§ 3–10 describe many of the main positions and ideas you will encounter in this book. In § 11 we list a few questions it will be useful to bear in mind as you read through the book and how you should approach metaethics. We end in § 12 with some general metaethical reading and some final advice.

SOME QUESTIONS AND TERMINOLOGY

3

We have had one central metaethical question, *Do moral properties exist?* Let us imagine we answer '*yes*'. If we do so, then in some sense of the phrase we will be *moral realists*. 'Realism' is often associated with two further terms that you will encounter, namely 'cognitivism' and 'descriptivism'. The former identifies a claim about the sort of mental state that a typical moral judgement is used to express. When I say, "John is kind", supposedly my words express a belief, a state that is a way of saying, "*This* is what the world is like". As such, we assume that I am trying to cognize or know what the world is like. It is clear what the relationship between realism and cognitivism is. If one assumes that there really are moral properties, then it is natural to think that beings such as ourselves have the ability to make knowledge claims about them, even if we might, at times, get things wrong. As we shall see throughout this collection, 'realism' and 'cognitivism' are sometimes used interchangeably, although strictly they express different ideas. 'Descriptivism' expresses a claim about the language that is typically used when people give moral judgements or, more accurately, is a philosophical claim about how moral language should best be understood, presumably based on much of our experience when we hear people making judgements. The claim is that just as moral judgements should best be understood as expressions of belief, so moral language should best be understood as an attempt to describe something about the world. When I say "John is kind" I am attempting to say something about what John is like. And in attempting this, I can, of course, speak correctly or incorrectly. My language reflects or expresses a supposed belief I have, that John is kind, and whether I speak truly or not depends on whether, in fact, John is kind.

This realism–cognitivism–descriptivism triumvirate is a classic position in meta-ethics, but as yet we have only scratched the surface. We have yet to appreciate how the different parts contrast with other philosophical claims and, thus, we have yet to appreciate what it is to be, say, a descriptivist. To begin with, however, let us focus our attention on realism, for that term is used in many complicated ways in metaethics and understanding it will help us a lot.

4

How might someone support the claim that moral properties exist? How might they support moral realism? Someone might begin by pointing to our normal everyday language and practices and claim that they reflect the idea that such properties exist. Just as we might say, "That person's hair is brown", we might say, "That person is wicked". We seem to be doing the same thing in both cases, namely ascribing properties to things. We ascribe properties with our language, and this includes moral language. As such, it makes sense to think that, in some fashion, moral properties exist. If we do not, then we are going to have to revise radically our understanding of moral language, and the arguments for this view will have to be very good. This train of thought might continue and people might emphasize some of the ideas from § 1 to show how integral to our lives it is to assume that moral properties exist. We naturally think that one can go right and wrong in one's judgements and that actions can be more or less appropriate, say. We think that there is, for instance, such a thing as moral progress – a moving closer to the moral truth. If we do not assume this, there would be no point to moral debate, or at least the point of moral debate would be revealed as being something radically different from what we ordinarily take it to be. Instead of it being an attempt to get at the truth and convince others that you speak truthfully, it is simply an exchange of people's personal opinions about the issue, or some power game where you try by various means to convince the other person to feel how you do. Likewise, if we do not assume the existence of moral properties and the standards based on them, then the whole system of law would break down, or at least change radically. Instead of thinking of punishment as being a legitimate activity following someone's breaking some moral or social rule, the law – that is any system of law – would be revealed as simply a system whereby people are punished *only because* they act differently from how the people in power (perhaps on a whim) want them to act. Normally we would think of such legal systems as being corrupt and the very opposite of just, but such moral claims could not be made about them if we do not assume the existence of moral properties and standards.

Notice that something important has emerged in this train of thought. Not only have we uncovered some starting reasons why moral properties might be thought to exist – why we should be moral realists – it seems that if they exist they better exist independently of any individual judge or group of judges or, indeed, anyone. After all, what seems important is that when moral properties generate moral standards, norms and rules, such resulting things are the arbiters of how people should act and think. It is no good basing such arbiters simply on what any and every individual thinks, for then the purpose of them being arbiters of correctness and incorrectness is lost and we return to a situation where 'anything goes'. It makes, in fact, little sense calling them arbiters at all. We will return to this idea in § 7.

Suffice it to say, this train of thought, or something like it, stands as the best positive argument in favour of thinking that moral properties exist. Any further thoughts in support tend to be directed against arguments and ideas provided by those who think differently.

5

However, being a moral realist invites further questions; for example, we might ask *What is the relationship between moral properties and nonmoral properties?* We deliberately word this question vaguely because it invites so many different answers and approaches. The general idea is this. We can talk of actions, and people, and other such things as being kind and cruel. But actions, say, have other features. They can be swift, and frequent, and pleasurable, and performed on a Tuesday. Supposedly, we can describe the world and all that it contains in nonmoral language. Indeed, not only can we describe the world and our actions using everyday nonmoral terms, we can also describe the world using more technical language, such as the language used by the natural and physical sciences. When we start to think like this, we might wonder what the relationship is between someone having an electro-chemical reaction in their brain that caused their limbs to move in such-and-such a manner at such-and-such a time, and the fact that we describe the resulting action as kind. (And we might wonder whether nonmoral features, such as swiftness, are reducible to properties studied by physics and biology.) Might it be that kindness is to be identified with, or reduced to, or constituted by, a nonmoral property or set of such properties? Or is the supposed property indicated by the term 'kindness' irreducible in this fashion? Of course, no one argues that this proposed sort of recharacterization is possible now. The supposition is only that it is possible in principle. Notice that even if one wishes to recharacterize the moral world in this fashion, some people might still count this as a realist and cognitivist position. There really are moral properties and there really are things in virtue of which "John is kind" turns out to be true. It is just that moral properties are not quite what we expected them to be. They are just nonmoral or natural properties. (However, some people feel uneasy with calling the resulting position moral realism precisely because this recharacterization requires such a radical change in our thought.)

What these initial thoughts give us is a way of introducing two broad families of realist position that go by the names *naturalism* and *nonnaturalism*. (We will assume, for argument's sake, that both sides can claim the label 'realism' and, although we have distinguished the nonmoral from the more narrow natural above, more often than not 'natural' is used as a synonym for all types of nonmoral feature and we use it in this way from now on.) Unfortunately, simply calling yourself a naturalist or a nonnaturalist is not enough to identify your position exactly. To explain, consider two possible positions on the extremes. The first is clearly nonnaturalist. The claim is that moral properties exist and are in no way, even in any individual situation, reducible to, or identifiable with, or constituted by any sort of natural property or set of such properties, such as swiftness or physical properties. Thus, goodness, say, is considered to be a metaphysically *sui generis* property. (This Latin phrase means 'of its own kind'.) The second position is clearly naturalist. The idea is simply that moral properties, either now or in the future, can be identified with a natural property or set of such properties. This reductionism might license our continued use of moral terminology, but this is only for convenience's sake. (Within this reductionist camp, there might be a further splintering of positions. One group might seek to say that whatever natural property goodness is, it is so for all groups and societies. Other reductionists might say that what we can do is identify the role or function that the term 'good' plays in moral thought generally and then allow that it is possible that different societies and groups could identify different specific natural properties that play the goodness role or function. Indeed, one could be a 'functionalist' in this sort of way and leave it open as to whether the thing that plays the goodness role has to be a natural property. It could be a religious or magical property such as 'Is commanded by God' or 'Is the work of Merlin'.)

Having got our two extreme positions, characterizing the middle ground is tricky. Consider the following possible position. One assumes that for any particular example of kindness there is some natural property or set of properties that one can isolate and identify as constituting the kindness. Perhaps the kindness simply is the sharing of sweets by an agent when she sees that someone is upset, or perhaps (to give an extreme example) the kindness is some complex physical state relating to atoms moving in various ways. But, the key idea is that across all situations and actions that are deemed kind there is no one natural thing, or even set of such things, that all of the kind things have in common. Kindness is multiply realizable, so much so that there is an infinite number of ways in which an action can have natural features that constitute its being kind. In other words, kindness is irreducibly complex. Notice that this is consistent with moral supervenience. Moral supervenience is roughly the claim that if something is a natural way, then it must be a moral way (one could not imagine that two actions could be naturally identical and not morally identical). It is clear we have consistency here since moral supervenience allows that two or more things could be morally identical (all are kind, say) without being naturally identical, that is they could be kind but for different reasons. Notice also that this middle position is different from the nonnaturalism described above, for this extreme position denies moral supervenience or any other such relation that ties the existence of moral properties into the existence of natural properties. Now, this middle position in its various guises is quite popular in metaethics. What is troublesome for the newcomer to the field is that some people call this general position 'naturalism' and some call it 'nonnaturalism'. And more troublesome is that there appears to be justification for both labels. After all, we are not assuming that moral properties are free-floating properties that exist independently of the natural world, hence why many people are concerned to make sure that such a position is consistent with supervenience. But it is also nonnaturalistic, since the idea is that the moral is *sui generis* in some respect, since it cannot be identified with one single natural property, nor even with a set of such properties. There is a particular way of conceptualizing the world that is of its own kind, and cannot be captured in a natural fashion. Is there any way of distinguishing further positions that are committed to irreducibility such that we can apply the labels 'naturalism' and 'nonnaturalism' sensibly? Rather than talk of possible positions, it is clear that writers who favour this sort of middle position have great differences of emphasis. Some theorists more than others might be impressed by what modern natural science, say, can do and might favour the label 'naturalism' because of this. Others who favour the label 'nonnaturalism' emphasize the complexity of human decision-making and valuing when persuading us of the irreducibility of the moral. They argue that such activity has to be assumed to be what makes us the free, rational creatures we are and if there is anything that resists capture and measure by the natural sciences it is this. Hence any values and moral properties we see the world as having should be thought to be nonnatural since it is only through expressing our human nature that the natural world takes on a moral shape, that we can discern what is kind and cruel. This is all very well, but is there any better way of distinguishing within this middle position so as to get clear ideas standing behind the two labels? We have suggested that the preceding thoughts are only matters of emphasis. But perhaps we are wrong about this and any of the above ideas can be described such that we get the difference required. We leave this to you to decide when reading our selections and pursuing further reading. Aside from this, here is one suggestion, with the promise of another, as to what might mark a difference. First, we might distinguish with reference to causation. The ability to cause effects is thought to be a mark of many natural properties and features, at least those studied by science. Perhaps it is important to being an irreducible-*naturalist*-realist that one's conception of moral properties is of things that have causal efficacy, despite being irreducible with respect to the natural. On the other hand, perhaps irreducible-*nonnaturalist*-realists are not so worried about causation and are content that something can exist and have no causal efficacy. A second suggestion, regarding moral motivation, we leave until § 10.

So far we have attempted only to characterize the various responses to the question that started § 3. What arguments might we give in favour of naturalism or nonnaturalism, or at least on the differences between reductionist and nonreductionist positions? Perhaps we reflect on what such a reduction would be like and we say, "Goodness simply is the maximization of pleasure". (We can assume here that 'maximization of pleasure' is a natural feature.) But this might cause us to worry. These two terms certainly seem to mean different things and, hence, we might think that they should be used to signify different things in the world. Doesn't it make sense to imagine that some action could maximize pleasure and yet not be morally good? On quick reflection we might say that this point will generalize. Any example we pick will have meanings and connotations different from 'moral goodness'. So, we might conclude by saying moral properties cannot be reduced to natural properties. Others are less convinced with this sort of argument. Just because two terms differ in meaning, this does not mean that they cannot pick out the same sort of stuff. After all, no one is suggesting that the success of the proposed reductionist move will depend on us agreeing that two terms previously thought to have different meanings will come to be seen by people to mean exactly the same thing. But it could be that after some investigation, perhaps some a posteriori scientific investigation guided by philosophers, we discover that goodness is, in fact, the maximization of pleasure, or some more complex natural property. Whether this reply, on behalf of reductionism, is successful will depend on a number of things, such as (a) what is meant by 'reduction' (and other terms we have loosely used as synonyms such as 'identification' and 'recharacterization') and whether reductionism can allow for there to be differences in meaning; and (b) how plausible it is to imagine that all of the morally good things, say, when viewed naturalistically, are not hopelessly disjointed and vary so hugely that it is simply silly to identify such a jumble as being the *single thing* moral goodness. Perhaps the various responses and further questions prompted by these issues will help us to distinguish more fine-grained versions of naturalism and nonnaturalism.

6

Let us return to our question from the start of § 3. Imagine we say, *"No, there are no moral properties"*. This leads to a range of possible arguments and positions. Recall earlier that we said that thinking about metaethics invites considerations in philosophy of language. Indeed, some people might say that many or all metaethical debates are best viewed as being primarily debates in the philosophy of language. (Despite our concentration on metaphysics in this introduction, we take no view on that matter here.) We said earlier that it is a good pretheoretical assumption that our everyday moral language is fact-stating or descriptive. Any typical moral utterance statement is best understood as signifying that its speaker is attempting to describe what the world is like. Just as we might say that someone's hair is brown and that an action is swift, so we might say that an institution is just and a person selfish. Two main families of positions can grow from a negative answer to our first question that can be understood by one's approach to this assumption about moral language. One could agree with the assumption that language should be interpreted as an attempt to describe the world but deny that there is any moral reality to so describe. Alternatively, one could disagree with the assumption to begin with and say that, if you think about it carefully, our moral language should not be conceived as being fact-stating despite first appearances. This leads us to see how our previous questions combine with a further question – *How should moral language be assumed to function?* – in order to generate different possible positions.

Let us take these two approaches in turn. Let us imagine that moral language is best understood as descriptive. Our first position claims that every time someone makes a moral judgement they are making a description, it is just that there is nothing in the world that answers to the description. It is easy to misunderstand this claim. The idea is not just that each and every person gets it wrong because each and every person is terrible at making moral judgements. For example, it is not just the idea that even though everyone thinks that human cloning is wrong, let's imagine, it just so happens that human cloning is right. Nor is it simply the idea that, for example, there is a moral property – 'blumberness', say – that no human has yet been able to pick out. The idea involves a conceptual claim about moral properties. Because of what we assume the nature of a moral property to be, nothing like that could ever exist. In which case, the idea is that each time anyone anywhere makes a moral judgement they are in systematic error. Positions of this type are called (unsurprisingly) *error theories*.

Why then should we believe that moral properties could not exist? Consider this idea. There are two common, prephilosophical intuitions that we seem to have about moral properties. First, we assume that they are prescriptive. This is clear in the case of some moral properties that wear their prescriptivity on their sleeve, properties such as 'rightness' or the clumsily worded 'moral obligatoriness'. Whereas other moral properties – particularly those that are more straightforwardly evaluative properties – are more circumspect in this way, but by some indirect way they can issue in prescriptions or demands. For example, we can assume for argument's sake that a proposed course of action's kindness or generosity generates a reason to pursue it. The second prephilosophical intuition about moral properties is that they are independent of what any individual judge, or society of judges, thinks. (This reflects the ideas in § 4.) The general worry is that combining these two ideas concerning moral properties shows them to be strange things. How could something that is directing us – that stands as a demand for us to act and think in certain ways – be independent, both in its existence and its content, of the very things that are the valuing creatures, that are the only things that can give and understand demands? Not only are such things metaphysically strange, but it would have to be a very strange faculty that humans had which was able to pick such things out. There is more to say about this argument, and we discuss it more in our introduction to Part 2. What is important to realize now though is that error theorists agree with part of the realist–cognitivist–descriptivist triumvirate, namely cognitivism and descriptivism. They agree that moral judgements that people typically make should be best understood as representing or expressing belief states and, correspondingly, that the moral language we typically employ should best be interpreted as descriptive. But they disagree that there are any moral properties.

Error theory is not immune to problems. Typically, error theorists do not wish to dismiss ethics as a hopelessly outdated and corrupt activity. Often they dismiss a commitment to a certain conception of moral properties and try to replace it with something else, whilst crucially hanging on to the notion that some thoughts and actions can be better than others. But this is a difficult tightrope to walk. It might be that they are asking us simply to revise our conception of moral properties, rather than do away with it entirely. They might build up the idea of ethics being a legitimate activity so much that the label 'error theory' smacks of false advertising. As mentioned, we return to error theory in Part 2.

Some people, whilst sharing error theorists' worries about a supposed moral reality, take a different view about the mental states that typically accompany moral judgements and the language that is used. After all, it is quite a claim to say that people

– the very people who make moral judgements every day – are in systematic error about what they are doing, and have been in such error, presumably, for countless generations.

One main way of opposing moral descriptivism is to adopt *moral expressivism*. To explain this difference, consider the varieties of function that language has. Imagine you want to put up a picture in your house and are using a hammer to hit a nail into the wall. Yet, you are very bad at DIY and you slip and hit your thumb with the hammer. "Ow!" you cry. However, after a while the pain fades and you have another go. But you slip again. "I've done it again!" you shriek. On the face of it, there is a big difference between these two utterances. The latter is fact-stating, since it stands as an attempt to describe something in the world. The former, however, does not have this function. (A good rule of thumb to see if something is fact-stating is to see if the whole phrase can replace 'p' in "It is true (or false) that p" and that larger utterance make grammatical sense. It doesn't make sense to say "It is false that ow".) However, if we think about it more, we might conclude that our two utterances in this example are, at bottom, both functioning in the same way. We might think that "I've done it again" is just a more sophisticated version of "Ow!". Both are used, primarily, as ways of expressing pain. Indeed, there might be a difference between two utterances of "I've done it again" and its cognates, such as those relating to past and future instances. Compare our previous example with a case where a few minutes later one points to one's bruise and says to a friend, in a calm fashion, "And then I did it again. Look". The former can plausibly be assumed to be expressing one's pain, whilst the latter seems not to be like that at all. One is reporting or describing an event.

It is important in all of this to realize that the difference being described is not between talking about something in the world and talking about something 'personal'. The difference is between describing and expressing. We can report that we are bored by explicitly saying, "I am bored". One way of understanding this is that it is a shorter form of the clumsy "I have investigated my mood at present and found that I am bored". But that is very different from yawning. Yawning does not describe anything, but can certainly express boredom. Things get more complicated because "I am bored" might be a more sophisticated form of expression in the right circumstances, just as "I've done it again!" from above might be. But the distinction between describing and expressing is a good one. (Furthermore, note that one can use language to do many things. One can ask questions, one can name and label objects, one can command and order people to act, and so on. It is perfectly possible to oppose moral descriptivism and think that much of what is going on with moral language is ordering, say, rather than expressing. In which case, by calling something good one would really be asking people to do it. We do not concentrate on this option here, but it is a viable one all the same.)

So what? People are impressed with this difference and are led to believe that moral language is primarily a matter of expression rather than description. When we say

"John is kind" we should not be interpreted as attempting to describe something about John's nature. Rather, we are expressing our approval of John. In a crude, simplified fashion, we are really saying "Hoorah for John!". Similarly, the associated mental states are not beliefs about what the world is like (my belief that John is kind), but are something else instead, something such as an attitude towards John, in this case an attitude of approval. Perhaps one is expressing a desire, a way in which one would like the world to change. So when I say of a possible course of action that it is kind I am really expressing (rather than describing) my desire that the action be performed, or somesuch. Very often the term 'noncognitivism' is used instead of expressivism, although strictly these two terms pick out different thoughts. 'Noncognitivism' is used because the mental state that is expressed by one's language is not assumed to be a representing, describing, belief-like state, but rather an attitude or a desire. Strictly, one cannot know anything – be in a state of knowing or cognizing the world – if one is desiring something or cheering something on. To repeat earlier thoughts, there is a difference between thinking that one's team is winning, which can be true and, if justified for the right reasons, can be a state of knowing, and hoping or desiring that they win. The latter cannot, strictly, be a candidate to be a state of knowing.

There are various reasons for being an expressivist, many of which we will meet in our selections (and primarily in Part 5). One might build on various arguments against moral reality, such as that above, and one might also be impressed with thoughts about moral motivation, of which more in §§ 9–10. However, expressivism faces many problems also. One that is worth indicating right now is this question: If moral language does not function descriptively, then why does it have a fact-stating grammatical form? Why did moral language not evolve in a different way? Even if expressivists can point out that some of our moral language is not descriptive – after all, commands such as "Don't do that!" and one word exclamations such as "Selfish!" seem to be as much a part of our moral language as fact-stating claims – and even if they can show that there are some power games going on in moral debate, we might still be suspicious that moral communication is not primarily descriptive.

We have so far assumed that an expression of attitude cannot be true or false, simply because there has to be some thing of which a statement is true. But this assumes a particular theory about what truth is, namely some form of the correspondence theory of truth. This theory of truth, though attractive, is not wholly accepted. Another theory, or family of theories, that has emerged in recent years as the main competitor has been deflationism. Deflationary theories of truth say, roughly, that although there are some truth-apt utterances, this does not entail that truth is a substantial property that utterances can have or lack and which philosophical reflection will reveal the nature of. Instead, in order for an utterance to be truth-apt it has to satisfy fairly minimal requirements. Metaethicists have therefore seen an opportunity to combine expressivism with a certain theory of truth, such that expressions of attitude can still be seen as true or false. This is important for modern expressivism. Just as error theorists typically say moral judgements are systematically and uniformly false, expressivists normally claim that ethics is not completely corrupt and we should stay committed to the idea that there are moral standards and norms. Some attitudes are better than others. Part 7 contains two pieces on expressivism and truth. We mention it here as this commitment to standards of some sorts pits error theorists and expressivists against a third sort of theorist, and this takes us to our next section.

Before that, we have left one thought hanging, which often does not get the coverage it deserves in metaethics. Descriptivism and expressivism are not simply empirical claims about how, in fact, every single moral judgement is used by its speaker. Rather they are philosophical claims, presumably based on some empirical evidence, about how best to understand judgements that are typical of ethics. The same thought is applicable to cognitivism and noncognitivism. But this raises an interesting issue. What about a particular judge who, because of her other normal judgements and language, is best understood as being atypical? Perhaps she is quite philosophically sophisticated and so explicitly resists the idea that her judgements are best understood as being expressions of attitude rather than descriptions. This is a delicate area. A perfectly possible position in metaethics – which blows much of the field open – is to resist *general* theories about matters of language and mental states, and then work through the (messy) implications of this for the metaphysics. Other people take a different tack and wish to hold that there is something important about having general theories and that we should try to strive to capture something that applies across all activity and thought. Our selections reflect this latter idea, but we are happy to note that there is this interesting question of philosophical commitment.

7

What if one rejects the sort of realism so far described by denying that there are any moral properties that generate standards and norms? Indeed, what if one rejects the idea of moral standards, norms of correctness and everything else? (Perhaps, unlike certain forms of expressivism, one thinks that moral norms of correctness make sense only if one assumes that there are full-blown moral properties that exist.) That is, perhaps one explicitly stands against the train of thought given in § 4. To do so is to embrace a form of *moral relativism*.

There are many forms of moral relativism, most of which we cannot do justice to here. But the main idea is this. Even if one is a moral realist it might well be that certain moral demands or standards do not apply to certain people. We might say that killing is wrong but make an exception for soldiers or for those that kill in self-defence. Or we might say that anyone who does not dive in to save a drowning child acts wrongly, apart from those that cannot swim, say, or those that are on the other side of the world. We still, supposedly, think that moral claims apply to all in principle, although there might well be some who are excused for good reason. Relativists typically make a different claim. They claim that moral claims and rules do not have a universal legitimate application and they make this claim without recourse to the idea of justified exceptions. Any legitimacy that a moral judgement has extends less than universally and, typically, will extend only to a local area. Relativists will then disagree amongst themselves about how far any moral claim's legitimacy extends and what sort of unit the legitimacy of the claim extends to or is based on (for example, the typical norms in a society, or membership of a group, or just one individual). In other words, one could have an extreme moral relativism. It could be that every single moral judgement would be legitimate only for one person, presumably the person who makes the judgement. Often this idea is cashed out by saying something such as, "Well, Jimmy might think it is true that murder is wrong, but it is only true-for-Jimmy, and possibly anyone else who agrees with him. There is no notion of moral truth and falsity, correctness and incorrectness, beyond this". A less extreme version might think that moral judgements are true and false, and actions correct and incorrect, whilst indexed to the ideas and standards of a social group unified in some fashion. But, again, there is no notion of truth beyond this.

Many people worry about moral relativism. Often we do want to condemn and praise and we think that such judgements go beyond merely what we – or the people we are criticizing – think. There really is something wrong with female circumcision, say, no matter what anyone thinks. Relativism in its many forms undercuts this idea. Indeed, so much so that many people think that it radically transforms or eradicates moral thought entirely since one of the essential aspects of moral thinking is the fact that judgements are universal in scope.

There is no single Part in this volume that covers moral relativism, but it hovers in the background of many of the debates we discuss. Many theorists try hard to distance themselves from it and show how their position does not commit themselves to it. We can locate relativism even better than we have done by discussing briefly two further terms that are often used in metaethics.

8

Those two terms are *objective* and *subjective*. These are used often in metaethics, and in everyday talk, but we should be careful how we use them as both can cover a number of different ideas. Consider 'objective' and two definitions we might give it. First, it can sometimes be used to reflect the idea that something (a property, a standard, whatever) is, in some fashion, 'mind-independent'. To say that something is mind-independent, or exists mind-independently, is to say that its existence does not depend at all on what humans (or any individual human) believes, desires, aims at, is committed to and the like (or could, in the future, believe, desire and the like). In contrast, to say that something is mind-dependent is to say that in some fashion there is some such dependency. So, to take some examples, the planet Pluto is (presumably) mind-independent. Its existence does not depend at all on what I, you or anyone has thought or will think. Of course, that a planet has been given the label 'Pluto' is dependent on what people say and think, but that's different.

The key question then is how moral properties should be characterized. Earlier, in § 4, we saw that initially we might be led to think of moral properties as being mind-independent. This was the natural move from thinking that it was a good thing if moral judgements are truth-apt to thinking that the thing that makes them true or false has to be something independent of how any individual or group thinks things are.

However, second, 'objective' can also be used to indicate a different idea. When we say that a given area of thought or discourse (ethics, say, or aesthetics or scientific thought) is objective we might well mean that it admits of standards of correctness, that certain activities are appropriate or inappropriate, that judgements typically made within the area are truth-apt. These two senses of objective are different. With the second sense we leave it open how we exactly characterize the thing that generates standards and makes judgements true. It doesn't commit us, we might say, to any one particular ontological account. The first sense of objective, on the other hand, gives us a very clear sense of how we should conceive of such things. And, we might say in addition, that thinking that a property is objective in the first sense strongly implies that the properties, and standards generated, typical of an area of thought are objective in the second sense. (If we claim that moral properties are mind-independent, then it naturally follows that these things generate standards of appropriateness and make judgements true or false.)

To illustrate this difference more, consider two important senses of 'subjective'. We might claim that something (a property, a standard, or whatever) is mind-dependent in a certain way. This is in opposition to the first sense of 'objective'. Similarly, we might give the contrary of the second sense of 'objective' and say that an area of thought and discourse is subjective if it does not admit of any standards of correctness or, perhaps, that no judgement that is typical of such an area is truth-apt. This type of subjectivism is really the relativism we discussed in the previous section. For example, we might think that there really is a matter of fact (as we might say) about whether there is a table in front of me right now. But is there really a matter of fact about which is the best tasting ice-cream? Possibly not. Aside from jokes we might make about chocolate being the best, we might well allow that in the area of ice-cream flavours judgements really are just a matter of taste, in both senses of the phrase. It really isn't appropriate to try to look for the best tasting ice-cream and criticize those that don't measure up. Of course, this is just an example. On further reflection we might say that there are *some* standards regarding ice-cream flavours. We might, after asking a number of people, draw up a league table of flavours. After all, even if there isn't a uniquely best flavour, we might think that some flavours – such as bleach flavour or earwig flavour – simply aren't right.

The important thing to get from this discussion is that, although the first sense of 'objective' is contrary to the first sense of 'subjective', and likewise for the second sense of each term, there is an interesting question as to whether a position can be objective in the second sense and subjective in the first sense. That is, is it possible that there be standards of appropriateness of activity and truth and falsity, but such things be based on properties or standards that are ultimately mind-dependent? As we shall see, quite a few people like this approach, partly because they find the other options unattractive. But there are worries. If we say that moral standards are based on what humans think or desire, how do we decide which humans, and which thoughts and desires, count? We could simply stipulate, without further justification, that a certain group or person gets it right, but such a move seems unwarranted in ethics. On the other hand, one could identify a certain sort of person or certain types of thought as being morally best. But to do this invites a regress, for how does one define 'morally best'? An answer to such a question could stop a regress, but it might not be accepted by everyone. To give up at this point and simply say, "Well, some people think that this sort of thing is acceptable, and others don't" is really to fall back to a relativistic position, which of course cuts against the second sort of objectivism we were trying to secure in the first place. There is more about this idea in Part 4.

9

In recent work in metaethics there has been a great deal of interest in moral psychology and in particular the nature of motivation and its relationship with moral judgement. This seems sensible for if moral life is about anything it is, at least in part, about being motivated to act or think in certain ways. Ethics is primarily a practical activity, it is said. This leads to two general questions, which themselves lead us to consider further specific issues.

The first main question that people have focused on is: *What is the relationship between moral judgement and motivation?* Some people think that if one makes a moral judgement then, crucially, one will feel motivated to some extent to act in a way that is consistent with that judgement. In other words, some people think that there is a necessary or internal connection between morally judging and moral motivation. Such people are called *motivational internalists*. Others – *motivational externalists* – disagree. One can perfectly well make a moral judgement and fail to feel any compunction to act. Notice that the debate between the two sides is not about the truth of any judgement. They are debating the relationship between what an agent *believes* is right and what motivation she should feel. Also notice that motivational internalists are not committed to thinking that an agent *will* act. Perhaps other conflicting judgements and their associated motivations get in the way. The idea is just that in making a moral judgement there is – necessarily – motivation of some strength.

Why should we believe either side? *Prima facie*, motivational externalism is the correct position. After all, it seems that amoralism is a perfectly consistent possibility. An amoralist is simply someone who makes moral judgements but who fails to feel any motivation. In other words, they can pick out any existing moral properties (supposing there are some) but are not moved at all to act in accordance with them. Indeed, not only is this a possibility, it seems that it is a common phenomenon. Think about the times when you have watched television, or read news reports, and discovered that somewhere countless children are dying from malnutrition or that some important part of our environment is being destroyed. We might well see that such things are terrible and that we should act. But many of us feel no motivation whatsoever and simply flick over the channel or move on and read the sports results. And it doesn't seem obvious that as such we aren't *really* making moral judgements.

How might internalists reply? First, they can add an important caveat. It might be that certain people and their judgements should not be considered when debating this issue. People can suffer from various types of depression or be weak-willed in certain ways and as such there is a mismatch between judgements and motivation almost by definition. It is supposed to be a common phenomenon that some depressed people can appreciate that something in their life – their family, their job – has value but remain entirely unmoved. In fact, this is often said to compound their depression. Internalists say that what they are really interested in is the central phenomenon of someone who is practically rational, someone who can make judgements where there is nothing obvious standing in the way of motivation following. When thinking about this central, normal case, what is the connection between judgement and motivation? When doing this, internalists ask us what is involved in making a legitimate or proper moral judgement and what it is to have mastery of moral concepts. By 'legitimate' they do not mean 'true'. Rather, they are asking us what is involved with making a moral judgement. Is it simply forming a suitably structured grammatical utterance in a particular context? Perhaps not. After all, a parrot or a robot could do that. Perhaps a moral judgement is legitimate only if accompanied by some form of appropriate motivation. After all, didn't we start by saying that if it was anything, ethics was a practical activity?

Internalism might start to look more attractive, but we might well have reached deadlock. Whilst internalists claim that a legitimate moral judgement in normal cases must involve some associated moral motivation, externalists disagree. At the very least, say externalists, the internalist thesis is a conceptual claim, one discoverable by a priori means. Why think that we can discover something like this without going out into the world? And, anyway, when we do go out into the world, we discover that people can perfectly well understand the claims they are making and their importance, whilst feeling no motivation. Furthermore, the internalist claim raises interesting questions about how similar the supposed 'practically rational' are to the supposed 'practically irrational'. Can we divide people – or people at different times – into two such distinct camps? What criteria are used to determine the practically rational? To say that people fall into this or that camp because they feel some suitable motivation seems arbitrary and appears to win the argument by mere stipulation. And, after all, why should we think that the normal cases are the practically rational agents?

These points are all good ones, and yet something attractive remains about the internalist claim. In Part 10 we have selected a piece that puts forward a very influential argument in favour of internalism.

10

But you might think we are getting ahead of ourselves. After all, the issue of moral motivation is wider than simply that between internalists and externalists. Nor are the issues surrounding motivation a separate topic within metaethics, cocooned from metaphysical ideas. Traditionally, expressivism has been thought to imply and be implied by motivational internalism. After all, if one assumes that one's moral judgement is an expression of a desire, then the internalist thesis seems to follow automatically: a desire is simply a state of being motivated. (Things are more complicated with the more general 'attitude', but the connection remains. To approve and cheer some person's action is to express one's motivation that that person's action is allowed to continue, say.) This connection between motivational internalism and expressivism has recently come under threat, but many still hold to it.

Certain sorts of realist and cognitivist have favoured motivational externalism, and there seems a nice connection here as well. The idea is just that moral properties exist, which one is trying to cognize and describe. Describing and cognizing seem to be the sorts of activity that do not require any sort of motivational aspect. My description 'The table is brown' does not entail or imply anything about what I will feel and do, be it judging that it is a nice colour or deciding to repaint it.

But now things get complicated, and this drags us back to the metaphysical issues from above. The specific question here is: *What sort of mental state is expressed by our moral judgements?* So far we have considered only two options: a representing belief state, or a desiring attitudinative state. The former is a picture of the world, whilst the other is a want to change the world in some way. Crucially it is assumed that this is a mutually exclusive division. A mental state can be one or the other but not both. This classic conception of matters is due to the eighteenth-century Scottish Enlightenment philosopher David Hume. Hume himself thought that moral judgements were, in our terminology, desire-like states. He thought that both sorts of state were needed for directed motivation and action, but he thought that desires were the 'senior partner'. For example, imagine I want some chocolate. That in itself is simply a desire. Without any beliefs (true or false) about where there is chocolate to be found, I might still be motivated to look for some. On the other hand, imagine I have a belief that there is some chocolate in a cupboard, but no desire. I will simply remain seated. Directed motivation comes when we combine desire – a state of being motivated – with inert, representing states, but it is clear that it is the desire that is what is doing the main work.

This classic account has come under threat in recent years. It is not so much that people deny that there can be desires, nor that they deny that there can be purely representational, inert states. The main question raised is why it is that desires have to be conceived as wholly noncognitive? That is, could there not be unitary mental states that were both states of being motivated and representing states at one and the same time? We discuss this more in Part 11. For now, notice the link between this and the earlier metaphysical thoughts. Some realist-cognitivists wish also to be motivational internalists. Challenging this Humean picture is important to them. If they can successfully argue against this picture, then they can claim that we can think of the mental states expressed by moral judgements as representations and from this argue that there really are moral properties to represent. But whilst these mental states are representations they are also states of being motivated and motivational internalism can be maintained.

This might explain why the labels 'naturalism' and 'nonnaturalism' are used as they are by people who agree that moral properties are irreducible. It just so happens that many of the people who are called nonnaturalists wish to challenge the Humean account of moral motivation. They do not think that our moral cognition should be thought of in the same way as our cognition and measure of everyday natural objects such as tables and the amount of pleasure. After all, they might say, is moral cognition such a cool and calm rational process? Perhaps moral judgements involve one seeing certain saliences such as the fact that the child is starving, or perhaps one can only see the injustice of chemical dumping if one has certain commitments in the first place. (Or, better, one's commitments are expressed precisely by how one sees the various features of a situation and which seem more important and pressing.) If such ideas can make good, the Humean belief–desire model might be rejected and we might argue that moral judgements stand for a third sort of mental state. On the other hand, and avoiding this complication, irreducible-naturalist-realists tend to favour motivational externalism. It is not obvious that moral judgements have to be an expression of a third sort of mental state.

This ends our brief tour of the main positions and questions you will read about in this book. We hope it has given you a flavour of what is to come. Now we turn our attention to some advice about how to use this book and what to ask when thinking about metaethics.

THINGS TO BEAR IN MIND WHEN USING THIS BOOK

11

Metaethics is riddled with terminology. One of the most important things to remember as you read our selections is:

> (1) What matters most in metaethics, as in all other areas of philosophy, are the ideas that stand behind the names of positions and arguments, not the names themselves.

It is certainly true that labels are important, not to mention convenient. But talking in labels is no substitute for good philosophical thinking. So, as we hope is obvious from our discussion above, simply stating that you are a moral realist, say, doesn't help someone else really understand what you believe. You should describe your position in detail, perhaps using examples and language that is as down to earth as you can make it. Following on from this, this might be good advice:

> (2) If you get confused about a particular position when you're reading, try to ignore the names of positions and summarize the key ideas of the author.

Of course there are countless other things which we could say about how to approach metaethics and philosophy in general, but in the end this is not a study skills book. A few further things, though, seem worth noting.

> (3) A number of the articles in our selection are tough; however, you should persist even if you fail to understand everything. At the end of the article it may all fall into place. Make use of the suggested future reading as other writers may give you a way into understanding what you've read.

> (4) We can't stress enough the importance of discussing these issues with others. We hope that this book will be used in group seminars and tutorials; but we are acutely aware that being in a group doesn't mean people talk to one another. However, the best way that you will come to understand and develop your *own* thoughts about metaethics is to get talking about the issues. We indeed urge you to argue about metaethics.

A number of questions struck us as being helpful to keep in mind when reading through this collection:

A   What is the *ontological* commitment of the writer? Do they think moral properties exist? If they do, what do they think they are like? And how do we come to know them?

B   What is the writer's account of moral *language*? Do they think that moral language is descriptive? Do they think that there is some good reason for treating moral language differently from other language?

C   What is the writer's account of the *psychology* of moral judgements and moral agents? Do they think there is something essentially practical about making a moral judgement? Do they think that motivation must include belief and appropriately related desire?

D   How do the answers I gave for A, B and C relate to one another? Are there any inconsistencies? How does the author address them, or how might they address them if they don't voice an opinion on this matter?

E   Where does the writer fit into the overall landscape of metaethics? Is their position similar to other positions I have read about? If so, which ones and why?

F   How might the writer's metaethical position influence their position in applied and normative ethics, if at all?

SOME FINAL ADVICE

12

At the end of each Part introduction we include a selection of what we deem to be the most important pieces on the issues. Note, first, that our selections in part repeat some, but not all, of the pieces cited in the bibliographies and footnotes of our selections. So, if you wish to investigate a topic further, you should check both our and our authors' suggestions. Second, our suggested further readings are only a selection. We can't include every-thing, or please everyone all of the time. However, we have suggested some of the *key* papers in each subject area that will hopefully be enough for the reader to develop their understanding and research. Third, we want to end with a very important point. As we have seen, metaethics has a number of interesting questions and draws upon a number of different areas in philosophy. Because of this, the area is rich. There are more questions to be raised and many more positions to be exploited than we have discussed here, and this is why metaethics remains such a vibrant area. For example, it might be that our language is best understood as expressing attitudes but this in no way means that that there could not be moral properties. Why think, then, that issues in language should imply anything metaphysical? Many are pursuing these sorts of question now. Additionally, we have already said that there is no distinct Part in this book on moral relativism, but we also do not have space to include distinct Parts on the different sorts of expressivism there are, or on the 'moral functionalist' account hinted at in § 5 above. The moral, then, is not to feel constrained – or constrain yourselves – to the selections we have made. We hope the selections in this book serve as an excellent introduction to the area and get you thinking about the many possible questions and answers we could ask regarding our moral lives. But this book is after all an introduction to metaethics, not an end.

FURTHER READING

The following are good introductions.

Darwall, Stephen, Gibbard, Allan and Railton, Peter (1992) 'Towards *fin de siècle* Ethics: Some Trends', *Philosophical Review*, vol. 101, pp. 115–89.

McNaughton, David (1988) *Moral Vision* (Oxford: Blackwell), [especially chapter 1].

Miller, Alexander (2003) *An Introduction to Contemporary Metaethics* (Cambridge: Polity Press), [especially chapter 1].

Smith, Michael (1984) *The Moral Problem* (Oxford: Blackwell), [especially chapter 1].

Part 1
THE OPEN
QUESTION ARGUMENT

Suppose that a friend tells you that he believes ethics should be demystified and that he has a plan to achieve this. He will, he informs you, demonstrate that moral properties such as goodness are identical with things which 'pull their weight' within the empirical sciences, properties such as pleasure and phenomena such as desire. He also informs you that he has made a start on this project by defining 'good' to mean 'pleasure'. If you judge that giving money to charity is good, then what you *really* mean, he claims, is that giving money to charity is pleasurable.

Presumably you would feel pretty uneasy and unhappy with your friend's proposal. Although you may feel it would be nice to have a manageable, more scientific approach to ethics, there seems to be something far too final and unhelpful about proceeding like this. You might want to challenge your friend on his definition of 'good'. For instance, surely the pleasure an alcoholic gets from 'falling off the wagon' is not good, and as such it can't be that 'good' simply means 'pleasurable'. This does not faze your friend. He admits that you have a good point, and his first definition may be a little off the mark. He reminds you that no one gets it right first time but insists that this means we have to search harder for a better definition. In the end, all moral terms are synonymous with nonmoral, natural terms. In light of your conversation, he suggests 'that which we desire to desire' as the definition of 'good'. Perhaps the alcoholic wishes that he did not want alcohol so much. However, you still feel uneasy – not about the details, but about his whole approach to ethics.

Before going any further, we need to notice that your friend's project – to identify moral properties with natural properties – may still be viable even if we could show that moral terms cannot be defined in this way. The term 'water' cannot be defined as 'H_2O'. For example, by 'water' we mean that clear, liquid stuff that humans can drink and splash in. H_2O has a more scientific air than that. But that need not mean, as we well know, that 'water' and 'H_2O' don't refer to the same stuff. However, let's leave the question whether there is a useful analogy to be had with theoretical identities, and focus on the stated version of your friend's project. (Part 3 deals with this naturalistic manoeuvre in more detail.)

This general issue should be familiar from § 5 of our Introduction (Chapter 1). The crucial question is why we have this attitude of unease about his proposal. We presumably don't want to keep ethics mysterious just for the sake of it. And most likely your friend's project would have a number of benefits if completed, such as the possibility of calculation and prediction within the moral domain. Yet, you feel that for any definition presented to you, however snazzy and sophisticated, you should be able to doubt it in a nontrivial, significant way, and that this somehow undermines the proposed definition. However, perhaps this resistance on your part is down to outdated beliefs about morality? And maybe with the proper approach your friend will help you come to see his definitions as correct?

In the first Part of this section G. E. Moore (Chapter 2) argues that this unease we feel is well founded, as *any* attempt to define 'good' in natural or metaphysical terms commits a fallacy, what he calls the 'naturalistic fallacy'. 'Good' he says is indefinable. Moreover, he thinks that our belief that we can always meaningfully question any proposed definition of 'good' is, in itself, a demonstration of there being such a fallacy.

Why does this ability to question demonstrate anything other than our own hang-ups and ignorance? Moore thought that if a definition – by which he means (roughly) the analysis of what is denoted by a term – is true, then it is analytic. And, if a definition is analytic, then we ought to be able to recognize its truth merely by grasping the meaning of the terms involved. Hence, he thought that all true definitions ought to be recognizable as such by grasping the meaning of the terms involved. If this is the case then answers to questions concerning proposed definitions that are correct ought to be obvious. Consider the question: 'Dr C. Little is an occultist, but is he also an eye doctor?' The answer, 'yes', ought to be obvious to us, since the question is 'closed'. It is obvious because the answer follows trivially from the meaning of the terms. Thus, if, after thinking about it, we don't find questions concerning a proposed definition obvious, but instead find such questions 'open', then Moore holds that the definition cannot be right. He claims that for any proposed definition of 'good' it will always be an open question if the definition is correct, and that this demonstrates that we cannot define 'good'. To ignore this fact is to commit the naturalistic fallacy. It is important to notice that Moore is not saying that if a question concerning a definition is closed then the definition is correct. He is claiming that if a definition is correct it ought not to be open for us to question the definition.

For Moore's 'open question' argument to work, for questions concerning true definitions to be closed, it seems he must be committed to the claim that true conceptual analyses are obvious. However, this seems on the face of it false. Surely a quick survey of the history of philosophy and mathematics will throw up a large number of true conceptual analyses that are not obvious. For example, it is open to the majority whether $\sin^2 x + \cos^2 x = 1$; however, it is (arguably) a conceptual truth of mathematics. This of course means that questions concerning true conceptual analysis could be open, and that Moore's argument fails. Having said this, if we found that everyone we asked doubted a proposed conceptual analysis then this seems like evidence to doubt that the analysis is true. (Frank Snare in Chapter 4 argues along these lines. He holds that the open question argument is best thought of as a linguistic test. See Further Reading below.)

Another question we might ask concerns Moore's ontological claims. Moore thinks that the naturalistic fallacy is committed if we define 'good' as a natural or a metaphysical property. And that as such good is a simple and nonnatural property. It seems then that there are (at least) two different things Moore means by the 'naturalistic fallacy', one is committed by defining the indefinable, and one is committed when identifying good with a natural or metaphysical property. We may wonder whether Moore's open question argument can cope with demonstrating *both* these claims. Can the open question argument secure both that 'good' is indefinable and that it is a simple, nonnatural property? Put in other words, can the open question argument rule out the possibility that good is a natural property that cannot be identified with any other property?

It is Moore's lack of precision concerning the naturalistic fallacy that is the focus of Chapter 3. In this article William Frankena attacks Moore's position by claiming that the naturalistic fallacy begs the question. (To beg the question is, roughly, to assume something when arguing that one's opponent will call into question, where the something assumed is often the very point at issue between the two opponents.) Frankena thinks that the naturalistic fallacy is a form of general fallacy – the 'definist fallacy' – that is committed when someone tries to define the indefinable. So, on this reading, Frankena thinks that what Moore means by the naturalistic fallacy is the defining of the indefinable 'good'. But, he claims, Moore provides no argument at all, for we must already know that good is indefinable before we can say that to define it is to commit a fallacy.

Frankena's article suggests an interesting defence of Moore's position. Perhaps we could provide independent justification of the position via Moore's intuitionism, the thought being that one could simply intuit – a sort of seeing without further justification – that goodness is indefinable. According to Frankena, though, this would be a mistake. For a start, on this account, people who did try to define goodness would be guilty of being 'morally blind', rather than, strictly, committing a fallacy. (We would not say, for instance, that the colour-blind person commits a fallacy when they fail to discriminate red and green.) These people simply do not realize that goodness is indefinable. More important, we might add, is whether this route provides any plausible defence. After all, can we provide further argument for thinking that goodness is indefinable? If we cannot, then claiming that it is just the sort of thing that 'those in the know' know might well fail to convince us.

Although there is some power to Frankena's thoughts, in response we might well wonder what role he assigns to the open question argument. Isn't the open question argument precisely Moore's reason for thinking that 'good' is indefinable in the first place? And, incidentally, although intuitionism was a much-derided position for much of the twentieth century, recently some people have tried to rehabilitate it as providing an important account of how we can know moral truths. Strictly intutionists claim that there is at least one moral claim, and possibly many, that are self-evidently justifiable. This does not automatically mean that they think that there are no other ways of justifying moral claims, for example, nor that they think that people are infallible. A more sophisticated version of intuitionism might well provide a structure in which our experience of and reflection on goodness might be such as to provide independent justification of the thought behind the open question argument. (For more on this, see the book edited by Philip Stratton-Lake (2002) and the piece by Jonathan Dancy (1991) listed in Further Reading below.)

Although most commentators hold that Frankena was right and that more generally the open question 'argument' is no argument at all, they also typically agree that Moore was onto something. What Moore did, it seems, was gesture towards a genuine challenge to the naturalist. Perhaps the most convincing way of constructing such a challenge would be to claim that as a matter of fact people find questions concerning proposed definitions of 'good' open, and then to give a reason for this. One such reason might be that proposed definitions will always fail to respect the *normativity* fundamental to the moral domain. Moral terms seem to have an intimate connection to motivation and practical reason which natural terms lack. Perhaps then it is this that grounds the pre-theoretical worries we have about our friend trying to reduce moral properties to naturalistic ones?

QUESTIONS TO CONSIDER AND TASKS TO COMPLETE

1   Exactly what is the connection between Moore's (Chapter 2) open question argument and the naturalistic fallacy?
2   How 'open' is the feeling you get when thinking about the claim that for something to be morally good is for it to be the thing that we typically desire to desire? How close in 'feeling' is this to the claim that water is H_2O?
3   Is Frankena (Chapter 3) right to dismiss the open question argument?
4   Try to construct Snare's (Chapter 4) characterization of Moore's argument in your own words. What do you think of Snare's arguments?
5   If you are reading this book systematically, come back to Part 1 at the end. People often claim that the open question argument and Moore's nonnaturalism were key to the development of the metaethical landscape of the twentieth century. How important do you think Moore's argument was?

FURTHER READING

For developments of the open question argument in relation to modern naturalism, please consult the further reading in Part 3.

Altman, Andrew (2004) 'Breathing Life into a Dead Argument: G. E. Moore and the Open Question Argument', *Philosophical Studies*, vol. 117, pp. 395–408.

Baldwin, Thomas (1990) *G. E. Moore* (London: Routledge).

Ball, Stephen (1991) 'Linguistic Intuitions and Varieties of Ethical Naturalism', *Philosophy and Phenomenological Research*, vol. LI, pp. 1–38.

Dancy, Jonathan (1991) 'Intuitionism', in Peter Singer (ed.) *A Companion to Ethics* (Oxford: Blackwell), pp. 411–20.

Darwall, Stephen, Gibbard, Allan and Railton, Peter (1992) 'Toward *fin de siècle* Ethics: Some Trends', *Philosophical Review*, vol. 101, pp. 115–89.

Kalderon, Mark (2004) 'Open Questions and the Manifest Image', *Philosophy and Phenomenological Research*, vol. 98, pp. 251–89.

Kolnai, Aurel (1980) 'The Ghost of the Naturalistic Fallacy', *Philosophy*, vol. 55, pp. 5–16.

Miller, Alexander (2003) *An Introduction to Contemporary Metaethics* (Cambridge: Polity Press), chapter 2.

Schilpp, P. (1942) *The Philosophy of G. E. Moore* (Evanston, IL and Chicago: Northwestern University Press).

Strandberg, Caj (2004) 'In Defence of the Open Question Argument', *The Journal of Ethics*, vol. 8, pp. 179–96.

Stratton-Lake, Philip (ed.) (2002) *Ethical Intuitionism: Re-evaluations* (Oxford: Oxford University Press).

2

THE OPEN QUESTION ARGUMENT

THE SUBJECT-MATTER OF ETHICS

G. E. Moore

1

It is very easy to point out some among our every-day judgments, with the truth of which Ethics is undoubtedly concerned. Whenever we say, 'So and so is a good man', or 'That fellow is a villain'; whenever we ask, 'What ought I to do?' or 'Is it wrong for me to do like this?'; whenever we hazard such remarks as 'Temperance is a virtue and drunkenness a vice' – it is undoubtedly the business of Ethics to discuss such questions and such statements; to argue what is the true answer when we ask what it is right to do, and to give reasons for thinking that our statements about the character of persons or the morality of actions are true or false. In the vast majority of cases, where we make statements involving any of the terms 'virtue', 'vice', 'duty', 'right', 'ought', 'good', 'bad', we are making ethical judgments; and if we wish to discuss their truth, we shall be discussing a point of Ethics.

So much as this is not disputed; but it falls very far short of defining the province of Ethics. That province may indeed be defined as the whole truth about that which is at the same time common to all such judgments and peculiar to them. But we have still to ask the question: What is it that is thus common and peculiar? And this is a question to which very different answers have been given by ethical philosophers of acknowledged reputation, and none of them, perhaps, completely satisfactory.

2

If we take such examples as those given above, we shall not be far wrong in saying that they are all of them concerned with the question of 'conduct' – with the question, what, in the conduct of us, human beings, is good, and what is bad, what is right, and what is wrong. For when we say that a man is good, we commonly mean that he acts rightly; when we say that drunkenness is a vice, we commonly mean that to get drunk is a wrong or wicked action. And this discussion of human conduct is, in fact, that with which the name 'Ethics' is most intimately associated. It is so associated by derivation; and conduct is undoubtedly by far the commonest and most generally interesting object of ethical judgments.

Accordingly, we find that many ethical philosophers are disposed to accept as an adequate definition of 'Ethics' the statement that it deals with the question what is good or bad in human conduct. They hold that its enquiries are properly confined to 'conduct' or to 'practice'; they hold that the name 'practical philosophy' covers all the matter with which it has to do. Now, without discussing the proper meaning of the word (for verbal questions are properly left to the writers of dictionaries and other persons interested in literature; philosophy, as we shall see, has no concern with them), I may say that I intend to use 'Ethics' to cover more than this – a usage, for which there is, I think, quite sufficient authority. I am using it to cover an enquiry for which, at all events, there is no other word: the general enquiry into what is good.

Ethics is undoubtedly concerned with the question what good conduct is; but, being concerned with this, it obviously does not start at the beginning, unless it is prepared to tell us what is good as well as what is conduct. For 'good conduct' is a complex notion: all conduct is not good; for some is certainly bad and some may be indifferent. And on the other hand, other things, beside conduct, may be good; and if they are so, then, 'good' denotes some property, that is common to them and conduct; and. if we examine good conduct alone of all good things, then we shall be in danger of mistaking for this property, some property which is not shared by those other things: and thus we shall have made a mistake about Ethics even in this limited sense; for we shall not know what good conduct really is. This is a mistake which many writers have actually made, from limiting their enquiry to conduct. And hence I shall try to avoid it by considering first what is good in general; hoping, that if we can arrive at any certainty about this, it will be much easier to settle the question of good conduct: for we all know pretty well what 'conduct' is. This, then, is our first question: 'What is good?' and 'What is bad?' and to the discussion of this question (or these questions) I give the name of Ethics, since that science must, at all events, include it.

3

But this is a question which may have many meanings. If, for example, each of us were to say 'I am doing good now' or 'I had a good dinner yesterday', these statements would each of them be some sort of answer to our question, although perhaps a false one. So, too, when A asks B what school he ought to send his son to, B's answer will certainly be an ethical judgment. And similarly all distribution of praise or blame to any personage or thing that has existed, now exists, or will exist, does give some answer to the question 'What is good?' In all such cases some particular thing is judged to be good or bad: the question 'What?' is answered by 'This'. But this is not the sense in which a scientific Ethics asks the question. Not one, of all the many million answers of this kind, which must be true, can form a part of an ethical system; although that science must contain reasons and principles sufficient for deciding on the truth of all of them. There are far too many persons, things and events in the world, past, present, or to come, for a discussion of their individual merits to be embraced in any science. Ethics, therefore, does not deal at all with facts of this nature, facts that are unique, individual, absolutely particular; facts with which such studies as history, geography, astronomy, are compelled, in part at least, to deal. And, for this reason, it is not the business of the ethical philosopher to give personal advice or exhortation.

4

But there is another meaning which may be given to the question 'What is good?' 'Books are good' would be an answer to it, though an answer obviously false; for some books are very bad indeed. And ethical judgments of this kind do indeed belong to Ethics; though I shall not deal with many of them. Such is the judgment 'Pleasure is good' – a judgment, of which Ethics should discuss the truth, although it is not nearly as important as that other judgment, with which we shall be much occupied presently – 'Pleasure *alone* is good.' It is judgments of this sort, which are made in such books on Ethics as contain a list of 'virtues' – in Aristotle's *Ethics* for example. But it is judgments of precisely the same kind, which form the substance of what is commonly supposed to be a study different from Ethics, and one much less respectable – the study of Casuistry. We may be told that Casuistry differs from Ethics, in that it is much more detailed and particular, Ethics much more general. But it is most important to notice that Casuistry does not deal with anything that is absolutely particular – particular in the only sense in which a perfectly precise line can be drawn between it and what is general. It is not particular in the sense just noticed, the sense in which this book is a particular book, and A's friend's advice particular advice. Casuistry may indeed be *more* particular and Ethics *more* general; but that means that they differ only in degree and not in kind. And this is universally true of 'particular' and 'general', when used in this common, but inaccurate, sense. So far a Ethics allows itself to give lists of virtues or even to name constituents of the Ideal, it is indistinguishable from Casuistry. Both alike deal with what is general, in the sense in which physics and chemistry deal with what is general. Just as chemistry aims at discovering what are the properties of oxygen, *wherever it occurs*, and not only of this or that particular specimen of oxygen; so Casuistry aims at discovering what actions are good, *whenever they occur*. In this respect Ethics and Casuistry alike are to be classed with such sciences as physics, chemistry and physiology, in their absolute distinction from those of which history and geography are instances. And it is to be noted that, owing to their detailed nature, casuistical investigations are actually nearer to physics and to chemistry than are the investigations usually assigned to Ethics. For just as physics cannot rest content with the discovery that light is propagated by waves of ether, but must go on to discover the particular nature of the ether-waves corresponding to each several colour; so Casuistry, not content with the general law that charity is a virtue must attempt to discover the relative merits of every different form of charity. Casuistry forms, therefore, part of the ideal of ethical science: Ethics cannot be complete without it. The defects of Casuistry are not defects of principle; no objection can be taken to its aim and object. It has failed only because it is far too difficult a subject to be treated adequately in our present state of knowledge. The casuist has been unable to distinguish, in the cases which he treats, those elements upon which their value depends. Hence he often thinks two cases to be alike in respect of value, when in reality they are alike only in some other respect. It is to mistakes of this kind that the pernicious influence of such investigations has been due. For Casuistry is the goal of ethical investigation. It cannot be safely attempted at the beginning of our studies, but only at the end.

5

But our question 'What is good?' may have still another meaning. We may, in the third place, mean to ask, not what thing or things are good, but how 'good' is to be defined. This is an enquiry which belongs only to Ethics, not to Casuistry; and this is the enquiry which will occupy us first.

It is an enquiry to which most special attention should be directed; since this question, how 'good' is to be defined, is the most fundamental question in all Ethics. That which is meant by 'good' is, in fact, except its converse 'bad', the *only* simple object of thought which is peculiar to Ethics. Its definition is, therefore, the most essential point in the definition of Ethics; and moreover a mistake with regard to it entails a far larger number of erroneous ethical judgments than any other. Unless this first question be fully understood, and its true answer clearly recognised, the rest of Ethics is as good as useless from the point of view of systematic knowledge. True ethical judgments, of the two kinds last dealt with, may indeed be made by those who do not know the answer to this question as well as by those who do; and it goes without saying that the two classes of people may lead equally good lives. But it is extremely unlikely that the *most general* ethical Judgments will be equally valid, in the absence of a true answer to this question: I shall presently try to show that the gravest errors have been largely due to beliefs in a false answer. And, in any case, it is impossible that, till the answer to this question be known, any one should know *what is the evidence* for any ethical judgment whatsoever. But the main object of Ethics, as a systematic science, is to give correct *reasons* for thinking that this or that is good; and, unless this question be answered, such reasons cannot be given. Even, therefore, apart from the fact that a false answer leads to false conclusions, the present enquiry is a most necessary and important part of the science of Ethics.

6

What, then, is good? How is good to be defined? Now, it may be thought that this is a verbal question. A definition does indeed often mean the expressing of one word's meaning in other words. But this is not the sort of definition I am asking for. Such a definition can never be of ultimate importance in any study except lexicography. If I wanted that kind of definition I should have to consider in the first place how people generally used the word 'good'; but my business is not with its proper usage, as established by custom. I should, indeed, be foolish, if I tried to use it for something which it did not usually denote: if, for instance, I were to announce that, whenever I used the word 'good', I must be understood to be thinking of that object which is usually denoted by the word 'table'. I shall, therefore, use the word in the sense in which I think it is ordinarily used; but at the same time I am not anxious to discuss whether I am right in thinking that it is so used. My business is solely with that object or idea, which I hold, rightly or wrongly, that the word is generally used to stand for. What I want to discover is the nature of that object or idea, and about this I am extremely anxious to arrive at an agreement.

But, if we understand the question in this sense, my answer to it may seem a very disappointing one. If I am asked 'What is good?' my answer is that good is good, and that is the end of the matter. Or if I am asked 'How is good to be defined?' my answer is that it cannot be defined, and that is all I have to say about it. But disappointing as these answers may appear, they are of the very last importance. To readers who are familiar with philosophic terminology, I can express their importance by saying that they amount to this: That propositions about the good are all of them synthetic and never analytic; and that is plainly no trivial matter. And the same thing may be expressed more popularly, by saying that, if I am right, then nobody can foist upon us such an axiom as that 'Pleasure is the only good' or that 'The good is the desired' on the pretence that this is 'the very meaning of the word'.

7

Let us, then, consider this position. My point is that 'good' is a simple notion, just as 'yellow' is a simple notion; that, just as you cannot, by any manner of means, explain to any one who does not already know it, what yellow is, so you cannot explain what good is. Definitions of the kind that I was asking for, definitions which describe the real nature of the object or notion denoted by a word, and which do not merely tell us what the word is used to mean, are only possible when the object or notion in question is something complex. You can give a definition of a horse, because a horse has many different properties and qualities, all of which you can enumerate. But when you have enumerated them all, when you have reduced a horse to his simplest terms, then you can no longer define those terms. They are simply something which you think of or perceive, and to any one who cannot think of or perceive them, you can never, by any definition, make their nature known. It may perhaps be objected to this that we are able to describe to others, objects which they have never seen or thought of. We can, for instance, make a man understand what a chimera is, although he has never heard of one or seen one. You can tell him that it is an animal with a lioness's head and body, with a goat's head growing from the middle of its back, and with a snake in place of a tail. But here the object which you are describing is a complex object; it is entirely composed of parts, with which we are all perfectly familiar – a snake, a goat, a lioness; and we know, too, the manner in which those parts are to be put together, because we know what is meant by the middle of a lioness's back, and where her tail is wont to grow. And so it is with all objects, not previously known, which we are able to define: they are all complex; all composed of parts, which may themselves, in the first instance, be capable of similar definition, but which must in the end be reducible to simplest parts, which can no longer be defined. But yellow and good, we say, are not complex: they are notions of that simple kind, out of which definitions are composed and with which the power of further defining ceases.

8

When we say, as Webster says, 'The definition of horse is "A hoofed quadruped of the genus Equus,"' we may, in fact, mean three different things. (1) We may mean merely: 'When I say "horse", you are to understand that I am talking about a hoofed quadruped of the genus Equus.' This might be called the arbitrary verbal definition: and I do not mean that good is indefinable in that sense. (2) We may mean, as Webster ought to mean: 'When most English people say "horse", they mean a hoofed quadruped of the genus Equus.' This may be called the verbal definition proper, and I do not say that good is indefinable in this sense either; for it is certainly possible to discover how people use a word: otherwise, we could never have known that 'good' may be translated by 'gut' in German and by 'bon' in French. But (3) we may, when we define horse, mean something much more important. We may mean that a certain object, which we all of us know, is composed in a certain manner: that it has four legs, a head, a heart, a liver, etc., etc., all of them arranged in definite relations to one another. It is in this sense that I deny good to be definable. I say that it is not composed of any parts, which we can substitute for it in our minds when we are thinking of it. We might think just as clearly and correctly about a horse, if we thought of all its parts and their arrangement instead of thinking of the whole: we could, I say, think how a horse differed from a donkey just as well, just as truly, in this way, as now we do, only not so easily; but there is nothing whatsoever which we could so substitute for good; and that is what I mean, when I say that good is indefinable.

9

But I am afraid I have still not removed the chief difficulty which may prevent acceptance of the proposition that good is indefinable. I do not mean to say that *the* good, that which is good, is thus indefinable; if I did think so, I should not be writing on Ethics, for my main object is to help towards discovering that definition. It is just because I think there will be less risk of error in our search for a definition of 'the good', that I am now insisting that *good* is indefinable. I must try to explain the difference between these two. I suppose it may be granted that 'good' is an adjective. Well 'the good', 'that which is good', must therefore be the substantive to which the adjective 'good' will apply: it must be the whole of that to which the adjective will apply, and the adjective must *always* truly apply to it. But if it is that to which the adjective will apply, it must be something different from that adjective itself; and the whole of that something different, whatever it is, will be our definition of *the* good. Now it may be that this something will have other adjectives, beside 'good', that will apply to it. It may be full of pleasure, for example; it may be intelligent: and if these two adjectives are really part of its definition, then it will certainly be true, that pleasure and intelligence are good. And many people appear to think that, if we say 'Pleasure and intelligence are good', or if we say 'Only pleasure and intelligence are good', we are defining 'good'. Well, I cannot deny that propositions of this nature may sometimes be called definitions; I do not know well enough how the word is generally used to decide upon this point. I only wish it to be understood that that is not what I mean when I say there is no possible definition of good, and that I shall not mean this if I use the word again. I do most fully believe that some true proposition of the form 'Intelligence is good and intelligence alone is good' can be found; if none could be found, our definition of *the* good would be impossible. As it is, I believe *the* good to be definable; and yet I still say that good itself is indefinable.

10

'Good', then, if we mean by it that quality which we assert to belong to a thing, when we say that the thing is good, is incapable of any definition, in the most important sense of that word. The most important sense of 'definition' is that in which a definition states what are the parts which invariably compose a certain whole; and in this sense 'good' has no definition because it is simple and has no parts. It is one of those innumerable objects of thought which are themselves incapable of definition, because they are the ultimate terms by reference to which whatever *is* capable of definition must be defined. That there must be an indefinite number of such terms is obvious, on reflection; since we cannot define anything except by an analysis, which, when carried as far as it will go, refers us to something, which is simply different from anything else, and which by that ultimate difference explains the peculiarity of the whole which we are defining: for every whole contains some parts which are common to other wholes also. There is, therefore, no intrinsic difficulty in the contention that 'good' denotes a simple and indefinable quality. There are many other instances of such qualities.

Consider yellow, for example. We may try to define it, by describing its physical equivalent; we may state what kind of light-vibrations must stimulate the normal eye, in order that we may perceive it. But a moment's reflection is sufficient to show that those light-vibrations are not themselves what we mean by yellow. *They* are not what we perceive. Indeed we should never have been able to discover their existence, unless we had first been struck by the patent difference of quality between the different colours. The most we can be entitled to say of those vibrations is that they are what corresponds in space to the yellow which we actually perceive.

Yet a mistake of this simple kind has commonly been made about 'good'. It may be true that all things which are good are *also* something else, just as it is true that all things which are yellow produce a certain kind of vibration in the light. And it is a fact, that Ethics aims at discovering what are those other properties belonging to all things which are good. But far too many philosophers have thought that when they named those other properties they were actually defining good; that these properties, in fact, were simply not 'other', but absolutely and entirely the same with goodness. This view I propose to call the 'naturalistic fallacy' and of it I shall now endeavour to dispose.

11

Let us consider what it is such philosophers say. And first it is to be noticed that they do not agree among themselves. They not only say that they are right as to what good is, but they endeavour to prove that other people who say that it is something else, are wrong. One, for instance, will affirm that good is pleasure, another, perhaps, that good is that which is desired; and each of these will argue eagerly to prove that the other is wrong. But how is that possible? One of them says that good is nothing but the object of desire, and at the same time tries to prove that it is not pleasure. But from his first assertion, that good just means the object of desire, one of two things must follow as regards his proof:

(1)   He may be trying to prove that the object of desire is not pleasure. But, if this be all, where is his Ethics? The position he is maintaining is merely a psychological one. Desire is something which occurs in our minds, and pleasure is something else which so occurs; and our would-be ethical philosopher is merely holding that the latter is not the object of the former. But what has that to do with the question in dispute? His opponent held the ethical proposition that pleasure was the good, and although he should prove a million times over the psychological proposition that pleasure is not the object of desire, he is no nearer proving his opponent to be wrong. The position is like this. One man says a triangle is a circle: another replies 'A triangle is a straight line, and I will prove to you that I am right: *for*' (this is the only argument) 'a straight line is not a circle.' 'That is quite true,' the other may reply, 'but nevertheless a triangle is a circle, and you have said nothing whatever to prove the contrary. What is proved is that one of us is wrong, for we agree that a triangle cannot be both a straight line and a circle: but which is wrong, there can be no earthly means of proving, since you define triangle as straight line and I define it as circle.' – Well, that is one alternative which any naturalistic Ethics has to face; if good is *defined* as something else, it is then impossible either to prove that any other definition is wrong or even to deny such definition.

(2)   The other alternative will scarcely be more welcome. It is that the discussion is after all a verbal one. When A says 'Good means pleasant' and B says 'Good means desired', they may merely wish to assert that most people have used the word for what is pleasant and for what is desired respectively. And this is quite an interesting subject for discussion: only it is not a whit more an ethical discussion than the last was. Nor do I think that any exponent of naturalistic Ethics would be willing to allow that this was all he meant. They are all so anxious to persuade us that what they call the good is what we really ought to do. 'Do, pray, act so, because the word "good" is generally used to denote actions of this nature': such, on this view, would be the substance of their teaching. And in so far as they tell us how we ought to act, their teaching is truly ethical, as they mean it to be. But how perfectly absurd is the reason they would give for it! 'You are to do this, because most people use a certain word to denote conduct such as this.' 'You are to say the thing which is not, because most people call it lying.' That is an argument just as good! – My dear sirs, what we want to know from you as ethical teachers, is not how people use a word; it is not even, what kind of actions they approve, which the use of this word 'good' may certainly imply: what we want to know is simply what *is* good. We may indeed agree that what most people do think good, is actually so; we shall at all events be glad to know their opinions: but when we say their opinions about what *is* good, we do mean what

we say; we do not care whether they call that thing which they mean 'horse' or 'table' or 'chair', 'gut' or 'bon' or 'ἀγαθός'; we want to know what it is that they so call. When they say 'Pleasure is good', we cannot believe that they merely mean 'Pleasure is pleasure' and nothing more than that.

12

Suppose a man says 'I am pleased'; and suppose that is not a lie or a mistake but the truth. Well, if it is true, what does that mean? It means that his mind, a certain definite mind, distinguished by certain definite marks from all others, has at this moment a certain definite feeling called pleasure. 'Pleased' *means* nothing but having pleasure, and though we may be more pleased or less pleased, and even, we may admit for the present, have one or another kind of pleasure; yet in so far as it is pleasure we have, whether there be more or less of it, and whether it be of one kind or another, what we have is one definite thing, absolutely indefinable, some one thing that is the same in all the various degrees and in all the various kinds of it that there may be. We may be able to say how it is related to other things: that, for example, it is in the mind, that it causes desire, that we are conscious of it, etc., etc. We can, I say, describe its relations to other things, but define it we can *not*. And if anybody tried to define pleasure for us as being any other natural object; if anybody were to say, for instance, that pleasure *means* the sensation of red, and were to proceed to deduce from that that pleasure is a colour, we should be entitled to laugh at him and to distrust his future statements about pleasure. Well, that would be the same fallacy which I have called the naturalistic fallacy. That 'pleased' does not mean 'having the sensation of red', or anything else whatever, does not prevent us from understanding what it does mean. It is enough for us to know that 'pleased' does mean 'having the sensation of pleasure', and though pleasure is absolutely indefinable, though pleasure is pleasure and nothing else whatever, yet we feel no difficulty in saying that we are pleased. The reason is, of course, that when I say 'I am pleased', I do *not* mean that 'I' am the same thing as 'having pleasure'. And similarly no difficulty need be found in my saying that 'pleasure is good' and yet not meaning that 'pleasure' is the same thing as 'good', that pleasure *means* good, and that good *means* pleasure. If I were to imagine that when I said 'I am pleased', I meant that I was exactly the same thing as 'pleased', I should not indeed call that a naturalistic fallacy, although it would be the same fallacy as I have called naturalistic with reference to Ethics. The reason of this is obvious enough. When a man confuses two natural objects with one another, defining the one by the other, if for instance, he confuses himself, who is one natural object, with 'pleased' or with 'pleasure' which are others, then there is no reason to call the fallacy naturalistic. But if he confuses 'good', which is not in the same sense a natural object, with any natural object whatever, then there is a reason for calling that a naturalistic fallacy; its being made with regard to 'good' marks it as something quite specific, and this specific mistake deserves a name because it is so common. As for the reasons why good is not to be considered a natural object, they may be reserved for discussion in another place. But, for the present, it is sufficient to notice this: Even if it were a natural object, that would not alter the nature of the fallacy nor diminish its importance one whit. All that I have said about it would remain quite equally true: only the name which I have called it would not be so appropriate as I think it is. And I do not care about the name: what I do care about is the fallacy. It does not matter what we call it, provided we recognise it when we meet with it. It is to be met with in almost every book on Ethics; and yet it is not recognised: and that is why it is necessary to multiply illustrations of it, and convenient to give it a name. It is a very simple fallacy indeed. When we say that an orange is yellow, we do not think our statement binds us to hold that 'orange' means nothing else than 'yellow', or that nothing can be yellow but an orange. Supposing the orange is also sweet! Does that bind us to say that 'sweet' is exactly the same thing as 'yellow', that 'sweet' must be defined as 'yellow'? And supposing it be recognised that 'yellow' just means 'yellow' and nothing else whatever, does that make it any more difficult to hold that oranges are yellow? Most certainly it does not: on the contrary, it would be absolutely meaningless to say that oranges were yellow, unless yellow did in the end mean just 'yellow' and nothing else whatever – unless it was absolutely indefinable. We should not get any very clear notion about things, which are yellow – we should not get very far with our science, if we were bound to hold that everything which was yellow, *meant* exactly the same thing as yellow. We should find we had to hold that an orange was exactly the same thing as a stool, a piece of paper, a lemon, anything you like. We could prove any number of absurdities; but should we be the nearer to the truth? Why, then, should it be different with 'good'? Why, if good is good and indefinable, should I be held to deny that pleasure is good? Is there any difficulty in holding both to be true at once? On the contrary, there is no meaning in saying that pleasure is good, unless good is something different from pleasure. It is absolutely useless, so far as Ethics is concerned, to prove, as Mr Spencer tries to do, that increase of pleasure coincides with increase of life, unless good *means* something different from either life or pleasure. He might just as well try to prove that an orange is yellow by showing that it always is wrapped up in paper.

13

In fact, if it is not the case that 'good' denotes something simple and indefinable, only two alternatives are possible: either it is a complex, a given whole, about the correct analysis of which there may be disagreement; or else it means nothing at all, and there is no such subject as Ethics. In general, however, ethical philosophers have attempted to define good, without recognising what such an attempt must mean. They actually use arguments which involve one or both of the absurdities considered in § 11. We are, therefore, justified in concluding that the attempt to define good is chiefly due to want of clearness as to the possible nature of definition. There are, in fact, only two serious alternatives to be considered, in order to establish the conclusion that 'good' does denote a simple and indefinable notion. It might possibly denote a complex, as 'horse' does; or it might have no meaning at all. Neither of these possibilities has, however, been clearly conceived and seriously maintained, as such, by those who presume to define good; and both may be dismissed by a simple appeal to facts.

(1)   The hypothesis that disagreement about the meaning of good is disagreement with regard to the correct analysis of a given whole, may be most plainly seen to be incorrect by consideration of the fact that, whatever definition be offered, it may be always asked, with significance, of the complex so defined, whether it is itself good. To take, for instance, one of the more plausible, because one of the more complicated, of such proposed definitions, it may easily be thought, at first sight, that to be good may mean to be that which we desire to desire. Thus if we apply this definition to a particular instance and say 'When we think that A is good, we are thinking that A is one of the things which we desire to desire', our proposition may seem quite plausible. But, if we carry the investigation further, and ask ourselves 'Is it good to desire to desire A?' it is apparent, on a little reflection, that this question is itself as intelligible, as the original question 'Is A good?' – that we are, in fact, now asking for exactly the same information about the desire to desire A, for which we formerly asked with regard to A itself. But it is also apparent that the meaning of this second question cannot be correctly analysed into 'Is the desire to desire A one of the things which we desire to desire?': we have not before our minds anything so complicated as the question 'Do we desire to desire to desire to desire A?' Moreover any one can easily convince himself by inspection that the predicate of this proposition – 'good' – is positively different from the notion of 'desiring to desire' which enters into its subject: 'That we should desire to desire A is good' is *not* merely equivalent to 'That A should be good is good.' It may indeed be true that what we desire to desire is always also good; perhaps, even the converse may be true: but it is very doubtful whether this is the case, and the mere fact that we understand very well what is meant by doubting it, shows clearly that we have two different notions before our minds.

(2)   And the same consideration is sufficient to dismiss the hypothesis that 'good' has no meaning whatsoever. It is *very* natural to make the mistake of supposing that what is universally true is of such a nature that its negation would be self-contradictory: the importance which has been assigned to analytic propositions in the history of philosophy shows how easy such a mistake is. And thus it is very easy to conclude that what seems to be a universal ethical principle is in fact an identical proposition; that, if, for example, whatever is called 'good' seems to be pleasant, the proposition 'Pleasure is the good' does not assert a connection between two different notions, but involves only one,

that of pleasure, which is easily recognised as a distinct entity. But whoever will attentively consider with himself what is actually before his mind when he asks the question 'Is pleasure (or whatever it may be) after all good?' can easily satisfy himself that he is not merely wondering whether pleasure is pleasant. And if he will try this experiment with each suggested definition in succession, he may become expert enough to recognise that in every case he has before his mind a unique object, with regard to the connection of which with any other object, a distinct question may be asked. Every one does in fact understand the question 'Is this good?' When he thinks of it, his state of mind is different from what it would be, were he asked 'Is this pleasant, or desired, or approved?' It has a distinct meaning for him, even though he may not recognise in what respect it is distinct. Whenever he thinks of 'intrinsic value', or 'intrinsic worth', or says that a thing 'ought to exist', he has before his mind the unique object – the 'unique property' of things – which I mean by 'good'. Everybody is constantly aware of this notion, although he may never become aware at all that it is different from other notions of which he is also aware. But, for correct ethical reasoning, it is extremely important that he should become aware of this fact; and, as soon as the nature of the problem is clearly understood, there should be little difficulty in advancing so far in analysis.

14

'Good', then, is indefinable; and yet, so far as I know, there is only one ethical writer, Professor Henry Sidgwick, who has clearly recognised and stated this fact. We shall see, indeed, how far many of the most reputed ethical systems fall short of drawing the conclusions which follow from such a recognition. At present I will only quote one instance, which will serve to illustrate the meaning and importance of this principle that 'good' is indefinable, or, as Professor Sidgwick says, an 'unanalysable notion'. It is an instance to which Professor Sidgwick himself refers in a note on the passage, in which he argues that 'ought' is unanalysable.[1]

'Bentham,' says Sidgwick, 'explains that his fundamental principle "states the greatest happiness of all those whose interest is in question as being the right and proper end of human action"'; and yet 'his language in other passages of the same chapter would seem to imply' that he *means* by the word 'right' 'conducive to the general happiness'. Professor Sidgwick sees that, if you take these two statements together, you get the absurd result that 'greatest happiness is the end of human action, which is conducive to the general happiness'; and so absurd does it seem to him to call this result, as Bentham calls it, 'the fundamental principle of a moral system', that he suggests that Bentham cannot have meant it. Yet Professor Sidgwick himself states elsewhere[2] that Psychological Hedonism is 'not seldom confounded with Egoistic Hedonism'; and that confusion, as we shall see, rests chiefly on that same fallacy, the naturalistic fallacy, which is implied in Bentham's statements. Professor Sidgwick admits therefore that this fallacy is sometimes committed, absurd as it is; and I am inclined to think that Bentham may really have been one of those who committed it. Mill, as we shall see, certainly did commit it. In any case, whether Bentham committed it or not, his doctrine, as above quoted, will serve as a very good illustration of this fallacy, and of the importance of the contrary proposition that good is indefinable.

Let us consider this doctrine. Bentham seems to imply, so Professor Sidgwick says, that the word 'right' *means* 'conducive to general happiness'. Now this, by itself, need not necessarily involve the naturalistic fallacy. For the word 'right' is very commonly appropriated to actions which lead to the attainment of what is good; which are regarded as *means* to the ideal and not as ends-in-themselves. This use of 'right', as denoting what is good as a means, whether or not it be also good as an end, is indeed the use to which I shall confine the word. Had Bentham been using 'right' in this sense, it might be perfectly consistent for him to *define* right as 'conducive to the general happiness', *provided only* (and notice this proviso) he had already proved, or laid down as an axiom, that general happiness was *the* good, or (what is equivalent to this) that general happiness alone was good. For in that case he would have already defined *the* good as general happiness (a position perfectly consistent, as we have seen, with the contention that 'good' is indefinable), and, since right was to be defined as 'conducive to *the* good', it would actually *mean* 'conducive to general happiness'. But this method of escape from the charge of having committed the naturalistic fallacy has been closed by Bentham himself. For his fundamental principle is, we see, that the greatest happiness of all concerned is the *right* and proper *end* of human action. He applies the word 'right', therefore, to the end, as such, not only to the means which are conducive to it; and, that being so, right can no longer be defined as 'conducive to the general happiness', without involving the fallacy in question. For now it is obvious that the definition of right as conducive to general happiness can be used by him in support of the fundamental principle that general happiness is the right end; instead of being itself derived from that principle. If right, by definition, means conducive to general happiness, then it is obvious that general happiness is the right end. It is not necessary now first to prove or assert that general happiness is the right end, before right is defined as conducive to general happiness – a perfectly valid procedure; but on the contrary the definition of right as conducive to general happiness proves general happiness to be the right end – a perfectly invalid procedure, since in this case the statement that 'general happiness is the right end of human action' is not an ethical principle at all, but either, as we have seen, a proposition about the meaning of words, or else a proposition about the *nature* of general happiness, not about its rightness or goodness.

Now, I do not wish the importance I assign to this fallacy to be misunderstood. The discovery of it does not at all refute Bentham's contention that greatest happiness is the proper end of human action, if that be understood as an ethical proposition, as he undoubtedly intended it. That principle may be true all the same; we shall consider whether it is so in succeeding chapters. Bentham might have maintained it, as Professor Sidgwick does, even if the fallacy had been pointed out to him. What I am maintaining is that the *reasons* which he actually gives for his ethical proposition are fallacious ones so far as they consist in a definition of right. What I suggest is that he did not perceive them to be fallacious; that, if he had done so, he would have been led to seek for other reasons in support of his Utilitarianism; and that, had he sought for other reasons, he *might* have found none which he thought to be sufficient. In that case he would have changed his whole system – a most important consequence. It is undoubtedly also possible that he would have thought other reasons to be sufficient, and in that case his ethical system, in its main results, would still have stood. But, even in this latter case, his use of the fallacy would be a serious objection to him as an ethical philosopher. For it is the business of Ethics, I must insist, not only to obtain true results, but also to find valid reasons for them. The direct object of Ethics is knowledge and not practice; and any one who uses the naturalistic fallacy has certainly not fulfilled this first object, however correct his practical principles may be.

My objections to Naturalism are then, in the first place, that it offers no reason at all, far less any valid reason, for any ethical principle whatever; and in this it already fails to satisfy the requirements of Ethics, as a scientific study. But in the second place I contend that, though it gives a reason for no ethical principle, it is a *cause* of the acceptance of false principles – it deludes the mind into accepting ethical principles, which are false; and in this it is contrary to every aim of Ethics. It is easy to see that if we start with a definition of right conduct as conduct conducive to general happiness; then, knowing that right conduct is universally conduct conducive to the good, we very easily arrive at the result that the good is general happiness. If, on the other hand, we once recognise that we must start our Ethics without a definition, we shall be much more apt to look about us, before we adopt any ethical principle whatever; and the more we look about us, the less likely are we to adopt a false one. It may be replied to this: Yes, but we shall look about us just as much, before we settle on our definition, and are therefore just as likely to be right. But I will try to show that this is not the case. If we start with the conviction that a definition of good can be found, we start with the conviction that good *can mean* nothing else than some one property of things; and our only business will then be to discover what that property is. But if we recognise that, so far as the meaning of good goes, anything whatever may be good, we start with a much more open mind. Moreover, apart from the fact that, when we think we have a definition, we cannot logically defend our ethical principles in any way whatever, we shall also be much less apt to defend them well, even if illogically. For we shall start with the conviction that good must mean so and so, and shall therefore be inclined either to misunderstand our opponent's arguments or to cut them short with the reply, 'This is not an open question: the very meaning of the word decides it; no one can think otherwise except through confusion.'

15

Our first conclusion as to the subject-matter of Ethics is, then, that there is a simple, indefinable, unanalysable object of thought by reference to which it must be defined. By what name we call this unique object is a matter of indifference, so long as we clearly recognise what it is and that it does differ from other objects. The words which are commonly taken as the signs of ethical judgments all do refer to it; and they are expressions of ethical judgments solely because they do so refer. But they may refer to it in two different ways, which it is very important to distinguish, if we are to have a complete definition of the range of ethical judgments. Before I proceeded to argue that there was such an indefinable notion involved in ethical notions, I stated (§ 4) that it was necessary for Ethics to enumerate all true universal judgments, asserting that such and such a thing was good, whenever it occurred. But, although all such judgments do refer to that unique notion which I have called 'good', they do not all refer to it in the same way. They may either assert that this unique property does always attach to the thing in question, or else they may assert only that the thing in question is *a cause or necessary condition* for the existence of other things to which this unique property does attach. The nature of these two species of universal ethical judgments is extremely different; and a great part of the difficulties, which are met with in ordinary ethical speculation, are due to the failure to distinguish them clearly. Their difference has, indeed, received expression in ordinary language by the contrast between the terms 'good as means' and 'good in itself', 'value as a means' and 'intrinsic value'. But these terms are apt to be applied correctly only in the more obvious instances; and this seems to be due to the fact that the distinction between the conceptions which they denote has not been made a separate object of investigation.

NOTES

1   *Methods of Ethics*, Bk. 1, Chap. iii, § 1 (6th edn).
2   *Methods of Ethics*, Bk. 1, Chap. iv, § 1.

3

THE NATURALISTIC FALLACY

William Frankena

The future historian of 'thought and expression' in the twentieth century will no doubt record with some amusement the ingenious trick, which some of the philosophical controversialists of the first quarter of our century had, of labelling their opponents' views 'fallacies'. He may even list some of these alleged fallacies for a certain sonority which their inventors embodied in their titles: the fallacy of initial predication, the fallacy of simple location, the fallacy of misplaced concreteness, the naturalistic fallacy.

Of these fallacies, real or supposed, perhaps the most famous is the naturalistic fallacy. For the practitioners of a certain kind of ethical theory, which is dominant in England and capably represented in America, and which is variously called objectivism, non-naturalism, or intuitionism, have frequently charged their opponents with committing the naturalistic fallacy. Some of these opponents have strongly repudiated the charge of fallacy, others have at least commented on it in passing, and altogether the notion of a naturalistic fallacy has had a considerable currency in ethical literature. Yet, in spite of its repute, the naturalistic fallacy has never been discussed at any length, and, for this reason, I have elected to make a study of it in this paper. I hope incidentally to clarify certain confusions which have been made in connexion with the naturalistic fallacy, but my main interest is to free the controversy between the intuitionists and their opponents of the notion of a logical or quasi-logical fallacy, and to indicate where the issue really lies.

The prominence of the concept of a naturalistic fallacy in recent moral philosophy is another testimony to the great influence of the Cambridge philosopher, G. E. Moore, and his book *Principia Ethica*. Thus Taylor speaks of the 'vulgar mistake' which Moore has taught us to call 'the naturalistic fallacy',[1] and G. S. Jury, as if to illustrate how well we have learned this lesson, says, with reference to naturalistic definitions of value, 'All such definitions stand charged with Moore's "naturalistic fallacy".'[2] Now, Moore coined the notion of the naturalistic fallacy in his polemic against naturalistic and metaphysical systems of ethics. 'The naturalistic fallacy is a fallacy,' he writes, and it

47

'must not be committed.' All naturalistic and metaphysical theories of ethics, however, 'are *based* on the naturalistic fallacy, in the sense that the commission of this fallacy has been the main cause of their wide acceptance'.[3] The best way to dispose of them, then, is to expose this fallacy. Yet it is not entirely clear just what is the status of the naturalistic fallacy in the polemics of the intuitionists against other theories. Sometimes it is used as a weapon, as when Miss Clarke says that if we call a thing good simply because it is liked we are guilty of the naturalistic fallacy.[4] Indeed, it presents this aspect to the reader in many parts of *Principia Ethica* itself. Now, in taking it as a weapon, the intuitionists use the naturalistic fallacy as if it were a logical fallacy on all fours with the fallacy of composition, the revelation of which disposes of naturalistic and meta-physical ethics and leaves intuitionism standing triumphant. That is, it is taken as a fallacy in advance, for use in controversy. But there are signs in *Principia Ethica* which indicate that the naturalistic fallacy has a rather different place in the intuitionist scheme, and should not be used as a weapon at all. In this aspect, the naturalistic fallacy must be proved to be a fallacy. It cannot be used to settle the controversy, but can only be asserted to be a fallacy when the smoke of battle has cleared. Consider the following passages: (a) 'the naturalistic fallacy consists in the contention that good *means* nothing but some simple or complex notion, that can be defined in terms of natural qualities'; (b) 'the point that good is indefinable and that to deny this involves a fallacy, is a point capable of strict proof'.[5] These passages seem to imply that the fallaciousness of the naturalistic fallacy is just what is at issue in the controversy between the intuitionists and their opponents, and cannot be wielded as a weapon in that controversy. One of the points I wish to make in this paper is that the charge of committing the naturalistic fallacy can be made, if at all, only as a conclusion from the discussion and not as an instrument of deciding it.

The notion of a naturalistic fallacy has been connected with the notion of a bifur-cation between the 'ought' and the 'is', between value and fact, between the normative and the descriptive. Thus D. C. Williams says that some moralists have thought it appropriate to chastise as the naturalistic fallacy the attempt to derive the Ought from the Is.[6] We may begin, then, by considering this bifurcation, emphasis on which, by Sidgwick, Sorley, and others, came largely as a reaction to the procedures of Mill and Spencer. Hume affirms the bifurcation in his *Treatise*: 'I cannot forbear adding to these reasonings an observation, which may, perhaps, be found of some importance. In every system of morality which I have hitherto met with, I have always remarked, that the author proceeds for some time in the ordinary way of reasoning, and establishes the being of a God, or makes observations concerning human affairs; when of a sudden I am surprised to find, that instead of the usual copulations of propositions, *is*, and *is not*, I meet with no proposition that is not connected with an *ought*, or an *ought not*. This change is imperceptible; but *is*, however, of the last consequence. For as this *ought*, or *ought not*, expresses some new relation or affirmation, it is necessary that it should be observed and explained; and at the same time that a reason should be given, for what seems altogether inconceivable, how this new relation can be a deduction from others, which are entirely different from it. But as authors do not commonly use this precaution, I shall presume to recommend it to the readers; and am persuaded, that this small attention would subvert all the vulgar systems of morality, and let us see that the distinction of vice and virtue is not founded merely on the relations of objects, nor is perceived by reason.'[7]

Needless to say, the intuitionists *have* found this observation of some importance.[8] They agree with Hume that it subverts all the vulgar systems of morality, though, of course, they deny that it lets us see that the distinction of virtue and vice is not founded on the relations of objects, nor is perceived by reason. In fact, they hold that a small attention to it subverts Hume's own system also, since this gives naturalistic definitions of virtue and vice and of good and evil.[9]

Hume's point is that ethical conclusions cannot be drawn validly from premises which are non-ethical. But when the intuitionists affirm the bifurcation of the 'ought' and the 'is', they mean more than that ethical propositions cannot be deduced from non-ethical ones. For this difficulty in the vulgar systems of morality could be remedied, as we shall see, by the introduction of definitions of ethical notions in non-ethical terms. They mean, further, that such definitions of ethical notions in non-ethical terms are impossible. 'The essential point,' says Laird, 'is the irreducibility of values to non-values.'[10]

But they mean still more. Yellow and pleasantness are, according to Moore, indefinable in non-ethical terms, but they are natural qualities and belong on the 'is' side of the fence. Ethical properties, however, are not, for him, mere indefinable natural qualities, descriptive or expository. They are properties of a different *kind* – non-descriptive or non-natural.[11] The intuitionist bifurcation consists of three statements:

1   Ethical propositions are not deducible from non-ethical ones.[12]
2   Ethical characteristics are not definable in terms of non-ethical ones.
3   Ethical characteristics are different in kind from non-ethical ones.

Really it consists of but one statement, namely, (3), since (3) entails (2) and (2) entails (1). It does not involve saying that any ethical characteristics are absolutely indefinable. That is another question, although this is not always noticed.

What, now, has the naturalistic fallacy to do with the bifurcation of the 'ought' and the 'is'? To begin with, the connexion is this: many naturalistic and metaphysical moralists proceed as if ethical conclusions can be deduced from premises all of which are non-ethical, the classical examples being Mill and Spencer. That is, they violate (1). This procedure has lately been referred to as the 'factualist fallacy' by Wheelwright and as the 'valuational fallacy' by Wood.[13] Moore sometimes seems to identify it with the naturalistic fallacy, but in the main he holds only that it involves, implies, or rests upon this fallacy.[14] We may now consider the charge that the procedure in question is or involves a fallacy.

It may be noted at once that, even if the deduction of ethical conclusions from non-ethical premises is in no way a fallacy, Mill certainly did commit a fallacy in drawing an analogy between visibility and desirability in his argument for hedonism; and perhaps his committing *this* fallacy, which, as Broad has said, we all learn about at our mothers' knees, is chiefly responsible for the notion of a naturalistic *fallacy*. But is it a fallacy to deduce ethical conclusions from non-ethical premises? Consider the Epicurean argument for hedonism which Mill so unwisely sought to embellish: pleasure is good, since it is sought by all men. Here an ethical conclusion is being derived from a non-ethical premise. And, indeed, the argument, taken strictly as it stands, *is* fallacious. But it is not fallacious because an *ethical* term occurs in the conclusion which does not occur in the premise. It is fallacious because any argument of the form 'A is B, therefore A is C' is invalid, if taken strictly as it stands. For example, it is invalid to argue that Croesus is rich because he is wealthy. Such arguments are, however, not intended to be taken strictly as they stand. They are enthymemes and contain a suppressed premise. And, when this suppressed premise is made explicit, they are valid and involve no logical fallacy.[15] Thus the Epicurean inference from psychological to ethical hedonism is valid when the suppressed premise is added to the effect that what is sought by all men is good. Then the only question left is whether the premises are true.

It is clear, then, that the naturalistic fallacy is not a logical fallacy, since it may be involved even when the argument is valid. How does the naturalistic fallacy enter such 'mixed ethical arguments'[16] as that of the Epicureans? Whether it does or not depends on the nature of the suppressed premise. This may be either an induction, an intuition, a deduction from a 'pure ethical argument', a definition, or a proposition which is true by definition. If it is one of the first three, then the naturalistic fallacy does not enter at all. In fact, the argument does not then involve violating (1), since one of its premises will be ethical. But if the premise to be supplied is a definition or a proposition which is true by definition, as it probably was for the Epicureans, then the argument, while still valid, involves the naturalistic fallacy, and will run as follows:

(a) Pleasure is sought by all men.
(b) What is sought by all men is good (by definition).
(c) Therefore, pleasure is good.

Now I am not greatly interested in deciding whether the argument as here set up violates (1). If it does not, then no 'mixed ethical argument' actually commits any factualist or valuational fallacy, except when it is unfairly taken as complete in its enthymematic form. If it does, then a valid argument may involve the deduction of an

50

ethical conclusion from non-ethical premises and the factualist or valuational fallacy is not really a fallacy. The question depends on whether or not (b) and (c) are to be regarded as ethical propositions. Moore refuses so to regard them, contending that, by hypothesis, (b) is analytic or tautologous, and that (a) is psychological, since it really says only that pleasure is sought by all men.[17] But to say that (b) is analytic and not ethical and that (a) is not ethical but psychological is to prejudge the question whether 'good' can be defined; for the Epicureans would contend precisely that if their definition is correct then (b) is ethical but analytic and (a) ethical though psychological. Thus, unless the question of the definability of goodness is to be begged, (b) and (a) must be regarded as ethical, in which case our argument does not violate (1). However, suppose, if it be not nonsense, that (b) is non-ethical and (c) ethical, then the argument will violate (1), but it will still obey all of the canons of logic, and it is only confusing to talk of a 'valuational logic' whose basic rule is that an evaluative conclusion cannot be deduced from non-evaluative premises.[18]

For the only way in which either the intuitionists or postulationists like Wood can cast doubt upon the conclusion of the argument of the Epicureans (or upon the conclusion of any parallel argument) is to attack the premises, in particular (b). Now, according to Moore, it is due to the presence of (b) that the argument involves the naturalistic fallacy. (b) involves the identification of goodness with 'being sought by all men', and to make this or any other such identification is to commit the naturalistic fallacy. The naturalistic fallacy is not the procedure of violating (1). It is the procedure, implied in many mixed ethical arguments and explicitly carried out apart from such arguments by many moralists, of defining such characteristics as goodness or of substituting some other characteristic for them. To quote some passages from *Principia Ethica*:

(a) '...far too many philosophers have thought that when they named those other properties [belonging to all things which are good] they were actually defining good; that these properties, in fact, were simply not "other", but absolutely and entirely the same with goodness. This view I propose to call the "naturalistic fallacy"....'[19]
(b) 'I have thus appropriated the name Naturalism to a particular method of approaching Ethics....This method consists in substituting for "good" some one property of a natural object or of a collection of natural objects....'[20]
(c) '...the naturalistic fallacy [is] the fallacy which consists in identifying the simple notion which we mean by "good" with some other notion.'[21]

Thus, to identify 'better' and 'more evolved', 'good' and 'desired', etc., is to commit the naturalistic fallacy.[22] But just why is such a procedure fallacious or erroneous? And is it a fallacy only when applied to good? We must now study § 12 of *Principia Ethica*. Here Moore makes some interesting statements:

51

... if anybody tried to define pleasure for us as being any other natural object; if anybody were to say, for instance, that pleasure *means* the sensation of red....Well, that would be the same fallacy which I have called the naturalistic fallacy.... I should not indeed call that a naturalistic fallacy, although it is the same fallacy as I have called naturalistic with reference to Ethics....When a man confuses two natural objects with one another, defining the one by the other ... then there is no reason to call the fallacy naturalistic. But if he confuses 'good', which is not ... a natural object, with any natural object whatever, then there is a reason for calling that a naturalistic fallacy....[23]

Here Moore should have added that, when one confuses 'good', which is not a metaphysical object or quality, with any metaphysical object or quality, as metaphysical moralists do, according to him, then the fallacy should be called the metaphysical fallacy. Instead he calls it a naturalistic fallacy in this case too, though he recognises that the case is different since metaphysical properties are non-natural[24] – a procedure which has misled many readers of *Principia Ethica*. For example, it has led Broad to speak of 'theological naturalism'.[25]

To resume: 'Even if [goodness] were a natural object, that would not alter the nature of the fallacy nor diminish its importance one whit.'[26]

From these passages it is clear that the fallaciousness of the procedure which Moore calls the naturalistic fallacy is not due to the fact that it is applied to good or to an ethical or non-natural characteristic. When R. B. Perry defines good 'as being an object of interest' the trouble is not merely that he is defining *good*. Nor is the trouble that he is defining an *ethical* characteristic in terms of *non-ethical* ones. Nor is the trouble that he is regarding a *non-natural* characteristic as a *natural* one. The trouble is more generic than that. For clarity's sake I shall speak of the definist fallacy as the generic fallacy which underlies the naturalistic fallacy. The naturalistic fallacy will then, by the above passages, be a species or form of the definist fallacy, as would the metaphysical fallacy if Moore had given that a separate name.[27] That is, the naturalistic fallacy, as illustrated by Perry's procedure, is a fallacy, not because it is naturalistic or confuses a non-natural quality with a natural one, but solely because it involves the definist fallacy. We may, then, confine our attention entirely to an understanding and evaluation of the definist fallacy.

To judge by the passages I have just quoted, the definist fallacy is the process of confusing or identifying two properties, of defining one property by another, or of substituting one property for another. Furthermore, the fallacy is always simply that two properties are being treated as one, and it is irrelevant, if it be the case, that one of them is natural or non-ethical and the other non-natural or ethical. One may commit the definist fallacy without infringing on the bifurcation of the ethical and the non-ethical, as when one identifies pleasantness and redness or rightness and goodness. But even when one infringes on that bifurcation in committing the definist fallacy, as when one identifies goodness and pleasantness or goodness and satisfaction, then the *mistake* is still not that the bifurcation is being infringed on, but only that two properties are being treated as one. Hence, on the present interpretation, the definist *fallacy* does not, in any of its forms, consist in violating (3), and has no essential connexion with the bifurcation of the 'ought' and the 'is'.

This formulation of the definist fallacy explains or reflects the motto of *Principia Ethica*, borrowed from Bishop Butler: 'Everything is what it is, and not another thing'. It follows from this motto that goodness is what it is and not another thing. It follows that views which try to identify it with something else are making a mistake of an elementary sort. For it *is* a mistake to confuse or identify two properties. If the properties really are two, then they simply are not identical. But do those who define ethical notions in non-ethical terms make this mistake? They will reply to Moore that they are not identifying two properties; what they are saying is that two words or sets of words stand for or mean one and the same property. Moore was being, in part, misled by the material mode of speech, as Carnap calls it, in such sentences as 'Goodness is pleasantness', 'Knowledge is true belief', etc. When one says instead, 'The word "good" and the word "pleasant" mean the same thing', etc., it is clear that one is not identifying two things. But Moore kept himself from seeing this by his disclaimer that he was interested in any statement about the use of words.[28]

The definist fallacy, then, as we have stated it, does not rule out any naturalistic or metaphysical definitions of ethical terms. Goodness is not identifiable with any 'other' characteristic (if it is a characteristic at all). But the question is: *which* characteristics are other than goodness, which names stand for characteristics other than goodness? And it is begging the question of the definability of goodness to say out of hand that Perry, for instance, is identifying goodness with something else. The point is that goodness is what it is, even if it is definable. That is why Perry can take as the motto of his naturalistic *Moral Economy* another sentence from Bishop Butler: 'Things and actions are what they are, and the consequences of them will be what they will be; why then should we desire to be deceived?' The motto of *Principia Ethica* is a tautology, and should be expanded as follows: Everything is what it is, and not another thing, unless it is another thing, and even then it is what it is.

On the other hand, if Moore's motto (or the definist fallacy) rules out any definitions, for example of 'good', then it rules out all definitions of any term whatever. To be effective at all, it must be understood to mean, 'Every term means what it means, and not what is meant by any other term'. Moore seems implicitly to understand his motto in this way in § 13, for he proceeds as if 'good' has no meaning, if it has no unique meaning. If the motto be taken in this way, it will follow that 'good' is an indefinable term, since no synonyms can be found. But it will also follow that no term is definable. And then the method of analysis is as useless as an English butcher in a world without sheep.

Perhaps we have misinterpreted the definist fallacy. And, indeed, some of the passages which I quoted earlier in this paper seem to imply that the definist fallacy is just the error of defining an indefinable characteristic. On this interpretation, again, the definist fallacy has, in all of its forms, no essential connexion with the bifurcation of the ethical and the non-ethical. Again, one may commit the definist fallacy without violating that bifurcation, as when one defines pleasantness in terms of redness or goodness in terms of rightness (granted Moore's belief that pleasantness and goodness are indefinable). But even when one infringes on that bifurcation and defines goodness in terms of desire, the *mistake* is not that one is infringing on the bifurcation by violating (3), but only that one is defining an indefinable characteristic. This is possible because the proposition that goodness is indefinable is logically independent of the proposition that goodness is non-natural: as is shown by the fact that a characteristic may be indefinable and yet natural, as yellowness is; or non-natural and yet definable, as rightness is (granted Moore's views about yellowness and rightness).

Consider the definist fallacy as we have just stated it. It is, of course, an error to define an indefinable quality. But the question, again, is: which qualities are indefinable? It is begging the question in favour of intuitionism to say in advance that the quality goodness is indefinable and that, therefore, all naturalists commit the definist fallacy. One must know that goodness is indefinable before one can argue that the definist fallacy *is* a fallacy. Then, however, the definist fallacy can enter only at the end of the controversy between intuitionism and definism, and cannot be used as a weapon in the controversy.

The definist fallacy may be stated in such a way as to involve the bifurcation between the 'ought' and the 'is'.[29] It would then be committed by anyone who offered a definition of any ethical characteristic in terms of non-ethical ones. The trouble with such a definition, on this interpretation, would be that an *ethical* characteristic is being reduced to a *non-ethical* one, a *non-natural* one to a *natural* one. That is, the definition would be ruled out by the fact that the characteristic being defined is ethical or non-natural and therefore cannot be defined in non-ethical or natural terms. But on this interpretation, too, there is danger of a *petitio* in the intuitionist argumentation. To assume that the ethical characteristic is exclusively ethical is to beg precisely the question which is at issue when the definition is offered. Thus, again, one must know that the characteristic is non-natural and indefinable in natural terms before one can say that the definists are making a mistake.

Moore, McTaggart, and others formulate the naturalistic fallacy sometimes in a way somewhat different from any of those yet discussed. They say that the definists are confusing a universal synthetic proposition about *the good* with a definition of *goodness*.[30] Abraham calls this the 'fallacy of misconstrued proposition'.[31] Here again the difficulty is that, while it is true that it is an error to construe a universal synthetic proposition as a definition, it is a *petitio* for the intuitionists to say that what the definist is taking for a definition is really a universal synthetic proposition.[32]

At last, however, the issue between the intuitionists and the definists (naturalistic or metaphysical) is becoming clearer. The definists are all holding that certain propositions involving ethical terms are analytic, tautologous, or true by definition, e.g., Perry so regards the statement, 'All objects of desire are good'. The intuitionists hold that such statements are synthetic. What underlies this difference of opinion is that the intuitionists claim to have at least a dim awareness of a simple unique quality or relation of goodness or rightness which appears in the region which our ethical terms roughly indicate, whereas the definists claim to have no awareness of any such quality or relation in that region, which is different from all other qualities and relations which belong to the same context but are designated by words other than 'good' and 'right' and their obvious synonyms.[33] The definists are in all honesty claiming to find but one characteristic where the intuitionists claim to find two, as Perry claims to find only the property of being desired where Moore claims to find both it and the property of being good. The issue, then, is one of inspection or intuition, and concerns the awareness or discernment of qualities and relations.[34] That is why it cannot be decided by the use of the notion of a fallacy.

If the definists may be taken at their word, then they are not actually confusing two characteristics with each other, nor defining an indefinable characteristic, nor confusing definitions and universal synthetic propositions – in short they are not committing the naturalistic or definist fallacy in any of the interpretations given above. Then the only fallacy which they commit – the real naturalistic or definist fallacy – is the failure to descry the qualities and relations which are central to morality. But this is neither a logical fallacy nor a logical confusion. It is not even, properly speaking, an error. It is rather a kind of blindness, analogous to colour-blindness. Even this moral blindness can be ascribed to the definists only if they are correct in their claim to have no awareness of any unique ethical characteristics and if the intuitionists are correct in affirming the existence of such characteristics, but certainly to call it a 'fallacy', even in a loose sense, is both unamiable and profitless.

On the other hand, of course, if there are no such characteristics in the objects to which we attach ethical predicates, then the intuitionists, if we may take them at their word, are suffering from a corresponding moral hallucination. Definists might then call this the intuitionistic or moralistic fallacy, except that it is no more a 'fallacy' than is the blindness just described. Anyway, they do not believe the claim of the intuitionists to be aware of unique ethical characteristics, and consequently do not attribute to them this hallucination. Instead, they simply deny that the intuitionists really do find such unique qualities or relations, and then they try to find some plausible way of accounting for the fact that very respectable and trustworthy people think they find them.[35] Thus they charge the intuitionists with verbalism, hypostatisation, and the like. But this half of the story does not concern us now.

What concerns us more is the fact that the intuitionists do not credit the claim of the definists either. They would be much disturbed, if they really thought that their opponents were morally blind, for they do not hold that we must be regenerated by grace before we can have moral insight, and they share the common feeling that morality is something democratic even though not all men are good. Thus they hold that 'we are all aware' of certain unique characteristics when we use the terms 'good', 'right', etc., only due to a lack of analytic clearness of mind, abetted perhaps by a philosophical prejudice, we may not be aware at all that they are different from other characteristics of which we are also aware.[36] Now, I have been arguing that the intuitionists cannot charge the definists with committing any fallacy unless and until they have shown that we are all, the definists included, aware of the disputed unique characteristics. If, however, they were to show this, then, at least at the end of the controversy, they could accuse the definists of the error of confusing two characteristics, or of the error of defining an indefinable one, and these errors might, since the term is somewhat loose in its habits, be called 'fallacies', though they are not logical fallacies in the sense in which an invalid argument is. The fallacy of misconstrued proposition depends on the error of confusing two characteristics, and hence could also on our present supposition, be ascribed to the definists, but it is not really a *logical* confusion,[37] since it does not actually involve being confused about the difference between a proposition and a definition.

Only it is difficult to see how the intuitionists can prove that the definists are at least vaguely aware of the requisite unique characteristics.[38] The question must surely be left to the inspection or intuition of the definists themselves, aided by whatever suggestions the intuitionists may have to make. If so, we must credit the verdict of their inspection, especially of those among them who have read the writings of the intuitionists reflectively, and, then, as we have seen, the most they can be charged with is moral blindness.

Besides trying to discover just what is meant by the naturalistic fallacy, I have tried to show that the notion that a logical or quasi-logical fallacy is committed by the definists only confuses the issue between the intuitionists and the definists (and the issue between the latter and the emotists or postulationists), and misrepresents the way in which the issue is to be settled. No logical fallacy need appear anywhere in the procedure of the definists. Even fallacies in any less accurate sense cannot be implemented to decide the case against the definists; at best they can be ascribed to the definists only after the issue has been decided against them on independent grounds. But the only defect which can be attributed to the definists, *if* the intuitionists are right in affirming the existence of unique indefinable ethical characteristics, is a peculiar moral blindness, which is not a fallacy even in the looser sense. The issue in question must be decided by whatever method we may find satisfactory for determining whether or not a word stands for a characteristic at all, and, if it does, whether or not it stands for a unique characteristic. What method is to be employed is, perhaps, in one form or another, the basic problem of contemporary philosophy, but no generally satisfactory solution of the problem has yet been reached. I shall venture to say only this: it does seem to me that the issue is not to be decided against the intuitionists by the application *ab extra* to ethical judgments of any empirical or ontological meaning dictum.[39]

NOTES

1 A. E. Taylor, *The Faith of a Moralist*, vol. I, p. 104n.
2 *Value and Ethical Objectivity*, p. 58.
3 *Principia Ethica*, pp. 38, 64.
4 E. Clarke, 'Cognition and Affection in the Experience of Value', *Journal of Philosophy*, 1938.
5 *Principia Ethica*, pp. 73, 77. See also p. xix.
6 'Ethics as Pure Postulate', *Philosophical Review*, 1933. See also T. Whittaker, *The Theory of Abstract Ethics*, pp. 19f.
7 Book III, part ii, § i.
8 See J. Laird, *A Study in Moral Theory*, pp. 16f.; Whittaker, op. cit., p. 19.
9 See C. D. Broad, *Five Types of Ethical Theory*, ch. iv.
10 *A Study in Moral Theory*, p. 94n.
11 See *Philosophical Studies*, pp. 259, 273f.
12 See J. Laird, op. cit., p. 318. Also pp. 12ff.
13 P. E. Wheelwright, *A Critical Introduction to Ethics*, pp. 40–51, 91f.; L. Wood, 'Cognition and Moral Value', *Journal of Philosophy*, 1937, p. 237.
14 See *Principia Ethica*, pp. 114, 57, 43, 49. Whittaker identifies it with the naturalistic fallacy and regards it as a 'logical' fallacy, op. cit., pp. 19f.
15 See ibid., pp. 50, 139; Wheelwright, loc. cit.
16 See C. D. Broad, *The Mind and its Place in Nature*, pp. 488f.; Laird, loc. cit.
17 See op. cit., pp. 11f.; 19, 38, 73, 139.
18 See L. Wood, loc. cit.
19 p. 10 (p. 38, this volume).
20 p. 40.
21 p. 58, cf. pp. xiii, 73.
22 Cf. pp. 49, 53, 108, 139.
23 p. 13 (p. 40, this volume).
24 See pp. 38–40, 110–12.
25 *Five Types of Ethical Theory*, p. 259.
26 p. 14 (p. 41, this volume).
27 As Whittaker has, loc. cit.
28 See op. cit., pp. 6, 8, 12 (p. 33, 35, 39, this volume).
29 See J. Wisdom, MIND, 1931, p. 213, n 1.
30 See *Principia Ethica*, pp. 10, 16, 38 (p. 37, 42–3, this volume); *The Nature of Existence*, vol. ii, p. 398.
31 Leo Abraham, 'The Logic of Intuitionism', *International Journal of Ethics*, 1933.

32 As Abraham points out, loc. cit.
33 See R. B. Perry, *General Theory of Value*, p. 30; cf. *Journal of Philosophy*, 1931, p. 620.
34 See H. Osborne, *Foundations of the Philosophy of Value*, pp. 15, 19, 70.
35 Cf. R. B. Perry, *Journal of Philosophy*, 1931, pp. 520ff.
36 *Principia Ethica*, pp. 17, 38, 59, 61 (p. 43, this volume).
37 But see H. Osborne, op. cit., pp. 18f.
38 For a brief discussion of their arguments, see ibid., p. 67; L. Abraham, op. cit. I think they are all inconclusive, but cannot show this here.
39 See *Principia Ethica*, pp. 124f., 140.

4

THE OPEN QUESTION AS A LINGUISTIC TEST

Frank Snare

Roger Hancock in a lucid paper called 'The Refutation of Naturalism in Moore and Hare' argues that a certain interpretation of Moore's open question argument against naturalism does not work because it tacitly assumes the falsehood of naturalism at the crucial point.[1] Although I do agree that some who have used this argument have been reasoning in circles, I want to argue that there is, nevertheless, an interpretation of the open question which saves this argument from circularity. This involves treating the open question as a kind of linguistic test and, although it is perhaps not what Moore had in mind, it seems to do justice to how many contemporary meta-ethicists do in fact use the open question. I also hope to shed light on the nature of the mistake involved in the 'naturalistic' or 'definist' fallacy and to suggest that from the mere elucidation of what this mistake is, we cannot deduce that any particular kind of meta-ethical theory (e.g. 'naturalistic') has committed this error; this can only be decided by the application of certain linguistic tests such as, for example, the open question test provides.

Hancock paraphrases Moore's open question argument against naturalism in the form of the following reductio:

1 If naturalism is true, then some sentence of the form 'Whatever is F is good' is analytic, where 'F' is replaceable by a non-ethical expression.
2 If ethical sentences of the form 'Whatever is F is good' are analytic then we cannot significantly ask 'Are F's good?'
3 But we can always significantly ask 'Are F's good?'
4 Therefore no sentence of the form 'Whatever is F is good' is analytic, and hence naturalism is false.[2]

Now it should be clear that this argument can't possibly be construed as a successful argument against every claim that can be put in the form: 'Whatever is F is good.' The argument can at most be successful in showing that for certain substitutions for 'F' or for certain kinds of substitutions for 'F' 'Whatever is F is good' is not analytic. Clearly it is the case that for some substitutions 'Whatever is F is good' *is* analytic. A trivial example would be the case where we substituted 'good' for 'F'. Or suppose we concocted an artificial constant symbol 'F_0' which we understood to stand for that simple, indefinable, non-natural property which Moore discusses in *Principia Ethica*. Moore argued it was 'indefinable' but this doesn't imply that it couldn't have a name. So of course Moore himself would have to say that the sentence 'Whatever is F_0 is good' is analytic. Now those who have used the open question argument have been aware of this need for some restriction on 'F' and have spoken of 'natural property' expressions or of 'descriptive predicate' expressions. But this leaves us with the further problem of furnishing an independent criterion of what, for example a 'natural property' is. I say 'independent' because to suppose that part of what makes an 'F' a natural property term is that its substitution in 'Whatever is F is good' would not make the latter analytic is to trivialize argument 1–4. Hancock sidesteps this issue in his formulation of the open question argument by restricting 'F' – in (1) – to 'non-ethical' expressions. This, however, might allow every conceivable view to get by the test since the 'naturalist', for example, could always argue that the substitution he was proposing for 'F' was an 'ethical' (even if also a 'naturalistic') expression in virtue of its alleged analytic connection with 'good' so that (1) would simply be denied and the argument would get no further.

However it is not really Hancock's problem to provide an independent criterion for the difference between 'naturalistic' and other kinds of theories. That problem belongs to the user of the open question argument, not to the critic of this argument. Fortunately we can completely ignore this problem, because Hancock's criticism of the argument 1–4 is at a much more basic level. We must distinguish two issues which come to be combined in argument 1–4. First, there is the issue of just who is and who is not making false claims of analyticity. But secondly, there is the issue, forgetting for the moment just who does and who doesn't make the mistake, whether the open question test is capable even in theory of exposing such a mistake. We will keep this distinction more clearly in mind if we just take a particular example of a proposed substitution for 'F': 'F_1' and not worry about whether it is 'naturalistic' or not, or 'non-ethical' or not. We shall further assume, for the sake of argument, that 'Whatever is F_1 is good' is *not* analytic. Hancock's contention is that the open question test is incapable, in theory, of exposing this mistake whoever it is that is making it. The reader might imagine 'F_1' to be the expression 'pleasant', since this is an example which both Moore and Hancock discuss and it does seem likely that 'Whatever is pleasant is good' is not analytic. But nothing would rest on that example and Hancock's point would be just as sound even if it were analytic since he is not making claims about what is or is not analytic but about the effectiveness of the open question test. Thus we might apply Hancock's interpretation of the open question argument to the particular example as follows:

1   'Whatever is F_1 is good' is analytic.
2   If the sentence 'Whatever is F_1 is good' is analytic, we cannot significantly ask 'Are F_1's good?'
3   But we can significantly ask 'Are F_1's good?'
4   Therefore (1) is false.

Hancock's criticism of the open question argument centres around what it is to 'significantly ask'. He rules out several trivial interpretations such as the one that a significant question is one which it is important for one to ask. He finally goes on to consider the possibility that to say we can significantly ask 'Are F_1's good?' is just to say that it is never contradictory to deny the sentence 'Whatever is F_1 is good.' But this is just another way of saying that 'Whatever is F_1 is good' is not analytic. Thus in affirming (3) we are assuming the falsehood of (1) and thus it is no surprise we get the conclusion in (4). But of course anyone who did hold (1) would deny we can significantly ask the question in (3) so the argument does not work. It begs the question. Hancock says:

> The hedonist, for example, will surely have no trouble with Moore's argument; having defined 'good' as 'pleasant' and holding that 'Whatever is pleasant is good' is analytic, he will simply reply that in point of fact it is self-contradictory to say that something is pleasant and yet not good. Moore would have no answer; at the very most his argument only pushes the dispute back a step, without doing anything to settle it.[3]

Now I think it's possible to extend Hancock's argument in certain respects to make it an argument against the possibility of any non-circular use of the open question argument in meta-ethics. One might argue that when a meta-ethicist uses the open question argument against his opponents he is, and can only be, proceeding in the following, circular fashion: First he accepts some account of the meaning of ethical terms and then he concludes that a certain set of questions are 'closed' and a certain set 'open' meaning that certain answers either are or are not necessarily wrong just in virtue of the meanings of the words – as he is determined to understand them. Then when such a meta-ethicist runs into an alternative theory he discounts it by pointing out how it 'closes' certain questions which are 'open' or else leaves 'open' certain questions which are 'closed'. But of course whether the question is 'open' or 'closed' will depend on one's meta-ethics to start with. For example, a non-cognitivist will conclude, given his theory of the meanings of ethical terms, that the sentence 'All pleasant things are good' is not true just in virtue of the meanings of the words and furthermore a negative reply to the question 'Are all pleasant things good?', whatever else it may be, is not even prima facie evidence that the person responding doesn't understand the meanings of the terms. Given this conclusion he will go on to exclude the meta-ethical theory of the naturalist who says that 'good' means 'pleasant' by pointing out that such a theory would have the conclusion that the sentence 'All pleasant things are good' would be true just in virtue of the meanings of the words and furthermore a negative reply to the question 'Are all pleasant things good?' would tend to indicate the person replying was confused about meanings. In short our non-cognitivist accuses the naturalist of 'closing' questions which are 'open'. But in fact he seems to be accusing the naturalist of little more than not being a non-cognitivist which is, we should think, something the naturalist can bear.

Now I do agree that the open question argument has, in some cases, been used in a manner just as circular as the above account. However, I wish to argue that there is such a thing as a mistaken view on the meanings of ethical terms and that there is a use of the open question argument which is sometimes capable of exposing such mistakes. Just which meta-ethical theories would be shown to be mistaken by such a technique is a further question. The question at hand is whether the open question argument is capable even in theory of exposing any such mistake without just begging the issue.

But in order to do this I must first make two points. The first is that meta-ethical theories have to be theories about what we ordinarily mean by ethical terms. I think it sufficient here to remind the reader of one of the reasons why philosophers are interested in meta-ethics to start with. There is a famous problem in ethics concerning whether it is possible to derive ethical judgments from descriptive judgments alone. Can 'good' follow from 'is'? Now some philosophers (certain naturalists) are reputed to answer that it can and does just in virtue of the meaning of the word 'good'. Others (for example, certain non-cognitivists) answer that it doesn't follow and this they know just in virtue of certain things they know about the meanings of words like 'good'. Such theories overtly claim to be true accounts of the ordinary meaning of 'good'. However, in any case, it's hard to see what else a meta-ethical theory would be doing since, if it has nothing to do with the ordinary meanings of terms like 'good', there is no real reason to suppose it is even about *goodness* or *ethics* at all (to put it in plain English). It would appear that it has merely changed the subject to something else which is called by the jargon term 'goodness' but which simply is not – to speak in ordinary English again – goodness. When we wonder whether a judgment about a thing's goodness can ever follow from any set of descriptive statements, we use the word 'good' in its ordinary sense in the very formulation of the problem and a discussion of the meaning the inscription 'good' might have in some jargon language is just irrelevant.

The second point I wish to make is that to know the ordinary meaning of a word like 'good' is not necessarily to know the answer to questions about what that meaning is. Any speaker of English knows what 'good' means but it does not follow that he knows the correct meta-ethical analysis of its ordinary meaning. This may seem paradoxical but it is not if we keep in mind Ryle's famous distinction between 'knowing how' and 'knowing that'. The speaker of English knows how to use the word but it doesn't follow that he knows that certain propositions which mention the word 'good' are true or even that he is aware of any such propositional claims. His knowledge of English need not be a propositional knowledge, it can be a matter of knowing how to use certain words even if he is incapable of explaining in a knowing-that sort of way, what that use is. This is why it is irrelevant to poll people on their views about what 'good' means.

I think this distinction is more plausible if we consider the analogous kind of knowledge which is involved in our knowledge of the rules of grammar of the language we speak. A native speaker of English 'knows' the rules of grammar of his language in a 'knowing-how' sort of way but it doesn't follow that he has any propositional (knowing-that) knowledge of the rules of grammar. Of course it is the latter, by contrast, that the foreigner learning the language acquires. But he is learning something quite explicit which the native speaker may not have encountered or be aware of. Indeed, when the native speaker encounters the rules of grammar for the first time in propositional form (I am assuming a grammar which seeks to describe his actual speech patterns rather than prescribe it), he is in a certain way acquiring a kind of knowledge he didn't have before even if these rules were in an implicit way something he already knew. Indeed, did we not distinguish these two ways in which one may be said to 'know' the grammar of his language, the whole project of descriptive grammar would seem paradoxical. For on one hand, if descriptive grammar merely seeks to describe the grammar I use, it will if successful only tell me things I already know; on the other hand, if it does tell me something I don't already know, it can't be a correct description of what I already know. Thus it would seem descriptive grammar must of necessity either be uninformative or false. But this paradox does not arise once we distinguish the implicit (knowing-how) knowledge of grammar any speaker of the language has from the explicit (knowing-that) knowledge the student of grammar acquires.

Notice that, although we can't discover the rules of grammar for a language by polling all the speakers for their views since they need not be explicitly aware of the rules they in fact operate on, theories of grammar, nevertheless, can be tested against the way people actually speak. Thus a theory of English grammar which had us saying things like 'There is three horses' or 'I have winning the game' just wouldn't be a correct description of our grammar. Now at this point a certain sophist might object that I am begging the question. If the proposed theory of grammar is correct then the above sentences are grammatical English sentences and by rejecting them I have merely assumed a different theory of English grammar. But the apt reply at this point is that I know the above sentences are not the way I speak, not because I have derived it from some propositions I already accept about the correct rules of English grammar, but because I know English and I just know that isn't the way I speak. Indeed I could have told you that even before I learned formal grammar. It might not be too misleading to call it a 'grammatical intuition', as long as it is seen that this is not a matter of having some mysterious faculty but merely a matter of having a practical knowledge which is not a propositional knowledge of the descriptive rules of grammar. It is against such 'grammatical intuitions' that any theory of English grammar is tested. It is not a matter of first having knowing-that theories about English grammar and deriving the result that the above sentences either are or are not grammatical; rather, it is the case that we first have the grammatical intuitions that such sentences are not in accord with the way we speak and any theory of the rules of English grammar must do justice to these brute intuitions.

Likewise, it seems to me that theories about the meanings of words must be tested by the ways we actually use the words in question, not by any preconceived theories about what the words must mean. Thus the question of what I mean by 'good' is not a question about what propositions I hold to be true about the meaning of 'good' for I may hold none or those I hold may be false theories, due to the pernicious influence of philosophy, of what I myself mean (just as I might have no views or mistaken views about the grammar I in fact implicitly use in speaking). Rather, seeing what I already mean by 'good' is a matter of proposing various theories to see how far they are consistent with how I use the word in actual discourse. And the only way I see of disproving a possible theory as to what I mean is to show that it would have me speaking in ways I do not; it is to appeal ultimately to my 'linguistic intuitions'. Thus if someone proposes the theory that by 'good' we mean 'pleasant', we can note that this would have the implication that the question 'Are all pleasant things good?' would be 'closed' in the sense that a serious negative reply would tend to be indicative that such a person wouldn't be understanding the expressions in the question at all in the ordinary way. Such a reply, it would be alleged, would be 'linguistically odd' analogous to the way in which 'There is three horses' is 'grammatically odd'. (Notice that the alleged 'oddness' here would be of a linguistic nature. It would not be the claim that a negative reply would be psychologically peculiar or unexpected, nor would it merely be the claim that a negative reply would be close to fantastic since the answer is so obviously 'Yes!' The claim has to be that such a reply would, in the straightforward case, show one to be deficient in the understanding of the language.) Now at this point I would want to say that such a negative response, contrary to the proposed theory, is *not* in any way linguistically odd even if it might be peculiar in other respects and I know this, not because I have already accepted some other meta-ethical theory from which this is a derived result, but simply and purely because I know English and that just isn't the way I speak. Indeed I could have told you that much without any meta-ethical theory at all. In much the same way I'm able to tell you that 'There are three horses' is not contrary to the grammar I use even if I couldn't tell you what the rules of that grammar are.

The point of the open question test, then, is to apply abstract theories about the meanings and meaning relations of words to concrete situations where, it is hoped, they can be tested against our natural feel for the language. If one didn't already know (in the knowing-how sort of way) the meaning of 'good', the open question test and indeed any linguistic test would be ineffectual. Now Hancock is surely right if his point is that sometimes philosophers have concluded that a certain question was 'open' or 'closed' not on the basis of their feel for the meanings of the words but as a direct result of their presupposed meta-ethical theories. That would make their arguments circular and they would refute no one. On the other hand, I have argued that, if the open question argument is construed as based on a linguistic test where the appeal is not to one's meta-ethical theory but to one's native understanding (knowing-how knowledge) of the language, the argument is not circular.

I don't wish to make any spectacular claims for this linguistic test. I don't think it is the only linguistic test nor do I think that as a linguistic test it is by itself all that conclusive. Nor can we deduce from the mere fact of its possibility as a test just who it refutes; we can only do that by applying the test to specific theories. For this reason I doubt it can be used to eliminate with one grand sweep whole classes of theories (e.g. naturalistic ones); it seems to me we can only proceed case by case. To show that 'good' does not mean 'pleasant' shows nothing about any other 'naturalistic' theory. We must suspect that those who use the open question argument to immediately conclude that all alternative meta-ethical theories are wrong are probably not using it as a linguistic test but, rather, are using it in the question-begging manner criticized by Hancock.

I am also quite aware of the fact that Moore himself did not think of the open question test as involving a linguistic test. However I am inclined to believe that the plausibility the open question argument had for Moore as well as for his readers was in large part due to the fact that it was in effect being used as a linguistic test even if not consciously so.

NOTES

1 *The Journal of Philosophy*, LVII (12 May 1960), 326–34; reprinted in E. D. Klemke (ed.), *Studies in the Philosophy of G. E. Moore* (Chicago, IL: Quadrangle Press, 1969), 44–52.
2 Hancock, op. cit., p. 327.
3 Hancock, op. cit., p. 329.

Part 2

ERROR THEORY AND MORAL REALISM

In § 6 of our Introduction (Chapter 1) we described error theory. Recall that error theorists agree with (typical) realists that ethical language is best understood as discourse that stands as an attempt to describe the world and, hence, describe some supposedly existing moral reality. However, error theorists believe that we are in systematic error because no such ethical reality exists; there are no moral properties. Recall also what this second claim amounts to. It is not simply a claim that, as it happens, every moral judgement is false because, perhaps, we all hold the same view about an issue but are all mistaken. (Perhaps it isn't wrong to murder innocent children at all.) Nor is the claim simply that there are types of moral property that no one has yet noticed as existing in our world. Rather the claim is a conceptual claim about our supposed common-or-garden conception of what moral properties are. The claim is that nothing like what we imagine moral properties to be exists.

Let us also repeat and recast one thought from the end of that § 6. Two things need to hold, amongst others, for an error theory about ethics to be correct. (i) It has to be true that people typically think of themselves as trying to describe moral properties; and (ii) no such properties, at least as people seem to be committed to, exist. There is good reason to think that people do typically think of themselves as trying to describe moral properties. Just think about the grammatical structure of the examples of moral judgements we gave in the Introduction. But there is one question to ask ourselves. Typically, non-philosophers do not worry about whether or not moral properties exist; it simply isn't an issue. So, if they have not thought about this, nor reflected on the grammatical structure of the judgements they typically make, to what extent are they 'committed' to there being moral properties? Are they committed simply in virtue of using a form of words, or can we speak of people having metaphysical commitments only if they have given the issue *some* thought?

This first concern does not tend to hold philosophers up too much. Most are happy to agree that much of our everyday moral thought embodies some level of realist commitment. But why do error theorists believe that there are no moral properties? In the first paper in this Part, John Mackie (Chapter 5) gives two arguments: the argument from relativity and the argument from queerness. The first starts with a claim that seemingly no one should deny: there is moral disagreement. Mackie then points out that, although disagreement occurs in other areas of our lives, for example in science, morality seems essentially to be about certain ways of living. This leads him to suggest that people adhere to certain moral beliefs because this is how they live, rather than people live certain ways only because they have certain beliefs about some supposedly existing properties. He then shows that the debate can become more complicated, but his essential point remains: it is easier to explain variation in moral thinking and activity without recourse to moral properties.

Mackie's second argument is more widely discussed. The main charge is that moral properties are 'queer', a charge we outlined in the Introduction. Mackie objects to the conjoining of two notions: prescriptivity and objectivity. (The conjunction is the key claim of 'moral objectivism', which is a type of moral realism.) There might be various ways of interpreting what Mackie means by objectivity, but we assume here that it is synonymous with mind-independence. We will see in a moment that there is a dispute about what exactly Mackie means by prescriptivity. We can assume, innocently enough in this context, that talk of value properties translates into talk about reasons, demands and prescriptions: if an action is valuable then this value generates a reason in favour of pursuing the action. We can then state Mackie's general worry. To say that there could be values and directives that exist independently of the humans who are the valuing creatures, and for whom the world is full of reasons and are motivated by reasons, seems strange. They would be things 'utterly different from anything else in the universe'. He goes further. We normally think that the moral aspects and properties of the world are linked in some way to the nonmoral, natural features of the world. We say that something is wrong *because* it is a piece of deliberate cruelty. (Mackie here assumes that 'deliberate cruelty' is a natural rather than a moral property. Whether it is or not is relatively unimportant to what he draws our attention to.) But, he thinks, just what in the world is signified by this 'because'? How can supposedly independently existing moral properties be linked to the natural features of the world? Surely the most plausible explanation is that humans interpret the natural world in moral ways. In which case, moral objectivism seems very implausible.

David Brink (Chapter 6) replies to both of Mackie's arguments, although we will confine our comments to the argument from queerness. The key section of Brink's reply to this argument is his § 2. He distinguishes two claims that one could read in Mackie's discussion: motives internalism (which we discussed in our Introduction, § 9, and Part 10, and which is roughly: if one judges that ϕ-ing is right then, necessarily, one will be motivated to ϕ); and reasons internalism (as Brink describes it, roughly: recognition of moral properties necessarily provides one with reason to perform the moral action). Brink then develops an argument for moral realism (moral objectivism) by showing that realists need not believe either claim and links that to a discussion of Mackie's worry about 'because' by trying to find partners in innocence. After all, plants photosynthesize because they are chemically and physically constituted in certain ways, and there's no worry there. Why not say that something is wrong because it is a certain natural way?

Brink is correct that Mackie's presentation is ambiguous. However, Richard T. Garner in Chapter 7 argues against Brink. There is a further doctrine that Brink does not examine that realists are committed to and which does seem queer. Independently of whether judges note that certain moral values and reasons exist, and whether they are motivated to act, a realist is committed to the bare fact that such things exist; there are directives out there, whether or not we know anything about them. And, isn't it queer to think that certain courses of action could have labels (metaphorically) attached to them that read 'Do me' – à la *Alice in Wonderland* – where the existence of such directives has nothing whatsoever to do with anything human? Isn't *that* odd enough? Garner goes on to wonder whether Brink's discussion of the 'because' worry is enough to answer the kernel of Mackie's complaint.

We leave readers to make up their own minds about how best to read Mackie. Aside from this debate, is the argument from queerness convincing in Garner's presentation of it? It is clear that on this reading we are left with things that are metaphysically unique. But why label them *queer*? They might seem queer in comparison to tables and people, unemployment and photosynthesis. But this can only be because they are queer in comparison to what we accept as normal. It seems as if the standard of normality being employed is that of natural science. But why privilege that? Indeed, on certain views of the natural sciences, people and their intentions are queer, or at least don't exist. And physics seems to throw up queer sorts of entity all the time. Why worry so much about reasons and values that exist independently of anything human?

Aside from this debate, one issue remains. What positive picture do error theorists give of our moral outlooks? Are they going to dabble in nihilist rhetoric and, as well as saying we are in error, accuse people of living a lie and perpetuating a corrupt and dangerous way of thinking? Perhaps not. Error theorists might explore the idea that, although there are no moral properties to speak of, the moral rules and values we typically speak of are used by us as a convenient fiction to help regulate our lives and the lives of others. (Mackie devotes much of the rest of his *Ethics* to doing this. One of the best recent explorations of this idea is Richard Joyce's book *The Myth of Morality* (2001) (see also, Joyce (2005) in Further Reading), which discusses 'moral fictionalism'. Moral fictionalism is also discussed by Kalderon, and Nolan *et al*. See Further Reading below.) There is a worry with this strategy though. In trying to explain how our moral activity and thought can be something other than corrupt and dangerous, and in trying to make the case for thinking and acting as we normally do, one runs the risk of constructing moral thought in a way which does not seem that different from how we ordinarily think it to be. In which case, is there so much of an error anymore? (See the pieces by Miller (1998) and Wright (1992, 1996) on this subject in Further Reading.)

QUESTIONS TO CONSIDER

1   Do people disagree morally? How wide is such disagreement? What is the link between there being disagreement and moral relativism, the claim (roughly) that there are no objective rights and wrongs? If there are just a few groups in our world that tolerate killing, say, does this mean we can assume that they are wrong rather than merely different?

2   What does Mackie (Chapter 5) mean by saying that typical moral thought is queer?

3   Are the editors of this volume right to think that what Mackie means by 'objectivism' is what they have referred to as 'mind-independence'?

4   Do you think that Garner's (Chapter 7) interpretation of Mackie's argument captures the

kernel of the problem for moral objectivism? Does this automatically mean that what Brink (Chapter 6) says misses the point or is there something worthwhile in his arguments against Mackie?

5   What does Garner say about Brink's 'partners in innocence' strategy?

6   To what extent should error theorists be worried about the problem, mentioned at the end of our introduction to this Part, regarding the reconstruction of moral thought into something that is no longer that erroneous?

7   Overall, what advantages does error theory hold over its rivals?

FURTHER READING

Black, Robert (1990) 'Moral Scepticism and Inductive Scepticism', *Proceedings of the Aristotelian Society*, vol. 90, pp. 65–82.

Blackburn, Simon (1985) 'Errors and the Phenomenology of Value', in Ted Honderich (ed.) *Ethics and Objectivity* (London: Routledge & Kegan Paul), pp. 1–22 (and also in Blackburn, Simon (1993) *Essays in Quasi-Realism* (Oxford: Oxford University Press), pp. 149–65).

Burgess, J. A. (1998) 'Error Theories and Values', *Australasian Journal of Philosophy*, vol. 76, pp. 534–52.

Honderich, Ted (ed.) (1985) *Ethics and Objectivity* (London: Routledge & Kegan Paul).

Joyce, Richard (2001) *The Myth of Morality* (Cambridge: Cambridge University Press).

——(2005) 'Moral Fictionalism', in Mark Kalderon (ed.) *Fictionalism in Metaphysics* (Oxford: Oxford University Press), pp. 287–313.

Kalderon, Mark (2005) *Moral Fictionalism* (Oxford: Oxford University Press).

Lillehammer, Hallvard (2004) 'Moral Error Theory', *Proceedings of the Aristotelian Society*, vol. 104, pp. 95–111.

Miller, Alexander (1998) 'Emotivism and the Verification Principle', *Proceedings of the Aristotelian Society*, vol. 98, pp. 103–24.

——(2002) 'Wright's Arguments Against Error-theories', *Analysis*, vol. 62, pp. 98–103.

——(2003) *An Introduction to Contemporary Metaethics* (Cambridge: Polity Press), chapter 6.

Nolan, Daniel, Restall, Greg and West, Caroline (2005) 'Moral Fictionalism versus the Rest', *Australasian Journal of Philosophy*, vol. 83, no. 3, pp. 307–30.

Smith, Michael (1993) 'Objectivity and Moral Realism: on the Significance of the Phenomenology of Moral Experience', in John Haldane and Crispin Wright (eds) *Reality, Representation and Projection* (Oxford: Oxford University Press), pp. 235–55.

Wright, Crispin (1992) *Truth and Objectivity* (Cambridge, MA: Harvard University Press), chapter 1.

——(1996) 'Truth in Ethics', in Brad Hooker (ed.) *Truth in Ethics* (Oxford: Blackwell), pp. 1–18.

5

THE ARGUMENTS FROM RELATIVITY AND QUEERNESS

John Mackie

THE ARGUMENT FROM RELATIVITY

The argument from relativity has as its premise the well-known variation in moral codes from one society to another and from one period to another, and also the differences in moral beliefs between different groups and classes within a complex community. Such variation is in itself merely a truth of descriptive morality, a fact of anthropology which entails neither first order nor second order ethical views. Yet it may indirectly support second order subjectivism: radical differences between first order moral judgements make it difficult to treat those judgements as apprehensions of objective truths. But it is not the mere occurrence of disagreements that tells against the objectivity of values. Disagreement on questions in history or biology or cosmology does not show that there are no objective issues in these fields for investigators to disagree about. But such scientific disagreement results from speculative inferences or explanatory hypotheses based on inadequate evidence, and it is hardly plausible to interpret moral disagreement in the same way. Disagreement about moral codes seems to reflect people's adherence to and participation in different ways of life. The causal connection seems to be mainly that way round: it is that people approve of monogamy because they participate in a monogamous way of life rather than that they participate in a monogamous way of life because they approve of monogamy. Of course, the standards may be an idealization of the way of life from which they arise: the monogamy in which people participate may be less complete, less rigid, than that of which it leads them to approve. This is not to say that moral judgements are purely conventional. Of course there have been and are moral heretics and moral reformers, people who have turned against the established rules and practices of their own communities for moral reasons, and often for moral reasons that we would endorse. But this can usually be understood as the extension, in ways which, though new and unconventional, seemed to them to be required for consistency, of rules to which they already adhered as arising out of an existing way of life. In short, the

75

argument from relativity has some force simply because the actual variations in the moral codes are more readily explained by the hypothesis that they reflect ways of life than by the hypothesis that they express perceptions, most of them seriously inadequate and badly distorted, of objective values.

But there is a well-known counter to this argument from relativity, namely to say that the items for which objective validity is in the first place to be claimed are not specific moral rules or codes but very general basic principles which are recognized at least implicitly to some extent in all society – such principles as provide the foundations of what Sidgwick has called different methods of ethics: the principle of universalizability, perhaps, or the rule that one ought to conform to the specific rules of any way of life in which one takes part, from which one profits, and on which one relies, or some utilitarian principle of doing what tends, or seems likely, to promote the general happiness. It is easy to show that such general principles, married with differing concrete circumstances, different existing social patterns or different preferences, will beget different specific moral rules; and there is some plausibility in the claim that the specific rules thus generated will vary from community to community or from group to group in close agreement with the actual variations in accepted codes.

The argument from relativity can be only partly countered in this way. To take this line the moral objectivist has to say that it is only in these principles that the objective moral character attaches immediately to its descriptively specified ground or subject: other moral judgements are objectively valid or true, but only derivatively and contingently – if things had been otherwise, quite different sorts of actions would have been right. And despite the prominence in recent philosophical ethics of universalization, utilitarian principles, and the like, these are very far from constituting the whole of what is actually affirmed as basic in ordinary moral thought. Much of this is concerned rather with what Hare calls 'ideals' or, less kindly, 'fanaticism'. That is, people judge that some things are good or right, and others are bad or wrong, not because – or at any rate not only because – they exemplify some general principle for which widespread implicit acceptance could be claimed, but because something about those things arouses certain responses immediately in them, though they would arouse radically and irresolvably different responses in others. 'Moral sense' or 'intuition' is an initially more plausible description of what supplies many of our basic moral judgements than 'reason'. With regard to all these starting points of moral thinking the argument from relativity remains in full force.

THE ARGUMENT FROM QUEERNESS

Even more important, however, and certainly more generally applicable, is the argument from queerness. This has two parts, one metaphysical, the other epistemological.

If there were objective values, then they would be entities or qualities or relations of a very strange sort, utterly different from anything else in the universe. Correspondingly, if we were aware of them, it would have to be by some special faculty of moral perception or intuition, utterly different from our ordinary ways of knowing everything else. These points were recognized by Moore when he spoke of non-natural qualities, and by the intuitionists in their talk about a 'faculty of moral intuition'. Intuitionism has long been out of favour, and it is indeed easy to point out its implausibilities. What is not so often stressed, but is more important, is that the central thesis of intuitionism is one to which any objectivist view of values is in the end committed: intuitionism merely makes unpalatably plain what other forms of objectivism wrap up. Of course the suggestion that moral judgements are made or moral problems solved by just sitting down and having an ethical intuition is a travesty of actual moral thinking. But, however complex the real process, it will require (if it is to yield authoritatively prescriptive conclusions) some input of this distinctive sort, either premises or forms of argument or both. When we ask the awkward question, how we can be aware of this authoritative prescriptivity, of the truth of these distinctively ethical premises or of the cogency of this distinctively ethical pattern of reasoning, none of our ordinary accounts of sensory perception or introspection or the framing and confirming of explanatory hypotheses or inference or logical construction or conceptual analysis, or any combination of these, will provide a satisfactory answer; 'a special sort of intuition' is a lame answer, but it is the one to which the clearheaded objectivist is compelled to resort.

Indeed, the best move for the moral objectivist is not to evade this issue, but to look for companions in guilt. For example, Richard Price argues that it is not moral knowledge alone that such an empiricism as those of Locke and Hume is unable to account for, but also our knowledge and even our ideas of essence, number, identity, diversity, solidity, inertia, substance, the necessary existence and infinite extension of time and space, necessity and possibility in general, power, and causation. If the understanding, which Price defines as the faculty within us that discerns truth, is also a source of new simple ideas of so many other sorts, may it not also be a power of immediately perceiving right and wrong, which yet are real characters of actions?

This is an important counter to the argument from queerness. The only adequate reply to it would be to show how, on empiricist foundations, we can construct an account of the ideas and beliefs and knowledge that we have of all these matters. I cannot even begin to do that here, though I have undertaken some parts of the task elsewhere. I can only state my belief that satisfactory accounts of most of these can be given in empirical terms. If some supposed metaphysical necessities or essences resist such treatment, then they too should be included, along with objective values, among the targets of the argument from queerness.

This queerness does not consist simply in the fact that ethical statements are 'unverifiable'. Although logical positivism with its verifiability theory of descriptive meaning gave an impetus to non-cognitive accounts of ethics, it is not only logical positivists but also empiricists of a much more liberal sort who should find objective values hard to accommodate. Indeed, I would not only reject the verifiability principle but also deny the conclusion commonly drawn from it, that moral judgements lack descriptive meaning. The assertion that there are objective values or intrinsically prescriptive entities or features of some kind, which ordinary moral judgements presuppose, is, I hold, not meaningless but false.

Plato's Forms give a dramatic picture of what objective values would have to be. The Form of the Good is such that knowledge of it provides the knower with both a direction and an overriding motive; something's being good both tells the person who knows this to pursue it and makes him pursue it. An objective good would be sought by anyone who was acquainted with it, not because of any contingent fact that this person, or every person, is so constituted that he desires this end, but just because the end has to-be-pursuedness somehow built into it. Similarly, if there were objective principles of right and wrong, any wrong (possible) course of action would have not-to-bedoneness somehow built into it. Or we should have something like Clarke's necessary relations of fitness between situations and actions, so that a situation would have a demand for such-and-such an action somehow built into it.

The need for an argument of this sort can be brought out by reflection on Hume's argument that 'reason' – in which at this stage he includes all sorts of knowing as well as reasoning – can never be an 'influencing motive of the will'. Someone might object that Hume has argued unfairly from the lack of influencing power (not contingent upon desires) in ordinary objects of knowledge and ordinary reasoning, and might maintain that values differ from natural objects precisely in their power, when known, automatically to influence the will. To this Hume could, and would need to, reply that this objection involves the postulating of value-entities or value-features of quite a different order from anything else with which we are acquainted, and of a corresponding faculty with which to detect them. That is, he would have to supplement his explicit argument with what I have called the argument from queerness.

Another way of bringing out this queerness is to ask, about anything that is supposed to have some objective moral quality, how this is linked with its natural features. What is the connection between the natural fact that an action is a piece of deliberate cruelty – say, causing pain just for fun – and the moral fact that it is wrong? It cannot be an entailment, a logical or semantic necessity. Yet it is not merely that the two features occur together. The wrongness must somehow be 'consequential' or 'supervenient'; it is wrong because it is a piece of deliberate cruelty. But, just what *in the world* is signified by this 'because'? And how do we know the relation that it signifies, if this is something more than such actions being socially condemned, and condemned by us too, perhaps through our having absorbed attitudes from our social environment? It is not even sufficient to postulate a faculty which 'sees' the wrongness: something must be postulated which can see at once the natural features that constitute the cruelty, and the wrongness, and the mysterious consequential link between the two. Alternatively, the intuition required might be the perception that wrongness is a higher order property belonging to certain natural properties; but what is this belonging of properties to other properties, and how can we discern it? How much simpler and more comprehensible the situation would be if we could replace the moral quality with some sort of subjective response which could be causally related to the detection of the natural features on which the supposed quality is said to be consequential.

It may be thought that the argument from queerness is given an unfair start if we thus relate it to what are admittedly among the wilder products of philosophical fancy – Platonic Forms, non-natural qualities, self-evident relations of fitness, faculties of intuition, and the like. Is it equally forceful if applied to the terms in which everyday moral judgements are more likely to be expressed – though still with a claim to objectivity – 'you must do this', 'you can't do that', 'obligation', 'unjust', 'rotten', 'disgraceful', 'mean' or talk about good reasons for or against possible actions? Admittedly not; but that is because the objective prescriptivity, the element a claim for whose authoritativeness is embedded in ordinary moral thought and language, is not yet isolated in these forms of speech, but is presented along with relations to desires and feelings, reasoning about the means to desired ends, interpersonal demands, the injustice which consists in the violation of what are in the context the accepted standards of merit, the psychological constituents of meanness, and so on. There is nothing queer about any of these, and under cover of them the claim for moral authority may pass unnoticed. But if I am right in arguing that it is ordinarily there, and is therefore very likely to be incorporated almost automatically in philosophical accounts of ethics which systematize our ordinary thought even in such apparently innocent terms as these, it needs to be examined, and for this purpose it needs to be isolated and exposed as it is by the less cautious philosophical reconstructions.

6

MORAL REALISM AND THE SCEPTICAL ARGUMENTS FROM DISAGREEMENT AND QUEERNESS

David Brink

1 INTRODUCTION

The most important kind of challenge to moral realism or moral objectivism argues that there is a *special* problem with realism in ethics. I shall defend moral realism against two influential versions of this challenge recently formulated by J. L. Mackie in his book *Ethics: Inventing Right and Wrong*.[1] According to standards of argument which Mackie himself sets, neither his argument from disagreement nor his argument from queerness shows any special problem for moral realism. Let me explain why.

Moral realism is best explained as a special case of a global realist thesis. The general thesis common to realist claims about a variety of disciplines is a two part metaphysical claim:

R: (a) there are facts of kind x, and
       (b) these facts are logically independent of our evidence, i.e. those beliefs which are our evidence, for them.[2]

Moral realism is then obtained by substituting 'moral' for the variable 'x'.

MR: (a) there are moral facts, and
       (b) these facts are logically independent of our evidence, i.e. those beliefs which are our evidence, for them.

Moral realism claims that there are objective moral facts and implies that there are true moral propositions.

Moral scepticism is technically an epistemological doctrine and so is officially neutral with respect to the metaethical thesis of moral realism. Moral scepticism claims that we have no moral knowledge and this claim is compatible with the existence of objective moral facts and true moral propositions. But while moral realism and moral scepticism are compatible (we may just have no cognitive access to moral facts), the standard and most plausible reason for claiming that we have no moral knowledge is the belief that there are no moral facts. This must be why Mackie construes moral scepticism as an anti-realist thesis. I shall follow Mackie in this and treat moral scepticism as a denial of the existence of objective values.[3]

There are two basic kinds of moral sceptic. The first kind applies general sceptical considerations to the special case of morality. On his view, there are no moral facts, but neither are there any other objective facts about the world. Of course, this first sort of sceptic is quite radical and has not been terribly influential as a source of moral scepticism. The second kind of moral sceptic claims that there is a special problem about realism in ethics, a problem which does not afflict realism about most other disciplines. This clearly has been the more popular and philosophically influential version of moral scepticism. Mackie is this second kind of moral sceptic.

As this second kind of moral sceptic, Mackie complains that belief in the existence of objective values is no part of a plausible realist world-view. (E: 17) Mackie's sceptical arguments, therefore, cannot turn on the application of general sceptical consider-ations. If it can be shown that the moral realist's metaphysical and epistemological commitments are no less plausible than those of, say, the physical realist, then Mackie's sceptical arguments will have been answered.

Although it is possible to *defend* moral realism against sceptical arguments without establishing any kind of presumption in its favour, there are, as Mackie recognises, general considerations which require the moral sceptic to bear a certain burden of proof. First, this second version of moral scepticism concedes a presumption in favour of moral realism. If, as this second sort of scepticism assumes, realism is plausible about a wide range of disciplines, then there must be some special justification for taking a different view about the existence and nature of moral facts. Of course, this establishes only a very weak presumption in favour of moral realism, but it is one which the moral sceptic must rebut.

Moreover, belief in moral realism is supported by certain features of our moral practice. In moral deliberation and moral argument we search for answers to our moral questions, answers whose correctness we assume to be independent of our means of arriving at them.[4] Of course, this presumption too is defeasible, but this takes some argument. As Mackie claims, moral scepticism must have the status of an error theory; it must explain how and why our commitment to the objectivity of moral values is mistaken. (E: 35)

Mackie distinguishes two arguments for the second version of moral scepticism. The first turns on the apparent unresolvability of many moral disputes and so is best thought of as an argument from disagreement,[5] while the second turns on the mysterious character objective values would seem to have to have and so represents an argument from queerness. Mackie presses both of these arguments against moral realism and in favour of moral scepticism and subjectivism.[6] In what follows, I shall examine and rebut Mackie's arguments from disagreement and queerness; I shall argue that neither argument establishes any special problem for moral realism. Although these two arguments may not exhaust the arguments for the second version of moral scepticism, they are sufficiently important both historically and philosophically that successfully rebutting them will go a long way towards defending moral realism.

2 MORAL OBJECTIVITY

Before discussing the details of the arguments from disagreement and queerness, we need to establish just which version of moral realism is or need be in question. In § 1 I described moral realism as the metaethical view that there are objective moral facts. However, in pressing the arguments from disagreement and queerness, Mackie employs a stronger or more committal version of moral realism according to which not only are there moral facts but also these moral facts are *objectively prescriptive*. (*E*: 23, 26–7, 29, 40, 42; *HMT*: 22, 53, 55, 134, 146; *MT*: 102, 104, 115–16) Indeed, although both the argument from disagreement and the argument from queerness apply to my formulation of moral realism, some of the special appeal of the argument from queerness derives from the assumption that moral facts would have to be objectively prescriptive. (*E*: 40–1 [pp. 78–9, this volume]; *HMT*: 61)

In claiming that moral facts would have to be objectively prescriptive, Mackie is claiming that moral realism requires the truth of *internalism*. Internalism is the a priori thesis that the recognition of moral facts itself either necessarily motivates or necessarily provides reasons for action. Internalism is an a priori thesis, because its proponents claim that the recognition of moral facts necessarily motivates or provides reasons for action no matter what the moral facts turn out to be. We can distinguish *motivational internalism* (MI) and *reasons internalism* (RI): MI holds that it is a priori that the recognition of moral facts itself necessarily motivates the agent to perform the moral action, while RI claims that it is a priori that the recognition of moral facts itself necessarily provides the agent with reason to perform the moral action. *Externalism*, by contrast, denies both MI and RI.[7]

Although Mackie is unclear as between MI and RI,[8] he clearly thinks that some version of internalism is required by moral realism. Both MI and RI make exceptionally strong claims. MI claims that – whatever the moral facts turn out to be and regardless of the psychological make-up of the agent – the mere recognition of a moral fact necessarily provides some motivation to perform the moral action, while RI claims that – whatever the moral facts turn out to be and regardless of the agent's interests or desires – the mere recognition of a moral fact necessarily provides the agent with at least some reason to perform the moral action. These claims are quite implausible, and it is unclear why moral realism is committed to either of them.

It is unlikely that the recognition of moral facts *necessarily* motivates or provides reasons for action; it is very unlikely that the recognition of moral facts *alone* necessarily motivates or provides reasons for action; and the mere recognition of moral facts almost certainly does not necessarily motivate or provide reasons for action *regardless of what the moral facts turn out to be*. Whether the recognition of moral facts motivates certainly depends upon what the moral facts are, and, at least on most plausible moral theories, whether recognition of these facts motivates is a matter of contingent (even if deep) psychological fact about the agent. Whether the recognition of moral facts provides reasons for action depends upon whether the agent has reason to do what morality requires. But this, of course, depends upon what morality requires, i.e. upon what the moral facts are, and, at least on standard theories of reasons for action, whether recognition of these facts provides reason for action will depend upon contingent (even if deep) facts about the agent's desires or interests. So, internalism is false; it is not something which we can know a priori, i.e. whatever the moral facts turn out to be, that the recognition of moral facts alone either necessarily motivates or necessarily provides reasons for action.[9]

It is hard to see why moral realism should be committed to the truth of internalism. Mackie claims both that moral realists have traditionally been internalists (*E*: 23) and that internalism is part of common sense moral thinking. (*E*: 35) But both claims seem false and would carry relatively little weight, even if true. Once we make clear the strength of the internalist claim – that we know a priori that *mere* recognition of moral facts *necessarily* motivates or provides reasons for action – it is less clear that the tradition of moral realism is a tradition of internalism. In particular, although I cannot argue the claims here, I doubt that Plato, Hume, or Sidgwick is, as Mackie claims, an internalist. And, of course, even if many moral philosophers have thought that internalism is true, it would not follow that they were right. Nor does common sense moral thinking seem to support belief in internalism; in fact, it seems extremely unlikely that any belief so recherche could be part of common sense moral thinking. Even if belief in internalism were part of common sense moral thinking, it would be revisable, especially if it could be shown that belief in internalism plays a social role such that it would persist even if mistaken.

So no good reason has been produced for thinking that internalism is true or for thinking that moral realism requires internalism. This means that the moral realist can defend externalism. In particular, determination of the motivational and reason-giving power of moral facts will have to await specifications of the moral facts and of the desires and interests of agents. In defending moral realism against the arguments from disagreement and queerness, I will offer what I call a functionalist theory of moral value according to which moral facts are facts about human well-being and flourishing as a model specification of moral realist claims. This account illustrates the kind of justification of morality which the externalist can provide, for this functionalist theory implies that moral facts will *as a matter of fact at least typically* provide agents with reasons to do the morally correct thing.

3 THE ARGUMENT FROM DISAGREEMENT

Mackie claims that the best explanation of inter- and intra-societal ethical disagreement is that there simply are no moral facts, only differences of attitude, commitment, or decision. (*E*: 36–7 [pp. 75–6, this volume]) Of course, disagreement does not entail scepticism. Mackie recognises that we do not infer from the fact that there are disagreements in the natural sciences that the natural sciences are not objective disciplines. Nor do we make what might appear to be the more modest inference from the fact that there is a specific dispute in some subject that there is no fact of the matter on the particular issue in question. For example, no one concluded from the apparently quite deep disagreement among astron-omers a short while ago about the existence of black holes that there was no fact of the matter concerning the existence of black holes. Mackie's claim is that disagreement in ethics is somehow more fundamental than disagreement in other disciplines. In particu-lar, realism about a discipline requires that its disputes be resolvable at least in principle, and, while most scientific disputes do seem resolvable, many moral disputes do not.

Mackie imagines the moral realist replying that moral disputes are resolvable, because deep moral disagreements are not really cases of disagreement. Rather, they are cases in which 'disputants' apply antecedently shared moral principles under different empirical conditions. (*E*: 37 [p. 76, this volume]) The resulting moral judgments are about different action types, so the 'disagreements' in question are really only apparent.

Mackie issues two rejoinders to this realist reply. His first rejoinder is that this realist response commits the realist to (a) claiming that necessity can only attach to general moral principles and (b) accepting the following counterfactual: 'if things had been otherwise, quite different sorts of actions would have been right'. (*E*: 37 [p. 76, this volume]) (a) and (b), Mackie claims, imply that many action types will be right or wrong only contingently.

Although this rejoinder does raise some interesting questions about the modal status of moral facts, it in no way threatens moral realism. First, certainly some moral facts are contingent, and, even if this realist reply requires the contingency of some moral facts, this shows nothing about how many moral facts the realist must regard as contingent. But, secondly and more importantly, Mackie's modal issue is a red herring. The truth of moral realism turns on the existence of moral facts, not their modal status.

Mackie's second rejoinder to the realist reply is simply that some moral disputes are real disputes. Not all putative moral disagreements can be explained away as the application of antecedently shared moral principles in different circumstances. (*E*: 38 [p. 76, this volume]).

Mackie is right that many moral disputes are genuine, and, if the realist had no account of these disputes, Mackie would have a strong argument against moral realism. But the realist can account for moral disputes.

As we have seen, not every apparent moral disagreement is a genuine dispute. But the realist need not maintain even that all genuine moral disputes are resolvable. He can maintain that some moral disputes have no uniquely correct answers. Moral ties are possible, and considerations, each of which is objectively valuable, may be incommensurable.[10] So the moral realist need only maintain that most genuine moral disputes are resolvable.[11]

Indeed, the realist can plausibly maintain that most genuine moral disputes are in principle resolvable. Mackie's discussion of the realist's reply shows that Mackie thinks moral disagreement is resolvable if and only if *antecedent* agreement on general moral principles obtains. This claim presupposes a one-way view of moral justification and argument according to which moral principles justify particular moral judgments but not vice versa. However, this view of moral justification is defective. As Goodman, Rawls, and other coherentists have argued, justification proceeds both from general principles to particular cases and from particular cases to general principles.[12] Just as agreement about general moral principles may be exploited to resolve disagreement about particular moral cases, so agreement about particular moral cases may be exploited to resolve disagreement about general moral principles. Ideally, trade-offs among the various levels of generality of belief will be made in such a way as to maximise initial commitment, overall consistency, explanatory power, etc. A coherentist model of moral reasoning of this sort makes it much less plausible that disagreements over moral principles are in principle unresolvable.[13]

Moreover, a great many moral disagreements depend upon disagreements over the non-moral facts. First, many disagreements over the non-moral facts result from culpable forms of ignorance of fact. Often, for moral or non-moral reasons, at least one disputant culpably fails to assess the non-moral facts correctly by being insufficiently imaginative in weighing the consequences for the relevant people of alternative actions or policies. This sort of error is especially important in moral disputes, since thought experiments (as opposed to actual tests) play such an important part in the assessment of moral theories. Thought experiments play a larger role in moral methodology than they do in scientific methodology, at least partly because it is often (correctly) regarded as immoral to assess moral theories by realising the relevant counterfactuals.

Second, many moral disagreements result from reasonable but nonetheless resolvable disagreements over the non-moral facts. The correct answers to moot moral questions often turn on certain non-moral facts about which reasonable disagreement is possible and which may in fact be known by no one. Correct answers to moral questions can turn at least in part upon correct answers to non-moral questions such as 'What (re)distribution of a certain class of goods would make the worst-off representative person in a particular society best-off?', 'Would public ownership of the means of production in the United States lead to an increase or decrease in the average standard of living?', 'What is the correct theory of human personality?', and 'What kind of life would my severely mentally retarded child lead (if I brought the pregnancy to term and raised the child), and how would caring for him affect my family and me?'. However difficult and controversial these questions are, the issues which they raise are in principle resolvable. Moral disputes commonly do turn on disagreement over issues such as these, and, insofar as they do, moral disputes are clearly resolvable in principle.

Mackie argues that if moral realism were true, all moral disputes should be resolvable, and since many seem irresolvable, he concludes that moral realism is false. But the moral realist need only claim that *most genuine* moral disputes are *in principle* resolvable. Not all apparent moral disagreements are genuine, because some apparent moral disputes merely reflect the application of antecedently shared moral principles under different circumstances. Not every genuine moral dispute need be even in principle resolvable, since moral ties are possible and some objective moral values may be incommensurable. Of those genuine moral disputes which the realist is committed to treating as in principle resolvable, some depend upon antecedent disagreement over moral principles, while others depend upon disagreement over the non-moral facts. The realist can claim that antecedent disagreement over moral principles is in principle resolvable by coherence arguments and that disagreement over the non-moral facts is always in principle resolvable.[14] The moral realist gives a plausible enough account of moral disagreement for us to say that Mackie has not shouldered the burden of proof for his claim that the falsity of moral realism is the best explanation of the nature of moral disagreement.

4 THE ARGUMENT FROM QUEERNESS

The rough idea behind the argument from queerness is that objective moral facts and properties would have to be so different from the sort of natural facts and properties for which we do have evidence that we have good a posteriori reason to reject moral realism[15] (E: 38–42 [pp. 76–9, this volume]; MT: 115–16). As I said in § 2, the argument from queerness is supposed to tell especially against the existence of moral facts conceived of as being objectively prescriptive. (E: 40–1 [pp. 77–8, this volume; HMT:

61) I claimed that in committing realism to objective prescriptivity Mackie is claiming that moral realism requires internalism. But I argued that internalism is implausible and that Mackie produces no good reason for committing realism to internalism. Instead, the realist can defend externalism; determination of whether agents have reason or motive to be moral will depend upon the content of morality and facts about agents. In explaining why objective values are not queer, I will offer a model specification of moral realism, which, together with plausible empirical assumptions, implies that agents generally do have reasons to be moral.

There are two limbs to the argument from queerness: one metaphysical, one epistemological. (*E*: 38 (pp. 76–7, this volume]) I turn to the metaphysical branch of the argument first. Mackie thinks that moral realism is a metaphysically queer doctrine, because he believes that moral facts or properties would have to be ontologically simple or independent. (*E*: 38 [p. 76, this volume]) The assumption is that moral properties would have to be *sui generis*, that is, ontologically independent of natural properties with which we are familiar. Although it is not inconceivable that there should be *sui generis* moral properties, we have very good a posteriori evidence for the truth of materialism and for the falsity of ontological pluralism.

However, Mackie's crucial assumption that moral facts and properties would have to be *sui generis* is false; moral realism does not require ontological pluralism. The moral realist has at least two options on the assumption that materialism is true: he can claim that moral properties are identical with certain physical properties, or he can claim that moral properties supervene upon certain physical properties. Because moral properties and their instances could be realised in non-physical as well as a variety of physical ways, neither moral properties nor their instances should be identified with physical properties or their instances.[16] For this reason, it is best for the moral realist to claim that moral properties supervene upon physical properties.

Mackie recognises the realist's claim about the supervenience of moral facts and properties on physical facts and properties but claims that the alleged supervenient relation is also metaphysically queer:

> Another way of bringing out this queerness is to ask about anything that is supposed to have some objective moral quality, how this is linked with its natural features. What is the connection between the natural fact that an action is a case of deliberate cruelty – say, causing pain just for fun – and the moral fact that it is wrong? It cannot be an entailment, a logical or semantic necessity. Yet it is not merely that the two features occur together. The wrongness must somehow be 'consequential' or 'supervenient'; it is wrong because it is a piece of deliberate cruelty. But just what *in the world* is signified by this 'because'?
>
> (*E*: 41 [p. 78, this volume])

Although I do not think that Mackie has really motivated a metaphysical worry about moral supervenience, I shall defend moral realism against the charge of metaphysical queerness by adopting the strategy which Mackie mentions of finding partners in guilt – although once it is clear what sort of company the realist is keeping it would only be perverse to regard them as partners in *guilt*.[17] I shall argue that the supervenient relation which the realist claims obtains between moral properties and natural or physical properties is neither uncommon nor mysterious.

Although it is an interesting question what the precise relation is between property identity and supervenience, it is fairly clear that one property can supervene upon another without those two properties being identical.[18] A supervenient relation obtains between two properties or sets of properties just in case the one property or set of properties is causally realised by the other property or set of properties; the former property or set of properties is the supervening property or set of properties, and the latter property or set of properties is the base property or set of properties. Supervenience implies that no change can occur in the supervening property without a change occurring in the base property, but it also asserts a claim of ontological dependence.[19] Assuming, as Mackie does, that materialism is true, all properties ultimately supervene on material or physical base properties.[20] Physical properties are basic then in the sense that all other properties are nothing over and above physical properties. Biological, social, psychological, and moral properties are all realised physically; they are simply different *kinds* of combinations and arrangements of matter which hang together explanatorily.[21]

Supervenience is a relation of causal constitution or dependence. There is nothing strange and certainly nothing unique about the supervenience of moral properties on physical properties. Assuming materialism is true, mental states supervene on physical states, yet few think that mental states are metaphysically queer (and those that do do not think that supervenience makes them queer). Social facts such as unemployment, inflation, and exploitation supervene upon physical facts, yet no one supposes that social facts are metaphysically queer. Biological states such as being an organism supervene on physical states, yet no one supposes that organisms are queer entities. Macro-scopic material objects such as tables supervene on micro-scopic physical particles, yet no one supposes that tables are queer entities. In short, it is difficult to see how the realist's use of supervenience in explaining the relationship between moral and physical properties makes his position queer. Moral properties are not ontologically simple or independent; but then neither are mental states, social facts, biological states, or macro-scopic material objects. It is unlikely that moral properties are identical with physical properties; moral properties could have been realised non-materially. But there is every reason to believe that in the actual world moral properties, like other natural properties, are realised materially.

This realist account of supervenience discharges any explanatory obligation which the argument from metaphysical queerness imposes. The details of the way in which moral properties supervene upon other natural properties are worked out differently by different moral theories. Determination of which account of moral supervenience is best will depend upon determination of which moral theory provides the best account of all our beliefs, both moral and non-moral. Although I obviously cannot do here what is needed to defend a particular account of moral supervenience, I will now offer a *model* specification of the moral realist's metaphysical claims.

When trying to determine the way in which moral properties supervene upon other natural properties, one might start by looking at plausible theories about other kinds of properties. Functional theories provide plausible accounts of a wide variety of kinds of properties; the nature of biological, psychological, social, and economic properties is profitably viewed in functional terms. Consider functionalist theories of mind as an example. Although functionalism is not without its critics,[22] it is fair to say that there are no rival *theories* in the philosophy of mind today.[23] What is essential to any particular mental state type, according to functionalism, is the causal role which that mental state plays in the activities which are characteristic of the organism as a whole. Mental states are identified and distinguished from other mental states in terms of the causal relations which they bear to sensory inputs, behavioural outputs, and other mental states. To take a hoary example, functionalist theories of mind claim that pain is identified and distinguished from other mental states by virtue of its tendency to result from tissue damage, to produce an injury-avoidance desire, and to issue in the appropriate injury-avoidance behaviour. The physical states which realise this functional state are the physical states upon which pain supervenes.

Similarly, the moral realist might claim that moral properties are functional properties. He might claim that what is essential to moral properties is the causal role which they play in the characteristic activities of human organisms.[24] In particular, the realist might claim that moral properties are those which bear upon the maintenance and flourishing of human organisms. Maintenance and flourishing presumably consist in necessary conditions for survival, other needs associated with basic well-being, wants of various sorts, and distinctively human capacities. People, actions, policies, states of affairs, etc. will bear good-making moral properties just insofar as they contribute to the satisfaction of these needs, wants, and capacities. People, actions, policies, states of affairs, etc. will bear bad-making moral properties just insofar as they fail to promote or interfere with the satisfaction of these needs, wants, and capacities.[25] The physical states which contribute to or interfere with the satisfaction of these needs, wants, and capacities are the physical states upon which, on this functionalist theory, moral properties ultimately supervene.

Although I cannot and do not need to defend here this functionalist model, it is worth pointing out how this model addresses two issues of concern to Mackie, namely, the justifiability of morality and the decidability of moral disputes. In § 2 I argued that internalism is implausible and that determination of whether agents have motivation or reason to be moral depends upon the content of morality and facts about agents. If this functionalist account of moral value which I have proposed as a realist model is plausible, then there is reason to think that moral facts will at least typically provide agents with reasons for action. Everyone has reason to promote his own well-being, and everyone has reason to promote the well-being of others at least to the extent that his own well-being is tied up with theirs. Presumably, any plausible theory of human needs, wants, and capacities will show that the satisfaction of these desiderata for any given individual will depend to a large extent on the well-being of others. People have needs and desires for friendship and love and for the benefits of cooperative activity; they also have capacities for sympathy, benevolence, and social intercourse. In order to satisfy these social needs, desires, and capacities, agents must develop and maintain stable social dispositions, and this means that they will often have reason to benefit others even when they do not otherwise benefit by their action. So, although there may be cases in which maintaining or promoting human well-being involves no benefit to the agent, there is good reason to suppose that human well-being and agent well-being will by and large coincide. As this functionalist theory of value illustrates, externalism allows a strong justification of morality.

This functionalist theory of moral value also helps to explain the nature of moral disagreement. Common sense and attention to the argument from disagreement tell us that moral disputes can be extremely difficult to resolve. This functionalist specification of moral realism explains why many moral disputes which are in principle resolvable are nonetheless so difficult to resolve even under favourable conditions. Because facts about human well-being and flourishing depend at least in part upon facts in such complex and controversial empirical disciplines as economics, social theory, and psychology, even disputants who share something like the functionalist theory of value and are well informed will often disagree about what morality requires.

In addition to the metaphysical complaint about 'what in the world' a supervenient relation is, Mackie lodges an epistemological complaint about how we could know when the appropriate supervenient relation obtains. (*E*: 41 [pp. 78–9, this volume]) We may know that certain natural facts or facts under a non-moral description obtain, but how do we know or go about finding out whether these physical facts realise any moral facts and, if so, which? Mackie claims that we could gain this kind of moral knowledge only if we had special faculties for the perception of moral facts of the sort ethical intuitionism ensures. But, Mackie argues, although moral intuitionism could have been true, there are good a posteriori grounds for believing that no such faculties exist. Therefore, barring the cognitive inaccessibility of moral facts, moral realism must be false (*E*: 38–9 [pp. 76–7, this volume]).

The epistemological belief that moral realism is committed to intuitionism rests at least in Mackie's case on the mistaken metaphysical assumption that moral values would have to be ontologically *sui generis*. If and only if moral facts were queer kinds of entities would we need some special faculty for cognitive access to them. But the realist denies that moral facts are *sui generis*; moral facts supervene on natural facts. One goes about discovering which natural facts moral facts supervene on by appeal to moral theories. (Of course, appeal to a particular moral theory is justified only if that theory coheres well with other moral and non-moral beliefs we hold.) For example, if the functionalist account of moral value sketched above can be defended, then we do know how to set about ascertaining which if any moral facts supervene on a particular set of natural facts. We ascertain whether the natural facts in question contribute to, interfere with, or are neutral with respect to the maintenance and promotion of human well-being. Granted, in many cases this will be no easy task, since completion of the task will depend in part upon answers to controversial empirical questions in such fields as economics, social theory, and psychology. But all this shows is that moral knowledge is sometimes hard to come by, not that it is queer or mysterious.

Mackie might complain that both acceptance and application of moral theories must be guided by other moral commitments. Not only does acceptance of the functionalist theory of value depend upon its coherence with, among other things, other moral beliefs, but also the findings of such disciplines as economics, sociology, and psychology cannot fully determine the extension of 'human well-being and flourishing'. Even if the special sciences can tell us something about human needs, wants, and capacities, and the effective ways of realising them, these sciences cannot rank these components of the good or adjudicate conflicts among them. Some irreducibly normative questions must be answered in determining what constitutes human well-being and flourishing.

But if the fact that some or all of our moral judgments are theory-dependent in this way is supposed to present a genuine epistemological problem for the moral realist which is not simply the result of applying general sceptical considerations to the case of morality, Mackie must claim that theory-dependence is a feature peculiar to moral methodology. Is this claim at all plausible?

Here, as before, the moral realist can find quite respectable partners 'in guilt'. It is a commonplace in the philosophy of science that scientific methodology is profoundly theory-dependent. Assessments of theoretical simplicity and theory confirmation as well as standards of experimental design and instrument improvement require appeal to the best available background theories in the relevant disciplines. For example, in theory confirmation there is an ineliminable comparative component. Theories count as well confirmed only if they have been tested against relevant rivals, and determination of which alternative theories are relevant or worth considering requires appeal to background bodies of accepted theory. Acceptance of normal scientific observations and judgments, as well as application of general methodological principles, is also theory-laden. For example, judgments about the acidity or alkalinity of a substance which are based on the results of litmus paper tests pre-suppose belief in the normality of the test conditions and acceptance of the relevant chemical theories explaining how litmus paper detects pH and how pH reflects acidity and alkalinity.

The fact that scientific method is heavily theory-dependent shows that science and ethics are on a par in being theory-dependent. Thus, the fact that moral commitments must be appealed to in the acceptance and application of moral theories poses *no special* epistemological problem for moral realism. Of course, although most of us do not draw non-realist conclusions from the theory-dependence of scientific method, one may wonder how the profoundly theory-dependent methodologies in science and ethics can be *discovery* procedures. The answer is that theory-dependent methodologies are discovery procedures just in case a sufficient number of background theories in the disciplines in question are approximately true.[26] And I have been arguing that Mackie has provided no good reason for doubting that some of our moral background theories are approximately true.

Mackie might respond that the moral and scientific cases are not in fact on a par and that there is reason to doubt the approximate truth of our moral theories, because while there is a good deal of consensus about the truth of the scientific theories appealed to, say, in the making of pH judgments, there is a notable lack of consensus about which moral theories to appeal to in making moral judgments. There are at least three reasons, however, for dismissing this response. First, this response probably overstates both the degree of consensus about which scientific theories are correct and the degree of disagreement about which moral theories are correct.[27] Second, the response probably also overstates the amount of antecedent agreement necessary to reach eventual moral agreement. Finally, this response just raises from a different perspective the argument from disagreement, and we saw that the moral realist has a plausible account of moral disputes.

These considerations show that moral realism is committed to nothing metaphysically or epistemologically queer. The realist holds that moral facts supervene upon other natural facts and that moral knowledge is acquired in the same theory-dependent way that other knowledge is. Moral realism is plausible enough both metaphysically and epistemologically to allow us to say that Mackie has again failed to shoulder the burden of proof.

5 CONCLUSION

Mackie follows an important sceptical tradition in attempting to show that there is a special problem about realism in ethics. He recognises that it is the sceptic who bears the burden of proof but claims that his arguments from disagreement and queerness satisfy this burden. I argued, however, that neither argument provides good reason for disbelieving moral realism; certainly neither argument successfully bears the sceptic's burden of proof. The moral realist has various resources with which to account for moral disputes, and neither his account of the supervenience of moral facts nor his account of the theory-dependence of moral knowledge is queer or uncommon. I also introduced and developed a functionalist theory of moral value according to which moral facts are facts about human well-being and flourishing. Although the truth of this functionalist theory is not essential to the defence of moral realism, it does provide a plausible model for a realist programme in ethics. Mackie's arguments from disagreement and queerness do not exhaust the sceptical challenges to moral realism. But both arguments are sufficiently important that by successfully rebutting them we have gone a long way towards defending moral realism.

NOTES

1 J. L. Mackie, *Ethics: Inventing Right and Wrong* (New York: Penguin Books, 1977) (hereinafter *E*). Mackie further discusses a number of features of these two arguments in *Hume's Moral Theory* (Boston, MA: Routledge & Kegan Paul, 1980) (hereinafter *HMT*) and *The Miracle of Theism* (New York: Oxford University Press, 1982) (hereinafter *MT*). Parenthetical references in the text to *E*, *HMT*, or *MT* are to pages in these books.

2 Cf. Michael Devitt, 'Dummett's Anti-Realism', *Journal of Philosophy* 80 (1983), pp. 75–6. For obvious reasons, the kind of dependence asserted in R is logical, not causal.

3 The simple denial of the existence of moral facts, accompanied by no positive account of the nature of moral values, is moral nihilism. But Mackie, like most moral sceptics, not only denies the existence of objective values but also adopts a constructivist or subjectivist position about the nature of value according to which we make or choose moral value.

4 See Thomas Nagel, 'The Limits of Objectivity', in S. McMurrin (ed) *The Tanner Lectures on Human Values I* (Salt Lake City, UT: University of Utah Press, 1980), p. 100. Cf. *E*: 35, 48–9; *HMT*: 34, 70–5, 136.

5 Mackie himself refers to this argument as 'the argument from relativity'. (*E*: 36 [p. 75, this volume]) But this label is at least misleading and on a natural reading of 'relativity' begs the question, since the argument in question alleges that moral relativity (or at least the denial of moral realism) is the best explanation of the facts about moral disagreement.

6 There is some question about whether Mackie's rejection of moral realism in chapter 1 of part I of *E* is consistent with his defence in part 11 of a mixed deontological/consequentialist ethical theory based on considerations of rational self-interest. I shall not pursue this issue here; it is the main topic of Jonathan Harrison, 'Mackie's Moral "Scepticism"', *Philosophy* 57 (1982), pp. 173–91.

7 The a priori character of the internalist thesis and the MI/RI distinction are often obscured. Cf. W. D. Falk, '"Ought" and Motivation', reprinted in W. Sellars and J. Hospers (eds) *Readings in Ethical Theory* (New York: Appleton-Century-Crofts, 1952); William Frankena, 'Obligation and Motivation in Recent Moral Philosophy', in A. I. Melden (ed) *Essays in Moral Philosophy* (Seattle, WA: University of Washington Press, 1958); and Thomas Nagel, *The Possibility of Altruism* (Princeton, NJ: Princeton University Press, 1970), pp. 7–12. Cf. *MT*: 115.

8 *E*: 23, 40 [p. 78, this volume], 49; *HMT*: 22, 53; and *MT*: 102 require Ml, while *MT*: 115 explicitly requires RI.

9 Cf. William Frankena, *Ethics* (Englewood Cliffs, NJ: Prentice-Hall, 1973), pp. 114–16.

10 Of course, the mere absence of a single fact or set of facts *in virtue of which* both considerations are valuable does not establish incommensurability.

11 A realist *could* maintain that most or even all genuine moral disputes are unresolvable, as long as he was willing to claim that moral ties and incommensurable values occurred frequently enough. Although these claims are compatible with his position, reliance on them would weaken his reply to the argument from disagreement.

12 See, e.g., Nelson Goodman, *Fact, Fiction, and Forecast* (Indianapolis: Hackett, 1979), p. 66; John Rawls, *A Theory of Justice* (Cambridge, MA: Harvard University Press, 1971), pp. 20, 46–51; Rolf Sartorius, *Individual Conduct and Social Norms* (Encino, CA: Dickenson, 1975), pp. 31–3; and Norman Daniels, 'Wide Reflective Equilibrium and Theory Acceptance in Ethics', *Journal of Philosophy* 76 (1979), pp. 256–82.

13 Although a coherentist theory of moral truth would be incompatible with moral realism, this part of the realist's reply requires only a coherence theory of moral justification.

14 Actually, the argument from disagreement presupposes that disagreement over non-moral facts is always in principle resolvable.

15 As Mackie himself observes (*MT*: 116), the queerness argument is a posteriori and not a priori as R. M. Hare, *Moral Thinking* (New York: Oxford University Press, 1981), pp. 82–6, insists.

16 Cf. Saul Kripke, 'Identity and Necessity', reprinted in S. Schwartz (ed) *Naming, Necessity, and Natural Kinds* (Ithaca, NY: Cornell University Press, 1977), pp. 76, 98–9 and *Naming and Necessity* (Cambridge, MA: Harvard University Press, 1980), p. 148; and Richard Boyd, 'Materialism without Reductionism: What Physicalism Does Not Entail', in N. Block (ed) *Readings in Philosophy of Psychology I* (Cambridge, MA: Harvard University Press, 1980).

17 Also, recall that Mackie advocates a selective and not a general kind of scepticism.

18 Cf. Boyd, 'Materialism without Reductionism: What Physicalism Does Not Entail'; and Jaegwon Kim, 'Causality, Identity, and Supervenience in the Mind–Body Problem', *Midwest Studies in Philosophy* IV (1979), pp. 31–49.

19 See Henry Sidgwick, *The Methods of Ethics*, seventh edition (New York: Macmillan, 1907), pp. 379–80; G. E. Moore, *Philosophical Studies* (Boston, MA: Routledge & Kegan Paul, 1922), pp. 260–1; C. D. Broad, *Five Types of Ethical Theory* (Boston, MA: Routledge & Kegan Paul, 1930), p. 223; W. D. Ross, *The Right and the Good* (New York: Oxford University Press, 1930), pp. 79, 89, 115, 155; Jaegwon Kim, 'Causality, Identity, and Supervenience in the Mind–Body Problem' and 'Supervenience and Nomological Incommensurables', *American Philosophical Quarterly* 15 (1978), pp. 149–56; and Donald Davidson, 'Mental Events', reprinted in Donald Davidson, *Essays on Actions and Events* (New York: Oxford University Press, 1980), p. 214. If, as these writers seem to suggest, the sufficiency of a change in the supervening property for a change in the base property were both a necessary and sufficient condition for supervenience, then supervenience would be compatible with epiphenomenalism. (An epiphenomenalist construal of supervenience might explain why Moore, Ross, and Broad, who are all non-naturalists and think that moral properties are *sui generis*, nonetheless claim that moral properties supervene on natural properties.) But the realist should construe supervenience as a relation of ontological dependence and so should count the sufficiency of a change in the supervening property for a change in the base property as only a necessary and not a sufficient condition for supervenience.

20 Supervenience is a transitive relation.

21 Although Mackie does not press Moore's open question argument or any of its cognates against moral realism, it is worth pointing out that property supervenience does not require any kind of syntactic or linguistic reductionism. Just as property identity does not require property predicate synonymy, so property supervenience does not require synonymy or meaning implications between supervening property predicates and base property predicates. For instance, whether or not human pains supervene on C-fibre firings, the truth of this claim does not depend upon whether there are synonymy relations or meaning implications between 'human pain' and 'C-fibre firing'. Thus, although biological, social, psychological, and moral properties all supervene on physical properties, biological, social, psychological, and moral terms need not be definable in the language of particle physics. This explains how moral realism can be true even if there are no reductive definitions of moral terms. Cf. Richard Boyd, 'Materialism without Reductionism: Non-Humean Causation and the Evidence for Physicalism', in Richard Boyd, *The Physical Basis of Mind* (Cambridge, MA: Harvard University Press); Jerry Fodor, 'The Special Sciences, or the Disunity of Science as a Working Hypothesis', reprinted in N. Block; Geoffrey Hellman and Frank Thompson, 'Physicalism: Ontology, Determination, and Reduction', *Journal of Philosophy* 72 (1975), pp. 551–64; and Hilary Putnam, 'On Properties', reprinted in Hilary Putnam, *Mathematics, Matter, and Method* (New York: Cambridge University Press, 1979), p. 312, *Reason Truth, and History* (New York: Cambridge University Press, 1981), pp. 84–5, 207, 'Possibility and Necessity', pp. 53–5, and 'Beyond Historicism', p. 291, both in Hilary Putnam, *Realism and Reason* (New York: Cambridge University Press, 1983).

22 See, e.g., Ned Block, 'Troubles with Functionalism', reprinted in N. Block.

23 The functionalist literature is quite extensive; I rely principally upon the following: David Armstrong, *A Materialist Theory of Mind* (Boston, MA: Routledge & Kegan Paul, 1968); Ned Block, 'What is Functionalism?', in N. Block; Ned Block and Jerry Fodor, 'What Psychological States Are Not', reprinted in N. Block; Richard Boyd, 'Materialism without Reductionism: What Physicalism Does Not Entail'; Austen Clark, *Psychological Models and Neural Mechanisms* (New York: Oxford University Press, 1980); Jerry Fodor, 'Materialism', in D. Rosenthal (ed) *Materialism and the Mind–Body Problem* (Englewood Cliffs, NJ: Prentice-Hall, 1971); Gilbert Harman, *Thought* (Princeton, NJ: Princeton University Press, 1973); Hilary Putnam, *Mind, Language, and Reality* (New York: Cambridge University Press, 1975), chapters 14, 16, 18, 20–2; and K. V. Wilkes, *Physicalism* (Boston, MA: Routledge & Kegan Paul, 1978).

24 A functionalist moral realist might claim that moral properties are properties which play a certain role in the activities which are characteristic of *sentient* organisms.

25 When suitably developed, this functionalist theory of moral value might be quite similar *in content* to the moral theory which Mackie himself defends in part II of *E*. However, Mackie and I would still disagree about *the status* of this theory. I am suggesting that it might be true; he is presumably doing something like recommending the adoption of his theory.

26 Boyd argues that because of the profound theory-dependence of scientific methodology, the instrumental reliability of scientific method can *only* be explained by assuming the truth of scientific realism. See Richard Boyd, 'Realism, Underdetermination, and a Causal Theory of Evidence', *Nous* 7 (1973), pp. 1–12 and 'Scientific Realism and Naturalistic Epistemology', *PSA 1980 Volume 2* (East Lansing, MI: Philosophy of Science Association, 1981).

27 Cf. Alan Gewirth, 'Positive "Ethics" and Normative "Science"', reprinted in J. Thomson and G. Dworkin (eds) *Ethics* (New York: Harper & Row, 1968).

7

ON THE GENUINE QUEERNESS OF MORAL PROPERTIES AND FACTS

Richard T. Garner

John Mackie described a 'second order moral view' as a 'view about the status of moral values and the nature of moral valuing, about where and how they fit into the world'.[1] He called his own second order moral view by two different names, 'moral subjectivism' and 'moral skepticism', but a less misleading designation might be 'anti-realism'.[2] In contrast to noncognitivists, Mackie claimed that moral judgments have a truth-value, and in contrast to moral realists and ethical naturalists, he held that each and every one of them is false. Moral judgments are false because they all involve the mistaken claim, or assumption, or presupposition, that there are objectively prescriptive moral properties or facts. The two arguments Mackie deployed to support this anti-realism, the argument from relativity and the argument from queerness, have been widely criticised, but I want to show that, when properly understood, they remain troublesome for moral realists.

I begin with some remarks about objective prescriptivity, because that is where the queerness of moral properties and facts is located. Then, I turn briefly to the argument from relativity, and at greater length to the argument from queerness. I defend clarified versions of both arguments against attacks by David Brink, and I show how Brink fails to confront the strongest version of the argument from queerness. He thinks that the real queerness lies in the power of moral judgments to motivate, and so he hopes to avoid queerness by moving to what he calls *externalist moral realism*. While properties that are intrinsically motivating would indeed be queer, queerness of a different magnitude would belong to any property or fact that by itself *called for* humans to act one way rather than another. Even the most vile of poisons does not say 'Don't drink me'. The genuine queerness of moral properties and facts, I shall claim, resides not, or not only, in their alleged power to motivate, but in their alleged intrinsic imperativeness.

It is this action-guiding or action-directing (rather than action-causing) feature that Mackie sometimes, but not always, has in mind when he speaks of objective prescriptivity.

1 OBJECTIVE PRESCRIPTIVITY

According to Mackie, it is a doctrine of Western moral theory and a dogma of common belief that moral values are objective, not subjective, and that moral judgments are 'partly prescriptive or directive or action-guiding' (p. 23). Morality is seen as having authority over us – its principles and rules are believed to be objective requirements, not ones we invent, imagine, or impose upon one another, and not ones we can avoid.

Mackie is not alone in identifying this cluster of puzzling beliefs as central to morality. Philippa Foot, commenting on Kant's idea that reason 'commands what ought to happen', identified *inescapability* as the mark of the categorical imperative. 'People talk about the "binding force" of morality,' she said, 'but it is not clear what this means if not that we *feel* ourselves unable to escape.'[3] Bernard Williams rejects what he calls the 'morality system' and, like Foot, sees inescapability as a fundamental feature of moral obligation. He says that this inescapability means that there is no opting out of morality, and he identifies *this* idea with Kant's claim that morality is categorical.[4]

Foot notes one way in which morality and etiquette are both inescapable – in societies where rules of morality and etiquette are in force, 'behaviour does not cease to offend against either morality or etiquette because the agent is indifferent to their purposes and to the disapproval he will incur by flouting them'.[5] That is, our own indifference to the imperatives of etiquette (Don't eat peas with a knife!) and to the imperatives of morality (Don't use people for selfish ends!) does not mean that our actions will not offend against the respective systems. But it is one thing for my behaviour to *offend against* a code (of etiquette or of morality), another thing for me to *feel bound* by that code, and yet a third thing for there to be some fact or circumstance beyond (or about) the code itself that *requires* me to obey the code, even if I desire and choose not to. We can escape the imperatives of etiquette by moving into a box on the street, but not even in a box on the street are we free of the imperatives of morality. Moral bondage, unlike the bondage that morality and etiquette share, is non-relative, non-derivative, and inescapable in some special and serious way.

It is clear why moralists claim that the judgments of morality are inescapable, but not at all clear what that claim means. Foot explores several ways of expressing the 'fugitive thought' that morality strongly binds us, that there are things we *must do*, or *have to do*. But she finds nothing standing behind the words, and concludes that there may not be such a form of bondage, and that our belief that there is results from our education and our training. 'Perhaps,' she suggests, 'it makes no sense to say that we "have to" submit to the moral law, or that morality is "inescapable" in some special way.'[6]

Even though the meaning of 'moral bondage' is unclear, the thought that we are inescapably bound is an indispensable part of the institution of morality, as it is understood by those who seriously participate in it. Herein, according to Mackie, lies the common failure of naturalist and non-cognitivist analyses of moral language. Both fail to capture or explain the apparent authority of ethics—naturalists by excluding 'the categorically imperative aspect' (the prescriptivity) and non-cognitivists by excluding 'the claim to objective validity or truth' (p. 33). Whether it is possible to combine these elements or not, our use of moral concepts requires the presence of both. If moral facts were neutral, then moral judgments would be *objective without being prescriptive*. They would make no demands and require nothing from us, but would merely express the information that an action belongs to the class of right or wrong actions. Learning that something is wrong would be like learning what time it is – its relevance would depend on other commitments. If, on the other hand, moral facts derive their value from subjective sources, then the commands of morality would be *prescriptive without being objective*. They would be expressions of what others want or demand, and while they may influence us, they would have no authority we have not given them.

2 THE ERROR THEORY

'Ordinary moral judgments,' says Mackie, 'include a claim to objectivity, an assumption that there are objective values' (p. 35). People who use ordinary moral judgments may not comprehend what this assumption involves, or how peculiar it is, nevertheless that is what they assume, and Mackie thinks that they are wrong every time. Obligations exist, but they are hypothetical and institutional. We value things, but not because we have discovered anything so peculiar as intrinsic value in them, and not because they meet intrinsic requirements. No matter how bound we feel, and no matter how bound others want us to be, we invent objective prescriptivity and intrinsic value and project them onto perfectly natural and intrinsically neutral items. The error pointed to in the 'error theory' is the error we make when we take our projections for independent features of what we are evaluating, or see our requirements, or the requirements of others, as lodged in reality itself. This error is made by all serious users of moral language; and even those who use it without making the error imply (to others) that they believe in objectively prescriptive moral facts or intrinsically evaluative properties.[7]

The idea that users of moral language are uniformly mistaken about the objectivity of morality (or about anything else) does go against ingrained assumptions and common sense. Mackie grants this and concedes that his form of anti-realism needs 'very solid support', much of which he finds in the arguments from relativity and queerness. I will deal briefly with the argument from relativity in the next section. The remaining sections will be devoted to the argument from queerness and related matters.

3 THE ARGUMENT FROM RELATIVITY (OR DISAGREEMENT)

Mackie offers the argument from relativity as an argument from moral diversity to the best explanation of that diversity. 'The actual variations in the moral codes,' he says, 'are more readily explained by the hypothesis that they reflect ways of life than by the hypothesis that they express perceptions, most of them seriously inadequate and badly distorted, of objective values' (p. 37 [p. 76, this volume]). In 'Moral Realism and the Sceptical Arguments from Disagreement and Queerness' (Chapter 6, this volume), David Brink acknow-ledges that this argument (which he calls the 'argument from disagreement') is an argument to the best explanation, but then he criticizes it as if it were a syllogism with a blatantly false premise. He says that Mackie 'argues that if moral realism were true, all moral disputes should be resolvable, and since many seem irresolvable, he concludes that moral realism is false'.[8] I can't find this terrible argument in Mackie's book, and if I could, I would ignore it in deference to the fact that he more than once insists that 'it is not the mere occurrence of disagreements that tells against the objectivity of values' (p. 36 [p. 75, this volume]).[9]

Moral realism could be true even if some moral disputes were not resolvable, and anti-realism could be true even if everyone agreed about what is right and wrong. As things stand, there is moral disagreement *and* agreement, both within and among cultures, and Mackie's argument from 'disagreement' says that the best explanation of both the agreement and the disagreement is in terms of human feelings, needs, interests, and traditions. Morality (with its claim to objective prescriptivity) enters the picture to limit egoism and to promote desired traits. We get agreement about morality and we have strong moral intuitions because we have learned our lessons, and we get disagree-ment because we haven't all learned the same lessons, and because our interests often conflict.

If we want to support anti-realism in morality and realism regarding the objects of everyday life and science, we dare not argue from bare disagreement, which occurs everywhere. We must look at the agreement and disagreement in the three areas, and then argue that the cases are different and that the best overall explanation of the actual patterns of agreement and disagreement leads to anti-realism about goodness and to realism about tables and quarks. When we try to say more about this difference, how-ever, we are forced to confront the claim that moral facts and properties are unique, and this leads directly to the next argument, the argument from queerness.

4 THE ARGUMENT FROM QUEERNESS

Mackie divides the argument from queerness into a metaphysical and an epistemo-logical part. The metaphysical part says that objective values would have to be 'entities or qualities or relations of a very strange sort, utterly different from anything else in the universe', and the epistemological part says that our awareness of these strange qualities 'would have to be by some special faculty of moral perception or intuition, utterly different from our ordinary ways of knowing everything else' (p. 38 [p. 77, this volume]). This argument is impressive when used against the wilder claims of some intuitionists.[10] If moral disagreement is disagreement about properties that are *really there*, then we do need to say something about them and about our apprehension of them. We learned our colour words in front of observable coloured objects, and properties like yellow are integrated into a network of beliefs about the relation of colour to light, paint, percep-tion, physiology, prisms, and photography. Intrinsic values and moral obligations don't fit into any system like this. We have no duty receptors or instruments to detect the presence of trace amounts of intrinsic value. So, the argument from queerness seems well-placed when directed against old-fashioned intuitionists like Moore or Richard Price, who think (or speak as if they think) that moral properties are there in the object itself.

Even without the queerness imported by objective prescriptivity, moral properties would present us with serious metaphysical and epistemological problems. But when we remember that a moral property is not inert, but 'involves a call for action or for the refraining from action', the queerness is compounded (p. 33). How could *any* feature of something outside us make it the case that we are objectively required to do something? It is not just that we don't need moral properties and facts to explain our moral experience, their queerness would undermine any explanation of moral experience that appealed to them.

5 INTERNALISM, EXTERNALISM AND MORAL REALISM

Brink's reply to the argument from queerness is based on his version of a distinction between *internalism* and *externalism*. He says that 'in claiming that moral facts would have to be objectively prescriptive, Mackie is claiming that moral realism requires the truth of *internalism*', which is the a priori thesis that 'the recognition of moral facts itself either necessarily motivates or necessarily provides reasons for action'.[11] Historic-ally, internalism has been a view about motivation. William Frankena characterized it as the belief that motivation is somehow 'built into' judgments of moral obligation. One who rejects this belief is an externalist. Externalists believe that one can 'recognize that one has [a moral obligation] and yet have no motivation to perform the required act'.[12] For the internalist, moral judgments state moral facts, and moral facts by themselves motivate those who are aware of them. The strongest form of internalism would say, for example, that when we see some course of action as a duty, we will choose it. Weaker forms say that we are inclined (a lot or a little) to choose what we identify as right, and to prefer what we acknowledge to be good.

Internalism offers us a thesis about motivation, but one that is both ambiguous and easy to criticise. This leads Brink to suggest that the moral realist abandon internalism and adopt externalism.[13] According to the externalist moral realist, motivation comes from the world (by way of desires, sanctions, and training) rather than from moral properties and facts themselves.

6 THE GENUINE QUEERNESS

Unfortunately for the moral realist, the queerness of being a property that is intrinsically motivating is not the only, or even the major, queerness moral facts exhibit. Another source of queerness emerges when we attend to the other half of Brink's formulation of internalism. In addition to 'motivational internalism', there is also what he calls 'reasons internalism', the thesis that 'it is a priori that the recognition of moral facts itself necessarily provides the agent with reasons to perform the moral action'.[14] Now the situation becomes more complicated due to a distinction, stressed by Frankena, between 'exciting reasons' and 'justifying reasons'.[15] If we are thinking of exciting reasons, then reasons internalism collapses into motivational internalism. But if we understand 'reasons' to mean 'justifying reasons', we are in a different dimension. It is hard to deny that the recognition of a moral fact (say the wrongness of an action), if such a thing were possible, would give us a justifying reason for refraining from performing that action. Recognizing such a moral fact, or even mistakenly believing that we recognize it, we would *have* such a reason, whether we were motivated by it or not.

Moral realists need not be saddled with motivational internalism, but they may have to embrace reasons internalism when 'reason' means 'justifying reason'. If we recognize a moral fact, then we recognize it *as* a moral fact, which is to say that we recognize it as directing us to be or act one way rather than another – and we recognize this whether or not we are moved to obey the directions. It is the peculiar combination of objectivity and prescriptivity, rather than any intrinsic motivational power, that makes moral facts and properties queer, and neither Brink nor anyone else can purge *that* from them to protect them from the argument from queerness.

Moral realists who acknowledge that moral facts are unique in possessing objective prescriptivity, often deny that this counts against them. Moral facts are not physical facts, they say, they are moral facts, different from other facts in just the way the anti-realist points out – they bind us objectively. They are indeed unusual, even queer, when we compare them to straightforward facts about observable features of objects, but why, the moral realist asks, should this count against them? There are, after all, many unusual things in the world.

It is not easy to know how seriously to take this defence. Moral facts are not just unusual in the way that facts about quarks and black holes are unusual, they are unusual in an unusual way – they demand. If a moral fact obtains, then we have a duty or a right to do something, which is to say that there is a legitimate and justifiable directive that *applies to* us, a directive that we can ignore or disobey, but one from which we cannot escape. The anti-realist says that this demand, however strongly felt, is no more than a projection of demands people make upon one another. The moral realist says that *this* is not enough, that the demands are in some sense independent of our moral feelings and beliefs, and responsible for them.

It is hard to believe in objective prescriptivity because it is hard to make sense of a demand without a demander, and hard to find a place for demands or demanders apart from human interests and conventions. We know what it is for our friends, our job, and our projects to make demands on us, but we do not know what it is for *reality* to do so. A black hole swallows everything, but it demands nothing. The only way to make sense of the demands of morality may be to see morality as a conventional social device, and its demands as ones we ourselves make.[16]

7 MACKIE'S SHARE OF THE BLAME

Brink's criticism of Mackie's use of the argument from queerness is not completely unwarranted. When explaining what it is for values to be both prescriptive and objective, Mackie alluded to Plato's Forms, and remarked that *seeing* them 'will not merely tell men what to do but will ensure that they do it, overruling any contrary inclinations' (pp. 23–4). This is certainly motivational internalism of the strongest sort, but independent moral facts with less power than that might still be held to be queer. Perhaps moral facts with *any* degree of intrinsic motivational power would be queer as well – the difference between a compulsion and a nudge may be only quantitative. This is why the only course for the externalist moral realist is to deny that moral properties and facts have *any* intrinsic motivational power.

Mackie describes the objective values that are the targets of his arguments as 'action-guiding' or 'action-directing' – but each of these expressions is ambiguous between motivational internalism and reasons internalism. By raising the possibility of externalist moral realism, Brink makes it clear that the important thing about moral facts and properties is that they are advanced as facts and properties that ought to move us. Morality has authority, and authority demands obedience, even if it doesn't always get it. If Mackie had concentrated more on the alleged authority of morality than on its alleged power, he would have fixed on a kind of queerness that remains even when we abandon motivational internalism. Since he did not, he left the way open for Brink to defend moral realism against the argument from queerness by assuming that the only queer thing about moral facts is their intrinsic power.

8 YET ANOTHER SOURCE OF QUEERNESS

Ethical naturalism can be seen as one response to the argument from queerness. If moral properties can be identified with natural properties, the naturalist thinks, then there will be no queerness, since natural properties are (by definition!) not queer. By identifying moral with natural properties, the naturalist emerges embracing either natural facts with intrinsic prescriptivity, or moral facts without it. But natural facts with intrinsic prescriptivity are at least as queer as moral facts with intrinsic prescriptivity, and for the same reason. On the other hand, moral facts without intrinsic prescriptivity are, if anything, even more queer than moral facts with it.

Brink doesn't accept the naturalist *identification* of moral properties with physical properties. Instead, he says that moral properties *supervene* upon physical properties. Mackie tried to deal with this possibility by attacking the purported relation between a natural fact (e.g. the fact that an act was a case of causing pain just for fun) and a moral fact (e.g. the fact that the act was wrong). It is, he says, not an entailment, a logical or semantic necessity, and yet the 'wrongness must somehow be "consequential" or "supervenient"; it is wrong because it is a piece of deliberate cruelty. But just what in the world is signified by this "because"?' (p. 41 [p. 78, this volume]). Brink fails to answer this question. What he says is that a supervenient relation 'obtains between two properties or sets of properties just in case the one property or set of properties is causally realised by the other property or set of properties'.[17] For materialists like Mackie and Brink, 'all properties ultimately supervene on material or physical base properties'. So, Brink argues, if we accept the supervenience of biological, social, and psychological properties, there is no reason not to accept the supervenience of moral properties as well.[18]

This move mirrors the strategy used against the argument from disagreement, and is a favourite tool in the realist's bag of tricks. One simply finds companions in guilt (or as Brink suggests, in innocence). But this ignores the special respect in which moral properties are queer. Projected or not, redness is inert, but wrongness forbids. The objective prescriptivity instantly (with or without intrinsic motivational power) distinguishes moral from biological, social, or psychological properties, and makes the supervenience of moral properties especially problematic.

9 COMMON SENSE AND QUEERNESS

Brink says that common sense doesn't support a belief in (motivational) internalism, since it is 'extremely unlikely that any belief so recherché could be part of common sense moral thinking'.[19] Motivational internalism is clearly not a part of common sense thinking, but common sense morality does involve a belief in objective prescriptivity. People believe that we are bound by moral considerations, that moral obligation is not optional, and that value is real rather than projected. R. M. Hare grants that many *philosophers* 'have thought that moral words connoted such objective, but at the same time prescriptive properties, and that the properties existed *in rerum natura* to make some of our moral judgments true', but he doesn't believe that 'ordinary people, innocent of any philosophy, are the whole time committing the same error'.[20] To be sure, ordinary people who manage to 'keep off philosophy' don't think or speak of their spontaneous moral intuitions as objective and prescriptive; nevertheless, beliefs that make no sense without the assumption of objective prescriptivity are common and entrenched. Ordinary people are so easily enticed into moral philosophy because the uses they make of morality require the very assumptions that the moral philosophers make explicit and debate.

10 TAKING THE AMORALIST SERIOUSLY

In his article 'Extemalist Moral Realism', Brink distinguishes between the moral skeptic, who is 'skeptical about the existence of moral facts', and the amoralist, 'who recognizes the existence of moral considerations and remains unmoved'.[21] One of the advantages Brink claims for externalist moral realism is that it permits us to take the amoralist's challenge seriously. 'Because externalism does not build motivational force into the concept of a moral consideration, it recognizes that we can imagine someone who recognizes moral considerations and remains unmoved.'[22]

One who 'recognizes moral considerations' must be understood to be one who is aware of the considerations people typically consider morally relevant, and who at the same time acknowledges the authority of morality, the legitimacy of its requirements, perhaps even its objective prescriptivity. Now, someone like *this* who 'remains unmoved' may remain unmoved by morality, or by the considerations moralists call moral (for convenience let us call these considerations of 'suffering'), or by both.

	Morality	Suffering
A	Moved	Unmoved
B	Unmoved	Moved
C	Unmoved	Unmoved

A is the Kantian *moralist* at his worst, moved by duty but not by suffering. Brink's amoralist, by contrast, is either B or C. B is unmoved by the morality of the moral considerations, but not by the facts themselves, by the suffering. C, on the other hand, is unmoved by moral appeals and by suffering. Amoralists like B acknowledge the authority of morality but (defiantly?) insist upon doing the moral thing for their own non-moral reasons. Amoralists like C also acknowledge the authority of morality, and not only are they unmoved by their own moral beliefs, they lack other, non-moral, inclinations to do what morality requires. One way *not* to take amoralism seriously is to suppose that all amoralists will be like C, and that someone who does not care about moral considerations will behave immorally. Brink comes close to doing this when he mentions the sociopath as an example of someone 'who does not care about moral considerations'.[23]

The *real* challenge to morality, however, comes from neither of Brink's amoralists, both of whom *accept* morality and its authority, but from the individual Brink calls the moral skeptic, and I call the anti-realist. The question is not whether there are *intrinsically motivating* moral facts, it is whether there are *objectively obligating* ones. When we separate obligation from motivation, and focus on the genuine queerness of moral facts and properties, then externalist moral realism looks no more plausible than internalist moral realism. It is the *realism* that is the problem.

NOTES

1 J. L. Mackie, *Ethics: Inventing Right and Wrong* (New York: Penguin Books, 1977), p. 16. Further references to this book will be given in parentheses in the text.

2 That is, 'anti-(moral) realism'. 'Subjectivism' and 'moral skepticism' are misleading because they have more familiar interpretations that differ from the position Mackie adopts. 'Moral realism' is now widely used to refer to a belief in moral facts.

3 Immanuel Kant, *Grounding for the Metaphysics of Morals* (Indianapolis: Hackett, 1981), p. 20; Philippa Foot, 'Morality as a System of Hypothetical Imperatives', in *Virtues and Vices* (Berkeley, CA: University of California Press, 1978), p. 162.

4 Bernard Williams, *Ethics and the Limits of Philosophy* (Cambridge, MA: Harvard University Press, 1985), pp. 177–8. Examples of the idea that this sort of bondage is central to morality are endless, but to cite one more example for the record, there is Alan Donagan's claim that 'the theory of morality is a theory of a system of laws or precepts binding upon rational creatures as such'. *The Theory of Morality* (Chicago, IL: Chicago University Press, 1977), p. 7.

5 Foot, op. cit., p. 162.

6 Ibid., p. 163.

7 Mackie says that if morality were not seen as objectively prescriptive, it would not be able to perform its function, which is to counteract impulses resulting from limited resources, information, intelligence, rationality, and sympathies (*Ethics*, p. 108). An *error* theory, by the way, is not necessarily a *falsity* theory. It is easy enough to propose some coherentist or

intersubjectivist account of 'truth' that allows us to say that moral judgments are sometimes true, even if those who make them imply something that we must admit is an error.

8 David O. Brink, 'Moral Realism and the Sceptical Arguments from Disagreement and Queerness', *Australasian Journal of Philosophy* 62 (1984), p. 117 [p. 86, this volume].

9 Thomas Nagel is attacking the same lame syllogism when he claims to find the popularity of the argument from disagreement surprising, and says that radical disagreement 'is a poor reason to conclude that values have no objective reality'. See *The View from Nowhere* (New York: Oxford University Press, 1986), pp. 147–8. But then he turns around and uses an argument from *agreement* to support the objectivity of morality (p. 148). The arguments, of course, neutralize each other, since there is both agreement and disagreement, and no serious way to say which we have more of.

10 Warnock uses it when he complains that intuitionism 'leaves it, at best, unclear how pieces of moral information are related to any other features of the world, and rather more than unclear how their truth can be established or confirmed'. See G. J. Warnock, *Contemporary Moral Philosophy* (New York: St Martin's Press, 1967), p. 15. More recently, David B. Wong has directed an epistemological version of the argument against neo-intuitionists like Mark Platts, John McDowell, and Alan Donagan. He says that 'there is no persuasive argument for the claim that we interact with moral properties and no explanation of the relation between ourselves and moral properties, in virtue of which we perceive them'. See David B. Wong, *Moral Relativity* (Berkeley, CA: University of California Press, 1984), pp. 103–4.

11 Brink, op. cit., p. 113 [p. 82, this volume].

12 William K. Frankena, 'Obligation and Motivation in Recent Moral Philosophy', in Kenneth E. Goodpaster (ed.) *Perspectives on Morality* (Notre Dame: University of Notre Dame Press, 1976), p. 50.

13 Brink, op. cit., pp. 114–15 [pp. 82–4, this volume].

14 Ibid., p. 113 [p. 82, this volume].

15 Frankena, op. cit., p. 51.

16 It was perhaps the realization that the world of the naturalist provided no binding obligation and no intrinsic value that led some moralists to adopt theological voluntarism, in the mistaken belief that only a divine being has what it takes to supply the objective prescriptivity that is missing from the natural world. See Elizabeth Anscombe's well-known paper, 'Modern Moral Philosophy', in Anscombe, *Ethics, Religion and Politics* (Minneapolis, MN: The University of Minnesota Press, 1981).

17 Brink, op. cit., p. 119 [p. 88, this volume].

18 Ibid., p. 120 [p. 88, this volume].

19 Ibid., p. 115 [p. 83, this volume].

20 R. M. Hare, *Moral Thinking* (Oxford: Clarendon Press, 1981), pp. 78–9.

21 Brink, 'Externalist Moral Realism', in *Spindel Conference 1985: Moral Realism* (ed. Norman Gillespie), Volume 24, Supplement, *The Southern Journal of Philosophy* (1985), p. 30.

22 Ibid., p. 31.

23 Ibid., p. 29.

Part 3

MORAL REALISM
AFTER MOORE

NATURALISM

Suppose you are drawn to moral realism – the claim that moral properties must exist. In that case, you'll need to consider the question, 'What are these properties like?' And also answer, 'Can I justify this?' In answering the first question, let us assume you are convinced by naturalism. Roughly you think that if empirical scientists were compiling a list of all the things that exist, moral properties would be included. How then are you going to respond to the second question? How can you justify that there exist moral facts that are natural? How do you give a good enough answer to the question that began § 5 of our Introduction (Chapter 1)?

Before this question even gets off the ground, you might worry that the position fails to take notice of the Moorean challenge in Part 1. Recall, Moore argued that moral terms cannot be defined as natural terms and as such moral properties are not reducible.

Sturgeon's paper in this Part (Chapter 8) defends naturalism and realism and responds to the Moorean challenge quite simply. Recall that Moore argued that good is irreducible. What he doesn't demonstrate though – although he doesn't recognize this – is that good is nonnatural. Sturgeon can then simply accept with Moore that good is irreducible but claim that it is a natural property. Of course, he has to prove it. Why think that good is an irreducible (*sui generis*) natural property?

Consider how we speak. We say things such as, "The President is in favour of torture because he is morally depraved", "What accounted for her actions was her moral compassion" and "On seeing the assault she recognized it was wrong". Sturgeon suggests we take these types of comment at face value. If we do this then it appears that 'moral facts' are something that we can *discover empirically* and *which provide causal explanations in the natural world*. For instance, it is the *fact* that the President is morally depraved that explains why we believe that he is morally depraved, and what explains his policy choices. And, Sturgeon continues, if moral facts do have these features, then they can quite correctly be called natural facts. After all, we argue that the physical, chemical or biological facts are natural facts precisely because they play an explanatory role in the best explanation of our experience.

Importantly, though, nothing follows from this metaphysical claim concerning moral facts about the possibility of giving *definitions* of moral facts in terms of natural facts. It just wouldn't matter to Sturgeon's account if moral terms couldn't be defined as natural terms. So Sturgeon has put forward a moral realist account, which is naturalist, and which can avoid the Moorean challenge. This type of realism has come to be known as Cornell Realism, after the US university philosophy department that was important for its development. (Richard Boyd is another example of a Cornell Realist. See Further Reading below.)

You may still worry that talk of *irreducible* natural properties is a little too odd, that it seems foreign to the naturalist project somehow. Railton's position in Chapter 9 then might seem attractive. It is both moral realist and naturalist but, unlike Sturgeon, holds that moral facts are *reducible* to natural facts. The first step to understand Railton is to think harder about what naturalism is. For Railton there is a vital distinction to be made between two different types of naturalism:

> *Methodological naturalism* holds that we shouldn't assume that we can discover truths about, say, ethics by purely thinking about it. Knowledge in ethics will come through a posteriori investigation rather than a priori 'armchair philosophy'.

> *Substantive naturalism* holds that we can give a *semantic interpretation* (NB. Nothing in this 'interpretation' demands that it be one of synonymy or analyticity) of moral concepts in terms of properties or relations that would 'pull their weight' within empirical science.

We could hold one without holding the other. We *could* give a semantic interpretation of moral concepts (substantive naturalism), but do this via a priori investigation (rejecting methodological naturalism). Or we could take an a posteriori approach to ethics (accepting methodological naturalism) and discover that you *can't* give a semantic interpretation of the moral concept. We could for instance end up as Cornell Realists (rejecting substantive naturalism).

Railton claims that we must approach ethics a posteriori and, if we do, then it will become clear that we ought to interpret moral concepts in terms of properties or relations that would 'pull their weight' within empirical science. He is then *both* a methodological and a substantive naturalist.

Railton's response to the Moorean challenge then is clear. Moore argues that moral terms can't be synonymous with natural terms and thus moral properties can't be natural properties. Railton claims via his methodological naturalism that moral terms don't need to be synonymous with natural terms for moral properties to be thought of as natural properties. Railton suggests that what we should do, as methodological naturalists, is to propose *reforming definitions* of moral terms in natural terms. Given that it is a reforming definition it will demand that we revise some of our understanding of moral facts – we will have to give up our idea that good is what is ordained by God, for example – but, obviously, we can't give up everything. For example, just think how odd it would be to define 'good' as something that doesn't explain anything, has no empirical role, doesn't motivate us to act and doesn't give us any reasons for action. In such a case we'd be inclined to think that the definition has, in Railton's terminology, eliminated 'good' rather than vindicated it. (Notice it doesn't matter for Railton that he can't provide a clear cut off point when a vindicating definition becomes an eliminating one). What, though, is essential for any reforming definition – what, as is were, is in the job description of any moral property – is, according to Railton, an *explanatory/empirical* and a *normative role*.

This seems fine. But what is Railton's suggested reforming definition? Well, you'll have to read his paper to find out. But one thing to keep in mind is that the fully informed agent plays a crucial role in accounting for Railton's vindicating reforming definition of both nonmoral and moral value (this is why his account is sometimes called a *full-information analysis*).

In Chapter 11 Frank Jackson puts forward another realist-naturalist position. He takes his cue from functionalism in the philosophy of mind. The functionalist in the philosophy of mind *defines* psychological terms in functional terms (inputs, internal connections, outputs, etc.). Although it is not that there is synonymy between the psychological terms and a description of their functional role. For the functionalist what in fact fulfils the functional role is left open – of course it is this 'multi-realizability' which makes functionalism so attractive to philosophers of mind. But importantly whatever does fulfil the role – if indeed anything does – will be what is referred to by the *psychological term*. It is not then that psychological terms refer to functional properties, they refer to what in fact plays the functional role stipulated by the definition. So what? What has this got to do with metaethics? Well, Jackson develops a form of *moral* functionalism (what he calls '*coherentism*'). This seems fine in theory, but in practice what does it amount to? The functional role of, say, pain is (sort of) clear. There is an input (burning your hand on the cooker), some internal stuff (the desire to move your hand away from the cooker, the belief that your body is injured, and so on) and the output (you might shout, swear, wince, jump backwards and the like). What of moral terms however? What are their functional roles? Well, Jackson only gives us a suggestion. He claims that whatever the functional role is, it is going to be decided a priori and will concern how people actually use moral terms. Moreover, it is not going to be how people *now* think and use moral terms, but what they would say once they had 'matured'. So the functional role of moral terms is set by what role they have in Mature Folk Morality. We should pause to consider what Jackson means by 'mature'. Obviously this doesn't mean Jackson is only concerned with what old people would say! By Mature Folk Morality Jackson means, roughly, people's common-or-garden moral judgements after there has been a lot of discussion and argument.

Let's grant that it makes sense to talk about Mature Folk Morality. What sort of thing do we mean when we talk about the 'roles' that moral terms would play? Well, for example, in Mature Folk Morality people may judge that causing suffering solely for fun is wrong (input), that considerations of what is wrong relates to considerations with blame (internal stuff) and claim that moral judgements give us reason to act in certain ways, or be motivated to act in certain ways (the output stuff).

Yet, this is not enough for Jackson who wants to develop a reductive naturalism. For this he has to provide a definition in non-evaluative terms. To this end he uses the work of Frank Ramsey and David Lewis (see Further Reading below). This is complicated, but the thing to hang onto when you are blurry eyed with the logic is this: it seems you can give the meaning of terms by stipulating what role they play in a bigger story. To adapt Lewis' famous example, imagine you're told a long and detailed story about how people X, Y and Z tricked the local TV network. The story might run, X, Y and Z conspire together to win a TV game show; X is in the audience and gives Y, who is the contestant, the answers on a certain cue from Z. X had discussed possible questions with Y over a pint the night before in the 'Quill and Quine'. X and Z bought a ticket to fly out of the country and drove straight to the airport after the TV show was recorded, Z had recorded a cover story onto a tape the night before . . . and so on.

In this story – a long and detailed story – three roles have been specified and it is claimed that they are occupied by X, Y and Z. Notice that in doing so we have specified the *meanings* of the three terms 'X', 'Y' and 'Z'. And, importantly, the meanings of X, Y and Z are fixed simultaneously by their role within the story as a whole.

This is the general strategy that Jackson takes. Moral terms have a general role with Mature Folk Morality. We should put all these roles in terms of moral properties (that is, instead of talking about it being wrong to steal we should say, "stealing has the property of being wrong") and then remove talk about *moral* properties. The idea then is we will have a massively complicated story about the roles 'X', 'Y', 'Z', etc. have in Mature Folk Morality. These roles are described in non-evaluative terms, with the meaning of all of the moral terms being fixed simultaneously by their role within Mature Folk Morality as a whole.

At the moment though (as we hope you have noticed) this is merely a conceptual claim. It could turn out that, in fact, Jackson is an error theorist. True, 'good' means whatever role it plays within Mature Folk Morality but it is just that there are no facts that fulfil that role. So there is no referent for 'good'. Clearly Jackson would be unhappy with this conclusion. After all, he is a realist! What then makes him so sure that there are facts that fulfil these roles? Moreover, what makes him so sure that these facts are going to be natural facts? Well, again, this is something you'll have to think about.

Before we leave the Jackson paper you might worry that if his account is taking this conceptual analysis approach it will be more vulnerable than Railton's and Sturgeon's to the open question challenge. However, Jackson says that this is no challenge at all. To think that once we have all the naturalistic information it could still be a substantive open question whether his account is correct is to be committed to (probably implicitly) an outdated Platonism with its accompanying queer ontology and problematic epistemology. The moral stuff just is the naturalistic stuff that plays the roles that it plays in our complicated moral thought and lives.

In Chapter 10 Terence Horgan and Mark Timmons attack those theories that claim that we should think of moral properties as natural properties, and that the best model of this identity is theoretical identities such as 'water = H_2O'. As such their paper doesn't speak to Jackson's or Railton's papers, as it is only Cornell Realists – including Sturgeon – who adopt this particular semantic framework. But, as well as thinking about what they say about Cornell Realism, thinking about how their points extend more generally is useful. (And, they have a similar argument against Jackson-type analytic moral functionalism. See Further Reading below.)

Cornell Realism has (generally speaking) a semantic framework that is based on the work of Saul Kripke and Hilary Putnam (see Further Reading below). Kripke and Putnam claim that some terms, including natural kind terms such as 'water', are rigid designators. That is, they refer to the same property across all worlds. It follows that if two natural kind terms flank an identity sign then this identity is *necessarily true* but *not analytic*, and it is a definition that reveals something essential about what is designated by a particular term. So 'water = H_2O' is a *synthetic* definition – we discovered it through empirical investigation – and the definition expresses the *essence* of water. This can be expressed in a conditional: *if* water is H_2O (and it possibly may not be) *then* it is *metaphysically necessary* that water is H_2O. Before we get into Horgan and Timmons' argument consider a parallel claim that the Cornell Realists would make:

> 'Good = N' (where N is a natural property(s)) is a *synthetic* definition discoverable through *empirical* investigation and the definition expresses the *essence* of good. This can be expressed in a conditional: *if* good is N (and it possibly may not be) *then* it is *metaphysically necessary* that good is N.

But why think that moral terms are rigid designators? Well, to answer this, Horgan and Timmons argue that we need to ask why we should think that natural kinds are rigid designators. The traditional way to answer this is via Hilary Putnam's famous Twin Earth thought experiment. Imagine there was a planet – Twin Earth – which is just like ours, except that the stuff that is a liquid at room temperature, which is colourless, odourless, which freezes at zero degrees, which falls from the sky, which is in the swimming pools and puddles, and so on, does *not* have the chemical structure H_2O but has some hugely complicated chemical structure which we'll abbreviate to XYZ. So the idea is that there are two substances that are, from all we can tell by looking, feeling and tasting, indistinguishable. We refer to both substances as 'water', but at the molecular level they are different. Further imagine that you have a doppelganger on Twin Earth and you swap with them while asleep and, given the similarities of the Earth and Twin Earth, you don't notice. You are suddenly very thirsty and so is your doppelganger and you both ask for a glass of water. Do you and/or your doppelganger think you've made a mistake? Putnam suggests and we would say, "yes", because if you asked for 'water' on Twin Earth you would intend to be referring to H_2O, not XYZ. (And, of course, our doppelganger has made the mirror image mistake, he intends to refer to XYZ and not H_2O.) What *you* meant was pass me a glass of water (H_2O) *not* pass me a glass of water (XYZ). So it seems that 'water' as we use it on Earth rigidly designates H_2O, and that this is what we *mean* when we talk about 'water'. To illustrate the point about *meaning* further just consider that for some bizarre reason you started to argue with the Twin Earthians about water. Now imagine that you discover that you were in fact on Twin Earth. The suggestion from Putnam is that you would cease to argue and accept that you were in fact talking at cross-purposes because, given the different molecular structures, 'water' on your lips means something different from 'water' on the Twin Earthians'. So let's agree with Putnam and conclude that this is very good evidence that 'water' rigidly designates H_2O.

Now essentially what Horgan and Timmons do to challenge Cornell Realism is show that a parallel thought experiment in the moral case considering what they call 'Moral Twin Earth' generates importantly *different intuitions*. Our intuitions don't justify the claim that moral terms are rigid designators that pick out natural properties. For instance, they suggest that if we get into a disagreement with someone about what is good and they (the Twin Earthian) use on Twin Earth 'good' in exactly the same way as us but it turns out that they are referring to a different natural property it's not obvious that we want to say in this case we are thus talking at cross-purposes. Our intuitions are just different; in the moral case, we want to hold there is genuine disagreement. Horgan and Timmons drive the point home by reintroducing a form of Open Question Argument to demonstrate that we have different intuitions in these cases. They conclude that if the moral terms are not rigid designators then it is hard to see how the Cornell Realists can defend their position.

QUESTIONS TO CONSIDER AND TASKS TO COMPLETE

1   What features must a naturalist position have?
2   List the similarities between the pieces by Sturgeon (Chapter 8), Railton (Chapter 9) and Jackson (Chapter 11).
3   What is a theory of reference? What is the difference between a descriptive (Jackson) and a causal (Cornell Realist) theory of reference? Which do you find most plausible?
4   What is 'Mature Folk Morality'?
5   Are there any important differences between the Twin Earth and Moral Twin Earth thought experiments?
6   What is scientism?
7   What do you think of the approach of studying theoretical identities as giving us an insight into ethics?
8   How do you understand these terms? 'Reductive', 'analytic', 'synonymous', 'conceptual analysis', 'a priori' and 'definition'. How does this compare with how the writers in this Part use them?

FURTHER READING

Boyd, Richard (1988) 'How to be a Moral Realist', in G. Sayre-McCord (ed.) *Essays on Moral Realism* (New York: Cornell University Press).

Copp, David (2000) 'Milk, Honey, and the Good Life on Moral Twin Earth', *Synthese*, vol. 124, pp. 113–37.

Gampel, Eric (1997) 'Ethics, Reference, and Natural Kinds', *Philosophical Paper*, vol. XXVI, no. 2, pp. 147–63.

Harman, Gilbert (1977) *The Nature of Morality* (Oxford: Oxford University Press).

——(1986) 'Moral Explanations of Natural Facts – Can Moral Claims be Tested Against Reality?', *Southern Journal of Philosophy*, vol. 24, suppl., pp. 57–68.

Hatzimoysis, Anthony (2002) 'Analytic Descriptivism Revisited', *Ratio*, vol. XV, pp. 11–22.

Horgan, Terence and Timmons, Mark (2000) 'Coping Out on Moral Twin Earth', *Synthese*, vol. 124, pp. 139–52.

——(forthcoming) 'Analytical Moral Functionalism Meets Moral Twin Earth', in I. Ravenscroft (ed.) *Essays on the Philosophy of Frank Jackson* (Oxford: Blackwell).

Kripke, Saul (1980) *Naming and Necessity* (Cambridge, MA: Harvard University Press).

Lewis, David (1970) 'How to Define Theoretical Terms', *Journal of Philosophy*, vol. 67, pp. 427–46.

——(1972) 'Psychophysical and Theoretical Identifications', *Australasian Journal of Philosophy*, vol. 50, 249–58.

Little, Margaret (1994) 'Moral Realism I: Naturalism', *Philosophical Books*, vol. 25, pp. 145–53.

Miller, Alexander (2003) *An Introduction to Contemporary Metaethics* (Cambridge: Polity Press), chapters 8 and 9.

Putnam, Hilary (1975) 'The Meaning of "Meaning"', in *Mind, Language, and Reality* (Cambridge: Cambridge University Press), pp. 215–71.

Railton, Peter (2003) *Facts, Values and Norms: Essays Toward a Morality of Consequence* (Cambridge: Cambridge University Press), [this contains most of Railton's key papers in metaethics].

Ramsey, Frank (1931) 'Theories', in F. Ramsey (ed.) *The Foundations of Mathematics* (London: Routledge & Kegan Paul).

Rosati, Connie (1995) 'Naturalism, Normativity, and the Open Question Argument', *Nous*, vol. 29, no. 1, pp. 46–70.

——(1995) 'Persons, Perspectives, and Full Information Accounts of the Good', *Ethics*, vol. 105, no. 2, pp. 296–325.

Sayre-McCord, Geoffrey (1997) '"Good" on Twin Earth', *Philosopical Issues*, vol. 8, pp. 267–332.

Smith, Michael (1994) *The Moral Problem* (Oxford: Blackwell), chapter 2.

Zangwill, Nick (2000) 'Against Analytic Moral Functionalism', *Ratio*, vol. 13, pp. 275–86.

8

MORAL EXPLANATIONS

Nicholas L. Sturgeon

There is one argument for moral skepticism that I respect even though I remain unconvinced. It has sometimes been called the argument from moral diversity or relativity, but that is somewhat misleading, for the problem arises not from the diversity of moral views, but from the apparent difficulty of *settling* moral disagreements, or even of knowing what would be required to settle them, a difficulty thought to be noticeably greater than any found in settling disagreements that arise in, for example, the sciences. This provides an argument for moral skepticism because one obviously possible explanation for our difficulty in settling moral disagreements is that they are really unsettleable, that there is no way of justifying one rather than another competing view on these issues; and a possible further explanation for the unsettleability of moral disagreements, in turn, is moral nihilism, the view that on these issues there just is no fact of the matter, that the impossibility of discovering and establishing moral truths is due to there not being any.

I am, as I say, unconvinced: partly because I think this argument exaggerates the difficulty we actually find in settling moral disagreements, partly because there are alternative explanations to be considered for the difficulty we do find. Under the latter heading, for example, it certainly matters to what extent moral disagreements depend on disagreements about other questions which, however disputed they may be, are nevertheless regarded as having objective answers: questions such as which, if any, religion is true, which account of human psychology, which theory of human society. And it also matters to what extent consideration of moral questions is in practice skewed by distorting factors such as personal interest and social ideology. These are large issues. Although it is possible to say some useful things to put them in perspective,[1] it appears impossible to settle them quickly or in any a priori way. Consideration of them is likely to have to be piecemeal, and, in the short run at least, frustratingly indecisive.

These large issues are not my topic here. But I mention them, and the difficulty of settling them, to show why it is natural that moral skeptics have hoped to find some quicker way of establishing their thesis. I doubt that any exist, but some have of course been proposed. Verificationist attacks on ethics should no doubt be seen in this light, and J. L. Mackie's "argument from queerness" is a clear instance (Mackie, 1977 [chapter 5, this volume]). The quicker argument on which I shall concentrate, however, is neither of these, but instead an argument by Gilbert Harman designed to bring out the "basic problem" about morality, which in his view is "its apparent immunity from observational testing" and "the seeming irrelevance of observational evidence" (Harman, 1977. Parenthetical page references are to this work). The argument is that reference to moral facts appears unnecessary for the *explanation* of our moral observations and beliefs.

Harman's view, I should say at once, is not in the end a skeptical one, and he does not view the argument I shall discuss as a decisive defense of moral skepticism or moral nihilism. Someone else might easily so regard it, however. For Harman himself regards it as creating a strong *prima facie* case for skepticism and nihilism, strong enough to justify calling it "the problem with ethics."[2] And he believes it shows that the only recourse for someone who wishes to avoid moral skepticism is to find defensible reductive definitions for ethical terms; so skepticism would be the obvious conclusion for anyone to draw who doubted the possibility of such definitions. I believe, however, that Harman is mistaken on both counts. I shall show that his argument for skepticism either rests on claims that most people would find quite implausible (and so cannot be what constitutes, for *them*, the problem with ethics); or else it becomes just the application to ethics of a familiar *general* skeptical strategy, one which, if it works for ethics, will work equally well for unobservable theoretical entities, or for other minds, or for an external world (and so, again, can hardly be what constitutes the distinctive problem with *ethics*). In the course of my argument, moreover, I shall suggest that one can in any case be a moral realist, and indeed an ethical naturalist, without believing that we are now or ever will be in possession of reductive naturalistic definitions for ethical terms.

I THE PROBLEM WITH ETHICS

Moral theories are often tested in thought experiments, against imagined examples; and, as Harman notes, trained researchers often test scientific theories in the same way. The problem, though, is that scientific theories can also be tested against the world, by observations or real experiments; and, Harman asks, "can moral principles be tested in the same way, out in the world?" (p. 4).

This would not be a very interesting or impressive challenge, of course, if it were merely a resurrection of standard verificationist worries about whether moral assertions and theories have any testable empirical implications, implications statable in some relatively austere "observational" vocabulary. One problem with that form of the challenge, as Harman points out, is that there are no "pure" observations, and in consequence no purely observational vocabulary either. But there is also a deeper problem that Harman does not mention, one that remains even if we shelve worries about "pure" observations and, at least for the sake of argument, grant the verificationist his observational language, pretty much as it was usually conceived: that is, as lacking at the very least any obviously theoretical terminology from any recognized science, and of course as lacking any moral terminology. For then the difficulty is that moral principles fare just as well (or just as badly) against the verificationist challenge as do typical scientific principles. For it is by now a familiar point about scientific principles – principles such as Newton's law of universal gravitation or Darwin's theory of evolution – that they are entirely devoid of empirical implications when considered in isolation.[3] We do of course base observational predictions on such theories and so test them against experience, but that is because we do *not* consider them in isolation. For we can derive these predictions only by relying at the same time on a large background of additional assumptions, many of which are equally theoretical and equally incapable of being tested in isolation. A less familiar point, because less often spelled out, is that the relation of moral principles to observation is similar in *both* these respects. Candidate moral principles – for example, that an action is wrong just in case there is something else the agent could have done that would have produced a greater net balance of pleasure over pain – lack empirical implications when considered in isolation. But it is easy to derive empirical consequences from them, and thus to test them against experience, if we allow ourselves, as we do in the scientific case, to rely on a background of other assumptions of comparable status. Thus, if we conjoin the act-utilitarian principle I just cited with the further view, also untestable in isolation, that it is always wrong deliberately to kill a human being, we can deduce from these two premises together the consequence that deliberately killing a human being always produces a lesser balance of pleasure over pain than some available alternative act; and this claim is one any positivist would have conceded we know, in principle at least, how to test. If we found it to be false, moreover, then we would be forced by this empirical test to abandon at least one of the moral claims from which we derived it.

It might be thought a worrisome feature of this example, however, and a further opening for skepticism, that there could be controversy about which moral premise to abandon, and that we have not explained how our empirical test can provide an answer to *this* question. And this may be a problem. It should be a familiar problem, however, because the Duhemian commentary includes a precisely corresponding point about the scientific case: that if we are at all cautious in characterizing what we observe, then the requirement that our theories merely be *consistent* with observation is an astoundingly weak one. There are always many, perhaps indefinitely many, different mutually inconsistent ways to adjust our views to meet this constraint. Of course, in practice we are often confident of how to do it: If you are a freshman chemistry student, you do not conclude from your failure to obtain the predicted value in an experiment that it is all over for the atomic theory of gases. And the decision can be equally easy, one should note, in a moral case. Consider two examples. From the surprising moral thesis that Adolf Hitler was a morally admirable person, together with a modest piece of moral theory to the effect that no morally admirable person would, for example, instigate and oversee the degradation and death of millions of persons, one can derive the testable consequence that Hitler did not do this. But he did, so we must give up one of our premises; and the choice of which to abandon is neither difficult nor controversial.

Or, to take a less monumental example, contrived around one of Harman's own, suppose you have been thinking yourself lucky enough to live in a neighborhood in which no one would do anything wrong, at least not in public; and that the modest piece of theory you accept, this time, is that malicious cruelty, just for the hell of it, is wrong. Then, as in Harman's example, "you round a corner and see a group of young hoodlums pour gasoline on a cat and ignite it." At this point, either your confidence in the neighborhood or your principle about cruelty has got to give way. But the choice is easy, if dispiriting, so easy as hardly to require thought. As Harman says, "You do not need to *conclude* that what they are doing is wrong; you do not need to figure anything out; you can *see* that it is wrong" (p. 4). But a skeptic can still wonder whether this practical confidence, or this "seeing," rests in either sort of case on anything more than deeply ingrained conventions of thought – respect for scientific experts, say, and for certain moral traditions – as opposed to anything answerable to the facts of the matter, any reliable strategy for getting it right about the world.

Now, Harman's challenge is interesting partly because it does not rest on these verificationist doubts about whether moral beliefs have observational implications, but even more because what it does rest on is a partial answer to the kind of general skepticism to which, as we have seen, reflection on the verificationist picture can lead. Many of our beliefs are justified, in Harman's view, by their providing or helping to provide a reasonable *explanation* of our observing what we do. It would be consistent with your failure, as a beginning student, to obtain the experimental result predicted by the gas laws, that the laws are mistaken. That would even be one explanation of your failure. But a better explanation, in light of your inexperience and the general success experts have had in confirming and applying these laws, is that you made some mistake in running the experiment. So our scientific beliefs can be justified by their explanatory role; and so too, in Harman's view, can mathematical beliefs and many commonsense beliefs about the world.

Not so, however, moral beliefs: They appear to have no such explanatory role. That is "the problem with ethics." Harman spells out his version of this contrast:

You need to make assumptions about certain physical facts to explain the occurrence of the observations that support a scientific theory, but you do not seem to need to make assumptions about any moral facts to explain the occurrence of the so-called moral observations I have been talking about. In the moral case, it would seem that you need only make assumptions about the psychology or moral sensibility of the person making the moral observation.

(p. 6)

More precisely, and applied to his own example, it might be reasonable, in order to explain your judging that the hoodlums are wrong to set the cat on fire, to assume "that the children really are pouring gasoline on a cat and you are seeing them do it." But there is no

> obvious reason to assume anything about "moral facts," such as that it is really wrong to set the cat on fire. ... Indeed, an assumption about moral facts would seem to be totally irrelevant to the explanation of your making the judgment you make. It would seem that all we need assume is that you have certain more or less well articulated moral principles that are reflected in the judgments you make, based on your moral sensibility.

(p. 7)

And Harman thinks that if we accept this conclusion, suitably generalized, then, subject to a possible qualification I shall come to shortly, we must conclude that moral theories cannot be tested against the world as scientific theories can, and that we have no reason to believe that moral facts are part of the order of nature or that there is any moral knowledge (pp. 23, 35).

My own view is that Harman is quite wrong, not in thinking that the explanatory role of our beliefs is important to their justification, but in thinking that moral beliefs play no such role.[4] I shall have to say something about the initial plausibility of Harman's thesis as applied to his own example, but part of my reason for dissenting should be apparent from the other example I just gave. We find it easy (and so does Harman [p.108]) to conclude from the evidence not just that Hitler was not morally admirable, but that he was morally depraved. But isn't it plausible that Hitler's moral depravity – the fact of his really having been morally depraved – forms part of a reasonable explanation of why we believe he was depraved? I think so, and I shall argue concerning this and other examples that moral beliefs commonly play the explanatory role Harman denies them. Before I can press my case, however, I need to clear up several preliminary points about just what Harman is claiming and just how his argument is intended to work.

121

II OBSERVATION, EXPLANATION, AND REDUCTION

1

For there are several ways in which Harman's argument invites misunderstanding. One results from his focusing at the start on the question of whether there can be moral *observations*.[5] But this question turns out to be a side issue, in no way central to his argument that moral principles cannot be tested against the world. There are a couple of reasons for this, of which the more important[6] by far is that Harman does not really require of moral facts, if belief in them is to be justified, that they figure in the explanation of moral observations. It would be enough, on the one hand, if they were needed for the explanation of moral beliefs that are not in any interesting sense observations. For example, Harman thinks belief in moral facts would be vindicated if they were needed to explain our drawing the moral conclusions we do when we reflect on hypothetical cases, but I think there is no illumination in calling these conclusions observations.[7] It would also be enough, on the other hand, if moral facts were needed for the explanation of what were clearly observations, but not moral observations. Harman thinks mathematical beliefs are justified, but he does not suggest that there are mathematical observations; it is rather that appeal to mathematical truths helps to explain why we make the physical observations we do (p. 10). Moral beliefs would surely be justified, too, if they played such a role, whether or not there are any moral observations.

So the claim is that moral facts are not needed to explain our having any of the moral beliefs we do, whether or not those beliefs are observations, and are equally unneeded to explain any of the observations we make, whether or not those observations are moral. In fact, Harman's view appears to be that moral facts aren't needed to explain anything at all: although it would perhaps be question-begging for him to begin with this strong a claim, since he grants that if there were any moral facts, then appeal to other moral facts, more general ones, for example, might be needed to explain *them* (p. 8). But he is certainly claiming, at the very least, that moral facts aren't needed to explain any nonmoral facts we have any reason to believe in.

This claim has seemed plausible even to some philosophers who wish to defend the existence of moral facts and the possibility of moral knowledge. Thus, Thomas Nagel has recently retreated to the reply that

> it begs the question to assume that *explanatory* necessity is the test of reality in this area. ... To assume that only what has to be included in the best explanatory picture of the world is real, is to assume that there are no irreducibly normative truths.[8]

But this retreat will certainly make it more difficult to fit moral knowledge into anything like a causal theory of knowledge, which seems plausible for many other cases, or to follow Hilary Putnam's suggestion that we "apply a generally causal account of reference ... to moral terms" (Putnam, 1975). In addition, the concession is premature in any case, for I shall argue that moral facts do fit into our explanatory view of the world, and in particular into explanations of many moral observations and beliefs.

2

Other possible misunderstandings concern what is meant in asking whether reference to moral facts is *needed* to explain moral beliefs. One warning about this question I save for my comments on reduction below; but another, about what Harman is clearly *not* asking, and about what sort of answer I can attempt to defend to the question he is asking, can be spelled out first. For, to begin with, Harman's question is clearly not just whether there is *an* explanation of our moral beliefs that does not mention moral facts. Almost surely there is. Equally surely, however, there is *an* explanation of our commonsense nonmoral beliefs that does not mention an external world: one which cites only our sensory experience, for example, together with whatever needs to be said about our psychology to explain why with that history of experience we would form just the beliefs we do. Harman means to be asking a question that will lead to skepticism about moral facts, but not to skepticism about the existence of material bodies or about well-established scientific theories of the world.

Harman illustrates the kind of question he is asking, and the kind of answer he is seeking, with an example from physics which it will be useful to keep in mind. A physicist sees a vapor trail in a cloud chamber and thinks, "There goes a proton." What explains his thinking this? Partly, of course, his psychological set, which largely depends on his beliefs about the apparatus and all the theory he has learned; but partly also, perhaps, the hypothesis that "there really was a proton going through the cloud chamber, causing the vapor trail, which he saw as a proton." We will *not* need this latter assumption, however, "if his having made that observation could have been equally well explained by his psychological set alone, without the need for any assumption about a proton" (p. 6).[9] So for reference to moral facts to be *needed* in the explanation of our beliefs and observations, is for this reference to be required for an explanation that is somehow *better* than competing explanations. Correspondingly, reference to moral facts will be unnecessary to an explanation, in Harman's view, not just because we can find some explanation that does not appeal to them, but because *no* explanation that appeals to them is any better than some competing explanation that does not.

Now, fine discriminations among competing explanations of almost anything are likely to be difficult, controversial, and provisional. Fortunately, however, my discussion of Harman's argument will not require any fine discriminations. This is because Harman's thesis, as we have seen, is *not* that moral explanations lose out by a small margin; nor is it that moral explanations, although sometimes initially promising, always turn out on further examination to be inferior to nonmoral ones. It is, rather, that reference to moral facts always looks, right from the start, to be "completely irrelevant" to the explanation of any of our observations and beliefs. And my argument will be that this is mistaken: that many moral explanations appear to be good explanations, or components in good explanations, that are not obviously undermined by anything else that we know. My suspicion, in fact, is that moral facts are needed in the sense explained, that they will turn out to belong in our best overall explanatory picture of the world, even in the long run, but I shall not attempt to establish that here. Indeed, it should be clear why I could not pretend to do so. For I have explicitly put to one side the issue (which I regard as incapable in any case of quick resolution) of whether and to what extent actual moral disagreements can be settled satisfactorily. But I assume it would count as a defect in any sort of explanation to rely on claims about which rational agreement proved unattainable. So I concede that it *could* turn out, for anything I say here, that moral explanations are all defective and should be discarded. What I shall try to show is merely that many moral explanations look reasonable enough to be in the running; and, more specifically, that nothing Harman says provides any reason for thinking they are not. This claim is surely strong enough (and controversial enough) to be worth defending.

3

It is implicit in this statement of my project, but worth noting separately, that I take Harman to be proposing an *independent* skeptical argument – independent not merely of the argument from the difficulty of settling disputed moral questions, but also of other standard arguments for moral skepticism. Otherwise his argument is not worth independent discussion. For *any* of these more familiar skeptical arguments will of course imply that moral explanations are defective, on the reasonable assumption that it would be a defect in any explanation to rely on claims as doubtful as these arguments attempt to show all moral claims to be. But if *that* is why there is a problem with moral explanations, one should surely just cite the relevant skeptical argument, rather than this derivative difficulty about moral explanations, as the basic "problem with ethics," and it is that argument we should discuss. So I take Harman's interesting suggestion to be that there is a *different* difficulty that remains even if we put other arguments for moral skepticism aside and *assume*, for the sake of argument, that there are moral facts (for example, that what the children in his example are doing is really wrong): namely, that these assumed facts *still* seem to play no explanatory role.

This understanding of Harman's thesis crucially affects my argumentative strategy in a way to which I should alert the reader in advance. For it should be clear that assessment of this thesis not merely permits, but *requires*, that we provisionally assume the existence of moral facts. I can see no way of evaluating the claim that *even if* we assumed the existence of moral facts they would still appear explanatorily irrelevant, without assuming the existence of some, to see how they would look. So I do freely assume this in each of the examples I discuss in the next section. (I have tried to choose plausible examples, moreover, moral facts most of us would be inclined to believe in if we did believe in moral facts, since those are the easiest to think about; but the precise examples don't matter, and anyone who would prefer others should feel free to substitute his own.) I grant, furthermore, that if Harman were right about the outcome of this thought experiment – that even after we assumed these facts they still looked irrelevant to the explanation of our moral beliefs and of other nonmoral facts – then we might conclude with him that there were, after all, no such facts. But I claim he is wrong: Once we have provisionally assumed the existence of moral facts, they *do* appear relevant, by perfectly ordinary standards, to the explanation of moral beliefs and of a good deal else besides. Does this prove that there *are* such facts? Well of course it helps support that view, but here I carefully make no claim to have shown so much. What I *show* is that any remaining reservations about the existence of moral facts must be based on those *other* skeptical arguments, of which Harman's argument is independent. In short, there may still be a "problem with ethics," but it has *nothing* special to do with moral explanations.

4

A final preliminary point concerns a qualification Harman adds himself. As I have explained his argument so far, it assumes that we could have reason to believe in moral facts only if this helped us "explain why we observe what we observe" (p. 13); but, he says, this assumption is too strong, for we can have evidence for the truth of some beliefs that play no such explanatory role. We might, for example, come to be able to explain color perception without saying that objects have colors, by citing certain physical and psychological facts. But this would not show that there are no colors; it would show only that facts about color are "somehow reducible" to these physical and psychological facts. And this leaves the possibility that moral facts, too, even if they ultimately play no explanatory role themselves, might be "reducible to certain other facts that can help explain our observations" (p. 14). So a crucial question is: What would justify a belief in reducibility? What makes us think color facts might be reducible to physical (or physical and psychological) facts, and what would justify us in thinking moral facts reducible to explanatory natural facts of some kind?

Harman's answer is that it is still the *apparent* explanatory role of color facts, or of moral facts, that matters; and hence that this qualification to his argument is not so great as it might seem. We know of no precise reduction for facts of either sort. We believe even so that reduction is possible for color facts because even when we are able to explain color perception without saying that objects are colored,

> we will still *sometimes* refer to the actual colors of objects in explaining color perception, if only for the sake of simplicity. ... We will continue to believe that objects have colors because we will continue to refer to the actual colors of objects in the explanations that we will in practice give.

But Harman thinks that no comparable point holds for moral facts. "There does not ever seem to be, even in practice, any point to explaining someone's moral observations by appeal to what is actually right or wrong, just or unjust, good or bad" (p. 22).

Now I shall argue shortly that this is just wrong: that sober people frequently offer such explanations of moral observations and beliefs, and that many of these explanations look plausible enough on the evidence to be worth taking seriously. So a quick reply to Harman, strictly adequate for my purpose, would be simply to accept his concession that this by itself should lead us to regard moral facts as (at worst) reducible to explanatory facts.[10] Concern about the need for, and the role of, reductive definitions has been so central to metaethical discussion in this century, however, and has also proved enough of a sticking point in discussions I have had of the topic of this essay, that I should say a bit more.

As a philosophical naturalist, I take natural facts to be the only facts there are.[11] If I am prepared to recognize moral facts, therefore, I must take them, too, to be natural facts: But which natural facts? It is widely thought that an ethical naturalist must answer this question by providing reductive naturalistic definitions[12] for moral terms and, indeed, that until one has supplied such definitions one's credentials as a *naturalist* about any supposed moral facts must be in doubt. Once such definitions are in hand, however, it seems that moral explanations should be dispensable, since any such explanations can then be paraphrased in nonmoral terms; so it is hard to see why an ethical naturalist should attach any importance to them. Now, there are several problems with this reasoning, but the main one is that the widely held view on which it is based is mistaken: mistaken about where a scheme of reductive naturalistic definitions would be found, if there were to be one, but also about whether, on a naturalistic view of ethics, one should expect there to be such a thing at all. I shall take up these points in reverse order, arguing first (a) that it is a mistake to require of ethical naturalism that it even promise reductive definitions for moral terms, and then (b) that even if such definitions are to be forthcoming it is, at the very least, no special problem for ethical naturalism that we are not *now* in confident possession of them.

(a) Naturalism is in one clear sense a "reductionist" doctrine of course, for it holds that moral facts are nothing but natural facts. What I deny, however, is that from this metaphysical doctrine about what sort of facts moral facts are, anything follows about the possibility of reduction in another sense (to which I shall henceforth confine the term) more familiar from the philosophical literature: that is, about whether moral expressions can be given reductive definitions in some distinctive nonmoral vocabulary, in which any plausible moral explanations could then be recast. The difficulty with supposing naturalism to require this can be seen by pressing the question of just what this distinctive vocabularly is supposed to be. It is common to say merely that this reducing terminology must be "factual" or "descriptive" or must designate natural properties; but unless ethical naturalism has already been ruled out, this is no help, for what naturalists of course contend is that moral discourse is *itself* factual and descriptive (although it may be other things as well), and that moral terms themselves stand for natural properties. The idea, clearly, is supposed to be that the *test* of whether these naturalistic claims about moral discourse are correct is whether this discourse is reducible to some other; but what other? I consider two possibilities.

(i) Many would agree that it is too restrictive to understand ethical naturalism as requiring that moral terms be definable in the terminology of fundamental physics. One reason it is too restrictive is that philosophical naturalism might be true even if physicalism, the view that everything is physical, is not. Some form of emergent dualism might be correct, for example. A different reason, which I find more interesting (because I think physicalism *is* true), is that physicalism entails nothing in any case about whether even biology or psychology, let alone ethics, is reducible to physics. There are a number of reasons for this, but a cardinality problem noted by Richard Boyd (1989, 1991) is sufficient to secure the point. If there are (as there appear to be) any continuous physical parameters, then there are continuum many physical states of the world, but there are at most countably many predicates in any language, including that of even ideal physics; so there are more physical properties than there are physical expressions to represent them. Thus, although physicalism certainly entails that biological and psychological properties (and ethical properties, too, if there are any) are physical, nothing follows about whether we have any but biological or psychological or ethical terminology for representing these particular physical properties.

(ii) Of course, not many discussions of ethical naturalism have focused on the possibility of reducing ethics to physics; social theory, psychology, and occasionally biology have appeared more promising possibilities. But that facts might be *physical* whether or not all the disciplines that deal with them are reducible to *physics*, helps give point to my question of why we should think that if all ethical facts are *natural* (or, for that matter, *social* or *psychological* or *biological*), it follows that they can equally well be expressed in some other, nonmoral idiom; and it also returns us to the question of just what this alternative idiom is supposed to be. The answer to this latter question simply assumed in most discussions of ethical naturalism, I think, is that there are a number of disciplines that we pretty well know to deal with a single natural world, for example, physics, biology, psychology, and social theory; that it is a matter of no great concern whether any of *these* disciplines is reducible to some one of the others or to anything else; but that the test of whether ethical naturalism is true *is* whether ethics is reducible to some (nonmoral) combination of *them*.[13]

But what rationale is there for holding ethics alone to this reductive test? Perhaps there would be one if ethics appeared in some salient respect strikingly dissimilar to these other disciplines: if, for example, Harman were right what whereas physics, biology, and the rest offer plausible explanations of many obviously natural facts, including facts about our beliefs and observations, ethics never does. Perhaps ethics could then plausibly be required to earn its place by some alternative route. But I shall of course argue that Harman is wrong about this alleged dissimilarity, and I take my argument to provide part of the defense required for a naturalistic but nonreductive view of ethics.

(b) A naturalist, however, will certainly want (and a critic of naturalism will likely demand) a fuller account than this of just where moral facts are supposed to fit in the natural world. For all I have shown, moreover, this account might even provide a scheme of reduction for moral discourse: My argument has been not that ethical naturalism could not take this form, but only that it need not. So where should one look for such a fuller account or (if it is to be had) such a reduction? The answer is that the account will have to be derived from our best moral theory, together with our best theory of the rest of the natural world – exactly as, for example, any reductive account of colors will have to be based on all we know about colors, including our best optical theory together with other parts of physics and perhaps psychology. If hedonistic act-utilitarianism (and enough of its associated psychology) turns out to be true, for example, then we can define the good as pleasure and the absence of pain, and a right action as one that produces at least as much good as any other, and that will be where the moral facts fit. If, more plausibly, some other moral theory turns out to be correct, we will get a different account and (if the theory takes the right form) different reductive definitions. It would of course be a serious objection to ethical *naturalism* if we discovered that the *only* plausible moral theories had to invoke supernatural facts of some kind, by making right and wrong depend on the will of a deity, for example, or by implying that only persons with immortal souls could have moral obligations. We would then have to choose between a naturalistic world view and a belief in moral facts. But an ethical naturalist can point out that there are familiar moral theories that lack implications of this sort and that appear defensible in the light of all we know about the natural world; and any of them, if correct, could provide a naturalistic account of moral facts and even (if one is to be had) a naturalistic reduction of moral discourse.

Many philosophers will balk at this confident talk of our discovering some moral theory to be correct. But their objection is just the familiar one whose importance I acknowledged at the outset, before putting it to one side: For I grant that the difficulty we experience in settling moral issues, including issues in moral theory, is a problem (although perhaps not an insuperable one) for any version of moral realism. All I contend here is that there is not, in addition to this acknowledged difficulty, any special further (or prior) problem of finding reductive definitions for moral terms or of figuring out where moral facts fit in the natural world. Our moral theory, if once we get it, will provide whatever reduction is to be had and will tell us where the moral facts fit. The suspicion that there must be more than this to the search for reductive definitions almost always rests, I believe, on the view that these definitions must be suited to a special epistemic role: for example, that they will have to be analytic or conceptual truths and so provide a privileged basis for the rest of our theory. But I am confident that moral reasoning, like reasoning in the sciences, is inevitably dialectical and lacks a priori foundations of this sort. I am also sure that no ethical naturalist need think otherwise.[14]

The relevance of these points is this: It is true that if we once obtained correct reductive definitions for moral terms, moral explanations would be in principle dispensable; so if ethical naturalism had to promise such definitions, it would also have to promise the eliminability in principle of explanations couched in moral terms. But note three points. First, it should be no surprise, and should be regarded as no special difficulty for naturalism even on a reductionist conception of it, that we are not now in possession of such definitions, and so not *now* in a position to dispense with any moral explanations that seem plausible. To be confident of such definitions we would need to know just which moral theory is correct; but ethics is an area of great controversy, and I am sure we do not yet know this. Second, if some moral explanations do seem plausible, as I shall argue, then one important step toward improving this situation in ethics will be to see what sort of theory emerges if we attempt to refine these explanations in the light both of empirical evidence and theoretical criticism. So it is easy to see, again even on a reductionist understanding of naturalism that promises the eliminability of moral explanations in the long run, why any naturalist will think that for the foreseeable short run such explanations should be taken seriously on their own terms.

The third and most important point, finally, is that the eliminability of moral explanations for *this* reason, if actually demonstrated, would of course not represent a triumph of ethical skepticism but would rather derive from its defeat. So we must add one further caution, as I promised, concerning Harman's thesis that no reference to moral facts is *needed* in the explanation of moral beliefs. For there are, as we can now see, two very different reasons one might have for thinking this. One – Harman's reason, and my target in the remainder of this essay – is that no moral explanations even seem plausible, that reference to moral facts always strikes us as "completely irrelevant" to the explanation of moral beliefs. This claim, if true, would tend to support moral skepticism. The other reason – which I have just been considering, and with which I also disagree – is that any moral explanations that *do* seem plausible can be paraphrased without explanatory loss in entirely nonmoral terms. I have argued that it is a mistake to understand ethical naturalism as promising this kind of reduction even in principle; and I think it in any case absurd overconfidence to suppose that anyone can spell out an adequate reduction now. But any reader unconvinced by my arguments should note also that this *second* reason is no version of moral skepticism: For what anyone convinced by it must think, is that we either are or will be able to say, in entirely nonmoral terms, exactly which natural properties moral terms refer to.[15] So Harman is right to present reductionism as an alternative to skepticism; part of what I have tried to show is just that it is neither the only nor the most plausible such alternative, and that no ethical naturalist need be committed to it.

III MORAL EXPLANATIONS

With these preliminary points aside, I turn to my arguments against Harman's thesis. I shall first add to my example of Hitler's moral character several more in which it seems plausible to cite moral facts as part of an explanation of nonmoral facts, and in partic-ular of people's forming the moral opinions they do. I shall then argue that Harman gives us no plausible reason to reject or ignore these explanations; I shall claim, in fact, that the same is true for his own example of the children igniting the cat. I shall conclude, finally, by attempting to diagnose the source of the disagreement between Harman and me on these issues.

My Hitler example suggests a whole range of extremely common cases that appear not to have occurred to Harman, cases in which we cite someone's moral character as part of an explanation of his or her deeds, and in which that whole story is then avail-able as a plausible further explanation of someone's arriving at a correct assessment of that moral character. Take just one other example. Bernard DeVoto, in *The Year of Decision: 1846*, describes the efforts of American emigrants already in California to rescue another party of emigrants, the Donner Party, trapped by snows in the High Sierras, once their plight became known. At a meeting in Yerba Buena (now San Francisco), the relief efforts were put under the direction of a recent arrival, Passed Midshipman Selim Woodworth, described by a previous acquaintance as "a great busy-body and ambitious of taking a command among the emigrants."[16] But Woodworth not only failed to lead rescue parties into the mountains himself, where other rescuers were counting on him (leaving children to be picked up by him, for example), but had to be "shamed, threatened, and bullied" even into organizing the efforts of others willing to take the risk; he spent time arranging comforts for himself in camp, preening himself on the importance of his position; and as a predictable result of his cowardice and his exercises in vainglory, many died who might have been saved, including four known still to be alive when he turned back for the last time in mid-March. DeVoto concludes: "Passed Midshipman Woodworth was just no damned good." I cite this case partly because it has so clearly the structure of an inference to a reasonable explanation. One can think of competing explanations, but the evidence points against them. It isn't, for example, that Woodworth was a basically decent person who simply proved too weak when thrust into a situation that placed heroic demands on him. He volunteered, he put no serious effort even into tasks that required no heroism, and it seems clear that concern for his own position and reputation played a much larger role in his motivation than did any concern for the people he was expected to save. If DeVoto is right about this evidence, moreover, it seems reasonable that part of the explanation of his believing that Woodworth was no damned good is just that Woodworth *was* no damned good.

DeVoto writes of course with more moral intensity (and with more of a flourish) than academic historians usually permit themselves, but it would be difficult to find a serious work of biography, for example, in which actions are not explained by appeal to moral character: sometimes by appeal to specific virtues and vices, but often enough also by appeal to a more general assessment. A different question, and perhaps a more difficult one, concerns the sort of example on which Harman concentrates, the explanation of judgments of right and wrong. Here again Harman appears just to have overlooked explanations in terms of moral character: A judge's thinking that it would be wrong to sentence a particular offender to the maximum prison term the law allows, for example, may be due in part to her decency and fairmindedness, which I take to be moral facts if any are. But do moral features of the action or institution being judged ever play an explanatory role? Here is an example in which they appear to. An interesting historical question is why vigorous and reasonably widespread moral opposition to slavery arose for the first time in the eighteenth and nineteenth centuries, even though slavery was a very old institution; and why this opposition arose primarily in Britain, France, and in French- and English-speaking North America, even though slavery existed throughout the New World.[17] There is a standard answer to this question. It is that chattel slavery in British and French America, and then in the United States, was much *worse* than previous forms of slavery, and much worse than slavery in Latin America. This is, I should add, a controversial explanation. But as is often the case with historical explanations, its proponents do not claim it is the whole story, and many of its opponents grant that there may be some truth in these comparisons, and that they may after all form a small part of a larger explanation.[18] This latter concession is all I require for my example. Equally good for my purpose would be the more limited thesis that explains the growth of antislavery sentiment in the United States, between the Revolution and the Civil War, in part by saying that slavery in the United States became a more oppressive institution during that time. The appeal in these standard explanations is straightforwardly to moral facts.

What is supposed to be wrong with all these explanations? Harman says that assumptions about moral facts seem "completely irrelevant" in explaining moral observations and moral beliefs (p. 7), but on its more natural reading that claim seems pretty obviously mistaken about these examples. For it is natural to think that if a particular assumption is completely irrelevant to the explanation of a certain fact, then the fact would have obtained, and we could have explained it just as well, even if the assumption had been false.[19] But I do not believe that Hitler would have done all he did if he had not been morally depraved, nor, on the assumption that he was not depraved, can I think of any plausible alternative explanation for his doing those things. Nor is it plausible that we would all have believed he was morally depraved even if he hadn't been. Granted, there is a tendency for writers who do not attach much weight to fascism as a social movement to want to blame its evils on a single maniacal leader, so perhaps some of them would have painted Hitler as a moral monster even if he had not been one. But this is only a tendency, and one for which many people know how to discount, so I doubt that our moral belief really is overdetermined in this way. Nor, similarly, do I believe that Woodworth's actions were overdetermined, so that he would have done just as he did even if he had been a more admirable person. I suppose one could have doubts about DeVoto's objectivity and reliability; it is obvious he dislikes Woodworth, so perhaps he would have thought him a moral loss and convinced his readers of this no matter what the man was really like. But it is more plausible that the dislike is mostly based on the same evidence that supports DeVoto's moral view of him, and that very different evidence, at any rate, would have produced a different verdict. If so, then Woodworth's moral character is part of the explanation of DeVoto's belief about his moral character.

It is more plausible of course that serious moral opposition to slavery would have emerged in Britain, France, and the United States even if slavery hadn't been worse in the modern period than before, and worse in the United States than in Latin America, and that the American antislavery movement would have grown even if slavery had not become more oppressive as the nineteenth century progressed. But that is because these moral facts are offered as at best a partial explanation of these developments in moral opinion. And if they really *are* part of the explanation, as seems plausible, then it is also plausible that whatever effect they produced was not entirely overdetermined; that, for example, the growth of the antislavery movement in the United States would at least have been somewhat slower if slavery had been and remained less bad an institution. Here again it hardly seems "completely irrelevant" to the explanation whether or not these moral facts obtained.

It is more puzzling, I grant, to consider Harman's own example in which you see the children igniting a cat and react immediately with the thought that this is wrong. Is it

true, as Harman claims, that the assumption that the children are really doing something wrong is "totally irrelevant" to any reasonable explanation of your making that
judgment? Would you, for example, have reacted in just the same way, with the thought
that the action is wrong, even if what they were doing *hadn't* been wrong, and could we
explain your reaction equally well on this assumption? Now, there is more than one
way to understand this counterfactual question, and I shall return below to a reading of
it that might appear favorable to Harman's view. What I wish to point out for now is
merely that there is a natural way of taking it, parallel to the way in which I have been
understanding similar counterfactual questions about my own examples, on which the
answer to it has to be simply: It depends. For to answer the question, I take it, we must
consider a situation in which what the children are doing is not wrong, but which is
otherwise as much like the actual situation as possible, and then decide what your
reaction would be in that situation. But since what makes their action wrong, what its
wrongness *consists* in, is presumably something like its being an act of gratuitious
cruelty (or, perhaps we should add, of intense cruelty, and to a helpless victim), to
imagine them not doing something wrong we are going to have to imagine their action
different in this respect. More cautiously and more generally, if what they are actually
doing is wrong, and if moral properties are, as many writers have held, supervenient on
natural ones,[20] then in order to imagine them not doing something wrong we are going
to have to suppose their action different from the actual one in some of its natural
features as well. So our question becomes: Even if the children had been doing something else, something just different enough not to be wrong, would you have taken
them even so to be doing something wrong?

Surely there is no one answer to this question: It depends on a lot about you,
including your moral views and how good you are at seeing at a glance what some
children are doing. It probably depends also on a debatable moral issue; namely, just
how different the children's action would have to be in order not to be wrong. (Is
unkindness to animals, for example, also wrong?) I believe we can see how, in a case in
which the answer was clearly affirmative, we might be tempted to agree with Harman
that the wrongness of the action was no part of the explanation of your reaction. For
suppose you are like this. You hate children. What you especially hate, moreover, is
the sight of children enjoying themselves; so much so that whenever you see children
having fun, you immediately assume they are up to no good. The more they seem to be
enjoying themselves, furthermore, the readier you are to fasten on any pretext for
thinking them engaged in real wickedness. Then it is true that even if the children had
been engaged in some robust but innocent fun, you would have thought they were
doing something wrong; and Harman is perhaps right[21] about you that the actual
wrongness of the action you see is irrelevant to your thinking it wrong. This is because
your reaction is due to a feature of the action that coincides only very accidentally with
the ones that make it wrong.[22] But, of course, and fortunately, many people aren't like

this (nor does Harman argue that they are). It isn't true of them that, in general, if the children had been doing something similar, although different enough not to be wrong, they would still have thought the children were doing something wrong. And it isn't true either, therefore, that the wrongness of the action is irrelevant to the explanation of why they think it wrong.

Now, one might have the sense from my discussion of all these examples – but perhaps especially from my discussion of this last one, Harman's own – that I have perversely been refusing to understand his claim about the explanatory irrelevance of moral facts in the way he intends. And perhaps I have not been understanding it as he wishes. In any case, I agree, I have certainly not been understanding the crucial counter-factual question, of whether we would have drawn the same moral conclusion even if the moral facts had been different, in the way he must intend. But I am not being perverse. I believe, as I said, that my way of taking the question is the more natural one. And more important, although there is, I grant, a reading of that question on which it will always yield the answer Harman wants – namely, that a difference in the moral facts would *not* have made a difference in our judgment – I do not believe this can support his argument. I must now explain why.

It will help if I contrast my general approach with his. I am addressing questions about the justification of belief in the spirit of what Quine has called "epistemology naturalized."[23] I take this to mean that we have in general no a priori way of knowing which strategies for forming and refining our beliefs are likely to take us closer to the truth. The only way we have of proceeding is to assume the approximate truth of what seems to us the best overall theory we already have of what we are like and what the world is like, and to decide in the light of *that* what strategies of research and reasoning are likely to be reliable in producing a more nearly true overall theory. One result of applying these procedures, in turn, is likely to be the refinement or perhaps even the abandonment of parts of the tentative theory with which we began.

I take Harman's approach, too, to be an instance of this one. He says we are justified in believing in those facts that we need to assume to explain why we observe what we do. But he does not think that our knowledge of this principle about justification is a priori. Furthermore, as he knows, we cannot decide whether one explanation is better than another without relying on beliefs we already have about the world. Is it really a better explanation of the vapor trail the physicist sees in the cloud chamber to suppose that a proton caused it, as Harman suggests in his example, rather than some other charged particle? Would there, for example, have been no vapor trail in the absence of that proton? There is obviously no hope of answering such questions without assuming at least the approximate truth of some quite far-reaching microphysical theory, and our knowledge of such theories is not a priori.

But my approach differs from Harman's in one crucial way. For among the beliefs in which I have enough confidence to rely on in evaluating explanations, at least at the outset, are some moral beliefs. And I have been relying on them in the following way.[24] Harman's thesis implies that the supposed moral fact of Hitler's being morally depraved is irrelevant to the explanation of Hitler's doing what he did. (For we may suppose that if it explains his doing what he did, it also helps explain, at greater remove, Harman's belief and mine in his moral depravity.) To assess this claim, we need to conceive a situation in which Hitler was *not* morally depraved and consider the question whether in that situation he would still have done what he did. My answer is that he would not, and this answer relies on a (not very controversial) moral view: that in any world at all like the actual one, only a morally depraved person could have initiated a world war, ordered the "final solution," and done any number of other things Hitler did. That is why I believe that, if Hitler hadn't been morally depraved, he wouldn't have done those things, and hence that the fact of his moral depravity is relevant to an explanation of what he did.

Harman, however, cannot want us to rely on any such moral views in answering this counterfactual question. This comes out most clearly if we return to his example of the children igniting the cat. He claims that the wrongness of this act is irrelevant to an explanation of your thinking it wrong, that you would have *thought* it wrong even if it wasn't. My reply was that in order for the action not to be wrong it would have had to lack the feature of deliberate, intense, pointless cruelty, and that if it had differed in this way you might very well *not* have thought it wrong. I also suggested a more cautious version of this reply: that since the action is in fact wrong, and since moral properties supervene on more basic natural ones, it would have had to be different in *some* further natural respect in order not to be wrong; and that we do not know whether if it had so differed you would still have thought it wrong. Both of these replies, again, rely on moral views, the latter merely on the view that there is *something* about the natural features of the action in Harman's example that makes it wrong, the former on a more specific view as to which of these features do this.

But Harman, it is fairly clear, intends for us *not* to rely on any such moral views in evaluating his counterfactual claim. His claim is not that if the action had not been one of deliberate cruelty (or had otherwise differed in whatever way would be required to remove its wrongness), you would still have thought it wrong. It is, instead, that if the action were one of deliberate, pointless cruelty, but this *did not make it wrong*, you would still have thought it was wrong. And to return to the example of Hitler's moral character, the counterfactual claim that Harman will need in order to defend a comparable conclusion about that case is not that if Hitler had been, for example, humane and fair-minded, free of nationalistic pride and racial hatred, he would still have done exactly as he did. It is, rather, that if Hitler's psychology, and anything else about his situation that could strike us as morally relevant, had been exactly as it in fact was, but this had *not constituted moral depravity*, he would still have done exactly what he did.

135

Now the antecedents of these two conditionals are puzzling. For one thing, both are, I believe, necessarily false. I am fairly confident, for example, that Hitler really was morally depraved,[25] and since I also accept the view that moral features supervene on more basic natural properties,[26] I take this to imply that there is no possible world in which Hitler has just the personality he in fact did, in just the situation he was in, but is not morally depraved. Any attempt to describe such a situation, moreover, will surely run up against the limits of our moral concepts – what Harman calls our "moral sensibility" – and this is no accident. For what Harman is asking us to do, in general, is to consider cases in which absolutely *everything* about the nonmoral facts that could seem morally relevant to us, in light of whatever moral theory we accept and of the concepts required for our understanding of that theory, is held fixed, but in which the moral judgment that our theory yields about the case is nevertheless mistaken. So it is hardly surprising that, using that theory and those concepts, we should find it difficult to conceive in any detail what such a situation would be like. It is especially not surprising when the cases in question are as paradigmatic in light of the moral outlook we in fact have as is Harman's example or as is, even more so, mine of Hitler's moral character. The only way we could be wrong about this latter case (assuming we have the nonmoral facts right) would be for our whole moral theory to be hopelessly wrong, so radically mistaken that there could be no hope of straightening it out through adjustments from within.

But I do not believe we should conclude, as we might be temped to,[27] that we therefore know a priori that this is not so, or that we cannot understand these conditionals that are crucial to Harman's argument. Rather, now that we have seen how we have to understand them, we should grant that they are true: that if our moral theory were somehow hopelessly mistaken, but all the nonmoral facts remained exactly as they in fact are, then, since we do *accept* that moral theory, we would still draw exactly the moral conclusions we in fact do. But we should deny that any skeptical conclusion follows from this. In particular, we should deny that it follows that moral facts play no role in explaining our moral judgments.

For consider what follows from the parallel claim about microphysics, in particular about Harman's example in which a physicist concludes from his observation of a vapor trail in a cloud chamber, and from the microphysical theory he accepts, that a free proton has passed through the chamber. The parallel claim, notice, is *not* just that if the proton had not been there the physicist would have thought it was. This claim is implausible, for we may assume that the physicist's theory is generally correct, and it follows from that theory that if there hadn't been a proton there, then there wouldn't have been a vapor trail. But in a perfectly similar way it is implausible that if Hitler hadn't been morally depraved we would still have thought he was: for we may assume that our moral theory also is at least roughly correct, and it follows from the most central features of that theory that if Hitler hadn't been morally depraved, he wouldn't have done what he did. The *parallel* claim about the microphysical example is, instead, that if there hadn't been a proton there, but there *had* been a vapor trail, the physicist would still have concluded that a proton was present. More precisely, to maintain a perfect parallel with Harman's claims about the moral cases, the antecedent must specify that although no proton is present, absolutely *all* the nonmicrophysical facts that the physicist, in light of his theory, might take to be relevant to the question of whether or not a proton is present, are exactly as in the actual case. (These macrophysical facts, as I shall for convenience call them, surely include everything one would normally think of as an observable fact.) Of course, we shall be unable to imagine this without imagining that the physicist's theory is pretty badly mistaken,[28] but I believe we should grant that, *if* the physicist's theory were somehow this badly mistaken, but all the macrophysical facts (including all the observable facts) were held fixed, then the physicist, since he does accept that theory, would still draw all the same conclusions that he actually does. That is, this conditional claim, like Harman's parallel claims about the moral cases, is true.

But no skeptical conclusions follow; nor can Harman, since he does not intend to be a skeptic about physics, think that they do. It does not follow, in the first place, that we have any reason to think the physicist's theory *is* generally mistaken. Nor does it follow, furthermore, that the hypothesis that a proton really did pass through the cloud chamber is not part of a good explanation of the vapor trail, and hence of the physicist's thinking this has happened. This looks like a reasonable explanation, of course, only on the assumption that the physicist's theory is at least roughly true, for it is this theory that tells us, for example, what happens when charged particles pass through a supersaturated atmosphere, what other causes (if any) there might be for a similar phenomenon, and so on. But, as I say, we have not been provided with any reason for not trusting the theory to this extent.

Similarly, I conclude, we should draw no skeptical conclusions from Harman's claims about the moral cases. It is true, I grant, that if our moral theory were seriously mistaken, but we still believed it, and the nonmoral facts were held fixed, we would still make just the moral judgments we do. But *this* fact by itself provides us with no reason for thinking that our moral theory *is* generally mistaken. Nor, again, does it imply that the fact of Hitler's really having been morally depraved forms no part of a good explanation of his doing what he did and hence, at greater remove, of our thinking him depraved. This explanation will appear reasonable, of course, only on the assumption that our accepted moral theory is at least roughly correct, for it is this theory that assures us that only a depraved person could have thought, felt, and acted as Hitler did. But, as I say, Harman's argument has provided us with no reason for not trusting our moral views to this extent, and hence with no reason for doubting that it is sometimes moral facts that explain our moral judgments.

I conclude with three comments about my argument.

(1) I have tried to show that Harman's claim – that we would have held the particular moral beliefs we do even if those beliefs were untrue – admits of two readings, one of which makes it implausible, and the other of which reduces it to an application of a general skeptical strategy, which could as easily be used to produce doubt about microphysical as about moral facts. The general strategy is this. Consider any conclusion C we arrive at by relying both on some distinguishable "theory" T and on some body of evidence not being challenged, and ask whether we would have believed C even if it had been false. The plausible answer, *if* we are allowed to rely on T, will often be no: for if C had been false, then (according to T) the evidence would have had to be different, and in that case we wouldn't have believed C. (I have illustrated the plausibility of this sort of reply for all my moral examples, as well as for the microphysical one.) But the skeptic intends us *not* to rely on T in this way, and so rephrases the question: Would we have believed C even if it were false *but* all the evidence had been exactly as it in fact was? Now the answer has to be yes, and the skeptic concludes that C is doubtful. (It should be obvious how to extend this strategy to belief in other minds, or in an external world.) I am of course not convinced: I do not think answers to the rephrased question show anything interesting about what we know or justifiably believe. But it is enough for my purposes here that no such *general* skeptical strategy could pretend to reveal any problems peculiar to belief in *moral* facts.

(2) My conclusion about Harman's argument, although it is not exactly the same as, is nevertheless similar to and very much in the spirit of the Duhemian point I invoked earlier against verificationism. There the question was whether typical moral assertions have testable implications, and the answer was that they do, so long as you include additional moral assumptions of the right sort among the background theories on which you rely in evaluating these assertions. Harman's more important question is whether we should ever regard moral facts as relevant to the explanation of nonmoral facts, and in particular of our having the moral beliefs we do. But the answer, again, is that we should, so long as we are willing to hold the right sorts of *other* moral assumptions fixed in answering counterfactual questions. Neither answer shows morality to be on any shakier ground than, say, physics: for typical microphysical hypotheses, too, have testable implications, and appear relevant to explanations, only if we are willing to assume at least the approximate truth of an elaborate microphysical theory and to hold this assumption fixed in answering counterfactual questions.

(3) Of course, this picture of how explanations depend on background theories, and moral explanations in particular on moral background theories, does show why someone already tempted toward moral skepticism on other grounds (such as those mentioned at the beginning of this essay) might find Harman's claim about moral explanations plausible. To the extent that you already have pervasive doubts about moral theories, you will also find moral facts nonexplanatory. So I grant that Harman may have located a natural symptom of moral skepticism; but I am sure he has neither

traced this skepticism to its roots nor provided any independent argument for it. His claim that we do not *in fact* cite moral facts in explanation of moral beliefs and observations cannot provide such an argument, for that claim is false. So, too, is the claim that assumptions about moral facts seem irrelevant to such explanations, for many do not. The claim that we *should* not rely on such assumptions because they *are* irrelevant, on the other hand, unless it is supported by some independent argument for moral skepticism, will just be question-begging: for the principal test of whether they are relevant, in any situation in which it appears they might be, is a counterfactual question about what would have happened if the moral fact had not obtained, and how we answer that question depends precisely upon whether we *do* rely on moral assumptions in answering it.

A different concern, to which Harman only alludes in the passages I have discussed, is that belief in moral facts may be difficult to render consistent with a naturalistic world view. Since I share a naturalistic viewpoint, I agree that it is important to show that belief in moral facts need not be belief in anything supernatural or "nonnatural." I have of course not dealt with every argument from this direction, but I *have* argued for the important point that naturalism in ethics does not require commitment to reductive definitions for moral terms, any more than physicalism about psychology and biology requires a commitment to reductive definitions for the terminology of those sciences.

My own view I stated at the outset: that the only argument for moral skepticism with any independent weight is the argument from the difficulty of settling disputed moral questions. I have shown that anyone who finds Harman's claim about moral explanations plausible must already have been tempted toward skepticism by some other considerations, and I suspect that the other considerations will always just be the ones I sketched. So that is where discussion should focus. I also suggested that those considerations may provide less support for moral skepticism than is sometimes supposed, but I must reserve a thorough defense of that thesis for another occasion.[29]

NOTES

1 As, for example, in Alan Gerwirth, "Positive 'Ethics' and Normative 'Science'," *Philosophical Review* 69 (1960), 311–30, in which there are some useful remarks about the first of them.
2 Harman's title for the entire first section of his book.
3 This point is generally credited to Pierre Duhem, *The Aim and Structure of Physical Theory*, trans. Philip P. Wiener (Princeton, NJ, 1954). It is a prominent theme in the influential writings of W. V. O. Quine. For an especially clear application of it, see Hilary Putnam, "The 'Corroboration' of Theories," in *Mathematics, Matter, and Method. Philosophical Papers*, vol. I, 2nd edn (Cambridge, 1977).
4 Harman is careful always to say only that moral beliefs *appear* to play no such role; and since he eventually concludes that there *are* moral facts (p. 132), this caution may be more than

stylistic. I shall argue that this more cautious claim, too, is mistaken (indeed, that is my central thesis). But to avoid issues about Harman's intent, I shall simply mean by "Harman's argument" the skeptical argument of his first two chapters, whether or not he means to endorse all of it. This argument surely deserves discussion in its own right in either case, especially since Harman himself never explains what is wrong with it.

5 He asks: "Can moral principles be tested in the same way [as scientific hypotheses can], out in the world? You can observe someone do something, but can you ever perceive the rightness or wrongness of what he does?" (p. 4).

6 The other is that Harman appears to use "observe" (and "perceive" and "see") in a surprising way. One would normally take observing (or perceiving, or seeing) something to involve knowing it was the case. But Harman apparently takes an observation to be *any* opinion arrived at as "a direct result of perception" (p. 5) or, at any rate (see next footnote), "immediately and without conscious reasoning" (p. 7). This means that observations need not even be true, much less known to be true. A consequence is that the existence of moral observations, in Harman's sense, would not be sufficient to show that moral theories can be tested against the world, or to show that there is moral knowledge, although this *would* be sufficient if "observe" were being used in a more standard sense. What I argue in the text is that the existence of moral observations (in either Harman's or the standard sense) is not *necessary* for showing this about moral theories either.

7 This sort of case does not meet Harman's characterization of an observation as an opinion that is "a direct result of perception" (p. 5), but he is surely right that moral facts would be as well vindicated if they were needed to explain our drawing conclusions about hypothetical cases as they would be if they were needed to explain observations in the narrower sense. To be sure, Harman is still confining his attention to cases in which we draw the moral conclusion from our thought experiment "immediately and without conscious reasoning" (p. 7), and it is no doubt the existence of such cases that gives purchase to talk of a "moral sense." But this feature, again, can hardly matter to the argument: Would belief in moral facts be less justified if they were needed only to explain the instances in which we draw the moral conclusion *slowly*? Nor can it make any difference for that matter whether the case we are reflecting on is hypothetical. So my example in which we, quickly or slowly, draw a moral conclusion about Hitler from what we know of him, is surely relevant.

8 Thomas Nagel, "The Limits of Objectivity," in Sterling M. McMurrin, ed., *The Tanner Lectures on Human Values* (Salt Lake City and Cambridge, 1980), p. 114n. Nagel actually directs this reply to J. L. Mackie.

9 It is surprising that Harman does not mention the obvious intermediate possibility which would occur to any instrumentalist: to cite the physicist's psychological set *and* the vapor trail, but say nothing about protons or other unobservables. It is *this* explanation that is most closely parallel to an explanation of beliefs about an external world in terms of sensory experience and psychological makeup, or of moral beliefs in terms of nonmoral facts together with our "moral sensibility."

10 And it is hard to see how facts could be reducible to explanatory facts without being themselves explanatory. Opaque objects often look red to normally sighted observers in white light because they *are* red; it amplifies this explanation, but hardly undermines it, if their redness turns out to be an electronic property of the matter composing their surfaces.

11 Some of what I say could no doubt be appropriated by believers in supernatural facts, but I leave the details to them. For an account I could largely accept, if I believed any of the

theology, see R. M. Adams, "Divine Command Metaethics as Necessary A Posteriori," in Paul Helm, ed., *Divine Commands and Morality* (Oxford, 1981), pp. 109–18.

12 Or, at any rate, a reductive scheme of translation. It surely needn't provide explicit term-by-term definitions. Since this qualification does not affect my argument, I shall henceforth ignore it.

13 *Nonmoral* because ethics (or large parts of it) will be trivially reducible to psychology and social theory if we take otherwise unreduced talk of moral character traits just to be *part* of psychology and take social theory to *include*, for example, a theory of justice. As an ethical naturalist, I see nothing objectionable or unscientific about conceiving of psychology and social theory in this way, but of course this is not usually how they are understood when questions about reduction are raised.

14 For more on this view of moral reasoning, see Nicholas L. Sturgeon, "Brandt's Moral Empiricism," *Philosophical Review* 91 (1982), 389–422. On scientific reasoning see Richard N. Boyd, "What Realism Implies and What It Does Not," *Dialectica* (1989) and "Realism, Anti-Foundationalism and the Enthusiasm for Natural Kinds," *Philosophical Studies* 61 (1991) 127–48.

   G. E. Moore, *Principia Ethica* (Cambridge, 1903) thought that the *metaphysical* thesis that moral facts are natural facts entailed that moral theory would have a priori foundations. For he took the metaphysical thesis to require not merely that there be a reductive scheme of translation for moral terminology, but that this reduction include explicit property-identities (such as "goodness = pleasure and the absence of pain"); and these he assumed could be true only if analytic. I of course reject the view that naturalism requires any sort of reductive definitions; but even if it required this sort, it is by now widely acknowledged that reductive property-identities (such as "temperature = mean molecular kinetic energy") can be true without being analytic. See Hilary Putnam, "On Properties," in *Mathematics, Matter and Method. Philosophical Papers*, vol. I., 2nd edn (Cambridge, 1977).

15 Nor does this view really promise that we can do without reference to moral facts; it merely says that we can achieve this reference without using moral terms. For we would surely have as much reason to think that the facts expressed by *these* nonmoral terms were moral facts as we would for thinking that our reductive definitions were correct.

16 DeVoto, B., *The Year of Decision: 1846* (Boston, 1942), p. 426; a quotation from the notebooks of Francis Parkman. The account of the entire rescue effort is on pp. 424–44.

17 What is being explained, of course, is not just why people came to think slavery wrong, but why people who were not themselves slaves or in danger of being enslaved came to think it so seriously wrong as to be intolerable. There is a much larger and longer history of people who thought it wrong but tolerable, and an even longer one of people who appear not to have got past the thought that the world would be a better place without it. See David Brion Davis, *The Problem of Slavery in Western Culture* (Ithaca, NY, 1966).

18 For a version of what I am calling the standard view about slavery in the Americas, see Frank Tannenbaum, *Slave and Citizen* (New York, 1947). For an argument against both halves of the standard view, see Davis, esp. pp. 60–1, 223–5, 262–3.

19 This counterfactual test no doubt requires qualification. When there are concomitant effects that in the circumstances could each only have been brought about by their single cause, it may be true that if the one effect had not occurred, then neither would the other, but the occurrence of the one is not relevant to the explanation of the other. The test will also be unreliable if it employs backtracking or "that-would-have-had-to-be-because" counter-

factuals. (I take these to include ones in which what is tracked back to is not so much a cause as a condition that partly constitutes another: as when someone's winning a race is part of what constitutes her winning five events in one day, and it is true that if she hadn't won five events, that would have had to be because she didn't win that particular race.) So it should not be relied on in cases of either of these sorts. But none of my examples falls into either of these categories.

20 What would be generally granted is just that *if* there are moral properties they supervene on natural properties. But, remember, we are assuming for the sake of argument that there are.

From my view that moral properties *are* natural properties, it of course follows trivially that they supervene on natural properties: that, necessarily, nothing could differ in its moral properties without differing in some natural respect. But I also accept the more interesting thesis usually intended by the claim about supervenience – that there are more basic natural features such that, necessarily, once they are fixed, so are the moral properties. (In supervening on more basic facts of some sort, moral facts are like *most* natural facts. Social facts like unemployment, for example, supervene on complex histories of many individuals and their relations; and facts about the existence and properties of macroscopic physical objects – colliding billiard balls, say – clearly supervene on the microphysical constitution of the situations that include them.)

21 Not *certainly* right, because there is still the possibility that your reaction is to some extent overdetermined and is to be explained partly by your sympathy for the cat and your dislike of cruelty, as well as by your hatred for children (although this last alone would have been sufficient to produce it).

We could of course rule out this possibility by making you an even less attractive character, indifferent to the suffering of animals and not offended by cruelty. But it may then be hard to imagine that such a person (whom I shall cease calling "you") could retain enough of a grip on moral thought for us to be willing to say he thought the action wrong, as opposed to saying that he merely pretended to do so. This difficulty is perhaps not insuperable, but it is revealing. Harman says that the actual wrongness of the action is "completely irrelevant" to the explanation of the observer's reaction. Notice that what is in fact true, however, is that it is *very hard* to imagine someone who reacts in the way Harman describes, but whose reaction is *not* due, at least in part, to the actual wrongness of the action.

22 Perhaps deliberate cruelty is worse the more one enjoys it (a standard counterexample to hedonism). If so, the fact that the children are enjoying themselves makes their action worse, but presumably isn't what makes it wrong to begin with.

23 W. V. O. Quine, "Epistemology Naturalized," in *Ontological Relativity and Other Essays* (New York, 1969), pp. 69–90. See also Quine, "Natural Kinds," in the same volume.

24 Harman of course allows us to assume the moral facts whose explanatory relevance is being assessed: that Hitler was depraved, or that what the children in his example are doing is wrong. But I have been assuming something more – something about what depravity *is*, and about what *makes* the children's action wrong. (At a minimum, in the more cautious version of my argument, I have been assuming that *something* about its more basic features makes it wrong, so that it could not have differed in its moral quality without differing in those other features as well.)

25 And anyway, remember, this is the sort of fact Harman allows us to assume in order to see whether, if we assume it, it will look explanatory.

26 It is about here that I have several times encountered the objection: but surely *supervenient*

properties aren't needed to explain anything. It is a little hard, however, to see just what this objection is supposed to come to. If it includes endorsement of the conditional I here attribute to Harman, then I believe the remainder of my discussion is an adequate reply to it. If it is the claim that, because moral properties are supervenient, we can always exploit the insights in any moral explanations, however plausible they may seem, without resort to moral *language*, then I have already dealt with it in my discussion of reduction: The claim is probably false, but even if it is true, it is no support for Harman's view, which is not that moral explanations are plausible but reducible, but that they are totally implausible. And doubts about the causal efficacy of supervenient facts seem misplaced in any case, as attention to my earlier examples (note 20) illustrates. High unemployment causes widespread hardship, and can also bring down the rate of inflation. The masses and velocities of two colliding billiard balls causally influence the subsequent trajectories of the two balls. There is no doubt some sense in which these facts are causally efficacious *in virtue of* the way they supervene on – that is, are constituted out of, or causally realized by – more basic facts, but this hardly shows them *in*efficacious. (Nor does Harman appear to think it does: for his *favored* explanation of your moral belief about the burning cat, recall, appeals to psychological facts (about your moral sensibility), a biological fact (that it's a cat), and macrophysical facts (that it's on fire) – supervenient facts all, on his physicalist view and mine.) If anyone does hold to a general suspicion of causation by supervenient facts and properties, however, as Jaegwon Kim appears to ("Causality, Identity and Supervenience in the Mind Body Problem," in *Midwest Studies* 4 (Morris, 1979), pp. 47–8), it is enough here to note that this suspicion cannot diagnose any special difficulty with *moral* explanations, any distinctive "problem with ethics." The "problem," arguably, will be with every discipline but fundamental physics. On this point, see Richard W. Miller, "Reason and Commitment in the Social Sciences," *Philosophy & Public Affairs*, 8 (1979), esp. 252–5.

27 And as I take it Philippa Foot, in *Moral Relativism*, the Lindley Lectures (Lawrence, KS, 1978), for example, is still prepared to do, at least about paradigmatic cases.

28 If we imagine the physicist *regularly* mistaken in this way, moreover, we will have to imagine his theory not just mistaken but hopelessly so. And we can easily reproduce the other notable feature of Harman's claims about the moral cases, that what we are imagining is *necessarily* false, if we suppose that one of the physicist's (or better, chemist's) conclusions is about the microstructure of some common substance, such as water. For I agree with Saul Kripke that whatever microstructure water actually has is essential to it, that it has this structure in every possible world in which it exists (S. A. Kripke, *Naming and Necessity* [Cambridge, MA, 1980], pp. 115–44). If we are right (as we have every reason to suppose) in thinking that water is actually H_2O, therefore, the conditional "If water were not H_2O, but all the observable, macrophysical facts were just as they actually are, chemists would still have come to *think* it was H_2O" has a necessarily false antecedent; just as, if we are right (as we also have good reason to suppose) in thinking that Hitler was actually morally depraved, the conditional "If Hitler were just as he was in all natural respects, but not morally depraved, we would still have *thought* he was depraved" has a necessarily false antecedent. Of course, I am not suggesting that in either case our knowledge that the antecedent is false is a priori.

These counterfactuals, because of their impossible antecedents, will have to be interpreted over worlds that are (at best) only "epistemically" possible; and, as Richard Boyd has pointed out to me, this helps to explain why anyone who accepts a causal theory of knowledge (or any theory according to which the justification of our beliefs depends on what explains our holding them) will find their truth irrelevant to the question of how much we know, either in chemistry or in morals. For although there certainly are counterfactuals that are relevant to questions about what causes what (and, hence, about what explains what), these have to be counterfactuals about real possibilities, not inertly epistemic ones.

29 This essay has benefited from helpful discussion of earlier versions read at the University of Virginia, Cornell University, Franklin and Marshall College, Wayne State University, and the University of Michigan. I have been aided by a useful correspondence with Gilbert Harman; and I am grateful also for specific comments from Richard Boyd, David Brink, David Copp, Stephen Darwall, Terence Irwin, Norman Kretzmann, Ronald Nash, Peter Railton, Bruce Russell, Sydney Shoemaker, and Judith Slein.

Only after this essay had appeared in print did I notice that several parallel points about *aesthetic* explanations had been made by Michael Slote in "The Rationality of Aesthetic Value Judgments," *Journal of Philosophy* 68 (1971), 821–39; interested readers should see that paper.

REFERENCES

Boyd, R. N., "Materialism without Reductionism: What Physicalism does not Entail," in N. Black (ed.) *Readings in Philosophy of Psychology*, vol. I (Cambridge: Harvard UP, 1980).

—— "What Realism Implies and What it does not," *Dialectica*, 1989, 5–29.

—— "Realism, Anti-Foundationalism and the Enthusiasm for Natural Kinds," *Philosophical Studies*, 61, 1991: 127–48.

Harman, G., *The Nature of Morality: An Introduction to Ethics* (New York, 1977), pp. vii, viii.

Mackie, J. L., *Ethics: Inventing Right and Wrong* (Harmondsworth, Middlesex, 1977), pp. 38–42.

Putnam, H., "Language and Reality," in *Mind, Language, and Reality. Philosophical Papers*, vol. 2 (Cambridge, 1975), p. 290.

9

MORAL REALISM

Peter Railton

Among contemporary philosophers, even those who have not found skepticism about empirical science at all compelling have tended to find skepticism about morality irresistible. For various reasons, among them an understandable suspicion of moral absolutism, it has been thought a mark of good sense to explain away any appearance of objectivity in moral discourse. So common has it become in secular intellectual culture to treat morality as subjective or conventional that most of us now have difficulty imagining what it might be like for there to be facts to which moral judgments answer.

Undaunted, some philosophers have attempted to establish the objectivity of morality by arguing that reason, or science, affords a foundation for ethics. The history of such attempts hardly inspires confidence. Although rationalism in ethics has retained adherents long after other rationalisms have been abandoned, the powerful philosophical currents that have worn away at the idea that unaided reason might afford a standpoint from which to derive substantive conclusions show no signs of slackening. And ethical naturalism has yet to find a plausible synthesis of the empirical and the normative: the more it has given itself over to descriptive accounts of the origin of norms, the less has it retained recognizably moral force; the more it has undertaken to provide a recognizable basis for moral criticism or reconstruction, the less has it retained a firm connection with descriptive social or psychological theory.[1]

In what follows, I will present in a programmatic way a form of ethical naturalism that owes much to earlier theorists, but that seeks to effect a more satisfactory linkage of the normative to the empirical. The link cannot, I believe, be effected by proof. It is no more my aim to refute moral skepticism than it is the aim of contemporary epistemic naturalists to refute Cartesian skepticism. The naturalist in either case has more modest aspirations. First, he seeks to provide an analysis of epistemology or ethics that permits us to see how the central evaluative functions of this domain could be carried out within existing (or prospective) empirical theories. Second, he attempts to show how traditional nonnaturalist accounts rely upon assumptions that are in some way incoherent, or that fit ill with existing science. And third, he presents to the skeptic a certain challenge, namely, to show how a skeptical account of our epistemic or moral practices could be as plausible, useful, or interesting as the account the naturalist offers, and how a skeptical reconstruction of such practices – should the skeptic, as often he does, attempt one – could succeed in preserving their distinctive place and function in human affairs. I will primarily be occupied with the first of these three aspirations.

One thing should be said at the outset. Some may be drawn to, or repelled by, moral realism out of a sense that it is the view of ethics that best expresses high moral earnestness. Yet one can be serious about morality, even to a fault, without being a moral realist. Indeed, a possible objection to the sort of moral realism I will defend here is that it may not make morality serious enough.

1 SPECIES OF MORAL REALISM

Such diverse views have claimed to be – or have been accused of being – realist about morality, that an initial characterization of the position I will defend is needed before proceeding further. Claims – and accusations – of moral realism typically extend along some or all of the following dimensions. Roughly put: (1) Cognitivism – Are moral judgments capable of truth and falsity? (2) Theories of truth – If moral judgments do have truth values, in what sense? (3) Objectivity – In what ways, if any, does the existence of moral properties depend upon the actual or possible states of mind of intelligent beings? (4) Reductionism – Are moral properties reducible to, or do they in some weaker sense supervene upon, nonmoral properties? (5) Naturalism – Are moral properties natural properties? (6) Empiricism – Do we come to know moral facts in the same way we come to know the facts of empirical science, or are they revealed by reason or by some special mode of apprehension? (7) Bivalence – Does the principle of the excluded middle apply to moral judgments? (8) Determinateness – Given whatever procedures we have for assessing moral judgments, how much of morality is likely to be determinable? (9) Categoricity – Do all rational agents necessarily have some reason to obey moral imperatives? (10) Universality – Are moral imperatives applicable to all rational agents, even (should such exist) those who lack a reason to comply with them? (11) Assessment of existing moralities – Are present moral beliefs approximately true, or do prevailing moral intuitions in some other sense constitute privileged data? (12) Relativism – Does the truth or warrant of moral judgments depend directly upon indi- vidually- or socially-adopted norms or practices? (13) Pluralism – Is there a uniquely good form of life or a uniquely right moral code, or could different forms of life or moral codes be appropriate in different circumstances?

Here, then, are the approximate coordinates of my own view in this multi- dimensional conceptual space. I will argue for a form of moral realism which holds that moral judgments can bear truth values in a fundamentally non-epistemic sense of truth; that moral properties are objective, though relational; that moral properties supervene upon natural properties, and may be reducible to them; that moral inquiry is of a piece with empirical inquiry; that it cannot be known a priori whether bivalence holds for moral judgments or how determinately such judgments can be assessed; that there is reason to think we know a fair amount about morality, but also reason to think that current moralities are wrong in certain ways and could be wrong in quite general ways; that a rational agent may fail to have a reason for obeying moral imperatives, although they may nonetheless be applicable to him; and that, while there are perfectly general criteria of moral assessment, nonetheless, by the nature of these criteria no one kind of life is likely to be appropriate for all individuals and no one set of norms appropriate for all societies and all times. The position thus described might well be called "stark, raving moral realism," but for the sake of syntax, I will colorlessly call it "moral realism." This usage is not proprietary. Other positions, occupying more or less different coordinates, may have equal claim to either name.

2 THE FACT/VALUE DISTINCTION

Any attempt to argue for a naturalistic moral realism runs headlong into the fact/value distinction. Philosophers have given various accounts of this distinction, and of the arguments for it, but for present purposes I will focus upon several issues concerning the epistemic and ontological status of judgments of value as opposed to judgments of fact.

Perhaps the most frequently heard argument for the fact/value distinction is epistemic: it is claimed that disputes over questions of value can persist even after all rational or scientific means of adjudication have been deployed, hence, value judgments cannot be cognitive in the sense that factual or logical judgments are. This claim is defended in part by appeal to the instrumental (hypothetical) character of reason, which prevents reason from dictating ultimate values. In principle, the argument runs, two individuals who differ in ultimate values could, without manifesting any rational defect, hold fast to their conflicting values in the face of any amount of argumentation or evidence. As Ayer puts it, "we find that argument is possible on moral questions only if some system of values is presupposed."[2]

One might attempt to block this conclusion by challenging the instrumental conception of rationality. But for all its faults and for all that it needs to be developed, the instrumental conception seems to me the clearest notion we have of what it is for an agent to have reasons to act. Moreover, it captures a central normative feature of reason-giving, since we can readily see the commending force for an agent of the claim that a given act would advance his ends. It would be hard to make much sense of someone who sincerely claimed to have certain ends and yet at the same time insisted that they could not provide him even *prima facie* grounds for action. (Of course, he might also believe that he has other, perhaps countervailing, grounds.)

Yet this version of the epistemic argument for the fact/value distinction is in difficulty even granting the instrumental conception of rationality. From the standpoint of instrumental reason, belief-formation is but one activity among others: to the extent that we have reasons for engaging in it, or for doing it one way rather than another, these are at bottom a matter of its contribution to our ends.[3] What it would be rational for an individual to believe on the basis of a given experience will vary not only with respect to his other beliefs, but also with respect to what he desires.[4] From this it follows that no amount of mere argumentation or experience could force one on pain of irrationality to accept even the factual claims of empirical science. The long-running debate over inductive logic well illustrates that rational choice among competing hypotheses requires much richer and more controversial criteria of theory choice than can be squeezed from instrumental reason alone. Unfortunately for the contrast Ayer wished to make, we find that argument is possible on scientific questions only if some system of values is presupposed.

However, Hume had much earlier found a way of marking the distinction between facts and values without appeal to the idea that induction – or even deduction – could require a rational agent to adopt certain beliefs rather than others when this would conflict with his contingent ends.[5] For Hume held the thesis that morality is practical, by which he meant that if moral facts existed, they would necessarily provide a reason (although perhaps not an overriding reason) for moral action to all rational beings, regardless of their particular desires. Given this thesis as a premise, the instrumental conception of rationality can clinch the argument after all, for it excludes the possibility of categorical reasons of this kind. By contrast, Hume did not suppose it to be constitutive of logic or science that the facts revealed by these forms of inquiry have categorical force for rational agents, so the existence of logical and scientific facts, unlike the existence of moral facts, is compatible with the instrumental character of reason.

Yet this way of drawing the fact/value distinction is only as compelling as the claim that morality is essentially practical in Hume's sense.[6] Hume is surely right in claiming there to be an intrinsic connection, no doubt complex, between valuing something and having some sort of positive attitude toward it that provides one with an instrumental reason for action. We simply would disbelieve someone who claimed to value honesty and yet never showed the slightest urge to act honestly when given an easy opportunity. But this is a fact about the connection between the values *embraced by* an individual and his reasons for action, not a fact showing a connection between moral evaluation and rational motivation.

Suppose for example that we accept Hume's characterization of justice as an artificial virtue directed at the general welfare. This is in a recognizable sense an evaluative or normative notion – "a value" in the loose sense in which this term is used in such debates – yet it certainly does not follow from its definition that every rational being, no matter what his desires, who believes that some or other act is just in this sense will have an instrumental reason to perform it. A rational individual may fail to value justice for its own sake, and may have ends contrary to it. In Hume's discussion of our "interested obligation" to be just, he seems to recognize that in the end it may not be possible to show that a "sensible knave" has a reason to be just. Of course, Hume held that the rest of us – whose hearts rebel at Sensible Knave's attitude that he may break his word, cheat, or steal whenever it suits his purposes – have reason to be just, to deem Knave's attitude unjust, and to try to protect ourselves from his predations.[7]

Yet Knave himself could say, perhaps because he accepts Hume's analysis of justice, "Yes, my attitude is unjust." And by Hume's own account of the relation of reason and passion, Knave could add "But what is that to me?" without failing to grasp the content of his previous assertion. Knave, let us suppose, has no doubts about the intelligibility or reality of "the general welfare," and thinks it quite comprehensible that people attach great significance in public life to the associated notion of justice. He also realizes that for the bulk of mankind, whose passions differ from his, being just is a source and a condition of much that is most worthwhile in life. He thus understands that appeals to justice typically have motivating force. Moreover, he himself uses the category of justice in analyzing the social world, and he recognizes – indeed, his knavish calculations take into account – the distinction between those individuals and institutions that truly are just, and those that merely appear just or are commonly regarded as just. Knave does view a number of concepts with wide currency – religious ones, for example – as mere fictions that prey on weak minds, but he does not view justice in this way. Weak minds and moralists have, he thinks, surrounded justice with certain myths – that justice is its own reward, that once one sees what is just one will automatically have a reason to do it, and so on. But then, he thinks that weak minds and moralists have likewise surrounded wealth and power with myths – that the wealthy are not truly happy, that the powerful inevitably ride for a fall, and so on – and he does not on this account doubt whether there are such things as wealth and power. Knave is glad to be free of prevailing myths about wealth, power, and justice; glad, too, that he is free in his own mind to pay as much or as little attention to any of these attributes as his desires and circumstances warrant. He might, for example, find Mae West's advice convincing: diamonds are very much worth acquiring, and "goodness ha[s] nothing to do with it."

We therefore must distinguish the business of saying what an individual values from the business of saying what it is for him to make measurements against the criteria of a species of evaluation that he recognizes to be genuine.[8]

To deny Hume's thesis of the practicality of moral judgment, and so remove the ground of his contrast between facts and values, is not to deny that morality has an action-guiding character. Morality surely can remain prescriptive within an instrumental framework, and can recommend itself to us in much the same way that, say, epistemology does: various significant and enduring – though perhaps not universal – human ends can be advanced if we apply certain evaluative criteria to our actions. That may be enough to justify to ourselves our abiding concern with the epistemic or moral status of what we do.[9]

By arguing that reason does not compel us to adopt particular beliefs or practices apart from our contingent, and variable, ends, I may seem to have failed to negotiate my way past epistemic relativism, and thus to have wrecked the argument for moral realism before it has even left port. Rationality does go relative when it goes instrumental, but epistemology need not follow. The epistemic warrant of an individual's belief may be disentangled from the rationality of his holding it, for epistemic warrant may be tied to an external criterion – as it is for example by causal or reliabilist theories of knowledge.[10] It is part of the naturalistic realism that informs this essay to adopt such a criterion of warrant. We should not confuse the obvious fact that in general our ends are well served by reliable causal mechanisms of belief-formation with an internalist claim to the effect that reason requires us to adopt such means. Reliable mechanisms have costs as well as benefits, and successful pursuit of some ends – Knave would point to religious ones, and to those of certain moralists – may in some respects be incompatible with adoption of reliable means of inquiry.

This rebuttal of the charge of relativism invites the defender of the fact/value distinction to shift to ontological ground. Perhaps facts and values cannot be placed on opposite sides of an epistemological divide marked off by what reason and experience can compel us to accept. Still, the idea of reliable causal mechanisms for moral learning, and of moral facts "in the world" upon which they operate, is arguably so bizarre that I may have done no more than increase my difficulties.

3 VALUE REALISM

The idea of causal interaction with moral reality certainly would be intolerably odd if moral facts were held to be *sui generis*;[11] but there need be nothing odd about causal mechanisms for learning moral facts if these facts are constituted by natural facts, and that is the view under consideration. This response will remain unconvincing, however, until some positive argument for realism about moral facts is given. So let us turn to that task.

What might be called "the generic stratagem of naturalistic realism" is to postulate a realm of facts in virtue of the contribution they would make to the a posteriori explanation of certain features of our experience. For example, an external world is posited to explain the coherence, stability, and intersubjectivity of sense-experience. A moral realist who would avail himself of this stratagem must show that the postulation of moral facts similarly can have an explanatory function. The stratagem can succeed in either case only if the reality postulated has these two characteristics:

1. *independence*: it exists and has certain determinate features independent of whether we think it exists or has those features, independent, even, of whether we have good reason to think this;
2. *feedback*: it is such – and we are such – that we are able to interact with it, and this interaction exerts the relevant sort of shaping influence or control upon our perceptions, thought, and action.

These two characteristics enable the realist's posit to play a role in the explanation of our experience that cannot be replaced without loss by our mere *conception* of ourselves or our world. For although our conceptual scheme mediates even our most basic perceptual experiences, an experience-transcendent reality has ways of making itself felt without the permission of our conceptual scheme – causally. The success or failure of our plans and projects famously is not determined by expectation alone. By resisting or yielding to our worldly efforts in ways not anticipated by our going conceptual scheme, an external reality that is never directly revealed in perception may nonetheless significantly influence the subsequent evolution of that scheme.

The realist's use of an external world to explain sensory experience has often been criticized as no more than a picture. But do we even have a picture of what a realist explanation might look like in the case of values?[12] I will try to sketch one, filling in first a realist account of non-moral value – the notion of something being desirable for someone, or good for him.[13]

Consider first the notion of someone's *subjective interests* – his wants or desires, conscious or unconscious. Subjective interest can be seen as a secondary quality, akin to taste. For me to take a subjective interest in something is to say that it has a positive *valence* for me, that is, that in ordinary circumstances it excites a positive attitude or inclination (not necessarily conscious) in me. Similarly, for me to say that I find sugar sweet is to say that in ordinary circumstances sugar excites a certain gustatory sensation in me. As secondary qualities, subjective interest and perceived sweetness supervene upon primary qualities of the perceiver, the object (or other phenomenon) perceived, and the surrounding context: the perceiver is so constituted that this sort of object in this sort of context will excite that sort of sensation. Call this complex set of relational, dispositional, primary qualities the *reduction basis* of the secondary quality.

We have in this reduction basis an objective notion that corresponds to, and helps explain, subjective interests. But it is not a plausible foundation for the notion of non-moral goodness, since the subjective interests it grounds have insufficient normative force to capture the idea of desirableness. My subjective interests frequently reflect ignorance, confusion, or lack of consideration, as hindsight attests. The fact that I am now so constituted that I desire something which, had I better knowledge of it, I would wish I had never sought, does not seem to recommend it to me as part of my good.

To remedy this defect, let us introduce the notion of an *objectified subjective interest* for an individual A, as follows.[14] Give to an actual individual A unqualified cognitive and imaginative powers, and full factual and nomological information about his physical and psychological constitution, capacities, circumstances, history, and so on. A will have become A+, who has complete and vivid knowledge of himself and his environment, and whose instrumental rationality is in no way defective. We now ask A+ to tell us not what *he* currently wants, but what he would want his non-idealized self A to want – or, more generally, to seek – were he to find himself in the actual condition and circumstances of A.[15] Just as we assumed there to be a reduction basis for an individual A's actual subjective interests, we may assume there to be a reduction basis for his objectified subjective interests, namely, those facts about A and his circumstances that A+ would combine with his general knowledge in arriving at his views about what he would want to want were he to step into A's shoes.

For example, Lonnie, a traveler in a foreign country, is feeling miserable. He very much wishes to overcome his malaise and to settle his stomach, and finds he has a craving for the familiar: a tall glass of milk. The milk is desired by Lonnie, but is it also desirable for him? Lonnie-Plus can see that what is wrong with Lonnie, in addition to homesickness, is dehydration, a common affliction of tourists, but one often not detectable from introspective evidence. The effect of drinking hard-to-digest milk would be to further unsettle Lonnie's stomach and worsen his dehydration. By contrast, Lonnie-Plus can see that abundant clear fluids would quickly improve Lonnie's physical condition – which, incidentally, would help with his homesickness as well. Lonnie-Plus can also see just how distasteful Lonnie would find it to drink clear liquids, just what would happen were Lonnie to continue to suffer dehydration, and so on. As a result of this information, Lonnie-Plus might then come to desire that were he to assume Lonnie's place, he would want to drink clear liquids rather than milk, or at least want to act in such a way that a want of this kind would be satisfied. The reduction basis of this objectified interest includes facts about Lonnie's circumstances and constitution, which determine, among other things, his existing tastes and his ability to acquire certain new tastes, the consequences of continued dehydration, the effects and availability of various sorts of liquids, and so on.

Let us say that this reduction basis is the constellation of primary qualities that make it be the case that the Lonnie has a certain *objective interest*.[16] That is, we will say that Lonnie has an objective interest in drinking clear liquids in virtue of this complex, relational, dispositional set of facts. Put another way, we can say that the reduction basis, not the fact that Lonnie-Plus would have certain wants, is the truth-maker for the claim that this is an objective interest of Lonnie's. The objective interest thus explains why there is a certain objectified interest, not the other way around.[17]

152

Let us now say that X is *non-morally good for A* if and only if X would satisfy an objective interest of A.[18] We may think of $A+$'s views about what he would want to want were he in A's place as generating a ranking of potential objective interests of A, a ranking that will reflect what is better or worse for A and will allow us to speak of A's actual wants as better or worse approximations of what is best for him. We may also decompose $A+$'s views into *prima facie* as opposed to "on balance" objective interests of A, the former yielding the notion of "*a good for A*", the latter, of "*the good for A*".[19] This seems to me an intuitively plausible account of what someone's non-moral good consists in: roughly, what he would want himself to seek if he knew what he were doing.[20]

Moreover, this account preserves what seems to me an appropriate link between non-moral value and motivation. Suppose that one desires X, but wonders whether X really is part of one's good. This puzzlement typically arises because one feels that one knows too little about X, oneself, or one's world, or because one senses that one is not being adequately rational or reflective in assessing the information one has – perhaps one suspects that one has been captivated by a few salient features of X (or repelled by a few salient features of its alternatives). If one were to learn that one would still want oneself to want X in the circumstances were one to view things with full information and rationality, this presumably would reduce the force of the original worry. By contrast, were one to learn that when fully informed and rational one would want oneself *not* to want X in the circumstances, this presumably would add force to it. Desires being what they are, a reinforced worry might not be sufficient to remove the desire for X. But if one were to become genuinely and vividly convinced that one's desire for X is in this sense not supported by full reflection upon the facts, one presumably would feel this to be a count against acting upon the desire. This adjustment of desire to belief might not in a given case be required by reason or logic; it might be "merely psychological." But it is precisely such psychological phenomena that naturalistic theories of value take as basic.

In what follows, we will need the notion of intrinsic goodness, so let us say that X is *intrinsically non-morally good for A* just in case X is in A's objective interest without reference to any other objective interest of A. We can in an obvious way use the notion of objective intrinsic interest to account for all other objective interests. Since individuals and their environments differ in many respects, we need not assume that everyone has the same objective intrinsic interests. *A fortiori*, we need not assume that they have the same objective instrumental interests. We should, however, expect that when personal and situational similarities exist across individuals – that is, when there are similarities in reduction bases – there will to that extent be corresponding similarities in their interests.

It is now possible to see how the notion of non-moral goodness can have explanatory uses. For a start, it can explain why one's actual desires have certain counterfactual features, for example, why one would have certain hypothetical desires rather than others were one to become fully informed and aware. Yet this sort of explanatory use – following as it does directly from the definition of objective interest – might well be thought unimpressive unless some other explanatory functions can be found.

Consider, then, the difference between Lonnie and Tad, another traveler in the same straits, but one who, unlike Lonnie, wants to drink clear liquids, and proceeds to do so. Tad will perk up while Lonnie remains listless. We can explain this difference by noting that although both Lonnie and Tad acted upon their wants, Tad's wants better reflected his interests. The congruence of Tad's wants with his interests may be fortuitous, or it may be that Tad knows he is dehydrated and knows the standard treatment. In the latter case we would ordinarily say that the explanation of the difference in their condition is that Tad, but not Lonnie, "knew what was good for him."

Generally, we can expect that what A+ would want to want were he in A's place will correlate well with what would permit A to experience physical or psychological well-being or to escape physical or psychological ill-being. Surely our well- or ill-being are among the things that matter to us most, and most reliably, even on reflection.[21] Appeal to degrees of congruence between A's wants and his interests thus will often help to explain facts about how satisfactory he finds his life. Explanation would not be preserved were we to substitute "believed to be congruent" for "are (to such-and-such a degree) congruent," since, as cases like Lonnie's show, even if one were to convince oneself that one's wants accurately reflected one's interests, acting on these wants might fail to yield much satisfaction.

In virtue of the correlation to be expected between acting upon motives that congrue with one's interests and achieving a degree of satisfaction or avoiding a degree of distress, one's objective interests may also play an explanatory role in the *evolution* of one's desires. Consider what I will call the *wants/interests mechanism*, which permits individuals to achieve selfconscious and unselfconscious learning about their interests through experience. In the simplest sorts of cases, trial and error leads to the selective retention of wants that are satisfiable and lead to satisfactory results for the agent.

For example, suppose that Lonnie gives in to his craving and drinks the milk. Soon afterwards, he feels much worse. Still unable to identify the source of his malaise and still in the grips of a desire for the familiar, his attention is caught by a green-and-red sign in the window of a small shop he is moping past: "7-Up," it says. He rushes inside and buys a bottle. Although it is lukewarm, he drinks it eagerly. "Mmm," he thinks, "I'll have another." He buys a second bottle, and drains it to the bottom. By now he has had his fill of tepid soda, and carries on. Within a few hours, his mood is improving. When he passes the store again on the way back to his hotel, his pleasant association with drinking 7-Up leads him to buy some more and carry it along with him. That night, in the dim solitude of his room, he finds the soda's reassuringly familiar taste consoling, and so downs another few bottles before finally finding sleep. When he wakes up the next morning, he feels very much better. To make a dull story short: the next time Lonnie is laid low abroad, he may have some conscious or unconscious, reasoned or superstitious, tendency to seek out 7-Up. Unable to find that, he might seek something quite like it, say, a local lime-flavored soda, or perhaps even the *agua mineral con gaz* he had previously scorned. Over time, as Lonnie travels more and suffers similar malaise, he regularly drinks clearish liquids and regularly feels better, eventually developing an actual desire for such liquids – and an aversion to other drinks, such as milk – in such circumstances.

Thus have Lonnie's desires evolved through experience to conform more closely to what is good for him, in the naturalistic sense intended here. The process was not one of an ideally rational response to the receipt of ideal information, but rather of largely unreflective experimentation, accompanied by positive and negative associations and reinforcements. There is no guarantee that the desires "learned" through such feedback will accurately or completely reflect an individual's good. Still less is there any guarantee that, even when an appropriate adjustment in desire occurs, the agent will comprehend the origin of his new desires or be able to represent to himself the nature the interests they reflect. But then, it is a quite general feature of the various means by which we learn about the world that they may fail to provide accurate or comprehending representations of it. My ability to perceive and understand my surroundings coexists with, indeed draws upon the same mechanisms as, my liability to deception by illusion, expectation, or surface appearance.

There are some broad theoretical grounds for thinking that something like the wants/interests mechanism exists and has an important role in desire-formation. Humans are creatures motivated primarily by wants rather than instincts. If such creatures were unable through experience to conform their wants at all closely to their essential interests – perhaps because they were no more likely to experience positive internal states when their essential interests are met than when they are not – we could not expect long or fruitful futures for them. Thus, if humans in general did not come to want to eat the kinds of food necessary to maintain some degree of physical well-being, or to engage in the sorts of activities or relations necessary to maintain their sanity, we would not be around today to worry whether we can know what is good for us. Since creatures as sophisticated and complex as humans have evolved through encounters with a variety of environments, and indeed have made it their habit to modify their environments, we should expect considerable flexibility in our capacity through experience to adapt our wants to our interests. However, this very flexibility makes the mechanism unreliable: our wants may at any time differ arbitrarily much from our interests; moreover, we may fail to have experiences that would cause us to notice this, or to undergo sufficient feedback to have much chance of developing new wants that more nearly approximate our interests. It is entirely possible, and hardly infrequent, that an individual live out the course of a normal life without ever recognizing or adjusting to some of his most fundamental interests. Individual limitations are partly remedied by cultural want-acquiring mechanisms, which permit learning and even theorizing over multiple lives and life-spans, but these same mechanisms also create a vast potential for the inculcation of wants at variance with interests.

The argument for the wants/interests mechanism has about the same status, and the same breezy plausibility, as the more narrowly biological argument that we should expect the human eye to be capable of detecting objects the size and shape of our predators or prey. It is not necessary to assume anything approaching infallibility, only enough functional success to hold our own in an often inhospitable world.[22]

Thus far the argument has concerned only those objective interests that might be classified as needs, but the wants/interests mechanism can operate with respect to any interest – even interests related to an individual's particular aptitudes or social role – whose frustration is attended even indirectly by consciously or unconsciously unsatisfactory results for him. (To be sure, the more indirect the association the more unlikely that the mechanism will be reliable.) For example, the experience of taking courses in both mathematics and philosophy may lead an undergraduate who thought himself cut out to be a mathematician to come to prefer a career in philosophy, which would in fact better suit his aptitudes and attitudes. And a worker recently promoted to management from the shop floor may find himself less inclined to respond to employee grievances than he had previously wanted managers to be, while his former co-workers may find themselves less inclined to confide in him than before.

If a wants/interests mechanism is postulated, and if what is non-morally good for someone is a matter of what is in his objective interest, then we can say that objective value is able to play a role in the explanation of subjective value of the sort the naturalistic realist about value needs. These explanations even support some qualified predictions: for example, that, other things equal, individuals will ordinarily be better judges of their own interests than third parties; that knowledge of one's interests will tend to increase with increased experience and general knowledge; that people with similar personal and social characteristics will tend to have similar values; and that there will be greater general consensus upon what is desirable in those areas of life where individuals are most alike in other regards (for example, at the level of basic motives), and where trial-and-error mechanisms can be expected to work well (for example, where esoteric knowledge is not required). I am in no position to pronounce these predictions correct, but it may be to their credit that they accord with widely-held views.

It should perhaps be emphasized that although I speak of the objectivity of value, the value in question is human value, and exists only because humans do. In the sense of old-fashioned theory of value, this is a relational rather than absolute notion of goodness. Although relational, the relevant facts about humans and their world are objective in the same sense that such non-relational entities as stones are: they do not depend for their existence or nature merely upon our conception of them.[23]

Thus understood, objective interests are supervenient upon natural and social facts. Does this mean that they cannot contribute to explanation after all, since it should always be possible in principle to account for any particular fact that they purport to explain by reference to the supervenience basis alone? If mere supervenience were grounds for denying an explanatory role to a given set of concepts, then we would have to say that chemistry, biology, and electrical engineering, which clearly supervene upon physics, lack explanatory power. Indeed, even outright reducibility is no ground for doubting explanatoriness. To establish a relation of reduction between, for example, a chemical phenomenon such as valence and a physical model of the atom does nothing to suggest that there is no such thing as valence, or that generalizations involving valence cannot support explanations. There can be no issue here of ontological economy or eschewing unnecessary entities, as might be the case if valence were held to be something *sui generis*, over and above any constellation of physical properties. The facts described in principles of chemical valence are genuine, and permit a powerful and explanatory systematization of chemical combination; the existence of a successful reduction to atomic physics only bolsters these claims.

We are confident that the notion of chemical valence is explanatory because proffered explanations in terms of chemical valence insert explananda into a distinctive and well-articulated nomic nexus, in an obvious way increasing our understanding of them. But what comparably powerful and illuminating theory exists concerning the notion of objective interest to give us reason to think – whether or not strict reduction is possible – that proffered explanations using this notion are genuinely informative?

I would find the sort of value realism sketched here uninteresting if it seemed to me that no theory of any consequence could be developed using the category of objective value. But in describing the wants/interests mechanism I have already tried to indicate that such a theory may be possible. When we seek to explain why people act as they do, why they have certain values or desires, and why sometimes they are led into conflict and other times into cooperation, it comes naturally to common sense and social science alike to talk in terms of people's interests. Such explanations will be incomplete and superficial if we remain wholly at the level of subjective interests, since these, too, must be accounted for.[24]

4 NORMATIVE REALISM

Suppose everything said thus far to have been granted generously. Still, I would as yet have no right to speak of *moral* realism, for I have done no more than to exhibit the possibility of a kind of realism with regard to nonmoral goodness, a notion that perfect moral skeptics can admit. To be entitled to speak of moral realism I would have to show realism to be possible about distinctively moral value, or moral norms. I will

157

concentrate on moral norms – that is, matters of moral rightness and wrongness – although the argument I give may, by extension, be applied to moral value. In part, my reason is that normative realism seems much less plausible intuitively than value realism. It therefore is not surprising that many current proposals for moral realism focus essentially upon value – and sometimes only upon what is in effect nonmoral value. Yet on virtually any conception of morality, a moral theory must yield an account of rightness.

Normative moral realism is implausible on various grounds, but within the framework of this essay, the most relevant is that it seems impossible to extend the generic strategy of naturalistic realism to moral norms. Where is the place in explanation for facts about what *ought* to be the case – don't facts about the way things *are* do all the explaining there is to be done? Of course they do. But then, my naturalistic moral realism commits me to the view that facts about what ought to be the case are facts of a special kind about the way things are. As a result, it may be possible for them to have a function within an explanatory theory. To see how this could be, let me first give some examples of explanations outside the realm of morality that involve naturalized norms.

"Why did the roof collapse? – For a house that gets the sort of snow loads that one did, the rafters ought to have been 2 × 8's at least, not 2 × 6's." This explanation is quite acceptable, as far as it goes, yet it contains an "ought." Of course, we can remove this "ought" as follows: "If a roof of that design is to withstand the snow load that one bore, then it must be framed with rafters at least 2 × 8 in cross-section." An architectural "ought" is replaced by an engineering "if … then …" This is possible because the "ought" clearly is hypothetical, reflecting the universal architectural goal of making roofs strong enough not to collapse. Because the goal is contextually fixed, and because there are more or less definite answers to the question of how to meet it, and moreover because the explanandum phenomenon is the result of a process that selects against instances that do not attain that goal, the "ought"-containing account conveys explanatory information.[25] I will call this sort of explanation *criterial*: we explain why something happened by reference to a relevant criterion, given the existence of a process that in effect selects for (or against) phenomena that more (or less) closely approximate this criterion. Although the criterion is defined naturalistically, it may at the same time be of a kind to have a regulative role in human practice – in this case, in house-building.

A more familiar sort of criterial explanation involves norms of individual rationality. Consider the use of an instrumental theory of rationality to explain an individual's behavior in light of his beliefs and desires, or to account for the way an individual's beliefs change with experience.[26] Bobby Shaftoe went to sea because he believed it was the best way to make his fortune, and he wanted above all to make his fortune. Crewmate Reuben Ramsoe came to believe that he wasn't liked by the other deckhands because he saw that they taunted him and greeted his frequent lashings at the hands of the First Mate with unconcealed pleasure. These explanations work because the action or belief in question was quite rational for the agent in the circumstances, and because we correctly suppose both Shaftoe and Ramsoe to have been quite rational.

Facts about degrees of instrumental rationality enter into explanations in other ways as well. First, consider the question why Bobby Shaftoe has had more success than most like-minded individuals in achieving his goals. We may lay his success to the fact that Shaftoe is more instrumentally rational than most – perhaps he has greater-than-average acumen in estimating the probabilities of outcomes, or is more-reliable-than-average at deductive inference, or is more-imaginative-than-average in surveying alternatives.

Second, although we are all imperfect deliberators, our behavior may come to embody habits or strategies that enable us to approximate optimal rationality more closely than our deliberative defects would lead one to expect. The mechanism is simple. Patterns of beliefs and behaviors that do not exhibit much instrumental rationality will tend to be to some degree self-defeating, an incentive to change them, whereas patterns that exhibit greater instrumental rationality will tend to be to some degree rewarding, an incentive to continue them. These incentives may affect our beliefs and behaviors even though the drawbacks or advantages of the patterns in question do not receive conscious deliberation. In such cases we may be said to acquire these habits or strategies because they *are* more rational, without the intermediation of any *belief* on our part that they are. Thus, cognitive psychologists have mapped some of the unconscious strategies or heuristics we employ to enable our limited intellects to sift more data and make quicker and more consistent judgments than would be possible using more standard forms of explicit reasoning.[27] We unwittingly come to rely upon heuristics in part because they are selectively reinforced as a result of their instrumental advantages over standard, explicit reasoning, that is, in part because of their greater rationality. Similarly, we may, without realizing it or even being able to admit it to ourselves, develop patterns of behavior that encourage or discourage specific behaviors in others, such as the unconscious means by which we cause those whose company we do not enjoy not to enjoy our company. Finally, as children we may have been virtually incapable of making rational assessments when a distant gain required a proximate loss. Yet somehow over time we managed in largely nondeliberative ways to acquire various interesting habits, such as putting certain vivid thoughts about the immediate future at the periphery of our attention, which enable us as adults to march ourselves off to the dentist without a push from behind. Criterial explanation in terms of individual rationality thus extends to behaviors beyond the realm of deliberate action. And, as with the wants/interests mechanism, it is possible to see in the emergence of such behaviors something we can without distortion call learning.

Indeed, our tendency through experience to develop rational habits and strategies may cooperate with the wants/interests mechanism to provide the basis for an *extended* form of criterial explanation, in which an individual's rationality is assessed not relative to his occurrent beliefs and desires, but relative to his objective interests. The examples considered earlier of the wants/interests mechanism in fact involved elements of this sort of explanation, for they showed not only wants being adjusted to interests, but also behavior being adjusted to newly adjusted wants. Without appropriate alteration of behavior to reflect changing wants, the feedback necessary for learning about wants would not occur. With such alteration, the behavior itself may become more rational in the extended sense. An individual who is instrumentally rational is disposed to adjust means to ends; but one result of his undertaking a means – electing a course of study, or accepting a new job – may be a more informed assessment, and perhaps a reconsideration, of his ends.

The theory of individual rationality – in either its simple or its extended form – thus affords an instance of the sort needed to provide an example of normative realism. Evaluations of degrees of instrumental rationality play a prominent role in our explanations of individual behavior, but they simultaneously have normative force for the agent. Whatever other concerns an agent might have, it surely counts for him as a positive feature of an action that it is efficient relative to his beliefs and desires or, in the extended sense, efficient relative to beliefs and desires that would appropriately reflect his condition and circumstances.

The normative force of these theories of individual rationality does not, however, merely derive from their explanatory use. One can employ a theory of instrumental rationality to explain behavior while rejecting it as a normative theory of reasons, just as one can explain an action as due to irrationality without thereby endorsing unreason.[28] Instead, the connection between the normative and explanatory roles of the instrumental conception of rationality is traceable to their common ground: the human motivational system. It is a fact about us that we have ends and have the capacity for both deliberate action relative to our ends and nondeliberate adjustment of behavior to our ends. As a result, we face options among pathways across a landscape of possibilities variously valenced for us. Both when we explain the reasons for people's choices and the causes of their behavior and when we appeal to their intuitions about what it would be rational to decide or to do, we work this territory, for we make what use we can of facts about what does-in-fact or can-in-principle motivate agents.

Thus emerges the possibility of saying that facts exist about what individuals have reason to do, facts that may be substantially independent of, and more normatively compelling than, an agent's occurrent conception of his reasons. The argument for such realism about individual rationality is no stronger than the arguments for the double claim that the relevant conception of instrumental individual rationality has both explanatory power and the sort of commendatory force a theory of *reasons* must possess, but (although I will not discuss them further here) these arguments seem to me quite strong.

Passing now beyond the theory of individual rationality, let us ask what criterial explanations involving distinctively moral norms might look like. To ask this, we need to know what distinguishes moral norms from other criteria of assessment. Moral evaluation seems to be concerned most centrally with the assessment of conduct or character where the interests of more than one individual are at stake. Further, moral evaluation assesses actions or outcomes in a peculiar way: the interests of the strongest or most prestigious party do not always prevail, purely prudential reasons may be subordinated, and so on. More generally, moral resolutions are thought to be determined by criteria of choice that are *non-indexical* and in some sense *comprehensive*. This has led a number of philosophers to seek to capture the special character of moral evaluation by identifying a *moral point of view* that is impartial, but equally concerned with all those potentially affected. Other ethical theorists have come to a similar conclusion by investigating the sorts of reasons we characteristically treat as relevant or irrelevant in moral discourse. Let us follow these leads. We thus may say that moral norms reflect a certain kind of rationality, rationality not from the point of view of any particular individual, but from what might be called a social point of view.[29]

By itself, the equation of moral rightness with rationality from a social point of view is not terribly restrictive, for, depending upon what one takes rationality to be, this equation could be made by a utilitarian, a Kantian, or even a non-cognitivist. That is as it should be, for if it is to capture what is distinctive about moral norms, it should be compatible with the broadest possible range of recognized moral theories. However, once one opts for a particular conception of rationality – such as the conception of rationality as efficient pursuit of the non-morally good, or as autonomous and universal self-legislation, or as a noncognitive expression of hypothetical endorsement – this schematic characterization begins to assume particular moral content. Here I have adopted an instrumentalist conception of rationality, and this – along with the account given of non-moral goodness – means that the argument for moral realism given below is an argument that presupposes and purports to defend a particular substantive moral theory.[30]

What is this theory? Let me introduce an idealization of the notion of social rationality by considering what would be rationally approved of were the interests of all potentially affected individuals counted equally under circumstances of full and vivid information.[31] Because of the assumption of full and vivid information, the interests in question will be objective interests. Given the account of goodness proposed in § 3, this idealization is equivalent to what is rational from a social point of view with regard to the realization of intrinsic non-moral goodness. This seems to me to be a recognizable and intuitively plausible – if hardly uncontroversial – criterion of moral rightness. Relative moral rightness is a matter of relative degree of approximation to this criterion.

The question that now arises is whether the notion of degrees of moral rightness could participate in explanations of behavior or in processes of moral learning that parallel explanatory uses of the notion of degrees of individual rationality – especially, in the extended sense. I will try to suggest several ways in which it might.

Just as an individual who significantly discounts some of his interests will be liable to certain sorts of dissatisfaction, so will a social arrangement – for example, a form of production, a social or political hierarchy, etc. – that departs from social rationality by significantly discounting the interests of a particular group have a potential for dissatisfaction and unrest. Whether or not this potential will be realized depends upon a great many circumstances. Owing to socialization, or to other limitations on the experience or knowledge of members of this group, the wants/interests mechanism may not have operated in such a way that the wants of its members reflect their interests. As a result they may experience no direct frustration of their desires despite the discounting of their interests. Or, the group may be too scattered or too weak to mobilize effectively. Or, it may face overawing repression. On the other hand, certain social and historical circumstances favor the realization of this potential for unrest, for example, by providing members of this group with experiences that make them more likely to develop interest-congruent wants, by weakening the existing repressive apparatus, by giving them new access to resources or new opportunities for mobilization, or merely by dispelling the illusion that change is impossible. In such circumstances, one can expect the potential for unrest to manifest itself.

Just as explanations involving assessments of individual rationality were not always replaceable by explanations involving individual *beliefs about* what would be rational, so, too, explanations involving assessments of social rationality cannot be replaced by explanations involving *beliefs about* what would be morally right. For example, discontent may arise because a society departs from social rationality, but not as a result of a belief that this is the case. Suppose that a given society is believed by all constituents to be just. This belief may help to stabilize it, but if in fact the interests of certain groups are being discounted, there will be a potential for unrest that may manifest itself in various ways – in alienation, loss of morale, decline in the effectiveness of authority, and so on – well before any changes in belief about the society's justness occur, and that will help explain why members of certain groups come to believe it to be unjust, if in fact they do.

In addition to possessing a certain sort of potential for unrest, societies that fail to approximate social rationality may share other features as well: they may exhibit a tendency toward certain religious or ideological doctrines, or toward certain sorts of repressive apparatus; they may be less productive in some ways (for example, by failing to develop certain human resources) and more productive in others (for example, by extracting greater labor from some groups at less cost), and thus may be differentially economically successful depending upon the conditions of production they face, and so on.

If a notion of social rationality is to be a legitimate part of empirical explanations of such phenomena, an informative characterization of the circumstances under which departures from, or approximations to, social rationality could be expected to lead to particular social outcomes – especially, of the conditions under which groups whose interests are sacrificed could be expected to exhibit or mobilize discontent – must be available. Although it cannot be known a priori whether an account of this kind is possible, one can see emerging in some recent work in social history and historical sociology various elements of a theory of when, and how, a persisting potential for social discontent due to persistently sacrificed interests comes to be manifested.[32]

An individual whose wants do not reflect his interests or who fails to be instru-mentally rational may, I argued, experience feedback of a kind that promotes learning about his good and development of more rational strategies. Similarly, the discontent produced by departures from social rationality may produce feedback that, at a social level, promotes the development of norms that better approximate social rationality. The potential for unrest that exists when the interests of a group are discounted is potential for pressure from that group – and its allies – to accord fuller recognition to their interests in social decision-making and in the socially-instilled norms that govern individual decision-making. It therefore is pressure to push the resolution of conflicts further in the direction required by social rationality, since it is pressure to give fuller weight to the interests of more of those affected. Such pressure may of course be more or less forceful or coherent; it may find the most diverse ideological expression; and it may produce outcomes more or less advantageous in the end to those exerting it.[33] Striking historical examples of the mobilization of excluded groups to promote greater representation of their interests include the rebellions against the system of feudal estates, and more recent social movements against restrictions on religious practices, on suffrage and other civil rights, and on collective bargaining.[34]

Of course, other mechanisms have been at work influencing the evolution of social practices and norms at the same time, some with the reverse effect.[35] Whether mechan-isms working on behalf of the inclusion of excluded interests will predominate depends upon a complex array of social and historical factors. It would be silly to think either that the norms of any actual society will at any given stage of history closely approximate social rationality, or that there will be a univocal trend toward greater social rationality. Like the mechanisms of biological evolution or market economics, the mechanisms described here operate in an "open system" alongside other mechan-isms, and do not guarantee optimality or even a monotonic approach to equilibrium. Human societies do not appear to have begun at or near equilibrium in the relevant sense, and so the strongest available claim might be that in the long haul, barring certain exogenous effects, one could expect an uneven secular trend toward the inclusion of the interests of (or interests represented by) social groups that are capable of some degree of mobilization. But under other circumstances, even in the long run, one could expect the opposite. New World plantation slavery, surely one of the most brutally exclusionary social arrangements ever to have existed, emerged late in world history and lasted for hundreds of years. Other brutally exclusionary social arrangements of ancient or recent vintage persist yet.

One need not, therefore, embrace a theory of moral progress in order to see that the feedback mechanism just described can give an explanatory role to the notion of social rationality. Among the most puzzling, yet most common, objections to moral realism is that there has not been uniform historical progress toward worldwide consensus on moral norms. But it has not to my knowledge been advanced as an argument against *scientific* realism that, for example, some contemporary cultures and subcultures do not accept, and do not seem to be moving in the direction of accepting, the scientific world view. Surely realists are in both cases entitled to say that only certain practices in certain circumstances will tend to produce theories more congruent with reality, especially when the subject matter is so complex and so far removed from anything like direct inspection. They need not subscribe to the quaint idea that "the truth will out" come what may. The extended theory of individual rationality, for example, leads us to expect that in societies where there are large conflicts of interest people will develop large normative disagreements, and that, when (as they usually do) these large conflicts of interest parallel large differences in power, the dominant normative views are unlikely to embody social rationality. What is at issue here, and in criterial explanations generally, is the explanation of certain patterns among others, not necessarily the existence of a single overall trend. We may, however, point to the existence of the feedback mechanisms described here as grounds for belief that we can make qualified use of historical experience as something like experimental evidence about what kinds of practices in what ranges of circumstances might better satisfy a criterion of social rationality. That is, we may assign this mechanism a role in a qualified process of moral learning.

The mechanisms of learning about individual rationality, weak or extended, involved similar qualifications. For although we expect that, under favorable circumstances, individuals may become better at acting in an instrumentally rational fashion as their experience grows, we are also painfully aware that there are powerful mechanisms promoting the opposite result. We certainly do not think that an individual must display exceptionless rationality, or even show ever-increasing rationality over his lifetime, in order to apply reason-giving explanations to many of his actions. Nor do we think that the inevitable persistence of areas of irrationality in individuals is grounds for denying that they can, through experience, acquire areas of greater rationality.

The comparison with individual rationality should not, however, be overdrawn. First, while the inclusion-generating mechanisms for social rationality operate through the behavior of individuals, interpersonal dynamics enter ineliminably in such a way that the criteria selected for are not reducible to those of disaggregated individual rationality. Both social and biological evolution involve selection mechanisms that favor behaviors satisfying criteria of relative optimality that are collective (as in prisoner's dilemma cases) or genotypic (which may also be collective, as in kin selection) as well as individual or phenotypic. Were this not so, it is hardly possible that moral norms could ever have emerged or come to have the hold upon us they do.

Second, there are rather extreme differences of degree between the individual and the social cases. Most strikingly, the mechanisms whereby individual wants and behaviors are brought into some congruence with individual interests and reasons operate in more direct and reliable ways than comparable mechanisms nudging social practices or norms in the direction of what is socially rational. Not only are the information demands less formidable in the individual case – that is the least of it, one might say – but the ways in which feedback is achieved are more likely in the individual case to serve as a prod for change and less likely to be distorted by social asymmetries.

Nonetheless, we do have the skeleton of an explanatory theory that uses the notion of what is more or less rational from a social point of view and that parallels in an obvious way uses of assessments of rationality from the agent's point of view in explanations of individual beliefs and behaviors. Like the individual theory, it suggests prediction- and counterfactual-supporting generalizations of the following kind: over time, and in some circumstances more than others, we should expect pressure to be exerted on behalf of practices that more adequately satisfy a criterion of rationality.

Well, if this is a potentially predictive and explanatory theory, how good is it? That is a very large question, one beyond my competence to answer. But let me note briefly three patterns in the evolution of moral norms that seem to me to bear out the predictions of this theory, subject to the sorts of qualifications that the existence of imperfections and competing mechanisms would lead one to expect. I do so with trepidation, however, for although the patterns I will discuss are gross historical trends, it is not essential to the theory that history show such trends, and it certainly is not part of the theory to endorse a set of practices or norms merely because it is a result of them.

Generality. It is a commonplace of anthropology that tribal peoples often have only one word to name both their tribe and "the people" or "humanity." Those beyond the tribe are not deemed full-fledged people, and the sorts of obligations one has toward people do not apply fully with regard to outsiders. Over the span of history, through processes that have involved numerous reversals, people have accumulated into larger social units – from the familial band to the tribe to the "people" to the nation-state – and the scope of moral categories has enlarged to follow these expanding boundaries. Needless to say, this has not been a matter of the contagious spread of enlightenment. Expanding social entities frequently subjugate those incorporated within their new boundaries, and the means by which those thus oppressed have secured greater recognition of their interests have been highly conflictual, and remain – perhaps, will always remain – incomplete. Nonetheless, contemporary moral theory, and to a surprising degree contemporary moral discourse, have come to reject any limitation short of the species.[36]

Humanization. Moral principles have been assigned various origins and natures: as commandments of supernatural origin, grounded in the will or character of a deity, to be interpreted by a priesthood; as formalistic demands of a caste-based code of honor; as cosmic principles of order; as dictates of reason or conscience that make no appeal to human inclinations or well-being; and so on. While vestiges of these views survive in contemporary moral theory, it is typical of almost the entire range of such theory, and of much of contemporary moral discourse, to make some sort of intrinsic connection between normative principles and effects on human interests. Indeed, the very emergence of morality as a distinctive subject matter apart from religion is an instance of this pattern.

Patterns of variation. In addition to seeing patterns that reflect some pressure toward the approximation of social rationality, we should expect to see greater approximation in those areas of normative regulation where the mechanisms postulated here work best, for example, in areas where almost everyone has importantly similar or mutually satisfiable interests, where almost everyone has some substantial potential to infringe upon the interests of others, where the advantages of certain forms of constraint or cooperation are highly salient even in the dynamics of small groups, and where individuals can significantly influence the likelihood of norm-following behavior on the part of others by themselves following norms. The clearest examples have to do with prohibitions of aggression and theft, and of the violation of promises.[37] By contrast, moral questions that concern matters where there are no solutions compatible with protecting the most basic interests of all, where there exist very large asymmetries in the capacity to infringe upon interests, where the gains or losses from particular forms of cooperation or constraint are difficult to perceive, and where individual compliance will little affect general compliance, are less likely to achieve early or stable approximation to social rationality. Clear examples here have to do with such matters as social hierarchy – for example, the permissibility of slavery, of authoritarian government, of caste or gender inequalities – and social responsibility – for example, what is the nature of our individual or collective obligation to promote the well-being of unrelated others?

Given a suitable characterization of the conditions that prevailed during the processes of normative evolution described by these patterns, the present theory claims not only that these changes could have been expected, but that an essential part of the explanation of their occurrence is a mechanism whereby individuals whose interests are denied are led to form common values and make common cause along lines of shared interests, thereby placing pressure on social practices to approximate more closely to social rationality.

These descriptions and explanations of certain prominent features of the evolution of moral norms will no doubt strike some as naive at best, plainly – perhaps even dangerously – false at worst. I thoroughly understand this. I have given impossibly sketchy, one-sided, simple-minded accounts of a very complex reality.[38] I can only hope that these accounts will seem as believable as one could expect sketchy, one-sided, simple-minded accounts to be, and that this will make the story I have tried to tell about mechanisms and explanation more plausible.

Needless to say, the upshot is not a complacent functionalism or an overall endorsement of current moral practice or norms. Instead, the account of morality sketched here emphasizes conflict rather than equilibrium, and provides means for criticizing certain contemporary moral practices and intuitions by asking about their historical genesis. For example, if we come to think that the explanation of a common moral intuition assigns no significant role to mechanisms that could be expected to exert pressure toward socially rational outcomes, then this is grounds for questioning the intuition, however firmly we may hold it. In the spirit of a naturalized moral epistemology, we may ask whether the explanation of why we make certain moral judgments is an example of a reliable process for discovering moral facts.

5 LIMITATIONS

Thus far I have spoken of what is morally best as a matter of what is instrumentally rational from a social point of view. But I have also characterized a genuinely moral point of view as one impartial with respect to the interests of all potentially affected, and that is not a socially-bounded notion. In fact, I have claimed that a trend away from social specificity is among the patterns visible in the evolution of moral norms. Part of the explanation of this pattern – and part, therefore, of the explanatory role of degrees of impartial rationality – is that the mechanisms appealed to above are not socially-bounded, either. Societies, and individuals on opposite sides of social boundaries, constrain one another in various ways, much as groups and individuals constrain one another within societies: they can threaten aggression, mobilize resistance to external control, withhold cooperation, and obstruct one another's plans; and they are prone to resort to such constraining activities when their interests are denied or at risk. As with intrasocial morality, so in intersocial morality, the best-established and most nearly impartially rational elements are those where the mechanisms we have discussed work most reliably: prohibitions on aggression are stronger and more widely accepted than principles of equity or redistribution. Of course, many factors make intersocietal dynamics unlike intrasocietal ones. ... But the reader will for once be spared more armchair social science. Still, what results is a form of moral realism that is essentially tied to a limited point of view, an impartial yet human one. Is this too limited for genuine moral realism?

A teacher of mine once remarked that the question of moral realism seemed to him to be the question whether the universe cares what we do. Since we have long since given up believing that the cosmos pays us any mind, he thought we should long since have given up moral realism. I can only agree that if this were what moral realism involved, it should – with relief rather than sorrow – be let go. However, the account offered here gives us a way of understanding how moral values or imperatives might be objective without being cosmic. They need be grounded in nothing more transcendental than facts about man and his environment, facts about what sorts of things matter to us, and how the ways we live affect these things.

Yet the present account is limited in another way, which may be of greater concern from the standpoint of contemporary moral theory: it does not yield moral imperatives that are categorical in the sense of providing a reason for action to all rational agents regardless of their contingent desires. Although troubling, this limitation is not tantamount to relativism, since on the present account rational motivation is not a precondition of moral obligation. For example, it could truthfully be said that I ought to be more generous even though greater generosity would not help me to promote my existing ends, or even to satisfy my objective interests. This could be so because what it would be morally right for me to do depends upon what is rational from a point of view that includes, but is not exhausted by, my own.

In a similar way, it could be said that I logically ought not to believe both a proposition p and a proposition that implies not-p. However, it may not be the case that every rational agent will have an instrumental reason to purge all logical contradictions from his thought. It would require vast amounts of cogitation for anyone to test all of his existing beliefs for consistency, and to insure that every newly acquired belief preserves it. Suppose someone to be so fortunate that the only contradictions among his beliefs lie deep in the much-sedimented swamp of factual trivia. Perhaps his memories of two past acquaintances have become confused in such a way that somewhere in the muck there are separate beliefs which, taken together, attribute to one individual logically incompatible properties. Until such a contradiction rears its head in practice, he may have no more reason to lay down his present concerns and wade in after it than he has to leave his home in suburban New Jersey to hunt alligators in the Okefenokee on the off chance that he might one day find himself stranded and unarmed in the backwaters of southeast Georgia.[39] What an individual rationally ought to do thus may differ from what logic requires of him. Still, we may say that logical evaluation is not subjective or arbitrary, and that good grounds of a perfectly general kind are available for being logical, namely, that logical contradictions are necessarily false and logical inferences are truth-preserving. Since in public discourse and private reflection we are often concerned with whether our thinking is warranted in a sense that is more intimately connected with its truth-conduciveness than with its instrumentality to our peculiar personal goals, it therefore is far from arbitrary that we attach so much importance to logic as a standard of criticism and self-criticism.

By parallel, if we adopt the account of moral rightness proposed above we may say that moral evaluation is not subjective or arbitrary, and that good, general grounds are available for following moral "ought's", namely, that moral conduct is rational from an impartial point of view. Since in public discourse and private reflection we are often concerned with whether our conduct is justifiable from a general rather than merely personal standpoint, it therefore is far from arbitrary that we attach so much importance to morality as a standard of criticism and self-criticism.

The existence of such phenomena as religion and ideology is evidence for the pervasiveness and seriousness of our concern for impartial justification. Throughout history individuals have sacrificed their interests, even their lives, to meet the demands of religions or ideologies that were compelling for them in part because they purported to express a universal – *the* universal – justificatory standpoint. La Rochefoucauld wrote that hypocrisy is the tribute vice pays to virtue,[40] but "hypocrisy" suggests cynicism. We might better say that ideology is the respect partisans show to impartiality. Morality, then, is not ideology made sincere and general – ideology is intrinsically given to heart-felt generalization. Morality is ideology that has faced the facts.

I suspect the idea that moral evaluations must have categorical force for rational agents owes some of its support to a fear that were this to be denied, the authority of morality would be lost. That would be so if one held onto the claim that moral imperatives cannot exist for someone who would not have a reason to obey them, for then an individual could escape moral duties by the simple expedient of having knavish desires. But if we give up this claim about the applicability of moral judgment, then variations in personal desires cannot license exemption from moral obligation.[41]

Thus, while it certainly is a limitation of the argument made here that it does not yield a conception of moral imperatives as categorical, that may be a limitation we can live with and still accord morality the scope and dignity it traditionally has enjoyed. Moreover, it may be a limitation we must live with. For how many among us can convince ourselves that reason is other than hypothetical? Need it also be asked: How many of us would find our sense of the significance of morality or the importance of moral conduct enhanced by a demonstration that even a person with the most thoroughly repugnant ends would find that moral conduct advanced them?

One implication of what has been said is that if we want morality to be taken seriously and to have an important place in people's lives – and not merely as the result of illusion or the threat of repression – we should be vitally concerned with the ways in which social arrangements produce conflicts of interest and asymmetries of power that affect the nature and size of the gap between what is individually and socially rational. Rather than attempt to portray morality as something that it cannot be, as "rationally compelling no matter what one's ends," we should ask how we might change the ways we live so that moral conduct would more regularly be rational given the ends we actually will have.

6 SUMMARY AND CONCLUSION

I have outlined a form of moral realism, and given some indication of how it might be defended against certain objections. Neither a full characterization of this view, nor full answers to the many objections it faces, can be given within the present essay. Perhaps then I should stop trying to say just a bit more, and close by indicating roughly what I have, and have not, attempted to show.

I have proposed what are in effect reforming naturalistic definitions of non-moral goodness and moral rightness. It is possible to respond: "Yes, I can see that such-and-such an end is an objective interest of the agent in your sense, or that such-and-such a practice is rational from an impartial point of view, but can't I still ask whether the end is good for him or the practice right?" Such "open questions" cannot by their nature be closed, since definitions are not subject to proof or disproof. But open questions may be more or less disturbing, for although definitional proposals cannot be demonstrated, they can fare better or worse at meeting various desiderata.

I have assumed throughout that the drawing up of definitions is part of theory-construction, and so is to be assessed by asking (1) whether the analyses given satisfy appropriate constraints of intelligibility and function, and (2) whether the terms as analyzed contribute to the formulation and testing of worthwhile theories. How do my proposals fit with these criteria?

(1) Beyond constraints of intelligibility, such as clarity and non-circularity, specifically naturalistic definitions of evaluative terms should satisfy two further analytic constraints arising from their intended function. (a) They should insofar as possible capture the normative force of these terms by providing analyses that permit these terms to play their central evaluative roles. In the present setting, this involves showing that although the definitions proposed may not fit with all of our linguistic or moral intuitions, they nonetheless express recognizable notions of goodness and rightness. Further, it involves showing that the definitions permit plausible connections to be drawn between, on the one hand, what is good or right and, on the other, what characteristically would motivate individuals who are prepared to submit themselves to relevant sorts of scrutiny. (b) The naturalistic definitions should permit the evaluative concepts to participate in their own right in genuinely empirical theories. Part of this consists in showing that we have appropriate epistemic access to these concepts. Part, too, (and a related part) consists in showing that generalizations employing these concepts, among others, can figure in potentially explanatory accounts. I have tried to offer reasonably clear definitions and to show in a preliminary way how they might meet constraints (a) and (b).

(2) However, a good deal more must be done, for it remains to show that the empirical theories constructed with the help of these definitions are reasonably good theories, that is, theories for which we have substantial evidence and which provide

plausible explanations. I have tried in the most preliminary way imaginable to suggest this. If I have been wholly unpersuasive on empirical matters, then I can expect that the definitions I have offered will be equally unpersuasive.

It is an attraction for me of naturalism in ethics and epistemology alike that it thus is constrained in several significant dimensions at once. One has such ample opportunities to be shown wrong or found unconvincing if one's account must be responsive to empirical demands as well as normative intuitions. Theorizing in general is more productive when suitably constrained; in ethics especially, constraints are needed if we are to have a clearer idea of how we might make progress toward the resolution of theoretical disputes. Of course, not just any constraints will do. A proposed set of constraints must present itself as both appropriate and useful. Let me say something about (1) the utility of the constraints adopted here, and then a final word about (2) their appropriateness.

(1) Consider three classes of competitors to the substantive moral theory endorsed above, and notice how criticisms of them *naturally* intertwine concerns about normative justification and empirical explanation. *Kantian* conceptions of morality are widely viewed as having captured certain intuitively compelling normative characteristics of such notions as rationality and moral rightness, but it seems they have done so partly at the expense of affording a plausible way of integrating these notions into an empirical account of our reasons and motives in action. Moreover, this descriptive difficulty finds direct expression on the normative side. Not only must any normative "ought" be within the scope of an empirical "can", but a normatively compelling "ought" must – as recent criticisms of Kantianism have stressed – reach to the real springs of human action and concern. *Intuitionist* moral theories also enjoyed some success in capturing normative features of morality, but they have largely been abandoned for want of a credible account of the nature or operation of a faculty of moral intuition. It is too easy for us to give a non-justifying psychological explanation of the existence in certain English gentlemen of something which they identified upon introspection as a faculty of moral insight, an explanation that ties this purported faculty more closely to the rigidity of prevailing social conventions than to anything that looks as if it could be a source of universal truth. *Social choice theories* that take occurrent subjective interests or revealed preferences as given fit more readily than Kantian or intuitionist theories with empirical accounts of behavior, and, unlike them, have found a place in contemporary social science. But they suffer well-known limitations as normative theories, some of which turn out to be bound up with their limitations as explanatory theories: they lack an account of the origin or evolution of preferences, and partly for that reason are unable to capture the ways in which we evaluate purportedly rational or moral conduct by criticizing ends as well as means.

(2) However, the issues at stake when we evaluate competing approaches to morality involve not only this sort of assessment of largish theories, but also questions about

which criteria of assessment appropriately apply to definitions and theories in ethics, and about whether definitional systematization and largish theorizing are even appropriate for ethics. I am drawn to the view that the development of theory in ethics is not an artificial contrivance of philosophers but an organic result of the personal and social uses of moral evaluation: time and again individuals and groups have faced difficult questions to which common sense gave conflicting or otherwise unsatisfactory answers, and so they have pressed their questions further and pursued their inquiry more systematically. The felt need for theory in ethics thus parallels the felt need for theory in natural or social science.[42] It does not follow from this alone that ethical theorizing must run parallel to or be integrable with theorizing in the natural and social sciences. Ethics might be deeply different. Although initially plausible and ultimately irrefutable, the view that ethics stands thus apart is one that in the end I reject. We are natural and social creatures, and I know of nowhere else to look for ethics than in this rich conjunction of facts. I have tried to suggest that we might indeed find it there.[43]

NOTES

1 Nineteenth-century evolutionary naturalism affords an example of the former, Dewey – and, on at least one reading, perhaps Mill as well – an example of the latter.

2 A. J. Ayer, *Language, Truth, and Logic* (New York: Dover, 1952), p. 111.

3 In saying this, I am insisting that questions about what it would be rational to believe belong to practical rather than theoretical reason. While results of theoretical reason – for example, conclusions of deductive inferences – are in general relevant to questions about rational belief, they are not determinative apart from the agent's practical reasons.

4 Of course, individual belief-formation is not typically governed by explicit means–end reasoning, but rather by habits of belief-formation and tendencies to invest varying degrees of confidence in particular kinds of beliefs. If we accept an instrumental account of rationality, then we can call such habits rational from the standpoint of the individual to the extent that they fit into a constellation of attitudes and tendencies that promote his ends. This matter will arise again in § 4.

5 Neither these remarks, nor those in subsequent paragraphs, are meant to be a serious exegesis of Hume's arguments, which admit of interpretations other than the one suggested here. I mean only to capture certain features of what I take Hume's arguments to be, for example, in Book III, Part I, § I of *A Treatise of Human Nature*, edited by L. A. Selby-Bigge (Oxford: Clarendon, 1973), esp. pp. 465–6, and in Appendix I of *An Inquiry Concerning the Principles of Morals*, edited by C. W. Hendel (Indianapolis: Bobbs-Merrill, 1957), esp. pp. 111–12.

6 Philippa Foot has questioned this thesis, although her way of posing and arguing the question differs enough from mine that I cannot judge whether she would be in agreement with the argument that follows. See her *Virtues and Vices* (Berkeley, CA: University of California Press, 1978), esp. Essay XI. The presentation of the issues here owes its main inspiration to William K. Frankena's distinction between the rational and the moral points of view.

7 See the *Inquiry Concerning the Principles of Morals*, Sec. IX, Pt. II, pp. 102–3.

8 The ancient criticism of noncognitivism that it has difficulty accounting for the difference between moral value and other sorts of desirability (so that Hume can speak in one breath of our approval of a man's "good offices" and his "well-contrived apartment"), gains some vitality in the present context. To account for such differences it is necessary to have a contentful way of characterizing criteria of moral assessment so that moral approval does not reduce to "is valued by the agent." (Such a characterization will be offered in § 4.) Value *sans phrase* is a generic, and not necessarily moral, notion. One sometimes hears it said that generic value becomes moral in character when we reach that which the agent prizes above all else. But this would invest pets and mementos with moral value, and have the peculiar effect of making amoralism a virtual conceptual impossibility. It seems more plausible to say that not all value is moral value, and that the highest values for an individual need not be, nor need they even seem to him to be, moral values. Once we turn to questions of duty, the situation should be clearer still: moral theorists have proposed quite different relations among the categories of moral rightness, moral goodness, and non-moral goodness, and it seems implausible to say that deeming an act or class of actions morally right is necessarily equivalent to viewing it personally as valuable *sans phrase*.

9 The character of moral imperatives receives further discussion in § 5.

10 Such theories are suitably externalist when, in characterizing the notions of *reliability* or *warrant-conferring causal process*, they employ an account of truth that does not resolve truth into that which we have reason to believe – for example, a nontrivial correspondence theory.

11 Or if moral facts were supposed to be things of a kind to provide categorical reasons for action. However, this supposition is simply Hume's thesis of practicality in ontological garb.

12 J. L. Mackie, in *Ethics: Inventing Right and Wrong* (Harmondsworth, Middlesex: Penguin, 1977), and Gilbert Harman, in *The Nature of Morality: An Introduction to Ethics* (New York: Oxford University Press, 1977), both challenge moral realism in part by questioning its capacity to explain. Nicholas L. Sturgeon, in "Moral Explanations," David Copp and David Zimmerman, eds, *Morality, Reason and Truth: New Essays in the Foundations of Ethics* (Totowa, NJ: Rowman and Allanhead, 1984 [Chapter 8, this volume]), takes the opposite side, using arguments different from those offered below.

13 A full-scale theory of value would, I think, show the concept of someone's good to be slightly different from the concept of what is desirable for him. However, this difference will not affect the argument made here.

14 It was some work by Richard C. Jeffrey on epistemic probability that originally suggested to me the idea of objectifying subjective interests. See note 17. I have since benefited from Richard B. Brandt's work on "rational desire," although I fear that what I will say contains much that he would regard as wrong-headed. See *A Theory of the Good and the Right* (Oxford: Clarendon, 1979), Part I.

15 We ask this question of A+, rather than what A+ wants for himself, because we are seeking the objectified subjective interests of A, and the interests of A+ might be quite different owing to the changes involved in the idealization of A. For example, A+ presumably does not want any more information for himself – there is no more to be had and he knows this. Yet it might still be true that A+ would want to want more knowledge were he to be put in the place of his less well-informed self, A. It may as a psychological matter be impossible for A+ to set aside entirely his desires *in his present circumstances* with regard to himself or to A in considering what he would want to want were he to be put *in the place of* his less-than-ideal self. This

reveals a measurement problem for objective interests: giving an individual the information and capacities necessary to "objectify" his interests may perturb his psychology in ways that alter the phenomenon we wish to observe. Such difficulties attend even the measurement of subjective interests, since instruments for sampling preferences (indeed, mere acts of reflection upon one's preferences) tend to affect the preferences expressed. For obvious reasons, interference effects come with the territory. Though not in themselves sufficient ground for skepticism about subjective or objective interests, these measurement problems show the need for a "perturbation theory," and for caution about attributions of interests that are inattentive to interference effects.

16 "Interest" is not quite the word wanted here, for in ordinary language we may speak of a want where we would not speak of a corresponding interest. See Brian Barry, *Political Argument* (London: Routledge & Kegan Paul, 1965), especially Chapter X, for discussion. A more accurate, but overly cumbersome, expression would be "positive-valence-making characteristic".

17 Suppose for a moment, contrary to what was urged above, that there is a workable notion of epistemic probability that determines rational degrees of belief independent of the contingent goals of the epistemic agent. Perhaps then the following analogy will be helpful. Consider a physically random process, such as alpha-decay. We can ask an individual what subjective probability he would assign to an event consisting in a certain rate of decay for a given sample of uranium; we can also ask what rational degree of belief the individual would assign to this event were he to become ideally informed about the laws of physics and the relevant initial conditions. Call the latter rational degree of belief the *objectified subjective probability* of the event, and suppose it to be equal to one fifth. (Cf. Richard C. Jeffrey, *The Logic of Decision* (New York: McGraw-Hill, 1964), pp. 190–6.) But now consider the physical facts that, in conjunction with the laws of quantum mechanics, ground the idealized individual's judgment. Call these the *reduction basis* of that judgment. This reduction basis is a complex set of primary qualities that can be said to bring it about that the event in question has an *objective probability* of one fifth. (It should be said that it is not part of Jeffrey's approach to posit such objective probabilities.) The existence of this objective probability can explain why an ideally informed individual would select an objectified subjective probability equal to one fifth, but the probability judgment of an ideally informed individual cannot explain why the objective probability is one fifth – that is a matter of the laws of physics. Similarly, the existence of an individual's objective interest can explain why his ideally informed self would pick out for his less-informed self a given objectified subjective interest, but not *vice versa*.

18 More precisely, we may say that X is non-morally good for A at time t if and only if X would satisfy an objective interest of A the reduction basis of which exists at t. Considerations about the evolution of interests over time raise a number of issues that cannot be entered into here.

19 A+, putting himself in A's place, may find several different sets of wants equally appealing, so that several alternatives could be equal-best for A in this sense. This would not make the notion of "the good for A" problematic, just pluralistic. However, a more serious question looms. Is there sufficient determinacy in the specification of A+'s condition, or in the psychology of desire, to make the notion of objective interest definite enough for my purposes? Without trying to say how definite *that* might be, let me suggest two ways in which an answer to the worry about definiteness might begin. (1) It seems that we do think that there are rather definite answers to questions about how an individual A's desires would change were his beliefs to change in certain limited ways. If Lonnie were to learn the consequences of drinking milk, he would no longer want his desire for milk to be effective. But a large change

in belief can be accomplished piecemeal, by a sequence of limited changes in belief. Thus, if (admittedly, a big "if") *order* of change is not in the end significant, then the facts and generalizations that support counterfactuals about limited changes might support an extrapolation all the way to A+. (2) Beliefs and desires appear to co-vary systematically. Typically, we find that individuals who differ markedly in their desires – for example, about careers or style of life – differ markedly, and characteristically, in their beliefs; as individuals become more similar in their beliefs, they tend to become more similar in their desires. This suggests that if (another big "if") the characterization given of A+ fixes the entire content of his beliefs in a definite way (at least, given a choice of language), then his desires may be quite comprehensively fixed as well. If we had in hand a general theory of the co-variation of beliefs and desires, then we could appeal directly to this theory – plus facts about A – to ground the counterfactuals needed to characterize A's objectified interests, eliminating any essential reference to the imaginary individual A+.

20 The account may, however, yield some counterintuitive results. Depending upon the nature and circumstances of given individuals, they might have objective interests in things we find wrong or repulsive, and that do not seem to us part of a good life. We can explain a good deal of our objection to certain desires – for example, those involving cruelty – by saying that they are not *morally* good; others – for example, those of a philistine nature – by saying that they are not *aesthetically* valuable; and so on. It seems to me preferable to express our distaste for certain ends in terms of specific categories of value, rather than resort to the device of saying that such ends could under no circumstances be part of anyone's non-moral good. People, or at least some people, might be put together in a way that makes some not-very-appetizing things essential to their flourishing, and we do not want to be guilty of wishful thinking on this score. (There will be wishful thinking enough before we are through.)

21 To put the matter in more strictly naturalistic terms, we can expect that evolution will have favored organisms so constituted that those behaviors requisite to their survival and flourishing are associated with positive internal states (such as pleasure) and those opposed to survival or flourishing with negative states (such as pain). "Flourishing" here, even if understood as mere reproductive fitness, is not a narrow notion. In order for beings such as humans to be reproductively successful, they must as phenotypes have lives that are psychologically sustainable, internally motivating, and effectively social; lives, moreover, that normally would engage in a wide range of their peculiarly human capacities. Humankind could hardly have been a success story even at the reproductive level were not pursuit of the sorts of things that characteristically have moved humans to action associated with existences of this kind. However, it must be kept in mind that most human evolution occurred under circumstances different in important ways from the present. It therefore is quite possible that the interaction of evolved human motivational potentials with existing circumstances will produce incongruities between what we tend to aim at, or to be driven by, and what would produce the greatest pleasure for us. That is one reason for doubting hedonism as a theory of motivation.

22 "Functional success" rather than "representational accuracy" for the following reason. Selection favors organisms that have some-or-other feature that happens in their particular environment to contribute to getting their needs met. Whether that feature will be an accurate representational capacity cannot be settled by an argument of this kind. Of course, it would be a very great coincidence if beings who rely as heavily upon representations as we do were able to construct only grossly inaccurate representations while at the same time managing successfully in a range of environments over a long period of time. But such coincidences cannot be ruled out.

23 Although some elements of their reduction basis depend upon our past choices, our objective interests are not therefore subjective in a sense damaging to the present argument. After all, such unproblematically objective facts about us as our weight, income, and spatial location depend in the same way upon past choices. The point is not that our subjective interests have no role in shaping the reduction basis of our objective interests, but rather that they can affect our objective interests only in virtue of their actual (rather than merely desired) effects upon this reduction basis, just as they can affect our weight, income, or spatial location only in virtue of actual (rather than merely desired) effects upon our displacement, employment, or movement.

24 In a similar way, it would be incomplete and superficial to explain why, once large-scale production became possible, the world's consumption of refined sugar underwent such explosive development, by mentioning only the fact that people liked its taste. Why, despite wide differences in traditional diet and acquired tastes, has sugar made such inroads into human consumption? Why haven't the appearance and promotion of other equally cheap foodstuffs produced such remarkable shifts in consumption? Why, even in societies where sugar is recognized as a health hazard, does consumption of sugars, often in concealed forms, continue to climb? Facts about the way we are constituted, about the rather singular ways sugar therefore affects us, and about the ways forms of production and patterns of consumption co-evolved to generate both a growing demand and an expanding supply, must supplement a theory that stops at the level of subjective preferences. See Sidney W. Mintz, *Sweetness and Power: The Place of Sugar in Modern History* (New York: Viking, 1985) for relevant discussion.

25 For a discussion of how informally expressed accounts may nonetheless convey explanatory information, see § II of my "Probability, Explanation, and Information," *Synthese* 48 (1981), pp. 233–56.

26 Such explanation uses a naturalized criterion when rationality is defined in terms of relative efficiency given the agent's beliefs and desires. A (more or less) rational agent is thus someone disposed to act in (more or less) efficient ways. There is a deep difficulty about calling such explanation naturalistic, for the constraints placed upon attributions of beliefs and desires by a "principle of charity" may compromise the claim that rational-agent explanations are empirical. Although I believe this difficulty can be overcome, this is hardly the place to start *that* argument.

27 For a survey of the literature, see Richard Nisbett and Lee Ross, *Human Inference: Strategies and Shortcomings of Social Judgment* (Englewood Cliffs, NJ: Prentice-Hall, 1980), where one unsurprisingly finds greater attention paid to drawbacks than advantages.

28 To recall a point from § 2: one may make assessments relative to particular evaluative criteria without thereby valuing that which satisfies them.

29 I realize that it is misleading to call a point of view that is "impartial, but equally concerned with all those potentially affected" a *social* point of view – some of those potentially affected may lie on the other side of an intersocial boundary. This complication will be set aside until § 5.

30 It also means that the relation of moral criteria to criteria of individual rationality has become problematic, since there can be no guarantee that what would be instrumentally rational from any given individual's point of view will coincide with what would be instrumentally rational from a social point of view.

31 A rather strong thesis of interpersonal comparison is needed here for purposes of social aggregation. I am not assuming the existence of some single good, such as happiness, underlying such comparisons. Thus the moral theory in question, although consequentialist, aggregative,

and maximizing, is not equivalent to classical utilitarianism. I *am* assuming that when a choice is faced between satisfying interest X of A vs. satisfying interest Y of B, answers to the question "All else equal, would it matter more to me if I were A to have X satisfied than if I were B to have Y satisfied?" will be relatively determinate and stable across individuals under conditions of full and vivid information. A similar, though somewhat weaker, form of comparability-across-difference is presupposed when we make choices from among alternative courses of action that would lead us to have different desires in the future.

32 See, for example, Barrington Moore, Jr., *The Social Origins of Dictatorship and Democracy: Lord and Peasant in the Making of the Modern World* (Boston, MA: Beacon, 1966) and *Injustice: The Social Bases of Obedience and Revolt* (White Plains, NY: M. E. Sharpe, 1978); E. P. Thompson, *The Making of the English Working Class* (New York: Pantheon, 1963); William B. Taylor, *Drinking, Homicide, and Rebellion in Colonial Mexican Villages* (Stanford, CA: Stanford University Press, 1979); Charles Tilly, *From Mobilization to Revolution* (Reading, MA: Addison-Wesley, 1978); and Charles Tilly *et al.*, *The Rebellious Century, 1830–1930* (Cambridge, MA: Harvard University Press, 1975).

33 A common theme in the works cited in note 32 is that much social unrest is re-vindicative rather than revolutionary, since the discontent of long-suffering groups often is galvanized into action only when customary entitlements are threatened or denied. The overt ideologies of such groups thus frequently are particularistic and conservative, even as their unrest contributes to the emergence of new social forms that concede greater weight to previously discounted interests. In a similar way, individuals often fail to notice irrationalities in their customary behavior until they are led by it into uncustomary difficulties, which then arouse a sense that something has gone wrong. For familiar reasons, a typical initial individual response is to attempt to retrieve the *status quo ante*, although genuine change may result from these restorative efforts.

34 It should be emphasized that these mechanisms do not presuppose a background of democratic institutions. They have extracted concessions even within societies that remained very hierarchical. See, for example, Taylor, *Drinking, Homicide, and Rebellion*.

35 Indeed, the mechanism just described may push in several directions at once: toward the inclusion of some previously excluded interests, and toward the exclusion of some previously included interests. To be sure, if interests come to be excluded even though their social and material basis remains more or less intact, a new potential for unrest is created. Some groups present a special problem, owing to their inherent inability to mobilize effectively, for example, children and future generations. To account for the pressures that have been exerted on behalf of these groups it is necessary to see how individuals come to include other individuals within their own interests. (Compare the way in which one's future selves, which can exert no pressure on their own behalf, come to be taken into account by one's present self in virtue of one's identification with them.) Unless one takes account of such processes of incorporation and identification, morality (or even prudence) will appear quite mysterious, but I will have little to say about them here. For some preliminary remarks, see § IX of my "Alienation, Consequentialism, and the Demands of Morality," *Philosophy and Public Affairs* 13 (1984), pp. 134–71.

36 Here and elsewhere, I mean by "contemporary moral theory" to refer to dominant views in the academies, and by "contemporary moral discourse" to refer to widespread practices of public moral argumentation, in those societies that have achieved the highest levels of development of empirical science generally. Again, the moral realist, like the scientific realist, is not committed to worldwide consensus.

37 However, such prohibitions historically have shown limitations of scope that are no longer recognized as valid. The trend against such limitations is an instance of the first sort of pattern, toward increased generality.

38 Moreover, the accounts are highly general in character, operating at a level of description incapable of discriminating between hypotheses based upon the particular account of moral rightness proposed here and others rather close to it. (Roughly, those characterizing moral rightness in terms of instrumental rationality relative to the non-moral good of those affected, but differing on details regarding instrumental rationality – for example, is it straight-forwardly maximizing or partly distributive? – or regarding non-moral goodness – for example, is it reducible to pleasure? For a discussion of not-very-close competitors, see § 6.) If the method I have employed is to be used to make choices from among close competitors, the empirical analysis must be much more fine-grained. Similar remarks apply to the weak and extended theories of individual rationality appealed to above.

39 It is of no importance whether we say that he has *no* reason to do this or simply a vanishingly small one. I suppose we could say that a person has a vanishingly small reason to do anything – even to expend enormous effort to purge minor contradictions from his beliefs or to purge alligators from distant swamps – that might *conceivably* turn out to be to his benefit. But then we would have no trouble guaranteeing the existence of vanishingly small reasons for moral conduct. This would allow naturalized moral rightness to satisfy a Humean thesis of practicality after all, but in a way that would rob the thesis of its interest.

40 François (duc de) la Rochefoucauld, *Reflexions, ou sentences et maximes morales suivi de reflexions diverses*, ed., Jean Lafond (Paris: Gallimard, 1976), p. 79. La Rochefoucauld apparently borrowed the phrase from the cleric Du Moulin. I am grateful to a remark of Barrington Moore, Jr. for reminding me of it. See his *Injustice*, p. 508.

41 Contrast Harman's relativism about "ought" in *The Nature of Morality*. Harman adopts the first of the two courses just mentioned, preserving the connection between an individual's moral obligations and what he has (instrumental) reason to do. He defends his approach in part by arguing that, if we suppose that Hitler was engaged in rational pursuit of his ends, an "internal" judgment like "Hitler (morally) ought not to have killed six million Jews" would be "weak" and "odd" compared to an "external" judgment like "Hitler was evil" (see pp. 107 ff.). I would have thought the opposite, namely, that it is too "weak" and "odd" to give an account of morality such that Hitler can be judged to be consummately evil (which Harman claims, without explanation, his brand of relativism *can* do) but in which "Hitler (morally) ought not to have acted as he did" is false.

42 This felt need is also reflected in the codification of laws, and in the development of legal theories. However contrived the law may at times seem, surely the general social conditions and needs that have driven its development are real enough. Indeed, the elaborate artifice of law and its language is in part an indication of how pressing the need to go beyond pre-theoretic common sense has been.

43 I am indebted to a great many people, including Peter Achinstein, Robert Audi, Annette Baier, Michael Bratman, Stephen Darwall, Allan Gibbard, Thomas Nagel, Samuel Scheffler, Rebecca Scott, Nicholas Sturgeon, Nicholas White, and the editors at *The Philosophical Review*, who have kindly provided comments on previous drafts or presentations of this paper.

10

TROUBLES FOR NEW WAVE MORAL SEMANTICS

THE OPEN QUESTION ARGUMENT REVIVED

Terence Horgan and Mark Timmons

G. E. Moore held that all forms of ethical naturalism rested on a fallacy – the so-called "naturalistic fallacy" which his open question argument was designed to expose. For a while anyway, the argument's persuasive appeal held a good many philosophers in its sway. Its appeal was felt by W. D. Ross (1930: 7–11, 92–3) and A. C. Ewing (1948: 41–2) who, like Moore, were led to espouse ethical nonnaturalism. Its appeal was also felt by A. J. Ayer (1952: 104–5) and R. M. Hare (1952: ch. 5) who, because they found the metaphysical and epistemological commitments of nonnaturalism unpalatable, were led to noncognitivist accounts of moral discourse.[1] But as it turned out, the persuasive appeal of Moore's argument lasted only as long as did the appeal of certain semantical views upon which ethical naturalism was presumed to rest. Once these semantical views were questioned and the philosophical soil was fertilized with more plausible views, a novel strain of ethical naturalism – a kind allegedly immune to Moorean open question arguments was bound to sprout forth. One now sees this new strain of ethical naturalism everywhere, though we think it first emerged in the hearty intellectual climate of upper New York state.

Our central aim in this paper is to cast doubt on the sort of new wave moral semantics that has recently been pressed into service on behalf of ethical naturalism. We argue that the currently popular version of naturalism, despite its immunity to Moore's version of the open question argument, succumbs to a newly fashioned open question argument. Since new wave moral semantics is at the heart of the recent strain of ethical naturalism, we take ourselves to be going for the jugular. We do all this in the second and third sections of the paper. But first, in order to bring things more clearly into focus, let us pause to remember Moore's open question argument.

1 MOORE'S OPEN QUESTION ARGUMENT REMEMBERED

Here we take ethical naturalism to be at bottom a metaphysical theory about the existence and nature of putative moral properties (like goodness and rightness) and moral facts involving such properties. The view can be put this way:

> MN *Metaphysical ethical naturalism*: There are moral properties (and facts); and these are identical with natural properties (and facts).[2]

One line of support for MN asserts that certain moral terms like "good" have analytically true naturalistic definitions; i.e., these terms are synonymous with natural terms or expressions referring exclusively to processes, states, or properties that are part of the subject matter of the sciences. Call this view "analytic semantic (ethical) naturalism", which can be expressed thus:

> ASN *Analytic semantic naturalism*: Fundamental moral terms like "good" have analytically true naturalistic definitions.

Traditionally, MN and ASN have been closely associated, so closely in fact, that one often finds authors assuming that MN and ASN are a package deal.[3] Call this package *analytic ethical naturalism*. The source of this close association seems to have been acceptance of a synonymy criterion of property identity, according to which two property referring expressions refer to the same property if and only if those expressions are synonymous – i.e. have the same meaning. Given this criterion, the truth of ASN is not merely sufficient for the truth of MN, but necessary as well.

Moore's open question argument was directed at analytic ethical naturalism. Given the assumption that MN requires ASN, Moore supposed that refuting the semantic thesis was sufficient for refuting the metaphysical thesis. His attempted refutation of ASN turned on what he took to be a crucial test of the theory, a test involving consideration of whether or not a certain form of question was open. A question is open if and only if it is possible for someone to completely understand the question, yet not know its answer; otherwise it is closed.[4] The rationale behind this test is clear. If ASN is true, then statements of the form "Anything which has natural property N is good" are analytically true. And any competent speaker (i.e., anyone who understands the statement, including of course, the meanings of the terms it contains) will know, merely upon attentive, clear-headed, reflection on the terms contained in the statement, that it is true. In other words, for a fully competent speaker, the statement will be knowable a priori. But if statements of the above form are a priori, then surely questions of the form:

> Q1 Entity e has natural property N, but is it good?

will be closed; any competent speaker will know, upon contemplating the meaning of the question, that if entity e does indeed have N, then the question's answer is affirmative. Of course, if Q1 is open, the hypothesis about the meaning of "good" expressed in ASN is false.

So Moore defended what we'll call the "open question thesis":

OQT *Open question thesis*: questions of the form Q1, for "good" and for other moral terms, are open questions.

Moore claimed, with a good deal of plausibility, that if Q1 were closed, then it should strike us intuitively as being on a par with the question, "Entity e has natural property N, but is it N?" But while this question is utterly trivial and its answer obvious, the same isn't true of questions having the form of Q1. As Moore remarked in connection with the suggestion that "good" just means "pleasure": "whoever will attentively consider with himself what is actually before his mind when he asks the question 'Is pleasure (or whatever it may be) after all good?' can easily satisfy himself that he is not merely wondering whether pleasure is pleasant" (1903: 16).

It is worth noting that although Moore focused on questions having the form of Q1, there is another kind of question equally relevant to the testing of ASN, viz., the converse of Q1:

Q2 Does entity e, which is good, have natural property N?

If ASN is correct then Q2 should also be closed. But it too is open; i.e., reflecting on meanings of our terms does not lead one to judge that the answer is trivially, "yes".

Moore's central argument against analytic ethical naturalism, then, was that MN requires the truth of ASN, but since this semantic thesis fails the open question test, it is false. Thus, Moore concluded, MN is likewise false. Schematically, his argument can be reconstructed this way:

1 $MN \rightarrow ASN$
2 $ASN \rightarrow \sim OQT$
3 OQT
Therefore,
4 $\sim MN$

Analytic ethical naturalism does seem to be a sitting duck for Moore's open question argument, but it is fairly clear that the argument fails as a refutation of all forms of ethical naturalism. The most obvious problem with the argument is the first premise. The claim that a moral property is identical with some natural property only if the terms designating these properties are synonymous derives, as we have already mentioned, from the synonymy criterion of property identity. But this criterion (which entails the claim that property identity requires synonymy of expressions designating the properties in question) is pretty implausible in light of numerous counterexamples from the sciences. The (sortal) property *being water* is identified with the property *being composed of H₂O molecules*; *being a cloud* is identified with *being a mass of water droplets*, temperature is identified with mean kinetic energy, and so on. But no one supposes that "being water" is synonymous with "being composed of H₂O molecules", or that "temperature" is synonymous with "mean kinetic energy", and so forth for many other scientific identities. Quite simply, it doesn't seem that, in general, property identity requires synonymy.

So it looks as if the best bet for the ethical naturalist is to grant that ASN is implausible but reject the first premise of the above (reconstructed) Moorean argument. The claim, then, is that moral properties (and the facts that involve them) are identical with natural properties even though expressions designating the relevant moral and natural properties involved in the identity are not synonymous. But then it is fair to ask just how the ethical naturalist proposes to understand the semantics of moral terms. Enter new wave moral semantics.

2 NEW WAVE MORAL SEMANTICS

What we are here calling "new wave moral semantics" is a view that has resulted from the attempt to extend relatively recent developments in the philosophy of language to the understanding of moral language. Three developments particularly deserve mention, since they have figured centrally in new wave moral semantics.

First, as mentioned already, in light of all sorts of counterexamples, particularly from the sciences, there has been widespread rejection of a synonymy criterion of property identity. Second, ever since the pioneering work of Kripke (1972) and Putnam (1975), there has been articulation and widespread acceptance of the idea that names and natural kind terms are *rigid designators* – rigid in the sense that such expressions designate the same entity with respect to every possible world in which that entity exists.[5]

Two facts are especially important about identity statements involving rigid designators flanking the identity sign. First, typically such statements are necessarily true without being analytic. Second, some such statements, such as "Water = H₂O", constitute definitions – not the kind that express meaning connections and thus are analytic, but rather *synthetic definitions* that give the real nature or essence of the entity, property, or kind designated by a particular term. Thus, if true, "Water = H₂O" expresses the real, underlying essence of water and provides us with a (synthetically true) definition of "water".

A third recent trend in philosophy of language is the widespread acceptance of so-called "causal" theories of reference for names and natural kind terms. In the simplest versions, such theories assert that the semantical property of reference is to be understood as essentially involving appropriate causal connections between speakers' use of a term and the thing to which the term refers. Such theories propose to explain (i) how the reference of a term is originally determined (e.g., there being some sort of baptism or dubbing ceremony through which speakers in causal contact with an item acquire the ability to refer to that item through the use of some expression used in the ceremony), and (ii) how the capacity to refer is spread throughout a linguistic community (again, by speakers' causally interacting with one another and with the item). Of course, this rather simple sketch can be elaborated in a number of ways, but the basic idea is clear: for some terms at least, reference is "grounded" by relevant causal hookups between speakers and the world.

New wave moral semantics has emerged in the context of these developments. One finds a representative version of this semantical view in the work of Richard Boyd (1988), who puts the view to work in his recent defense of (a naturalistic version of) moral realism. All three of the above mentioned ideas are present in Boyd's semantic views about such moral terms as "right" and "good".

First, he contends that "good", like many other terms, has a synthetic or what he calls a "natural" definition[6] that reveals the essence of the property that term expresses.[7] And, of course, this claim implies the rejection of the synonymy criterion of property identity: the property goodness is identical with such and such natural property even though the term "good" is not synonymous with any naturalistic term or phrase designating the relevant natural property.[8]

Second, in claiming that moral terms admit of synthetic definitions, Boyd evidently takes these terms to be rigid. Like natural kind terms, moral terms allegedly rigidly designate the properties (natural properties for the ethical naturalist) to which they refer. As explained above, it is rigidity that underlies the necessity possessed by synthetic definitions.[9]

Third, Boyd maintains that for moral terms, just as for names and natural kind terms, reference is a matter of there being certain causal connections between the use of moral terms and the relevant natural properties. According to Boyd's own version of the causal theory of reference, reference is essentially an epistemic notion and so the relevant causal connections constituting reference are just those causal connections involved in knowledge gathering activities:

> *Roughly*, and for nondegenerate cases, a term *t* refers to a kind (property, relation, etc.) *k* just in case there exist causal mechanisms whose tendency is to bring it about, over time, that what is predicated of the term *t* will be approximately true of *k* (excuse the blurring of the use-mention distinction). Such mechanisms will

typically include the existence of procedures which are approximately accurate for recognizing members or instances of *k* (at least for easy cases) and which relevantly govern the use of *t*, the social transmission of certain relevantly approximately true beliefs regarding *k*, formulated as claims about *t* (again excuse the slight to the use-mention distinction), a pattern of deference to experts on *k* with respect to the use of *t*, etc. ... When relations of this sort obtain, we may think of the properties of *k* as *regulating* the use of *t* (via such causal relations) ...

(1988: 195)

Extending this version of the causal theory of reference to moral terms, as Boyd proposes to do, commits him to what we'll call the "causal regulation thesis":

CRT *Causal regulation thesis*: For each moral term t (e.g., "good"), there is a natural property N such that N alone, and no other property, causally regulates the use of t by humans.

(We shall say, of such an N, that it "uniquely" causally regulates the use of t by humans.) On Boyd's view then, the fact that humankind's uses of moral terms are regulated in the way described in CRT is what allows one to conclude that moral terms like "good" behave semantically like natural kind terms: they rigidly refer to certain natural properties and hence possess synthetic definitions. So we can encapsulate what we are calling new wave moral semantics (at least as developed by Boyd) as the following thesis:

CSN *Causal semantic naturalism*: Each moral term t rigidly designates the natural property N that uniquely causally regulates the use of t by humans.

If CSN is true, then each moral term t should have a synthetically true natural definition whose definiens characterizes, in purely naturalistic vocabulary, the natural property that uniquely causally regulates the use of t by humans.[10] (In addition, CRT is a corollary of CSN, since CSN cannot be true unless each moral term t is indeed causally regulated by some unique natural property N.)

Let us call the combination of MN with CSN, *causal ethical naturalism*. This new strain of ethical naturalism entirely avoids Moore's open question argument, since any force that that argument has is only good against ASN, and ASN is no part of new wave ethical naturalism. Nevertheless, Boyd's semantical views seem to commit him to the view that if MN is true then CSN is also true.

Our project here is to develop a new open question argument which, we claim, casts serious doubt on CSN and thereby on MN. For purposes of the present discussion, we are willing to grant CRT for argument's sake.[11] Our central claim will be this: even if CRT is true, nevertheless moral terms do *not* rigidly refer to the natural properties that causally regulate their use by humans. Although causal regulation may well coincide with – or even constitute – reference for certain terms (e.g., names and physical natural-kind terms), we claim that for *moral* terms anyway, causal regulation does not coincide with reference. I.e., moral terms do not refer to the natural properties that (we are supposing) causally regulate their use by humans.[12] A newly formulated version of the open question argument, we claim, supports our main contention.

3 TWIN EARTH SCENARIOS AND CLOSED QUESTIONS

It will be instructive to approach this matter by first considering the analogous issue concerning terms like "water". Suppose someone grants that the use of "water" by humans is causally regulated by some specific physico-chemical natural kind, but then questions the claim that "water" *rigidly designates* the natural kind (viz., H_2O) which happens to fill this role. (This skeptic might believe, for instance, that "water" designates a more general physical natural kind – a genus which has H_2O as only one of its various actual or physically possible species.) What kind of evidence can be put forth to support the contention that "water" really does rigidly designate the sortal kind-property H_2O?

When philosophers defend such semantic theses with respect to, e.g., names and physical natural kind terms, a particular type of thought experiment looms very large: the Putnam-style Twin Earth scenario. Recall how those go. In one of Putnam's stories, we are to imagine Twin Earth – a planet pretty much like Earth except that the oceans, lakes, and streams are filled with a liquid whose outward, easily observable, properties are just like those of water, but whose underlying physico-chemical nature is not H_2O, but some other molecular structure XYZ. Despite outward similarities and the fact that speakers of twin English apply the word "water" to this liquid composed of XYZ, reflection on this scenario yields a very strong intuition that Twin Earthlings don't mean by their twin-English term "water" what we mean by "water", and that their term is not translatable by our orthographically identical term. And along with this judgment come two further intuitive judgments: (i) that the meaning of the English term "water" is such that in any possible world w where this term designates at all, it designates the same physical natural kind in w that it actually designates on Earth (viz., H_2O); and (ii) that this fact explains why the English and twin-English terms differ in meaning.

Competent speakers have a strong intuitive mastery of both the syntactic and the semantic norms governing their language. Consequently, the intuitive judgments just described concerning the Twin Earth scenario constitute important (though of course defeasible) empirical evidence for the hypothesis that "water" rigidly designates the specific physico-chemical physical kind that happens to causally regulate the use of this term by humans, viz., the kind H_2O.[13]

The form of argument just canvassed can be called a *semantic competence argument*.[14] It is importantly related to Moore-style considerations concerning open and closed questions, as we shall now explain. First, we need a characterization of the closed/open distinction that suitably updates Moore's. So let us say that a question is *closed* just in case most any semantically competent speaker who considers the question carefully, and who properly brings his semantic competence to bear on the question, will judge both that the answer to the question is obviously "yes" (or obviously "no").[15] The idea is that semantic competence alone, apart from any specific empirical knowledge the speaker might or might not possess, is the likely source of the judgment; and that the intuitive obviousness of the answer is evidence that this is its source. Let us say that a question is *open* just in case it is not closed. Here the idea is that semantic competence alone does not yield an intuitive judgment about the question's answer; those who do form a judgment probably are relying on additional knowledge, as evidenced by their not regarding the answer as obvious in light of how terms are employed.

The statement "Water = H_2O" is held to be a synthetic definition that gives the real essence of water, not an analytic definition that gives a synonym for "water". Since a person linguistically competent with the terms "water" and "H_2O" need not know that the stuff humans call "water" is composed of H_2O molecules, the following two questions are open:

Q3   Liquid L is H_2O, but is it water?
Q4   Liquid L is water, but is it H_2O?

But the relevant analogs to the Moorean questions Q1 and Q2 are not Q3 and Q4, but rather the following questions, which have built into them the appropriate empirical hypothesis about causal regulation:

Q5   Given that the use of "water" by humans is causally regulated by the natural kind H_2O, is liquid L, which is H_2O, water?
Q6   Given that the use of "water" by humans is causally regulated by the natural kind H_2O, is liquid L, which is water, H_2O?

Now, a competent speaker who reflects on Q5 and Q6, and who taps into his own linguistic competence by reflecting carefully on Putnam's Twin Earth scenario, will judge (i) that the twin-English term "water" differs in meaning from the corresponding English term, enough so that the two terms are not intertranslatable; (ii) that the twin human term "water" rigidly designates the physical natural kind that causally regulates its use by twin humans (viz., XYZ); (iii) that the human term "water" rigidly designates the physical natural kind that causally regulates its use by humans (viz., H_2O); and (iv) that in virtue of facts (i)–(iii), the answer to both Q5 and Q6 is obviously "yes". Thus,

Q5 and Q6 are *closed* questions – a fact providing strong empirical evidence in favor of the claim that "water" rigidly designates the specific physical natural kind that causally regulates the use of this term by humans.

4 TROUBLES FOR NEW WAVE MORAL SEMANTICS: THE OPEN QUESTION ARGUMENT REVIVED

Competent speakers, as we said, have substantial intuitive mastery of the syntactic and semantic norms governing the proper use of terms in their language. Mastery of the semantic workings of "water", for instance, is reflected in people's strong intuitions about Putnam's Twin Earth scenario, and in the fact that Q5 and Q6 are closed questions. Presumably, competent speakers have a comparable intuitive mastery of the semantic workings of "good" and other fundamental moral terms. So if causal semantic naturalism is correct, then things should go the same way they go with "water". That is, if indeed the term "good" rigidly designates the unique natural property (if there is one) that causally regulates the use of "good" by humankind in general, then it should be possible to construct a suitable Twin Earth scenario with these features: (i) reflection on this scenario generates intuitive judgments that are comparable to those concerning Putnam's original scenario; (ii) these judgments are accompanied by the more general intuitive judgment that "good" does indeed work semantically as CSN says it does; and (iii) in light of this latter judgment, the relevant analogs of Q5 and Q6 are closed questions.

Conversely, if the appropriate Twin Earth scenario does *not* have these features – i.e., if the semantic intuitions of competent speakers turn out not to be what they should be if CSN is true – then this will mean that CSN is probably false. We say "probably" false because the inference to CSN's falsity would be inductive, an inference to the best explanation. Speakers' semantic intuitions about Twin Earth scenarios are *empirical* evidence about matters of semantics (just as their syntactic intuitions about grammaticality are empirical evidence about matters of syntax). Such intuitions, especially when robustly present among most all competent speakers, are quite *powerful* evidence; *ceteris paribus*, a semantic hypothesis that respects the intuitions is preferable to, and is more likely to be correct than, a semantic hypothesis that repudiates them.[16]

We plan to mount an argument against CSN (and MN) by arguing that things go the latter way – i.e. one's intuitive judgments concerning a suitable Twin Earth scenario go contrary to CSN, and the following two questions are both open:

Q7 Given that the use of "good" by humans is causally regulated by natural property N, is entity e, which has N, good?

187

Q8   Given that the use of "good" by humans is causally regulated by natural property N, does entity e, which is good, have N?

What is wanted is a Twin Earth where things are as similar to Earth as possible, consistent with the hypothesis that twin-moral terms are causally regulated, for twin humans in general, by certain natural properties *distinct from* those natural properties which (as we are here granting for argument's sake) regulate the use of moral terms by humans in general.

So let's begin by supposing that, as Boyd maintains, human uses of "good" and "right" are regulated by certain *functional* properties; and that, as a matter of empirical fact, these are consequentialist properties whose functional essence is captured by some specific consequentialist normative theory; call this theory T^c.[17] We further suppose that there is some reliable method of moral inquiry which, if properly and thoroughly employed, would lead us to discover this fact about our uses of moral terms.

Now consider Moral Twin Earth, which, as you might expect, is just about like good old Earth: same geography and natural surroundings, people who live in the twin United States by and large speak twin English; there is a state they call "Tennessee" that is situated directly south of a state they call "Kentucky" and every year a fairly large number of Twin Earthlings make a pilgrimage to Twin Memphis to visit the grave site of Twin Elvis.[18] You get the idea. Of particular importance here is the fact that Moral Twin Earthlings have a vocabulary that works much like human moral vocabulary; they use the terms "good" and "bad", "right" and "wrong" to evaluate actions, persons, institutions and so forth (at least those who speak twin English use these terms, whereas those who speak some other twin language use terms orthographically identical to the terms for good, etc., in the corresponding Earthian dialects). In fact, were a group of explorers from Earth ever to visit Moral Twin Earth they would be strongly inclined to translate Moral Twin Earth terms, "good", "right" and the rest as identical in meaning to our orthographically identical English terms. After all, the uses of these terms on Moral Twin Earth bear all of the "formal" marks that we take to characterize moral vocabulary and moral practice. In particular, the terms are used to reason about considerations bearing on Moral Twin Earthling well-being; Moral Twin Earthlings are normally disposed to act in certain ways corresponding to judgments about what is "good" and "right"; they normally take considerations about what is "good" and "right" to be especially important, even of overriding importance in most cases, in deciding what to do, and so on.

Let us suppose that investigation into twin English moral discourse and associated practice reveals that their uses of twin-moral terms are causally regulated by certain natural properties distinct from those that regulate English moral discourse. The properties tracked by twin English moral terms are also functional properties, whose essence is functionally characterizable by means of a normative moral theory. But these are *non-consequentialist* moral properties, whose functional essence is captured by some specific deontological theory; call this theory T^d.[19] These functional properties are similar enough to those characterizable via T^c to account for the fact that twin-moral discourse operates in Twin Earth society and culture in much the manner that moral discourse operates on Earth. (We've already noted that if explorers ever visit Moral Twin Earth, they will be inclined, at least initially, to construe Moral Twin Earthlings as having beliefs about good and right, and to translate twin English uses of these terms into our orthographically identical terms.) The differences in causal regulation, we may suppose, are due at least in part to certain species-wide differences in psychological temperament that distinguish Twin Earthlings from Earthlings. (For instance, perhaps Twin Earthlings tend to experience the sentiment of *guilt* more readily and more intensively, and tend to experience *sympathy* less readily and less intensively, than do Earthlings.)[20] In addition, suppose that if Twin Earthlings were to employ in a proper and thorough manner the same reliable method of moral inquiry which (as we are already supposing) would lead Earthlings to discover that Earthling uses of moral terms are causally regulated by functional properties whose essence is captured by the consequentialist normative theory T^c, then this method would lead the Twin Earthlings to discover that their own uses of moral terms are causally regulated by functional properties whose essence is captured by the deontological theory T^d.

Given all these assumptions and stipulations about Earth and Moral Twin Earth, what is the appropriate way to describe the differences between moral and twin-moral uses of "good" and "right"? Two hermeneutic options are available. On the one hand, we could say that the differences are analogous to those between Earth and Twin Earth in Putnam's original example, to wit: the moral terms used by Earthlings rigidly designate the natural properties that causally regulate their use on Earth, whereas the twin-moral terms used by Twin Earthlings rigidly designate the *distinct* natural properties that causally regulate their use on Twin Earth; hence, moral and twin-moral terms *differ in meaning*, and are not intertranslatable. On the other hand, we could say instead that moral and twin-moral terms do *not* differ in meaning or reference, and hence that any apparent moral disagreements that might arise between Earthlings and Twin Earthlings would be *genuine* disagreements – i.e., disagreements in moral belief and in normative moral theory, rather than disagreements in meaning.[21]

We submit that by far the more natural mode of description, when one considers the Moral Twin Earth scenario, is the second. Reflection on the scenario just does not generate hermeneutical pressure to construe Moral Twin Earthling uses of "good" and "right" as not translatable by our orthographically identical terms. But if CSN were true, and the moral terms in question rigidly designated those natural properties that causally regulate their use, then reflection on this scenario ought to generate intuitions analogous to those generated in Putnam's original Twin Earth scenario. That is, it should seem intuitively natural to say that here we have a difference in meaning, and that twin English "moral" terms are not translatable by English moral terms. But when it comes to characterizing the differences between Earthlings and Twin Earthlings on this matter, the natural-seeming thing to say is that the differences involve belief and theory, not meaning.[22]

One's intuitions work the same way if, instead of considering the Moral Twin Earth scenario from the outside looking in, one considers how things would strike Earthlings and Twin Earthlings who have encountered each other. Suppose that Earthlings visit Twin Earth (or vice versa), and both groups come to realize that different natural properties causally regulate their respective uses of "good", "right", and other moral terms. If CSN were true, then recognition of these differences ought to result in its seeming rather silly, to members of each group, to engage in inter-group debate about goodness – about whether it conforms to normative theory T^c or to T^d. (If, in Putnam's original scenario, the two groups learn that their respective uses of "water" are causally regulated by different physical kind-properties, it would be silly for them to think they have differing views about the real nature of water.) But such inter-group debate would surely strike both groups not as silly but as quite appropriate, because they would regard one another as differing in moral beliefs and moral theory, not in meaning.[23]

Since semantic norms are tapped by human linguistic competence, and since the relevant linguistic competence is presumably reflected in one's intuitive judgments concerning Twin Earth scenarios, this outcome constitutes strong empirical evidence against CSN.[24] And since it is a highly non-trivial issue whether the basic good-making natural property is the one (if there *is* just one) that causally regulates the use of "good" by humans, or instead is the one that causally regulates this term's use by twin-humans, or instead is some natural property distinct from either of these, the outcome of the Moral Twin Earth thought experiment also undergirds the following "revised open question thesis":

> ROQT   *Revised open question thesis*: Questions of the form Q7 and Q8, for "good" and for other moral terms, are open questions.

But this thesis ought to be false if CSN is true. So we have arrived at an open question argument against causal semantic naturalism similar to the one we take Moore to have given against analytic semantic naturalism: (1) CSN → ~ ROQT; (2) ROQT; therefore, (3) ~ CSN.

What is the import of all this for MN, the thesis of metaphysical ethical naturalism? In addressing this question one should notice that CSN is a species of the following more generic semantic thesis:

> SSN   *Synthetic semantic naturalism*: Fundamental moral terms like "good" have synthetic naturalistic definitions.

Now it might be thought that even if CSN is not tenable because of Moral Twin Earth, there remains a serious possibility that some other species of SSN still might be tenable – perhaps a version of SSN that nobody has yet articulated. But Moral Twin Earth is more than a specific thought experiment directed at the specific semantic thesis CSN. It is, in addition, a *recipe* for thought experiments. For any potential version of SSN that might be proposed, according to which (i) moral terms bear some relation R to certain natural properties that collectively satisfy some specific normative moral theory T, and (ii) moral terms supposedly *refer* to the natural properties to which they bear this relation R, it should be possible to construct a Moral Twin Earth scenario suitably analogous to the one constructed above – i.e., a scenario in which twin-moral terms bear the same relation R to certain natural properties that collectively satisfy some specific normative theory T, incompatible with T. The above reasoning against CSN should apply, *mutatis mutandis*, against the envisioned alternative version of SSN.

So Moral Twin Earth provides strong grounds for rejecting not only CSN, but also the more generic thesis SSN. The generic scope of Moral Twin Earth also undergirds the following "general revised open question thesis":

> GROQT   *General revised open question thesis*: Questions analogous in form to Q7 and Q8, for "good" and for other moral terms, are open questions.

(A question will be analogous in form to Q7 or Q8, in the intended sense, if its "given"-clause mentions, in place of Boyd's posited relation of causal regulation, whatever relation R supposedly grounds the reference of moral terms according to the particular version of SSN one is considering.) But if there is any version of SSN that is true, then the corresponding instance of ROQT should be false. We have thus arrived at the following open question argument against metaphysical ethical naturalism, a version that plugs the hole left open by Moore's original open question argument:

1 MN → (ASN v SSN)
2 ASN → ~ OQT
3 SSN → ~ GROQT
4 OQT
5 GROQT
Therefore,
6   ~ MN

5 CONCLUSION

No doubt various defensive stratagems are possible, in response to this postmodern version of the open question argument. The principal options, listed in order of increasing retreat against the force of Moral Twin Earth, appear to be the following:

(1) *Bold denial*: Claiming that the Moral Twin Earth thought experiment does not describe a genuinely possible scenario.

(2) *Avoidance*: Claiming that although people's semantic intuitions about Moral Twin Earth are not suitably analogous to their intuitions about Putnam's original Twin Earth scenarios, these semantic intuitions are just mistaken and hence do not really undermine causal semantic naturalism at all. After all, brute intuitions don't settle the matter by themselves; they can be overruled by a semantical theory that best accommodates all relevant data, including data about the workings of moral discourse and inquiry.[25] Once all relevant data are considered, the new waver might argue, Boydian semantics has a lot going for it and recalcitrant intuitions should be dismissed.

(3) *Betting on the future*: Granting that Moral Twin Earth and the revised open question thesis refute Boyd-style causal semantic naturalism, but claiming that there may yet be some other version of synthetic semantic naturalism that does not succumb to a similar Moral Twin Earth scenario.

(4) *Relativism*: Granting the above open question argument against MN, and retreating to a relativist version of naturalism; i.e., claiming that although there are no moral properties or moral facts *simpliciter*, nevertheless (i) there are moral properties (and facts) *relative to a person or social group*; and (ii) that these relativized properties (and facts) are natural properties. (One might claim, for instance, that on Earth the terms "good", "right", etc. refer *nonrigidly* to functional properties whose essence is captured by the consequentialist normative theory T^c, whereas on Moral Twin Earth these terms refer nonrigidly to different functional properties whose essence is captured by the deontological theory T^d.)

Option (1) incurs an overwhelmingly heavy burden of proof, because of two inter-related facts. First, in order for a Twin Earth thought experiment to serve its intended purpose, the relevant scenario need not be a genuine *metaphysical* possibility, but only a broadly *conceptual* possibility. (Suppose, for instance, that Putnam's original Twin Earth scenarios turn out to be metaphysically impossible: i.e., no physically possible substance other than H_2O can have all the features that Putnam attributes to the mythical natural kind XYZ. This outcome would not alter the *conceptual* coherence of Putnam's thought experiments, and hence would not alter their relevance to the semantics of "water".) Second, the *prima facie* intelligibility of the above Moral Twin Earth story constitutes very strong evidence that the scenario is indeed conceptually possible – whether it is metaphysically possible or not.[26]

Option (2) also carries an enormous burden of proof. Admittedly, brute intuitions of the sort revealed by Moral Twin Earth are defeasible; thus people's semantic intuitions might be just mistaken. But the ethical naturalist who claims that they are has some hard explaining to do. First, we are talking about not just any old intuitively strong beliefs involving morality, but intuitive beliefs about *meaning*, surely an important kind of data when one is considering theoretical accounts of meaning, not easily dismissed.[27] Second, even allowing that such intuitions could be overridden by an otherwise plausible semantics of moral discourse, nevertheless, *ceteris paribus*, a semantical account that respects the meaning-intuitions of competent language users is to be preferred over one that does not. Third, and most important for present purposes, the evidential import of such intuitions becomes stronger – they become more than mere isolated, brute data bearing on semantical views – if they can be embedded in a wider semantic theory that provides them with a strong rationale. We think semantic theories that provide just such a rationale can be developed.

Although this is not the place to elaborate such a theory, the sort of rationale any such theory might be expected to provide for our meaning-intuitions can be briefly outlined as follows. (1) One of the defining characteristics of a moral code is that it performs an action-guiding role for members of the community in which it is in force. (2) This normative aspect thus amounts to a semantic constraint for interpreting the practices of a community as moral practices, and so is plausibly taken to be built in to the meaning of moral terms like "good" and "right".[28] (3) This action-guiding, normative feature of the meanings of moral terms helps explain why our intuitions engaged by the Moral Twin Earth thought experiment go the way they do: essential to the meaning of moral terms like "good" and "right" is their action-guiding function, which both Earthian usage of moral terms and twin Earthian usage of moral terms share. Hence, despite the fact that the use of moral terms by the two groups is regulated by different natural properties, the (orthographically identical) moral terms of the two groups mean the same, contrary to Boydian semantics and consistent with the results of reflection on questions Q7 and Q8. With such an explanation available for why our intuitions go the way they do, the avoidance option lacks any genuine plausibility.

Option (3) looks unreasonably optimistic, for two reasons. First, no interesting version of synthetic semantic naturalism, significantly different from Boyd-style causal semantic naturalism, is currently even remotely in sight. Second, as explained at the close of § 4, there are already strong grounds for believing that any such version of SSN would indeed succumb to its own Moral Twin Earth scenario, and thus to its own revised open question argument.

Option (4) will be very unattractive to new wave metaethical naturalists like Boyd. These philosophers espouse *moral realism*, an adamantly non-relativist position. And in any case, relativism is the last defensive ditch against Moral Twin Earth. If ethical naturalism gets forced into that ditch, there it deserves to die.

Grim as the situation looks for new wave naturalism, resourceful moves are to be expected – especially from the dialectically vigorous region of upstate New York, from whence the latest strain of moral realism first began to spread like ragweed. But in the end, all defensive strategies are likely to prove futile against Moral Twin Earth. The new wavers are defending (to borrow terminology from the chess world) a lost position.[29]

NOTES

1 The writers just mentioned were all somewhat less sanguine about the use of the open question argument, and some, most notably Hare, only endorsed a suitably modified version of the argument. Still, for all of the above-mentioned moral philosophers, their rejection of ethical naturalism was due in large part to Moorean open question considerations.

2 Naturalists hold that moral properties (and facts) are a species of natural properties (and facts). Materialistically minded naturalists don't necessarily hold that they are *physical* properties in a narrow sense, properties of the kind posited by physics. Instead, they can hold that moral properties are (identical to) properties that are *realized* by, or *constituted* by, physical properties and whose essence is characterizable in non-normative terminology (though not necessarily directly in the terminology of physics). So even realization/constitution versions of ethical naturalism are presumably committed to an identity thesis, involving identities between moral properties and properties whose essence is characterizable in non-normative terms. Thus, such views are not really rivals to identity views. Rather, given that moral properties are natural properties, there is the further metaphysical issue about whether all natural properties are identical with physical properties (in the narrow sense).

3 It has been fairly standard to take ethical naturalism as a thesis about the meaning of moral terms, with very little care taken to sort out metaphysical ethical naturalism and related semantic views like analytic semantic (ethical) naturalism. See, for example, Brandt (1959: ch. 7).

4 If the question has any empirical assumptions then knowing the answer amounts to knowing what answer *would* be correct if the assumptions were all true.

5 One important source of support for the rigidity view is Putnam's famous Twin Earth thought experiments. More on these below.

6 See Boyd (1988: 194–5, 209–12). Boyd contrasts natural definitions – definitions of, e.g., natural kinds that purport to express the scientific essence or nature of the kind that is the referent of the term – with conventional definitions – the sort of meaning-giving definitions that purport to be analytically true. The distinction between synthetic or natural definitions on the one hand, and analytic or conventional definitions on the other, corresponds to the traditional distinction (made by Locke, for instance) between "real" and "nominal" definition.

7 Boyd's own suggestion about a correct natural or synthetic definition of "good" is in teams of what he calls "homeostatic consequentialist properties" of actions, institutions, and so forth. Of course, even if the suggestion is incorrect, this would not necessarily affect his central claim, viz., that the term "good" admits of a synthetic definition.

8 Boyd's view, as we understand it, is that the essence of goodness, rightness, and other moral properties consists primarily in certain *relational* connections they bear to one another and to other properties, actions, institutions, and so forth. So we take it that for Boyd, moral properties are *functional* properties whose essential relations and interconnections are captured by

some specific normative moral theory. It is an empirical question, on this view, which normative theory has this status. (Boyd thinks that the relevant theory is probably some version of consequentialism.) This functionalist construal of moral properties is articulated more explicitly by Brink (1984, 1989), whose version of moral realism is quite similar to Boyd's.

9 Admittedly, Boyd is not as explicit as one would like about the rigidity of moral terms. But this view fits well with his claim that moral terms have "natural" definitions, and also helps fend off a form of relativism which, of course, runs counter to the realist form of ethical naturalism Boyd defends. We briefly take up the rigidity issue in note 17, and again in § 5.

10 In the present context, the notion of purely naturalistic vocabulary should be understood broadly enough to encompass *causal/functional* vocabulary. Boyd, as we understand him, holds that moral terms rigidly designate certain functional properties, whose essence is their causal role in a system of causally interrelated properties. Cf. note 7, and § 4.

11 Of course, even if one grants that "good" refers to a natural property N only if N causally regulates the use of this term, it can be questioned whether any genuine natural property really does play such a role for "good" or other moral terms. Not all natural-kind terms succeed in tracking a natural property – as illustrated by terms like "caloric" and "phlogiston". Also, even if one grants causal regulation of moral terms by natural properties, it is still quite contentious whether any *single* natural property causally regulates the use of "good" for humankind in general; likewise for other moral terms. But here we are granting this highly optimistic assumption because we want to show that even if it is true, CSN is incorrect anyway.

12 Does this claim entail that causal theories cannot provide a fully *general* account of reference? Not necessarily. That depends upon what one requires of such an account. The claim does entail that in general, even if an entity e bears to a term t the relation Boyd calls "causal regulation", this is not *sufficient* for t to refer to e; hence, the reference relation cannot be simply *identical* to Boyd's (putative) causal-regulation relation. However, reference still might be just a *species* of causal regulation; this could be true if moral terms don't really refer at all, either to properties that might happen to causally regulate them or to any other properties.

13 Some philosophers who espouse causal theories of reference, and who hold that statements like "Water = H_2O" constitute synthetic definitions, tend to regard the use of thought experiments and appeals to intuition as part of an outmoded, unduly aprioristic, philosophical methodology. This tendency is both ironic and misplaced: ironic, because of the key role that Twin Earth thought experiments have played in convincing the philosophical community that names and natural-kind terms are rigid designators; and misplaced, because thought experiments and speakers' intuitions about them often constitute an important kind of *empirical* evidence concerning philosophical theses about language and about language/world relations.

14 This label is intended to suggest a relevant analogy between such arguments and a common form of reasoning within empirical linguistics: viz., the appeal to speakers' intuitions about the grammaticality and/or syntactic ambiguity of certain sentence-like strings of words, as evidence for or against various empirical hypotheses about natural-language syntax. The latter kind of argument rests on the (empirically plausible) background assumption that syntactic intuitions normally reflect what Noam Chomsky has called speakers' "linguistic competence". For further discussion of semantic competence arguments and their relation to the methodology of linguistics, see Horgan and Graham (1990).

15 The proviso mentioned in note 4 applies again here. Also, we are construing a question as an interrogative *sentence* of a particular language; and we are talking about semantically competent speakers *of that language.*

16 We will return to this dialectical point in § 5, in connection with the second of four defensive stratagems we will consider for trying to evade the revived "open question argument" we present in the present section.

17 As we explained in note 8, we find it natural to construe Boyd as a moral functionalist, as is Brink. This construal will be built into the specific Twin Earth thought experiment we shall now set forth. But if it should turn out that Boyd is better interpreted some other way – say, as holding that moral terms (nonrigidly) designate, in a given socio-cultural situation, whatever first-order physical properties (or property clusters) happen to collectively satisfy T^c (in that situation) – then our Twin Earth story could be modified appropriately. This would not change the moral we shall draw from the story.

18 Moral Twin Earth made its first appearance in Horgan and Timmons (1992).

19 Since standard deontological normative theories are internally consistent and conceptually cogent, there is no particular reason to doubt that such a theory characterizes a family of *genuine* functional properties. (For discussions of how functional properties whose essence is captured by a theory are explicitly characterizable by means of (the Ramsey sentence of) that theory, see Block (1978) and Horgan (1984); these papers adapt a format originally proposed by Lewis (1972).) And since deontological functional properties are reasonably similar, overall, to the kinds of functional properties characterized by consequentialist normative theories, there is also no particular reason to doubt that deontological functional properties are *physically realizable* by certain first-order physical properties (or by certain "homeostatic clusters" of first-order physical properties).

20 Those who were raised Catholic, as we both were, should have little difficulty envisioning this kind of psychological temperament vis-à-vis matters moral. Indeed, we doubt that there is really any single characteristic temperament – any single profile of sentiments – that operates, for Earthlings generally, in matters of morals. But for present purposes one can suppose there is. This supposition fits naturally with the optimistic (though implausible) empirical assumption, which we are already granting for argument's sake, that there is some single set of natural properties that causally regulate the use of moral terms by Earthlings generally. (One could bring the Moral Twin Earth scenario down to Earth by supposing, more realistically but less congenially with Boyd's assumption, that the kinds of temperamental differences we describe actually obtain among different Earthlings themselves.)

21 It should be stressed that differences in normative moral theory, between Earthlings and Twin Earthlings, do not constitute different claims about which property is identical to goodness, or to rightness, etc. For, normative theories do not make such property-identity claims. Rather, they make claims, for instance, about which natural property is the fundamental good-making property, which is the fundamental right-making natural property, etc. Normative theories *per se* are neutral between the metaethical claims (i) that moral properties are identical with these natural properties; (ii) that moral properties are nonnatural properties that supervene upon the natural ones without being identical to them; or (iii) that moral properties do not exist at all.

22 Some time after we thought up the Moral Twin Earth story, we discovered that Hare uses a similar story to criticize ethical naturalism (though, of course, his target is analytic ethical naturalism). He has his readers imagine a group of missionaries landing on a cannibal island

and discovering that by sheer coincidence "good" in Cannibalese is apparently a correct translation of "good" in English. However, whereas the missionaries apply the English term to people of genteel spirit, the cannibals use their term "good" to commend people who, among other things, collect more scalps than the average. Hare finds it natural to interpret disagreements between missionaries and cannibals as disagreements in the standards used by these different groups in evaluation rather than as mere disagreements in the meanings of the English and cannibal uses of "good". He writes:

> Even if the qualities in people which the missionary commended had nothing in common with the qualities which the cannibals commended, yet they would both know what the word "good" meant. If "good" were like "red", this would be impossible; for then the cannibals' word and the English word would not be synonymous. If this were so, then when the missionary said that people who collected a lot of scalps were good (cannibal), they would not be disagreeing, because in English (at any rate missionary English), "good" would mean among other things "doing no murder", whereas in the cannibals' language "good" would mean something quite different, among other things "productive of maximum scalps".
>
> (Hare 1952: 148–9)

23 At any rate, this is how they would regard the matter insofar as they rely on their *pretheoretic* semantic intuitions. Intuitions can become skewed for those who are sufficiently in the grip of a philosophical theory. Some new-wave moral realists, for instance, may by now have become so strongly gripped by the Boydian conception of moral reference as causal regulation by natural properties that their own intuitions about Moral Twin Earth actually fall into line with their intuitions about Putnam's original case. For them some philosophical therapy may be necessary, to get them back into touch with their semantically true selves.

24 It is worth noting that the Moral Twin Earth thought experiment does not depend for its outcome on the hypothetical assumption that a *consequentialist* normative moral theory characterizes the essence of the functional properties that (as we are granting for argument's sake) causally regulate human moral judgments. This was only for concreteness and vividness. It makes no substantive difference if one supposes instead that the functional essence of the causally regulating properties is characterizable, say, by some deontological theory, or by some mixed consequentialist/deontological theory. Rather, the crucial features of the thought experiment are (i) that the twin-moral judgments of Twin Earthlings track *distinct* functional properties than those allegedly causally tracked by the moral judgments of Earthlings; (ii) that twin-moral judgments made by Twin Earthlings coincide largely, but not completely, with moral judgments that would be made by Earthlings; and (iii) that twin-moral and moral judgments, respectively, play comparable roles in the social and institutional lives of Twin Earthlings and of Earthlings, respectively.

25 New wavers are fond of claiming that features of our moral discourse and moral inquiry rest on realist assumptions and so demand some sort of realist metaphysics and associated semantics. See Brink (1989: ch. 2) and Boyd (1988). But see Blackburn (1980; 1984, ch. 6), Copp (1991: 613–14) and Timmons (1993) for doubts about this claim.

26 In addition, we see no particular reason to doubt that Moral Twin Earth is metaphysically possible anyway. Cf. note 17.

27 At the very least, the ethical naturalist who would go the avoidance route must plausibly explain (i) why people's meaning-intuitions about moral terms are so strong and so

widespread even though they are allegedly mistaken, and (ii) why those intuitions don't work the same way they do in Putnam's original cases.

28 Exactly how a semantic theory should explain this built-in normative dimension of moral terms is not obvious. Ethical internalism, the semantic thesis according to which (roughly) the meaning of moral terms is such that it is not possible (consistent with what moral terms mean) for anyone to judge that some action is, say, wrong, and yet fail to be motivated (or have reason) to avoid performing that action, has been quite typical of semantic views that attempt to incorporate the action-guiding feature into a semantic story about moral discourse. But as critics like Brink (1989: ch. 3) have pointed out, because this sort of *local* internalist thesis would require, for each and every member of a community who was competent with moral language, that she be relevantly motivated (or have reason for action) on each occasion of her sincere utterance of a moral judgment, it is unduly strong in dismissing the conceptual possibility of the amoralist. But the intrinsic action-guiding feature of moral terms need not be understood in this rather crude way. For one thing, one might opt for a *global* form of internalism that would allow for all of the members of a community to be amoralists some of the time, and for some of the members to be moralists all of the time, but would only deny that all of the members could be amoralists all of the time. Global internalism would tie the action-guiding feature of moral discourse to the activities and motivations of the members of a community in a global, community-wide way. (The global internalist might handle the case of the amoralist by adapting, *mutatis mutandis*, the treatment by David Lewis (1980) of scenarios involving people who undergo so-called "mad pain".)

29 This paper is fully collaborative; order of authorship is alphabetical. An earlier version was presented at the Mark Overvold Memorial Conference at St. Olaf College, October, 1990, where Erik Kraemer commented. It was also presented at the 1991 APA Pacific division meetings in San Francisco (Philip Clarke commented), and at the 1991 Spring Colloquium (by Terence Horgan). We thank our conference commentators and also Tom Carson, Seumas Miller, Mark Sainsbury, Nick Sturgeon, Corliss Swain, and John Tienson for their helpful comments. We dedicate the paper to the memory of Mark Overvold.

REFERENCES

Ayer, A. J. (1952) *Language, Truth, and Logic*, Second Edition (New York: Dover).
Blackburn, S. (1980) "Truth, Realism and the Regulation of Theory," *Midwest Studies in Philosophy* 5.
—— (1984) *Spreading the Word* (Oxford: Oxford University Press).
Block, N. (1978) "Troubles with Functionalism," in C. Savage, ed., *Minnesota Studies in the Philosophy of Science*, IX (Minneapolis, MN: University of Minnesota Press).
Boyd, R. (1988) "How to Be a Moral Realist," in G. Sayre-McCord, ed., *Essays on Moral Realism* (Ithaca, NY: Cornell University Press).
Brandt, R. (1959) *Ethical Theory* (Englewood Cliffs, NJ: Prentice-Hall).
Brink, D. (1984) "Moral Realism and Skeptical Arguments from Disagreement and Queerness," *Australasian Journal of Philosophy* 62 [Chapter 6, this volume].
—— (1989) *Moral Realism and the Foundations of Ethics* (Cambridge: Cambridge University Press).
Copp, D. (1991) "Moral Realism: Facts and Norms," *Ethics* 101.
Ewing, A. C. (1948) *The Definition of Good* (London: Routledge & Kegan Paul).
Hare, R. M. (1952) *The Language of Morals* (Oxford: Oxford University Press).
Horgan, T. (1984) "Functionalism and Token Physicalism," *Synthese* 59.

Horgan, T. and Graham, G. (1990) "In Defense of Southern Fundamentalism," *Philosophical Studies* 49.

Horgan, T. and Timmons, M. (1992) "Trouble on Moral Twin Earth: Moral Queerness Revived," *Synthese* 92.

Kripke, S. (1972) "Naming and Necessity," in D. Davidson and G. Harman, eds, *Semantics of Natural Language* (Dordrecht: Reidel).

Lewis, D. (1972) "Psychophysical and Theoretical Identifications," *Australasian Journal of Philosophy* 50.

——(1980) "Mad Pain and Martian Pain," in Ned R. Block, ed., *Readings in the Philosophy of Psychology*, Volume I (Cambridge, MA: Harvard University Press).

Moore, G. E. (1903) *Principia Ethica* (Cambridge: Cambridge University Press).

Putnam, H. (1975) "The Meaning of 'Meaning'," in K. Gunderson, ed., *Minnesota Studies in the Philosophy of Science*, VII (Minneapolis, MN: University of Minnesota Press).

Ross, W. D. (1930) *The Right and the Good* (Oxford: Oxford University Press).

Timmons, M. (1993) *Philosophia*. "Irrealism and Error in Ethics."

11

CRITICAL NOTICE
OF HURLEY

Frank Jackson

Hurley, S. L., *Natural Reasons: Personality and Polity* (Oxford: Oxford University Press, 1989), pp. xii, 462.

This rich, long and complex book discusses and interconnects issues in ethics, decision theory, philosophy of mind, philosophy of law, and political theory. I am going to concentrate on the substantial and interesting things Susan Hurley has to say in ethics. After describing her position and making some passing comments, I will argue that there is a problem with her treatment of ethical scepticism. I will conclude by taking the liberty of suggesting what in my view she should, and consistently with her overall position could, have said about scepticism.

1 HURLEY'S ETHICAL THEORY

Hurley espouses cognitivism, non-centralism, coherentism and realism. What does all this amount to in words rather than labels?

She is a cognitivist in the usual sense. For her, to assert that slavery is wrong is to make a claim about how things are (and a true one we take it). The statement 'Slavery is wrong' is truth-valued in the substantial sense that the statement purports to represent how things are, and counts as true precisely when it gets the way things are right, that is, when slavery does indeed have the property of being wrong.

She is a non-centralist in the sense that she denies the conceptual priority of the central ethical concepts of good, bad, right, and wrong – those sometimes called the 'thin' ethical concepts – by contrast with the 'thick', specific ethical concepts like courageous, inequitable, just, dishonest, and so on. Her concern is not so much to deny that, say, being inequitable is equivalent to the conjunction of (a) being a certain purely-naturalistically-describable skewed way with (b) being wrong, but to deny that such an analysis would reveal that being wrong was the conceptually prior notion: '*Non-centralism* about reasons for action rejects the view that the general concepts such as *right* and *ought* are conceptually prior to and independent of specific reason-giving concepts such as *just* and *unkind*' (11).

She holds a coherence theory of the right: 'to say that a certain act ought to be done is to say that it is favoured by the theory, whichever it may be, which gives the best account of the relationships among the specific values that apply to the alternatives in question ... ' (11). This coherence theory of the right is developed at length as the book proceeds, but I take it that the central idea can be put briefly but not too misleadingly as follows. Coherentism about the right is an approach to ethics akin to the commonsense functionalist approach to the mind.[1] In the case of the mind we have folk psychology, a body of folk opinion about the mind encapsulated in: input clauses telling us what sorts of situations typically cause what sorts of mental states; internal role clauses telling us how various mental states typically inter-connect; and output clauses telling us what sort of behaviour various combinations of mental states typically give rise to. In the case of ethics we have what we might call 'folk morality', a body of folk opinion encapsulated in: input clauses telling us what sorts of situations naturalistically described typically warrant what sorts of moral descriptions ('If an action increases suffering and has no other effects, it is wrong', for example); internal role clauses telling us about the internal connections between matters ethically described ('Rights generate duties of respect'; 'One ought to promote what is good', for example); and output clauses telling us about the actions and motivations associated with moral judgements ('If someone believes that they ought to do something, then they will typically be motivated to some extent to do it', for example). According to the coherentist, the task of one who seeks an ethical theory is to construct from the folk beginnings the best theory which makes sense of it all. In particular, as Hurley emphasises, we have a pre-analytic apprehension that acts which are friendly, just, deserved, benevolent, the honouring of a promise, and the like typically ought to be done; and acts which are cowardly, insensitive, reckless, and the like ought not to be done. As she plausibly sees it, we move from the various specific values displayed by the actions we may be contemplating to verdicts in terms of the general values of rightness and wrongness. But in tricky cases we have to weigh up competing claims. Perhaps the choice is between courageously telling the truth at the cost of losing a friend, or keeping a friend by prevarication. And the principal theoretical business of ethics on her conception, as I read it, is the development of a theory that articulates the inter-relations between potentially competing specific values in a way that enables us to arbitrate between them, and so arrive at all-things-considered judgements of rightness and wrongness. The right action then is by definition the action recommended by the theory with the best credentials to be the arbitrator; and the theory with the best credentials to be the arbitrator is the theory that best articulates the inter-relations between the various specific values. Hurley has a lot to say (mainly in chapter 11: 'Deliberation') about how theories which articulate the inter-connections and adjudicate between the claims of specific values may be arrived at. The general idea, though, is familiar from, for instance, John Rawls and Henry Sidgwick. We consider various actual and possible cases together with intuitively appealing general moral principles and their underlying rationales, and seek 'considered judgement in reflective equilibrium'[2] or a 'harmonious system'.[3] Hurley works out the idea in very much her own way and gives interesting discussions of some detailed case histories.

It is, incidentally, no part of her theory that the best theory – the theory whose verdicts settle what is right and wrong – must be *irreducibly* pluralistic. Her coherentism leaves open the possibility that it might turn out as Sidgwick held (hoped?) that the theory which best articulates and makes sense of the inter-connections between the various specific values and the naturalistically described facts sees them as having a common underlying utilitarian vindication. It is however clear that she does not think that it is at all likely that this will turn out to be the case. She has her money on pluralism about values. Also, although Hurley talks (as we will) of the best theory, I take it that she would allow that it might turn out that we should talk of the best *theories*, that a number of similar but not identical theories might turn out to have equal claims to be the arbitrator, in which case to be *definitely* obligatory would presumably be to come out obligatory on *all* the best theories.

Hurley's non-centralism is a more or less immediate consequence of her coherentism about the right. If what is right is settled by what is the best theory, and the best theory is the one we would end up with in the limit of inquiry if we took folk morality and refined it into a harmonious system à la Rawls, Sidgwick or Hurley, the various ethical concepts, specific and general, are all interconnected. None forms the conceptual bedrock. No ethical concept gets its sense in isolation from the other ethical concepts and the relevant naturalistic ones. We have a great big package deal of inter-related concepts, and mastery of any one concept requires mastery of the system to some significant extent. 'Non-centralism' on this reading is importantly distinct from the doctrine that the specific or thick concepts cannot be analysed out into a purely naturalistic component combined with a general or thin component. Being a wife and being a husband are logically inter-connected and neither concept is prior to the other; nevertheless, being a wife is analysable as having a husband, and being a husband is analysable as having a wife.

I agree with Hurley that coherentism and non-centralism are very attractive doctrines, and that the general coherentist picture which I have described in terms of what we might call 'matured folk morality' is a very appealing one. Indeed, it is hard from the cognitivist perspective to see how else the various ethical concepts could get their sense other than through their positions in a network. The only alternative would seem to be a kind of platonism about the values which Hurley rightly dismisses briskly

(14–15). In any case I will be following Hurley in accepting the coherentist picture, and will be addressing the issue of realism and scepticism from this vantage point.

2 HURLEY'S TREATMENT OF SCEPTICISM

Hurley is well aware that cognitivism and realism are distinct doctrines in ethics (see especially 185–6). The cognitivist holds that ethical statements make claims about how things are. Realism holds in addition that the claims so made are on the appropriate occasions true: things really are the way they are claimed to be. A pressing question thus becomes how to justify moving from a cognitivist position to a realist one; or to put the matter in terms of personalities, how to show that J. L. Mackie was wrong to move from cognitivism to scepticism.[4] Mackie could have agreed with the coherentist's way of articulating cognitivism, namely, that the right or obligatory is identified by a position in the network of matured folk morality; he could simply add that nothing falls under the concept so identified.

Hurley identifies three principal challenges to moral realism as she sees it from her coherentist perspective. One is the claim that there is no coherent theory to be had. Her model is Kenneth Arrow's impossibility proof in social choice theory.[5] Arrow proved that no social choice function could simultaneously satisfy a set of individually appealing principles. This was a surprising result. Perhaps a similar surprise awaits us in ethics. We cannot award the role of arbitrator of the right to the best theory interconnecting the specific values because there is no such theory. Every theory which captures enough to be a contender captures enough to be inconsistent. She argues against this possibility in chapters 12 ('Coherence') and 13 ('Commensurability').

A second challenge is the position on moral conflict most particularly associated with Bernard Williams. If, as the realist maintains, there is a property of being obligatory, and an action is right precisely if it possesses that property, no action can be simultaneously what ought to be done and what ought not to be done. A property cannot be both had and not had. But Williams has argued that a proper respect for the reality of moral conflict shows that an action can be both what ought to be done and what ought not to be done.[6] If I am under an obligation to do A and an obligation to do B, and learn that I cannot fulfil both obligations, both obligations typically survive the discovery that they cannot both be honoured. Otherwise there would be no such phenomenon as being unable to honour all one's obligations. (If only that were true!) According to Williams there is only one way to accommodate this insight about the reality of moral conflict, namely, by allowing that sometimes it is simultaneously the case that one ought to do A, and ought not to do A.

Hurley's interesting reply to this threat to moral realism is to distinguish *prima facie* from *pro tanto* reasons for performing some action. *Pro tanto* reasons are like forces.

(As I see it. Do not hold Hurley responsible for the illustration.) A force F_1 acting on a particle can be such that by itself it would accelerate the particle towards North. At the same time there may be another force F_2 which by itself would accelerate the particle towards South. Perhaps F_1 is greater than F_2 so that there is a resultant force towards North. Nevertheless, F_2 still exists; it explains why the particle does not accelerate more briskly towards North. The overwhelmed force is still there. Similarly, when *pro tanto* reasons clash, the overwhelmed reason survives. When justice requires giving the money to Smith, whereas benevolence requires giving the money to Jones, and benevolence has (let us suppose) the greater claim in the particular case, the *single* answer to what ought to be done all things considered is that Jones ought to get the money. But it is still the case that an injustice has been committed; an injustice that ought to be committed but an injustice nevertheless. The injustice done survives as a morally relevant feature of the situation and as an appropriate object of regret. The detailed, and to my mind very appealing, case for this treatment of moral conflict is developed in chapter 7 ('Conflict').

It is the third challenge to moral realism that I want to discuss in a little detail. This is the challenge of finding a plausible place for the moral properties in our picture of the world. It is mentioned a number of times through the book but takes centre stage in chapter 14 ('Skepticism'), which is the longest chapter in the book.

For the moral realist, ethics and metaphysics are not separate areas of philosophical inquiry. To be a moral realist is to take a position on what the world is like. Thus, among the objections to Moore's claim[7] that goodness is a non-natural, unanalysable, sometimes instantiated property, there is the objection from metaphysical plausibility. We have no reason to think that there is any such property instantiated by anything. Moorean goodness is like the redness of naive commonsense, that putative property of surfaces that is quite distinct from their disposition to look red, and quite distinct from any complex of their primary properties.

Hurley's question in chapter 14 is whether something we know about how the world is and works rules out the existence, in the sense of instantiation, of moral properties. The chapter is devoted to stating various ways you might seek, and many have sought, to argue from such information to the falsity of moral realism, and rebutting them in turn. I think that her rebuttals succeed, or at the worst leave the issue stalemated. Thus Hurley (279–87) considers the following style of argument: (i) we know enough about the world to know that all the causal-explanatory work is done by the kinds of properties that figure in the scientific picture of the world; (ii) moral properties are not among the kinds of properties that figure in the scientific picture of the world; (iii) we should only believe in properties that earn their causal-explanatory keep. Hence, we should not believe in moral properties. Her reply, reasonably enough, is to deny the premise that we should only believe in properties that earn their causal-explanatory keep. There are other ways of paying the bill – for instance, by supervening on properties that earn their causal-explanatory keep.[8]

The fact remains, though, that in the course of giving her various replies she never specifies precisely the relationship she thinks holds between moral properties and natural properties, and between statements about how things are naturalistically and how things are ethically. My impression is that she regards this as a hard question she does not need to address for the purposes at hand. I think that this is a mistake. How natural properties and ethical properties inter-connect, how the way things are naturalistically and the way things are ethically relate one to another, is it seems to me a compulsory question for the realist. Without an answer to it, the question of scepticism cannot be addressed adequately.

The reason is not to do with what science tells us about the causal-explanatory character of our world. Our justification for believing in goodness, rightness, justice and so on is quite different from our justification for believing in redness. They are not posited as what explains our sensory responses to the world, or as the occupiers of some causal-explanatory role. The analogy we bruited above between folk psychology and matured folk morality was that both theories specified their key concepts by locating them in a complex network. Only in the folk psychology case is that network largely composed of causal principles. The reason the moral realist should be explicit about how moral and naturalistic properties inter-connect is that there is a strong case for saying (a) that moral properties are one and all natural properties, and (b) that total naturalistic information about how things are includes *inter alia* all there is to know about the way things are morally, that is, about moral properties.[9] It follows that to be a moral realist is to take a position about the naturalistic way our world is, and until we know what that position is, or is in broad outline, we cannot identify what it is that we are committing ourselves to when we espouse moral realism. We are without a handle with which to grasp the issue between realist and sceptic.

Although Hurley does not describe the kind of position the moral realist is taking about the naturalistic nature of our world, she could have. Her book contains the essential ideas that enable an explicit account of moral properties, and of moral discourse in general, in purely naturalistic terms.[10] But first I should outline the case for (a) and (b), and here too the essential idea is to be found in her book.

3 HURLEY'S TREATMENT OF SUPERVENIENCE

At a number of points Hurley addresses the supervenience of the moral on the natural. Here is a typical passage:

> Consistent with the denial that ethical truths are conceptually necessary is the conceptual doctrine that the evaluative characteristics of alternatives supervene on, or are some function of, their non-evaluative characteristics. It is not a conceptually

necessary truth that slavery, as identified by its non-evaluative characteristics, is wrong, all things considered (though it may be necessary in some other sense), but supervenience requires that if it weren't wrong there would be some further difference between slavery in our world and slavery in the close conceptually possible world we've imagined.

(296)

This passage, and her discussions of supervenience elsewhere in the book, commit Hurley to what is sometimes called the *inter-world* as opposed to the *intra-world* supervenience of the ethical on the natural. The intra-world supervenience of the ethical on the natural is: in every possible world, if x and y are naturalistically exactly alike, they are ethically exactly alike. The inter-world (global) supervenience of the ethical on the natural is: any two possible worlds which are naturalistically exactly alike are ethically exactly alike.[11] In both cases the relevant notion of a possible world should be thought of in the wide sense Hurley indicates by her use of the prefix 'conceptually'.[12] Both theses are put forward as conceptual truths graspable by anyone who has the relevant concepts.

In the quoted passage Hurley is committing herself to the inter-world version (though I have no doubt that she holds the intra-world version also). Intra-world supervenience tells us that anything in our world naturalistically exactly like slavery is wrong, but says nothing about the naturalistic nature of worlds where slavery is *not* wrong. Hence, in order to insist that such worlds must differ naturalistically from ours she must be interpreting the supervenience doctrine in the inter-world way. And fair enough. The doctrine is very plausible when understood in either way. I will understand it in the inter-world way from now on.

To avoid possible misunderstanding I should emphasise the difference between the inter-world supervenience of the ethical on the natural and the inter-world supervenience of the psychological on the physical. The inter-world supervenience of the psychological on the physical is *false*. Let w_1 be a world containing one electron and nothing else. Let w_2 be a world containing one electron and many thoughtful 'angels' – thinkers realised entirely in non-physical stuff – and nothing else. Materialist and dualist agree that both worlds are possible, and that they are physically exactly alike. They are physically exactly alike because in each the one electron exhausts their physical nature (though it does not exhaust their naturalistic nature, for in the sense relevant here the angels have naturalistic natures). Nevertheless, w_1 and w_2 differ psychologically.[13]

The inter-world supervenience of the ethical on the natural provides a strong reason for thinking that moral properties are a species of naturalistic properties, that the moral way of being is some one or another, more or less complex, natural way of being. Think of the vast mosaic of instantiated naturalistic properties and relations which constitutes the total naturalistic nature of our world. If there is another possible world, exactly alike with respect to this vast mosaic but differing ethically, we would have clear reason to hold that moral properties are distinct from natural properties. As we go from one world to the other the ethical properties, or some of them, vary, whereas the naturalistic properties do not. But inter-world supervenience tells us that this never happens. Hence, the only way we can hold that ethical properties are distinct from natural properties is by holding that they are distinct but necessarily connected. This anti-Humean stance is possible but unattractive.[14] A way to bring out its unattractiveness is to consider the task of the interpreter of our language required to justify assigning these mysteriously distinct-but-necessarily-connected-to naturalistic properties as being the properties our moral predicates really attach to. Corresponding to any such assignment there will be a more mundane assignment of the purely naturalistic to the very same predicates; and because moral nature makes no distinctions among the possibilities that are not made by naturalistic nature, this more mundane assignment will obey the canons of good interpretation to the very same extent. Or rather, it will obey, in addition to all the canons obeyed by the exotic assignment to the moral predicates of the allegedly distinct but necessarily connected moral properties, the canon that counsels assigning to that whose instantiation is most beyond question.

It might be objected that I have overlooked the distinction between the meta-physically possible worlds and the conceptually or analytically possible worlds. Every metaphysically possible world is conceptually or analytically possible but not conversely. Consider one who holds that God exists necessarily.[15] Such a person typically does not think that God exists as a matter of analytic or conceptual necessity, that the necessity that God exists is deducible from reflection on concepts alone. She thinks that it is synthetic a priori (as it used to be said) or that it is synthetic necessary (as it is better said, particularly post *Naming and Necessity*[16]) that God exists. The view of such a person might be captured by saying that they hold that 'God exists' is true at every metaphysically possible world, but not at every conceptually possible world. Similarly, it might be (has been) held that 'Water = H_2O' is true at every metaphysically possible world, but not at every conceptually possible world. It might then be claimed, though not I think by Hurley, that inter-world supervenience is only plausible when the worlds in question are understood as metaphysically possible worlds. Among the *conceptually* possible worlds, there are naturalistic duplicates which are not ethical duplicates, and hence moral properties are distinct from naturalistic ones.

I think that it is a mistake to hold that the analytically or conceptually necessary on the one hand, and the synthetically necessary and the necessary a posteriori on the other, differ in the kind of necessity they possess. To think that they differ in the kind of necessity they possess is to make the same kind of mistake that Quine famously identified over existence.[17] The difference between the existence of numbers (if indeed they do exist) and the existence of tables is in the nature of what exists, not in the kind of existence possessed. Similarly, the necessity possessed by 'Water = H_2O' is the same kind of necessity as that possessed by 'Water = water'.[18] The difference is in how we ascertain that they are necessary, not in what we ascertain when we ascertain that they are necessary. Indeed, to suppose that there is a conceptually possible world C where water is not H_2O but instead is, say, XYZ, would commit one to holding that being water is a different property from being H_2O; for being water and being H_2O would differ in that the first would have, and the second would not have, XYZ in its extension in C. But what we are supposed to have learned from Kripke and Putnam is precisely that being water and being H_2O is one and the same property, despite the fact that it took empirical work to show it.

Moreover, the inter-world supervenience of the ethical on the natural is, as we noted following Hurley, a conceptual truth.[19] Someone who includes in their list of all the possibilities two or more naturalistically identical but ethically distinct ones reveals an inadequate grasp of the relevant concepts. Similarly, it is part of our concept of water that it is the very same stuff in every possible world, and so it is a conceptual mistake to think that it is both possible that water is H_2O, and possible that water is XYZ. What is true is that our concept of water does not reveal which of water's being H_2O and water's being XYZ is possible (and if possible necessary), and which is not a possibility at all.[20]

There is therefore a good case from inter-world supervenience for holding that moral properties are natural properties. But it is one thing to use inter-world supervenience to show that ethical properties are naturalistic properties, and quite another to show that enough knowledge of naturalistic facts yields in itself knowledge of moral properties, or to show that, in the limit, total information about how things are naturalistically includes all there is to know about how things are morally. Facts about water fix or logically determine facts about H_2O. For instance, the way water is distributed fixes or logically determines the way H_2O is distributed in the following sense: any possible world where water is distributed thus and so is a possible world where H_2O is distributed thus and so. However, knowing water facts is not enough for knowing H_2O facts. Information about how things are as far as water is concerned is not *per se* information about how things are as far as H_2O is concerned. This is of course a reflection of the a posteriori, albeit necessary, nature of 'Water is H_2O'. Accordingly, it might be suggested that although inter-world supervenience shows that the total naturalistic picture fixes the ethical way our world is down to the last detail, and so makes it plausible that ethical properties (and relations) are naturalistic, we cannot move a priori from the total way things are naturalistically to the total way they are ethically, and so information, total or otherwise, about naturalistic facts does not constitute information about the ethical facts.

I think, however, that the water-H_2O example is very different from the ethics-natural properties case. Exactly how to explain the necessary a posteriori is controversial. But the general picture is reasonably non-controversial. The necessary a posteriori truths are ones where in order to know that they are necessary you need to know something about the actual world which is itself contingent and a posteriori. The concept of water is not that of that which falls from the sky, is essential to life, is odourless and colourless, and so on; it is the concept of that which *actually* falls from the sky, is essential to life, is odourless and colourless, and so on.[21] Water in any given possible world is the stuff which does the falling and so on in the *actual* world regardless of whether it does the falling and so on in the given world. It is this fact which simultaneously makes it necessary that water is H_2O, and makes the fact that it is necessary an a posteriori matter. For in order to know that it is necessary, you have to know which stuff it is which falls from the sky and so on in the actual world. This means that whenever we have a case where some contingent body of information I fixes some body of information I^*, but we cannot move a priori from I to I^* – a case, that is, where every I-world is an I^*-world, but it is necessary a posteriori that if I then I^* – there will be some additional, contingent bit of information which if conjoined to I would enable us to move a priori from the conjunction of that information with I to I^*. The additional information will be precisely the relevant facts about the actual world which reveal the necessary status of 'if I then I^*'. The reason we cannot move a priori from the way water is distributed to the way H_2O is distributed relates to the *partial* nature of the information that water is distributed thus and so. Supplement the information suitably and all will be well. For instance, although you cannot move a priori from the fact that water is distributed thus and so hereabouts, to the fact that H_2O is distributed thus and so hereabouts; you can move a priori from the fact that water is distributed thus and so hereabouts conjoined with the fact that it is H_2O which falls from the sky, is essential to life, is odourless and colourless, and so on, to the fact that H_2O is distributed thus and so hereabouts.

The crucial point about the ethics-natural properties case is that enough information about the naturalistic nature of a world fixes the position of the world uniquely in logical space. It is not just that it fixes the ethical nature of the world. It fixes all there is to fix. It is not partial information. Any two naturalistically exactly alike worlds are exactly alike *simpliciter*. (This would not of course be true if 'naturalistic' meant 'physicalistic' as it sometimes does in the philosophy of mind.) This means that full information about the naturalistic nature of our world will constitute full information about the ethical nature of our world. It won't just fix the ethical nature; it will reveal it. Of course there may well be necessary a posteriori truths of the form 'If N then E', in which case knowing that N will fix that E but not in itself enable the deduction of E. But the contingent fact about the actual world needed to reveal the necessary nature of 'If N then E' will itself be capturable naturalistically – if it couldn't be, naturalistic nature would not fix position in logical space without remainder – and from the additional piece of information together with N, it will be possible to deduce E.

There are, that is, two distinguishable things the inter-world supervenience of the ethical on the natural tells us. One is that the total naturalistic story fixes the *ethical* position of a world in logical space. This is the result which supports ontological naturalism in ethics. The other and stronger message is that the total naturalistic story fixes the position of a world in logical space *simpliciter*. It is this result which supports informational naturalism in ethics – the doctrine that all there is to tell about moral nature can be told in naturalistic terms.

4 FROM COHERENTISM TO ANALYTIC NATURALISM

If informational naturalism is true, there should be a way to give the meanings of ethical expressions in purely naturalistic terms. Our language is a remarkably powerful instrument for describing how things are, for giving information about the way our world is. If all the information about the ways things are ethically can be given naturalistically, it should be possible to do this, or to sketch the general way it might be done, in our language in a way which makes it explicit that it is naturalistic information that is being given.[22] Hurley's coherentism spelt out in the way we have suggested combined with David Lewis's method of defining theoretical terms via Ramsey sentences gives us a way of doing exactly this, and so a way of stating a species of *analytic naturalism*.

We noted at the beginning that we can think of coherentism in ethics as holding that the various ethical concepts, specific and general, are identified by their place in the complex network which constitutes matured folk morality. If this is right, naturalistic definitions of the ethical terms drop out in the way made familiar by Lewis for theoretical terms in general, and for mental state terms in particular.[23] Here is the story in outline.

Let **M** be matured folk morality written out as a long conjunction, with the moral predicates written in property-name style. For example, 'Killing someone is typically morally wrong' becomes 'Killing typically has the property of being morally wrong'. Replace each distinct moral property term by a distinct variable to give '$M(x_1, \ldots, x_n)$'. Then '$(Ex_1)(Ex_2) \ldots M(x_1, x_2, \ldots)$' is the Ramsey sentence of **M**, and

$$(Ex_1)(Ex_2) \ldots (y_1)(y_2) \ldots [M(y_1, y_2, \ldots) \text{ iff } x_1 = y_1 \,\&\, x_2 = y_2 \ldots]$$

is the modified Ramsey sentence of **M** which says that there is a unique realisation of **M**. If coherentism is true, **M** and the modified Ramsey sentence of **M** say the same thing. For that is what holding that the ethical concepts are fixed by their place in the network comes to (of course, the elements in a unique realisation may themselves be disjunctive). Justice is what plays the justice role. Now we can specify what it is for some action *a* to be, say, right, thus:

a is right iff $(Ex_1)(Ex_2) \ldots \{a$ has $x_r \,\&\, (y_1)(y_2) \ldots [M(y_1, y_2, \ldots)$ iff $x_1 = y_1 \,\&\, x_2 = y_2 \ldots]\}$

where 'x_r' replaced 'being right' in **M**. The right hand side will be framed entirely in naturalistic terms because each and every moral term in **M** was replaced by an existentially bound variable. Hence we have derived from the coherentist picture a specification of the meaning of 'right' in the sense of a specification of the truth conditions of 'a is right' in naturalistic terms as required by analytic naturalism.[24] The same could of course be done for 'good', 'just', 'courageous' and so on.

There is much that might be said about the story I have just outlined, but I will restrict myself to our topic set from Hurley: its bearing on the debate between moral realism and scepticism. I said earlier that we need to be explicit about the naturalistic nature of the ethical in order to get a handle on that debate. We now have the needed handle. Rightness will be instantiated, some actions will indeed be right and scepticism will be false, just if '$(Ex_1)(Ex_2) \ldots \{-$ has $x_r \,\&\, (y_1)(y_2) \ldots [M(y_1, y_2, \ldots)$ iff $x_1 = y_1 \,\&\, x_2 = y_2 \ldots]\}$' is true of some actions. And that in turn will depend both on the nature of **M**, and on the naturalistic nature of our world. **M** specifies the naturalistic conditions that need to be met for an action to be right, and whether or not they are in fact satisfied will depend on how things actually are.

This specifies the question that needs to be addressed but not the answer. We have not said enough about **M** to give the answer. If Mackie is right, if it is an essential part of **M** that there be properties which of *necessity* attract anyone who contemplates them, no doubt nothing is right. But more moderate views about **M** are possible.[25] The answer Hurley should give is, I think, clear from her remarks (24–5, 50–2 and 86–8, for example) about the importance of the principle of charity in interpretation. Any account of **M** which makes it all but impossible for any actions in the world as it is actually constituted, to be right must be mistaken. It is a constraint on interpreting our moral discourse that some actions have the moral properties our discourse putatively ascribes to them.

So that is the story about how Hurley's interesting, and to my mind plausible, account of ethical theory could provide an answer to moral scepticism.

5 POSTSCRIPT: THE OPEN QUESTION

Analytic naturalism is often taken to be refuted by the open question argument. If analytic naturalism is true, then if I know all there is to know about the naturalistic facts and have *per impossibile* properly got my mind around this enormous body of information, any given moral judgement is analytically determined. The only sense in which the matter can still be open is semantic – I might for example waver about what judgement to make in the way I might waver about what to say about an object on the borderline between red and pink, or whether someone has lost enough hair to count as bald. But, runs the objection, it is intuitively evident that the matter might still be open in a substantial sense.

There is (notoriously) much to say about this objection but I think that Hurley tells us the most important thing to say. In many places in the book, but most particularly in chapters 3 and 5, she forcefully attacks the idea of 'mythically intrinsically self-interpreting entities' (84) and the idea that 'there could be a residual content to our concepts which transcends all the uses to which we put them' (51). To find it *evident* in the face of supervenience that any given moral matter might remain open in a substantial sense despite total naturalistic information, is to be a captive of the idea that somehow we internally fix on the senses of the moral terms. It is a kind of platonism but without the dubious ontology.[26]

NOTES

1 See Lewis (1972) and Shoemaker (1981).
2 Rawls (1972, p. 46), though, as Philip Pettit reminded me, the best parallel for the cognitivist would be the role of reflective equilibrium in discussions of rationality.
3 Sidgwick (1907, p. 13).
4 In his error theory, Mackie (1977).
5 Arrow (1963).
6 Williams (1981).
7 Moore (1903, ch. 1).
8 Her overall position seems closest to that of McDowell (1985) and opposed to those of Blackburn (1985a) and Harman (1977).
9 In discussions of moral realism, moral properties are moral 'ways to be'. To adopt moral realism is not of course to repudiate nominalism *per se*.
10 Or so I will argue: her remarks on pp. 196–200 suggest that she would resist this conclusion.
11 For a discussion of the various forms of supervenience and their implications, see Oddie (1991). It is compatible with inter-world supervenience that x in w_1 and y in w_2 be naturalistically exactly alike in all the properties and relations people typically have in mind when they talk of the 'right making' properties of actions and yet x be right in w_1 and y wrong in w_2, provided w_1 and w_2 differ appropriately in naturalistic nature elsewhere.
12 The remark in parentheses suggests that Hurley thinks that 'Slavery is wrong all things considered' might be necessary though not conceptually necessary. However, it seems to be straightforwardly contingent. Slavery in a world where perpetual torment is the only alternative, is right all things considered. The status of 'Slavery is *pro tanto* wrong' is, of course, another matter.
13 Of course some more or less complicated and more or less substantial modification of the claim that the psychological supervenes on the physical may be true, or at least may express what materialists believe. See, e.g., Horgan (1982) and Lewis (1983). The point is that the modifications are not called for in the ethics-natural properties case.

14 One way to pay the price is to hold that the moral properties are properties of properties, see Forrest (1988).

15 I take the example and the possibility of the objection from Forrest (1992). The objection is also considered by Blackburn (1984, p. 221).

16 Kripke (1980).

17 See Quine (1960, § 27).

18 I am taking for granted here the view, widely accepted as a result of Kripke (1980) and Putnam (1975) that, modulo worlds where there is no water, 'Water = H_2O' is necessary a posteriori. I am in fact agnostic on the question of whether 'water' as used by the person in the street is a rigid designator. But clearly it is a rigid designator in the mouths and from the pens of many philosophers alive today, and for the purposes of the discussion here and below we will give it that meaning.

19 A point emphasised in this connection by Blackburn (1985b).

20 For one way of making this way of looking at the issue formally precise see Stalnaker (1978). In this treatment, and in general in treatments in the style of two-dimensional modal logic, there is a *single* set of possible worlds.

21 To put the matter in the terms of Davies and Humberstone (1980).

22 Some recent expositions of naturalism in ethics have emphasised that though they hold the ontological doctrine that moral properties and facts are one and all natural properties and facts, they do not hold that moral terms can be analysed naturalistically: see Boyd (1988, p. 199), and Sturgeon (1988, p. 240). It would be easy to see how moral properties could be natural properties without ethical terms being analysable naturalistically if those natural properties which are moral properties had themselves non-natural features which we used to secure reference to those natural properties when we used ethical terminology. But according to ontological naturalists themselves, *all*, or at least all contingent, properties are natural. How ethical terms pick out those natural properties which are moral properties cannot depend on non-natural properties simply because there are none such to depend on. (A similar point is made by Charles Pigden (1991a, b).)

23 See Lewis (1970, 1972). I am grateful to Ian Ravenscroft and David Lewis for help in spotting two (!) blunders in an earlier presentation of what follows.

24 We can think of the meaning specification in two different ways. We can think of it as giving the meaning of 'right' in the traditional sense. An action is right in a possible world iff it has the property, if any, which occupies the 'x_r' position in that world. Or we can (less plausibly, it seems to me) think of it as fixing the reference of 'right' in the sense of Kripke (1980). An action is right in a possible world iff it has the property which occupies the 'x_r' position in the actual world, whether or not the action has that property in the world in question.

25 See Lewis (1989, p. 137).

26 Some of the ideas in this notice were presented at a conference at Monash University in 1991. I am greatly indebted to discussion on that occasion. I am also very much indebted to many discussions before and after that conference with Peter Railton, David Lewis, Lloyd Humberstone, Michael Smith (who pointed out a serious confusion in an earlier version of the final section), Charles Pigden and Philip Pettit, and to reading Pargetter and Campbell (1986).

REFERENCES

Arrow, Kenneth J. (1963) *Social Choice and Individual Values* (New Haven, CT: Yale University Press).
Blackburn, Simon (1984) *Spreading the Word* (Oxford: Oxford University Press).
——(1985a) 'Errors and the Phenomenology of Value', in Ted Honderich (ed.) *Morality and Objectivity* (London: Routledge & Kegan Paul).
——(1985b) 'Supervenience Revisited', in Ian Hacking (ed.) *Exercises in Analysis* (Cambridge: Cambridge University Press).
Boyd, Richard (1988) 'How to be a Moral Realist', in Geoffrey Sayre-McCord (ed.) *Essays on Moral Realism* (Ithaca, NY: Cornell University Press), pp. 181–228.
Davies, M. K. and I. L. Humberstone (1980) 'Two Notions of Necessity', *Philosophical Studies* 38, pp. 1–30.
Forrest, Peter (1988) 'Supervenience: The Grand Property Hypothesis', *Australasian Journal of Philosophy* 66, pp. 1–12.
——(1992) 'Universals and Universalisability', *Australasian Journal of Philosophy* 70, pp. 93–8.
Harman, Gilbert (1977) *The Nature of Morality* (New York: Oxford University Press).
Horgan, Terence (1982) 'Supervenience and Microphysics', *Pacific Philosophical Quarterly* 63, pp. 29–43.
Kripke, Saul (1980) *Naming and Necessity* (Oxford: Blackwell).
Lewis, David (1970) 'How to Define Theoretical Terms', *The Journal of Philosophy* 67, pp. 427–46.
——(1972) 'Psychophysical and Theoretical Identifications', *Australasian Journal of Philosophy* 50, pp. 291–315.
——(1983) 'New Work for a Theory of Universals', *Australasian Journal of Philosophy* 61, pp. 343–77.
——(1989) 'Dispositional Theories of Value', *Proceedings of the Aristotelian Society*, Suppl. Vol. LXIII, pp. 113–37.
Mackie, J. L. (1977) *Ethics: Inventing Right and Wrong* (Harmondsworth: Penguin).
McDowell, John (1985) 'Values and the Secondary Qualities', in Ted Honderich (ed.) *Morality and Objectivity* (London: Routledge & Kegan Paul) [Chapter 12, this volume].
Moore, G. E. (1903) *Principia Ethica* (Cambridge: Cambridge University Press).
Oddie, Graham (1991) 'Supervenience and Higher-Order Universals', *Australasian Journal of Philosophy* 69, pp. 20–47.
Pargetter, Robert and John Campbell (1986) 'Goodness and Fragility', *American Philosophical Quarterly* 23, pp. 155–66.
Pigden, Charles R. (1991a) *The Reluctant Nihilist* (manuscript).
——(1991b) 'Naturalism', in Peter Singer (ed.) *A Companion to Ethics* (Oxford: Blackwell).
Putnam, Hilary (1975) 'The Meaning of "Meaning"', in *Mind, Language and Reality* (Cambridge: Cambridge University Press).
Quine, W. V. O. (1960) *Word and Object* (Cambridge, MA: MIT Press).
Rawls, John (1972) *A Theory of Justice* (Oxford: Oxford University Press).
Shoemaker, Sydney (1981) 'Some Varieties of Functionalism', *Philosophical Topics* 12, pp. 83–118.
Sidgwick, Henry (1907) *Methods of Ethics* (London: Macmillan), p. 13.
Stalnaker, Robert C. (1978) 'Assertion', in P. Cole (ed.) *Syntax and Semantics*, Vol. 9 (New York: Academic Press), pp. 315–32.
Sturgeon, Nicholas L. (1988) 'Moral Explanations', in Geoffrey Sayre-McCord (ed.) *Essays on Moral Realism* (Ithaca, NY: Cornell University Press), pp. 229–55 [Chapter 8, this volume].
Williams, Bernard (1981) 'Ethical Consistency', in *Problems of the Self* (Cambridge: Cambridge University Press).

Part 4

MORAL REALISM AFTER MOORE

MODERN NONNATURALISM

What happens if you wish to remain a realist, but suspect that trying to characterize moral properties as natural properties is fishy? The obvious answer, so far at least for those reading this collection in order, is to adopt a position like Moore's. But many modern commentators have turned their backs on much of what Moore said as his position, rightly or wrongly, is thought to be committed to thinking that moral properties are mind-independent properties. In recent times, modern versions of nonnaturalism – encompassing a wide variety of positions – have emerged and become very popular.

The attractions of a mind-dependent version of nonnaturalist realism are obvious. One can assert that moral properties are, in some sense of the term, real and that moral judgements are to be understood descriptively and are truth-apt. Furthermore, this position puts at its heart the lasting sense many feel that ethics is special and cannot be reduced to a collection of natural, nonmoral parts. When we describe an action as being kind it seems that we are, essentially, referring to the kindness of the action and not to a collection of natural parts that make it up. (There will be more on this line of thought in Part 8.) And, in all of this, a key feature of this position is that typical human sensibility – or judging ability – is seen as the marker of what it is for an action to be, say, kind. That's how the position makes good on its claims to mind-dependence. For many, this idea has to be right because ethics, that is *our* ethics, is by definition a human phenomenon.

All of this sounds wonderful. But there are problems, many of which stem from trying to see how the position can make good on all its hopes and, in doing so, how it can steer a clear path away from opposing positions. We are supposed to imagine that these properties are mind-dependent. In itself, this is fine. But the hope is not that every person uniquely has a set of properties in the world that exist for them and which make their judgements true. (Which effectively would be a form of relativism.) The idea is that there is one set of properties that are there to be experienced by all and that people can go right and wrong in their judging. In which case, we have to adopt some standards, some ways of conceiving of judges and judging conditions, which eventually will tell us not just what it is to be a good judge but what the nature of moral properties is and which ones exist when and where. The idea behind the previous thought being that if moral properties are mind-dependent, then their nature is heavily influenced by the types of person who react in a certain way and who have a certain sensibility. So, the focus on human sensibility is important because it isn't simply an epistemological matter, telling us (only) what sort of person can pick out the properties that exist, but is a metaphysical matter and tells us which moral properties there are: something is kind if it is judged to be so by a judge of such-and-such a sort. But, how do we conceive of the judges, their judging conditions (whether they have all of the relevant information, say) and the other criteria that determine what a good judgement is? We could conceive them in moral or, more broadly, evaluative terms (so, not just kind and just, but 'credible', 'reliable', 'imaginative' and the like) and assume that such terms indicate *sui generis* categories. Alternatively, we could give a naturalistic account of what it is to be a good judge and give scientifically respectable conceptions of, say, kindness and reliability. The thought then is that, assuming we have filled in the details in the right sort of way, we would have given a naturalistic account of moral properties. Nonnatural moral realists, as one might expect, choose the former option. But the problem then is that it seems as if we might well have some infinite regress or vicious circle. (A number of metaphors might be appropriate.) We want to know which moral properties exist when and where. We can discern whether an action is kind by asking the best judge. "How will we know which is the best judge?", we might then ask. The answer is that the best judge is the person who is kind, and just and whatever else. We seem to have got no further, not only because people will have different ideas about who is kind (and this lead to relativism), but we wish to understand what kindness is and the only response we get presupposes that we already have such understanding. Perhaps, then, we are better off being naturalists if we wish to be realists. But in defence, we might say that this circularity might not be vicious. After all, the central thought of the account is that one cannot reduce kindness and other evaluative categories to natural categories, one cannot put evaluative understanding in a nonevaluative idiom, and perhaps this situation is simply an expression of this thought. What makes this circularity seem problematic is a yearning for something outside of the evaluative that will justify our evaluative claims, and such a yearning represents a vain hope. We might additionally say that relativists go wrong because, as it happens, there is enough shared understanding across individuals and groups as to what makes one thing kind and another wicked.

It is worth saying here that expressivists often make a different move having considered the debate. Because of these worries, perhaps it makes better sense to claim that a metaethical account, whilst having mind-dependence at its heart, should claim that moral judgements are better interpreted as expressions of human attitude rather than descriptions of mind-dependently existing properties. Again, there will be more on the debate between nonnatural moral realism and expressivism in Part 8.

One of the classic papers in support of the general account above is John McDowell's 'Values and Secondary Qualities' (Chapter 12), which is the first paper of this Part. McDowell devotes much of the piece to arguing for there being logical space for his position with the hope that in doing so he makes it attractive. His paper is primarily written in opposition to Mackie's error theory and specifically the argument from queerness. McDowell argues that Mackie can swiftly reject moral realism because he conceives of moral properties incorrectly. Following John Locke, McDowell outlines two conceptions of moral properties: as primary qualities and as secondary qualities. (As an aside, there is some debate as to how Locke did, and how anyone should, understand the distinction between the two sorts of quality or property. But, McDowell's way of distinguishing matters has some appeal.) A primary quality is something that exists in the object independently of how humans experience that object.

A classic Lockean example here is size. Intuitively, no matter how I or anyone else experiences a ball, it has a certain size. Secondary qualities, in contrast, are qualities of the object that in some way depend on how humans experience them. So, the ball's redness crucially depends on how humans with good eyesight in the right sorts of lighting condition view the object because of the structure of their eyes and the like. In contrast, a goldfish or a Martian might have a very different sort of experience so colours seem far more dependent on the experiencing subject. In effect, McDowell is drawing a distinction between mind-independent and mind-dependent conceptions of moral properties. He augments this by describing two ways of thinking about objectivity and two ways of thinking about subjectivity, reflecting the discussion in § 8 of our Introduction (Chapter 1). From all of this, McDowell claims that one can be a moral realist and conceive moral properties to be subjective in a certain sense – namely that they are dependent on us in an interesting fashion – and not threaten the fact that they exist, in some way at least. This is just like arguing for the existence of colours whilst agreeing that they depend on human perception. McDowell then argues that Mackie was wrong to dismiss moral properties as queer. Mind-independent moral properties and other phenomena (specifically for Mackie, objective prescriptions) are metaphysically strange things. But mind-dependent moral properties are not queer in the same way.

As well as drawing his conclusions against Mackie, McDowell makes other points throughout his paper, some of which we consider below. One thing worth highlighting at this point is, again, a thought about expressivism. In his § 5 McDowell claims that a failure to appreciate that moral realists can remain realists whilst rejecting a primary quality view of moral properties supplies much of the explanation as to why people (erroneously) adopt expressivism. Whether or not this is true remains for the reader to consider.

In his detailed paper, which is our second selection in this Part, David Sosa (Chapter 13) tackles McDowell's position and argues that it comes unstuck. After first discussing Mackie's argument from queerness he concentrates on a number of interconnected problems for McDowell, three of which we mention. First, he worries that McDowell attempts to get too much from the phenomenology of experience. This is important since many of the intuitions that McDowell uses to support his position stem from his comments about our moral phenomenology. Essentially, Sosa worries that McDowell assumes too readily that philosophical claims can be 'read off' from our pre-philosophical moral and colour phenomenology. For example, Sosa claims that McDowell thinks that our experiences of things looking red are experiences of things being such as to look red and that such a claim is erroneous. According to Sosa, I can have an experience of something being red without thinking at all that it has to be red (to certain sorts of subject) let alone experience it, pre-philosophically, in this way. In other words, people typically do not experience the world under the descriptions that philosophers often use to characterize and explain it. McDowell requires this sort of move, according to Sosa, because Mackie agrees that our colour and moral phenomenology is such that we are led to believe that colours and values really exist. For Mackie, however, this is a projective error that requires philosophical correction. McDowell, according to Sosa, needs the phenomenology to tell us more so that he can draw philosophical ideas from it that are more in keeping with his position.

Is this fair on McDowell? This is a question you should ask yourself as you read both pieces and think about your everyday moral phenomenology. Perhaps a better way of supporting his nonnaturalism, and what McDowell is trying to get at anyway, is to say that a secondary quality account of moral properties 'sits best with' our everyday moral phenomenology; the claim that we pre-philosophically experience moral properties as secondary qualities *is* too extreme. Whoever is right, we should be clear that the worry is not so much with McDowell's position (although it leads to scrutiny of it), but rather with the intuitions that McDowell trades on to try to convince us of its plausibility.

Sosa's second worry concerns a key comment McDowell makes about evaluative responses that threatens the plausibility of the position itself. According to McDowell, certain situations and actions are such as to *merit* an evaluative response. What does he mean here? He contrasts the case of value responses, such as moral ones, with both those that are the upshot of a mechanical or 'para-mechanical' process and with the specific example of the disgusting. The response that something is disgusting is, according to McDowell, something that we project onto the object itself. There is no notion that something is disgusting *per se*, no objective property of disgustingness. In contrast, we can talk of something being fearful *per se* and people can be right and wrong in their judgement about it. Sosa tries to understand this contrast between the disgusting and the fearful. If McDowell is right, the difference seems to be judging that something is to be feared is open to rational revision, but this does not apply to the disgusting. Even if this particular conclusion is right, Sosa worries that McDowell does not give us more detailed ideas as to how we would decide which type of response is open to rational revision and which is not so. After all, don't people argue about which foods are disgusting, just as they argue about which films are scary? The worry is that if we cannot capture what it is for something to be a correct value response and what it means to say that an action merits a response, then we cannot distinguish responses that are projections onto the world and those that are descriptions of properties of the world. It could be that moral responses are just like responses of disgust.

Perhaps thinking about the contrast with responses of para-mechanical processes will help McDowell here. (This is something Sosa does not explicitly do.) There is some difference between value responses and colour responses. No matter what I think, I cannot help but see a red patch (in certain lighting conditions) as having a certain colour. I cannot decide to change what I think and, in future, consciously try to respond differently. Value responses are different. Even if we initially respond to an action as being cruel, we can reflect on that response afterwards and try to justify it to ourselves and others as cruel. If no good justification is forthcoming, then we can change our judgement about that particular action and, over time, often change our natural, initial reaction to similar actions in the future. The same might well be true of disgusting, of course, but then perhaps McDowell is wrong to think of disgust and the response that something is selfish as being so different.

This raises a new worry, however. There are clearly some sorts of response that are argued about, but which we do not think so important and are more inclined to be subjective, in the everyday sense meaning 'akin to relativism'. To repeat our example from § 8 of our Introduction, we can argue about which is the best tasting ice-cream flavour and, in the end, we might say that chocolate is better than bleach flavour. But if someone does quite like bleach flavour ice-cream, we might just shrug our shoulders and laugh at the richness of life's tapestry. But in ethics surely there is more at stake and we wish our moral judgements to be more objective than this. But is there anything to help us mark a dividing line and stop our account of what is happening from becoming relativistic? Possibly not.

And this is a point Sosa continues to make as he spells out his third worry, the worry we have already considered above concerning circularity. Is there any way, outside of what we value and justify as being legitimate and kosher, normal or best, for us to say that *this* is the correct response? If we keep to the ideals of McDowell's position – at least as presented in this one paper – it seems there is not. (McDowell has developed his view in a series of papers; many of which are collected in his *Mind, Value and Reality* (1998). See Further Reading below.) In the remaining parts of his paper Sosa describes how other writers – Crispin Wright and Mark Johnston – have tried to grapple with these problems and develop better versions of sensibility theory, theories that, broadly, put human responses centre stage in our account of moral properties. (Often such positions are called 'response-dependent' accounts.) We leave it to the reader to decide whether his criticisms are good ones. One thing is certain. Even though modern versions of nonnaturalism, such as sensibility theory and response-dependent accounts, have their problems, they are still one of the most popular metaethical positions. People continue to think that, given that all philosophical positions have their problems, these are the sorts of problem with which they are most comfortable.

QUESTIONS TO CONSIDER AND TASKS TO COMPLETE

1   Try to explain in your own words, and with your own examples, the two senses of 'objectivity' and the two senses of 'subjectivity' that McDowell (Chapter 12) uses.
2   Think about your everyday moral experiences and the judgement you might draw. Based on these experiences and McDowell's distinctions concerning objectivity and subjectivity, how would you characterize morality?
3   Do you think that McDowell provides enough justification for a rejection of error theory?
4   What do you understand by McDowell's contrast between colour and value when he talks about the latter *meriting* responses?
5   Make a list of all of Sosa's (Chapter 13) worries with McDowell's position. Which is the most powerful and why?

6   You might not have read anything on this topic by Wright and Johnston, but from what Sosa says do you find what they say appealing? Is it more appealing than McDowell's position? Why?

7   Overall, do you think it is possible to combine (i) the aim of characterizing and grounding standards to which people should conform if they want to act and judge properly with (ii) the aim that such standards should be based on what people think and feel?

FURTHER READING

Ayers, Michael (1991) *Locke: Epistemology* (London: Routledge).

Boghossian, Paul and Velleman, David (1989) 'Colour as a Secondary Quality', *Mind*, vol. 98, pp. 81–103.

Dancy, Jonathan (1986) 'Two Conceptions of Moral Realism', *Proceedings of the Aristotelian Society,* suppl. vol. 60, pp. 167–87.

Hookway, Christopher (1986) 'Two Conceptions of Moral Realism', *Proceedings of the Aristotelian Society,* suppl. vol. 60, pp. 189–205.

Hume, David (1742) 'Of the Standard of Taste', in *Essays: Moral, Political, and Literary* (London: Grant Richards, 1903), pp. 231–55.

Johnston, Mark (1989) 'Dispositional Theories of Value', *Proceedings of the Aristotelian Society*, suppl. vol. 63, pp. 139–74.

——(1993) 'Objectivity Refigured: Pragmatism without Verification', in J. Haldane and C. Wright (eds) *Reality Representation and Projection* (Oxford: Oxford University Press), pp. 85–130.

——(1998) 'Are Manifest Qualities Respose-Dependent?', *The Monist*, vol. 81, pp. 3–43.

Kirchin, Simon (2003) 'Ethical Phenomenology and Metaethics', *Ethical Theory and Moral Practice*, vol. 6, no. 3, pp. 241–64.

Leiter, Brian (2001) 'Objectivity, Morality and Adjudication', in B. Leiter (ed.) *Objectivity in Law and Morals* (Cambridge: Cambridge University Press), pp. 66–98.

Lewis, David (1989) 'Dispositional Theories of Value', *Proceedings of the Aristotelian Society*, suppl. vol. 63, pp. 113–37.

Little, Margaret (1994) 'Moral Realism II: Non-Naturalism', *Philosophical Books,* vol. 25, pp. 225–33.

Locke, John (1690) *An Essay Concerning Human Understanding*, P. H. Nidditch (ed.) (Oxford: Oxford University Press, 1975).

McDowell, John (1998) *Mind, Value and Reality* (Cambridge, MA: Harvard University Press).

McNaughton, David (1988) *Moral Vision* (Oxford: Blackwell).

Miller, Alexander (2003) *An Introduction to Contemporary Metaethics* (Cambridge: Polity Press), chapters 7 and 10.

Pettit, Philip (1991) 'Realism and Response-Dependence', *Mind*, vol. 100, pp. 597–626.

Smith, Michael (1989) 'Dispositional Theories of Value', *Proceedings of the Aristotelian Society*, suppl. vol. 63, pp. 89–111.

Wiggins, David (1996) 'Objective and Subjective in Ethics, with Two Postscripts about Truth', in B. Hooker (ed.) *Truth in Ethics* (Oxford: Blackwell), pp. 35–50.

——(1998) *Needs, Values, Truth* (Oxford: Oxford University Press, 3rd edn), especially chapters 3 and 5.

Wright, Crispin (1988) 'Moral Values, Projection and Secondary Qualities', *Proceedings of the Aristotelian Society*, suppl. vol. 62, pp. 1–26.

——(1996) 'Truth in Ethics', in B. Hooker (ed.) *Truth in Ethics* (Oxford: Blackwell), pp. 1–18.

12

VALUES AND SECONDARY QUALITIES

John McDowell

1

J. L. Mackie insists that ordinary evaluative thought presents itself as a matter of sensitivity to aspects of the world.[1] And this phenomenological thesis seems correct. When one or another variety of philosophical non-cognitivism claims to capture the truth about what the experience of value is like, or (in a familiar surrogate for phenomenology[2]) about what we mean by our evaluative language, the claim is never based on careful attention to the lived character of evaluative thought or discourse. The idea is, rather, that the very concept of the cognitive or factual rules out the possibility of an undiluted representation of how things are, enjoying, nevertheless, the internal relation to 'attitudes' or the will that would be needed for it to count as evaluative.[3] On this view the phenomenology of value would involve a mere incoherence, if it were as Mackie says – a possibility that then tends (naturally enough) not to be so much as entertained. But, as Mackie sees, there is no satisfactory justification for supposing that the factual is, by definition, attitudinatively and motivationally neutral. This clears away the only obstacle to accepting his phenomenological claim; and the upshot is that non-cognitivism must offer to correct the phenomenology of value, rather than to give an account of it.[4]

In Mackie's view the correction is called for. In this paper I want to suggest that he attributes an unmerited plausibility to this thesis, by giving a false picture of what one is committed to if one resists it.

2

Given that Mackie is right about the phenomenology of value, an attempt to accept the appearances makes it virtually irresistible to appeal to a perceptual model. Now Mackie holds that the model must be perceptual awareness of *primary* qualities (see *HMT*, pp. 32, 60–1, 73–4). And this makes it comparatively easy to argue that the appearances are misleading. For it seems impossible – at least on reflection – to take seriously the idea of something that is like a primary quality in being simply *there*, independently of human sensibility, but is nevertheless intrinsically (not conditionally on contingencies about human sensibility) such as to elicit some 'attitude' or state of will from someone who becomes aware of it. Moreover, the primary-quality model turns the epistemology of value into mere mystification. The perceptual model is no more than a model: perception, strictly so called, does not mirror the role of reason in evaluative thinking, which seems to require us to regard the apprehension of value as an intellectual rather than a merely sensory matter. But if we are to take account of this, while preserving the model's picture of values as brutely and absolutely *there*, it seems that we need to postulate a faculty – 'intuition' – about which all that can be said is that it makes us aware of objective rational connections: the model itself ensures that there is nothing helpful to say about how such a faculty might work, or why its deliverances might deserve to count as knowledge.

But why is it supposed that the model must be awareness of primary qualities rather than secondary qualities? The answer is that Mackie, following Locke, takes secondary-quality perception, as conceived by a pre-philosophical consciousness, to involve a projective error: one analogous to the error he finds in ordinary evaluative thought. He holds that we are prone to conceive secondary-quality experience in a way that would be appropriate for experience of primary qualities. So a pre-philosophical secondary-quality model for awareness of value would in effect be, after all, a primary-quality model. And to accept a philosophically corrected secondary-quality model for the awareness of value would be simply to give up trying to go along with the appearances.

I believe, however, that this conception of secondary-quality experience is seriously mistaken.

3

A secondary quality is a property the ascription of which to an object is not adequately understood except as true, if it is true, in virtue of the object's disposition to present a certain sort of perceptual appearance: specifically, an appearance characterizable by using a word for the property itself to say how the object perceptually appears. Thus an object's being red is understood as obtaining in virtue of the object's being such as (in certain circumstances) to look, precisely, red.

This account of secondary qualities is faithful to one key Lockean doctrine, namely the identification of secondary qualities with 'powers to produce various sensations in us.'[5] (The phrase 'perceptual appearance,' with its gloss, goes beyond Locke's unspecific 'sensations,' but harmlessly; it serves simply to restrict our attention, as Locke's word may not, to properties that are in a certain obvious sense perceptible.[6])

I have written of what property-ascriptions are understood to be true in virtue of, rather than of what they are true in virtue of. No doubt it is true that a given thing is red in virtue of some microscopic textural property of its surface; but a predication understood only in such terms – not in terms of how the object would look – would not be an ascription of the secondary quality of redness.[7]

Secondary-quality experience presents itself as perceptual awareness of properties genuinely possessed by the objects that confront one. And there is no general obstacle to taking that appearance at face value.[8] An object's being such as to look red is independent of its actually looking red to anyone on any particular occasion; so, notwithstanding the conceptual connection between being red and being experienced as red, an experience of something as red can count as a case of being presented with a property that is there anyway – there independently of the experience itself.[9] And there is no evident ground for accusing the appearance of being misleading. What would one expect it to be like to experience something's being such as to look red, if not to experience the thing in question (in the right circumstances) as looking, precisely, red?

On Mackie's account, by contrast, to take experiencing something as red at face value, as a non-misleading awareness of a property that really confronts one, is to attribute to the object a property which is 'thoroughly objective' (*PFL*, p. 18), in the sense that it does not need to be understood in terms of experiences that the object is disposed to give rise to; but which nevertheless resembles redness as it figures in our experience – this to ensure that the phenomenal character of the experience need not stand accused of misleadingness, as it would if the 'thoroughly objective' property of which it constituted an awareness were conceived as a microscopic textural basis for the object's disposition to look red. This use of the notion of resemblance corresponds to one key element in Locke's exposition of the concept of a primary quality.[10] In these Lockean terms Mackie's view amounts to accusing a naive perceptual consciousness of taking secondary qualities for primary qualities (see *PFL*, p. 16).

According to Mackie, this conception of primary qualities that resemble colours as we see them is coherent; that nothing is characterized by such qualities is established by merely empirical argument (see *PFL*, pp. 17–20). But is the idea coherent? This would require two things: first, that colours figure in perceptual experience neutrally, so to speak, rather than as essentially phenomenal qualities of objects, qualities that could not be adequately conceived except in terms of how their possessors would look; and, second, that we command a concept of resemblance that would enable us to construct notions of possible primary qualities out of the idea of resemblance to such neutral elements of experience. The first of these requirements is quite dubious. (I shall return to this.) But even if we try to let it pass, the second requirement seems impossible. Starting with, say, redness as it (putatively neutrally) figures in our experience, we are asked to form the notion of a feature of objects which resembles that, but which is adequately conceivable otherwise than in terms of how its possessors would look (since if it were adequately conceivable only in those terms it would simply be secondary). But the second part of these instructions leaves it wholly mysterious what to make of the first: it precludes the required resemblance being in phenomenal respects, but it is quite unclear what other sense we could make of the notion of resemblance to redness as it figures in our experience. (If we find no other, we have failed to let the first requirement pass; redness as it figures in our experience proves stubbornly phenomenal.)[11] I have indicated how we can make error-free sense of the thought that colours are authentic objects of perceptual awareness; in face of that, it seems a gratuitous slur on perceptual 'common sense' to accuse it of this wildly problematic understanding of itself.

Why is Mackie resolved, nevertheless, to convict 'common sense' of error? Secondary qualities are qualities not adequately conceivable except in terms of certain subjective states, and thus subjective themselves in a sense that that characterization defines. In the natural contrast, a primary quality would be objective in the sense that what it is for something to have it can be adequately understood otherwise than in terms of dispositions to give rise to subjective states. Now this contrast between objective and subjective is not a contrast between veridical and illusory experience. But it is easily confused with a different contrast, in which to call a putative object of awareness 'objective' is to say that it is there to be experienced, as opposed to being a mere figment of the subjective state that purports to be an experience of it. If secondary qualities were subjective in the sense that naturally contrasts with this, naive consciousness would indeed be wrong about them, and we would need something like Mackie's Lockean picture of the error it commits. What is acceptable, though, is only that secondary qualities are subjective in the first sense, and it would be simply wrong to suppose that this gives any support to the idea that they are subjective in the second.[12]

More specifically, Mackie seems insufficiently whole-hearted in an insight of his about perceptual experiences. In the case of 'realistic' depiction, it makes sense to think of veridicality as a matter of resemblance between aspects of a picture and aspects of what it depicts.[13] Mackie's insight is that the best hope of a philosophically hygienic interpretation for Locke's talk of 'ideas,' in a perceptual context, is in terms of 'intentional objects': that is, aspects of representational content – aspects of how things seem to one in the enjoyment of a perceptual experience. (See *PFL*, pp. 47–50.) Now it is an illusion to suppose, as Mackie does, that this warrants thinking of the relation between a quality and an 'idea' of it on the model of the relation between a property of a picture's subject and an aspect of the picture. Explaining 'ideas' as 'intentional objects' should direct our attention to the relation between how things are and how an experience represents them as being – in fact identity, not resemblance, if the representation is veridical.[14] Mackie's Lockean appeal to resemblance fits something quite different: a relation borne to aspects of how things are by intrinsic aspects of a bearer of representational content – not how things are represented to be, but features of an item that does the representing, with particular aspects of its content carried by particular aspects of what it is intrinsically (non-representationally) like.[15] Perceptual experiences have representational content; but nothing in Mackie's defence of the 'intentional objects' gloss on 'ideas' would force us to suppose that they have it in that sort of way.[16]

The temptation to which Mackie succumbs, to suppose that intrinsic features of experience function as vehicles for particular aspects of representational content, is indifferent to any distinction between primary and secondary qualities in the representational significance that these features supposedly carry. What it is for a colour to figure in experience and what it is for a shape to figure in experience would be alike, on this view, in so far as both are a matter of an experience's having a certain intrinsic feature. If one wants, within this framework, to preserve Locke's intuition that primary-quality experience is distinctive in potentially disclosing the objective properties of things, one will be naturally led to Locke's use of the notion of resemblance. But no notion of resemblance could get us from an essentially experiential state of affairs to the concept of a feature of objects intelligible otherwise than in terms of how its possessors would strike us. (A version of this point told against Mackie's idea of possible primary qualities answering to 'colours as we see them'; it tells equally against the Lockean conception of shapes.)

If one gives up the Lockean use of resemblance, but retains the idea that primary and secondary qualities are experientially on a par, one will be led to suppose that the properties attributed to objects in the 'manifest image' are all equally phenomenal – intelligible, that is, only in terms of how their possessors are disposed to appear. Properties that are objective, in the contrasting sense, can then figure only in the 'scientific image.'[17] On these lines one altogether loses hold of Locke's intuition that primary qualities are distinctive in being both objective and perceptible.[18]

If we want to preserve the intuition, as I believe we should, then we need to exorcize the idea that what it is for a quality to figure in experience is for an experience to have a certain intrinsic feature: in fact I believe that we need to reject these supposed vehicles of content altogether. Then we can say that colours and shapes figure in experience, not as the representational significance carried by features that are – being intrinsic features of experience – indifferently subjective (which makes it hard to see how a difference in respect of objectivity could show up in their representational significance); but simply as properties that objects are represented as having, distinctively phenomenal in the one case and not so in the other. (Without the supposed intrinsic features, we should be immune to the illusion that experiences cannot represent objects as having properties that are not phenomenal – properties that are adequately conceivable otherwise than in terms of dispositions to produce suitable experiences.[19]) What Locke unfelicitously tried to yoke together, with his picture of real resemblances of our 'ideas,' can now divide into two notions that we must insist on keeping separate: first, the possible veridicality of experience (the objectivity of its object, in the second of the two senses I distinguished), in respect of which primary and secondary qualities are on all fours; and, second, the not essentially phenomenal character of some properties that experience represents objects as having (their objectivity in the first sense), which marks off the primary perceptible qualities from the secondary ones.

In order to deny that a quality's figuring in experience consists in an experience's having a certain intrinsic feature, we do not need to reject the intrinsic features altogether; it would suffice to insist that a quality's figuring in experience consists in an experience's having a certain intrinsic feature *together with* the quality's being the representational significance carried by that feature. But I do not believe that this yields a position in which acceptance of the supposed vehicles of content coheres with a satisfactory account of perception. This position would have it that the fact that an experience represents things as being one way rather than another is strictly additional to the experience's intrinsic nature, and so extrinsic to the experience itself (it seems natural to say 'read into it'). There is a phenomenological falsification here. (This brings out a third role for Locke's resemblance, namely to obviate the threat of such a falsification by constituting a sort of intrinsic representationality: Locke's 'ideas' carry the representational significance they do by virtue of what they are like, and this can be glossed both as 'how they are intrinsically' and as 'what they resemble.') In any case, given that we cannot project ourselves from features of experience to nonphenomenal properties of objects by means of an appeal to resemblance, it is doubtful that the metaphor of representational significance being 'read into' intrinsic features can be spelled out in such a way as to avoid the second horn of our dilemma. How could representational significance be 'read into' intrinsic features of experience in such a way that what was signified did not need to be understood in terms of them? How could a not intrinsically representational feature of experience become imbued with objective significance in such a way that an experience could count, by virtue of having that feature, as a direct awareness of a not essentially phenomenal property of objects?[20]

How things strike someone as being is, in a clear sense, a subjective matter: there is no conceiving it in abstraction from the subject of the experience. Now a motive for insisting on the supposed vehicles of aspects of content might lie in an aspiration, familiar in philosophy, to bring subjectivity within the compass of a fundamentally objective conception of reality.[21] If aspects of content are not carried by elements in an intrinsic structure, their subjectivity is irreducible. By contrast, one might hope to objectivize any 'essential subjectivity' that needs to be attributed to not intrinsically representational features of experience, by exploiting a picture involving special access on a subject's part to something conceived in a broadly objective way – its presence in the world not conceived as constituted by the subject's special access to it.[22] Given this move, it becomes natural to suppose that the phenomenal character of the 'manifest image' can be explained in terms of a certain familiar picture: one in which a confronted 'external' reality, conceived as having only an objective nature, is processed through structured 'subjectivity,' conceived in this objectivistic manner. This picture seems to capture the essence of Mackie's approach to the secondary qualities.[23] What I have tried to suggest is that the picture is suspect in threatening to cut us off from the *primary* (not essentially phenomenal) qualities of the objects that we perceive: either (with the appeal to resemblance) making it impossible, after all, to keep an essentially phenomenal character out of our conception of the qualities in question, or else making them merely hypothetical, not accessible to perception. If we are to achieve a satisfactory understanding of experience's openness to objective reality, we must put a more radical construction on experience's essential subjectivity. And this removes an insidious obstacle – one whose foundation is summarily captured in Mackie's idea that it is not simply wrong to count 'colours as we see them' as items in our minds (see the diagram at *PFL*, p. 17) – that stands in the way of understanding how secondary-quality experience can be awareness, with nothing misleading about its phenomenal character, of properties genuinely possessed by elements in a not exclusively pheno-menal reality.

4

The empirical ground that Mackie thinks we have for not postulating 'thoroughly objective features which resemble our ideas of secondary qualities' (*PFL*, pp. 18–19) is that attributing such features to objects is surplus to the requirements of explaining our experience of secondary qualities (see *PFL*, pp. 17–18). If it would be incoherent to attribute such features to objects, as I believe, this empirical argument falls away as unnecessary. But it is worth considering how an argument from explanatory superfluity might fare against the less extravagant construal I have suggested for the thought that secondary qualities genuinely characterize objects: not because the question is difficult or contentious, but because of the light it casts on how an explanatory test for reality – which is commonly thought to undermine the claims of values – should be applied.

A '*virtus dormitiva*' objection would tell against the idea that one might mount a satisfying explanation of an object's looking red on its being such as to look red. The weight of the explanation would fall through the disposition to its structural ground.[24] Still, however optimistic we are about the prospects for explaining colour experience on the basis of surface textures,[25] it would be obviously wrong to suppose that someone who gave such an explanation could in consistency deny that the object was such as to look red. The right explanatory test is not whether something pulls its own weight in the favoured explanation (it may fail to do so without thereby being explained away), but whether the explainer can consistently deny its reality.[26]

Given Mackie's view about secondary qualities, the thought that values fail an explanatory test for reality is implicit in a parallel that he commonly draws between them (see, for instance, *HMT*, pp. 51–2; *E*, pp. 19–20). It is nearer the surface in his 'argument from queerness' (*E*, pp. 38–42; pp. 76–9 this volume), and explicit in his citing 'patterns of objectification' to explain the distinctive phenomenology of value experience (*E*, pp. 42–6).[27] Now it is, if anything, even more obvious with values than with essentially phenomenal qualities that they cannot be credited with causal efficacy: values would not pull their weight in any explanation of value experience even remotely analogous to the standard explanations of primary-quality experience. But reflection on the case of secondary qualities has already opened a gap between that admission and any concession that values are not genuine aspects of reality. And the point is reinforced by a crucial disanalogy between values and secondary qualities. To press the analogy is to stress that evaluative 'attitudes,' or states of will, are like (say) colour experience in being unintelligible except as modifications of a sensibility like ours. The idea of value experience involves taking admiration, say; to represent its object as having a property which (although there in the object) is essentially subjective in much the same way as the property that an object is represented as having by an experience of redness – that is, understood adequately only in terms of the appropriate modification of human (or similar) sensibility. The disanalogy, now, is that a virtue (say) is conceived to be not merely such as to elicit the appropriate 'attitude' (as a colour is merely such as to cause the appropriate experiences), but rather such as to *merit* it. And this makes it doubtful whether merely causal explanations of value experience are relevant to the explanatory test, even to the extent that the question to ask is whether someone could consistently give such explanations while denying that the values involved are real. It looks as if we should be raising that question about explanations of a different kind.

For simplicity's sake, I shall elaborate this point in connection with something that is not a value, though it shares the crucial feature: namely danger or the fearful. On the face of it, this might seem a promising subject for a projectivist treatment (a treatment that appeals to what Hume called the mind's 'propensity to spread itself on external objects').[28] At any rate the response that, according to such a treatment, is projected into the world can be characterized, without phenomenological falsification, otherwise than in terms of seeming to find the supposed product of projection already there.[29] And it would be obviously grotesque to fancy that a case of fear might be explained as the upshot of a mechanical (or perhaps para-mechanical) process initiated by an instance of 'objective fearfulness.' But if what we are engaged in is an 'attempt to understand ourselves,'[30] then merely causal explanations of responses like fear will not be satisfying anyway.[31] What we want here is a style of explanation that makes sense of what is explained (in so far as sense can be made of it). This means that a technique for giving satisfying explanations of cases of fear – which would perhaps amount to a

satisfactory explanatory theory of danger, though the label is possibly too grand –
must allow for the possibility of criticism; we make/sense of fear by seeing it as a
response to objects that *merit* such a response, or as the intelligibly defective product
of a propensity towards responses that would be intelligible in that way.[32] For an
object to merit fear just is for it to be fearful. So explanations of fear that manifest
our capacity to understand ourselves in this region of our lives will simply not
cohere with the claim that reality contains nothing in the way of fearfulness.[33] Any
such claim would undermine the intelligibility that the explanations confer on our
responses.

The shared crucial feature suggests that this disarming of a supposed explanatory
argument for unreality should carry over to the case of values. There is, of course, a
striking disanalogy in the contentiousness that is typical of values; but I think it would
be a mistake to suppose that this spoils the point. In so far as we succeed in achieving
the sort of understanding of our responses that is in question, we do so on the basis of
preparedness to attribute, to at least some possible objects of the responses, properties
that would validate the responses. What the disanalogy makes especially clear is that
the explanations that preclude our denying the reality of the special properties that are
putatively discernible from some (broadly) evaluative point of view are themselves
constructed from that point of view. (We already had this in the case of the fearful, but
the point is brought home when the validation of the responses is controversial.)
However, the critical dimension of the explanations that we want means that there is
no question of just any actual response pulling itself up by its own bootstraps into
counting as an undistorted perception of the relevant special aspect of reality.[34] Indeed,
awareness that values are contentious tells against an unreflective contentment with the
current state of one's critical outlook, and in favour of a readiness to suppose that there
may be something to be learned from people with whom one's first inclination is to
disagree. The aspiration to understand oneself is an aspiration to change one's
responses, if that is necessary for them to become intelligible otherwise than as defective. But although a sensible person will never be confident that his evaluative outlook
is incapable of improvement, that need not stop him supposing, of some of his
evaluative responses, that their objects really do merit them. He will be able to back up
this supposition with explanations that show how the responses are well-placed; the
explanations will share the contentiousness of the values whose reality they certify, but
that should not stop him accepting the explanations any more than (what nobody
thinks) it should stop him endorsing the values.[35] There is perhaps an air of boot-
strapping about this. But if we restrict ourselves to explanations from a more external
standpoint, at which values are not in our field of view, we deprive ourselves of a kind
of intelligibility that we aspire to; and projectivists have given no reason whatever to
suppose that there would be anything better about whatever different kind of self-
understanding the restriction would permit.

5

It will be obvious how these considerations undermine the damaging effect of the primary-quality model. Shifting to a secondary-quality analogy renders irrelevant any worry about how something that is brutely *there* could nevertheless stand in an internal relation to some exercise of human sensibility. Values are not brutely there – not there independently of our sensibility – any more than colours are: though, as with colours, this does not stop us supposing that they are there independently of any particular apparent experience of them. As for the epistemology of value, the epistemology of danger is a good model. (Fearfulness is not a secondary quality, although the model is available only after the primary-quality model has been dislodged. A secondary-quality analogy for value experience gives out at certain points, no less than the primary-quality analogy that Mackie attacks.) To drop the primary-quality model in this case is to give up the idea that fearfulness itself, were it real, would need to be intelligible from a standpoint independent of the propensity to fear; the same must go for the relations of rational consequentiality in which fearfulness stands to more straightforward proper-ties of things.[36] Explanations of fear of the sort I envisaged would not only establish, from a different standpoint, that some of its objects are really fearful, but also make plain, case by case, what it is about them that makes them so; this should leave it quite unmysterious how a fear response rationally grounded in awareness (unproblematic, at least for present purposes) of these 'fearful-making characteristics' can be counted as being, or yielding, knowledge that one is confronted by an instance of real fearfulness.[37]

Simon Blackburn has written, on behalf of a projectivist sentimentalism in ethics, that 'we profit ... by realizing that a training of the feelings rather than a cultivation of a mysterious ability to spot the immutable fitnesses of things is the foundation of how to live.'[38] This picture of what an opponent of projectivism must hold is of a piece with Mackie's primary-quality model; it simply fails to fit the position I have described.[39] Perhaps with Aristotle's notion of practical wisdom in mind, one might ask why a train-ing of the feelings (as long as the notion of feeling is comprehensive enough) cannot *be* the cultivation of an ability – utterly unmysterious just because of its connections with feelings – to spot (if you like) the fitnesses of things; even 'immutable' may be all right, so long as it is not understood (as I take it Blackburn intends) to suggest a 'platonistic' conception of the fitnesses of things, which would reimport the characteristic ideas of the primary quality model.[40]

Mackie's response to this suggestion used to be, in effect, that it simply conceded his point.[41] Can a projectivist claim that the position I have outlined is at best a notational variant, perhaps an inferior notational variant, of his own position?

It would be inferior if, in eschewing the projectivist metaphysical framework, it obscured some important truth. But what truth would this be? It will not do at this point to answer 'The truth of projectivism.' I have disarmed the explanatory argument for the projectivist's thin conception of genuine reality. What remains is rhetoric expressing what amounts to a now unargued primary-quality model for genuine reality.[42] The picture that this suggests for value experience – objective (value-free) reality processed through a moulded subjectivity – is no less questionable than the picture of secondary-quality experience on which, in Mackie at any rate, it is explicitly modelled. In fact I should be inclined to argue that it is projectivism that is inferior. Deprived of the specious explanatory argument, projectivism has nothing to sustain its thin conception of reality (that on to which the projections are effected) but a contentiously substantial version of the correspondence theory of truth, with the associated picture of genuinely true judgment as something to which the judger makes no contribution at all.[43]

I do not want to argue this now. The point I want to make is that even if projectivism were not actually worse, metaphysically speaking, than the alternative I have described, it would be wrong to regard the issue between them as nothing but a question of metaphysical preference.[44] In the projectivist picture, having one's ethical or aesthetic responses rationally suited to their objects would be a matter of having the relevant processing mechanism functioning acceptably. Now projectivism can of course perfectly well accommodate the idea of assessing one's processing mechanism. But it pictures the mechanism as something that one can contemplate as an object in itself. It would be appropriate to say 'something one can step back from,' were it not for the fact that one needs to use the mechanism itself in assessing it; at any rate one is supposed to be able to step back from any naively realistic acceptance of the values that the first-level employment of the mechanism has one attribute to items in the world. How, then, are we to understand this pictured availability of the processing mechanism as an object for contemplation, separated off from the world of value? Is there any alternative to thinking of it as capable of being captured, at least in theory, by a set of principles for superimposing values on to a value-free reality? The upshot is that the search for an evaluative outlook that one can endorse as rational becomes, virtually irresistibly, a search for such a set of principles: a search for a *theory* of beauty or goodness. One comes to count 'intuitions' respectable only in so far as they can be validated by an approximation to that ideal.[45] (This is the shape that the attempt to objectivize subjectivity takes here.) I have a hunch that such efforts are misguided; not that we should rest content with an 'anything goes' irrationalism, but that we need a conception of rationality in evaluation that will cohere with the possibility that particular cases may stubbornly resist capture in any general net. Such a conception is straightforwardly available within the alternative to projectivism that I have described. I allowed that being able to explain cases of fear in the right way might amount to having a theory of danger, but there is no need to generalize that feature of the case; the explanatory capacity that certifies the special objects of an evaluative outlook as real, and certifies its responses to them as rational, would need to be exactly as creative and case-specific as the capacity to discern those objects itself. (It would be the same capacity: the picture of 'stepping back' does not fit here.)[46] I take it that my hunch poses a question of moral and aesthetic taste, which – like other questions of taste – should be capable of being argued about. The trouble with projectivism is that it threatens to bypass that argument, on the basis of a metaphysical picture whose purported justification falls well short of making it compulsory. We should not let the question seem to be settled by what stands revealed, in the absence of compelling argument, as a prejudice claiming the honour due to metaphysical good taste.

NOTES

1 See *E*, pp. 31–5. I shall also abbreviate references to the following other books by Mackie: *Problems from Locke* (Clarendon Press, Oxford, 1976: hereafter *PFL*); and *Hume's Moral Theory* (London: Routledge & Kegan Paul, 1980; hereafter *HMT*).

2 An inferior surrogate: it leads us to exaggerate the extent to which expressions of our sensitivity to values are signalled by the use of a special vocabulary. See my 'Aesthetic Value, Objectivity, and the Fabric of the World', in Eva Schaper, ed., *Pleasure, Preference, and Value* (Cambridge: Cambridge University Press, 1983), pp. 1–16, at pp. 1–2.

3 I am trying here to soften a sharpness of focus that Mackie introduces by stressing the notion of prescriptivity. Mackie's singleness of vision here has the perhaps unfortunate effect of discouraging a distinction such as David Wiggins has drawn between 'valuations' and 'directives or deliberative (or practical) judgments' (see 'Truth, Invention, and the Meaning of Life,' *Proceedings of the British Academy* 62 (1976): 331–78, at pp. 338–9). My topic here is really the former of these. (It may be that the distinction does not matter in the way that Wiggins suggests: see note 35 below.)

4 I do not believe that the 'quasi-realism' that Simon Blackburn has elaborated is a real alternative to this. (See p. 358 of his 'Truth, Realism, and the Regulation of Theory', in Peter A. French, Theodore E. Uehling, Jr. and Howard Wettstein, eds, *Midwest Studies in Philosophy V: Studies in Epistemology* (Minneapolis, MN: University of Minnesota Press, 1980), pp. 353–71.) In so far as the quasi-realist holds that the values, in his thought and speech about which he imitates the practices supposedly characteristic of realism, are *really* products of projecting 'attitudes' into the world, he must have a conception of genuine reality – that which the values lack and the things on to which they are projected have. And the phenomenological claim ought to be that *that* is what the appearances entice us to attribute to values.

5 *An Essay concerning Human Understanding*, II. viii. 10.

6 Being stung by a nettle is an actualization of a power in the nettle that conforms to Locke's description, but it seems wrong to regard it as a perception of that power; the experience lacks an intrinsically representational character which that would require. (It is implausible that looking red is intelligible independently of being red; combined with the account of secondary qualities that I am giving, this sets up a circle. But it is quite unclear that we ought to have the sort of analytic or definitional aspirations that would make the circle problematic. See Colin McGinn, *The Subjective View* (Oxford: Clarendon Press, 1983), pp. 6–8.)

7 See McGinn, op. cit., pp. 12–14.

8 Of course there is room for the concept of illusion, not only because the senses can mal-function but also because of the need for a modifier like my '(in certain circumstances),' in an account of what it is for something to have a secondary quality. (The latter has no counterpart with primary qualities.)

9 See the discussion of (one interpretation of the notion of) objectivity at pp. 77–8 of Gareth Evans, 'Things Without the Mind', in Zak van Straaten, ed., *Philosophical Subjects: Essays Presented to P. F. Strawson* (Oxford: Clarendon Press, 1980), pp. 76–116. Throughout the present section I am heavily indebted to this most important paper.

10 See *Essay*, II. viii. 15.

11 Cf. pp. 56–7 of P. F. Strawson, 'Perception and Its Objects', in G. F. Macdonald, ed., *Perception and Identity: Essays Presented to A. J. Ayer* (London: Macmillan, 1979), pp. 41–60.

12 This is a different way of formulating a point made by McGinn, op. cit., p. 121. Mackie's phrase 'the fabric of the world' belongs with the second sense of 'objective' but I think his arguments really address only the first. *Pace* p. 103 of A. W. Price, 'Varieties of Objectivity and Values,' *Proceedings of the Aristotelian Society* 82 (1982–3): 103–19, I do not think the phrase can be passed over as unhelpful, in favour of what the arguments do succeed in establishing, without missing something that Mackie wanted to say. (A gloss on 'objective' as 'there to be experienced' does not figure in Price's inventory, p. 104. It seems to be the obvious response to his challenge at pp. 118–19.)

13 I do not say it is correct: scepticism about this is very much in point. (See Nelson Goodman, *Languages of Art* (London: Oxford University Press, 1969), chap. 1.)

14 When resemblance is in play, it functions as a palliative to lack of veridicality, not as what veridicality consists in.

15 Intrinsic features of experience, functioning as vehicles for aspects of content, seem to be taken for granted in Mackie's discussion of Molyneux's problem (*PFL*, pp. 28–32). The slide from talk of content to talk that fits only bearers of content seems to happen also in Mackie's discussion of truth, in *Truth, Probability, and Paradox* (Oxford: Clarendon Press, 1973), with the idea that a formulation like 'A true statement is one such that the way things are is the way it represents things as being' makes truth consist in a relation of correspondence (rather than identity) between how things are and how things are represented as being; pp. 56–7 come too late to undo the damage done by the earlier talk of 'comparison,' e.g., at pp. 50, 51. (A subject matter for the talk that fits bearers is unproblematically available in this case; but Mackie does not mean to be discussing truth as a property of sentences or utterances.)

16 Indeed, this goes against the spirit of a passage about the word 'content' at *PFL*, p. 48. Mackie's failure to profit by his insight emerges particularly strikingly in his remarkable claim (*PFL*, p. 50) that the 'intentional object' conception of the content of experience yields an account of perception that is within the target area of 'the stock objections against an argument from an effect to a supposed cause of a type which is never directly observed.' (Part of the trouble here is a misconception of direct realism as a surely forlorn attempt to make perceptual knowledge unproblematic: *PFL*, p. 43.)

17 The phrases 'manifest image' and 'scientific image' are due to Wilfrid Sellars; see 'Philosophy and the Scientific Image of Man', in *Science, Perception and Reality* (London: Routledge & Kegan Paul, 1963).

18 This is the position of Strawson, op. cit. (and see also his 'Reply to Evans', in van Straaten, ed., op. cit., pp. 273–82). I am suggesting a diagnosis, to back up McGinn's complaint, op. cit., p. 124n.

19 Notice Strawson's sleight of hand with phrases like 'shapes-as-seen,' at p. 280 of 'Reply to Evans'. Strawson's understanding of what Evans is trying to say fails altogether to accommodate Evans's remark ('Things Without the Mind', p. 96) that 'to deny that ... primary properties are *sensory* is not at all to deny that they are *sensible* or *observable*'. Shapes as seen are *shapes* – that is, non-sensory properties; it is one thing to deny, as Evans does, that experience can furnish us with the concepts of such properties, but quite another to deny that experience can disclose instantiations of them to us.

20 Features of physiologically specified states are not to the point here. Such features are not apparent in experience; whereas the supposed features that I am concerned with would have to be aspects of what experience is like for us, in order to function intelligibly as carriers for aspects of the content that experience presents to us. There may be an inclination to ask why it should be any harder for a feature of experience to acquire an objective significance than it is for a word to do so. But the case of language affords no counterpart to the fact that the objective significance in the case we are concerned with is a matter of how things (e.g.) *look* to be; the special problem is how to stop that 'look' having the effect that a supposed intrinsic feature of experience get taken up into its own representational significance, thus ensuring that the significance is phenomenal and not primary.

21 See Thomas Nagel, 'Subjective and Objective', in *Mortal Questions* (Cambridge: Cambridge University Press, 1979), pp. 196–213.

22 Cf. Bernard Williams, *Descartes: The Project of Pure Enquiry* (Harmondsworth: Penguin, 1978), p. 295.

23 Although McGinn, op. cit., is not taken in by the idea that 'external' reality has only objective characteristics, I am not sure that he sufficiently avoids the picture that underlies that idea: see pp. 106–9. (This connects with a suspicion that at pp. 9–10 he partly succumbs to a temptation to objectivize the subjective properties of objects that he countenances: it is not as clear as he seems to suppose that, say, redness can be, so to speak, abstracted from the way things strike *us* by an appeal to relativity. His worry at pp. 132–6, that secondary quality experience may after all be phenomenologically misleading, seems to betray the influence of the idea of content-bearing intrinsic features of experience.)

24 See McGinn, op. cit., p. 14.

25 There are difficulties over how complete such explanations could aspire to be: see Price, op. cit., pp. 114–15, and my 'Aesthetic Value, Objectivity, and the Fabric of the World', op. cit., pp. 10–12.

26 Cf. pp. 206–8, especially p. 208, of David Wiggins, 'What Would Be a Substantial Theory of Truth?', in van Straaten, ed., op. cit., pp. 189–221. The test of whether the explanations in question are consistent with rejecting the item in contention is something that Wiggins once mooted, in the course of a continuing attempt to improve that formulation: I am indebted to discussion with him.

27 See also Simon Blackburn, 'Rule-Following and Moral Realism', in Steven Holtzman and Christopher Leich, eds, *Wittgenstein: To Follow a Rule* (London: Routledge & Kegan Paul, 1981), pp. 163–87 [Chapter 24, this volume]; and the first chapter of Gilbert Harman, *The Nature of Morality* (New York: Oxford University Press, 1977).

28 *A Treatise of Human Nature*, I. iii. 14. 'Projectivist' is Blackburn's useful label: see 'Rule-

Following and Moral Realism', op. cit., and 'Opinions and Chances', in D. H. Mellor, ed., *Prospects for Pragmatism* (Cambridge: Cambridge University Press, 1980), pp. 175–96.

29 At pp. 180–1 of 'Opinions and Chances', Blackburn suggests that a projectivist need not mind whether or not this is so; but I think he trades on a slide between 'can ... only be understood in terms of' and 'our best vocabulary for identifying' (which allows that there may be an admittedly inferior alternative).

30 The phrase is from p. 165 [p. 471, this volume] of Blackburn, 'Rule-Following and Moral Realism'.

31 I do not mean that satisfying explanations will not be causal. But they will not be *merely* causal.

32 I am assuming that we are not in the presence of a theory according to which no responses of the kind in question *could* be well-placed. That would have a quite unintended effect. (See *E*, p. 16.) Notice that it will not meet my point to suggest that calling a response 'well-placed' is to be understood only quasi-realistically. Explanatory indispensability is supposed to be the test for the *genuine* reality supposedly lacked by what warrants only quasi-realistic treatment.

33 Cf. Blackburn, 'Rule-Following and Moral Realism', op. cit., p. 164 [pp. 470–1, this volume].

34 This will be so even in a case in which there are no materials for constructing standards of criticism except actual responses: something that is not so with fearfulness, although given a not implausible holism it will be so with values.

35 I can see no reason why we should not regard the contentiousness as ineliminable. The effect of this would be to detach the explanatory test of reality from a requirement of convergence (cf. the passage by Wiggins cited in note 26 above). As far as I can see, this separation would be a good thing. It would enable resistance to projectivism to free itself, with a good conscience, of some unnecessary worries about relativism. It might also discourage a misconception of the appeal to Wittgenstein that comes naturally to such a position. (Blackburn, 'Rule-Following and Moral Realism', pp. 170–4 [pp. 475–8, this volume], reads into my 'Non-cognitivism and Rule-Following', in Holtzman and Leich, eds, op. cit., pp. 141–62 [Chapter 23, this volume], an interpretation of Wittgenstein as, in effect, making truth a matter of consensus, and has no difficulty in arguing that this will not make room for hard cases: but the interpretation is not mine.) With the requirement of convergence dropped, or at least radically relativized to a point of view, the question of the claim to truth of directives may come closer to the question of the truth status of evaluations than Wiggins suggests, at least in 'Truth, Invention, and the Meaning of Life', op. cit.

36 Mackie's question (*E*, p. 41 [p. 78, this volume]) 'Just what *in the world* is signified by this "because"?' involves a tendentious notion of 'the world'.

37 See Price, op. cit., pp. 106–7, 115.

38 'Rule-Following and Moral Realism', p. 186 [p. 492, this volume].

39 Blackburn's realist evades the explanatory burdens that sentimentalism discharges, by making the world rich (cf. p. 181) and then picturing it as simply setting its print on us. Cf. *E*, p. 22: 'If there were something in the fabric of the world that validated certain kinds of concern, then it would be possible to acquire these merely by finding something out, by letting one's thinking be controlled by how things were.' This saddles an opponent of projectivism with a picture of awareness of value as an exercise of pure receptivity, preventing him from deriving any profit from an analogy with secondary-quality perception.

40 On 'platonism', see my 'Non-Cognitivism and Rule-Following', op. cit., at pp. 156–7 [pp. 464–5, this volume]. On Aristotle, see M. F. Burnyeat, 'Aristotle on Learning To Be Good', in

Amelie O. Rorty, ed., *Essays on Aristotle's Ethics* (Berkeley, CA: University of California Press, Los Angeles, London, 1980), pp. 69–92.

41 Price, op. cit., p. 107, cites Mackie's response to one of my contributions to the 1978 seminar (see Acknowledgment below).

42 We must not let the confusion between the two notions of objectivity distinguished in § 3 above seem to support this conception of reality.

43 Blackburn uses the correspondence theorist's pictures for rhetorical effect, but he is properly sceptical about whether this sort of realism makes sense (see 'Truth, Realism, and the Regulation of Theory', op. cit.). His idea is that the explanatory argument makes a counterpart to its metaphysical favouritism safely available to a projectivist about values in particular. Deprived of the explanatory argument this projectivism should simply wither away. (See 'Rule-Following and Moral Realism', p. 165 [pp. 471–2, this volume]. Of course I am not saying that the thin conception of reality that Blackburn's projectivism needs is unattainable, in the sense of being unformulable. What we lack is reasons of a respectable kind to recognize it as a complete conception of *reality*.)

44 Something like this seems to be suggested by Price, op. cit., pp. 107–8.

45 It is hard to see how a rational *inventing* of values could take a more piecemeal form.

46 Why do I suggest that a particularistic conception of evaluative rationality is unavailable to a projectivist? (See Blackburn, 'Rule-Following and Moral Realism', pp. 167–70 [pp. 472–5, this volume].) In the terms of that discussion, the point is that (with no good explanatory argument for his metaphysical favouritism) a projectivist has no alternative to being 'a *real* realist' about the world on which he thinks values are superimposed. He cannot stop this from generating a quite un-Wittgensteinian picture of what *really* going on in the same way would be; which means that *he* cannot appeal to Wittgenstein in order to avert, as Blackburn puts it, 'the threat which shapelessness poses to a respectable notion of consistency' (p. 169 [p. 475, this volume]). So, at any rate, I meant to argue in my 'Non-Cognitivism and Rule-Following', to which Blackburn's paper is a reply. Blackburn thinks his projectivism is untouched by the argument, because he thinks he can sustain its metaphysical favouritism without appealing to '*real* realism', on the basis of the explanatory argument. But I have argued that this is an illusion. (At p. 181 [pp. 483–4, this volume], Blackburn writes: 'Of course, it is true that our reactions are "simply felt" and, in a sense, not rationally explicable.' He thinks he can comfortably say this because our conception of reason will go along with the quasi-realist truth that his projectivism confers on some evaluations. But how can one restrain the metaphysical favouritism that a projectivist must show from generating some such thought as 'This is not *real* reason'? If that *is* allowed to happen, a remark like the one I have quoted will merely threaten – like an ordinary nihilism – to dislodge us from our ethical and aesthetic convictions.)

This paper grew out of my contributions to a seminar on J. L. Mackie's *Ethics: Inventing Right and Wrong* (Harmondsworth, Middlesex, Penguin: 1977: I refer to this as *E*) which I had the privilege of sharing with Mackie and R. M. Hare in 1978. I do not believe that John Mackie would have found it strange that I should pay tribute to a sadly missed colleague by continuing a strenuous disagreement with him.

13

PATHETIC ETHICS

David Sosa

The battle for territory between subjectivist and objectivist ideologies is ultimately global war: truth itself is under siege.[1] One theater in which the fighting has been elegantly fierce is ethics. But it is not always clear for whom or what the troops are fighting. If your flag is just realism, for example, you could be Swiss about the engagement. But realists are reasonably suspicious of the antirealist *tendencies* of subjectivism (however this is ultimately defined) – it introduces a significant discontinuity between ethics and, for example, physics (which can be taken as paradigmatically *real*). A different realist may worry rather that objectivity in ethics will commit us to "queer" properties and lead ultimately to an error theory or to eliminativism. So realists enter the fray, on either side.

So-called sensibility theories[2] seek to negotiate a cease-fire. They grow with the thought that ethics must have *something* important to do with agents and their sensibilities. And they develop on analogy with views of secondary qualities, proposing a variety of analytic connections between moral properties and subjective states. What the proposals have in common is that in them the instantiation of ethical properties is viewed as not entirely independent of human psychological reactions. Still, such instantiation, when it occurs, is there to be cognized. There is nothing queer about ethical properties: they are intelligibly rooted in ethical thought or feeling. An ethical reaction, however, is not itself merely the expression of preference or the issuance of an imperative. It is an essentially cognitive response to ethical properties.

I think there is something importantly wrong with sensibility theories. Ultimately, their flaw is that they are, in a word, pathetic.[3] One way to bring this out is to review how these theories arise in response to John Mackie's error theory. Part of the problem, it seems to me, is that Mackie has been rejected for the wrong reasons. Though I too find his view problematic, sensibility theorists have been misled by an under appreciation of Mackie. Reviewing his contribution, we better understand and more effectively resist the appeal of the proffered alternative.

Explaining the persistence of our allegedly erroneous commitment to objectivity in ethics, Mackie appeals to Hume's remark about the mind's "propensity to spread itself on external objects."[4] Compare the "pathetic fallacy": "If a fungus, say, fills us with disgust, we may be inclined to ascribe to the fungus itself a non-natural quality of foulness" (*Ethics*, 42).[5] This inclination can lead us into error. The features of the object that produce our disgust in no way *resemble* that experience. They are simply natural qualities. The relevant features (or even their conjunction) do not, it seems, have "to-be-disgusted-by" built in intrinsically. And moreover, our actually being disgusted is a product of our own sensibility as much as it is a result of the natural qualities of the fungus that lead to our disgust. Here the idea of an illegitimate spreading of our own feelings onto the external object is clear. The question is whether ethical properties are another case in point.

To preview, our dialectic will proceed as follows. First, we review Mackie's seminal metaethical statement. Some of McDowell's early development of sensibility theory, to which we proceed, was explicitly in response to Mackie. Where Mackie saw ordinary morality committed to an error, in virtue of its commitment to objectivity, McDowell finds ordinary morality innocent, in spite of recognizing that commitment. The question is whether the commitment to objectivity stands a chance of being satisfied. Mackie does not think so; and given *Mackie's* interpretation of the commitment, McDowell would agree that it is unsatisfiable. But according to McDowell, that interpretation is optional. Properly understood, the commitment to objectivity implicit in commonsense moral discourse and practice *can* be satisfied. This requires a reconceptualization of the variety of objectivity in play. As we'll see, David Wiggins too develops, apparently simultaneously, a position similar to McDowell's.

But their position suffers at least two important disadvantages. First, the sensibility theories offered are circular. They appeal to the very moral notions under analysis. Does the circularity vitiate the account? I will argue that it does. Second, Mackie's interpretation of commonsense morality's commitment to objectivity is the more plausible. Accordingly, unless moral value is after all objective in Mackie's sense, we appear to be forced to an error theory.

Since the late 1980s there has been a second wave of the *kind* of theory McDowell and Wiggins proposed. Crispin Wright and Mark Johnston,[6] sensitive to criticisms of McDowell made by Simon Blackburn,[7] have developed versions of sensibility theory that take seriously the analogy with secondary qualities but qualify it in order to avoid difficulties of the McDowell/Wiggins view. We will see, however, that these new versions also come with their own new problems.

I propose, then, to challenge the rejection of the variety of objectivity (commitment to which) Mackie feared would lead inevitably to an error theory. Because sensibility theories cannot effect the desired truce, a view of moral value according to which it is in relevant respects more like a *primary* quality merits further development. Admittedly I do not develop a positive proposal as an alternative.[8] But if such a view is ultimately incoherent, an error theory, or skepticism, and some post hoc revisionism, are our lot.

The point of the present chapter is to reintroduce the possibility of a more robust objectivity in ethics by challenging an increasingly popular class of views that reject it. Sensibility theories proceed from an implausible interpretation of moral phenomenology and appear unpromising if not empty. In their understanding of morality, they give the wrong role to human subjective response.

1 PROBLEMS FROM MACKIE

A. A fertile idea

Although the locus classicus may be Hume,[9] contemporary sensibility theories develop in response to Mackie. Mackie begins *Ethics: Inventing Right and Wrong* with a "bald statement of the thesis" of his Chapter 1: "There are no objective values" (*Ethics*, 15). And he articulates his basic anti-objectivist metaethical claim in relation to moral reasoning: made fully explicit, moral reasoning must contain as input something that cannot be objectively validated, something whose truth, validity, or authority "is constituted by our choosing or deciding to think in a certain way" (*Ethics*, 30).

Pay close attention to Mackie's drawing (*Ethics*, 19) of a close "analogy with colours." He draws the analogy with a specific purpose in mind: to clarify the distinction between conceptual and factual analysis in ethics. But he found the productive vein tapped earlier by Hume.

Boyle and Locke claimed that "colours as they occur in material things consist simply in patterns of arrangement and movement of minute particles on the surfaces of objects, which ... enable these objects to produce colour sensations in us; but that colours *as we see them* do not literally belong to the surfaces of material things" (cited in *Ethics*, 18–19; emphasis added). Mackie makes the point that whether Locke and Boyle were right cannot be settled merely by linguistic inquiry. Whatever the nature of our color claims, there is a residual question about the nature of the colors themselves. The development of color science and more detailed knowledge about the mechanism of color vision has had a significant impact on the question. Beside the specific use to which he puts it, Mackie's analogy also provides a useful model by which to understand him. His position with respect to moral value is akin to Locke's on color. Ethical value, *as we understand it* (viz. objectively), does not literally belong to anything. What ethical value things have is not as we ordinarily understand it.

B. Queerness

Mackie deploys two arguments for the view that there are no objective values. The first is a familiar argument from relativity. But there is also a second, the argument from queerness. The substance of this objection was already, I would argue, a part of his rejection of any "naturalist descriptivist" position. Mackie's idea is that a naturalist can hold that moral claims are committed to *something* objective, some natural descriptive facts, but not that they are committed to objective value. Such a view misses, Mackie claims, the categorical imperative force of moral assertion: if moral claims assert only that some natural state of affairs obtains, then no prescription is forthcoming except relative to subjective desires, preferences, and so forth. This presupposes, what he now makes explicit in the argument from queerness, that no natural entity or feature can be intrinsically prescriptive. Objective values, if there were any, would be "utterly different from anything else in the universe" (*Ethics*, 38 [p. 77, this volume]).

Mackie cannot understand the idea of an end having "to-be-pursuedness" built in, independently of any subjective desire or preference. Hume famously argued that reason (we can generalize to all of what we might call the "cognitive attitudes") cannot motivate the will. Only desires (generalize to the "conative attitudes") have that force. To suppose that some objects of cognition can, after all, influence the will independently of any conation is to postulate something "of quite a different order from anything else with which we are acquainted" (*Ethics*, 40 [p. 77, this volume]). It is hard to see how such a thing, a categorically prescriptive characteristic, could be related to the natural. According to Mackie, and before him Moore, there must be *some* supervenience of the ethical on the natural. But if value is objective, what could that relation be?

So far I have emphasized only the metaphysical edge of the argument from queerness. But the argument has an epistemological edge too. In accord with their being metaphysically extraordinary, objective values would apparently require an extraordinary epistemology. If we are aware of moral value, then, it seems, it is not in the mundane way by which we become aware of anything else. According to Mackie, our ordinary forms of perception cannot make us aware of the "authoritative prescriptivity" (*Ethics*, 39) of value, so they cannot make us aware of value. We need some special sort of intuition; this need is a disadvantage of the view that espouses objective moral value.

Worse, "[i]t is not even sufficient to postulate a faculty which 'sees' the wrongness: something must be postulated which can see at once the natural features that constitute the cruelty, and the wrongness, and the mysterious consequential link between the two" (*Ethics*, 41 [p. 78, this volume]). I must confess, however, that I don't know why Mackie says this. Why must we postulate such a super-faculty? Why wouldn't a faculty that can appreciate categorical prescriptivity when it sees it suffice? The faculty that sees the natural features that constitute the cruelty could just be our standard sensory capacity. Moral sense could be sensitivity to the imperatives that might arise. And it may be philosophical reflection that's needed to understand the categorical link between the natural features and the wrongness. Perhaps most moral agents would never "see" the "mysterious link." Why should they?

C. A slide to avoid

There is the threat of a slide in the above reasoning concerning queerness. I'm not sure that Mackie makes it. But I want to raise the issue if only to be able to refer back to it later. No one denies that moral claims involve an element of *intensionality*. From claims like "it is (would be) wrong for S to do A" or "S should not do A," it follows neither that S does A, nor that S fails to do A. Similarly from the fact, if it were one, that feature F has "to-be-pursuedness" built in, it does not follow that F is in fact pursued. All that follows is that F is *to be* pursued. The slide to avoid (at least without further argument) is *from* a kind of intensionality, *out of* it. Consider the following quotation from Mackie. "An objective good would be sought by anyone who was acquainted with it, not because of any contingent fact that this person, or every person, is so constituted that he desires this end, but just because the end has to-be-pursuedness somehow built into it" (*Ethics*, 40 [p. 78, this volume]). This seems to make the slide. Whether an objective good *would* be sought by anyone who was acquainted with it need *not* be independent of that person's desires, preferences, and so forth. What is independent of that person's subjectivity is its "to be" pursuedness. The imperative, the categorical demand (the satisfaction of which cannot be inferred), that the subject pursue the good obtains whatever the agent's attitudes toward it. But whether the agent actually seeks the good or would seek the good depends on what she wants or prefers or would want or prefer.

If objective value is queer, it is not because its existence would entail the existence of motivations that are independent of conative attitudes. The existence of objective value would, given the considerations that have been adduced so far, entail the existence only of *demands for* motivation (indeed, perhaps for something else: for action) – demands that obtain independently of the conative attitudes. Watch the scopes: (i) demand for (motivation that is independent of conative attitudes), (ii) (demand for motivation) that is independent of conative attitudes. It's the demand that's independent, not the motivation.

Now it may be that Mackie finds unintelligible even the existence of a *demand* for action that is independent of conative attitudes. But insofar as his view inherits the plausibility of Hume's observation that beliefs cannot, by themselves, motivate, the view is not entitled to reject the existence of objective moral value. Perhaps motivation is always, even in some sense is necessarily, a product of affective attitudes. But that doesn't entail that nothing could *call* for a motivation or for a course of action independently of any conative attitude. The Humean observation simply does not apply directly. And the notion of a *demand* here is not extravagant: it is just a reflex of the categorical imperative force of moral assertion – a point Mackie himself stresses. That the imperative force is categorical is tantamount to its desire independence; that the categorical is an imperative is tantamount to its making a demand. Once we are clear about what would *not* follow from the postulation of objective moral values, however (no spooky desire-independent motivations), is it still so clear that they are queer? The issue will re-arise significantly below toward the end of this chapter.

2 MCDOWELL'S SECONDARY QUALITIES

A. Problematic

McDowell begins his "Values and Secondary Qualities" (Chapter 12, this volume, cited hereafter as VSQ)[10] by trying to reintroduce us to a problematic: Mackie insisted, and McDowell agrees, that ordinary evaluative thought "presents itself as a matter of" sensitivity to aspects of the world. Noncognitivists, for whom moral judgments are not truth evaluable, cannot thereby capture the nature of moral *experience*. The experience of making a moral judgment is as of making a truth-evaluable judgment – it is as of attributing a real (moral) property. Noncognitivists do not, admittedly, base their view on any phenomenology; their idea is that the truth evaluable cannot, by itself, be motivational. McDowell now claims that this noncognitivist view (the truth-evaluable can't be motivational), combined with Mackie's view about how value "presents itself," makes the phenomenology of evaluation involve a "mere incoherence." Why?

Evaluative thought would be "presenting itself" as what it cannot possibly be. It would be presenting itself as *evaluative* and hence necessarily motivational; but it would also be presenting itself as truth evaluable. And the noncognitivist view is that nothing could be both. Mackie sees that some kinds of truth-evaluable claims *can*, after all, be motivational. Only claims of "objective" fact cannot be. According to McDowell, this insight (that some instances of the truth evaluable *can* be motivational) "clears away the only obstacle to accepting [Mackie's] phenomenological claim" (VSQ, p. 110 [p. 225, this volume]) by removing the implication that the phenomenology of evaluation [necessarily] involves an incoherence. Noncognitivism must now be seen, says McDowell, as offering a *correction* to the phenomenology: it is misleading of evaluative thought to present itself as sensitivity to aspects of the world. In fact, evaluative thought is a matter of *expression*. And so it should present itself that way. We should attempt to alter the phenomenology accordingly. Finally, according to McDowell, "In Mackie's view, the correction is called for" (VSQ, p. 110 [p. 225, this volume]).

A problem with McDowell's analysis is that Mackie need not call for a *noncognitivist* correction. It is a different correction to the phenomenology of evaluation, one that has not yet been so much as implicated by McDowell's discussion, that Mackie's view requires. What needs fixing is just our *objectifying* tendency. Moreover, McDowell's putting the point by referring to Mackie's *removal* of an incoherence in the phenomenology of evaluation may be obfuscatory. Mackie's own view of unreconstructed moral phenomenology incorporates the incoherence. According to Mackie too, ordinary evaluative thought presents itself as what it cannot possibly be. It presents itself as a matter of sensitivity to objective aspects of the world. And Mackie admits that claims of objective fact cannot be motivational. The correction called for by Mackie is simply the removal of the objectifying tendency: a recognition that moral value is ultimately *invented* and is not built in to the fabric of the world.

McDowell will suggest that Mackie attributes an unmerited plausibility to the thesis that the phenomenology of value needs correcting. The reason for Mackie's mistake, according to McDowell, is a "false picture of what one is committed to if one resists" (VSQ, p. 110 [p. 225, this volume]) the thesis. According to McDowell, we can in a way agree with Mackie about the phenomenology while rejecting the error theory: the phenomenology, in representing the evaluative as objective, need not be committing an error.

B. A false picture

It is thus agreed that evaluative judgment appears to be an exercise of sensitivity to aspects of the world. Assuming we accept that appearance, what is the nature of this sensitivity? According to McDowell, a perceptual "model" is "virtually irresistible" (VSQ, p. 110 [p. 225, this volume]). But to what does that model commit us? Mackie implicitly held that the model is perceptual awareness of *primary* qualities. This, according to McDowell, stacks the deck in favor of Mackie's error theory – this is the crux of the allegedly "false picture of what one is committed to if one resists" Mackie's view.

Following Locke, Mackie takes secondary-quality perception, untutored, to involve a projective error. According to McDowell, Locke and Mackie hold that "we are prone to conceive secondary-quality experience in a way that would be appropriate for experience of primary qualities" (VSQ, p. 111 [p. 226, this volume]). But McDowell is at least misleading here. The error that Locke and now Mackie point to is not in our "conception of secondary-quality experience." Until Locke, we probably had nothing so robust as a *conception* of secondary-quality experience. Even now most secondary-quality perceivers probably have no distinct conception of secondary-quality experience. What we do have is the phenomenology of secondary-quality experiences. We have the experiences; and they involve a phenomenology. And according to Locke, that phenomenology is misleadingly indistinct from the phenomenology of primary-quality experience.

When we see the color of an object, the experience is relevantly akin to seeing the object's shape. In each case there is the sense that the experience is a response to a feature of the object that the object has independently of that or any other similar experience – a feature the experience *resembles* but in no way *constitutes*. In the case of primary-quality experience, that sense is correct. Not so for secondary-quality experience. In any case, it seems, McDowell finds this conception of secondary-quality experience "seriously mistaken." That is, apparently, McDowell thinks it is wrong to suppose that, untutored, the phenomenology of primary- and secondary-quality experience is similar in the way Locke and Mackie do.

C. Self-consciously-secondary-quality experience

"A secondary quality is a property the ascription of which to an object is not adequately understood except as true, if it is true, in virtue of the object's disposition to present a certain sort of perceptual appearance" (VSQ, p. 111 [p. 226, this volume]). This incorporates an ambiguity: what variety of *understanding* is in question? If McDowell meant only that the (philosophical) fact of the matter is that secondary qualities are dispositions to produce certain sorts of perceptual experience, then there need be no disagreement with Locke and Mackie. Mackie, you recall, favors a correction to our phenomenology. Untutored, it involves a projective error; but when we discover that objects have no quality that resembles our untutored experience thereof, then we can correct our experience. McDowell: "a predication *understood* only in [terms of some microscopic textural property of the object's surface] – not in terms of how the object would look – would not be an ascription of a secondary quality" (VSQ, p. 112 [p. 227, this volume] emphasis added). Again, what is the nature of the understanding in question?

McDowell has an answer. The understanding is phenomenological. According to McDowell, the ascription or predication of a secondary quality presents itself as the predication of a property that is essentially a matter of being disposed to look a certain way. "What would one expect it to be like to experience something's being such as to look red, if not to experience the thing in question (in the right circumstances) as looking, precisely, red?" (VSQ, p. 112 [p. 227, this volume]). In other words, our experiences of things' looking red *are* experiences of things' being such as to look red. This is a troubling feature of McDowell's view.

For my part, I would expect the experience of something's being such as to look red (if I could possibly have such an experience, about which I remain unsure) to be quite different from the experience of something's looking red. For example, couldn't a color-blind person, who in one good sense cannot experience anything as looking red, still experience some things as being such as to look red? Maybe he has some reliable way of distinguishing red objects. And (switching to different sense modalities) experiencing the *smell* of a fresh lime might serve better than any tasting as the experience of something's being *such as* to *taste* tart. So McDowell may illegitimately eliminate an important phenomenological distinction in his attempt to introduce another.

The phenomenological distinction he is trying to introduce is between secondary-quality experience and primary-quality experience. In Mackie's Lockean view, naive perceptual consciousness stands accused of (mis)taking secondary qualities for primary qualities. We have secondary-quality ideas that are phenomenologically indistinguishable, in respect of primacy, from primary-quality ideas: but while primary-quality ideas resemble their objects, secondary-quality ideas do not. McDowell finds this view not only wrong but incoherent. According to him the view requires two things:

> First, that colours figure in perceptual experience neutrally, so to speak, rather than as essentially phenomenal qualities of objects, qualities that could not be adequately *conceived* except in terms of how their possessors would look; and second, that we command a concept of resemblance that would enable us to construct notions of possible primary qualities out of the idea of resemblance to such neutral elements of experience.
>
> (VSQ, p. 113 [p. 227, this volume] emphasis added)

As we've seen, he denies that the first condition is satisfied. (Notice the switch to the terminology of "conception" from that of "understanding.") But at this point he focuses on the second condition. He finds it "quite unclear" (VSQ, p. 113 [p. 228, this volume]) what sense we could make of a notion of resemblance to redness-as-it-figures-in-our-experience other than in phenomenological respects. If the notion of resemblance is analyzed in phenomenological respects, then we have no conception of the possible primary qualities other than in terms of how they would look; redness as it figures in our experience would prove to be "stubbornly phenomenal." For McDowell, the property that an object is represented as having, already in secondary-quality *experience*, is "distinctively phenomenal."

Claiming to find something unclear, even quite unclear, is insufficient argument. The concept of resemblance that would enable us to construct a notion of (what is in fact a secondary quality but is) a possible primary quality from "neutral" elements of experience is just that notion of resemblance involved in the claim that primary-quality ideas resemble their objects. Perhaps this notion needs further elucidation; but it has not been shown incoherent. Secondary qualities are supposed to resemble our ideas in just the way primary qualities actually do resemble our ideas. In both cases the property figures in experience neutrally, in the sense that it does *not* (*contra* McDowell) present itself as essentially subjective. In both cases the phenomenology is as of a property that *resembles* the experience. And, so far as I can tell, there is no incoherence in this prephilosophical conception of secondary-quality experience. According to Locke and Mackie, our phenomenology, does, however, turn out to have been misleading: as a matter of fact (but not simply as a matter of logic), there are no properties of objects that resemble our ideas of secondary qualities (in the sense in which there *are* properties of objects that resemble our ideas of primary qualities).

McDowell thinks that "no notion of resemblance could get us from an *essentially* experiential state of affairs to the concept of a feature of objects intelligible otherwise than in terms of how its possessors would strike us" (VSQ, p. 115 [p. 229, this volume] emphasis added). I'm not sure what (other than possibly begging a question) the "essentially" is doing in this claim. If it is just redundant, if all experiential states are essentially experiential, then it may be innocent. But if it is supposed to somehow make the resemblance impossible, then it begs the question. Redness-as-it-figures-in-experience is an experiential property; perhaps it is even essentially experiential. And the nature of the resemblance claimed is a matter for investigation. But why *can't* something that is essentially experiential resemble something that is not (other than in respect of subjectivity)? This is not addressed.

It is instructive that McDowell notes, in passing, that a version of this point "tells ... against the Lockean conception of *shapes*" (VSQ, p. 115 [p. 229, this volume] emphasis added). So McDowell would apparently reject the use of resemblance altogether. He says that "[e]xplaining 'ideas' as 'intentional objects' should direct our attention to the relation between how things are and how an experience represents them as being – in fact identity, not resemblance" (VSQ, p. 114 [p. 228, this volume]). He wants properties of objects to be the very elements of experience. It is not that we have subjective phenomena that *resemble* (except in the limiting sense of identity) the properties that are their objects; no, our experiences are simply constituted by properties that ordinary objects can instantiate. At least this seems to be the view McDowell is bruiting.

This contrasts with an alternative "picture": "a confronted 'external' reality, conceived as having only an objective nature, is processed through a structured 'subjectivity,' conceived in [an] objectivistic manner" (VSQ, p. 117 [p. 231, this volume]). The objectivistic conception in question is supposed to consist in taking phenomenological representation to be a matter of experience being constituted by intrinsically representational elements. Redness-in-experience, in virtue of its intrinsic nature, represents redness itself.

It thus becomes clearer that it's nothing particular about its account of *secondary*-quality experience that inclines McDowell to reject this picture. What he means to suggest (unsuccessfully, I think, to this point), is that this picture threatens to "cut us off" from even the *primary* qualities of the objects we perceive (VSQ, p. 117 [p. 231, this volume]). Primary-quality experience too is essentially subjective; its elements can no more *resemble* their objects, if these are to be fully *objective*, than can the elements of secondary-quality experience.

It is not easy, however, to view McDowell's recommendation as a real alternative. Although the elements of experience, because they are essentially subjective, allegedly cannot *resemble* what is objective, they can nevertheless be *identical* to what is not essentially subjective. Primary-quality experience is partly constituted by not-exclusively-phenomenal properties. The constitution of secondary-quality experience, by contrast, is by phenomenal properties. But this seems to undermine the earlier argument: if there is no problem with not-essentially-phenomenal properties *constituting* subjective experience, there should be still less of a problem about the elements of subjective experience *resembling* not-essentially-phenomenal properties.

250

McDowell's opponent may believe that experience is constituted by intrinsically representational elements. It is another step, though one we may well want to take, to hold that experience is constituted by *essentially* representational elements. Not everything intrinsic is essential. The target view is, perhaps, that the elements of experience are "individuated" by their representational character. What it is to be one of these elements is just to represent as it does; and again, they represent as they do in virtue of what they are intrinsically like. Experience is thus supposed, by McDowell's opponents, to be intrinsically representational, essentially representational, and essentially phenomenological – *what it is* amounts to *what it is like to have it*. If experience is both essentially representational and essentially phenomenological, then it must be that its representational character just *is* what it is like to have it.

McDowell rejects this view because he finds it "hard to see how a difference in respect of objectivity [between primary and secondary qualities] could show up in their representational significance" (VSQ, p. 115 [p. 229, this volume]). But why should it show up *there*? What's the argument for the idea that perceptual experience must disclose the *nature* of its objects? Why can't reasoning, philosophical analysis, and even scientific theorizing all be necessary – perception providing only some input to the question and even some-times providing misleading input, input that must be corrected by the other epistemic faculties? That the situation is otherwise appears simply to be asserted.

This is a general problem with the position McDowell is trying to develop. It is as if everything we might come to know about some objective matters is already present in a corresponding experience. We can *perceive* natures. Phenomenology discloses essences. This is deeply problematic. Though McDowell calls it a "gratuitous slur on perceptual 'common sense' to accuse it of [what he considers] a wildly problematic understanding of itself" (VSQ, p. 113 [p. 228, this volume]), the fact is that perception, at least, has no *understanding* of itself at all. Common sense does have a (rather superficial and subject to correction) understanding of perception: in some cases experience is misleading. Sometimes the properties of objects are not exactly as they seemed; and sometimes, perhaps, there really aren't any such properties at all (and the line between these two cases is notoriously difficult to draw). Although the discovery that perception has misled us can result from additional experience, the contents of the original experience may have been simply erroneous.

When we look at a color picture in the newspaper, we have the experience as of a fully "dissectably" colored area. That experience is misleading. Look closer, with a magnifying glass for example, and you discover that the color of the area is not fully dissectable. Not every part of the area has the color that the area as a whole appears from a distance to have. The ordinary phenomenology represents the area as having a uniformly dissectable color, as being such that each sub-area has the same color as the whole. Does this indicate some wildly problematic understanding of itself by perceptual common sense? No. It indicates a kind of illusion we are subject to in experience.

251

Secondary-quality experience is supposed to be a similar phenomenon (the analogy is quite apt). We are under the illusion that the object has a property that resembles our experience (in the way primary qualities actually often do resemble our experiences). As a matter of fact, the property of the object which our experience is *of* (and this needs to be explicated – though McDowell does not explicitly raise a problem here) does not resemble it.

D. Reality

In § 4 of "Values and Secondary Qualities," McDowell challenges Mackie's reason for rejecting the objectivity of secondary qualities. Of course, given McDowell's recommended revision of our conception of secondary qualities, Mackie's skeptical reasoning would have to apply in a different way, to take account of the "less extravagant construal [McDowell has] suggested for the thought that secondary qualities genuinely characterize objects" (VSQ, p. 117 [p. 231, this volume]) – less extravagant because it is no longer required, for objectivity, to be independent of human sensibility in general. Objectivity is now understood simply as a matter of being there to be experienced, an aspect of the world rather than a figment of the experience supposed to be *of* it, a property genuinely possessed by objects that confront us. But all this is compatible with some of these properties having an essentially phenomenal character in the sense that experiencing them is necessarily an experience as of something's being disposed to present a certain sort of perceptual appearance.

The skeptical argument McDowell attributes to Mackie appeals to explanatory idleness. We don't need to affirm that an object actually has any property resembling what it is taken in experience to have in order to explain that experience. I'm not sure this really is Mackie's argument, at least not in *Ethics*. It does not seem to me to be near the surface in the argument from queerness, as McDowell suggests (VSQ, p. 118 [p. 231, this volume]). In any case, McDowell points out a weakness in the argument: "the right explanatory test is not whether something pulls its own weight in the favoured explanation … but whether the explainer can consistently deny its reality" (VSQ, p. 118 [p. 231, this volume]). The fact that a property does not appear in the best explanation of a phenomenon does not suffice to impugn its reality; it must be the case, at least, that accepting the best explanation is consistent with denying its existence. The existence of many properties that do not *appear in* the best explanation may still be *implied by* the properties that do appear. So even if a property is explanatorily idle, it may still be objectively real, so long as it is implied by the best explanation of corresponding phenomena.

Still, McDowell does think there is after all an important disanalogy between the case of secondary qualities and the case of values. Although these features (secondary qualities and values) are said to be alike in that experiences of them are unintelligible except as experiences as of essentially subjective properties – except as experiences as of properties that can be "understood adequately only in terms of the appropriate modification of human (or similar) sensibility" (VSQ, p. 118 [p. 231, this volume]) – they are also distinct in that value experiences are also experiences as of properties that *merit* the appropriate sensible reaction. This introduces a significant new element into the issue.

McDowell attempts to "elaborate" this point in connection with "danger or the fearful." Setting aside the obvious difference between danger and the fearful, let's focus on the fearful. Sometimes, when we are experiencing fear, we also have the sense that the situation merits it: The situation *is* fearful, and as a justifiable result, we are afraid. (There are also cases, which we can ignore, of diffuse but recalcitrant anxiety accompanied by the depressing sense that the situation does not merit it.) So the fearful is like the good in this sense. And though it may be coherent to suppose that the fearful is best understood as a property of situations that is not independent of human sensibility – that what is fearful is so in virtue of being such as to produce fear in subjects like us – there is the question of how to make appropriate room for the possibility of *criticism*. Our experiencing a situation as *to be feared* appears to be subject to rational revision. We might, while continuing to be afraid, come to think that in fact there is nothing to fear. We may come to feel that our fear is misplaced. How to make room for rational disagreement about what is in fact fearful?

Recall the pathetic fallacy. Is the disgusting like the fearful? Do we make sense of disgust by "seeing it as a response to objects that *merit* such a response, or as the intelligibly defective product of a propensity towards responses that would be intelligible in that way" (VSQ, p. 119 [p. 233, this volume])? Presumably not. Unlike the fearful, and unlike the good, the disgusting lacks what McDowell wants to call "objectivity." McDowell is suggesting that for the disgusting the image of projection is appropriate, but that not so for ethics. The problem, however, is that we still have not been told what this *meriting* of a response amounts to.[11] So we do not know how to capture the difference in a way that will rule *in* the fearful and the good and rule *out* the disgusting. The most natural way to accommodate this consideration is by means of the rejected primary-quality model.

By the end of "Values and Secondary Qualities," McDowell sees himself as having begun to sketch an intermediate position. He rejects both intuitionistic Platonism and projectivist sentimentalism (and of course the idea that there is an exhaustive opposition between them). He has no patience for what he appears to consider the burlesque of an epistemology offered by the Platonist, and anyway cannot take seriously the idea of primary-quality-like properties *demanding* human affective responses. What is right about intuitionist Platonism, however, is its view of evaluative experience as a matter of *sensitivity* to aspects of the world rather than of *projection* of sentiment (by means of an erroneous attribution of a property to which the sentiment is anyway supposed to be a response). Projectivist sentimentalism, on the other hand, gets this wrong. Mackie, and since him Blackburn, are said to have a *thin* conception of reality, a conception on which there is nothing in the world that *answers* to our experience of value. Evaluative experience involves an erroneous projection onto a value-free reality. According to McDowell, reality does have values built in; those built-in values are, essentially, subjective-response producers.

In § 3 of "Values and Secondary Qualities," McDowell had distinguished two conceptions of objectivity (VSQ, pp. 113–14 [p. 228, this volume]: (i) "what it is for something to have [the quality] can be adequately understood otherwise than in terms of dispositions to give rise to subjective states," and (ii) "[the quality] is there to be experienced, as opposed to being a mere figment of the subjective state that purports to be an experience of it." An important thrust of McDowell's paper is that a quality can be objective in sense (ii) without needing to be objective in sense (i). McDowell alleges that it is confusion on this score that leads Mackie to skepticism about objective moral value and to the error theory.

Later, however, McDowell draws the distinction slightly differently. (i) is redrawn (VSQ, pp. 115–16 [pp. 229–30, this volume]) so that whether a quality is objective depends on whether *experience* represents it as being essentially phenomenal. Mackie would *insist* that value is objective according to the redrawn sense (i) – evaluative experience does not represent value properties as essentially phenomenal. Mackie, recall, claims to be engaging in a kind of ontological analysis; and because value is subjective in the *original* sense (i), its being objective in this *redrawn* sense (i) leads precisely to his error-theory. Only now do we locate the heart of the disagreement between Mackie and McDowell. If we accept McDowell's redrawing of the first kind of objectivity, so that whether a quality is objective depends on whether experience represents it as being essentially phenomenal, then Mackie finds qualities to be objective and McDowell holds them to be subjective.

This is ironic because it is Mackie whose overall position is the *denial* of objective moral value and McDowell whose position is to affirm a kind of objectivity. But that's because although Mackie believes value is objective in the redrawn sense of (i), he finds nothing in the world that actually answers to the objective conception implicit in our experience. We might say he finds value to be *objective* in experience and in implicit conception, but *subjective*, using the original sense (i), in independent reality. McDowell by contrast emphasizes the objectivity of value in sense (ii). But he claims that our evaluative experience is already constituted by the essential phenomenality of value. So McDowell would hold that value is subjective in experience subjective in the redrawn sense (i). That experience is not mistaken, however: value *is* subjective in the original sense (i). Our evaluative experience is thus objective in representing value as (as subjective as) it is.

E. A projection of error into metaethics

Simon Blackburn claims that his own "quasi-realism"[12] coherently combines projectivism with an earned right to a standard deployment of the notion of truth. Projectivism does *threaten* to lead to noncognitivism: if "ethical remarks … express attitudes or sentiments"[13] it is hard to see how they are even *apt* for truth evaluability. Blackburn tries to find room for truth evaluability, in something other than an error-theoretic way, in the projectivist paradigm. Because the attitudes expressed in ethical remarks are the "upshot" of sensibilities that are themselves "subject to attitudes of approbation or disapprobation" and "a matter for argument and criticism," truth "can now be explained in terms of the fact that the sensibility from which the attitude issues stands up to the appropriate kind of criticism" (PTE, p. 217 [p. 491, this volume]). Although McDowell finds it "hard to imagine that anyone would explicitly deny that if truth in ethics is available, it needs to be earned," he will argue that "a crucial issue opens up when one sets out to be less schematic" about "an account of the nature of the criticism to which ethical sensibilities are subject" (PTE, p. 216 [p. 491, this volume]).

> The point of the image of projection is to explain certain seeming features of reality as reflections of our subjective responses to a world that really contains no such features. Now this explanatory direction seems to require a corresponding priority, in the order of understanding, between the projected response and the apparent feature: we ought to be able to focus our thought on the response without needing to exploit the concept of the apparent feature that is supposed to result from projecting the response. … The question, now, is this: if in connection with some range of concepts whose application engages distinctive aspects of our subjective make-up in the sort of way that seems characteristic of evaluative concepts, we reject the kind of realism that construes subjective responses as perceptions of associated features of reality … , are we entitled to assume that the responses enjoy this kind of explanatory priority, as projectivism seems to require?
>
> (PTE, p. 218 [p. 493, this volume])

McDowell thinks the answer is no. And since projectivism does reject that kind of realism, it cannot satisfy the requirement about explanatory priority. McDowell recommends his own alternative. Remain realist (i.e. do not accept projectivism), thereby avoiding the requirement of an explanatorily *prior* understanding of our subjective responses, and nourish the realist aspiration by observing that ethical sensibility is susceptible to *reason* (all this while admitting the essentially response-dependent character of ethical value itself).

McDowell's alternative is developed on analogy to the comic and its associated response, amusement. We can be realists about comedy: amusement can be understood as a response to the comic qualities of a joke, for example. Jokes that are funny really do have comic qualities that are there for us to respond to. But those qualities are not wholly prior to the sentiment of amusement: what it is to be funny is, precisely, to be disposed to produce amusement. Neither, however, is the sentiment in question prior to the quality: there is no understanding the relevant response, amusement, independently of its being a matter of finding something *funny*. *Laughter*, for example, would not suffice because, as we know, we laugh at things that are not funny and fail to laugh at what is funny.

This is the essence of the "no-priority view" that McDowell seeks to defend: "a position which says that the extra features are neither parents nor children of our sentiments, but – if we must find an apt metaphor from the field of kinship relations – siblings" (PTE, p. 219 [p. 495, this volume]). This view, rejecting the idea that value is *projected onto* a fundamentally value-free world, dodges the demand, otherwise implicit in earning a right to truth, for a corresponding explanatory priority. We need not seek "a conception of what it is for things to be really funny on the basis of principles for ranking senses of humor which would have to be established from outside the propensity to find things funny" (PTE, p. 220 [p. 495, this volume]). Instead we focus on the funny itself in discriminating between more or less refined senses of humor; and we do this while admitting that the funny is a matter of producing amusement in refined senses of humor. Our conception of greater and less refinement and discrimination in senses of humor will be "derivative from an understanding of what it is for things to be really funny" (PTE, p. 223 [p. 499, this volume]). At the same time, what it is for things to be funny will be conceived in terms of their producing amusement in people with a good sense of humor.

McDowell's position is threatened by vicious circularity. It is impossible to explain a feature F in terms of a feature G and at the same time explain (in the same sense of explanation) feature G in terms of feature F. Nothing can *derive* from itself; and no two things can both be derivative from each other. If G-ness derives from F-ness, then F-ness does not derive from G-ness. McDowell is not unaware of the threat. But he is not impressed: "understanding the genesis of the 'new creation' [ethics] may be understanding an interlocking complex of subjective and objective or response and feature responded to" (PTE, p. 223 [p. 499, this volume]). Some kinds of "interlocking," however, are incompatible with understanding.

Blackburn raises a similar issue. He says that McDowell's suggestion shirks a plainly necessary explanatory task. We want to fit the commitments implicit in our "activity of moralizing, or reaction of finding things funny ... into a metaphysical view which can properly be hostile to an unanalysed and *sui generis* area of moral or humorous ... facts" (PTE, p. 221 [p. 497, this volume], citing Blackburn). Blackburn worries that McDowell's position provides no connection between such truths and devices whereby we might know about them.

McDowell responds, a bit gnomically, that his aim is to "locate" the activity and reactions in the "appropriate region of the space of reasons" (PTE, p. 221 [p. 497, this volume]). He admits that no particular judgment is a sacrosanct starting point, immune to critical scrutiny; but he denies that we must earn the right to truth from an initial position "in which *all* such verdicts or judgments are suspended at once" (PTE, p. 222 [p. 498, this volume]). The issue, however, is whether, if we allow *any* such judgments or verdicts, and discriminate better or worse senses of humor on that basis, we can then use the resulting conception of comic sensibility in an *explanation of* or in *understanding* (McDowell's terms) something's humor.

The same issue re-arises in connection with McDowell's view that we can protect our right to conditionals of the form "if it had not been the case that the act was wrong, I would not have become committed to the belief that the act was wrong" (our having a right to such conditionals serving as a mark of objectivity) by establishing that one would not have arrived at (become committed to?) the belief that the act was wrong

> had it not been for good reasons for it, *with the excellence of the reasons vindicated from within the relevant way of thinking.* ... We have no point of vantage on the question what can be the case, that is, what can be a fact, external to the modes of thought and speech we know our way around in, with whatever understanding of what counts as better and worse execution of them our mastery of them can give us.
>
> (PTE, p. 222 [p. 498, this volume] emphasis added)

McDowell's position thus aims at "an epistemology that centers on the notion of susceptibility to reasons" (PTE, p. 221 [p. 496, this volume]) where the reasons in question can themselves be partly constituted by ethical concepts. Critical scrutiny need not involve stepping outside the point of view constituted by an ethical sensibility.

Another, perhaps sharper, way of putting the point about the threat of circularity is in terms of the resulting *weakness* of the condition for objectivity. According to McDowell's view, it seems, truth and objectivity can be earned through susceptibility to reasons. But what is *that*? What kind of susceptibility? What kinds of reason? What distinguishes a "reason-susceptible" ethical stance from one that is deeply arbitrary? The difference should have something to do with the relevance of (good) reasons to take the ethical stance. But now what makes something a good ethical reason? What makes a reason relevant? If these questions will be answered from within the ethical sensibility at issue, it is unclear how to avoid the arbitrary.

Imagine: my ethical stance is the result of overwhelming oppression. My ethical beliefs, as well as my belief that an act is right just in case my oppressors approve, have been forcefully *required* of me. My ethical sensibility is affected only by alterations in what my oppressors sanction; no other considerations touch me. Is my stance susceptible to *ethical* reasons? Certainly it is subject to the will of my oppressors. This does not look much like susceptibility to ethical reasons; but then *that* appears to be a judgment from outside the moral system in question. The idea that "susceptibility to reasons" might suffice to objectify a domain builds a lot into the variety of susceptibility in question. In particular, it may need to build in (surreptitiously) what it is trying to leave out: an *external* grounding for ethics.

McDowell mentions Alasdair MacIntyre's claim that, as things stand, we cannot distinguish, "among methods of inducing people to change their minds on ethical matters, between making reasons available to them on the one hand and manipulating them in ways that have nothing in particular to do with rationality on the other" (PTE, p. 217 [p. 492, this volume]). He holds that "if there is enough substance to [our understanding of better and worse execution of ethical thought and speech] to enable us to rule out a position like MacIntyre's with a clear conscience, that is what it is for truth to be attainable in such thought and speech" (PTE, p. 222 [p. 498, this volume]). Unfortunately, unless whether a manipulation has anything "in particular to do with rationality" is determined from *outside* an ethical sensibility, and it certainly seems that McDowell would be opposed to any such view, we cannot rule out a position like MacIntyre's with a clear conscience. We might rule it out; but our conscience should be shadowed by the realization of the parochialism of that ruling. And we should be dissatisfied by an objectivity that we recognize to be so deeply self-centered.

3 A PREHENSILE SUBJECTIVISM

Attention to the threat of circularity in McDowell is preparatory: Wiggins is faced with the same threat. We'll proceed by focusing, intermittently, on key passages.

> What traditional subjectivists [those that preceded "Moore's celebrated and influential critique of subjectivism"[14]] have really wanted to convey is not so much definition as commentary. Chiefly they have wanted to persuade us that, when we consider whether or not *x* is good or right or beautiful, there is no appeal to anything that is more fundamental than actually possible human sentiments.
>
> (SS, 188)

This is, in the first instance, a comment about what there is *appeal to* when we *consider* whether *x* is good or right or beautiful. But the notion of what might be appealed to in a consideration is somewhat obscure. An opponent of subjectivism need not deny that, in some sense, actually possible human sentiments are appealed to in considerations of value. The objectivist might still insist that these sentiments have no role in the *constitution* of ethical properties themselves. Compare what are agreed to be primary qualities: shape, for example. When we consider whether or not *x* is round, is there appeal to anything more fundamental than sensory experience? One needn't be a radical empiricist to accept that we have no a priori access to the shapes of objects. But that our consideration of an object's shape can ("appeal to" or) be based on, ultimately, only our sensory experience does not amount to, or force, the conclusion that shape is a subjective quality.[15]

Wiggins, like McDowell and Mackie, finds the analogy with color suggestive. According to him, "it is simply obvious that colour is something subjective" (SS, 189). Although this may be premature, the issue for Wiggins is "to develop and amplify the subjectivist claim that x is good if and only if x is such as to arouse/such as to make appropriate the sentiment of approbation" without "traducing" that claim or "treating it unfairly as a definition or an analysis" (SS, 190).

He urges that there are "two main ways." The first is Hume's projectivism. Wiggins himself aims to provide the second way to develop the subjectivist claim (SS, §§ 8–9). The crucial difference, between Hume's way and Wiggins' alternative, is that Hume, holding that "values are merely phantasms of the feelings, or gildings or stainings with colours borrowed from internal sentiment[,] ... must never look to objects and properties themselves in characterizing the difference between good and bad judgments in taste and morals" (SS, 192–3). Ultimately, unacceptably, this leads Hume to a "*non-subjective foundation*" for his subjectivism as well as to a "substantial conception of a nearly homogeneous human nature" (SS, 193).

This "paradox" leads Wiggins away from Hume's "official theory." Wiggins seizes upon a different sort of Humean suggestion concerning "qualities in objects that are fitted by nature to produce particular ... feelings."

> Suppose that objects that regularly please or help or amuse us ... or harm or annoy or vex us ... in various ways come to be grouped together by us under various categories or classifications to which we give various avowedly anthropocentric names; and suppose they come to be grouped together as they are precisely *because* they are such as to please, help, amuse us, ... or harm, annoy, vex us ... in their various ways. There will be then no saying, very often, what properties these names stand for independently of the reactions they provoke. (The point of calling this position subjectivism is that the properties in question are explained by reference to the reactions of human subjects.) But equally – at least when the system of properties and reactions diversifies, complicates, and enriches itself – there will often be no saying exactly *what* reaction a thing with the associated property will provoke without direct or indirect allusion to the property itself.
>
> (SS, 195)

This passage clearly exhibits a deep problem with early sensibility theories: if the objects come to be grouped together as they are *because* they are such as to please, help, amuse, harm, annoy, or vex us, then there is some *priority* of the sentiments in question with respect to the groupings. It is because of their production of certain sentiments that the objects *come to be* grouped together under categories to which we give anthropocentric names. And again the "point of calling this position subjectivism is that the properties in question are *explained by* reference to the reactions of human subjects" [emphasis added]. Explanation, recall, is necessarily asymmetric. But then we cannot accept that there is "no saying exactly *what* reaction a thing with the associated property will provoke without direct or indirect allusion to the property itself."

If there is no identifying the reaction in question without at least implicit reference to the property, then objects cannot be understood to be grouped together as instances of the properties as a result of their tendency to produce reactions in us. What I mean to suggest is that Wiggins's account of the properties' *derivation* gives a kind of priority to human reactions that he cannot then eliminate by insisting that the reactions cannot be identified except by alluding to those same properties.

Wiggins's "sensible" subjectivism, like McDowell's self-styled objectivism, is developed on analogy with the comic.

> [W]hen we dispute whether x is really funny, there is a whole wealth of considerations and explanations we can adduce, and by no means all of them have to be given in terms simply synonymous or interdefinable with "funny." ... [Even if "funny" is an irreducibly subjective predicate,] [t]hese diverse and supporting considerations will ... serve [a] purpose. By means of them, one person can improve another's grasp of the concept of the funny; and one person can improve another's focus or discrimination of what *is* funny.
>
> (SS, 195–6)

Of course, this is all supposed to provide a model for the moral case. How satisfactory a model is it? Wiggins suggests that considerations – not all of which need be given in terms interdefinable with "funny" – can be adduced in order to *improve* one another's discrimination of what is funny. So improvement with respect to comic sensibility is supposed to be possible. But what, on the model Wiggins is developing, can such improvement amount to? Is the improvement in question anything other than more-faithful adherence to a more-widely-popular way of responding? Wiggins helps himself to a language of "improvement," "refinement," and "keenness"; so far, however, this is to assert, not to explicate, the compatibility of his subjectivism with concepts that cohere more naturally with objectivist positions.

One question concerns the standard of refinement. Improvement is improvement along a dimension; what defines the relevant dimension? The objectivist has a view; the dimension is defined by the properties themselves. Our reactions, because they are not metaphysically *prior to* the properties, can be more or less *sensitive to* them. Wiggins wants the same idea to apply to his subjectivism. But if the properties are *derivative* from our reactions, if things have the properties only *because* we have the reactions we do, if the properties are *explained* by our reactions, then the metaphor of our reactions' being better or worse approximations of what is anyway there is ruled out. A given reaction may still be more or less faithful to the reactions, taken generally, that determine the properties; so there is room for criticism of any individual reaction in terms of others. But refinement is then, presumably, a matter of blending in perfectly, having the average reactions, lack of individuality or uniqueness: accuracy becomes, essentially, *compliance*.

Wiggins argues that

> we must keep faith in another way with Hume's desire to maintain the sovereignty of subjects simultaneously with the distinction between sound and mistaken judgment. We shall do this by insisting that *genuinely* [funny/appalling/shocking/consoling/reassuring/disgusting/pleasant/delightful/ ...] things are things that not only [amuse/appall/shock/console/reassure/disgust/please/delight/ ...] but have these effects precisely because they *are* [funny/appalling/shocking/consoling/reassuring/disgusting/pleasant/delightful/ ...] – at the same time insisting that this "because" introduces an explanation that both explains and justifies.
>
> (SS, 199–200)

Again, subjects are sovereign (!). Nonetheless, we can distinguish between sound and mistaken judgment. And we can do this, Wiggins urges, by insisting that the genuinely funny is that which not only amuses, but does so *because* it is funny. The comic properties of genuinely funny things justify and explain our amusement; when we are amused by what is not funny, our amusement cannot be so explained. So, explanatorily idle "comic properties" do not, when instantiated, yield genuine instances of the funny.

But the problem of circularity that besets McDowell is, ironically, highlighted by Wiggins's bracketing of funny/appalling/shocking/consoling/reassuring/disgusting/pleasant/delightful. What, indeed, is the difference between the appalling and the consoling? Appalling things appall; and consoling things console. But to be appalled is to find something appalling and to be consoled is to find something consoling. The genuinely appalling appalls because it is appalling; the genuinely consoling consoles because it is consoling. Similarly for the other property/response pairs that Wiggins lists. If there is no "object-independent and property-independent, 'purely phenomenological' or 'purely introspective' account of amusement" (SS, 195) or of these other responses, then Wiggins has not yet said enough for us to distinguish the matched pairs in his list from one another.[16]

It is striking that immediately after the passage quoted above, Wiggins uses an especially inapt analogy for how the various effects can be explained and justified: "in *something* like the way in which 'there is a marked tendency for us all to think that 7 + 5 = 12, and this tendency exists because there is really nothing to think about what 7 + 5 is' explains a tendency *by* justifying it" (SS, 200). What's striking is that arithmetic facts appear to be an extreme example of the *non*-subjective. There being nothing else to think about what 7 + 5 equals is independent of what any of us, or all of us, might be, or have been, disposed to think. Ultimately, the tendency is explained by the arithmetic facts; and, of course, the arithmetic facts are not in turn explained or justified by the tendency.

Wiggins does worry that an opponent of his view might protest that he is (in a phrase, for a different purpose, of Bernard Williams's) confusing resonance with reference. Wiggins is trying to formulate a variant upon "classical" (presumably Humean) subjectivism. The opponent objects that he is "trying to ground ... a distinction between what is really ø and not really ø upon what are by [his] own account mere responses – upon a convergence in the inclinations various people feel or do not feel to say that *x* is ø or that *x* is not ø" (SS, 204). Wiggins answers that the reactions he has been "speaking of are not 'mere' responses. They are responses that are correct when and only when they are occasioned by what has the corresponding property ø and are occasioned by it because it *is* ø" (SS, 204–5). But this makes matters worse.

If Wiggins is trying to ground a distinction between what is really ø and not really ø upon *correct* responses, where responses are correct when and only when they are occasioned by what [really] has the corresponding property ø and are occasioned by it because it *is* ø, then his task is clearly hopeless. There can be no grounding, no explanation, in terms that presuppose what is to be grounded or explained. What is to be explained is the difference between really being ø and not really being ø. This is explained in terms of a kind of response. What kind of response? Those that are occasioned by things that are really ø and because those things are really ø. But the difference between things that are really ø and those that aren't was what was to be explained. We have made no progress.

In a revealing statement, Wiggins insists that subjectivism does not "insulate from criticism the attitudes and responses that sustain glib, lazy, or otherwise suspect predications" (SS, 207). But to what *variety* of criticism does it leave those predications open? If the standards for refinement are to be found from within the moral system in question, perhaps only glib, lazy, or otherwise suspect criticisms will be applicable. The predicative practice will survive (take on a "life of its own" – see SS, 196) and evolve. Intuitively "mistaken" reactions – for example, glib and lazy indifference in the face of gross injustice – may "catch on and survive, and then ... evolve further, and generate further [mistaken?] property, response pairs." It is not clear that a pathologically glib and lazy ethical system is differentially less *fit*, evolutionarily. Indeed, it would seem to be at least as self-supporting and self-perpetuating as preferred alternatives. A superficial look at the history of civilization may support this view (though I would not draw any definite conclusions). Given conceivable relations among antecedent distributions of resources and a disposition to such systems, there is reason to suppose such systems will show greater adaptive advantage. In short, for all we know, Wiggins's position may be a meta*un*ethics rather than a metaethics.

4 THE WRIGHT STUFF

A. Basics

Sensibility theories themselves have evolved since their early development. Crispin Wright has sketched[17] a position that, while opposed to sensibility theories like those of McDowell and Wiggins, retains some of their basic features. His opposition to their view is based on the idea that moral judgment has no distinctive phenomenology. Moral judgment, according to Wright, does not encompass any distinctive kinds of psychological effect. It's true that valuing is necessarily linked to the state of *caring*; but Wright thinks valuing is dispassionate and has the caring as a consequence, not as a constitutive aspect. In any case, the caring in question is not a particular kind of caring.

This is a striking point on the part of Wright because, as we know, McDowell and Wiggins themselves deny that there is a distinctive moral phenomenology. That's why they define the responses that are to ground evaluative properties in terms of those same properties. There is no independent way of identifying the response of *amusement*, for example, according to McDowell, except that it is a matter of finding something *funny*. But Wright may think, plausibly, that this nevertheless points up a disanalogy between secondary qualities and evaluative properties. For the experience of red *does* have a distinctive phenomenology, qualitatively identifiable independently of the secondary quality itself.

Wright deepens this by connecting it to what he considers a more basic point. "If our experience of secondary qualities provides a model of anything, then it is of a notion of experience which is, up to a point at least, *raw*" (MVP, 12). Not every aspect of a color experience is a deployment of conceptual resources. Even when it is affected and conditioned by concepts, phenomenology maintains a degree of independence. Wright doubts that there is anything of sufficient rawness in the phenomenology of moral judgment to give the notion of "moral experience" any work to do. We cannot make sense of someone's finding something phenomenologically to be immoral while possessing no moral concepts.

This is where the dialectic becomes especially complex. Wright now thinks he has shown a certain view to be bankrupt. The unacceptable view exploits the secondary-quality analogy in a specific way. We cannot view our appreciation of moral value as modeled by our perception of secondary qualities. That perceptual model demands a kind of phenomenology that has a "raw" element – the model demands the availability of a kind of phenomenology that is potentially preconceptual. And this is what the evaluative will not provide. There is no distinctive evaluative phenomenology, or so Wright urges. Therefore the "perceptualist" application of the secondary-quality analogy fails. But the insight embedded in drawing the analogy, Wright believes, can still be preserved. The insight consists in the idea that the subjectivity of moral *judgment* can be "harmonised" with moral realism in the way that a proper understanding of secondary qualities and secondary-quality experience can yield a harmonious mix of realism and subjectivism.

Importantly, Wright's development of the analogy will jettison the notion of a distinctively moral *experience* and replace it with the notion of distinctively moral *beliefs* – beliefs whose formation is analytically tied to a disposition to certain sorts of practical concern (MVP, 13). How does Wright's development proceed? He starts with what he calls, using a term of Mark Johnston's, the "*basic equation*" for "red":

> x is red ↔ for any S: if S were perceptually normal and were to encounter x in perceptually normal conditions, S would experience x as red.
>
> (MVP, 14)

Wright imagines modifying this by replacing the condition involving a distinctive experience ("S would experience x as red") with a condition demanding a distinctive belief.

Red

> x is red ↔ for any S: if S knows which object x is, and knowingly observes it in plain view in normal perceptual conditions; and is fully attentive to this observation; and is perceptually normal and is prey to no other cognitive disfunction; and is free of doubt about the satisfaction of any of these conditions – *then* if S forms a belief about x's colour, that belief will be that x is red.
>
> (MVP, 15)

The strategy is promising; but raises a question. This new equation (like the basic equation before it) involves the notion of *normality*. How is that to be understood?

Wright distinguishes (MVP, 15–16) a *conduciveness* interpretation of normality from a *statistical* interpretation. On the conduciveness interpretation, the amended basic equation appears to hold true a priori. On the statistical interpretation, things are a bit more complicated.

> It would, I think, subserve the correctness of *Red* if we glossed the notion of normal perceptual function as: perceptual function of a kind which is actually typical of human beings. But it will not do so to gloss "normal perceptual circumstances." The conditions which actually usually prevail during winter in Spitzbergen, for

instance, or in a normal photographic dark-room, are not suited for colour appraisal. A good description of conditions which are, optimally, so suited would be: conditions of illumination like those which actually typically obtain at noon on a cloudy summer's day out of doors and out of shadow. Even here "typically" is required because such conditions are sometimes disturbed by solar eclipses, nuclear explosions, dust storms and volcanic discharges. So there is still an element of statisticality. But notice: when both uses of the notion of normality are so interpreted, in broadly statistical terms, *Red* continues not merely to hold true but to hold true a priori. For our knowledge that typical visual functioning and conditions of illumination like those I just broadly statistically characterised are conducive for the appraisal of colour is not a posteriori knowledge.

(MVP, 16)

I think Wright is too quick in making these claims about color. He thinks our knowledge that certain conditions are conducive to color appraisal might be a priori. It might be an a priori truth that, for example, illumination like that *typically* obtaining at noon on a cloudy summer's day is conducive to color appraisal. But I'm skeptical. For all we might have known a priori, couldn't it have been the case that color appraisal is best carried out in photographic darkrooms? Conditions conducive to color appraisal come to be known to us only through experience, it seems; our knowledge that certain conditions are so conducive can be justified only empirically. Wright's opposing opinion is, according even to him, "crucial in what follows" (MVP, 16).

At this point, Wright marks an alleged disanalogy between secondary and primary qualities. The contrast, ultimately, involves the possibility of producing a priori true basic equations for primary qualities on the model of those we have seen for secondary qualities. His contention is that the analogous basic equations would not be true a priori – not even after judicious refinement (or if they were, there would still be another crucial disanalogy concerning the independence of the concepts used in specifying the relevant conditions and the concepts under analysis).

He considers a "canonical biconditional" for "approximately square."

x is approximately square $\leftrightarrow$ if the four sides and four interior angles of x were to be correctly measured, and no change were to take place in the shape or size of x during the process, then the sides would be determined to be approximately equal in length, and the angles would be determined to approximate right angles.

(MVP, 19)

He considers this in order to bring out the fact that:

[I]t is not a priori true, but merely a deep fact of experience, that our (best) judgements of approximate shape, made on the basis of predominantly visual

265

observations, usually "pan out" when appraised in accordance with more refined operational techniques. ... It is not a priori true that the world in which we actually live allows reliable perceptual appraisal of approximate shape – is not, for example, a world in which the paths travelled by photons are subject to grossly distorting forces.

(MVP, 20)

The problem is that this is supposed to be by way of contrast with the case of secondary qualities. As I noted above, however, it's not clear that the contrast holds. Isn't it also knowable only a posteriori that the world in which we actually live allows reliable perceptual appraisal of color? that it is not, for example, a world in which the paths traveled by photons are subject to grossly distorting forces? Actually, I don't feel certain whether these are a priori or a posteriori; but I do not in any case see the alleged variation between the case of primary qualities and that of secondary qualities.

The upshot for Wright is that we have "a satisfying account of what is subjective and what is objective in secondary quality ascription, and how the element of subjectivity is compatible with objectivity" (MVP, 21). And "[t]he question is, do ascriptions of moral quality provide another illustration?" His answer, ultimately, is that the ascription of moral qualities is fundamentally different from secondary-quality ascription, but that the latter may point us in the direction of a related way of harmonizing a subjective element with objectivity in ethics.

Moral experience, unlike secondary-quality experience, has no distinctive phenomenology. But by substituting moral beliefs for moral experience in a nonreductive account of evaluative properties, we can produce a priori true basic equations that characterize evaluative properties. Even so, the satisfaction of the relevant conditions in *Moral* cannot be independent of the extension of moral concepts themselves.

Moral

P ↔ for any *S*: if *S* scrutinises the motives, consequences, and for Jones, foreseeable consequences in the context of the remark; and does this in a fashion which involves no error concerning nonmoral fact or logic, and embraces all *morally-relevant* considerations; and if *S* gives all this the fullest attention, and so is victim to no error or oversight concerning any relevant aspect of his/her deliberations; and if *S* is a *morally-suitable* subject – accepts *the right moral principles*, or has *the right moral intuitions or sentiments*, or whatever; and if *S* has no doubt about the satisfaction of any of these conditions, *then* if *S* forms a moral evaluation of Jones' remark, that evaluation will be that *P*.

(MVP, 22–3, emphasis added)

Here we find a fundamental breakdown in the analogy between moral and secondary qualities:

> [P]roper pedigree for visual appraisals of colour is a matter of meeting conditions whose satisfaction in a particular case does not directly depend on what the extension of colour predicates is; proper pedigree for moral judgments, by contrast, is a matter of meeting conditions the satisfaction of some of which is, irreducibly, a moral question.
>
> (MVP, 23–4)

This is now a familiar problem for sensibility theories. Wright draws two important consequences. First, "the extension of the truth predicate among ascriptions of moral quality may not be thought of as determined by our best beliefs" and second, "judgments of moral quality cannot *inherit* objectivity in the way in which ... judgments of secondary quality can" (MVP, 24). These consequences *appear* to favor a projectivist view (or even an error theory) over a view like that of McDowell and Wiggins's, Wright admits. But he thinks it would be premature to recoil from the analogy with secondary qualities directly into a projectivist or an error theory. Another possibility is to see moral epistemology as *"self-contained"* – an idea that Wright thinks, controversially, has a prima facie analog in mathematical judgment. Wright appears optimistic that we will accordingly find harmony at last. I worry about emptiness.

B. Struth!

Later, in "Truth in Ethics,"[18] Wright attempts to substantiate his optimism. Like McDowell, he too I think subtly misunderstands the import of Mackie's error theory.[19] He finds that theory "unlikely ... [to] serve [as] a satisfactory moral theory" because it "relegates moral discourse to bad faith." If there is something to this, so far I think Wright's case for it (TE, 2–3) is insufficient.

The critical point for Wright, to begin with, is that the error theory forgoes any conception of a *"proper basis"* for moral sentiment – "the world is unsuited to confer truth on any of our claims about what is right." (TE, 2). But we see that Wright bases this criticism on the idea that according to the error theory, "it is of the essence of moral judgment to aim at the truth" even when "there is no moral truth to hit" (TE, 2). This understanding of the error theory's predicament, however, may conflate two ideas from Mackie.

Mackie is almost certainly a cognitivist. He does think that moral judgments aim at the truth. And he might well think that it is of the essence of moral judgments that they aim at the truth. But it is not clear that Mackie would support the idea that there are no truths of the sort that it is of the essence of moral judgments to aim at. He denies that there are any *objective* moral truths; and he thinks that moral judgments do, *in fact*, aim at objectivity. But it is not clear, to me at least, that he thinks *it is of the essence of* moral judgments to aim at objective truth. It is not clear that he would think anything that did not aim at objectivity was ipso facto not a moral judgment. His claim about the objectivity to which moral judgment aims appears to be more of an observation, a generalization from introspection. Indeed, refraining from attributing to him the stronger claim would make sense of his readiness, in later chapters, to make moral judgments. Mackie might view cognitivism as a nonnegotiable feature of morality, while consistently maintaining that the implicit commitment to objectivity of our actual moral practice is in principle separable.

In any case, Wright canvasses a possible response to his criticism, a response in support of Mackie's position: perhaps there is some subsidiary norm relative to which moral judgments, all of which are equally false, can be assessed. The making of moral judgments can be rendered reasonable by appeal to this subsidiary norm and the charge of bad faith could be dissolved. But this strategy invites what Wright considers a good question.

> [I]f, among the welter of falsehoods which we enunciate in moral discourse, there is a good distinction to be drawn between those which are acceptable in the light of some such subsidiary norm and those which are not ... then why insist on construing *truth* for moral discourse in terms which motivate a charge of global error, rather than explicate it in terms of the satisfaction of the putative subsidiary norm, whatever it is?
>
> (TE, 3)

Indeed. Simply substitute "objectively true" for "true" (and analogously for the cognates) and let some form of subjective truth constitute the subsidiary norm and you get a question to which Mackie could answer as follows: "only because doing so would be revisionary of what is implicit in our actual moral phenomenology; nevertheless, the revision may be called for." In other words, what there is a welter of, according to Mackie, is claims to *objective* moral truth. No claim to objective moral truth can be made good; and all such claims are thus false. But such claims may satisfy certain, admittedly ultimately subjective, standards. It may then be appropriate to *redefine* moral truth in terms of the satisfaction of those standards. But such an account would be revisionary: ordinary moral practice is, as a matter of contingent fact, implicitly committed to the objectivity of moral judgments. The charge of global error is appropriate – but the error has not been alleged as *pathological*.

Summarizing broadly, Wright is attempting to show that antirealists need not give up the notion of truth in ethics. Some but not all moral judgments will still be *superassertible* (TE, 9): "superassertible" will effectively function as a truth predicate, a predicate that validates the basic platitudes about truth that Wright elsewhere argues[20] are constitutive of the notion of truth.

Superassertibility is "an absolute notion: a statement is superassertible if it is assertible in some state of information and then remains so no matter how that state of information is enlarged upon or improved" (TE, 10). And assertibility is a matter of meeting the standards (the "discipline" in Wright's terminology) that govern the discourse in question. These standards are "*language-game internal*," internal to the discourse. We thus dispense with the notion of *correspondence* (though we could innocently retain the locution, if we chose). Truth is ultimately defined from *within* the discourse. Wright's discussion here hearkens back to his earlier ideas about the "self-containment" of moral epistemology.

But Wright misses at least *my* inclinations when he claims: "What those whose intuitive inclination is to moral realism really want, I suggest, is not truth as representation – realism as properly understood – but a certain kind of objectivity in moral appraisal: ideally, precisely that a tendency towards convergence in the conception of what is morally important and how much importance it has, be indeed intrinsic to moral thinking itself" (TE, 18).

Intersubjectivity (or even "that a tendency towards convergence be intrinsic") will not satisfy the intuitive demand for realism and objectivity. If I am concerned that a particular agent might, even in ideal conditions of "information," make errors in moral judgment, why should I think it metaphysically impossible that we *all* make moral errors, even that we all *tend* to make moral errors, even under conditions of increasing (nonmoral) information? One needn't be so pessimistic as to think that what is true in morality is "altogether beyond our ken" (TE, 13) in order to hold that what is true in morality is always, even in conditions of full nonmoral information (even if a judgment is superassertible), independent of what we judge – though we may often judge correctly. What is *potentially* beyond our ken might fail actually to be beyond our ken. Of course, Wright's tendentious characterization of the realist alternative ("the idea that ... the connection between prosecution of best method and getting at the truth is, at bottom, 'serendipitous'" [TE, 9]) makes that an easier target. But to hold that two things are metaphysically independent is far from holding that they might not overlap in *systematic*, rather than merely serendipitous, ways. So we set Wright's sensibility theory aside too, as we proceed.

5 HYPERTHALAMIC ETHICS?

A.

Mark Johnston begins his discussion[21] with Hume. In a pair of quotations, Hume first compares "vice and virtue" to colors and other secondary qualities, which "according to the modern philosophy [e.g., Locke's] are not qualities in the object but perceptions in the mind." But in the second quotation Hume expresses some hesitation in connection with the error-theoretic aspect of "modern philosophy," comparing the claim that "snow is neither cold nor white" to a "paradox." If we admit the analogy with secondary qualities and deny the view that such qualities are not "in the object," we get what might be the "motto" for "analogists" such as McDowell and Wiggins.

With what conception of secondary qualities might the analogists be operating? Johnston begins with a simple "dispositional conception":

> x is red iff x is disposed to look such and so (ostended) way to standard perceivers as they actually are under standard conditions as they actually are.
>
> (DTV, 140)

Such an account would have three virtues. First, predications involving 'x is red' would be truth-evaluable in a straightforward way. Second, "predicating 'x is red' could be part of straightforward causal/dispositional explanations of why those things look red to perceivers" (DTV, 140). And third, the dispositional account does not devolve into a "simple subjectivism or idealism": the phrase "as they actually are" enables the biconditional to count x as red even if, standard perceivers or standard conditions being different, it were not disposed to look such and so (ostended) way to standard perceivers under standard conditions (just so long as it *were* disposed to look that way to standard perceivers *as they actually are* ...).

These three virtues allow the dispositional conception to "confound" three kinds of theories: noncognitivism about color, error theories about color, and "delayed-reaction" color realism that sees "a problem about how remarks of the form 'x is red' could be truth evaluable given their causal origin in our responses, a problem which requires a substantial explanation of how we come to 'earn the right' to express our experiences in terms of judgments about external things" (DTV, 141).

The analogy between the evaluative and the colored thus holds out the promise of a corresponding effect on noncognitivism, error theory, or quasi-realism in ethics. But Johnston insists that this promise is conditioned by just which analogy is deployed. There are important disanalogies.

First, in the evaluative domain (at least once we go beyond the sensuous aesthetic values) there is no very good analog of our ordinary perception of secondary qualities. "[V]alues are not in general the object of any perceptual or quasi-perceptual faculty or sense" (DTV, 142).[22] Second, according to Johnston, "talk about red, colour or secondary qualities, while talk of determinables, is still relatively detailed talk. However, talk about value is talk at a level of almost fantastic abstraction" (DTV, 143). I worry that the disanalogy claimed by Johnston may be the product of an unfair comparison: redness is in some sense a more specific property than simply being valuable. But can we say the same for *having a secondary quality*? Is talk about value really talk at a level of more fantastic abstraction than talk of being a secondary quality? I'm not yet convinced.

In any case, Johnston claims other disanalogies. According to him, the prospects for an analysis or definitional reduction are brighter in the case of colors than they are with respect to the evaluative.

> [W]e can rely upon the neophyte's quality space and a cannily chosen collection of foils and paradigms to make salient a way things look ... we could [accordingly] give a substantive specification of standard perceivers and standard conditions without even covertly using the notions of being red ... [and] we would here have defined a colour concept ostensively and without relying upon any colour concept as opposed to colour sample.
>
> However, nothing like this will be plausible in the case of the concept of being a valuable state of affairs. ... There is a colour (appearance) solid but no value (appearance) solid.
>
> (DTV, 143–4)

Finally fourth, and this further supports the differential prospects for definitional reduction in the two domains, the concept of finding good reason to value a state of affairs appears to depend on the concept of value itself: x is a good reason for valuing y only if valuing y because of x is itself *valuable*. *Good reason* is itself an evaluative concept: noticing this forces us to give up the "analytically reductive game with respect to the universal predicate of favourable assessment of states of affair" (DTV, 144).

But, Johnston goes on to claim, that is not the only game suggested by the analogy. "The most plausible, if highly generalizing, way of taking the analogy is this: evaluational concepts, like secondary quality concepts as understood by the analogists, are 'response-dependent' concepts" (DTV, 144). What is response-dependence? Johnston defines this as a matter of a concept's being "interdependent with or dependent upon the concept of certain subjects' responses under certain conditions" (DTV, 145).[23] With respect to any such concept something of the following form will hold a priori:

> x is C iff In K, S's are disposed to produce x-directed response R (or [iff] x is such as to produce R in S's under conditions K).
>
> (DTV, 145)

Some obvious examples of response-dependent concepts would be the *nauseating*, the *embarrassing*, the *irritating*, and the *credible* (DTV, 146). And the best examples of response-*in*dependent concepts are from theoretical science, logic, and mathematics. Johnston cautions us not to confuse the concept of a subject's employing a concept with the concept so employed (DTV, 146).

Now, Johnston thinks that "[m]any pivotal issues in philosophy … can be cast in terms of whether and in what way the central concepts in those areas are response-dependent" (DTV, 146). This is because philosophers often seek a "qualified realism" about the relevant areas of discourse. A qualified realism would assert that "the discourse in question serves up genuine candidates for truth and falsity, and that, nonetheless, the subject matter which makes statements of the discourse true or false is *not wholly independent of* the cognitive or affective responses of the speakers of the discourse" (DTV, 144; emphasis added). The "basic problem" is to explain the variety of *dependence*, contemplated by such a qualified realism without reducing the view to some kind of idealism. Opposing Dummett's semantic antirealism and Putnam's internal realism,[24] Johnston prefers *local* and *topic-specific* qualified realisms and rejects a response-dependent conception of truth.

Johnston stresses that the characterization of response-dependent concepts does not imply that they admit of a *reductive* definition in terms of subjects' responses, and he reminds us of the "explicit allowance for conceptual interdependence." He notes, moreover, the possibility that the biconditional that shows a concept to be response-dependent might be, strictly speaking, circular. If our aim is only the exhibition of conceptual connections, however, this circularity is no vice (DTV, 147).

We thus see how a response-dependent account of the central concepts of a given area of discourse can amount to a qualified realism about that area. It can be a realist (as opposed to *irrealist*) conception of the area because it can allow genuine instances of the relevant concepts to exist, realist (as opposed to *idealist*) conception because it can allow that instances of the concept could exist even if the relevant conditions and responders had been different, and a realist (as opposed to *antirealist*, *internal realist*, or *pragmatist*) conception because it can deny those views' commitment to a response-dependent conception of truth. But the realism is nevertheless qualified precisely in its denial that the concepts in question are independent of the concept of subjects' responses under specified conditions.

This much smartly sets the stage for Johnston's central concern: whether "the notion of value, the all purpose notion of favourable assessment of states of affair, is a response-dependent notion" (DTV, 148). He is not prepared to endorse just any response-dependent account of value (indeed in his next section he subtly critiques David Lewis's elegant proposal); but he will ultimately propose an alternative of his own.

B.

Johnston's proposal proceeds in stages. First, we must broaden our conception of reasonableness to encompass that more substantive variety "which we look for in both practical and theoretical matters" (DTV, 162). Accordingly, Johnston offers the following:

(1) x is a value iff substantive reason is on the side of valuing x.

(DTV, 162)

This is supposed to be uncontroversial. The right-hand side may be a kind of para-phrase of the left. But we can articulate the claim, and make it more controversial, by adding the following:

(2) y is a substantive reason for/against valuing x iff we are disposed stably to take it to be so under conditions of increasing information and critical reflection.

(DTV, 162)

If under some conditions we take y to be a substantive reason for valuing x, and if critical reflection on more inclusive states of information yields the same result (with respect to y's being a substantive reason for valuing x), then we are disposed stably to take y to be a substantive reason for valuing x. (2) raises a question about which methods for weighing substantive reasons are acceptable. Surely not just any method for weighing substantive reason, such that relative to it, we are stably disposed to take y to be a substantive reason for valuing x, suffices to make y in fact a substantive reason for valuing x. Johnston suggests the following:

(3) A method for weighing substantive reasons is an acceptable method for determining whether the weight of substantive reason is on the side of valuing x iff we are stably disposed to take it to be so under conditions of increasing information and critical reflection.

(DTV, 163)

I worry about the adequacy of (3) as a response to the possible difficulty with (2). After all, surely not just any method for considering the acceptability of methods for weighing substantive reasons will do. There may be methods for judging the accept-ability of a method for weighing substantive reasons such that, relative to them, we are stably disposed to judge the method acceptable when in fact it is not. At least, this seems no less likely than the analogous claim with respect to (2), to which Johnston himself appears to be sensitive in offering us (3). In any case, we are led immediately to (4):

(4) Substantive reason is on the side of valuing x iff this is so according to one and all [acceptable] methods of weighing the reasons for and against valuing x.

(DTV, 163–4)

Together, (1) through (4) constitute Johnston's (dispositional and) response-dependent account of value. The notion of substantive reason used in the account of value given by (1) is response-dependent as made explicit by (2) and (3). "There are no

273

substantive reasons which we cannot get to in principle from here, although getting to them may involve a gradual but thorough reworking of what we take to be substantive reasons, the appropriate methods of weighing them and perhaps also the correct styles of critical reflection" (DTV, 164).

A worry I expressed above re-arises here: couldn't arriving at substantive reasons sometimes involve a reworking of our methods of reworking? If so, might not such reasons be in principle inaccessible to us? Couldn't we be wrong *all the way down*? Johnston says (DTV, 164), "[i]f we think of our present system of substantive reasonableness on the model of Neurath's ship, not only may the ship require considerable overhaul but so also may our methods of overhauling it." But so also might our way of changing our method of overhauling the ship, and so also might our process for changing the way we change the method by which we overhaul the ship, and so on and on without end. If there is no level of our system of practical reason that is not in need of overhaul, then it may be that some substantive reasons are, after all, *hyper-external*.[25]

After a discussion of the variety of relativism entrained by the response-dependent account he favors (DTV, § VI, 166–70), Johnston returns (DTV, § VII, 170–4) to the residual appeal of response-independent accounts of value. He admits that a response-dependent account should be offered as a "partly revisionary account." But I question his sympathetic use of the quotation from Wittgenstein:

> The right road is the road which leads to an *arbitrarily* predetermined end and it is quite clear to us all that there is no sense in talking about the right road apart from such a predetermined goal ... I think it would have to be the road which *everybody* on seeing it would, *with logical necessity* have to go or feel ashamed for not going.[26]
>
> (cited by Johnston, DTV, 170–1)

While Johnston finds something in this sort of robust objectivity, he holds that Mackie successfully stigmatized it as an error at the heart of our thought about value. And Johnston's account is meant to "eliminate precisely this error of supposing that the demands of value or substantive practical reason are thoroughly independent of our tendency to respond to such demands" (DTV, 171). I am troubled because Wittgenstein is stressing the kind of *internalism* that Johnston himself has earlier (DTV, 160–1) in effect rejected. Why should a defender of a response-independent account, of all positions, be viewed as committed to such a strong variety of internalism?

According to a response-independent conception of value, there are evaluative demands built into the world in such a way that any responsible agent *should*, on pain of evaluative error, respect. The evaluative, to be response independent, need not be thought of as a product of rationality.[27] Did Mackie successfully stigmatize *this* view of "the objectively prescriptive"? Not if, as I suggest, he commits the slide to avoid. The fact that we can make no sense of a demand for a motive-independent-motivation (these would be queer) does not entail that we can make no sense of a motive-independent-demand for a motivation. The response-independent theorist is committed only to the latter.

We might consider other possible manifestations of the projective error Mackie finds embedded in our ordinary moral discourse and practice. Take Plato's *Euthyphro*. The Socratic argument exhibited there (at 10B–11B) is, Johnston admits, "the characteristic bugbear of response-dependent accounts" (DTV, 172). Johnston points out that his account will "allow many instances of this form of argument as showing that *certain* dependencies are not relevant to the correct account of value. . . . Something is valued by the ideal observer because it is valuable, i.e., in accord with substantive practical reason. It is not valuable because it is valued by the ideal observer" (DTV, 172).

But at the next level, when we consider the nature of substantive reasons, Johnston must "take care" and "dig in." He can admit an "explanatory element in the remark that we take something to be a reason because it is a reason" (DTV, 172); but he will insist that whatever is a reason is so precisely because we would take it to be so as we approach ideal conditions. Otherwise we illegitimately require *hyper-external* reasons.

It is not easy to see how to argue about this. But Johnson offers (DTV, 172–3) one argument in support of his view. If there were hyper-external reasons, by what consideration could we be led to believe that we have ever been in contact with one? Given a response-independent conception of substantive reason, the following claim

(H)   The substantive reasons are to be discovered by taking into account relevant information and critically reflecting on it.

appears to be a merely contingent empirical hypothesis. And, according to Johnston there is something "essentially bogus" (DTV, 173) about the idea of finding empirical support for the claim that we discover the substantive reasons through reflection on information.

If a response-independent conception of substantive reason must regard (H) as contingent, then perhaps Johnston has a powerful argument. But I'm not convinced the position is committed to that. Notice that (H) is a thesis about how substantive reasons are to be *discovered*, not about what they *are*. It may be a priori that a set of facts are to be discovered in some way, even though perfect exercise of the recommended method is no *guarantee* of success. Johnston himself wants to allow some response-independent concepts – he rejects (DTV, 145) one kind of response-dependent account of *truth*. Is he now prevented from maintaining a priori theses about how the instantiation of those concepts is to be discovered? I don't see why. Facts about how discoveries occur *when they do* may be knowable a priori even while the possibility of error is persistent. Our metaethics had better not manifest a *hypo*-objectifying, hyperthalamic error.[28]

6 FORWARD TO THE PAST

To recapitulate briefly, sensibility theories are troubled. There needs to be some constraint on the subjective reactions that properly count as constituting ethical value. But no noncircular account appears plausible – for two reasons. First, there seems to be no way to characterize the *kind* of reaction that is relevant – unlike color experience, moral experience is not phenomenologically distinctive. But if moral experience is constituted by cognitive states, and the relevant individuation of cognitive states is in terms of their *contents*, then specification of the relevant kind of reaction will presuppose the concept whose nature is under investigation. Second, even assuming there were no circularity in defining the notion of a moral judgment and then using it to understand moral proper-ties, not just any exercise of moral judgment should be relevant to the determination of moral properties. Presumably only *good* (or appropriate, or morally or ethically sensitive) uses of moral judgment should qualify. But this is a small circle of concepts. Can we be confident that it will distinguish ethics from etiquette?

More recently, Wright and Johnston have tried to rehabilitate sensibility theory, reducing its reductive ambition and jettisoning the perceptualist metaphor implicit in McDowell and Wiggins's development of the secondary-quality analogy. Wright's discussion relies ultimately on the possibility of a substantive "self-contained" moral epistemology. His talk of standards that are "language-game internal," however, is reminiscent of the McDowell/Wiggins view, if now shorn of its perceptualist trappings. And though such a view need not be *false*, I have tried to raise a doubt about its explanatory adequacy.

Johnston's introduction of the general notion of a "response-dependent concept" is promising. Like Wright's idea of concepts for which a characteristic sort of bicon-ditional – one making essential reference to human subjective responses – is a priori, response-dependence bids fair to give us an understanding of how the normative might both *demand* certain attitudes from us while, in another sense, being *constituted* by those very attitudes. Of course Johnston faces an analog of the issue that threatens other sensibility theories. According to him, the relevant concepts are response-dependent *all the way down*: value is defined in terms of the balance of substantive reason, substantive reason is defined in terms of our disposition to find a reason substantive (according to an acceptable method for weighing reasons), and the acceptability of methods for weighing reasons is defined in terms of our disposition to find such methods acceptable.

The opposing attitude is suspicious of making the metaphysical depend on the epistemic in this way. A healthy modesty about our epistemic capacity nourishes the worry that we just *might* be wrong all the way down. This modesty finds expression in an echo of *Euthyphro*. Isn't the practice of finding something a good reason itself "answerable" to an independent reality in the following sense: in the best cases we find something a good reason for something else *because it is*?

If sensibility theory's heroic effort to reconceptualize objectivity fails, we are thrown back on Mackie's interpretation. According to Mackie, and according to his conception of objectivity, ethics is not objective. Our commonsense conception of it is in error. We go wrong in seeing ethical properties as objective, *that is* – for this is now what objectivity will be – as built into the fabric of the world independently of any subjective responses to those properties. To correct the error, we must slough off these objectivist tendencies and face the subjectivist reality squarely. This need not force us to non-cognitivism – just to a better appreciation of the nature of what is cognized. We are not noncognitivist about the disgusting, or about the funny, appalling, and so on. Neither should we be noncognitivist about the ethical. But we cannot be objectivist without error.

On the other hand, any sort of projectivism will have its own disadvantages. Indeed, it is partly recoil from Hume's "gilding and staining" metaphor that leads to sensibility theory in the first place. Again, Mackie himself points out that ordinary moral phenomenology is committed to the objectivity of morality. Our sense of moral outrage upon witnessing some act of wanton cruelty is experienced as a response to features of the situation that are anyway there. McDowell finds an important difference between evaluative properties and their secondary-quality cousins (not siblings) in the fact that evaluative properties can be said to *merit* the very responses in terms of which they are conceived. And Wiggins doubts that life can be meaningful if value is not seen as, in some sense, *transcending* our valuations: "no attempt to make sense of the human condition can make sense of it if it treats the objects of psychological states as unequal partners or derivative elements in the conceptual structure of values and states and their objects."[29] We are referred to Aristotle (though unsympathetically, by Wiggins, who finds it an overreaction): "We desire the object because it seems good to us, rather than the object's seeming good to us because we desire it."[30]

Perhaps it is time to reconsider the rejection of a full-blooded, *hardcore* objectivity, this notwithstanding various derogatory claims about whether the position can be "taken seriously," "is intelligible," or "incoherent."

> Of all the possible objectivist positions available in the logical space left by the denial of subjectivism, Platonism is one of the least tempting. Hardly anyone holds it, there is little point in arguing against it, and there is not very much to say about it. Any subjectivists who take it to be their most serious opposition are wasting their time on a straw man, and underestimating the strength of their objectivist opposition. . . . [I] assume that in ethics, at least, Platonism is not a live option.[31]

Exactly *why*, however, can't evaluative properties be more like primary qualities than they are like either projections or secondary qualities?

It should be admitted right away that there is a bit (or perhaps a *variety*) of subjectivism that is right. Never mind ethical properties – the very *bearers* of ethical properties depend on the existence of subjective agents. Whatever we take as the primary bearers of ethical property, whether these be intentional actions, complexes involving subjects, or just subjects individually, subjectivity is an essential element in the very constitution of the bearers of ethical properties. So the field of ethics is bound up with subjectivity in an intimate way. Notice that this seems different from, say, physics generally. There is a kind of discontinuity brought on simply in virtue of the metaphysics of the subject matter. Ethical properties are significantly different from physical properties because, whatever their nature, the former, though not the latter, could in no way obtain without the existence of agents – what could have them? Of course, if we are ultimately physicalist about the mind, this distinction dissolves.

Ethics is intimately bound up with subjectivity in a further way: part of what makes an action right has *something* to do with how that action relates to subjective agents. Such notions as intent, happiness, pleasure and pain, duty, and rights appear to be inseparable from subjectivity (as do the virtues of courage, loyalty, generosity, justice, benevolence, etc.). To the extent that those notions are relevant to the ethical status of an act, that status is not independent of subjectivity. Whatever the final form of our normative theory, it seems antecedently clear that what makes an action ethically right or good will have *something* to do with how things stand (or stood or will stand) with subjective agents. It will be some properties of subjects – either the agent herself or the agent together with various affected parties – that will make the agent's action have the ethical status it does. Exactly which properties of which subjects is a matter for normative theory. But no plausible normative theory leaves subjectivity out of the picture entirely.

These two roles for subjectivity mark an interesting division, incidentally, between ethics and aesthetics, it seems to me. The subject matter of aesthetics *need not* involve subjectivity. Beautiful things need not have any mentality as a constituent part. Consider the following passage from Putnam's *Reason, Truth, and History*.

> An ant is crawling along a patch of sand. As it crawls, it traces a line in the sand. By pure chance the line that it traces curves and recrosses itself in such a way that it ends up looking like a recognizable caricature of Winston Churchill. Has the ant traced a picture of Winston Churchill, a picture that *depicts* Churchill?[32]

Putnam doubts the pattern produced would be *meaningful*. Whatever we think of Putnam's point, there should be little doubt that the ant might produce a *beautiful* pattern. That we might value more a duplicate pattern produced by intentional agency shows only that we have more values than the purely aesthetic, it seems to me. The natural majesty of the Grand Canyon does not depend on a divine provenance; and we delight, when Voyager sends back pictures of Jupiter's surface, at the discovery of so much beauty, so far from home. We may say then, perhaps surprisingly, that aesthetics is in this way *more* objective than ethics.

The existence of subjects is thus a precondition on the obtaining of ethical properties; and how things stand with subjects will be in some way relevant to the determination of the ethical status of actions. So much forces us toward a particular sort of subjectivism in ethics. But sensibility theories press for something else. They see the nature of ethical properties as significantly interrelated with ethical *attitudes* – a specifically *cognitive* response is singled out as distinctively relevant. We have an incipient *epistemicism*[33] associated with sensibility theories. Subjective evaluations are held to be interdependent with ethical value. It is this element for which I do not see sufficient justification.

Sensibility theories appear to represent an unholy matrimony between two quite different ideas. First, the idea implicit in the analogy with secondary qualities is that the features in question are *constituted* by subjective reactions, objects have the properties *in virtue of* subjects' having those reactions, the features have no reality *beyond* that given them by the existence of the relevant subjective reactions. This idea alone is insufficient to sustain a "sensible" subjectivism, objectivity of the sort McDowell pursues, mainly because there is no independently specifiable variety of subjective reaction in terms of which to analyze the evaluative properties.

A second, very different idea is borrowed from an antirealist current (whose roots are in verificationism). That current is opposed to the idea that there might be truths that will outrun all of our best theories, no matter how much those theories are improved. This is the central idea of, for example, Putnam's "internal" or "pragmatic" realism, and whatever we may think of that so-called realism, there is an important difference between it and the central idea of the analogy with secondary qualities. Sensibility theories in ethics in this way go beyond subjectivism to a form of epistemicism. In admitting that evaluative properties are subjective in the two ways discussed above – the existence of subjects is a precondition of the obtaining of ethical properties and the ethical status of an act is not independent of the subjective states of the agents involved – we in no way commit ourselves to the epistemicism implicit in latter-day subjectivism.

The alternative floated here, then, is that ethics is subjective insofar as its subject matter essentially involves subjects and insofar as the applicability of its characteristic properties and predicates is not independent of the distribution of subjective states among the subjects involved in the ethically evaluable situation. What I allege to be irrelevant, however, is how things stand with subjects who are not involved in the ethically evaluable state: how things stand (or would stand, under specified conditions, or are disposed to stand) with actual or potential *evaluators* (that do not themselves figure in the situation) is independent of the ethical status of actions. Given that certain agents act from a vicious character, or a bad will, or produce a balance of pain over pleasure or unhappiness over happiness, the ethical status of their act is settled, and any potential evaluator's disposition to *judge* the act bad, or to have a con- or pro-attitude toward it, simply reflects their ethical acumen. Ethics is accordingly objective while still reflecting a kind of subjectivity. What could be wrong with such a view?

Recall an important passage in McDowell. "[I]t seems impossible – at least on reflection – to take seriously the idea of something that is like a primary quality in being simply *there*, independently of human sensibility, but is nevertheless intrinsically (not conditionally on contingencies about human sensibility) *such as to* elicit some 'attitude' or state of will from someone who becomes aware of it" (VSQ, p. 111 [p. 226, this volume] emphasis added). McDowell will have to do much better, in rejecting this view, than to report his inability to take it seriously. In the meanwhile, be aware of the threat of what I earlier called the "slide to avoid." Can a quality be "such as to" elicit a state of will even if many who are, in some sense, aware of it, do not acquire the state? The wording is, I think, critically indeterminate. Certainly I can elicit a response (to a party invitation, for example, I can add 'RSVP') and not get one. It is not at all impossible, or even difficult, to take seriously (indeed, to *accept*) the idea that something that is like a primary quality in being simply there, independently of human sensibility, is nevertheless intrinsically such as to elicit a state of will from someone who becomes aware of it (perhaps the state of will is in some sense demanded even of those who are *not* aware of it). Why couldn't a primary quality in the relevant sense *demand* an affective attitude?

The issue of internalism is confusing because it encompasses not only the question (i) of whether the obtaining of a property could possibly demand, independently of any subjective reactions, an affective state, but also the question (ii) of whether a subject could *judge* that a property obtains without being in the relevant affective state.[34] The case of color is again instructive. Even if it were the case that an object's being red were analytically tied to the obtaining of certain independently specifiable subjective states, it would not follow that someone could not judge that something is red without being in or even having a tendency to be in that subjective state. Color-blind people, exploiting testimony, can judge and even know that things have certain colors, colors they cannot see.

For evaluative properties too, there is the possibility that ethical value be analytically tied to the obtaining of certain independently specifiable subjective states, but that someone judges that a circumstance has positive value without being positively motivated toward it. "There is a name for not being motivated by what one judges valuable. It is of course 'weakness of will' ... [w]eakness of will ... can disrupt the expected connection between judging something valuable and desiring it in the extended sense" (DTV, 161).

Avoiding the slide, and appreciating the weakness of any plausible internalism, we see that Platonism[35] has less against it than might be supposed. The demand that ethical properties be partly constituted by subjective responses may be guided by an exaggerated internalism. Objective properties can demand responses, responses that for one reason or another they may not get. And disaffection, alienation, weakness, self-deception, and other psychological phenomena can disjoin an agent's psyche so that her cognitive and conative states do not march in lockstep. Some may be inclined to call this, when it occurs, a form of irrationality. But I for one find that too simple – for one thing, finding oneself with a recalcitrant will can rationally lead one to alter one's judgments.[36]

My purpose in this chapter has been to reflect critically on a kind of metaethical view that has been growing in popularity since at least the early 1980s. Sensibility theories emphasize, in one way or another, an analogy with secondary qualities. Ethical judgments can be objective in a manner not unlike color judgments. While the differences may be as important as the similarities (and what these differences might be is, as we've seen, a matter of some controversy), a common thread is that the ethical facts are not independent of our best judgments about what those facts are. This enables a "qualified realism" according to which we can make sense of *error* in ethical judgment while still capturing the sense that the ethical facts are in some important sense *up to us*.

I think the sense in which the ethical facts are up to us is far weaker than sensibility theory claims. The ethical facts are fixed by features of the ethical situation. Some of these will include, of course, whether agents are in pain, whether agents intend to do harm, whether agents are acting in expression of a virtuous character, and so on. But given those facts, the ethical status of the act is fixed and whatever anyone might think, no matter what their state of non-moral information, is beside the point. Of course, if they are morally sensitive, they will likely judge correctly. But to the extent there is a real issue between sensibility theory and the kind of opponent I have been trying to give content, it is better understood in connection with the following quotation from Wright.

> One basic form of opposition between realist and anti-realist views of a discourse will be between those who think of the truth of a statement as constituted in some substantial relation of fit or representation – the traditional imagery of the mirror – and those who conceive, or might as well conceive, of truth as superassertibility, as durable satisfaction of the discourse's internal disciplinary constraints.
>
> (TE, 11)

There is an important difference between supposing that moral reality is independent of human subjectivity (of course it is not – whether an act is wrong is not utterly independent of who gets hurt) and supposing that moral reality owes something to "the standards that inform our conception of responsible discourse about it" (TE, 17). Standards, and conceptions of responsible discourse, are ultimately epistemic notions. We commit the pathetic fallacy when we mistake features of our own responses to a situation for features of the situation itself. There is *some* property defined by sensibility theory. It is a relational property that a situation has (very roughly) just in case we would be disposed, under conditions understood as ideal (in nonmoral respects), to have a certain kind of pro-attitude toward it. My worry is that a theory that takes that to be an *ethical* property commits the pathetic fallacy. We are mistaking features (defined in terms) of our own responses to the situation for features of the situation itself. And in ethics, as in so many other areas, though it's not certain we'll always get it wrong, there's also no metaphysical guarantee that we must eventually get it right.[37]

NOTES

1 See, for example, Hilary Putnam's *The Many Faces of Realism* (1987).

2 Apparently originally by Stephen Darwall, Allan Gibbard, and Peter Railton, "Toward *Fin de Siècle* Ethics: Some Trends," *Philosophical Review* 101 (1992): 115–89. Page references to its reprinting as chap. 1 of Darwall *et al.* (eds) *Moral Discourse and Practice: Some Philosophical Approaches* (New York: Oxford University Press, 1997).

3 In the sense of definition 4 in the *OED*, 2nd ed., Oxford University Press (1989): "4. Pertaining or relating to the passions or emotions of the mind." Cf. definition 3 of "pathos": "In reference to art, especially ancient Greek art: The quality of the transient or emotional, as opposed to the permanent or ideal: see *ethos* 2." The referenced entry 2 for "ethos" is remarkable: "In reference to ancient aesthetic criticism and rhetoric; Aristotle's statement that Polygnotus excelled all other painters in the representation of 'ethos' apparently meant simply that his pictures expressed 'character'; but as Aristotle elsewhere says that this painter portrayed men as nobler than they really are, some modern writers have taken *ethos* to mean 'ideal excellence.' The opposition of *ethos* and *pathos* ('character' and 'emotion'), often wrongly ascribed to Aristotle's theory of art as expounded in the *Poetics*, really belongs only to Greek rhetoric." And consider the accompanying quotation: "1881 *Q. Rev*. Oct. 542 The real is preferred to the ideal, transient emotion to permanent lineaments, pathos to ethos."

4 Cited in John L. Mackie, *Ethics: Inventing Right and Wrong* (Harmondsworth, Middlesex: Penguin, 1977) [hereafter cited as *Ethics*], p. 42.

5 The phrase "pathetic fallacy" was first used by John Ruskin to label a different sort of peccadillo: 1856 Ruskin *Mod. Paint*. III. iv. xii. § 5. 160 "All violent feelings ... produce ... a falseness in ... impressions of external things, which I would generally characterize as the 'Pathetic fallacy'." But Eliot gave Ruskin's point a twist: 1856 Geo. Eliot in *Westm. Rev*. Apr. 631 "Mr. Ruskin ... enters on his special subject, namely landscape painting. With that intense interest in landscape, which is a peculiar characteristic of modern times, is associated the 'Pathetic Fallacy' – the transference to external objects of the spectator's own emotions." In any case, Mackie's use is slightly different again: we do not suspect the fungus itself has feelings of disgust; rather that it has some property to which our disgust is a direct and appropriate response.

6 Also David Lewis ("Dispositional Theories of Value," *Proceedings of the Aristotelian Society*, supp. vol. 63 [1989]: 113–37) and Michael Smith ("Dispositional Theories of Value," *Proceedings of the Aristotelian Society*, supp. vol. 63 [1989]: 89–111), whose views, however, have specific features that take them outside the scope of the present essay.

7 Simon Blackburn, "Errors and the Phenomenology of Value," in T. Hondereich (ed.) *Morality and Objectivity* (London: Routledge & Kegan Paul, 1985).

8 Moreover, I attend to projectivist and eliminativist alternatives only obliquely.

9 See, for example, Appendix I to Hume's *Enquiry Concerning the Principles of Morals*.

10 John McDowell, "Values and Secondary Qualities," in T. Hondereich (ed.) *Morality and Objectivity* (London: Routledge & Kegan Paul, 1985) [Chapter 12, this volume. Cited hereafter as VSQ].

11 McDowell's attempt to address this concern is clearest in his later "Projection and Truth in Ethics," in S. Darwall *et al.* (eds) *Moral Discourse and Practice: Some Philosophical Approaches* (Oxford: Oxford University Press, 1997) [Chapter 25, this volume], which we will discuss below.

12 See his *Essays in Quasi-Realism* (New York: Oxford University Press, 1993).

13 Cited in John McDowell, "Projection and Truth in Ethics," p. 216 [p. 490, this volume, cited hereafter as PTE].

14 David Wiggins, "A Sensible Subjectivism?" [cited hereafter as SS], in *Needs, Values, and Truth: Essays in the Philosophy of Value* (Oxford: Blackwell, 1987), p. 186.

15 Compare Mark Johnston's point about verificationism. Mark Johnston, "Dispositional Theories of Value," *Proceedings of the Aristotelian Society*, supp. vol. 63 (1989): 139–74, p. 146.

16 In a similar vein, Darwall *et al.* note, "A peg that fits a round hole has a particular shape; so does a hole that fits a square peg; but what shape in particular do an otherwise unspecified peg and hole have thanks to the fact that they fit each other?" "*Fin de Siècle* Ethics," p. 21.

17 Crispin Wright, "Moral Values, Projection, and Secondary Qualities" [cited hereafter as MVP], *Proceedings of the Aristotelian Society*, supp. vol. 62 (1988): 1–26; Wright, *Truth and Objectivity* (Cambridge, MA: Harvard University Press, 1992) [cited hereafter as TO].

18 Crispin Wright, "Truth in Ethics" [cited hereafter as TE], in B. Hooker (ed.) *Truth in Ethics* (Oxford: Blackwell, 1996).

19 Together with Blackburn's discussion ("Errors," pp. 1–4), which I do not address here, this may constitute a third such failure.

20 In, *inter alia*, *Truth and Objectivity* (1992).

21 Johnston, "Dispositional Theories of Value," [cited hereafter as DTV], p. 139.

22 This sort of criticism is made by others too. See Blackburn, "Errors," p. 14.

23 Actually at first he gives this only as a necessary condition; but in the following paragraph he affirms its sufficiency.

24 His arguments against those overambitious responses to the basic problem are spelled out in detail in his "Objectivity Refigured: Pragmatism Without Verificationism," in J. Haldane and C. Wright (eds) *Reality, Representation, and Projection* (New York: Oxford University Press, 1993).

25 "[H]yper-external reasons, reasons which could in principle outrun any tendency of ours to accept them as reasons, even under conditions of increasing information and critical reflection" (DTV, 172).

26 From Ludwig Wittgenstein, "Lecture on Ethics," *Philosophical Review* 74 (1965): 3–11.

27 Though this is one way, indeed Kant's, of securing the result. It is also, differently, Michael Smith's. Michael Smith, *The Moral Problem* (Cambridge, MA: Blackwell, 1994). Smith's contribution to the Aristotelian Society symposium on dispositional theories of value appears with Lewis's and Johnston's. Smith, "Dispositional Theories of Value."

28 It's worth noting that Johnston has begun developing an attractive and more qualified conception of the scope of response-dependent accounts. "Are Manifest Qualities Response-

Dependent?" *Monist* 81 (1998): 3–43. It is not clear whether this new conception remains susceptible to the critical considerations adduced here: if what substantive reason is on the side of valuing is (in his terms) "manifest," then it would seem Johnston has revised his view in a way that would make it immune to the worries I raise (and more sympathetic to the alternative implicated here).

29 David Wiggins, "Truth, Invention, and the Meaning of Life," *Proceedings of the British Academy* 62 (1976): 331–78. Reprinted in his *Needs, Values, and Truth*, pp. 87–137. See p. 106 (page references to its reprinting in *Needs, Values, and Truth*).

30 Ibid.

31 Susan Hurley, *Natural Reasons* (New York: Oxford University Press, 1989).

32 Hilary Putnam, *Reason, Truth, and History* (New York: Cambridge University Press, 1981), p. 1.

33 Say that "epistemicism" with respect to an area is a matter of holding that the truth of claims in that area depends on our tendency to find them true.

34 Cf. also Darwall's distinction between *existence internalism* and *judgment internalism*, Stephen Darwall, *Impartial Reason* (Ithaca, NY: Cornell University Press, 1983), pp. 54–5; and Brink's distinction between "agent" and "appraiser" internalism, David Brink, *Moral Realism and the Foundations of Ethics* (Cambridge: Cambridge University Press, 1989), p. 40.

35 "Platonism" might be inapt: there need be no commitment to an intuitionistic epistemology, and the view that ethical properties occupy an abstract Platonic realm is optional. The position is constituted by holding ethical properties to be akin to primary qualities in their independence from subjective judgment (though with the qualifications noted). If sensibility theories constitute a "reactionary" realism, perhaps "Anti-Reactionary Realism" is a better term.

36 Such a view put me at odds with Michael Smith's well-developed view (e.g., Smith, "Dispositional Theories of Value"; Smith, *The Moral Problem*; Smith, "Internalism's Wheel," in Hooker (ed.) *Truth in Ethics*) of the consequences for ethical theory of internalism. His work is part of a significant literature on that subject. Considerations of space prohibit a discussion that takes account of it. I hope to pursue the issue elsewhere.

37 My thanks to Mark Johnston, conversations with whom shaped some of my thinking on these issues, to Brian Leiter for useful comments, written and oral, throughout the development of this essay (and for making it possible in the first place), to Dan Bonevac and Cory Juhl for critical discussion, and to the participants in my metaphysics seminar here at Austin in Spring 1998.

Part 5

EXPRESSIVISM

Our moral language is often fact-stating, or seemingly so. We often hear people say, "Those people are so kind", "That was a wicked thing to do" and "This regime is unjust". These are as much attempts to describe the world – the world of people, actions and institutions – as utterances such as "This table is brown". For an utterance to be fact-stating and descriptive is for it to stand as an attempt to describe the world and to get things right. Such utterances are normally assumed to be truth-apt, that is there is something about the world such that the utterance describes things correctly or does not, it is either true or false. (This idea of truth-aptness will be discussed in more detail in Part 7.) But, when one thinks about things carefully, is moral language descriptive in this fashion? After all, we often use language that is more suited to commands. "Don't do that!" is a common refrain, as is "Give her some of your sweets". But these aren't the sorts of utterance that can be truth-apt at all. (It does not make sense to say, "It is true that don't do that", and placement in such a larger sentence that still makes grammatical sense is one of the hallmarks of an utterance being descriptive.) Now, we could easily imagine that with a little bit of jiggery-pokery we could transform such commands into descriptive utterances. For example, "Charity-giving is a good thing" is straightforwardly descriptive. But this should make us pause. Perhaps we can just as easily transform seemingly descriptive utterances into commands or, even, expressions of attitude or preference. Sometimes when we see a lovely bowl of strawberries we might say "Mmmm, strawberries". This isn't a descriptive utterance. We aren't describing anything in the world, be it the strawberries we are looking at or our taste preferences. The linguistic expression is just that, an expression of a personal attitude, rather than our attempt to describe something about ourselves or something in the world. Perhaps, then, moral language functions not to describe things about the world but is, at heart, functioning to give commands or to express responses and attitudes to the world, or something else. So, when we say that charity-giving is good we are really saying "Hoorah for charity-giving!" or somesuch. And, if we decide that moral language does function, at bottom, in this way, this has huge ramifications for our moral metaphysics. It looks likely that if ethical language is fundamentally expressive, then there is no moral reality that exists and which we could attempt to describe. The moral world is really a nonmoral world to which people express positive or negative attitudes. (Strictly, of course, it could be that moral properties exist even if ethical language works in an expressive fashion. Perhaps humans simply do not have the right linguistic and conceptual traditions to do justice to how the world is. Many people put this option aside and assume that, in this context, our best guess about what the metaphysics is should be informed by our arguments for how our language should be assumed to function. We leave the reader to reflect on whether this is a justified assumption.)

Much of this should be familiar from § 6 of our Introduction (Chapter 1). We are leaving the possibility of moral language being primarily a matter of commanding aside. (But see Hare (1952) in Further Reading below.) In this Part and the next few we concentrate on expressivism, the claim that moral language is best understood as an attempt to express our attitudes towards a nonmoral world rather than as an attempt to describe an assumed-to-exist moral world. The question facing us now is: What reason do we have for being expressivists? In the first selection in this Part, Simon Blackburn (Chapter 14) – one of the leading exponents of modern expressivism – valuably situates expressivism in a variety of options available to us before he outlines what expressivism is and provides reasons for being an expressivist. We pick out two reasons he provides for being an expressivist.

First, if one is any sort of moral naturalist, then one faces a problem. Imagine that two people who (seemingly) disagree about some moral matter – Blackburn's example is contraception – have different standards or nonmoral conceptions of what it is for something to be morally good. In that case, what each means by 'moral goodness' is different; for a utilitarian 'moral goodness' is to be identified with that which is useful to society, whereas a priest might cast moral goodness as that which God has willed. When one says that contraception is morally good and the other says otherwise then they are not, strictly, *disagreeing* with each other but rather talking past each other. Although they are using the same words, this shouldn't blind us to the fact that what they mean by those words are very different things. It is the same as one person saying, "Contraception is good" and the other saying, "No, contraception is yellow". It makes no sense to call this a disagreement. But this theoretical explanation of what is happening surely cannot be right since we think that such disputes are real things and that people aren't talking past each other. The alternative, then, is to say that there is just one nonmoral standard as to what moral goodness is. But the difficulty then is to get everyone to agree to what it is. Of course, even if we do not reach such agreement it could well be that moral goodness really is one nonmoral thing, let's say 'usefulness' for argument's sake. But in that case what do we say of the priest, or someone else who has a different conception of moral goodness? If they are speaking erroneously how do we explain how they can disagree with others, our original problem? How do we explain that there can be anything like a clash of descriptions as there should be if we are thinking in descriptive terms?

Adopting expressivism short-circuits these problems, although it raises others. Because people are not making a descriptive claim about the value of something such as contraception, then we can say that we should not expect any sort of direct contradiction between them about the moral nature of the thing in question. Rather there is a clash – unlike in the scenario above – but it is a clash of attitudes that they have expressed. It's true that this does not give us a characterization of moral disagreement that we might have wanted at the start – one by where they are both in the business of describing the world and where they are not talking past each other – but often philosophers will transform ordinary phenomena into something other than we expected. Adopting expressivism at least lets us say that there is a clash and the pair are not trying to dispute using completely different conceptions of a word.

This reason given by Blackburn is part of a wider reason for favouring expressivism. Essentially, one can wonder why it is that nonmoral stuff gets to be moral, one can wonder how the moral 'enters' the world. Why is pleasure, or happiness, or usefulness, morally good? (Or – more specifically – why is it that using condoms, or not using condoms, or picking up shopping for old ladies who have stumbled, are considered by people as morally good things?) This is one of the key questions in metaethics. The expressivist answer is that the moral enters the world because people evaluate the world in a certain way, and expressivists put this act of evaluation – this expression of attitude – at the centre of their theory. (Note: this is different from putting the *reporting* of such an evaluation at the centre of a theory. That could well lead to a realist account.)

A second reason that Blackburn gives for preferring expressivism comes at the end of the excerpt. He claims that it is a better alternative to realism than error theory is. His reasoning is roughly that if one follows through on the central claims of error theory then one is committed to viewing ethical activity as completely mistaken (and, perhaps, corrupt, hypo-critical and other worse things). But this is a large mistake in itself and something we should not commit ourselves to. Expressivism gives us an alternative because expressivists view ethical activity as perfectly legitimate, but simply not the sort of realist activity that one might have expected it was at the start. And one can massage our worries there by marrying to one's position about moral language what Blackburn calls 'quasi-realism'. The idea behind this is that one uses the resources the expressivist identifies – attitudes and other noncognitive states had towards a nonevaluative world – and build up near-realist conceptions of truth, moral reality and the like. As mentioned, we think about expressivism and truth in Part 7. But for now, the idea in brief is that we can talk as if there is a moral reality and sets of moral standards, simply because many people have similar sorts of response to things and similar ways of thinking. But we should not confuse this – as, say, sensibility theorists might do – with the idea that our responses are picking out a moral reality, a moral reality that comes into being by some complicated combination of natural world and human response. This is confused and confusing. It is safer to treat human responses as, at bottom, expressions of attitude towards a nonmoral world. (For more on quasi-realism start with Blackburn (1993) listed below in Further Reading.)

Expressivism, however, is a controversial doctrine and faces many problems. We encountered a few of them in our Introduction. We might ask why moral language has a descriptive form if it does not function in this way. We also raised the question of what we should do with someone who is quite sophisticated and insists that she is trying to describe the moral world even if philosophers think that she is expressing attitudes. (Recall that this is not so much a problem for expressivism, but rather an issue facing all metaethicists when thinking about how general to make their theories.) There are other problems as well that we shall meet in the next few Parts. In this Part we concentrate on one problem that has been advanced recently. In this Part's second selection, Frank Jackson and Philip Pettit (Chapter 15) argue that expressivists will find it hard, if not impossible, to prevent their position becoming a type of descriptivist position and that this, obviously, is fatal for the hope of making expressivism an internally coherent and plausible position.

Jackson and Pettit present their problem thus. Expressivism consists of two main claims. The first, negative claim is that moral utterances lack truth conditions. The second, positive claim is that moral utterances are expressions of attitude rather than reports or descriptions of facts. (They claim also that the second idea is supposed to explain the first.) Jackson and Pettit argue that expressivists do not have a plausible story about how it is that moral utterances express rather than describe attitudes. They use thoughts from John Locke in order to do this. Assuming, as expressivists do, that words such as 'good' and 'wicked' are used, when they are used, in some sort of intentional, non-accidental way (unlike, say, involuntary yawns), then we must assume, argued Locke, that they are 'conventional signs'. They are used to signify ideas that all mature speakers in a linguistic community can understand. That certain words are used to signify certain ideas is something fairly arbitrary; we could have used 'schmicked' rather than 'wicked' in English. Yet communication happens all the time so there must be some measure of agreement, however implicit and historically rich, that serves to underpin why it is that the word 'fairness', say, is used in the way it is. But, in which case, if there is agreement then people must know what it is that such linguistic entities stand for and how they are used. Then, to cut a long story short, it would seem odd that we could use words – both generally and on particular occasions – if we failed to recognize or even assume that we had the appropriate feeling that is thought by all linguistic speakers to lie behind the word in question. So, when someone says, "Charity-giving is good", if we assume that she is trying to communicate with typical English speakers (and is speaking sincerely), we must assume that she recognizes that she has a certain sort of attitude, or feeling of whatever, that is the typical thing that stands behind the word 'good'. If we did not assume that an utterer herself had to assume this, we could not assume that she was trying to speak English and communicating (and speaking sincerely rather than trying to convey something other than what attitude she had towards charity-giving). As Jackson and Pettit put it in their § 2, 'We regulate our linguistic behaviour under the presumption that our fellows are doing likewise as part of our membership of a common linguistic community.' The killer blow is that if all this is right, then it seems that what we are doing is reporting our attitudes rather than expressing them. We are reporting to our fellow speakers that we believe that we have the attitudes that stand behind the linguistic terms that we are using when we are communicating with them.

As Jackson and Pettit point out, claiming that moral utterances report attitudes is compatible with claiming that they express attitudes. Indeed, a good way to express an attitude is to report that you have it. (It would be odd to say that you had failed to express your approval of charity-giving because you had only reported that you had such an attitude.) But, they claim, once you allow that there is reporting of attitudes occurring, then you lose your right to make the first, negative claim from above. It appears that moral utterances do have truth conditions. In which case, a central claim of expressivism is lost. In fact, expressivism has become a certain sort of subjectivism. By 'subjectivism' here they mean a descriptivist position which claims that ethical utterances are truth-apt and where the thing making such utter-ances true and false are the moral beliefs of a particular subject, in this case a special sort of subject, namely the utterer themselves. (So, notice that 'subjectivism' here is not a sort of moral relativism. Relativism says, roughly, that no claims are truth-apt *per se*, that is true or false no matter who you are and what you think. Subjectivism here is the claim that such utterances are truth-apt, for all people, but they are indexed to a particular person.)

One of the most interesting challenges to Jackson and Pettit's arguments comes from Michael Smith and Daniel Stoljar (Chapter 16). They argue that Jackson and Pettit do not notice an important distinction between for-agreements and when-agreements. Sometimes when we use words, we agree to use them *for* something. To take Smith and Stoljar's example, in the case of 'square' we agree to use it to stand for, or to truly apply to, square things. In the case of 'good', though, we have agreed to use it *when* we are in a certain psychological state. But these two types of agreement are different, or can be. It is an open matter what the psychological state is referred to in the case of the second type of agree-ment. Perhaps we have agreed to use 'good' when we have a certain approving attitude towards things. The crucial thought is that we could then communicate (sincerely and successfully) by using the word 'good' without having to refer to (or report, or describe) the psychological state that stands behind it. And this means that one could keep the expressivist claim that ethical utterances are not truth-apt (or, as Smith and Stoljar say, truth-evaluable). Smith and Stoljar bolster their argument by thinking about indicative conditionals and by considering objections and replies to what they say. Similarly, Jackson and Pettit discuss various ways in which expressivists might argue against their conclusion. All of these thoughts depend, unsurprisingly, on *how* language works and *what* is conveyed by certain utterances in certain circumstances, and then what we can assume about the moral case. We leave the reader to read these thoughts and to make their mind up about the various points made. What we wish you to think about, generally, is how moral language (and other evaluative language) should be assumed to function and then, further to that, what philosophical claims can be built on such assumptions. Such thoughts are crucial not just to the fortunes of expressivism, but many other metaethical positions.

As a coda to all of this, note in Further Reading that Jackson and Pettit (2003) reply to Smith and Stoljar's argument where they put pressure on the distinction between the two supposed types of agreement. Ira Schnall's (2004) article provides commentary on this debate, and Jackson and Pettit (1999) also debate their paper with Michael Ridge.

QUESTIONS TO CONSIDER AND TASKS TO COMPLETE

1   Try to explain, in your own words, what expressivism is. Do you think it captures much of the phenomena of everyday moral language?

2   How might an alternative non-descriptivist position to expressivism work, such as one based on assuming that moral language comprises commands?

3   What do you think of the various alternatives that Blackburn (Chapter 14) describes to expressivism and his comments about them? Do you think he motivates the need for expressivism well?

4   Can you think of advantages for expressivism that Blackburn does not mention?

5   Try to state Jackson and Pettit's (Chapter 15) argument in your own words. How convinced by it are you? What do you think of Smith and Stoljar's (Chapter 16) reply?

FURTHER READING

There are a variety of expressivist positions. Earlier advocates normally mentioned are A. J. Ayer and C. L. Stevenson. The two most prominent modern defenders of the position are Simon Blackburn and Allan Gibbard.

Ayer, A. J. (1936) *Language, Truth and Logic* (London: Gollancz).

Barker, Stephen (2006) 'Truth and the Expressing in Expressivism', in *Metaethics After Moore* (eds) Terence Horgan and Mark Timmons (Oxford: Oxford University Press).

Blackburn, Simon (1992a) 'Gibbard on Normative Logic', *Philosophy and Phenomenological Research*, vol. 52, no. 4, pp. 947–52.

——(1992b) 'Wise Feelings, Apt Readings', *Ethics*, vol. 102, pp. 342–56.

——(1993) *Essays in Quasi-Realism* (Oxford: Oxford University Press).

——(1996) 'Securing the Nots', in Walter Sinnott-Armstrong and Mark Timmons (eds) *Moral Knowledge* (New York: Oxford University Press), pp. 82–100.

——(1998) *Ruling Passions* (Oxford: Oxford University Press).

——(2002) 'Replies', *Philosophy and Phenomenological Research*, vol. 65, pp. 164–76.

Carson, Thomas (1992) 'Gibbard's Conceptual Scheme for Moral Philosophy', *Philosophy and Phenomenological Research*, vol. 52, no. 4, pp. 953–6.

Gibbard, Allan (1990) *Wise Choices, Apt Feelings* (Oxford: Oxford University Press).

——(1992) 'Reply to Blackburn, Carson, Hill and Railton', *Philosophy and Phenomenological Research*, vol. 52, no. 4, pp. 969–80.

——(1993) 'Reply to Sinnott-Armstrong', *Philosophical Studies*, vol. 69, pp. 315–27.

——(1996) 'Projection, Quasi-Realism and Sophisticated Realism: Critical Notice of Blackburn's *Essays in Quasi-Realism*', *Mind*, vol. 105, pp. 331–5.

——(2003) *Thinking How to Live* (Cambridge, MA: Harvard University Press).

Hare, R. M. (1952) *The Language of Morals* (Oxford: Oxford University Press).

Hill, Thomas (1992) 'Gibbard on Morality and Sentiment', *Philosophy and Phenomenological Research*, vol. 52, no. 4, pp. 957–60.

Horwich, Paul (1993) 'Gibbard's Theory of Norms', *Philosophy and Public Affairs*, vol. 22, pp. 67–78.

Jackson, Frank and Pettit, Philip (1999) 'Reply to Ridge', at: www.brown.edu/departments/philosophy/bears/homepage.htm

——(2003) 'Locke, Expressivism, Conditionals', *Analysis*, vol. 63, no. 1, pp. 86–92.

Kalderon, Mark (2005) *Moral Fictionalism* (Oxford: Oxford University Press).

Locke, John (1690) *An Essay Concerning Human Understanding* (ed.) P. H. Nidditch (Oxford: Oxford University Press, 1975).

Miller, Alexander (2003) *An Introduction to Contemporary Metaethics* (Cambridge: Polity Press), chapters 3, 4 and 5.

Railton, Peter (1992) 'Nonfactualism and Normative Discourse', *Philosophy and Phenomenological Research*, vol. 52, no. 4, pp. 961–8.

Ridge, Michael (1999) 'A Solution for Expressivists', at: www.brown.edu/departments/philosophy/bears/homepage.htm

Schnall, Ira (2004) 'Philosophy of Language and Meta-ethics', *Philosophical Quarterly*, vol. 54, no. 217, pp. 587–94.

Sinnott-Armstrong, Walter (1993) 'Some Problems for Gibbard's Norm-expressivism', *Philosophical Studies*, vol. 69, pp. 297–313.

Smith, Michael (2001) 'Some Not-Much-Discussed Problems for Non-cognitivism in Ethics', *Ratio*, vol. 14, pp. 93–115.

——(2002) 'Which Passions Rule?', *Philosophy and Phenomenological Research*, vol. 65, pp. 157–63.
Stevenson, C. L. (1944) *Ethics and Language* (New Haven, CT: Yale University Press).
Van Roojen, Mark (1996) 'Expressivism and Irrationality', *Philosophical Review,* vol. 105, pp. 311–35.
Wright, Crispin (1988) 'Realism, Antirealism, Irrealism, Quasi-Realism', *Midwest Studies in Philosophy*,
    vol. 12, pp. 25–49.

14

REALISM AND VARIATIONS

Simon Blackburn

The one discovers objects as they really stand in nature, without addition or diminution: the other has a productive faculty, and gilding or staining all natural objects with the colours, borrowed from internal sentiment, raises in a manner a new creation.

David Hume, Appendix 1 of the *Enquiry Concerning the Principles of Morals*

1 OPPOSITIONS TO REALISM

Hume's description of the different offices of reason and taste sets a challenge. How do we tell when we are discovering objects "as they really stand in nature", and when we are doing some other thing, such as projecting onto them our own subjective sentiments? Which side of this divide do we fall on when we describe objects as good or bad, nice or nasty, hot or cold, red or blue, square or round? Echoing Hume the scientist Heinrich Hertz says that "the rigour of science requires that we distinguish well the undraped figure of nature itself from the gay-coloured vesture with which we clothe it at our pleasure".[1] How do we know where to draw this distinction, or what counts as an argument for putting a given saying on one side or the other? This is the issue between realists and their opponents. It takes a bewildering variety of forms, for philosophers have seen it very differently. Realists are contrasted with a variety of alleged opponents: reductionists, idealists, instrumentalists, pragmatists, verificationists, internalists, neo-Wittgensteinian neutralists, and no doubt others. They also form obscure alliances with, and hostilities towards, various views about truth: correspondence, coherence, pragmatic, redundancy, semantic, theories. To swim at all in this swirl of cross-currents we need a better lifeline than any which these mysterious labels provide.

My strategy will be to follow through a variety of possible attitudes to some particular area of commitments. This will give us a sense of the options *locally*. But by coming to appreciate local issues, arising, say, in the philosophy of value, or of mathematics, we can work our way into more general problems of realism and truth, and get a sense of why the *global* issues fall out as they do. I prefer this to a top-down strategy, which would approach highly general issues of the nature of truth first, and then apply the results to particular cases, because the general issues are more or less unintelligible unless given particular applications.

When discussing meaning in 2.1 I introduced the possibility of a perspective from which facts about meaning appeared utterly mysterious – a perspective from which the world could not contain any such facts. Similar doubts pepper the whole of philosophy. Hume could not see what kind of thing a causal connection between distinct events could be; mathematical, moral, and aesthetic facts seem suspicious to many people; semantic, psychological, conditional facts invite scepticism, and so on. Once such doubts are felt – motivated in whatever way – a number of attitudes are possible. We might *reject* the whole area, advocating that people no longer think or speak in the terms which seem problematic. Or, we might seek to give a *reductive analysis* of it, advocating that the problematic commitments be put in other terms, and claiming that when this is done the problems disappear. We can try to see the commitments not as beliefs with *truth-conditions* but as expressions of other sorts. We can query whether the commitments are *mind-dependent* – not really describing a mind-independent reality at all, but as in some sense creating the reality they describe. And at each choice-point there will be a jumble of issues and of suggestions about what the debate hinges upon. In particular there can be the attitude which I christen *quietism* or *dismissive neutralism*, which urges that at some particular point the debate is not a real one, and that we are only offered, for instance, metaphors and images from which we can profit as we please. Quietism is a relative newcomer to the philosophical world, owing much of its inspiration to the positivist mistrust of metaphysics, and to the belief of the later Wittgenstein that such problems required therapy rather than solution.

Views about truth will be particularly relevant where we discuss whether some commitment is best regarded as a belief with a truth-condition, or in some other light. For this contrast seems to hinge upon our view of what it is for a commitment to have a truth-condition, and it is here that the various lights in which truth is put – correspondence, coherence, and so on – affect the issue. Thus, to take a simple example, moral commitments are often thought of as not really beliefs, but as more like attitudes, emotions, or prescriptions: this contrast in turn may look very different if we think of beliefs in pragmatic or instrumental terms rather than in terms of correspondence with facts.

Putting together the positions I have suggested we then get the map illustrated in Figure 14.1. But, as I have said, the issue need not be clear-cut at any of these choice-points: there will be different suggestions as to what the decision hinges upon, and, from the quietist, the general disenchantment with discussing the issue at all. Quietism

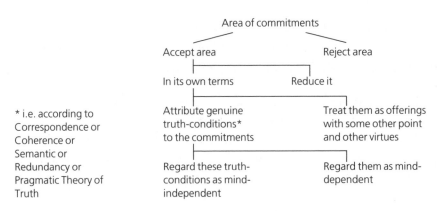

Figure 14.1

is currently expressed by denials that there is a "god's-eye view" or an "external" or "Archimedean" point from which we can discover whether some commitment is, as it were, describing the undraped figure of nature or imposing clothing. Perhaps we either accept the sayings in a given area, and "from that standpoint" suppose that they describe reality, or we do not accept them, and of course think that they do not. In other words, an overall quietist is only interested in the first choice-point, and ignores the rest. We shall see that this is unduly short-winded. I shall now introduce the various options at greater length.

2 REJECTION

We might want to reject a given commitment within an area without rejecting the whole area. We do not accept that 2 + 2 = 5, but we do, of course, accept many beliefs about numbers. Rejecting a whole kind of commitments is more sweeping. Until relatively recently it seemed to raise few problems. If a remark in some area (e.g. a moral remark) is meaningful it must have a definite content. If it does, either things are as it says they are, and it is true, or they are not, and it is false. If it does not have a definite content it is meaningless, or at least vague and defective on that score. How is there any room for subtlety here?

The only subtleties arise because the neat division between attributing a definite, false, content to a remark and rejecting it in some other way is, in practice, impossible to rely upon. I can introduce the problems this causes with a simple example.[2] Consider the use of the term "Kraut" as a term of contempt for Germans. If someone describes Franz as a Kraut, I want to reject his remark. Do I say it is *meaningless*? Hardly. I know what I am being asked to think, and it is because I know this that I find the remark offensive. Is the remark *false*? We usually accept an equivalence between "it is false that *p*" and "it is true that not-*p*". But I do not want to *say* that it is true that Franz is not a

Kraut. That is the remark made by someone who has the contemptuous attitude towards Germans, but believes that Franz is not a German. So I do not want to say that on two counts. So should I say that the remark is true or even half-true? Uncomfortable, again.

One theory would be that the remark is a conjunction: "Franz is a German *and* on that account he is a fit object of derision." A conjunction is false if either part is. Since I regard the second conjunct as false I should maintain that the whole remark is false. In this spirit we would say things like "there are no Krauts," or "nobody is a Kraut." This is a way of construing the remark, and thence of disowning the attitude. But a different option is to regard the remark as true, but to disown the phrasing. A parallel would be "Franz is a *German*" said with a derisive intonation on the last word. Here we suppose that what was strictly said was true but reject the overtone. The convention would be that you only put beliefs about Germans using that overtone (or the derisory word) if you have the contemptuous attitude. If this is the right account then it is in fact true that there are lots of Krauts (although I would not put it that way myself).

Each proposal is "semantically coherent": in other words, a population could properly speak a language L_1 in which the first analysis is right, and the remark is false, or L_2, in which the second is right, and the remark is rejected, although what it strictly says is true. Is there bound to be a fact determining whether English operates like L_1 or L_2? If not, then there is no uniquely right way of expressing rejection of the utterance. Since we are left with a slight sense of discomfort with either of the sharp options, perhaps there is this indeterminacy. The vocabulary belongs to people who accept a certain attitude – that being a German is enough to make someone a fit object of derision. Rejecting the attitude we reject the vocabulary. But if the way the attitude is expressed is indeterminate, it will also be indeterminate whether remarks made by people using it are true or false. In other words, people using a certain vocabulary tend to have clusters of belief, some true and some not, or clusters of attitudes, some acceptable and some not, and tendencies to favor certain inferences, some reliable and some not. But there may be no conventions determining how many of these habits we are endorsing by accepting some remark as true, nor how many we are rejecting by regarding it as false. The overall rejected theory may have distributed its content in no very secure way over the various sentences involved. It will then be unsettled how to express the rejection.

The problem arises in more serious areas. In writing the history of science (or any other body of thought) we want to express what was right and wrong about particular doctrines. But the vocabulary people had may offer no particular way of doing this. Terms will have been used in the context of clusters of beliefs, attitudes, habits of reasoning and inference. Some of these we will accept, and others we will reject. But how could the people have formed conventions determining that some particular thing is the *right* thing to say, in the face of *unforeseen* disruptions of beliefs, attitudes, and habits? There is no cause to worry whether we are speaking L_1 or L_2 just so long as the views and attitudes remain intact. But when they are disrupted, then from the later standpoint it may be indeterminate *which* sayings, expressed in the earlier vocabulary, can be thought of as true, and which as false. For instance, Newtonian mass was a concept central to classical physical theory, and integral to the enormous success and near-truth (as we now see it) of that theory. Unfortunately amongst the things believed in that theory is that the mass of an object is quite independent of its velocity – its rest mass and moving mass are always identical. When this thesis is abandoned, and we consider other sayings of classical physics, such as "force applied is proportional to mass times change in velocity," it is simplistic to regard them either as definitely true, or as definitely false. They were part of a theory or overall web of belief which involved false views; how much of the falsity is to be read into an individual saying is often indeterminate. The reason we can put up with this indeterminacy is *not* that in any sense we cannot express what the old theory held. We can express it very easily, in our own terms, just as we can say what people think when they describe Germans as Krauts. We do not have to share the views and attitudes in order to know what they are. What we cannot easily or determinately do is describe things in *their* terms (are there or are there not Krauts?) because there is *no unique way* in which the rejected views can be pinned onto individual sayings, and insulated from others. We cannot neatly partition truth and falsity, sentence by sentence, across their individual sayings.

The point deserves attention whenever we consider how to describe our distance from other theories, or webs of views and attitudes. Was there such a stuff as phlogiston? Can a Marxist believe in human rights? Using our terms we can distinguish what was true and false in the beliefs held by phlogiston theorists. Using his scheme of values the Marxist can say what is acceptable and what not so in the (bourgeois) conception of rights. But it is quite hopeless to try to express that distance by allowing that individual theses of the rejected theories express uncontaminated truths, or uncontaminated falsities. That requires *using* the old vocabulary (there are or are not *Krauts*; are or are not human *rights*), and this is something which, from the opposed point of view, it will be undesirable to do.

There is a temperament which would dismiss this as an unfortunate product of the vagueness of ordinary thought, contrasted with some ideal language with the precision to give every remark definite, indubitable conditions of truth and falsity. If we met this ideal, then whatever the changes in belief and attitude, we could always look back and attribute definite truth or falsity to each individual saying in the old terms. But how could such an ideal language be speakable? The significance of remarks has to be one which we are capable of giving them. That capacity is a function of our beliefs, attitudes, of the things we have been exposed to and the habits of thought, reasoning, and inference in which we indulge. We cannot possibly foresee how these may be improved, or what strange possibilities will disrupt them. When they are changed, previous usages will pull in different ways, and there is no reason to expect previous sentences to express individual propositions, isolatable as truths or falsities in the new scheme of thought. To paraphrase Wittgenstein, when we start to abandon a way of thought, the lights do not go out one by one, but darkness falls gradually over the whole.

3 REDUCTION

A different attitude to a theory, which yet shades into outright rejection of it, is that its theses can be accepted, but their content can be expressed in other ways, using a different kind of vocabulary. Thus we might find some particular set of terms awkward or puzzling in various ways; the demand becomes that we can give an "account" – an analysis, or reduction, or reinterpretation – of the things said using them. The analysis supposedly reveals the true or proper content of remarks in the area. For example, if moral commitments appear particularly puzzling, attempts might be made to reinterpret them in some other terms: perhaps "X is something which ought to be done" means the same as "X will produce more happiness than any alternative". The moral vocabulary would then turn out to be just a different way of putting ordinary, natural, or psychological truths. In that case it would import no particular problems of its own – such as ones of what kind of thing moral facts can be, of how we can know about them, or how they relate to underlying natural facts, and so on. If the moral vocabulary demanded a distinct type of moral fact these questions would arise, but since, according to the analysis, it does not, they resolve themselves. We know about what ought to be done in whatever way we know about the creation of happiness, since it is a proposition about this which gives the real content of the moral statement.

Famous positions in philosophy which are based on the claim that analyses and reductions are possible include:

Phenomenalism:	the analysis of propositions about external reality into ones about actual and possible experiences;
Positivism:	the analysis of propositions about theoretical entities into ones about regularities in experience;
Behaviourism:	the analysis of propositions about mental states into ones about dispositions to behavior;
Logicism:	the analysis of propositions about numbers into truths of (elementary) logic, thought of as describing no especial, abstract, subject-matter;
Naturalism:	the position in ethics already described.

And there are many other local analyses – of propositions about causation into ones merely describing successions of events, of ones about the meanings of terms into ones about peoples' intentions when they use the terms, and so on. Indeed, so many philosophical problems centre around the possibility and desirability of providing analyses of various kinds that in the early part of this century the philosopher's role became identified with this (*analytical* philosophy). Naturally in an empiricist and verificationist time attempts are made to reveal in terms especially close to experience the true content of statements which appear to concern esoteric subjects. The idea behind the verification principle is that the real meaning of any assertion can be found by analysing the difference in sense-experience which its truth would make.

The motivation for reductive analyses is based on a contrast. The commitments expressed in some original vocabulary (the A-vocabulary, or A-commitments) must be felt to introduce some apparent puzzle, either of meaning, or of epistemology, or of metaphysics, not introduced by statements made in the analysing, B-vocabulary. An analysis represents a piece of imperialism on behalf of the concepts expressed in B-terms, and will be motivated if the A-statements are in some particular way puzzling, or if there is a background view that everything which it is possible to say truly can be said in B-terms. If only we did not have the additional A-commitments, the puzzles would go: the solution is to propose that in the relevant sense we do not have them – they are not additional, because their true content can be revealed entirely in B-terms. Examples on a local scale, suggesting the kind of relief which reductive analysis can bring, are quite persuasive. Suppose I tell you that Henry's prestige is enormous. Suppose that you are attached to an ontological doctrine – roughly that everything which exists has a place in space and time, and has scientifically measurable properties of weight, charge, velocity, etc. Then Henry's prestige seems an odd kind of object: you cannot put it into a bucket or weigh it or measure it – what kind of *thing* is it? Your problem is removed by analysing the original A-remark so as to remove reference to this mysterious thing: it means nothing different from this B-remark: other people admire Henry enormously. If your world-view allows for this kind of fact, then there is nothing further to jib at in talking of prestige. Notice of course that other problems might still remain – problems with the kind of statement to which the original was reduced. Your world-view might make it difficult to accommodate people admiring one another; in which case you have to continue the analysis until you find statements which you can put up with. B-statements might need reduction to C . . . W which is respectable.

In itself the claim that one statement has the same content as another is quite symmetrical: this suggests that the problems affecting the first must also affect the second. But, as the example about prestige shows, this is not inevitable. The problem might arise only because of a feature of the original which is not shared by the analysing statement. In this example the feature was the *apparent* reference to a non-physical thing. Once it is accepted that this feature is not essential, since the same content can be expressed without it, the problem resolves itself. Usually, however, it is not so obvious whether the analysis does more than draw other statements into the problematic class. For instance, a *counterfactual* analysis of causal remarks is quite attractive: to say that X causes Y is, perhaps, to say something like "if X had not happened, and other things had been the same, Y would not have happened". But even if this equation works, its significance is debatable. What is the contrast which motivates such a reduction? What problem of meaning, epistemology, or metaphysics, does the initial statement have, which is removed if we can see its content as the same as that of the second? Or does the counterfactual come to seem just as problematic, in terms of what makes it true or what shows it to be true, as the original causal statement? A prominent example of this difficulty is the equation of arithmetical with set-theoretical remarks. Propositions about numbers may be reduced to propositions about sets in various ways. But even if one of these is taken to really give us the meaning of the original arithmetical statements, the question is whether sets then take on a good deal of the mystery of numbers, posing substantially the same problems of existence, mind-independence, and of knowledge and logic, which originally make arithmetical statements into desirable objects of analysis.

So for a successful reduction we need an A-discourse which poses some problem, a B-vocabulary used to say things which do not pose this problem, and an equation between any propositions expressed in the first and some set of judgments expressed in the second. Now, however, we can see that there can be considerable tension between the disappearance of the problem, and the equation of meaning. If the original problem is a substantive or persistent one, then the fact that A-statements are subject to it *by itself* suggests that we take them to mean something different from the B-statements, so that the equation fails. This is a kind of Catch 22: if the reduction is really well motivated, then it cannot be true. For example, we have given our moral vocabulary a meaning which results in moral statements posing characteristic problems of proof or verification, of truth and objectivity. For this very reason, we might urge, they cannot be identical in meaning with other statements which do not pose these problems. Moralizing is a specific activity, so how could these other statements give us a non-moral way of doing it? The reply has to be that the problems prompting the reductions are in some sense only apparent – in other words, they arise only because we misapprehend the true content of A-statements. When these are seen for what they are – in B-terms – the temptation to puzzle over the problems disappears (as with prestige). However, this reply in turn raises a query: what right has anyone to separate out the reduced content as the only true content of the original, if our practices, including our doubts, problems of verification and proof, and so on, all suggest that we take those statements to have a further or different content?

A sharp formulation of this problem comes with the classical "paradox of analysis". Consider as an example the proposal that "*X* ought to be done" means the same as "*X* would bring about more happiness than any alternative". Now it is quite intelligible to describe someone as wondering, or doubting, or thinking, whether all and only things which ought to be done would bring about more happiness than any alternative. Indeed, faced with the proposal the first thing to do is exactly to try the thought-experiment of finding a counterexample – a thing which satisfies the one concept, but not the other. But how is this possible, if the analysis is correct? If the two notions just mean the same, then it would seem that the doubt or wonderment can have no content – it would be the same as doubting whether all and only things which ought to be done ought to be done, or whether all and only things which bring about more happiness than any alternative bring about more happiness than any alternative. The paradox (which has other forms) gives rise to quite difficult technical problems, some of which I discuss under the general heading of difficulties over substitution of synonyms for one another elsewhere. Here it illustrates the general point, that frequently one set of terms is *given* a sufficiently different role by us, as witnessed by our beliefs, doubts, queries, etc., for the claim that it has the same role as some reducing set of terms to seem implausible from the beginning. A common aspect of this is an asymmetry in the way we regard A-truths and B-truths, in respect of explanation and evidence. Frequently the B-truths (e.g. about sense experience, or behaviour, or non-moral states of affairs) are regarded as evidence for the A's but not vice versa. This asymmetry is incompatible with the view that the content of the A-statements is identical with that of some suitable set of B-statements. Now reductionism often has just this kind of asymmetry as its target: it is sceptical whether there is a legitimate inference from B-truths to a *different* set of A-truths. This is why it prefers to reduce the A's down, meaning that the inference is no longer vulnerable. It leads nowhere different, outside the B-range. But since this *revises* the natural belief, it hardly gives the meaning of the original concepts, but suggests substitutes.

Because of this problem, there is a tendency for reductionist programs to take on a revisionist air. It becomes tempting to shelve the question of whether the reductions mean the same as the original statements. Suppose our doubts, puzzles, or other practices illustrate a way in which we take A-statements as having more content than B-statements. Still, perhaps the B-statements exhaust the legitimate content of the A's. In that case the extra can be dismissed as the product of muddle, of "prehistoric metaphysics" and failure to see the A-vocabulary's only legitimate role. The extra that we add is to be pruned away, in a program of reconstruction. Reductionists from Berkeley right to Russell have tended to uncertainty over the relation of their analyses to the original discourse. One part of them wants to *accept* the original discourse – the A-statements – because, of course, they have identical content with quite legitimate

B-statements. But another part wants to voice *suspicion* of the A-statements, because along with the pure content, there is the intruding illegitimate element which disguises it. Thus Berkeley presents himself as siding in all things with the mob: his analysis of the world as a community of spirits and ideas allows us to think that there exist tables, chairs etc. However, in another mood he will insist that it is a vulgar *error* to suppose, for example that anything is ever both touched and seen (since the ideas of touch and those of sight are quite different from each other, and his idealism disallows any common object). Yet chairs and tables are ordinarily thought to be both seen and touched. So Berkeley havers over whether the reduced, legitimate content exhausts the actual meaning we can give to statements, or whether in the actual meaning there is additional, false material, arising because of our misunderstanding of the idealist truth, and resulting in statements which ought to be rejected. Russell too presents an uncertain attitude towards statements of the A-kind: a phenomenalist analysis means, on his view, that chairs and tables become "logical fictions", but whether this allows us to say that there really are tables and chairs (surely something the mob, the vulgar, want to say) is not certain.[3] The one line would be that we can say this (meaning by it something susceptible of expression in terms of actual or possible sense-experience), the other line would be that we cannot, because it involves views which are themselves impugned by the phenomenalist reduction.

Not that it is too discreditable to sit on this particular fence. From the reductionist point of view the legitimate content is given by the B-statements. Whether the A-statements have a meaning which supplies them with more, but illegitimate, content, may be left relatively indeterminate. Suppose, for example, that false views about the relation between A-sayings and B-states of affairs have prevailed – prehistoric metaphysics which supply us with images and metaphors, ways of taking A-statements which serve to separate them from B's. Then it may be indeterminate to what extent we accept these particular views when we accept A-statements. If we do, then the B-statements should be seen as replacements. If we do not, they may be analyses revealing the real content. A phenomenalist may happily admit that ordinary people are so infected by false views about the independence of objects from our sense-experience, that there is something of a shock in his analyses. And, according to me, given that the shock is one of realizing that some of our thoughts about objects and ourselves were wrong; he need not try to settle whether these thoughts were part of the content of our ordinary remarks, so that the proposal is to replace these, or whether on the other hand these thoughts were mere accidental sideshows, not part of what we ever said, so that the full content of this is revealed in the reducing B-statements.

A nice example comes from moral theory. Suppose people are naturally drawn to the realist options when they think about moral remarks. Then the realist thoughts might become so associated with the vocabulary that anti-realist theory is no longer perceived as giving an analysis or reduction of the original content (or as treating it in some other anti-realist way) but as proposing to replace that content by some purged substitute. An anti-realist who accepts that realist views were "part of the meaning" of the original saying will have an "error view" of these, and urge replacement not reduction: someone who denies this may regard himself as merely revealing the meaning. As we have already seen, if we grow up to use a given vocabulary *and* have various views about the subject matter, there is no likelihood of definite conventions determining how many of those views are properly part of the content of statements made in the vocabulary. This does not take the interest out of reductionist claims. The interest remains in whether sufficient approximations to A-statements can be made in the B-vocabulary, for us to regard any differences as in effect detachable – the product of erroneous ways of thinking of the area. Serious questions can still remain about the adequacy of a B-vocabulary, as either a reconstruction or substitute for an A-vocabulary, even if we remain agnostic about which of these it is best taken to be.

4 EXPRESSIVE THEORIES: CONTRASTS WITH TRUTH

This brings us to the third point of departure for anti-realism: the attempt to explain the practice of judging in a certain way, by regarding the commitments as *expressive* rather than *descriptive*. The commitments in question are contrasted with others – call them judgments, beliefs, assertions, or propositions – which have genuine truth-conditions.

Two classic examples of such theories are instrumentalism, as a philosophy of science, and emotivism in ethics. According to this latter, the commitment that a thing is good or bad, right or wrong, permissible or impermissible, is not a judgment with truth-conditions of its own (probably irreducible to other terms, by the argument of the last section, and therefore highly mysterious). It is a commitment of a different sort, maintained not by *believing* something but by having an *attitude towards* it. The theory was expressed with characteristic vigor by A. J. Ayer:

> The presence of an ethical symbol in a proposition adds nothing to its factual content. Thus if I say to someone, "You acted wrongly in stealing that money," I am not stating anything more than if I had simply said, "You stole that money." In adding that this action is wrong I am not making any further statement about it. I am simply evincing my moral disapproval of it. It is as if I had said "You stole that money," in a peculiar tone of horror, or written it with the addition of some special exclamation marks.[4]

Emotivism is sometimes dubbed the "boo-hooray" theory of ethics. Ayer here presents it by a contrast between what is *stated* and what it *evinced*. The same contrast can be put in terms of what it is to accept a moral remark; it is to concur in an attitude to its subject, rather than in a belief. Alternatively we might say that the speech-act of putting forward a moral opinion is not one of asserting that some state of affairs obtains, but one of evincing or expressing an attitude, or perhaps of exhorting or encouraging others to share an attitude.

In the heyday of linguistic philosophy similar suggestions were applied to a wide range of commitments:

Saying that X causes Y	=	Offering X as an instrument or recipe for obtaining Y
Saying that action X is voluntary	=	Expressing willingness to blame or commend the agent
Saying that you know X	=	Allowing other people to take your word for it
Saying that a statement is true	=	Endorsing it
Saying that a statement is probable	=	Expressing guarded assent to it
Saying that a statement is possible	=	Refusing to endorse ruling it out of consideration.

Expressive theories contrast with reductions. On an expressive account there is a considerable difference between saying, for instance, that X causes Y, and saying anything which might be a plausible candidate for a reductive analysis – e.g. that events similar to X are always followed by events similar to Y. You might only offer the recipe if you believed this latter thing. You might be open to criticism if you offered it when this latter thing was false. In other words, the regularity might provide a *standard* for endorsing the recipe. Nevertheless the standard might, in principle, be variable or displaced by something more subtle, but this would not be a change in the meaning of the causal saying. This is particularly important in the moral case. Naturalism finds it impossible to say how disputants with different standards mean the same by moral remarks. On the account according to which the meaning of such a remark is given by the standard for saying it which the speaker has, people with different standards mean different things. But that makes it impossible to see how they are expressing conflicting opinions. If a utilitarian says that contraception is an excellent thing, he would mean that it promotes happiness; if a priest says that it is an awful thing, he might mean that it is against the wishes of the creator of the universe. But in that case each remark could be true, and there would be no contradiction between them. The expressive theory avoids this undesirable consequence. It locates the disagreement where it should be, in the clash of attitudes towards contraception.

Expressive theories must be sharply distinguished from more naïve kinds of subjectivism. An expressive theory does not give a moral utterance a truth-condition which concerns the speaker. A man saying "Hitler was a good thing" is expressing or evincing an appalling attitude. But he is not *saying that* he has got this attitude. If he were, what he said would be true, provided that he is sincere. But we do not regard his remark as true; we allow that he is sincere, if he is, without accepting his remark (which, on the expressive theory, would mean endorsing the attitude it expresses).

The point of expressive theories is to avoid the metaphysical and epistemological problems which realist theories of ethics, and of the other commitments in the list, are supposed to bring with them. Again it is important to remember the overall motivation. This is to explain the practice of moralizing, using causal language, and so on, in terms only of our exposure to a thinner reality – a world which contains only some lesser states of affairs, to which we respond and in which we have to conduct our lives. Unless this is borne in mind, it is easy to charge expressive theories with irrelevant mistakes. For instance, it is frequently pointed out that a term may occur in an utterance which *both* is a description of how things are, *and* expresses an attitude. If I say that there is a bull in the next field I may be threatening you, or warning you, or expressing timidity, or challenging you to cross, or doing any of a range of other things, and expressing any of a range of subtle attitudes and emotions. But none of these doings has any bearing on the meaning or content of my remark, which is true or false in a determinate range of circumstances, and is a paradigm of a saying with a truth-condition. If I say that someone is a Kraut, or blotto, I may express an attitude of contempt towards Germans, or of wry amusement at drunkenness, but I also say something true or false about their nationality or sobriety. In the bull example the attitudes expressed are incidental to the conventional meaning of the remark. In these other examples they attach to the vocabulary as a matter of convention. You should not use those terms unless you sympathize with those attitudes. But in each case it would be wrong to infer that *no* description is given from the fact that an attitude is *also* expressed. Similarly, critics have pointed out, it is wrong to infer that there is no strict and literal content, capable of truth and falsity, in the remark that X causes Y, or X knows the truth about Y, or X ought to be done, from the fact that when these things are said, attitudes are expressed. This "speech-act fallacy" has been widely accepted as the root mistake of expressive theories.[5]

However, the fallacy need not be committed (and I rather doubt if it ever was). There are two reasons why not. First of all, an expressive theory should not infer that the attitude gives the role of the saying, simply from the fact that it is expressed when the saying is made. So long as the attitude *may* give the role, the argument for saying that it does is the superior explanation of the commitments which we then arrive at. There is no inference of the form "this attitude is expressed, *so* these remarks have no truth-conditions", but only "this attitude is expressed; if we see the remark as having no truth-conditions the philosophy improves; so let us see the remark as expressive rather than descriptive". There is no fallacy there. And there is a second point. Remembering the anti-realist motivation, we can see that it does not matter at all if an utterance is descriptive as well as expressive, provided that its *distinctive* meaning – the aspect which separates it from any underlying B-descriptions – is expressive. It is obviously a useless argument against anti-realism about values to point out that the word "Kraut" has a descriptive element. That is quite acceptable. It is the *extra import* making the term evaluative as well as descriptive, which must be given an expressive role. It is only if that involves an extra truth-condition that expressive anti-realism about values is impugned. But perhaps there is no good reason for supposing that it does: the natural thing to say about such terms is that the extra ingredient is emotive, expressive.

There are, however, much more respectable arguments surrounding expressive theories. These concern the extent to which they can explain the appearance that we are making judgments with genuine truth-conditions. Ultimately it is the attempt to explain this which introduces the need for a wider theory of truth, and enables us to appreciate the point of the different contenders. We should realize that expressive theories, like reductive theories, may be uncertain about how much they need to explain. Suppose that we say we *project* an attitude or habit or other commitment which is not descriptive onto the world, when we speak and think as though there were a property of things which our sayings describe, which we can reason about, know about, be wrong about, and so on. Projecting is what Hume referred to when he talks of "gilding and staining all natural objects with the colors borrowed from internal sentiment", or of the mind "spreading itself on the world". Then expressive theorists often tend to the view that this projection is a *mistake* – that itself it involves flirting with a false realism. (Ayer entitled his chapter from which I quoted, "A *Critique* of Ethics and Theology".) John Mackie believed that our ordinary use of moral predicates involved an *error*, because the underlying reality was as the expressive view claims, whilst in using those concepts we claim more.[6] For this reason he denied that emotivism gives the actual *meaning* of moral terms, and this claim is frequently put forward as almost self-evident. But it is not. The issue is whether the projection is only explicable if we mistake the origins of our evaluative practices. The idea would be that were we aware of these origins we would give up some or all of our tendency to practice as if evaluative commitments had truth-conditions, and were not expressive in origin and in their essential nature. But perhaps there is no mistake. I call the enterprise of showing that there is none – that even on anti-realist grounds there is nothing improper, nothing "diseased" in projected predicates – the enterprise of *quasi-realism*. The point is that it tries to earn, on the slender basis, the features of moral language (or of the other commitments to which a projective theory might apply) which tempt people to realism. The issues are complicated enough to deserve a chapter to themselves. It is only when we have understood them that we can properly assess the final divisions between realists and their opponents, over mind-dependence and over truth.

5 METAPHOR AND TRUTH

There is one other overtly expressive phenomenon of interest to the philosophy of language: metaphor. Metaphor has not commanded the respect of many mainstream theorists of meaning: it can appear to be merely a poor relation of proper judgment, arising only when language is on holiday, and the appropriate attitude is that voiced by Hobbes:

> In Demonstration, in Councell, and all rigorous search of Truth, Judgement does all; except sometimes the understanding have need to be opened by some apt similitude; and then there is so much use of Fancy. But for Metaphors, they are in this case utterly excluded. For seeing they openly professe deceipt; to admit them into Councell, or Reasoning, were manifest folly.[7]

By contrast with this stark hostility we can mention Nietszche's attitude that truth itself is merely good dead metaphor. Those who appreciate a good metaphor certainly seem to acquire a gain of *some* sort. So we should at least ask how this gain compares with that of acquiring a true belief. I can best organize this issue by comparing four different positions, in ascending order of the importance they attach to metaphor.

(1) The prosaic end of things. Some metaphors scarcely deserve the name: they are close to being dead metaphors, or idioms. If I tell you not to cross the path of someone who is prickly, steaming, or up in arms, you understand my language, for all its figurative nature, as immediately and certainly as if I had chosen more literal ways of expressing myself. The words I use are customarily associated with features of things which I could have expressed directly. Let us say that the figurative language *yields* an interpretation if the interpretation is customarily given, and customarily expected. If the custom has hardened into a convention we have a case of an *idiom*, and it will be right to say that we have a new or extended literal meaning. Perhaps "prickly" in this context means "easily aggravated." In that case a dictionary ought to report the fact, and a learner ought to be taught it. And someone could fully understand sentences in which people are described as prickly, without knowing that the word has a use in which it applies to cacti and hedgehogs. But a term may yield an interpretation reliably enough without this having happened: the yield is given firstly by the literal meanings of the terms, and secondly because some feature of the original thing meant is "salient," or an associated commonplace. In other words it is a feature people think of when they think of the original, and which in the context is a likely feature to apply to the subject-matter. "Bert is a real gorilla" yields that Bert is strong, rough, and fierce. It does this because the word "gorilla" has its normal meaning, and because people (wrongly) associate these features with gorillas.[8] Any hearer aware of this can follow the metaphor to its intended interpretation.

In these first-level cases the metaphor has an intended interpretation which is reliably given. But the mechanism goes via the ordinary meaning of the terms, to the suggested meaning: we have only an indirect way of suggesting some definite truth by saying some definite falsehood (for Bert is not really a gorilla). There can be some debate about how we fit these facts into other theoretical categories. Is it right to describe the speaker as having asserted falsely that Bert is a gorilla? Is it right to describe him as having asserted truly the yielded propositions, that Bert is strong and rough and fierce? Because of our analysis of convention and tone we need not find these questions too hard. The speaker said that Bert is a gorilla, but did not assert it: he did not intend anyone to believe that this was the truth, and would not normally be taken to have displayed that it is. He did, on the other hand, intend people to believe that Bert is strong, rough, and fierce, and chose a reliable method of transmitting this belief, and of being taken to do so. But the method was one of reliable suggestion, and we do not allow that people assert everything that they reliably suggest, and are known to be reliably suggesting. However, the responsibility the speaker bears is much the same as if he had said straight out what he transmits only indirectly. He has chosen a customary and certain way of representing to his audience that Bert is strong, rough, and fierce: if he is not, Bert has an equal right to feel aggrieved (if he is really like a gorilla, perhaps he will not do much about it).

(2) The next cases differ from the previous ones in that they maintain an open-ended or creative element. The range of features indicated remains indefinite: both speaker and listener are able to explore the comparison or image suggested, and find new features of the subject matter as a result. The critic I. A. Richards talked of poetic language as a "movement among meanings": there is no single literal truth which the figure or metaphor yields, and no single class of such truths. Thus when Romeo says that Juliet is the sun we can profit from the metaphor indefinitely: we can move among respects in which someone's lover is like the sun: warm, sustaining, comforting, perhaps awesome, something on which we are utterly dependent ... This process is quite open-ended. Shakespeare need have had no definite range of comparisons which he intended, and it is quite wrong to substitute some definite list and suppose that the exploration is complete. The metaphor is in effect an invitation to explore comparisons. But it is not associated with any belief or intention, let alone any set of rules, determining when the exploration is finished.

This is the first sense in which metaphor is both valuable and ineliminable. It is valuable because it directs our attention towards aspects of things which we might not otherwise have thought of. It is ineliminable because there is no single list of literal thoughts which cashes it in. In this respect the metaphor may work like a picture (we talk in the same breath of metaphorical and figurative uses of language, or uses of imagery). Possessing a picture I may think of the subject pictured, and the picture may lead me to think of all kinds of things. But no list of these things substitutes for the picture, just because the picture has an unlimited potential for directing me to further

310

aspects of the subject, whereas the list does not. As Davidson puts it, "Joke or dream or metaphor can, like a picture or a bump on the head, make us appreciate some fact – but not by standing for, or expressing, the fact."[9]

(3)   The preceding level is enough to defend and in a way to explain the value of metaphor. It gets us beyond the crass thought that using metaphor is always an indirect and inferior way of putting what would best be put directly (although it can be this, and at the first level often is). Still, at the second level the value of a metaphor is essentially that of a means to an end. The end product is appreciation of a literal truth or several literal truths. The metaphor suggests how to go about finding some such truth or truths. Its success is dependent upon their value to us, and perhaps too upon providing us pleasure in the exploration. (There is pleasure in exploring the metaphor of the Church as a hippopotamus even if we do not believe anything about the Church at the end that we did not believe at the beginning.) So far, however, the only way that a metaphor can provide a gain in understanding is by provoking a quest which may end up in our grasping some new strict and literal truths. The third level of description queries this. It alleges that there is a distinct, intrinsically metaphorical, way of understanding. The appreciation of the metaphor constitutes a different, distinctive success of its own: the success of seeing one thing *as* another. Seeing history as a tidal wave, or architecture as frozen music, is doing something different from believing, and different from accepting an invitation to search for a range of beliefs. But it is a gain in understanding, a success, of its own kind.

It is absolutely vital to see that this kind of description is not forced on us by level (2) facts. And it is a defect of some of the best literature on the subject that it does not clearly separate the two ideas. Some even explain the ineliminability of metaphor *via* its alleged level (3) powers. Davidson, at the end of his highly illuminating paper on the subject, says: "Since in most cases what the metaphor prompts or inspires is not entirely, or even at all, recognition of some truth or fact, the attempt to give literal expression to the content of the metaphor is simply misguided." But the attempt to give literal expression would be misguided even if we accepted only the *second* level of description, where the metaphor *does* prompt or inspire a search for literal truths or facts. It is quite another question whether it can prompt or inspire a mode of insight all of its own, so that the appreciation of one thing *as* another or *in the light of* another is a distinctive metaphorical way of understanding. It is this idea which Hobbes was opposing.

The sheer psychology of coming to appreciate a good metaphor, like seeing a joke or seeing the point of a comparison, may suggest this way of describing things: If I suddenly see architecture as frozen music, or history as a tidal wave, it feels like a gain which is quite akin to acquiring a new piece of knowledge. It seems like possession of a self-sufficient *thought*. It doesn't seem just like accepting an invitation to explore the comparison, because I may relish the metaphor and yet have no sense at all that anything remains to be done, which is the distinctive aspect according to (2) descriptions. In support of this we can notice how often we assent to a remark without realizing that there is metaphor buried in it. A large amount of philosophy consists in unravelling how much is metaphorical, and how much literal, when we talk of: the *foundations* of knowledge; bodies *acting* upon one another; the *flow* of time; propositions *corresponding* to facts; the mental *realm*, and so on. Suppose we decide that there is a large amount of metaphor involved when we talk, say, of the foundations of knowledge. What then do we say of someone who passionately believes that knowledge has foundations, and in no sense realizes the degree of metaphor? He does not realize how much exploration needs to be done to arrive at some literal truth about knowledge, so he does not see himself as someone who has just accepted an invitation to look for such truths. And he is not someone who has come to a literal belief about knowledge, because he may have no non-metaphorical way of expressing himself. Are we to credit him with a metaphorical piece of understanding (or misunderstanding, if knowledge needs no foundations)?

The opposing view would be that there is no distinctive understanding here. The man says the words supposing that they mean something true, and that he knows what it is. More thought would disillusion him. So he simply believes he has a belief, when in fact he has none. He thinks he is rich when he has a cheque which he cannot actually cash. But he has not therefore come into possession of a different kind of currency. Consider too the exercises of imagination involved in seeing history as a tidal wave, or architecture as frozen music. We present ourselves with images; we put a sense of the inexorable sweep of a tidal wave alongside our thoughts of the progress of historical events, or our sense of the structure of a cathedral alongside a sense of the structure of a piece of music, suddenly stopped in time. Such exercises are pleasurable, even marvelous. But the ability to conduct them is not itself the exercise of a distinctive piece of understanding. A historian who performs the exercise every so often may enjoy the idea; he may even find that in some way it guides his writings or his attitudes to events. But it is what he then says which means that he understands history well or badly. In short, it is not necessary to postulate a distinctive success which the metaphor provides. Its virtue lies in prompting insights, but the insights themselves are strict and literal truths.

(4) This rebuttal of level (3) descriptions of metaphor may leave some dissatisfaction. I would express it like this: the rebuttal takes for granted the kind of success involved in acquiring a (strict and literal) *belief*. But what right have we got to contrast this with seeing one thing *as* another? We have seen how ordinary belief involves the transference of a term from one set of things to another, and it was the business of chapter 3 to search for some conception of the rules and intentions which govern this process. In that chapter we met the idea that only natural propensities to find things similar underlie any kind of description of things. Why shouldn't a natural propensity to see

one thing as another or in the light of another, which yet falls short of applying the same predicate to them in the same meaning, not serve to found a self-standing piece of metaphorical insight? I take it that this is why Nietzsche describes literal truth as worn-out metaphor. Is belief perhaps just one end of a spectrum of attitudes which can go with the new application of a term: at this end, pure prose, and at the other end, pure metaphor?

To think of this, compare two populations. Each of them is taught a certain term initially in connection with a certain range of cases or range of procedures. In one population they find it natural to describe some new cases by the same term. In the other they find it natural to see the new cases in the light of the old, or see them *as* possessing the feature, but they view this as irreducibly a case of "seeing as." These think of the extension as metaphorical, whereas the others think of it as a simple case of belief. What is the difference?

A plausible example might help. Consider the way in which we use terms which also describe physical affairs to describe psychological affairs. We talk of matches in boxes, and thoughts in the head; of being pulled by ropes, or being pulled by desires; of jumping to attention, or jumping to a conclusion. Metaphorical, of course. Or is it? We most probably cannot cash the metaphors, either by giving a single literal way of saying something which they yield or even by indicating a range of comparisons which they suggest. On the other hand we should not be happy with just postulating two different senses of the terms: it is not pure accident that we talk of thoughts in the heads, for example. If it were simply a case of the word "in" being ambiguous we might just as well have planted the ambiguity on some other term, and talked of thoughts being *on* the head, for instance. Yet we should also be unhappy with the idea that there is a smooth or natural extension of the terms from the physical to the mental. Someone who understands what it is for one thing to be in another physically has a definite range of capacities: he can find things, obey instructions, perform a range of tasks which exhibit or exercise that understanding. These tasks are not the same as any (whichever they might be!) which exercise an understanding of thoughts being in the head.

It is profitable here to recall the bent learners. Imagine a bent learner who responds perfectly well to some range of cases, but whose capacity to exercise his concept involves odd bends and blind spots. From our point of view his capacity is flawed or partial. From the point of view of the population which finds it natural to spread a term over a larger range, people who do not find it natural, but who regard the extension in the spirit of a metaphor, would similarly be flawed or partial. Now if we sympathize with either conventionalist or even naturalist responses to the bent learner it will seem that such reactions are all that there is to go on: it is then a matter merely of our reactions which determine whether an affirmation expresses a belief or only a metaphor. But if the opposition to nominalism is roughly right, we do not get this result. According to me there is a distinctive fact whether the extension over new cases is, or is not, an exercise of the same capacities that are involved in applying the term to the original kind of case. This ought to give determinancy to the issue of whether a new kind of application is metaphorical or not.

But even if the issue is determinate, it is often not easy. Remember the examples of philosophical descriptions/metaphors, and the difficulty of disentangling the literal from the metaphorical which they illustrate. I suggested that the man affirming that knowledge has foundations may only think he is expressing a literal belief, but not be doing so; similarly for someone saying that thoughts are in the head, or that we are often pulled by desire. If such a person recognizes no obligation to find a better way of putting it and insists on resting content with his way, what can we urge? We show the way the *practice* differs: what verifies whether a building has foundations, whether one thing is inside another, whether one thing is pulling another. We show how in the ordinary cases these truths influence things which, for example, we want; beliefs in them therefore couple with our desires to have consequences for action. Since the practice is different in the disputed case, however much we sympathize with the passive acceptance of the same terminology, the obligation to look for the points of similarity and difference remains.

Sadly, then, I incline to Hobbes's view that understanding things metaphorically is not understanding them at all, although it may often immediately yield understanding, and guide it and increase it. On this account a good metaphor at the open-ended level is expressed by an utterance which does not say that such-and-such is the case, but rather expresses an invitation or suggestion that a certain comparison be followed up. In this respect such an utterance is like the other speech-acts listed in the last section. It does not have truth conditions, but is successful or not in a different dimension. In the next chapter I explore this contrast a little more, and consider objections which such accounts tend to meet.

NOTES

1 Quoted in van Fraassen, *The Scientific Image*, p. 6.
2 In the nature of the case, the following example employs offensive terms with which I do not associate myself.
3 E.g. Russell, "The Philosophy of Logical Atomism," in *Logic and Knowledge*, pp. 272–3. Berkeley, *Principles of Human Knowledge*, §§ 38–51.
4 A. J. Ayer, *Language, Truth and Logic*, ch. 6, p. 107.
5 J. Searle, *Speech Acts*, p. 139. H. Putnam, *Reason, Truth and History*, pp. 208–10.
6 J. Mackie, *Ethics: Inventing Right and Wrong*, pp. 30–5.
7 Hobbes, *Leviathan*, p. 44.
8 People may think of these features although they do not believe gorillas to have them. But in a population which comes to realize this, the metaphor will begin to die out, or degenerate into

an idiom. For consider children learning. They will only realize the intended yield by learning that it is a distinct custom to use "gorilla" as if fierceness were a feature of the animal, when natural history has told them it is not. This is not readily distinguishable from learning a distinct convention, or meaning.

9   "What Metaphors Mean," in Platts (1980), p. 253.

BACKGROUND NOTES

§ 3 Reductionism in the Philosophy of Science deserves much more discussion than I have been able to give it here. A good literature would include:

A. J. Ayer, *The Foundations of Empirical Knowledge*.
I. Scheffler, *The Anatomy of Inquiry*, pt. II.
R. Carnap, "The Methodological Status of Theoretical Concepts," *Minnesota Studies in the Philosophy of Science*, vol. i (1956).
B. van Fraassen, *The Scientific Image*, ch. 2.

§ 4 The most comprehensive recent collection on metaphor is: A. Ortony (ed.), *Metaphor and Thought*. However, I think nobody would claim that the study of metaphor has been one of analytical philosophy's brighter achievements. In particular, a number of discussions seem to presuppose that the problem is one of how we "compute," according to rules and principles, a non-literal meaning from a literal one. I hope that the stress in the text on the dynamic and open-ended exploration of metaphor removes the idea that we do any such thing.

15

A PROBLEM FOR EXPRESSIVISM

Frank Jackson and Philip Pettit

1 INTRODUCTION

Language, Truth and Logic added expressivism to the inventory of substantive positions in meta-ethics, and the recent defences of versions of it by Simon Blackburn and Allan Gibbard have enhanced its status as a major position.[1] Ayer presented the doctrine as an improvement on subjectivism – that is, on the doctrine that ethical sentences serve to report attitudes of approval and disapproval – and it is widely supposed to be an internally coherent and interesting position. We argue, however, that there is a serious problem that expressivists, unlike subjectivists, have to face which has not been adequately addressed in the development of the doctrine.

Expressivism is a bipartite theory. It holds, first, that ethical sentences lack truth conditions – they are not truth apt, truth assessable etc. – and do not serve to report anything that the speaker believes to be so. And it holds, second, that ethical sentences express certain distinctive pro and con *attitudes*, and express them without in any sense reporting them: without reporting them even in the broad sense in which 'The present King of France is bald' reports the existence of the King as well as his baldness.[2] The first clause is a negative, semantic claim; it denies that ethical sentences have truth conditions. The second is a positive claim: it informs us about the function – that of expressing attitudes – served by ethical sentences.

The second, positive clause is supposed to underpin the first, semantic claim in the following sense. If ethical sentences reported the presence of attitudes rather than merely expressing them – if they expressed beliefs that the attitudes were present – then, problems of vagueness aside, they would automatically be true or false. They would be true just when the beliefs they expressed were true, just when the attitudes they reported obtained. The reason, according to expressivists, that ethical sentences lack truth conditions is precisely that they express attitudes without reporting them.

The problem that we raise for expressivism is that expressivists do not have a persuasive story to tell about how ethical sentences can express attitudes without reporting them and, in particular, without being true or false. We think that they cannot satisfactorily explain how the two clauses in their theory can obtain together: how, without being true or false, as the first clause maintains, ethical sentences can yet serve to express certain attitudes, as the second clause insists that they do. Although there are (of course) interpretations that might be given to the claim that ethical sentences express attitudes which would mean that ethical sentences lack truth conditions, we shall see that they are not interpretations that expressivists can afford to embrace.

Most of our paper is given to presenting this problem but a final section is devoted to the issue, as it is often described, of the persistence of moral disagreement. Expressivists argue that, precisely because they deny truth conditions to ethical sentences, they are especially well-placed to make sense of persisting moral disagreement. This, indeed, is the argument with which Gibbard launches *Wise Choices, Apt Feelings*.[3] In the final section, we argue that this is a mistake: the denial of truth conditions to ethical sentences is not merely hard to maintain for the reasons we will be presenting, it does not buy a solution to the puzzle that so often motivates it.

One further remark before the main business. We said above that expressivism holds that ethical sentences serve to express attitudes. This is a simple version of expressivism. More complex versions might talk of expressing higher-level attitudes, or attitudes formed after due deliberation or negotiation with others, or the properties to which the attitudes are expressed, and so on. In the same way, we can distinguish simple versions of subjectivism that hold that ethical sentence report the attitudes of the utterer from more sophisticated (and plausible) versions that focus on higher level attitudes, properties of actions inasmuch as they prompt attitudes in us and others, and so on. We shall continue to frame our discussion in terms of the simple versions. The argument is more easily developed in relation to them and extends *mutatis mutandis* to the more complex ones.

2 LOCKE ON VOLUNTARY SIGNS

The crux of the problem we raise for expressivism is that a point of Locke's about language makes it very hard for expressivists to hold onto their view that ethical sentences express attitudes in a way that prevents those sentences from having truth conditions.

In holding that ethical sentences serve to express attitudes, expressivists do not suggest that this occurs in an unintentional or accidental manner: in the manner in which a natural response like a gasp may express admiration, or a yawn boredom. They regard words and phrases like 'good', 'ought to be done', 'just', and 'morally bad' as conventional signs which we learnt when we learnt English. And they maintain that when we use such terms we intentionally express the attitudes of approval and disapproval with which they are associated.

Now there is a serious problem with the claim that certain words and expressions are conventional, intentionally used signs and yet generate sentences that lack truth conditions. The problem goes back to Locke's observations about voluntary signs.[4]

Locke observes that, because it is contingent and fundamentally arbitrary that we use the words we do for the things we do use them for, our ending up with the conventions or arrangements we have in fact ended up with is to be understood in terms of our, explicitly or implicitly, entering into agreements for the use of these words for these things.[5] However, entering such agreements requires that we *know* what it is that we are using the words for. As Locke puts it, 'Words being voluntary signs, they cannot be voluntary signs imposed by him *on things he knows not.* ... they would be signs of he knows not what, which is in truth to be *the signs of nothing.*'[6] In other words, because the word 'square' is a voluntary, agreed-on conventional sign of the property we use it for, the explanation of how it is that we come to use it for that property requires that, on certain occasions, we *take* something to be square, and use this fact to found the convention of using the word 'square' for that property. To make the point vivid, consider your reaction to being asked to enter an agreement to use the word 'Fred' for a certain shape by someone *who won't let you see which shape it is.*[7]

If this line of thought is right, then any explanation of how we English speakers came to use the voluntary sign 'good' for the attitude we do use it to express, according to expressivists, must allow that we *recognize* the attitude in question in us. For, to follow Locke, we could hardly have agreed to use the word for an attitude we did not recognize and failed to believe we had, since that would be to use the word for 'we know not what'. But that is to say that expressivists must allow that we use the word sincerely only when we *believe* that we have a certain kind of attitude. And then it is hard to see how they can avoid conceding truth conditions to 'That is good', namely, those of that belief. Not only will the sentence 'That is good' express the attitude alleged, it will be true just in case the attitude is present and false otherwise: it will in some sense, however broad, report the presence of that attitude. Expressivism will have become a variety of subjectivism.

Here is a way to put the point. The attitudes that expressivists hold are expressed by the use of ethical terms in sentences had better be attitudes we (and our potential audiences) recognize as those it is correct, according to the conventions of English (or French or ...), to use the ethical words for, and it had better be that we use the ethical words just when we believe that we have the attitudes. We are not ostriches when we give voice to our attitudes. Moreover, when we follow the conventions for the use of the ethical vocabulary, we seek to conform to them, and know, or at least very much hope, that those we are communicating with are seeking to conform to them. We regulate our linguistic behaviour under the presumption that our fellows are doing likewise as part of our membership of a common linguistic community. Would it be better, according to expressivists, to use the ethical vocabulary when we thought we had quite different attitudes, or had no opinion at all on the matter, and would it be better if we ignored the usage patterns of our fellow language speakers? How then, runs our challenge, can *expressivists* fail to count our uses of the ethical terms in sentences like 'That is right' as reports of those attitudes?[8]

The view that ethical terms serve to report attitudes is compatible, it should be noted, with the view that they express the attitudes. Indeed, a good way to express an attitude is to report that you have it. It would be absurd to tell someone who says 'I dislike George a good deal' that they failed to express their dislike because they reported it. But if 'That is right' and the like are reports as well as expressions of the attitudes, then they have truth conditions, contrary to the central claim of expressivists.

Ayer half-sees the difficulty that this observation raises for expressivists in his discussion of a 'complication' concerning the crucial distinction between expressing and asserting.

> The distinction between the expression of feeling [his term for the relevant attitudes] and the assertion of feeling is complicated by the fact that the assertion that one has a certain feeling often accompanies the expression of that feeling, and is then, indeed, a factor in the expression of that feeling. Thus I may simultaneously express boredom and say that I am bored, and in that case my utterance of the words, 'I am bored', is one of the circumstances which make it true to say that I am expressing or evincing boredom. But I can express boredom without actually saying that I am bored. I can express it by my tone and gestures, …, or by an ejaculation, or without uttering any words at all.[9]

Ayer sees that saying that one has a certain attitude counts as expressing it but observes (rightly) that there are ways of expressing an attitude that do not involve saying that you have it. But his examples are ejaculations and gestures, and cases that do not involve 'uttering any words at all'. This hardly helps with sentences like 'This is good' and 'That is wrong', which involve words, are not typically ejaculations, and, more-over, are part of the voluntary convention we English speakers entered into concerning what words stood for what when we mastered the language.

Blackburn also notes that one way of expressing an attitude is to say that you have it.[10] He is explicit that his view is not that expressing attitudes, on the one hand, and reporting them, describing them or saying that you have them, on the other, are incompatible; it is simply that you can have the former without the latter. We agree. The problem is, as we have been arguing, that the cases where you can have the former without the latter differ in a crucial respect from the way we use ethical words and sentences.

It might be objected that the production of a sentence like 'That is wrong' is much more like an exclamation – or ejaculation, as Ayer puts it – than we are allowing: we contemplate some situation and simply find the words 'That is wrong', as it might be, coming to our lips. The attitude 'outs' itself without any conscious cognitive processing, and so, expressivists might argue, there is no truth-assessable claim being made when we produce the sentence. What happens is almost like wincing. This seems to us a highly implausible account of our moral psychology. It is a commonplace that we argue about and reflect on which ethical judgements to make. We do not typically 'give out' with the first thing that pops into our head. This is a point that Blackburn is explicit about when he talks about 'taking *all possible opportunities* for improvement of attitude'.[11] Moreover, even if some relatively simple kind of 'outing' story were true, this would not support the view that ethical sentences lack truth conditions. Face recognition is mostly not a conscious cognitive process, which is why verbal descriptions of suspects are often of little use to the police. Nevertheless, judgements of facial identity have truth conditions – obviously. In the same way, even if ethical sentences are prompted by an ability to recognize certain attitudes, they would still have truth conditions; they would simply be claims about the recognized attitudes.

This completes the presentation of our main challenge to expressivists. In the next three sections we consider three replies that they may (do) make and try to show that none is satisfactory.

3 FIRST REPLY: EXPRESSING VERSUS REPORTING BELIEF

Expressivists, and philosophers in general, often rightly distinguish expressing what you believe from reporting what you believe. The sentence 'Snow is white', uttered in the right context, expresses your belief that snow is white, and is true iff snow is white. It does not report your belief. If you want to report your belief that snow is white, you need to use the sentence 'I believe that snow is white' (if you are speaking English), and this sentence is true iff you have the belief.

Expressivists often suggest that we can apply this distinction to other psychological states, including especially the 'ethical' attitudes, and that when we do, we get the account they need of the sense in which ethical sentences express attitudes. They observe that we can distinguish the doctrine that 'X is right' reports a certain pro-attitude to X, from the doctrine that it expresses that pro-attitude to X. The first view is subjectivism; the second, they claim, is expressivism.[12] They may argue, then, that the availability of this distinction shows that there has to be something wrong with the argument from Locke. There has to be a sense of 'express' which ensures that 'X is right', and the like, express attitudes without reporting them and without having truth conditions.

Sometimes it almost seems as if the argument on offer here is supposed to run as follows: if 'X is right' reports an attitude, 'X is right' has truth conditions; therefore, if it expresses an attitude instead, it lacks truth conditions. But this would, of course, be to commit a fallacy: a version of denying the antecedent. What we need to do, in order to give the argument a fair hearing, is ask about the sense in which 'Snow is white' expresses a belief, apply this sense to the claim that 'X is right' might express an attitude, and see whether that will really help expressivists. We maintain that it will not.

The trouble for expressivists is that, although there is an important difference between reporting and expressing a belief, it is plausibly a difference in what is reported. It is not a difference between reporting something and not reporting at all. When you express your belief that snow is white by producing, in the right context, the sentence 'Snow is white', you are not avoiding the business of reporting altogether. You are not reporting the fact that you believe that snow is white but you are reporting the content of that belief; you are reporting that snow is white. This is how the sentence gets to be true iff the belief is true.

If we take the distinction as drawn for beliefs, then, and apply it to attitudes, we do not get a result that can help expressivists. What we get is that 'X is right' expresses a certain pro-attitude iff 'X is right' reports the content of the attitude. And this is not at all what expressivists are after. First, it makes 'X is right' out to have truth conditions, namely, those of the content; and, second, it is very implausible in itself. The relevant content will be something like *that X happens* – for that is what we are favourably disposed towards, according to expressivists, when we assert that X is right – and that is very different from X being right (unfortunately).

4 SECOND REPLY: THE EXCLAMATION ANALOGUE

There are plausible examples of intentionally delivered, more or less conventional signs of psychological states that seem to lack truth conditions and both the second and third replies to the argument from Locke take their starting point from these. The second reply starts from examples that expressivists themselves often cite: exclamations like 'Boo' and 'Hurrah'. Such exclamations do not have truth conditions and are not used to make claims about how things are – so at least it appears – and yet they are conventional, intentionally employed signs of psychological states. The suggestion often made by expressivists is that 'X is good' is very roughly like 'Hurrah', and 'X is bad' very roughly like 'Boo'. In particular, these sentences are like the relevant exclamations in not having truth conditions and so in not making claims about how things are.

We are prepared to grant that exclamations like 'Boo' and 'Hurrah' do not have truth conditions. But we insist that that possibility very much calls for explanation, particularly in the light of the argument from Locke. And the only available explanation, we will argue, is not one that can be plausibly extended to explain how ethical sentences might lack truth conditions.

Even if 'Boo' and 'Hoorah' do not have truth conditions, they could have had them. We could, for example, have used 'Boo' simply to mean that the producer of 'Boo' does not like what they are here and now acquainted with, in which case 'Boo' would have had truth conditions; it would have been true in S's mouth at t iff S did not like what S was acquainted with at t. What then could stop 'Boo' from having these, or indeed any, truth conditions? The reason does not lie in the fact that 'Boo' lacks the right syntax – it would be strange if syntax alone stopped us making claims about how things are. The only possible explanation is that, as it happens, 'Boo' has a rather erratic, highly personal connection to our feelings.

The situation we have in mind is like that which obtains with the word 'but'. It is standard doctrine that 'P and Q' and 'P but Q' have the same truth conditions, but it might, of course, have been the case that their truth conditions differed. It might have been that the contrast signalled by 'but' was part of the literal meaning of 'P but Q', in which case the existence of a contrast would have been a necessary condition for the truth of 'P but Q'. The reason it isn't is that the convention of using 'but' when there is a contrast is not sufficiently entrenched and clear cut.[13] (And, as you would expect if this is right, the minority who think that 'but' does affect truth conditions are those who insist that the convention *is* sufficiently well-entrenched and clear cut.)

Why does the convention need to be so well-entrenched and clear cut? This is a controversial issue in the philosophy of language, but the essential point is reasonably uncontroversial. When we produce sentences to say how we take things to be, there will typically be a whole web of beliefs lying behind their production. The problem is to isolate the ones that matter for what is literally said, in the sense of determining truth conditions, by using the sentences. For instance, typically, an English speaker only says 'Snow is white' when they believe that there is someone around to hear what they are saying, but that is not part of what they intend to convey and is not a necessary condition for what they say being true. It is the nature of the complex set of conventions for the use of the sentence that serves to filter out the 'wrong' candidates. We are using the phrase 'well-entrenched and clear cut' to mark out the conventions that do the trick. For example, followers of the 'Gricean programme' should hear this as marking out the conventions that suffice for an audience to recognize the primary communicative intentions of a producer of the sentence: as marking out the conventions that are up to the kind of job that Grice sees as crucial.[14]

We can now say why examples like 'Boo' and 'Hurrah' are of no use to expressivists. If these exclamations do not report (in the broad sense operative in this paper) that the speaker has the attitudes they express, that can only be because the conventions whereby they are linked to those attitudes are not sufficiently entrenched or clear-cut; the exclamations may suggest the presence of suitable attitudes, in the way in which the use of 'but' suggests a sense of contrast between the matters it conjoins, but they do not report those attitudes. It follows that if expressivists are to use the exclamation analogue, they have to take the view that ethical sentences serve only in a very loose fashion to signal the presence of the attitudes they express. And that means trouble.

Expressivism is not the view that there is only a rough, unclear, insufficiently-entrenched-for-truth-aptness connection between ethical words and the attitudes that lead to their production. Expressivists think that ethical terms are well-suited for the task of discussing the attitudes they hold ethical sentences express; if the ethical terms were not well-suited, expressivists would have trouble telling us what their books and articles are about. But this means that they cannot say that the reason ethical sentences lack truth conditions is the same as the reason 'Boo' does, namely, that we have not settled the usages precisely enough.

You might, of course, advance a version of expressivism that was a kind of subjectivism-except-that-we-speak-loosely view. This would be an expressivism that holds that all that stops subjectivism being true is that 'right' and the other ethical terms are rather like 'but', and it would secure the doctrine that ethical sentences lack truth conditions. But then the very moment that you make suitably precise in words the attitudes you wish to place at the centre of your account of ethics, you will automatically give ethical sentences containing them truth conditions. This highlights the difference between this bizarre style of expressivism, and standard expressivism. Standard expressivists do not hold that once they have made clear in words which attitudes are central in ethical theory on their view, ethical sentences thereby acquire truth conditions. They do not hold that they can only be precise at the cost of refuting themselves.

5 THIRD REPLY: THE COMMAND ANALOGUE

Some expressivists take as a model of ethical sentences, not exclamations, but rather commands or recommendations.[15] This suggests a further reply that they may make to the argument from Locke. They may try to elucidate the needed sense of expressing – the sense in which ethical sentences express attitudes without thereby having truth conditions – by saying that it is like the relation between the desires and attitudes that lead to an order or a recommendation: they may hold that my 'ethical' pro-attitude to X stands to 'X is right' as my desire that the door is shut stands to the order 'Shut the door'. As orders and recommendations express the desire for certain states of affairs to be realized, and yet apparently lack truth conditions, so they will argue that ethical sentences may have a similar expressive but not truth-conditional role.

The trouble for this suggestion is that it is very plausible that orders have truth conditions in the relevant sense – the same is true of recommendations but we will make the argument in terms of orders. The issue as to whether orders have truth conditions bears on what we are doing when we produce the words 'Shut the door' in the right circumstances (production in a play or a philosophy of language tutorial doesn't count). Every competent English speaker knows that producing the words 'Shut the door' in the right circumstances is *ipso facto* to command that the door be shut; that's what is being done. And that is to say that it makes no difference whether I say 'Shut the door' or I say 'I command that the door be shut' – a point which is independently plausible. But 'I command that the door be shut' obviously has truth conditions. And so it follows that 'Shut the door' has truth conditions too: it is true in S's mouth at *t* just if S did indeed command at *t* that the door be shut.

It might be objected that it is 'crook' English to talk of orders as true or false, but our topic is not what is or is not good English. It might be objected that this fact about English usage points to a deep feature of orders. We would disagree, but the point could in any case hardly help someone who holds that ethical sentences lack truth conditions, for it is good English to talk of them as true or false. It might be objected that 'Shut the door' and 'I command that the door be shut' cannot have the same truth conditions on the grounds that only the latter sentence can appear in certain contexts; for example, as the antecedent of a conditional. This would be an awkward point for expressivists to press for, as everyone agrees, ethical sentences can appear in such contexts. Moreover, there is a plausible explanation for why 'Shut the door' cannot figure as the antecedent of a conditional: its syntax signals that whenever it is used in serious speech, it is being used to *give* an order and it makes no sense for a sentence within the antecedent of a conditional to be used in that way. This means that, in a wide sense of meaning, 'Shut the door' and 'I command that the door be shut' do not mean the same, because they behave differently in certain contexts; but it does not mean that 'Shut the door' in my mouth in 'simple' contexts does not have the same truth conditions as 'I command that the door be shut'.

We can also argue for the conclusion that orders have truth conditions from Locke's observations on voluntary signs. Ordering is something we learn to do, and recognize one another as doing, through our shared mastery of the voluntary conventions that settle when we are, and when we are not, ordering. The possibility of this rests on our *knowing* when we are ordering and when not. And so it is plausible that when I use a sentence like 'Shut the door', I believe that I am giving an order and that I am intentionally producing the sentence as a conventional sign of giving an order. Of course, producing the sentence 'Shut the door' – and, equally, the sentence 'I command that the door be shut' – in the right circumstances *is* to order you to shut the door; the sentences are performatives. But, as many have observed against J. L. Austin, this does not stop them having truth conditions; instead, it makes it easy to make them true.[16]

6 EXPRESSIVISM AND MORAL DISAGREEMENT

Many expressivists with whom we have discussed the problem raised here for their position remind us that philosophy is hard. They insist that because there is an overwhelming argument – the argument from the persistence of moral disagreement – for the view that ethical sentences lack truth conditions, we should simply look harder for the account they need; namely, the account that denies truth conditions to ethical sentences without running afoul of Locke's point and without turning expressivism into subjectivism-except-that-we-speak-loosely.[17]

In this final section, we seek to undermine this motivation by arguing that expressivists are no better placed than anyone else to handle the problem posed by the alleged persistence of moral disagreement. In arguing this, we are arguing against many non-expressivists, as well as against nearly all expressivists. Many non-expressivists concede, grudgingly, that expressivism is especially well-placed to handle the persistence problem.

The argument from the persistence of moral disagreement starts from the observation that two claims are independently plausible. The first is that if you utter the words 'X is right' and I utter the words 'X is wrong', we are in disagreement. It is *not* like my saying that I like X, and your saying that you dislike X. The second is that this disagreement might survive our agreeing about all the relevant facts concerning X, including all facts about psychological responses to X. An example might be the disagreement between us if one of us is a total utilitarian and the other an average utilitarian, in a case where the difference matters for whether or not X is the right thing to do. We might agree about the effects of X on, say, happiness; we might agree that only effects on happiness matter for rightness and wrongness; and we might know all about our difference in attitudes. Still, it seems, we could be in genuine disagreement – it seems, for example, wrong to infer that you and I must be giving the word 'right' a slightly different meaning. But then, it follows, urge expressivists, that 'X is right' and 'X is wrong' do not make claims about the facts, about how things are, for we agree completely about how things are. And if they do not make claims about how things are, they lack truth conditions and must be construed along expressivist lines.

There is a large literature devoted to this argument, and there is no doubting the interest of the issues it raises. Our concern here, though, is simply to point out that it is no kind of argument for the view that ethical sentences lack truth conditions, and no kind of argument for expressivism.

The key question that needs to be addressed is what is meant by *disagreement* in the argument. Often, what is meant when it is observed that if I produce S and you produce T, we are in disagreement is that S and T cannot be true together. This, though, cannot be what expressivists mean, because, for them, *no* ethical sentences can be true together as they cannot be true to start with.

However, if you say 'I believe that Chicago will win the championship' and I say 'I believe that Boston will win the championship', we count as disagreeing, despite the fact that the sentences we produce can be, and most likely are, true together. But if a difference in belief can count as a disagreement, why not a difference in certain sorts of attitude? So, expressivists can fairly count your assertion that X is right and mine that X is wrong as disagreement by virtue of the difference in our moral attitudes. And this, of course, is what they mostly do.[18]

But *if* disagreement in moral attitude counts as disagreement, then the persistence of moral disagreement is no reason to favour expressivism over a subjectivism that holds that our assertions report our moral attitudes. The difference between expressivists and subjectivists over the semantics of ethical sentences is neither here nor there as far as our having different moral attitudes go. Indeed, almost every party to the debate in meta-ethics believes that if I sincerely assert that X is right and you sincerely assert that X is wrong, we must have different moral attitudes; so, if *that* counts as our disagreeing, as expressivists who are not eliminativists about moral disagreement must allow, almost every party to the meta-ethical debate can respond to the problem of moral disagreement simply by noting that a difference in moral attitudes can survive agreement over all the facts.

We think that the result that expressivism does not help with the problem of moral disagreement is no surprise. Moral disagreement, and indeed disagreement in general, is a psychological phenomenon. The production of sentences makes public our disagreements; it does not create them. Your disagreement with Hitler's moral outlook did not come into existence when you remarked on it in language. This means that a thesis whose essential distinction from other theses lies in a certain claim about the semantics of sentences cannot be in a privileged position when it comes to giving a good account of moral disagreement.[19]

NOTES

1 A. J. Ayer, *Language, Truth and Logic*, London: Gollancz, 2nd. ed. 1946, Simon Blackburn, *Spreading the Word*, Oxford: Clarendon Press, 1984, and Allan Gibbard, *Wise Choices, Apt Feelings*, Oxford: Clarendon Press, 1990.

2 For a view according to which ethical sentences report attitudes but only in this wide sense – in a sense in which the presence of the attitudes is not the focus of attention – see James Dreier, 'Internalism and Speaker Relativism', *Ethics* 101: 6–26.

3 See chapter 1, esp. pp. 11–18; see also Blackburn, *Spreading the Word*, p. 168 [p. 306, this volume], and chapter 1 of C. L. Stevenson, *Ethics and Language*, New Haven, CT: Yale University Press, 1944.

4 John Locke, *An Essay Concerning Human Understanding*, book III, chapter 2.

5 For more on this, see, e.g., H. P. Grice, 'Meaning', *Philosophical Review*, 66 (1957): 377–88, David Lewis, *Convention*, Cambridge, MA: Harvard University Press, 1969, and Jonathan Bennett, *Linguistic Behaviour*, Cambridge: Cambridge University Press, 1976.

6 *Essay*, III.ii.2. Our emphasis.
7 The issue of whether we start with words or (one word) sentences does not affect the points we make here; the key point is simply that we perforce start out with *belief*. According to Lewis, *Convention*, in order to found the convention, we need much more than the belief that something is square; we need a whole web of beliefs about beliefs including those of our fellow speakers of the language. For our purposes here, the crucial point is that we need *at least* to regulate our use of the word via belief.
8 The issue here is quite separate from whether the attitudes reported are themselves in the general category of beliefs. Expressivists are typically internalists and Humeans – they argue that moral judgements have internal connections to motivation that Hume taught us no cognitive state can have. This would mean that moral judgements are not beliefs proper but that does not negate our point that ethical sentences had better, in that case, express subjects' beliefs about their allegedly non-cognitive judgements. This point was overlooked by one author (FJ) in Frank Jackson, Michael Smith and Graham Oppy, 'Minimalism and Truth Aptness', *Mind*, 103 (1994): 287–302. 'Minimalism and Truth Aptness', but he stands by the critique of minimalism about truth aptness in that paper.
9 *Language, Truth and Logic*, p. 109.
10 Blackburn, *Spreading the Word*, pp. 169–70 [pp. 306–7, this volume]. In his view, you can, in addition, express attitudes by making claims about how things are other than the claim that you have the attitude in question.
11 Blackburn, *Spreading the Word*, p. 198 [p. 35, this volume], our emphasis.
12 See, e.g., Blackburn, *Spreading the Word*, p. 169 [p. 307, this volume], and Gibbard, *Wise Choices, Apt Feelings*, p. 84.
13 This account of why 'but' signals a contrast without altering truth conditions is essentially the one Michael Dummett, *Frege*, London: Duckworth, 1973, offers on p. 86. Incidentally, as he points out, the contrast signalled need not be between 'P' and 'Q'.
14 For detailed accounts, see Grice, 'Meaning', *Philosophical Review*, 66 (1957): 377–88, Lewis, *Convention*, Cambridge, MA: Harvard University Press, 1969, and Bennett, *Linguistic Behaviour*, Cambridge: Cambridge University Press, 1976.
15 See, e.g., Stevenson, *Ethics and Language*. Incidentally, it might be argued that the reason 'boo' and 'hurrah' lack truth conditions is not that the conventions governing their use are not 'good' enough, but rather that they belong with commands and recommendations. In this case, we would not have different models for understanding the expressivist view, but the same model approached in slightly different ways.
16 See esp. Lewis, 'General Semantics', reprinted in *Philosophical Papers*, Vol. I, New York: Oxford University Press, 1983. The view that a sentence cannot both be a performative and have truth conditions is prominent in J. L. Austin, *How to do Things with Words*, Oxford: Clarendon Press, 1962, see esp. Lecture I.
17 Blackburn has especially urged this on us.
18 Ayer is a notable exception. In *Language, Truth and Logic*, around p. 110, he argues that expressivists should be eliminativists about ethical disagreement. Of course, expressivists who hold that a difference in attitude counts as disagreement, will construe attitude here in a special sense – perhaps as one designed to *spread*, somewhat as belief is designed to fit the facts and desire *simpliciter* is designed to make the facts fit it.
19 We are indebted to many discussions with many audiences, mention Michael Smith, Martin Davies, Susan Wolf, Peter Railton, and apologize to those whom we should have remembered.

16

IS THERE A LOCKEAN ARGUMENT AGAINST EXPRESSIVISM?

Michael Smith and Daniel Stoljar

1 INTRODUCTION

It is sometimes suggested that expressivism in meta-ethics is to be criticized on grounds which do not themselves concern meta-ethics in particular, but which rather concern philosophy of language more generally.[1] Frank Jackson and Philip Pettit (Chapter 15, this volume; see also Jackson and Pettit 1999, and Jackson 2001) have recently advanced a novel version of such an argument. They begin by noting that expressivism in its central form[2] makes two claims – that ethical sentences are not truth evaluable, and that to assert an ethical sentence is to express one's desires or feelings rather than to report a fact. They then argue that, given some plausible premises in the philosophy of language emanating mainly from Locke, the two central claims of expressivism are contradictory: when combined with the plausible premises, they say, the second claim refutes the first. The purpose of this paper is to formulate Jackson and Pettit's Lockean argument, and to suggest that it fails.

2 THE ARGUMENT FORMULATED

The place to start is the main passage in which Jackson and Pettit present their argument (Chapter 15, p. 318, this volume):

> Locke observes that, because it is contingent and fundamentally arbitrary that we use the words we do for the things we do use them for, our ending up with the conventions or arrangements we have in fact ended up with is to be understood in

terms of our, explicitly or implicitly, entering into agreements for the use of these words for these things. However, entering such agreements requires that we *know* what it is that we are using the words for. As Locke puts it, 'Words being voluntary signs, they cannot be voluntary signs imposed by him *on things he knows not* ... they would be signs of he knows not what, which is in truth to be *the signs of nothing*.' In other words, because the word 'square' is a voluntary, agreed-on conventional sign of the property we use it for, the explanation of how it is that we come to use it for that property requires that, on certain occasions, we *take* something to be square, and use this fact to found the convention of using the word 'square' for that property ... If this line of thought is right, then any explanation of how we English speakers came to use the voluntary sign 'good' for the attitude we do use it to express, according to expressivists, must allow that we *recognize* the attitude in question in us. For, to follow Locke, we could hardly have agreed to use the word for an attitude we did not recognize and failed to believe we had, since that would be to use the word for 'we know not what'. But that is to say that expressivists must allow that we use the word sincerely only when we *believe* that we have a certain kind of attitude. And then it is hard to see how they can avoid conceding truth conditions to 'That is good', namely, those of that belief. Not only will the sentence 'That is good' express the attitude alleged, it will be true just in case the attitude is present and false otherwise: it will in some sense, however broad, report the presence of that attitude. Expressivism will have become a variety of subjectivism.

The central ideas about philosophy of language here can be brought out by considering the word 'square', and asking why a sentence such as '*x* is square' is truth-evaluable (which of course it is).

To begin with, since '*x* is square' might have meant anything at all, it is plausible to suppose, with Locke, that the fact that it means what it does must somehow be owing to a convention or implicit agreement about how to use the word.[3] Moreover, it is surely true that when we enter into this agreement – that is, when we act on it more generally – we cannot but believe that something is square when we assert that *x* is square. That is, if we have agreed to use 'square' for square things, then, on those occasions when we do use the sentence '*x* is square' of some object *x*, we must believe that *x* is square. A consequence of this – a consequence that is quite explicitly drawn in the last section of the passage – is that '*x* is square' is truth evaluable (or has truth conditions or is truth apt etc.). And of course, this is exactly as it should be, because '*x* is square' *is* truth evaluable.

We might focus the issues more directly by concentrating on two claims, which we will call the 'agreement claim' and the 'belief claim'. In the case of 'square', the agreement claim and the belief claim are these:

Agreement Claim (square):
We agreed to (sincerely) use '*x* is square' for *x*'s being square.
Belief Claim (square):
Acting on this agreement means using '*x* is square' when we believe that *x* is square.

According to Jackson and Pettit, the Agreement Claim (square) and the Belief Claim (square) together conspire to show that '*x* is square' is truth evaluable. And certainly initially this *is* a plausible thing to say – though later we will examine the argument for this claim in more detail.

We are now in a position to state the Lockean argument against expressivism. The key point is that in the case of evaluative words such as 'good' and 'right' there are parallel agreement and belief claims, and that, since these claims lead to truth evaluability in the case of 'square', they should likewise do so for the evaluative case. Taking 'good' as our example, the agreement claim and the belief claim would be these:

Agreement Claim (good):
We agreed to (sincerely) use '*x* is good' when we approve of *x*.
Belief Claim (good):
Acting on this agreement means using '*x* is good' when we believe that we approve of *x*.

Since these two claims are analogous to the claims we isolated in the case of 'square', there is no choice but to assume that claims such as '*x* is good' are truth evaluable just as '*x* is square' is. However, since expressivists are committed to denying that '*x* is good' is truth evaluable they must give up either the Agreement Claim (good) or the Belief Claim (good). However – and there is the nub of the argument – neither of these can be legitimately rejected by expressivists, or at least cannot if they want to maintain both expressivism and the Lockean philosophy of language.

One might put the point in terms of the two central claims of expressivism distinguished earlier – the claim that ethical sentences are not truth evaluable, and the claim that we assert such sentences in order to express our feelings or desires and not to report a fact. According to the Lockean argument, the Agreement Claim (good) and the Belief Claim (good) together entail that '*x* is good' is truth evaluable. But this contradicts the first claim of expressivism, viz. that such sentences are not truth evaluable. Expressivists cannot give up the Agreement Claim (good) without compromising their position, for that is a formulation in Lockean terms of (part of) their second claim[4] – that in asserting such sentences one is expressing one's feelings or desires. And nor can expressivists respond by giving up the Belief Claim (good) – for that claim is sanctioned by Lockean philosophy of language.

However, if this *is* the argument offered by Jackson and Pettit, there is at least the following ground on which it can be criticized. The argument neglects the fact that the Agreement Claim (square) and the Agreement Claim (good) are different.[5] In the first case, we have an agreement to use 'square' *for* something – and the 'for' here seems to indicate that we have agreed to use it to *stand for* something, or *to truly apply to* square things. In the second case, we have an agreement to use 'good' *when* we are in a certain psychological state. But on the face of it these two agreements – *for-agreements* and *when-agreements*, as we might call them – are different. And this opens up the possibility of a response to the Lockean argument. The response is this. In the case of 'square' we have a for-agreement and this explains why assertions of '*x* is square' are truth evaluable. On the other hand, in the case of 'good' all we have is a when-agreement. But we have so far been given no reason to suppose that when-agreements by themselves generate truth evaluability. Unless the distinction between when- and for-agreements can be shown to be illegitimate or irrelevant there is no cause for alarm here for the expressivist.[6]

3 INDICATIVE CONDITIONALS

The distinction between for-agreements and when-agreements provides only a prima facie objection to the Lockean argument. But the objection can be bolstered by considering a view mentioned by Jackson in another connection (Jackson 2001): the view that indicative conditionals are not truth evaluable – CANT, as we may call this view.[7]

CANT closely parallels expressivism in that it makes two claims: that indicative conditionals – sentences of the form 'If it rains, the match is cancelled' – are not truth evaluable; and, second, that we assert such sentences when we have a particular ratio of credences, but not to report any conditional facts. That is, it is appropriate to assert 'If it rains, the match is cancelled' when – to put it rather roughly – (i) you believe that it rains to some degree d, and (ii) you believe the match is cancelled to some degree d^* and (iii) d and d^* stand in the right sort of relation.

The first point to make is that in the case of indicative conditionals we can likewise formulate an agreement claim and a belief claim.

> *Agreement claim (If it rains, the match is cancelled)*:
> We agree to use 'if it rains, the match is cancelled' when we have the appropriate ratio of credences.
> *Belief claim (If it rains, the match is cancelled)*:
> When we act on this agreement we must believe that we have this ratio of credences.[8]

If the Lockean argument that Jackson and Pettit are mounting works in the case of 'good', then it must likewise work in the case of 'If it rains, the match is cancelled'. But – as at least Jackson makes clear (2001: 16) – it does *not* work in the case of 'If it rains, the match is cancelled'. For – he says – it is in fact quite possible to hold that 'If it rains, the match is cancelled' is not truth-evaluable but is only used *when* we have the appropriate ratio of credences. So at this point we face two important questions: why does the argument not work against CANT, and what does its not working against CANT tell us about whether it works against expressivism?

Our answer to the first of these questions has to do with the distinction between when- and for-agreements. If CANT is true, we have in the case of indicative conditionals an agreement to assert 'If it rains, the match is cancelled' *when* we have a certain ratio of credences. But we do not have an agreement to assert 'If it rains, the match is cancelled' *for* a certain conditional fact, and neither do we have an agreement to assert the sentence *for* that ratio of credences. This seems to be the reason that the Lockean Argument fails in the case of CANT. However – and this is our answer to the second question – if this is the reason that it fails in the case of CANT, it should likewise fail in the case of expressivism. For if expressivism is true, the case of 'good' presents us with a when-agreement, not a for-agreement. In short, the problem for Jackson and Pettit is that, by their own lights – or, at any rate, by the lights of Jackson – the Lockean argument works in the case of 'square' but does not work in the case of 'If it rains, the match is cancelled'. But the case of 'good' is, on the parameter we have isolated, more like 'If it rains, the match is cancelled', and this suggests that there is no Lockean argument against expressivism.

There is also a further point to make about the analogy between CANT and expressivism. Expressivists have traditionally sought to distinguish themselves from another position, subjectivism, which is the view that sentences of the form '*x* is good' mean 'I approve of *x*', and thus that when one asserts this sentence one reports one's psychological state. Part of the rhetorical power of Jackson and Pettit's argument is that, if successful, it shows that expressivists will not be able to distinguish themselves from subjectivism in the way that they have wanted. Since subjectivism looms large for expressivism this, if true, is an extremely effective point. It is thus worth pointing out, in this connection, that there is a position which stands to CANT just as subjectivism stands to expressivism – though, we hasten to add, a position that nobody has endorsed, to our knowledge. According to this view, in asserting an indicative conditional one is reporting oneself as having a particular ratio of credences. The question for Jackson and Pettit is why they do not suppose that the Lockean Argument, if it succeeds in establishing that expressivism cannot distinguish itself from subjectivism, does not likewise establish that CANT cannot distinguish itself from this position. We can think of no answer to this question.[9]

4 OBJECTIONS AND REPLIES

So far we have suggested that the Lockean argument fails because it fails to distinguish when-agreements from for-agreements, a point that receives considerable support from the case of indicative conditionals. How might one move to defend the argument from this criticism? There are three main objections to the line of thought we have been considering.

> *Objection #1.* The distinction between for-agreements and when-agreements is beside the point because both sorts of agreement lead to the relevant claims about truth evaluability.

However, the response to this objection is straightforward. The case of indicative conditionals shows that one can have a when-agreement without truth evaluability, so there seems to be no easy inference here.

> *Objection #2.* While there is a difference between for-agreements and when-agreements, the distinction is irrelevant to the Lockean argument, since it is the belief claim, and not the agreement claim, which guarantees the truth evaluability of the relevant sentences. And we have the belief claim in both cases.

One reply to this objection appeals again to indicative conditionals. In this case, we seem to have a belief claim without truth evaluability. However, there is a further point to be mentioned in this connection. For Jackson and Pettit *do* often suggest that the belief claim shows that assertions of the relevant sentences are truth evaluable. In short, they appear to move from 'A asserts S when A believes that p' to 'In asserting S, A expresses the belief that p' and then finally to 'S is truth evaluable'. However, this two-step inference is mistaken. The expressivist should agree that when asserting 'x is good' one believes certain things, among them that one approves of x. But they should not agree that it follows that 'x is good' is truth evaluable.

The point can be developed by distinguishing two things one might mean when one says that a person expresses his or her beliefs in asserting some sentence or other.

> *Expression (weak sense)*
> In asserting a sentence S, A expresses the belief that p just in case there is an agreement that A asserts S when A believes that p.
> *Expression (strong sense)*
> In asserting a sentence S, A expresses the belief that p just in case there is an agreement that A asserts when (i) A believes that p; and (ii) A intends the assertion of S to report the content of the belief that p.

Taking expression of belief in its weak sense, we do indeed have an inference from 'A asserts S when A believes that p' to 'In asserting S, A expresses the belief that p'. But on that interpretation, there is no reason to draw the further conclusion that S is truth evaluable. On the other hand, taking expression of belief in its strong sense, we do indeed have an inference from 'In asserting S, A expresses the belief that p' to 'S is truth evaluable', but we no longer have a reason to move from 'A asserts S when A believes that p' to 'In asserting S, A expresses the belief that p'. The trouble for Jackson and Pettit is that they seem to have confused the weak sense of belief expression with the strong sense.

> *Objection #3.* The distinction between when-agreements and for-agreements is unimportant because what the belief claim does is transform a when-agreement into a for-agreement and vice versa. Hence, if you agree that a for-agreement guarantees truth evaluability, and if you agree with the belief claim, you must agree that you have truth evaluability if you have a when-agreement.

What is true about this objection is that the belief claim *does* seem to transform a for-agreement into a when-agreement. For example, in the case of '*x* is square' we start with a for-agreement, we notice the Belief Claim (square) and we immediately seem to have a when-agreement. However, it's hard to see how the reverse is true – and it is this claim that is required if the objection is going to work. For how can a belief claim all by itself turn a when-agreement into a for-agreement? We might concede that 'good' could not be used when we have certain attitudes if we did not believe that we had these attitudes. But the mere fact that we must have this belief does nothing to suggest that we have implicitly agreed to use 'good' *for* these attitudes. Consider indicative conditionals again. Suppose it is true that we must believe that we have a certain ratio of credences to use 'If it rains, the match is cancelled' when we have that ratio of credences. Would that show that we have agreed implicitly to use 'If it rains, the match is cancelled' *for* that ratio of credences? Surely not – but if not, it cannot be true, contrary to the objection, that the belief claim transforms a when-agreement into a for-agreement.[10]

5 CONCLUSION

We have suggested that the Lockean argument fails, but we have said little so far about what might have led Jackson and Pettit to mistakenly suppose that it is successful, nor have we considered a distinction that looms large in their discussion, the distinction between reporting and expressing. We will close by speaking briefly to the diagnostic issue and saying something about the reporting/expressing distinction.

In our view, Jackson and Pettit's mistake comes right at the beginning when they explain why '*x* is square' is truth evaluable. Jackson and Pettit emphasize the truth of the Belief Claim (square), and they are certainly right to do so. However, they also suggest that the Belief Claim (square) plays a crucial role in explaining why '*x* is square' is truth evaluable. But, as we in effect saw previously in our discussion of expression of belief, there is no reason to move from '*A* asserts *S* when *A* believes that *p*' to '*S* is truth evaluable'. What this suggests in turn is that the Belief Claim (square), while true, is in fact completely irrelevant in securing the conclusion that '*x* is square' is truth evaluable. What secures that conclusion is not the Belief Claim (square) but rather the nature of the agreement entered into – in our terminology, that the agreement in question is a for-agreement, and not merely a when-agreement. In particular, what secures the fact that '*x* is square' is truth evaluable is that we agreed to use 'square' for squares, or, if you like, to use '*x* is square' to report the fact that *x* is square. Hence, while the belief claim might perfectly well be true – not only in the case of 'square' but also in the case of 'good' and 'If it rains, the match is cancelled' – it is not *this* claim that guarantees truth evaluability.

Similar considerations tell against what Jackson and Pettit say about the reporting/expressing distinction. The Lockean argument is presented by them as a challenge to the expressivists to explain their use of this distinction. As we have noted, expressivists say that assertions of '*x* is good' express feelings or desires and do not report anything. Jackson and Pettit ask what can possibility be meant by 'express' in this context. On the one hand, they say, one might mean 'expression' as it occurs in 'his wincing expressed his pain'. But that belies the conventional nature of the words such as '*x* is good'. On the other hand, one might mean 'expression' as it occurs in talk of expression of belief. But from this, Jackson and Pettit argue, it follows that evaluative sentences are truth evaluable after all. The distinctions we have introduced show the mistake in this line of thought. We may agree with Jackson and Pettit that expression always involves expression of belief. But it does not follow that expressing always involves reporting. The crucial thing is what, if anything, you agreed to use your words *for*, not what you believe when you use your words.[11]

NOTES

1 The *locus classicus* is Geach 1956. For some more recent discussion see Horwich 1993.
2 Some expressivists resist this formulation and seek to respond to Jackson and Pettit in that way – see e.g. Ridge 1999 – but the formulation will not be questioned here. See also Jackson and Pettit 1999.
3 See Locke 1689, Book III, Chapter 2. As Jackson and Pettit note, the modern incarnation of the Lockean view is the Gricean tradition of Grice 1957, Lewis 1969, Schiffer 1973 and Bennett 1975. One might respond to the Lockean argument by rejecting this tradition – but again that is not a strategy we will adopt here.

4 Part of, because the second claim of expressivism itself divides into two: the claim that in asserting an ethical sentence one is expressing one's desires or feeling, and the claim that in asserting an ethical sentence one is not reporting a fact. The agreement claim is a formulation in Lockean terms of the first part of this second claim.

5 The line of argument we are about to develop concedes both the Belief Claim (good) and the Belief Claim (square). However, it is worth noting that one might well resist the Belief Claim (good) even if one agrees that the Belief Claim (square) is plausible. See note 8.

6 It is important here to reconsider a part of the passage quoted at the beginning (emphasis added): 'any explanation of how we English speakers came to use the voluntary sign "good" *for* the attitude we do use it to express, according to expressivists, must allow that we *recognize* the attitude in question in us. For, to follow Locke, we could hardly have agreed to use the word *for* an attitude we did not recognize and failed to believe we had, for that would be to use the word *for* "we know not what"'. Note that Jackson and Pettit here ascribe to expressivists the view that we agree to use 'good' *for* certain attitudes, not *when* we have certain attitudes. Our suggestion, if you like, is that expressivists should reject this formulation of their view. They should insist that Jackson and Pettit provide some argument that moves them (i.e. the expressivists) from a when-agreement to a for-agreement.

7 Cf. Adams 1975.

8 Again, while we are agreeing with the various belief claims discussed in the text, it is worth asking whether the defender of CANT should accept the Belief Claim (if it rains the match is cancelled). Mightn't the defender of CANT insist that in order to act in accordance with our agreement to use 'If it rains, the match will be cancelled' when we have a certain ratio of credences it suffices that we have that ratio of credences, that our use of the sentence 'If it rains, the match is cancelled' conveys that ratio of credences, and that we believe of such uses that they accord with our agreement? In order to see that these conditions do not entail the Belief Claim (if it rains the match is cancelled), note that it seems at least possible that someone could believe of his uses of 'If it rains, the match is cancelled' that they accord with the agreement he made about how to use that sentence – which, as it happens, was an agreement to use that sentence when he has a certain ratio of credences – even while admitting that he has forgotten the details of that agreement.

9 What if there were telling independent reasons for supposing that a position on indicative conditionals parallel to subjectivism in ethics is false? Would that provide the needed explanation? We think that that would make things worse for Jackson and Pettit, not better. For their argument against expressivism has the same form as the argument for the collapse of CANT into a position on indicative conditionals parallel to subjectivism in ethics. If, for some reason, the latter argument doesn't go through, then that would suffice to show that arguments of that form are not in general persuasive.

10 In saying that a belief claim does not transform a when-agreement into a for-agreement, we do not mean to deny that there might be when-agreements which are also for-agreements. For example, consider the agreement to assert a sentence *when* one intends that assertion to report a fact – such an agreement is in fact implicit in Expression (Strong Sense). In this case, we seem to have a when-agreement which is also a for-agreement. However, this possibility is irrelevant to the main point we want to make. What is at issue is not whether there might be when-agreements which are also for-agreements, what is at issue is whether there are when-agreements which are *not* for-agreements. In effect, Jackson and Pettit are suggesting that *any* when-agreement, when combined with a belief claim, yields a for-agreement. It is precisely this last point which we think is mistaken.

11 We would like to thank Simon Blackburn, Frank Jackson and Philip Pettit for useful discussion.

REFERENCES

Adams, E. 1975. *The Logic of Conditionals*. Dordrecht: Reidel.

Bennett, J. 1976. *Linguistic Behaviour*. Cambridge: Cambridge University Press.

Geach, P. T. 1956. Assertion. Repr. in his *Logic Matters*, 254–69. Oxford: Blackwell, 1972.

Grice, H. P. 1957. Meaning. *Philosophical Review* 66: 377–88.

Horwich, P. 1993. Gibbard's theory of norms. *Philosophy and Public Affairs* 22: 67–78.

Jackson, F. 2001. What is expressivism? *Philosophical Books* 42: 10–17.

Jackson, F. and P. Pettit. 1999. Reply to Ridge. *Brown Electronic Article Review Service*, ed. J. Dreier and D. Estlund. www.brown.edu/Departments/Philosophy/

Lewis, D. 1969. *Convention*. Cambridge, MA: Harvard University Press.

Locke, J. 1689. *An Essay Concerning Human Understanding*. Oxford: Clarendon Press.

Ridge, M. 1999. Ridge reviews Jackson and Pettit. *Brown Electronic Article Review Service*, ed. J. Dreier and D. Estlund. www.brown.edu/Departments/Philosophy/

Schiffer, S. 1973. *Meaning*. Oxford: Oxford University Press.

Part 6

EXPRESSIVISM AND THE FREGE–GEACH PROBLEM

There is a problem with expressivistic theories of moral language, normally referred to as the Frege–Geach problem. It is so named because Peter Geach provided the touchstone exposition of the problem, but he claimed that he was developing an objection from Gottlob Frege. Some people see this as the key problem for expressivism and think it so troublesome that it is fatal to the whole project. Others are less convinced and, indeed, expressivists have devised ways in which to combat the problem in recent times. After reading the selections in this Part – and some of the further reading – you need to make up your own mind. A word of caution at the start: some of the twists and turns of the debate can get very complicated, particularly as logic is involved, so those new to this debate should tread carefully.

The best way of understanding the problem is by thinking about examples. Let us build up to one. Recall that, so far at least, expressivists are committed to the idea that ethical language is fundamentally an expression of attitude, or noncognitive state generally, rather than an expression of a cognitive, representing state. That is all very well in cases when a speaker is clearly asserting something they sincerely hold to (strictly, the phrase ' ... sincerely *believe*' is out of bounds to an expressivist). But there are many cases when we use moral words and do not assert the claim that we are making. For example, we might say, "If it is wrong to belch in public, then Geoff shouldn't have belched just then". In this case, we are not strictly asserting that public belching is wrong (that is, we are not expressing our negative attitude towards belching). Rather we are putting forward a hypothetical claim or link: if so-and-so, then such-and-such. But someone could make such a claim – Geoff himself, perhaps – and not believe (or hold to) the wrongness of belching. In other words, the moral claim is unasserted, or embedded in a larger claim, and someone can voice it and not be committed to the first part – the antecedent – of the hypothetical.

Why does this matter? Because the object moral phrase can be unasserted in this way, we must give an account of its semantic function – what it really means and how it operates – that is different from cases when the object phrase appears on its own, asserted. (Or, in other words, we must account for the fact that Geoff – if he is being sincere, non-hypocritical and normal in other ways – can voice the moral phrase when it is in an unasserted context, but cannot do so when it would be a plain assertion.) But then we encounter a problem. Consider a classic, simple and everyday piece of reasoning such as a *modus ponens* argument. (And, for argument's sake, let's assume that belching in public is just not on!)

(P1) It is wrong to belch in public
(P2) If it is wrong to belch in public, then Geoff shouldn't have belched in public.
(C) Therefore, Geoff shouldn't have belched in public.

(Whether we carry out such a piece of reasoning in this explicit form in our everyday reasoning is highly dubious. The idea is that it is just supposed to characterize clearly our supposed thought processes.) Now, we normally think that such a piece of reasoning is valid. After all, the structure of *modus ponens* is 'P, If P then Q, therefore Q' and that type of structure strikes us as intuitively right. (Whether the conclusion is true in addition depends, of course, on whether our premises are true to start with.) But in order for there to be validity, we need to make sure that we can make the transition, as it were, from P1 and P2 to our conclusion. The worry – the Frege–Geach worry – about expressivism is that on an expressivistic reading we cannot. If P1 and P2 are really operating in a different way, despite their surface grammatical form, then we cannot move from P1 and P2 to get to our conclusion. This worry – although particularly pointed when considering moral *modus ponens* arguments – works whenever one is reasoning and combining asserted and unasserted grammatical phrases. And this is supposed to be devastating for expressivism since combining asserted and unasserted instances of moral phrases is so frequent that it forms the basis of most of our moral reasoning.

Some people explain the problem as one of equivocation. To equivocate is to use words or phrases across premises in order to reach one's conclusion, which are seemingly the same but, in fact, operate differently. An example would be when we move from talking about the various branches of a financial institution to use 'branch' in a different sense, as in 'The bank has branches. If something has branches, it must also have twigs. So, the bank must have twigs'. In the present case, the phráse 'It is wrong to belch in public' could well be operating differently on an expressivistic understanding. However, we have to tread carefully. No one is suggesting that 'belch' means something different across the premises in a way similar to the 'branch' case. So what is going on? As we've said, the worry seems to be the difference in function of the phrase, between asserted and unasserted. But now consider this:

(P1) Grass is green
(P2) If grass is green, then *p*.
(C) Therefore, *p*.

Here we have an argument where a crucial phrase occurs both asserted and unasserted. (P2 does not – or need not – contain an assertion that grass is green, but need only be an assertion that something is the case if grass is green.) Now, we normally don't worry about this type of reasoning, even though we have switched from asserted to unasserted contexts. But, so far, this is supposedly the exact problem about the moral case. So, some people think that equivocation isn't quite the issue. (Or, better, we need to say something else about the type of 'switch' that is happening between the premises in the moral case that means we don't have a valid argument if the whole argument is interpreted expressively.) The real issue might be one of truth, or more specifically truth-aptness. It is seemingly easy in the argument involving grass to go from P1 to P2, since both parts of the hypothetical in P2 are truth-apt.

EXPRESSIVISM AND THE FREGE–GEACH PROBLEM

They are used in a descriptive fashion. (So, if we were constructing a truth table of classic logic, we could easily see whether the argument was valid.) But, it is obviously the case with expressivistic readings of moral *modus ponens* arguments that some crucial phrases are not truth-apt. Perhaps this is the problem.

We do not take sides on how exactly to set up the problem. We introduce this issue merely to get you thinking about what the problem is, and to introduce the issue of truth that comes up in this Part and the next. However one sets up the problem, it seems that it is a good one that forces two general options on us. Either expressivism is correct, in which case we need to radically rethink what we are doing when we reason morally and, perhaps, accept that what intuitively seem to be perfectly valid pieces of moral reasoning are fundamentally flawed. Or our reasoning practices are as they seem to be and expressivism fails as an explanation of them. In which case, because reasoning is such an important part of our moral practices, we might as well give up altogether on expressivism. Many people adopt the latter option.

In this Part's first selection, Simon Blackburn (Chapter 17) – in an excerpt from his *Spreading the Word* – outlines the problem in more detail than we have and then provides a solution to it. In effect, Blackburn's solution dispenses with the idea that unasserted contexts, and specifically hypothetical claims, are truth-assessable at all in order for reasoning to take place. When we say, "If belching in public is wrong, Geoff shouldn't have belched then" we are expressing our positive attitude towards a moral sensibility – a general moral viewpoint if you like – that combines two attitudes: a disapproval of belching in public with a disapproval of Geoff's belching in public. Blackburn introduces some new logical notation to get at this idea. Traditionally, we might represent our above moral (P2) thus:

(P2′)   It is wrong to belch in public → It is wrong for Geoff to belch in public

Blackburn's new notation represents it thus:

(P2″)   H! [[B!(belching in public)]; [B!(Geoff's belching in public)]]

H! (or 'Hoorah for') indicates that one approves of the thing in brackets whilst B! ('Boo for') indicates one's disapproval. Instead of the traditional arrow, we have ";", which simply represents a joining of commitments, in this case two disapprovals. In other words, just as one can approve or disapprove of actions and institutions, one can also approve and disapprove of other attitudes and combinations of attitude.

How does this solve the Frege–Geach problem? Blackburn says that if someone disapproves of belching in public, and also that that person approves of those sensibilities that combine a disapproval of belching in public with disapproval of a particular person belching in public, then we would expect that someone to disapprove of the belching of the particular person named. If they didn't – if they were indifferent to Geoff's belching, let's say – then that would be a very strange result and we would think of them as having a very

343

strange moral sensibility. Blackburn refers to such a sensibility as 'fractured' involving as it does a 'clash of attitudes'. It simply isn't committed in the right sort of way. And this is what is going on when someone is reasoning in a strange fashion. So, the expressivist can explain our moral reasoning practices. When our moral reasoning is valid and correct what is happening is that we are expressing the commitments that we would intuitively think people should have given their other commitments. When we don't do that – when we express commitments that are not in keeping with our other ones – our reasoning is flawed. Of course, things aren't quite as we took them to be since we are dealing with expressions of attitude. But the expressivistic characterization isn't so radically different from what we might assume we are doing.

Many are unimpressed with this response to the problem. G. F. Schueler in Chapter 18 puts the worry well. (And see also Hale (1986), Wright (1988) and Zangwill (1992) in Further Reading below.) In essence the concern is how one should characterize what goes wrong when there is a clash of attitudes as described above. Viewed traditionally and non-expressivistically, someone who says, "P, If P then Q" but then fails to say Q or even says not-Q strikes us as the height of being logically inconsistent, no matter what the content of the thoughts. One might as well just say P and not-P. But would someone be failing logically if they expressed approval of P (rather than asserted something truth-apt), expressed approval of those people that both approved of P and approved of Q and then failed to express approval of Q? Nothing worth calling straightforward inconsistency is going on here, and some think this is simply because we are viewing these things as expressions of attitude. When someone fails to have every combination of attitudes that she herself approves of seems to be a *moral* failing, not a *logical* one.

Many find this compelling (although not all; see Miller (2003) in Further Reading below). In fact, Blackburn himself, in a response to Schueler called 'Attitudes and Contents' that is included as Chapter 19 in this book, agrees that his solution in *Spreading the Word* is flawed. He thus offers a different solution, with different logical notation (which reverts back to the more traditional '→' as a logical connective for conditionals). In essence, his new solution claims that we should not interpret conditional claims as overall or higher-order expressions of attitude towards combinations of attitudes, but rather interpret them as ways in which we tie ourselves to trees of commitments.

Does this do the job? Bob Hale says it does not. In the fourth piece included here (Chapter 20), he argues that the 'Attitudes and Contents' solution results in a dilemma for the expressivists: *either* conditional claims such as that involving Geoff above are to be read as we normally read them, that is as truth-functional, but then their evaluative components require a descriptive, non-expressivistic reading; or we read such conditionals in an expressivistic fashion. But this second alternative is no good. In order for Blackburn's new 'tree-tying' account to work, he needs a speaker's commitment to conditionals not to distribute across the disjunction. (That is, on the new interpretation, the speaker has to be committed only to, say, [either denying that it is wrong to belch in public or to endorsing that it is wrong for

Geoff to do so], rather than committed to either [denying that it is wrong to belch in public] or to [endorsing that it is wrong for Geoff to do so]. This is often referred to as the difference between a single disjunctive commitment and a disjunction of commitments.) Why does an expressivist need this interpretation? If we assume that there is a disjunction of commitments, then it looks as if we are back to a non-expressivistic reading. Assuming a disjunction of commitments goes along with assuming that each part is individually truth-evaluable, and this obviously runs counter to expressivism. But in that case, how exactly are we to interpret what is happening? If we assume a single disjunctive commitment, as expressivism dictates, then it seems that we cannot proceed logically in our everyday arguments from premises to conclusion. If we follow as logic normally dictates, it seems that we no longer have an expressivistic reading.

You might have to read Hale's paper a few times in order to understand why the above dilemma is a dilemma and why Hale thinks it so important. As you read you'll see that Hale covers a lot of ground, including reflection on what it is to be a 'quasi-realist'. (Recall our short characterization of this in our introduction to Part 5.) As you consider this, you might want to ask yourself whether expressivists can defend their whole enterprise by being 'modest' rather than 'ambitious' quasi-realists, to use Hale's (and Crispin Wright's) terms. Perhaps expressivists who adopt quasi-realism should not be in the ambitious business of exactly replicating realist truth, realist characterizations of reasoning and the like, but rather be more modestly trying to mimic things somewhat. Perhaps only trying to mimic things somewhat will lead to a change in our everyday understanding of what is happening when we judge and reason with moral terms. But this might be acceptable given expressivism's advantages. In which case, perhaps we could return to something like Blackburn's first solution to the Frege–Geach problem. Perhaps what is happening is that we are failing morally. Perhaps the idea of failing logically simply doesn't apply in the moral case. Even though the reasoning is superficially similar between moral and nonmoral cases, we should give different philosophical characterizations.

As you read, this idea might appeal. Alternatively, some people – including expressivists – hold that moral reasoning is still reasoning and hence needs to be viewed in pretty much the same way as we view nonmoral reasoning. What is clear is that the debate is far from over, and we have only scratched the surface, both in this introduction and in our selections. For a start, Blackburn (1993) is a response to Hale's dilemma and Hale himself responds further in his (1993). Further to that, Blackburn repeats much of his second solution in his (1998), which is then discussed by Hale again in his (2002). Aside from this, Allan Gibbard (1990, 2003), the other notable modern writer working in the expressivist tradition, has developed a response to the problem. As we said at the start, we leave it to you to make your minds up whether expressivism can answer the Frege–Geach problem successfully, and whether it is such an important problem anyway. Thinking about this topic should, more generally, get you to think about what is going on when we reason morally.

QUESTIONS TO CONSIDER AND TASKS TO COMPLETE

1 Explain in your own words the difference between an asserted and an unasserted context. Give some examples.
2 Again, explain in your own words how the Frege–Geach problem is supposedly so damaging for expressivism.
3 What is Blackburn's (Chapter 17) first solution to the problem? How successful is it?
4 What is the difference between a logical failing and a moral failing, the distinction employed by many opponents of Blackburn's first solution? Do you think this distinction is ultimately a good one? Does it ultimately show Blackburn's first solution to fail?
5 Explain Blackburn's (Chapter 19) second solution in your own words. What is Hale's (Chapter 20) worry about it? What dilemma does he create?
6 Before you carry on any further reading, how do you think Blackburn might respond to Hale?
7 Think about your everyday moral reasoning and the logical structures that underlie it. Which metaethical theory best characterizes what is going on and why?

FURTHER READING

Blackburn, Simon (1993) 'Realism, quasi or queasy?', in John Haldane and Crispin Wright (eds) *Reality, Representation and Projection* (Oxford: Oxford University Press), pp. 365–83.

—— (2002) 'Replies', *Philosophy and Phenomenological Research*, vol. 65, pp. 164–76.

Geach, P. T. (1960) 'Ascriptivism', *Philosophical Review*, vol. 69, pp. 221–5.

—— (1965) 'Assertion', *Philosophical Review*, vol. 74, pp. 449–65.

Gibbard, Allan (1990) *Wise Choices, Apt Feelings* (Oxford: Clarendon Press).

—— (2003) *Thinking How to Live* (Cambridge, MA: Havard University Press), chapter 3.

Hale, Bob (1986) 'The Compleat Projectivist', *Philosophical Quarterly*, vol. 36, pp. 65–84.

—— (1993) 'Postscript', in John Haldane and Crispin Wright (eds) *Reality, Representation and Projection* (Oxford: Oxford University Press), pp. 385–8.

—— (2002) 'Can Arboreal Knotwork Help Blackburn out of Frege's Abyss?', *Philosophy and Phenomenological Research*, vol. 65, pp. 144–9.

Kolbel, Max (2002) *Truth Without Objectivity* (London: Routledge), chapter 4.

Miller, Alexander (2003) *An Introduction to Contemporary Metaethics* (Cambridge: Polity Press), sections 3.5, 4.3 to 4.6 and 5.1 to 5.3.

Van Roojen, Mark (1996) 'Expressivism and Irrationality', *Philosophical Review*, vol. 105, pp. 311–35.

Wedgwood, Ralph (1997) 'Noncognitivism, Truth and Logic', *Philosophical Studies*, vol. 86, pp. 73–91.

Wright, Crispin (1988) 'Realism, Antirealism, Irrealism, Quasi-Realism', *Midwest Studies in Philosophy*, vol. 12, pp. 25–49.

Zangwill, Nick (1992) 'Moral *Modus Ponens*', *Ratio,* vol. 5, pp. 177–93.

17

THE FREGE–GEACH PROBLEM

Simon Blackburn

1 FREGE'S ARGUMENT

In a very influential article, P. T. Geach used a point of Frege's to block expressive theories.[1] The 'Frege point' is very simple. Sentences containing given predicates may occur in utterances by which we are claiming the predicates to apply, as when I call something good, true, probable, a cause of something else, and so on. But such sentences may also occur unasserted, inside the context provided by other words, making up larger sentences. I may assert: 'It is wrong to tell lies.' But I may also assert: 'If *it is wrong to tell lies*, then it is wrong to get your little brother to tell lies.' In this latter occurrence the italicized sentence is not asserted. It is the antecedent of a conditional – in other words, it is put forward to introduce an hypothesis or supposition. The Frege point is that nevertheless the sentence *means the same* on each occurrence. The proof of this is simple and decisive. The two sentences mate together to make up the premises of a valid argument:

> It is wrong to tell lies.
> If it is wrong to tell lies, it is wrong to get your little brother to tell lies.
> *So*   It is wrong to get your little brother to tell lies.

This is a valid argument, illustrating the general form: *P*; if *P* then *Q*; so *Q*. But the argument is only of this form because the sentence 'It is wrong to tell lies' means the same on each occurrence. If it did not there would be a fallacy of equivocation, as in: 'He is working at the bank; if he is working at the bank he must have his feet in the river; so he must have his feet in the river.' Here the second premise is true only if 'bank' is taken in a different sense from that in which, we might imagine, it makes the first premise true, and if so the argument does not illustrate the valid form. The question now is: how does an expressive theory explain the identity of meaning? For anyone asserting the second, hypothetical premise is *not* expressing an attitude of condemnation towards telling lies. He commits himself to no attitude towards it at all. He just says: 'If telling lies is wrong … ' without offering any indication of whether he thinks it is. Let us call contexts in which a sentence occurs like this, an *unasserted* context. Then the question is whether expressive theories can cope with unasserted contexts in such a way as to allow sentences the same meaning within them, as they have when they are asserted.

It is a nice sharp problem. It might seem to provide a swift refutation of expressive theories. In unasserted contexts no attitude, etc. is evinced when the sentence is uttered; the meaning is the same as in direct contexts when such an attitude is evinced; therefore this (variable) feature does not give the (constant) meaning. But before quasi-realism surrenders it needs to see whether expressive theories can give any account at all of these contexts.

There are in fact two distinct aspects to this problem. Firstly, can we explain what we are up to when we make these remarks? Unasserted contexts show us treating moral predicates like others, *as though* by their means we can introduce objects of doubt, belief, knowledge, things which can be supposed, queried, pondered. Can the projectivist say why we do this?

Here he faces two questions. Consider the fact that we can conjoin evaluations and ordinary expressions of belief 'It is wrong to tell lies and your mother is going to be annoyed'. Now it is surely not surprising that we might link together two commitments, even if one expresses an attitude, and the other a belief. The one sentence conjoins the two disparate commitments, and since we often want to communicate that we have both, it is hardly surprising that we have a way of doing it. That gives us an idea of *what we are up to* in offering the conjunction. But it does not fully answer the second question: why do we have this *particular* sentence to serve that purpose? For we might want to say other things about 'and', which make it difficult to see why it is serving this function. For instance, we might explain the semantic function of 'and' like this: it stands between two sentences to make one large sentence out of them; the large sentence is true if and only if each smaller one is true. Otherwise it is false. Now this little semantic theory fits badly, initially at any rate, with the occurrence of the evaluation as a conjunct. For suppose, according to the expressive theory, the evaluation is not susceptible of truth or falsity. Then it should not mingle with an operator which needs truths and falsities to work on. But there are ways of easing around this obstacle. One is to expand the way we think of 'and'. We have to do this anyway, for it can link utterances when they certainly do not express beliefs which are genuinely susceptible of truth-value – e.g. commands: 'hump that barge and tote that bale'. We would instead say something like this: 'and' links commitments to give an overall commitment which is accepted only if each component is accepted. The notion of a commitment is then capacious enough to include both ordinary beliefs, and these other attitudes, habits, and prescriptions.

So to tackle Frege's problem the first thing we need is a view of what we are up to in putting commitments into conditionals. Working out their implications, naturally. But how can attitudes as opposed to beliefs have implications? At this point we must turn again to the projective picture. A moral *sensibility*, on that picture, is defined by a function from *input* of belief to *output* of attitude.[2] Now not all such sensibilities are admirable. Some are coarse, insensitive, some are plain horrendous, some are conservative and inflexible, others fickle and unreliable; some are too quick to form strict and passionately held attitudes, some too sluggish to care about anything. But it is extremely important to us to rank sensibilities, and to endorse some and to reject others. For one of the main features affecting the desirability of the world we live in is the way other people behave, and the way other people behave is largely a function of their sensibility. So much is obvious enough. And amongst the features of sensibilities which matter are, of course, not only the actual attitudes which are the output, but the interactions between them. For instance, a sensibility which *pairs* an attitude of disapproval towards telling lies, and an attitude of calm or approval towards getting your little brother to tell lies, would not meet my endorsement. I can only admire people who would reject the second action as strongly as they reject the first. It matters to me that people should have only this pairing because its absence opens a dangerous weakness in a sensibility. Its owner would have the wrong attitude to indirect ways of getting lies told (and for that matter the wrong attitude to his little brother).

The conditional form shows me expressing this endorsement. Of course, it is an endorsement which is itself the expression of a moral point of view. Some casuistry might lead people to the other commitment, that there is a great difference between telling lies and getting your little brother to do so (am I my brother's keeper?).[3] Such people would reject the conditional. But it is quite satisfactory that the conditional expresses a moral point of view. The task was not to show that it does not, but to explain what it does at all. Other conditionals have the same general role:

> If lying makes you feel good, then it's all right.
> If you ought to give him £10, then you ought to give him something.

The latter is held on logical grounds. I can only endorse a sensibility which, in the presence of the antecedent attitude, also has the consequent one, because it is logically impossible that the action specified in the antecedent can be done without giving the man something. I could not endorse at all an illogical sensibility, which itself paired approval of an action with disapproval of a logical implication of the performance of the action. The former conditional is the expression of a repulsive *standard*: it endorses a function from an input of knowledge that a lie has made you feel good to an output of satisfaction with it. Finding better descriptions of admirable input/output functions is the task of moral philosophy.

This account of what we are up to when we use the conditional form with evaluative components now needs supplementing by a semantic theory. We can put the need this way. Imagine a language unlike English in containing no evaluative predicates. It wears the expressive nature of value-judgements on its sleeve. Call it E_{ex}. It might contain a 'hooray!' operator and a 'boo!' operator (H!, B!) which attach to descriptions of things to result in expressions of attitude. H! (the playing of Tottenham Hotspur) would express the attitude towards the playing. B! (lying) would express the contrary attitude towards lying, and so on. For the reasons I have developed, we would expect the speakers of E_{ex} to want another device, enabling them to express views on the structure of sensibilities. They would need a notation with which to endorse or reject various couplings of attitudes, or couplings of beliefs and attitudes. Suppose we talk *about* an attitude or belief by putting its expression inside bars: |H! (X)| refers to approval of (X). And suppose we use the semi-colon to denote the view that one attitude or belief involves or is coupled with another. Then the speakers of E_{ex} will need to express themselves thus:

H! (|H! (Tottenham)|;| H! (Arsenal)|)

H! (|B! (lying)|;|B! (getting little brother to lie)|)

The first endorses only sensibilities which, if they endorse Tottenham, also endorse Arsenal, and this is what we express by saying that if Tottenham is a good team, so is Arsenal. The second is our old friend.

E_{ex} will naturally want further constructions. We want to say things like 'X used to be a good thing, but now it is not', in which evaluations connect with tenses. Notice that this does not mean the same as 'I used to approve of X but now I do not': it implies that X has changed, not that I have. The favourable evaluation attaches to X as it was, so E_{ex} will need a device to express this: perhaps an index indicating that the past state is the object of evaluation. Again, consider our different attitudes to our own attitudes. Since I have the concept of improvement and deterioration in a sensibility, I know that I am vulnerable to argument that in forming a particular attitude I am myself falling victim to a flawed input/output function. I may be exhibiting dispositions which I do not endorse, or committing myself to pairings of attitude and attitude, or attitude and belief, which I also cannot endorse. So in some cases I can be uncertain not only of the facts of the case, but of how to react to them. I will need to explore the other aspects of my moral commitments, and see whether, when they are brought to bear, one attitude or another begins to settle itself. And when I have taken up an attitude, I might be uncomfortably aware that it may turn out to be vulnerable to criticism. So E_{ex} will need a way of signalling different degrees of robustness in our attitudes: different ways in which they can be regarded as likely or unlikely to succumb to an improved perspective. H!(X) can co-exist with something like ? H! (|H! (X)|): uncertainty that one's own attitude of approval can itself be endorsed.

E_{ex} will be spoken by people who need to signal and respect consistencies and inconsistencies. Consider:

B! (lying)
H! (|B! (lying)|;|B! (getting little brother to lie)|)

Disapproval of lying, and approval of making (disapproval of getting little brother to lie), follow upon (disapproval of lying). Anyone holding this pair must hold the consequential disapproval: he is committed to disapproving of getting little brother to lie, for if he does not his attitudes clash. He has a fractured sensibility which cannot itself be an object of approval. The 'cannot' here follows not (as a realist explanation would have it) because such a sensibility must be out of line with the moral facts it is trying to describe, but because such a sensibility cannot fulfil the practical purposes for which we evaluate things. E_{ex} will want to signal this. It will want a way of expressing the thought that it is a logical mistake that is made, if someone holds the first two commitments, and not the commitment to disapproval of getting your little brother to lie.

In short, E_{ex} needs to become an instrument of serious, reflective, evaluative practice, able to express concern for improvements, clashes, implications, and coherence of attitudes. Now one way of doing this is to become like ordinary English. That is, it would invent a predicate answering to the attitude, and treat commitments as if they were judgements, and then use all the natural devices for debating truth. If this is right, then our use of indirect contexts does not prove that an expressive theory of morality is wrong; it merely proves us to have adopted a form of expression adequate to our needs. *This is what is meant by 'projecting' attitudes onto the world.*

What I have done here is to explain how conditionals can be regarded as ways of following out implications, although it is not imperative that the commitments whose implications they trace have 'truth-conditions'. Now you might say: even if this can be done, hasn't the quasi-realist a very dreary task in front of him? For remember that the Frege point was entirely general; it could cite any unasserted context. So mightn't others arise which require separate and ingenious explanations, and is the quasi-realist faced with an endless task? Isn't he like Ptolemaic astronomers, having to bolster his theory with ever more complex or *ad hoc* epicycles, whereas by comparison there is a simple, common-sense view that moral predicates are just the same as more ordinary ones, so that there is nothing to explain about the way they function in unasserted contexts?[4]

Questions of what does or does not require explanation involve delicate matters of philosophical judgement, but the objection here is surely overdrawn. For what plays the role of Copernicus to the allegedly Ptolemaic complexities? What was wrong with Ptolemaic astronomy (by the end of its reign) was that there was a better way of explaining the same things. But this better way did not just take those things for granted. It was not the stultifying position that everything is just in order without our bothering to explain it. We have seen enough of why projectivism is a plausible moral philosophy. And this being so it is extremely important to tell whether it is blocked by arguments from the philosophy of language. Nobody denies that the surface phenomena of language – the fact that we use moral predicates, and apply truth or falsity to the judgements we make when we use them – pose a problem for projectivism. This is why they tempt people into realism. But by overcoming the problem projectivism also steals a march on its rivals. For it removes the temptation to think that our surface forms of expression embody a mistake, that they are 'fraudulent' or 'diseased': it *protects* our ordinary thinking, in a way that mere reminders of the way we do actually proceed cannot do. It solves Kant's question of the *right* to our concepts, as well as the question of what they are actually like.

But now a new and rather surprising vista is opened. For if this is right, might 'it is true that ...' also be given this quasi-realist explanation? Initially an expressive theory stands in stark contrast to one giving moral remarks truth-conditions. But if we sympathize with the pressures I have described, we come to appreciate why it should be natural to treat expressions of attitude as if they were similar to ordinary judgements. We come to need a predicate, whose behaviour is like that of others. Why not regard ourselves as having *constructed* a notion of moral truth? If we have done so, then we can happily say that moral judgements are true or false, only not think that we have sold out to realism when we do so.

2 CONSTRUCTING TRUTH

The arguments of the last section may give us a right to a notion of an *improved* set of attitudes; they give us some right to a notion of the *coherence* and *consistency* of such a set. But do they suffice to build all that we need from a conception of truth, applicable to moral judgements?

The root disquiet here runs very deep. In effect, quasi-realism is trying to earn our right to talk of moral truth, while recognizing fully the subjective sources of our judgements, inside our own attitudes, needs, desires, and natures. The sense of subjectivity triggers all kinds of wild reactions. Can the projectivist take such things as obligations, duties, the 'stern daughter of the voice of God', seriously? How can he if he denies that these represent external, independent, authoritative requirements? Mustn't he in some sense have a schizoid attitude to his own moral commitments – holding them, but also holding that they are ungrounded? And when the tension comes out, shouldn't he become frivolous, amoral? A recent influential book even believes that an emotivist should approve of manipulating people, bullying and lying and brainwashing as we please, rather than respecting their independence.[5] Words like 'relativism' and 'subjective' focus these fears; books and sermons alike pronounce that the projectivist should, if consistent, end up with the morals of a French gangster.

Fortunately, all this is ridiculously beside the point. Just as the senses constrain what we can believe about the empirical world, so our natures and desires, needs and pleasures, constrain much of what we can admire and commend, tolerate and work for. There are not so many livable, unfragmented, developed, consistent, and coherent systems of attitude. A projectivist, like anyone else, may be sensitive to the features which make our lives go well or badly; to the need for order, contracts, sources of stability. If his reflection on these things leads him to endorse a high Victorian love of promises, rectitude, contracts, conventional sexual behaviour, well and good: there is nothing in his meta-ethic to suggest otherwise. For instance, a proper respect for promises, the kind of respect which sees them as making requirements, as bounds on conduct, is certainly a good attitude to foster. But it may, for all that, be just that: an attitude.

The problem is not with a subjective source for value in itself, but with people's inability to come to terms with it, and their consequent need for a picture in which values imprint themselves on a pure passive, receptive witness, who has no responsibility in the matter. To show that these fears have no intellectual justification means developing a concept of moral truth out of the materials to hand: seeing how, given attitudes, given constraints upon them, given a notion of improvement and of possible fault in any sensibility including our own, we can construct a notion of truth. The exercise is important. For one moral of the brush with Goodman's paradox and the rule-following considerations is that judgement never involves quite the pure passivity which is supposed to be an untainted source of objectivity and truth. We have to see our concepts as the product of our own intellectual stances: how then are they suitable means for framing objectively correct, true, judgement, describing the mind-independent world as it in fact is? It is not only moral truth which starts to quake. But we can learn how to approach the general problems of truth by starting with it.

The simplest suggestion is that we define a 'best possible set of attitudes', thought of as the limiting set which would result from taking all possible opportunities for improvement of attitude. Saying that an evaluative remark is true would be saying that it is a member of such a set, or is implied by such a set.[6] Call the set M^*. Then if m is a particular commitment, expressing an attitude U;

m is true = U is a member of M^*

To test this suggestion we must find conditions which truth obeys, and see whether they square with it. In particular, does the definition justify the constraint of *consistency* (m cannot be true and false)? The first hurdle is to define the idea of a unique best possible sensibility. Certainly there is improvement and deterioration. But why should not improving sensibilities diverge in various ways? An imperfect sensibility might take any of several different trajectories as it evolves into something better. We might imagine a tree (see Figure 17.1). Here each node (point at which there is branching) marks a place where equally admirable but diverging opinion is possible. And there is no unique M^* on which the progress of opinion is sighted. So there is no truth, since the definition lapses. More precisely, truth would shrink to only those commitments which are shared by all the diverging systems: truth belongs to the trunk.

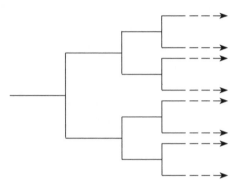

Figure 17.1

This is the deep problem of *relativism*. It is not the vague and unfounded disquiet that I have no right to judge unfavourably people with any other opinion – those who practice human sacrifice, or murder Jews, for instance. Of course I have. My attitudes, and those involved in any system I could conceive of which might be superior to mine, alike condemn them. The deep problem is the suspicion that other, equally admirable sensibilities, over which I can claim no superiority of my own, lead to divergent judgements. This does take away my right to think of mine as true, which is equivalent to unsettling my commitments.

The classic introduction of the problem is Hume's superb and neglected essay 'Of the Standard of Taste'. He introduces 'such diversity in the internal frame or external situation as is entirely blameless on both sides'. He illustrates it with the difference between 'a young man, whose passions are warm' and 'a man more advanced in years, who takes pleasure in wise, philosophical reflections concerning the conduct of life and the moderation of the passions'. The former prefers the amorous and tender images of Ovid, the latter the wisdom of Tacitus; in the twenty-first century no doubt the one reads *Playboy* and the other *The Economist*. Now we imagine the young man's literary sensibility improved and refined into a system M^*_o and the old man's into a system M^*_t, and one containing the commitment that Ovid is a better writer than Tacitus, whilst the other contains the reverse. How can we recover a notion of truth for either judgement? Hume's answer is subtle: it consists in expanding the difference between a (mere) matter of predilection, and a fit object of literary comparison: 'it is plainly an error in a critic, to confine his approbation to one species or style of writing, and condemn all the rest.' The point of this emerges if we ask the question: who is to adopt the following three views:

(1) $M^*_o \rightarrow$ it is true that Ovid is better than Tacitus
(2) $M^*_t \rightarrow$ it is true that Tacitus is better than Ovid
(3) There is no possible improvement on either M^*_o or M^*_t

(where '$M^* \rightarrow$ it is true that m' means that M^* contains an attitude which is expressed by the sentence m).

How can you have each of these? Think of the detail. Is someone who has either of the two sensibilities aware of the other? If not, it would surely be an improvement if he were. But if so, then quite what is the combination of attitudes required? It surely begins to seem wrong to hold, straight out, that Ovid is better than Tacitus, or vice versa. If we admit a really developed rival way of looking at it, are we not required to soften the opposition – to say, for instance, that Ovid and Tacitus are of equal merit, although each has features which appeal to different people? In short, as soon as I hold that a case begins to look as though the tree structure applies, I also hold that there is a truth about the subject on which the divergent attitudes are held, and, holding that, I would also judge that one or both of the rival sensibilities is capable of improvement, until it yields my own attitude. Hume's case depends upon the audience accepting that Ovid and Tacitus actually are of equal merit – otherwise it would not be just the different tastes of different ages which result in the different rankings. But if we think this, then each of the two systems is flawed. The young but able literary critic is insensitive to the virtues which appear to the older man, and which in truth result in the two writers coming out equally; similarly for the older literary critic.

What does this mean? It means that an evaluative system should contain the resources to *transcend the tree structure*: evidence that there is a node *itself* implies that it is wrong to maintain either of the conflicting commitments. It is itself a signal that the right attitude – the truth about the relative merits of Ovid and Tacitus – is not that expressed by either of these partial perspectives. The better perspective may judge the merits equal, or it may award the prize to just one view, or it may regret and change the terms of the discussion, by losing interest in the simplistic question of whether Ovid is a better writer than Tacitus, and concentrating upon different merits of each, with no intention of finding a summary comparison. In that case the system of *each* of these literary critics is defective, by containing too many crude comparisons. So in practice evidence that there is a node is just treated as a signal that the truth is not yet finally argued, and it goes into discussions as part of the evidence. We are constrained to argue and practise as though the truth is single, and this constraint is defensible in spite of the apparent possibility of the tree-structure.

It is as though the trunk – the core of opinion to which there is no admirable alternative – contains the power to grow through any of the choices of opinion which lead to branching: the choices become themselves part of the knowledge which the progress of attitude must use to form its course.[7] In so far as acquaintance with another value-system makes me respect it, then it properly makes me rethink both systems, transcending the tree-structure.

One common element of 'relativism' is the thought that if we can conceive of different, equally admirable systems, then that must weaken our own in favour of *toleration*. It seems to be particularly the attitudes associated with *obligation* which are vulnerable to worries about rival systems. The explanation of this is quite pleasant, although perhaps slightly peripheral to language.

Suppose we symbolize 'it is obligatory to do A' by OA, and 'it is permissible to avoid A' by 'P¬A'. P¬A contradicts OA. Now imagine:

(1) $M^*_1 \rightarrow OA$
(2) $M^*_2 \rightarrow$ P¬A
(3)   There is no possible improvement on either M^*_1 or M^*_2.

This is the tree structure. One way of transcending it goes:

(4)   (3) implies that it is permissible to hold M^*_2; this implies that it is permissible to hold that ¬A is permissible, which in turn implies that ¬A is permissible;
(5)   So any view, such as M^*_1 which implies the reverse, is wrong, and *ipso facto* capable of improvement.

This transcends the tree by showing that if we suppose that the choice leading to M^*_2 is permissible, then we must dislike the other. We cannot maintain the even-handed, Olympian stance which finds them each blameless. But now notice that if we have a *prima facie* case of (1), (2), and (3), it is *likely to be the obligation* which is the more threatened. Suppose we try to transcend the tree by the reverse argument:

(4')   (3) implies that it is permissible to hold M^*_1; this implies that it is permissible to hold that A is obligatory, which in turn implies that A is obligatory;

we need the different reduction principle that if it is permissible to hold that A is obligatory, then A *is* obligatory, and that is not nearly so intuitive.[8] Evidence of a permissible system which permits ¬A is evidence that ¬A is permissible; evidence of a permissible system which obligates A is not so plausibly thought of as evidence that A is obligatory. So here, once we have an initial inclination to each of the three propositions, we are more likely to escape the inconsistency by seeing M^*_1 as capable of improvement.

So on this account it is correct, as well as natural, to find faith in particular obligations shaken, if what seems to be admirable sensibilities do not recognize them. This is why travel broadens the mind.

NOTES

1   'Assertion', *Philosophical Review* (1964).
2   Or, more generally, an input of *awareness* rather than belief. A man may respond to perceived features without realizing that they are the ones responsible for his reactions. For example, we often do not know what we find funny in a situation.
3   Examples of genuinely controversial commitments of the form may help: 'if something ought to be done, any means to it ought to be allowed'; 'if a group has been discriminated against, it is now right to give it better treatment'.
4   This response was made to me by Professor Geach.
5   A. MacIntyre, *After Virtue*, p. 22, and throughout.
6   Although this is the simplest projectivist account of truth, and is one used by many anti-realists, I do not myself think it is the best. It is only a first approximation, but serves to make the immediate points.
7   Readers may be reminded of the Hegelian three-step (look left, look right, and then cross over) of thesis, antithesis, synthesis, by which we lurch towards the Absolute.
8   Formally the reduction principles differ in a way analogous to the difference between the modal system S4 and the stronger system S5. If 'it is permitted to permit A' implies 'A is permitted', we have PP$x \rightarrow$ Px, which corresponds to S4. This does not demand that 'it is permitted to obligate x' implies 'x is obligatory', for which S5 is needed. The comparison is suggestive, and indicates a respectable side of worries about relativism.

18

MORAL *MODUS PONENS* AND MORAL REALISM*

G. F. Schueler

Moral realism holds that our moral judgments are "about the world" in much the way our other judgments are. Antirealists deny this, holding that in making moral judgments we are projecting our own attitudes onto things, or expressing these attitudes, or the like. As usually stated the issue between these two views is thus a linguistic one, about the meaning of moral judgments. It is not the parallel metaphysical or ontological issue of whether there *are* any "moral facts" or "objective values." Thus, one might, like J. L. Mackie, hold that while moral judgments are indeed intended to be "about the world" (as realism holds), there are in fact no objective values and hence anyone who makes moral judgments is committed to a claim which is false.[1]

In the realism/antirealism debate, realism seems to have a strong initial advantage since, as Simon Blackburn says, "Nobody denies that the surface phenomena of language – the fact that we use moral predicates, and apply truth or falsity to the judgments we make when we use them – pose a problem for projectivism."[2] The task for an antirealist then will be to push through what Blackburn calls "the quasi-realist project," which is to show that the features of our moral language which appear to commit us to the idea that there are objective moral truths and the like are really neutral as between realism and antirealism, that is, that these features can be explained adequately by the view that in making moral judgments we merely express our attitudes toward things. One such feature of moral language which has been thought to commit us to realism is the use of *modus ponens* in reasoning about moral issues.

The problem for antirealists is that there are obvious examples of valid reasoning with sentences using moral terms (i.e. examples which all sides agree are valid) but which, on the antirealist theory, do not have or at least do not seem to have the correct logical form to allow us to say that it is, for example, *modus ponens*, which justifies them, that is, shows them to be valid. To adapt one of Blackburn's examples, the following argument seems obviously valid.

(A)   Courage is an intrinsically good thing.

(H)   If courage is an intrinsically good thing, then organized games should be a part of school curricula.

(C)   Organized games should be a part of school curricula.

On the face of it this seems to be of the form

$$P$$
$$P \rightarrow Q$$
$$Q$$

The problem which Geach and others have pointed out[3] is that if we take sentence *A* as (merely) expressing an attitude and as having the form *P*, then this seems to leave us totally in the dark about the form of *H* since one might seriously utter *H* without having the attitude toward courage supposed to be expressed by anyone seriously uttering *A*. If *A* is "nothing but" the expression of an attitude (when seriously uttered) then it is hard to make any sense of a sentence like *H* where the same string of words appears in the antecedent "unasserted." In particular it is not at all obvious that, without an equivocation on "*P*," *H* can be held to be of the form $P \rightarrow Q$. But if it isn't, then this argument is not an instance of *modus ponens* after all, and we are left without a reason for thinking that it is valid. Since it is agreed that *C* does obviously follow from *A* and *H*, this cannot apparently be the correct understanding of *A* to begin with.

In this paper I will examine Simon Blackburn's attempt to deal with this problem on behalf of antirealism. The main elements of his solution are stated twice, a number of years ago in a paper entitled "Moral Realism" (MR)[4] and more recently in his book *Spreading the Word* (STW, chap. 6). For clarity I will concentrate first on the earlier version before moving to the more recent restatement.

In MR, Blackburn attempts to solve this problem by giving an analysis of hypotheticals such as *H* such that the "validity of *modus ponendo ponens* as a rule of inference is preserved" (MR, p. 121). The idea is that rather than expressing attitudes, hypotheticals of this sort "refer to" or "mak(e) claims about" (MR, p. 119) the attitudes in question. On this account, then, *H* is to be understood as the claim "that an attitude of approval to courage itself involves an attitude of approval to organized games as part of the curriculum in every school" (MR, p. 120). Premise *H* is thus to be understood as what is called a "propositional reflection" of a claim about moral attitudes. "By a propositional reflection," Blackburn says he means "roughly any statement which, while appearing to make a factual claim about states of affairs, their interrelations and their logic, is actually making claims about attitudes, *although* none of the propositions involved in the statement is to be analyzed into one whose subject is an attitude" (MR, p. 119). So this theory tells us "that anybody asserting '*P* and if *P* then Q' where P attributes worth to a thing *expresses* his attitude to that thing, and *asserts* that that attitude involves a further attitude or belief. There is, when that has been done, a logical inconsistency in not holding the further attitude or belief. It is this logical inconsistency which is expressed by saying that *modus ponendo ponens* is valid" (MR, p. 121).

The first thing to say about this theory is that it does not in fact "preserve *modus ponens* as a valid rule of inference" if by this is meant "show that the reasoning from premises A and H to conclusion C is valid by showing it to be an instance of *modus ponens*." This is because, on the MR account, though it is not clear what exactly the logical form of H is supposed to be, it is clear that it cannot be $P{\to}Q$. Blackburn says the following things which bear on the logical form of H:

1 Even though H "appears to be making a claim that one state of affairs exists if another does," it "must be taken as a propositional reflection of a claim about attitudes" (MR, p. 120). But none of the sentences involved in such a propositional reflection has a subject which is an attitude (MR, p. 119).

2 He gives a straight "reading" or "gloss" of the claim of which H is a "propositional reflection": "The claim is that an attitude of approval to courage in itself involves an attitude of approval to organized games as part of the curriculum in every school" (MR, p. 120).

3 In explaining how his theory of moral hypotheticals preserves the validity of *modus ponens*, he says that anyone who asserts sentences like both A and H "*expresses* his attitude to (some)thing, and *asserts* that that attitude involves a further attitude or belief" (MR, p. 121).

What do these tell us about the logical form of H? Points 1 and 3 together seem to be saying that, appearances to the contrary notwithstanding, A and H are not of the forms P and $P{\to}Q$ and indeed that H cannot be taken as analyzable into sentences connected by the truth functional connective "$\to$" at all. This is confirmed by 2 since the reading of H contained in 2 does not even appear to have a form which could be represented by "$\to$" as its main connective. The reading of H given in 2 seems to have the logical form

(x) $((x$ has an attitude of approval toward courage$){\to}(x$ has an attitude of approval toward organized games as part of the curriculum in every school$))$.

But not only does this not present H as having the form $P{\to}Q$, even after instantiation it would leave the original problem unresolved since the antecedent of the resulting hypothetical would still "talk about" an attitude, where A, according to Blackburn, merely "expresses" one. And of course on this reading of H, its logical form, for the purposes of propositional logic, is just R, that is, it must be taken as "simple," not truth functionally compound.

In short, Blackburn's idea is that, though *H* appears to represent a hypothetical connecting the sentences labeled *A* and *C* above, in fact it is a claim about one attitude "involving" another. But on this reading the logical form of the reasoning from *A* and *H* to *C* will just be *P*, *R*, *Q*, that is, not *modus ponens*. So Blackburn has not shown that, on his version of antirealism, the reasoning which goes from *A* and *H* to *C* can be shown to be valid as an instance of *modus ponens*.

This is not the whole story, however, since one might want to argue that even though an antirealist such as Blackburn cannot claim that the reasoning from *A* and *H* to *C* is valid because it is an instance of *modus ponens*, he can still claim that his theory lets him show that this reasoning is valid (i.e. on some other grounds). If he can do that he might claim that he has done all that really needs to be done here since what is agreed on all sides is only that the reasoning from *A* and *H* to *C* is valid, not the explanation of why it is valid.

I suspect that if we recall the quasi-realist project, we will see that this last is not correct. For quasi-realism, as Blackburn says, is "the enterprise of showing how much of the apparently 'realist' appearance of ordinary moral thought is explicable and justifiable on an anti-realist picture."[5] On the "realist picture," the reasoning from *A* and *H* to *C* is straightforwardly an instance of *modus ponens*. So if a "projectivist" such as Blackburn has to deny this, quasi-realism would seem to suffer. Still, I am not going to pursue this question here because I think Blackburn cannot even show the reasoning from *A* and *H* to *C* to be valid at all.

What might make one think that Blackburn can show the reasoning from *A* and *H* to *C* to be valid after we admit that this reasoning is not an instance of *modus ponens* on his account? So far as I can see, the only other reason he gives for thinking this reasoning is valid is his claim that in asserting hypotheticals such as *H* we are asserting that the attitude normally expressed by the antecedent "involves" the attitude normally expressed by the consequent. To do this, he says, is itself to "express a moral standard, to make a moral claim" (MR, p. 122). Such hypotheticals therefore "express commitments."[6] So the thought here is that in asserting *A* I express an attitude and in asserting *H* I express a commitment to the idea that this attitude "involves a further attitude or belief" (MR, p. 121). He then says, "There is, when that has been done, a logical inconsistency in not holding the further attitude or belief" (MR, p. 121).

But why? This seems just flatly false. If I fail to do what I have committed myself to do then, presumably, I do wrong. I fail to do what I ought to do. In that sense (if there is such a sense) I act "inconsistently." But this is a far cry from saying that I involve myself in any logical inconsistency. As these words are standardly used I am involved in logical inconsistency if I believe (or assert, etc.) a set of sentences which are such that, as a matter of logic, not all of them can be true. But the whole point of Blackburn's antirealist account of moral language is that in uttering sentences such as *A*, *H*, and *C* we are not doing these sorts of things, we are "expressing attitudes or commitments" and the like.[7] And it is just false to say that violating or failing to keep a commitment involves any *logical* inconsistency in the standard sense of these words. But so far as I can see, once we have removed the idea that the reasoning from *A* and *H* to *C* is an instance of *modus ponens*, the whole weight of the claim that this reasoning is valid rests on the claim that there is a logical inconsistency here. (Referring to just this sort of case, Blackburn says, "It is this logical inconsistency which is expressed by saying that *modus ponendo ponens* is valid" (MR, p. 121)). If that is so, then nothing Blackburn says is even enough to show that the reasoning from *A* and *H* to *C* is valid, let alone that it is an instance of *modus ponens*.

Of course this by itself does not show that on Blackburn's antirealist theory the reasoning involved in going from *A* and *H* to *C* is *not* valid, since there may be something in his theory which his MR account fails to exploit. But once we have gotten this far it is easy to see that the same sort of problem will arise for the antirealist's use of "valid" that we just saw in his use of "logical inconsistency." As it is standardly used in logic, an argument is said to be valid just in case it is not possible for its premises to be true and its conclusion false.[8] This notion of validity employs the idea that sentences (premises and conclusions) have truth values independently of whether they are asserted or believed. That is, this notion of validity is the notion of a certain relation among sentences (or sets of sentences) themselves, in some sense, and depends on the idea that, thus considered, they can be either true or false. But, again, this is just exactly the sort of "picture" the antirealist about morals wants to reject. According to him it is not true that a sentence such as *A* is true or false "in itself." It is rather that when people assert or deny that courage is intrinsically good they express a certain attitude toward courage, or the like. So on this view it is hard to see what sense can be made of the claim that an argument is valid in the standard sense of this term. What the antirealist owes us is an account of validity for moral arguments which is not the same as the standard realist account but which is enough like it to show how the two might get confused. Or rather, what he owes us is a separate account of the whole "family" of logical terms ("valid," "logically inconsistent," "entails," etc.) as they apply to moral arguments. It will do the antirealist no good to explain one member of this family in terms of another, as Blackburn does in the quotation above when he tries to explain "valid" in terms of "logical inconsistency," if he leaves the second with its usual, realist connotations.[9]

Thus the account in MR. In *STW* Blackburn takes up the challenge of trying to give an account of what it is for moral arguments to be valid which does not covertly depend on unexplained realist terms. Following Geach, the example used is this:

> It is wrong to tell lies.
> If it is wrong to tell lies, it is wrong to get your little brother to tell lies.
> *So*   It is wrong to get your little brother to tell lies.
>
> (STW, p. 190 [p. 349, this volume])

In *STW* Blackburn's "expressive theory" account of this reasoning is put in terms of an "expressive" language which he calls "E$_{ex}$" which "wears the expressive nature of value judgments on its sleeve" (*STW*, p. 193 [p. 352, this volume]). For this a symbolism is introduced. First: he defines "a 'horray!' operator and a 'boo!' operator (H!, B!) which attach to descriptions of things to result in expressions of attitude" (*STW*, p. 193 [p. 352, this volume]). Next: "we talk about an attitude or belief by putting its expression inside bars: (H! (X)) refers to approval of (X)" (*STW*, p. 194 [p. 352, this volume]). Finally, "we use the semi-colon to denote the view that one attitude or belief involves or is coupled with another" (*STW*, p. 194 [p. 352, this volume]). Given this symbolism, the first two steps of the reasoning given above are represented as follows:

   B! (lying)
   H! ([*B*! (lying)]; [*B*! (getting little brother to lie)]).

These are explained as: "Disapproval of lying, and approval of making (disapproval of getting little brother to lie), follow upon (disapproval of lying)" (*STW*, p. 195 [p. 353, this volume]).

The antirealist explanation Blackburn gives for the validity of this argument, though it uses some unexplained realist-sounding terms, does not depend essentially on them. So we will need to look at the plausibility of the explanation itself. First a couple of small points. In the MR version the hypothetical was claimed to be asserting something, only not what a realist thought it was. Instead of a connection between two sentences (to be legitimately symbolized by "→"), the utterance of the hypothetical was claimed to be the assertion that one attitude "involved" another (or a belief). In the *STW* version, this has changed. Now the claim is that the hypothetical (when seriously uttered, presumably) is itself the expression of an attitude toward "the view that one attitude or belief involves or is coupled with another" (*STW*, p. 194 [p. 352, this volume]).

This change has the effect of making less plausible, in a way already familiar, a claim which is carried over from MR to *STW*, namely, that the hypothetical is the expression of or involves one in a "commitment." This is another one of those terms which seem to entail the realist picture. If I am committed to, say, paying my nephew's way through school, or to the claim that a Republican succeeded Carter, then this seems something objective, forced on me by a promise I have made or other views I hold. It is not at all clear that it has anything to do with whether I approve or disapprove of anything. So in taking the hypothetical as an expression of an attitude it becomes problematic whether Blackburn can also say that it expresses a "commitment" in the usual sense. And if a different sense is intended then an explanation of it is needed. We will return to this point in a moment.

Another change between the MR version and the *STW* version of his theory is this. Though the *STW* explanation of his theory is put in the context of the "*modus ponens* objection" with which this paper began, nowhere in this version does Blackburn actually claim that his theory can show how the argument he is considering can be shown to be an instance of *modus ponens*. In fact he does not even claim that his theory shows this argument to be valid. This may or may not be significant, but in any case it is worth looking at what he does claim his theory does.

Here is the relevant passage, which follows immediately after the gloss he gives for the two symbolically represented sentences above:

> Anyone holding this pair must hold the consequential disapproval: he is committed to disapproving of getting little brother to lie, for if he does not his attitudes clash. He has a fractured sensibility which cannot itself be an object of approval. The "cannot" here follows not (as a realist explanation would have it) because such a sensibility must be out of line with the moral facts it is trying to describe, but because such a sensibility cannot fulfill the practical purposes for which we evaluate things. E_{ex} will want to signal this. It will want a way of expressing the thought that it is a logical mistake that is made, if someone holds the first two commitments, and not the commitment to disapproval of getting your little brother to lie.
>
> (*STW*, p. 195 [p. 353, this volume])

On its face the last claim here seems open to the same objection made above against the MR version of this theory. Having clashing attitudes, or failing to do something which one has committed oneself to do (even on a realist account of commitment), are not the same things as making logical mistakes, at least in the ordinary sense of those words. But this is probably unfair. Blackburn in this passage can best be taken as simply giving what he regards as the antirealist account of a term such as "logical mistake" as it applies to moral arguments, an account which does not depend in an essential way on any unexplained realist-sounding term such as "commitment." After all, one might say, hasn't he at least shown that there is some kind of mistake here? Isn't there something automatically untoward in the sort of clash of attitudes which would be involved in disapproval of lying and approval of the idea that disapproval of lying involves disapproval of getting one's little brother to lie, while still not disapproving of getting one's little brother to lie? Won't this involve, as Blackburn says, a kind of "fractured sensibility"?

One question to ask here is why exactly Blackburn thinks that in such a situation one's attitudes "clash." Suppose I have the following attitudes: I disapprove of lying. I approve of the view that disapproval of lying "involves" disapproving of getting one's little brother to lie. And (to make it simple) I approve of getting my little brother to lie. Here are three different attitudes. What is supposed to make us think that they somehow "clash"? We cannot say (or anyway Blackburn cannot say) that disapproval of lying "clashes" with approval of getting my little brother to lie, period. Even though there is a sense of "disapprove" in which that seems true, it is not a point Blackburn can use since appeal to it would simply circumvent the hypothetical premise in this argument and, clearly, that has to do at least some of the work if this whole account of *modus ponens* isn't to just fall apart.

So it must be that if there is to be a "clash" of attitudes here, it has to be produced in part by my attitude of approval toward the view that disapproval of lying involves disapproval of getting my little brother to lie. And clearly the operative term here is "involves" (or perhaps the "approval" of the one attitude "involving" the other). That is, so to speak, what takes the place of the "→" here. So what does this mean? In the quoted passage Blackburn speaks of a "commitment" to holding the "consequent disapproval." As we have already seen, however, talk of "commitments" is problematic for an antirealist. This term itself seems to bring in a realist picture and hence, without a further antirealist gloss, cannot be leaned on here without begging the essential question at issue.

The other phrases Blackburn uses in place of "involves" are "is coupled with" (*STW*, p. 194 [p. 352, this volume]) and "follow upon" (*STW*, p. 195 [p. 353, this volume]) but these do not provide much help. He cannot presumably be thinking that the connection between disapproval of lying and disapproval of getting little brother to lie is somehow a psychological (or even physical) one, as if anyone who had the one attitude couldn't help but have the other. That is clearly false, and anyway it would not explain why approval of the "involvement" of the one attitude with the other was important. So I conclude that, at least without further explanation, it is mysterious why Blackburn even thinks that there is a "clash" of attitudes here. The most he seems entitled to say is that there are just some different attitudes, but that is all.

This brings us to the final point. Suppose that Blackburn were able to meet this last objection completely. To take the strongest case, suppose that he were able to show that on the antirealist theory he proposes, accepting the premises and rejecting the conclusion of the argument in question left one both approving and disapproving of getting one's little brother to lie. What is it about this that, on his theory, is supposed to involve a mistake? He says that such a clash would involve a "fractured sensibility which cannot itself be an object of approval" since "such a sensibility cannot fulfill the practical purposes for which we evaluate things" (*STW*, p. 195 [p. 353, this volume]).

But why not? Once we disallow appeal to a realist explanation (which could back up the claim of a mistake here with an account of the contradictory nature of the relevant sentences) and disallow covert appeals to realist-sounding terms, it is not at all clear where the mistake is supposed to lie in the mere clash of attitudes. So far as I can see, people have such "clashes" all the time without being "mistaken" about anything (or otherwise having their practical purposes thwarted by "fractured sensibilities"). Almost every time I walk past the cookie jar, for instance, I experience such a conflict of attitudes. On the one hand, I approve of my eating a cookie since, from long experience, I know I will enjoy it. On the other hand, I also disapprove of eating one since, from equally long experience, I know what it does to my waistline. So here is a clash of attitudes, but where is the "mistake" (or "fractured sensibility") that is supposed to be involved? The fact that I cannot act on or satisfy both attitudes just means that I have to figure out what to do here, not that there is anything untoward or fishy about having both attitudes. Yet without some account of how there is something untoward or mistaken in a mere clash of attitudes of this sort, Blackburn cannot claim even to have shown that, on the antirealism theory he is advocating, a person who asserts the premises and denies the conclusion of the argument above has made any mistake at all, let alone any sort of logical mistake in the usual sense.

NOTES

*   Thanks are due to Donald Hubin, James Klagge, Kevin Lavelle, Andrzej Zabludowski, and an anonymous reader for the journal *Ethics* for help on this paper.

1   Mackie's position is explained in J. L. Mackie, *Ethics: Inventing Right and Wrong* (Harmondsworth: Penguin Books, 1977), chap. 1.

2   S. W. Blackburn, *Spreading the Word* (Oxford: Oxford University Press, 1984), p. 196 [p. 354, this volume]. References to this work will be cited in the text as *STW*.

3   P. T. Geach, "Assertion," *Philosophical Review* 74 (1965): 449–65; see also J. R. Searle, "Meaning and Speech Acts," *Philosophical Review* 71 (1962): 423–32; and Paul Ziff, *Semantic Analysis* (Ithaca, NY: Cornell University Press, 1960), chap. 6.

4   S. W. Blackburn, "Moral Realism," in *Morality and Moral Reasoning*, ed. John Casey (London: Methuen, 1971). References to this essay in the text will be cited as MR.

5   S. W. Blackburn, "Errors and the Phenomenology of Value," in *Morality and Objectivity*, ed. T. Honderich (London: Routledge & Kegan Paul, 1985), p. 4.

6   S. W. Blackburn, "Rule Following and Moral Realism," in *Wittgenstein: To Follow a Rule*, ed. S. Holtzman and C. Leich (London: Routledge & Kegan Paul, 1981), p. 177 [Chapter 24, this volume, p. 481].

7   One might, presumably, want to expand or change the meaning of a term such as "logical inconsistency" so as to cover the violating of commitments. We would then have to decide whether I would be, in this new sense, "logically inconsistent" were I to promise to weed your garden and then not do so.

8   Of course, there are other senses of "valid," as when I claim to have a valid passport, but presumably these are not relevant here.

9   Earlier attempts by antirealists to explain what it means to call moral arguments valid or the like have also helped themselves to realist-sounding terms which were then left unexplained. Explaining "entails" in *The Language of Morals*, Hare says, "A sentence P entails a sentence Q if and only if the fact that a person assents to P but dissents from Q is *sufficient criterion* for saying that he has misunderstood one or other of the sentences" (R. M. Hare, *The Language of Morals* (New York: Oxford University Press, 1964), p. 25; emphasis added).

19

ATTITUDES AND CONTENTS

Simon Blackburn

GENERAL CONSIDERATIONS

G. F. Schueler's paper (Chapter 18, this volume) puts in a forceful way various reservations about my treatment of indirect contexts, on behalf of the position I have called "quasi-realism."[1] His opposition is, I think, as complete as could be: it is not only that my treatment has been incomplete, which I happily concede, or that its formulation has been defective, which I am prepared to believe, but also that nothing like it could possibly succeed. That at least is the proper consequence of some of his views – on logical form, and on validity, and on the nature of commitment. For example, if to show that an inference has "the logical form" or "is an instance" of *modus ponens* involves taking it as "the realist picture" has it, then no attempt to explain it in other terms will be compatible with its having that form. Again, if validity is ("as it is used in logic") defined in terms of the impossibility of premises being true and conclusions false, then persons reluctant to apply truth and falsity to any of the elements of an inference will have to admit that the inference is not valid, as the term is used in logic. Third, if "talk of 'commitments' is problematic for the antirealist" then antirealism will make no headway by thinking of a more general class of commitments than those with representative or realistic truth conditions. Fortunately, none of these contentions seems to me correct. Since the survival of quasi-realism even in spirit demands their rebuttal, I shall start by considering them in turn.

1

It is not too clear what it is for an argument to have the logical form of *modus ponens*. If that is a remark about syntactical form, then obviously having that logical form is compatible with any number of deep and different semantics for the components. To show this compare "*P, P→Q*, so *Q*" with the implication taken as truth-functional, with the same seeming argument taken as some suppose the English take it: *P→Q* is the commitment of one who attributes a high probability to *Q* conditional upon *P*. Which is the true *modus ponens*? If we plump for either exclusively, we face the uncomfortable consequence that it becomes controversial whether natural English contains any inferences of the form. If we embrace both, then being of the form *modus ponens* is compatible with any number of deep and different *explanations* of the semantics of the components: how it comes about that we have here elements describable as true or false, or a connective properly represented by some → or other. The same point could be made with any connective: knowing even when to interpret the negation sign of a logic as meaning negation is no easy matter.[2] If quasi-realism, in the form in which I tried to develop it, is right, the "deep" semantics of a surface example of *modus ponens* is to be explained in a particular, and perhaps initially surprising, way. But it is *modus ponens*, for all that. Or, if we say it is not, then we have no effective procedure for telling when anything is.

2

Perhaps the best way to answer the restrictive view of validity is by appeal to authority. One might cite imperative logic. Or, one might cite the approach to propositional inference in terms of coherent subjective probability functions, where validity corresponds to there being no coherent function attributing a lesser probability to the conclusion than to the premises, and coherence is defined in terms of immunity to Dutch book.[3] (This is the approach which would best marry with the probabilistic view of conditionals above.) Or one could cite the view of Stig Kanger, that in interpreting a deontic logic the extension of the truth predicate to the formulae, which could equally be regarded as imperatives or expressions of attitude, is a conventional matter.[4] A further reply would draw the usual distinction between an algebraic, mathematical, pure, or uninterpreted semantics – itself sufficient to yield notions of satisfaction, validity, and completeness – versus an applied or interpreted semantics, in which the valuation clauses reflect something about the use or meaning of the connectives.[5] Formal studies are content with the first, so that truth-in-a-structure, or satisfiability defined in terms of (for instance) sets of open sets in the topology of the real line defines validity.[6] But even when we turn to the second, the question of priorities still arises. It does not go without saying that we interpret the propositional connectives by drawing on an antecedent understanding of (classical) truth and falsity. Falsity and negation go hand in hand, and it should not be obvious which is the dominant partner. The view that it is by knowing how to *use* the connectives in proofs that we come to understand them, and hence gain what understanding we have of the truth tables, is perfectly open. In Prawitz's words: "Presumably, the observational consequences that can be drawn from the assumption that a person knows the condition for the truth of a sentence can also be drawn from the assumption that he knows how to use the sentence in proofs."[7] The whole philosophy of intuitionistic interpretations of the logical constants and of those who give priority to sequent calculi and natural deduction systems opposes the simple assumption that an antecedent understanding of "representative" truth and falsity affords the only road to understanding validity. A more plausible view and one which nicely fits quasi-realism is that attributions of validity and application of the truth predicate go hand in hand: I expand on this below.

3

Schueler finds the very notion of a commitment "problematic for the anti-realist." His argument that it is one of "those terms which seem to entail a realist picture" is this: "If I am committed to, say, paying my nephew's way through school, or to the claim that a Republican succeeded Carter, then this seems something objective, forced on me by a promise I have made or other views I hold." Well it might be, if we could suitably cash the metaphor of forcing, and suitably interpret objectivity – although whether the objectivity forced by, say, promises has anything to do with realism is another matter. But equally, the commitment might not be forced by anything, like the commitment to go for a jog once a week or to improve one's golf. It does not matter, because "commitment" I simply use as a general term to cover mental states which may be beliefs, but also those which gain expression in propositional form, but which for various reasons philosophers such as Hume, Ramsey, Wittgenstein, Stevenson, Ayer, Hare, and I have seen in terms of such things as acceptance of rules, changes in disposition, possession of attitudes, which are worth separating from beliefs. Some commitments will have nothing to do with approval: these include the change in one who accepts a rule of inference, or treats a proposition as necessary, or accords a high subjective probability to Q upon P, and so on, as well as Schueler's example of his belief that a Republican succeeded Carter. In the sphere of ethics, approval and attitude are natural terms to work with, but it would not matter if neither fitted exactly, or if better terms for the state in question existed. What is important is the theoretical issue of whether and why the state is worth distinguishing from belief, or at least from belief with representational truth conditions thought of realistically, but since I have written extensively on this elsewhere, I shall pass that over.[8]

FAST-TRACK AND SLOW-TRACK QUASI-REALISM

So far I have simply dissented from Schueler's reasons for general pessimism about the approach, intending to show that the ideas behind quasi-realism survive his onslaught. But he is on stronger ground in attacking the detail of my treatment. I shall turn to that after taking stock for a moment.

The problem is that of embedding of sentences which primarily express attitude, in contexts which might appear to admit only sentences which in some contrasting way express propositions. When I say that these sentences primarily express attitude I have never intended to deny that they can be regarded as expressing beliefs or propositions. This opposition would be going beyond anything I embrace. But I do mean that the right way of theorizing about them identifies them, in the first instance, as expressing states of mind whose function is not to represent anything about the world. They express something more to do with attitudes, practices, emotions, feelings arising in contemplating some kinds of conduct, with goal seeking, with insistence upon normative constraints on conduct, and nothing to do with representing the world. In the familiar metaphor, their "direction of fit" with the world is active – to have the world conform to them, rather than descriptive or representational. I call someone who approves both of this contrast, and with this direction of theorizing, a projectivist. Projectivism may seem to be automatically opposed to the view that in saying that something is good (etc.) we give voice to a real belief about it, and it is often so introduced (as labels like "noncognitivism" suggest). But this opposition is not automatic. Subtlety with the concept of belief, or with the concept of truth or fact, may enable the expressivist to soften this opposition. Theory may enable us to understand how a commitment with its center in the expression of subjective determinations of the mind can also function as expressing belief, or be capable of sustaining the truth predicate – properly called "true" or "false." I tried to herald this development with the notion of a "propositional reflection" in the older paper "Moral Realism," and it was the point of the last pages of chapter 6, and of chapter 7, of *Spreading the Word*.[9] It means separating truth (in this application at least) from "represents" and its allies, but nobody has ever pointed out the harm in that.

It did, however, seem to me that, before this happy result could be secured, work had to be done. It had to be shown *why* a sentence with this role could *properly* function in the ways ethical sentences do – why it sustains a fully propositional role. I now think we should distinguish a slow track to this result and a fast track. The slow track involves patiently construing each propositional context as it comes along. This is the line I took in trying to meet Geach's problem. Its advantage is that of honest toil over what might seem like theft; its disadvantage if Schueler is right is that it does not work. But before judging that I should admit not only that it threatens to look Ptolemaic but also that it seems not to correspond to any obvious cognitive processes we go through. It is not as though construing (say) conditionals with evaluative components comes harder to us than construing them with ordinary components, and this will need explanation.

Fast-track quasi-realism would get there in better style. It would make sufficient remarks about truth to suggest that we need a comparable notion to regulate evaluative discourse (even although that is nonrepresentational) and then say that our adherence to propositional forms needs no further explanation than that. The adoption of propositional form and style meets a need because we need to share and discuss and dissent from attitudes or other stances. It involves only philosophers in error, and little more need be said. That sounds cavalier, but it was the line of, for instance, Kant and Nietzsche and probably Wittgenstein,[10] none of whom found any particular trouble in imagining the emergence of a predicate with a nondescriptive role. Nietzsche puts it roundly:

> The pathos of nobility and distance, as aforesaid, the protracted and domineering fundamental total feeling on the part of a higher ruling order in relation to a lower order, to a *below – that* is the origin of the antithesis "good" and "bad" (the lordly right of giving names extends so far that one should allow oneself to conceive the origin of language itself as an expression of power on the part of the rulers: they say "this *is* this and this," they seal every thing and event with a sound, and, as it were, take possession of it).

Perhaps our general propensity to seal things with sounds needs no detailed explanation or justification (cf. "this is nice" as a way of voicing pleasure, and immediately giving rise to compounds "if it's nice, two would be nicer," etc.). But compromises are possible: the fast track can benefit from some of the security achieved on the slow, and the slow track can make use of some of the short cuts of the fast. Or so I shall argue. Notice that, whichever track we favor, the point is to *earn* our right to propositional forms – including the use of a truth predicate. If this is done, any conventional concept of validity tags along – there is a level of analysis at which *modus ponens* and the rest are no different when their components are evaluative and when they are not.

EMBEDDING

A parallel to the idea that a certain sentence expresses an attitude – "Hooray for the Bears" – would be the obvious truth that some others express commands – "Go to see the Bears" – and questions – "Are the Bears doing well?" Now when imperatives and questions give rise to subordinate clauses, the linguistic forms typically maintain an indication of the original mood, even if there is another syntactic change: "he told me *to* go to see the Bears, he asked me *whether* the Bears are doing well, if *I am to* go to see the

Bears, I had better have some tea first." Here the right thing to say is that the subordinate clause maintains the mood of the original, but that it is not uttered with the *force* that a direct utterance of the sentence has (nothing is commanded or questioned). Nevertheless, mood is in some sense primarily an indicator of force. It is only by understanding what a question or command is that one understands the function of the interrogative or imperative mood.

There is a prima facie puzzle here. Mood is primarily an indicator of force, force is lost in subordinate clauses, but mood is not.

I do not think, however, that the puzzle is very deep, although its formal representation can be difficult. The subordinate clause in "He said that *P*" identifies which proposition he asserted; the clauses in "he told me to go to see the Bears" or "he asked whether the Bears are doing well" identify which order he gave or which question he asked. Mood indicates that a question or command is still part of the topic, even when the overall communication is not itself a question or command. Technically, I therefore agree with Michael Pendlebury that mood (or at least the presence of the indicator "to go..," "whether ...") affects the sense of such clauses: the embedding does not cancel the semantic significance of the mood indicator, which is to maintain some connection with an original command or question.[11] It can matter that a question or command is still in this sense part of the *topic*. Perhaps the nicest illustration of this is the difference between "he knew that the Bears had won" and "he knew whether the Bears had won" where the first simply gives us the content of his knowledge, but the mood in the second shows that what he is said to have known is the answer to a question – which might have been yes or no. Of course, saying that in this way a command or question is part of the topic is not implying that one was ever actually uttered – one can know the answer to questions that have never been asked.

We do not have a mood which in this way indicates that an attitude is part of the topic. The nearest approximation is in indirect reportage of wishes expressed in the optative: "would I were in Grantchester!" can perhaps be reported: he said that he would be in Grantchester, but there is at least a slight sense of strain. Normally, if I make plain to you what I feel, say about the Bears, I will most probably do so using a sentence with an "expressive" predicate: "the Bears are great!" The report of what I said in indirect speech is then easy: he said that the Bears are great. According to projectivism, the item of vocabulary shows that the original utterance was expressive of attitude. In the subordinate clause, it remains to make attitude the topic just as overt mood indicators do. The person who said that the Bears are great expressed just that attitude about the Bears. Saying that this is what he did is not of course endorsing or subscribing to the view, any more than reporting a command or question involves reissuing it in propria persona.

Suppose we spoke an "emotivist" language, in which expressions of attitude wore this function on their faces. We would not have the predicative form, to keep such expressions in the indicative mood, but an ejaculatory mood, corresponding to that of "Hooray for the Bears." It would then be necessary to have a construction of subordinate clauses corresponding to words such as "that … ," "to … ," and "whether …," which marks the original attitude as the topic. There seems no problem of semantic principle about this; "that!" "whether!" and so on might be introduced, so that "he said that! hooray for the Bears" tells us which attitude he expressed, "he wondered whether! hooray for the Bears" tells us which attitude he was pondering, and so on.

If natural languages have chosen not to register expressive force by a particular mood, they may have chosen to do it in other ways. And taking other cases of mood and force as our model, there might be no great difficulty about imagining it done by an expressive mood and yielding a smooth interpretation of at least some subordinate clauses. Here there is room for the compromise between fast- and slow-track quasi-realism: see how far you get in imagining an overtly expressive language developed in such ways, and diminish (even if not to zero) the gap between what it achieves and what we do with predication, and talk of truth.

A LOGIC

Geach concentrated upon the special case of the antecedent of conditionals in his original article. My suggestion involved first describing what we are up to in embedding what is primarily an expression of attitude in a context, making it intelligible that the context should have a function. Second, it involved giving sufficient semantic theory to show why we have the way we do of meeting that need. Thus in the case of Geach's original conditional, my suggestion of what we are up to involved taking up an attitude to an involvement of attitude with attitude, or attitude with belief. Such "second-order" stances seemed to me both needed in themselves and plausible candidates for the import of a conditional with evaluative elements. If we use '⇒' to signify the *involvement* of one mental state with another, the result was that a simple conditional "if lying is wrong, then getting your little brother to lie is wrong" came out as:

H! (*B*!*L*\ ⇒*B'GBL*\),

where the \ … \ notation shows that our topic is the attitude or belief whose normal expression occurs within the slashes. Involvement is not a logical notion, but neither should it seem mysterious. I tried to explain it by introducing the idea of a sensibility as a function from belief to attitude, attitude to attitude, and so on: it is what we would overtly talk about by saying things like "I really approve of *making* approval of an action depend on its consequences" or "believing that *should* increase your approval of this." Endorsing or rejecting such an involvement of commitments one with another is an important thing to do; it is therefore not surprising that we have a simple English form with which to do it.

Let us now consider *modus ponens*. We have

$$B!L$$
$$H!(\backslash B!L\backslash \Rightarrow \backslash B!GBL\backslash)$$
$$\text{So: } B!GBL.$$

Schueler and others rightly raise doubts about the kind of inconsistency in avowing the two initial attitudes and refusing endorsement of the conclusion.[12] In *Spreading the Word* I talked of a "fractured sensibility" which could not be a proper object of approval. Schueler reasonably asks why it could not be an object of approval and whether in any case this smacks more of a moral or evaluative problem than of a logical one. Yet *modus ponens* with these components is surely logically valid, and a proper semantics for expressions of attitude ought to explain why.

How do attitudes become things which enter into logical relationships, which *matter* in the theory of inference? It is well known that logical relationships between imperatives can be studied by thinking of joint satisfiability – seeing whether there is a consistent world in which each of a set of imperatives is obeyed. Similarly deductive relationships between norms can be studied by thinking of ideal or relatively ideal worlds in which the norms are met. If we have here the basis for a logic, it extends to attitude. For $H!p$ can be seen as expressing the view that p is to be a goal, to be realized in any perfect world. A world in which $\sim p$ is less than ideal, according to this commitment. The contrary attitude $B!p$ would rule p out of any perfect world, and corresponding to permission we can have $T!p$, which is equivalent to not hooraying $\sim p$, that is, not booing p.

Putting attitude to the fore, instead of the more usual obligations and permissions of deontic logic, promises two gains. The first is that writers on deontic logic usually interpret "Op" and "Pp" as purely propositional by making them describe what is obligated or permitted by some supposed background set of norms (the most notable exception to this generalization is Hector-Neri Castañeda).[13] But this divorces them from their ordinary expressive use, which is not to describe what some (possibly alien) system of norms yields but to insist upon or permit various things. If the apparatus of deontic logic can be taken over while this use is kept primary, so much the better. But there is another gain in taking the portmanteau term "attitude" rather than the particular, restricted notion of "obligation" and "permission." This is that the logical apparatus should apply wherever we have the idea of a goal or aim, and corresponding idea of something to be avoided, or not to be avoided. We need not be in the realm of the obligatory, or of *requirements*, but merely in that of the needed or even just the desirable. Consistency in goals is still a desideratum whose logic needs development.

And in fact the deductive apparatus of deontic logic does not depend in any way on taking obligations and permissions as fully fledged deontic notions. The same structure exists if "Op" is interpreted as any kind of view that p be true ideally and "Pp" as any kind of toleration of p.

There is nothing surprising about using realization of goals or ideals as the final test for consistency. The ordinary notion of finding whether recommendations are consistent just is to imagine them carried out and see if that can be consistently done. But Schueler rightly raises a problem which might affect the extension to attitude. This is that consistency in attitude is not a particular virtue. I may wish that p and wish that $\sim p$ without particular shame. I may desire that p, and desire that q, but not desire that p & q: I want to spend the evening at the theater, and I want to read my book, but I do not want to read my book at the theater. There is a sense in which my goals are inconsistent – they cannot all be realized – but, if this does not matter, then it is not sufficiently *like* the vice of inconsistency in belief to form the basis of a logic.

My comment on this is threefold. First of all, I think part of the objection comes from confusing desires with wishes. Inconsistent wishes may not matter because in wishing or daydreaming we are spinning fictions, and inconsistent fictions do not matter. This is because there is no connection with action. But for all that, inconsistency in real desire may matter. Incompatible and therefore unrealizable goals are bad in a way quite analogous to that in which inconsistent beliefs are. The latter cannot represent the world properly. But the former cannot represent how to behave in the world properly: they cannot mate together with beliefs, in the usual belief-desire psychological framework, to direct effective action. The man who believes that it is raining and that it is not is badly placed to act if he wants, say, to avoid getting wet. But so is the man who believes that it is raining but wants to get wet and not to get wet.

The second point to notice is that attitude and desire are capable of qualification. I may be subject to some desires, or some pressures (tiredness, mood) which suggest reading a book and others which suggest visiting the theater. Do I both want to read a book and want to go to the theater? It is a crude way of representing my state. Perhaps I want to read a book *inasmuch as* I am tired, want to go to the theater *inasmuch as* I like company. I feel the different pressures, but it is at least as natural to say that I don't know what I want to do as it is to say that I want to do both. I can indeed say that I would like to do both, but that takes us back to the realm of wishes (I would like them not to conflict somehow). So one way of diminishing the attraction of inconsistent desires is to remember the difference between full-scale, all-in desires, and attractions or pressures which are not yet resolved.

Even if this point were contested, a third defense is waiting. Although I have urged the advantage of thinking in terms of a catholic conception of attitude rather than of strict deontological notions, we could restrict ourselves to concepts of being for or against or neither for nor against things where consistency *does* matter. If this is a more limited range than the full spectrum of desire, this need not matter. If, for instance, it embraced only desires which one was inclined to submit to public scrutiny, or translate into practical advice, then there would be a corresponding restriction of the interpretation of notions such as "goal" or "ideal." That is fine, provided the relevant attitudes satisfy the constraints when it comes to interpreting the logic in a domain such as ethics. Since ethics is at bottom a practical subject, this is to be expected.

In the usual metaphor, the direction of fit between desires and the world is opposite to that between beliefs and the world. The desire that p dictates action if it is deemed likely, but avoidable, that ~p, whereas the belief that p needs abandoning if it is deemed likely that ~p.[14] But since belief and desire do each have a direction of fit and a content, then each should be fitted to play a role in a logic of consistency. A person may flout the demand of consistency in complicated or demanding situations, but only at the cost of tension: his goals cannot be realized, or if he has inconsistent beliefs, the world cannot be as he represents it. It may be admirable that we sometimes get into states where we feel that tension, but this is so for belief as well as desire. It could not be admirable in general, and it could not be true in general, for these states are essentially characterized by responsibility either to the world, in the case of beliefs, or in our response to the world, in the case of attitude.

I therefore reject Schueler's contention that there is no legitimate notion of inconsistency. But it remains to be seen whether it ratifies my assault on *modus ponens*, or any other natural inference pattern. Meanwhile, there is another natural worry about my proposal. As it stands it yields no smooth extension to other propositional contexts. For instance, simple disjunction with an evaluative component does not yield an obvious second-order attitude. "Either Johnny has done something wrong, or Freddy has" is not well represented as $H!(\backslash B! J \backslash$ OR $\backslash B! F \backslash)$ where "OR" introduces a kind of disjunctive relation between attitudes. Because even if the idea of a disjunctive relation between attitudes makes sense, one might know that one of them has done something wrong but quite disapprove of taking up a negative attitude to *either* of them – if neither has yet been proved guilty, for instance. The stance that $H!$ $(\backslash B! J \backslash$ OR $\backslash B! F \backslash)$ expresses seems to be that of someone who endorses only psychologies which contain at least one of the embedded attitudes (this would be the natural interpretation of disjunction), but this is not at all the same as the stance of someone who thinks that either Johnny has done something wrong or Freddy has. One could interpret disjunction by first translating it into the associated conditional and then using the account of conditionals on that. But there is something ad hoc about such procedures. They take the theory too far from anything which seems necessary for the ordinary truth-functional disjunction, and their very unnaturalness raises again the question of adequacy. Even if the notion of involvement gives a reasonable surrogate for implication, there may be no such notion naturally available in each case of potential embedding.

Suppose then we take the theory of inference as primary. If we ask what these embeddings are *for*, the immediate answer is that they mediate inference. They show us the deductive relationships between our commitments, and between our commitments and our beliefs. So rather than *replace* logical constants, as in the approach I just gave, we might try to *retain* them and to provide an interpretation of embeddings of attitude in the contexts the deductive system is to treat: in the first place, contexts provided by the truth functors.

We know, or think we know, what the negation, disjunction, and conjunction of an ordinary proposition is. It needs showing that we have any right to extend those notions to cover expressions of a different kind. Thus in the language to come $H!p$ is to be treated as a well-formed formula capable of entering the same embeddings as p. Even if this provides a language which is formally workable, it still needs showing that it provides one which is interpretable – in which $H!p$ can still be regarded as fundamentally expressive of attitude.

Consider first negation. What can $\sim H!A$ mean? Schueler might say: nothing much to do with truth or falsity, and since that reversal is the fundamental effect of negation, it cannot mean anything to apply the notion here. But I have already remarked that it might go the other way round: falsity of p is the truth of the negation of p. Ordinary negation is expressive of denial: $\sim p$ is that proposition whose expression denies p. There is a clear corresponding relation between attitudes: there exists that attitude which "denies," or rejects, having p as an aim or goal. If $H!p$ expresses the attitude of endorsing the goal p, $\sim H!p$ then expresses that of opposition: tolerating $\sim p$ or allowing it as consistent with an ideal world. So we can say that $T!A$ is substitutable for $\sim H!A$, and $H!A$ for $\sim T!A$. Such a conversion drives external "negations" on attitudes inward. So even if the original occurrence of the external negation made us uneasy, *formally* the unease is dissipated by the conversion, and *philosophically* dissipated by recognizing sufficient analogy between conflict of attitude and conflict of belief.

What of other truth functional contexts? It is an important feature of inference using propositional calculus embeddings that they can all be represented by the normal forms of conjunction and disjunction. In a tableau development each move either adds to the string (as when A, B, are appended under $A \& B$) or divides the string (as when A makes one branch, and B another, under $A \vee B$). Now let us suppose that we are involved with an evaluative commitment, $H!A$ or $T!A$ in a propositional calculus embedding. We can see what this means if we can interpret the strings in which it issues. This reduces then to the problem of interpreting these two elements in a tree structure. But it is easy to see what a string represents if, underneath this embedding, we get $H!p$ occurring alone (e.g. under $p \& H!p$ we get $H!p$). This means that the initial complex commits us to the attitude, and this is not hard to interpret. Being against clergymen and for free love commits one to being against clergymen, and the notion of consistent realization of aims or goals shows us why.

There remains the case in which a tableau under a complex branches and $H!p$

belongs to one of the branches. The interpretation is that one potential route to drawing out the consequences of the complex involves this commitment, although another may not. Thus $p \lor H!q$ issues in a branch; it is the commitment of one who is what I shall call *tied to a tree*. That is, tied to (*either* accepting that p, or endorsing q), where the brackets show that this is not the same as (being tied to accepting p) or (being tied to endorsing q). Rather, the commitment is to accepting the one branch should the other prove untenable. The essential point is that this is a quite intelligible state to be in. Philosophically we justify the procedure by analogy with the ordinary notion of accepting a disjunction, which similarly ties one to a tree of possibilities, and formally the language admits of identical deductive procedures.

How does this relate to the original proposal for treating the conditional? Under a material conditional $A \to B$ we get the tree with $\sim A$ in one branch and B in the other. Suppose then we treat Geach's conditional "if lying yourself is wrong getting your little brother to lie is wrong" this way. Someone asserting it is tied to the tree of (either assenting to "lying yourself is not wrong" or to "getting your little brother to lie is wrong"). What was right about my original proposal is that being so tied is in this case characteristic of a particular value system or set of attitudes. Only someone with a certain view of the relation between doing things directly and doing them indirectly is apt to assent to the conditional. This represents the reason for his being tied. What was inelegant about the original proposal, I now think, was putting that directly into the content of the conditional itself. The assent to the conditional itself does not tell us why someone is tying himself to that tree – it only tells us that he is tied and that we can use this fact in assessing the consistency of his position. I return to this below, after detailing the logic a little.

I do not want to claim finality for the semantics I shall now sketch, but it illustrates how a logic might be developed, and it shows that notions of inconsistency and satisfiability can be defined (it also bears out Kanger's remarks mentioned above). It uses Hintikka's notion of a set of "deontic alternatives."[15] In Hintikka's semantics the central notion is that of norms obtaining in a possible world, and of the deontic alternatives to that world being the possible worlds which are in accordance with those norms. Hintikka compares this notion to Kant's "Kingdom of Ends" (*Reich der Zwecke*): it represents a "mere ideal" (Kant: "freilich nur ein Ideal") which is not realized but which we nevertheless must be able to think of consistently.

In Hintikka's development we work in terms of a model system or set of model sets. A model set is a partial description of a possible world or alternative. A set of sentences including oughts and permissions will be satisfiable if it is embeddable in such a set. This means that a set of sentences L is satisfiable if and only if there is a model system S and a model set $m \in S$, such that L is a subset of m. Logical truth of A is unsatisfiability of the negation of A; B is a logical consequence of A if and only if $A \to B$ is valid, that is, $(A \,\&\, \sim B)$ is unsatisfiable.

Where we are not concerned with attitudes the notion of a model set m is defined in a standard way:

If $p \in m$, then not $\sim p \in m$;

if $p \,\&\, q \in m$, then $p \in m$ and $q \in m$;

if $p \lor q \in m$, then $p \in m$ or $q \in m$ or both;

if $(Ex)p \in m$ then $p\,(a/x) \in m$ for some individual constant a;

if $(Ax)p \in m$ and if the free singular term b occurs in the sentences of m, then $p\,(b/x)$ $\in m$;

$p\,(a/x)$ is the result of replacing the variable x by the singular term z everywhere in p.

Henceforward I shall depart somewhat from Hintikka's terminology, in order to separate some of the main ideas more obviously. Suppose we add to a standard first-order language operators $H!$ and $T!$ subject to the condition that if A is a well-formed formula $H!A$ is well formed and $T!A$ is well formed. Suppose now we start with a set of sentences L, which may contain sentences with these operators among them. We begin by defining a *next approximation to the ideal*, L^* of L.

(Ii)   If $H!A \in L$, then $H!A \in L^*$;

(Iii)   If $H!A \in L$, then $A \in L^*$;

(Iiii)   If $T!p \in L$, then a set L^* containing p is to be added to the set of next approximations for L.

(Iiv)   If L^* is a next approximation to the ideal relative to some set of sentences L, then, if $A \in L^*$, $A \in$ subsequent approximations to the ideal $L^{**}, L^{***} \ldots$

We can say that a set of *final ideals*, $\{L^{***} \ldots\}$ of L is obtained when further use of these rules produces no new sentence not already in the members $L^{***} \ldots$ of the set.

The set of sentences L may contain disjunctions or conditionals ready to be treated as disjunctions in the deductive apparatus. We can say that to each branch of a disjunction there corresponds a *route* to an ideal.

We can then define:

A set of sentences L is unsatisfiable iff each route to a set of final ideals S results in a set of sentences S one of whose members contains both a formula and its negation.

These rules need a little gloss. Obviously Iii embodies the aim that an ideal relative to a starting set of attitudes is obtained by specifying that the goals expressed are met. Rules Ii and Iii merely ensure that the attitudes specified originally remain in the subsequent realizations (if it is good that people are kind, it remains good in a world in which they are kind). The statement $T!A$ gets handled slightly differently. It sees A as compatible with perfection, but not mandatory. When tolerations are in play we have to consider both developments in which they are realized, but also developments in which they are not. One next approximation for $(T!p$ & $T!\sim p)$ should contain p, and another $\sim p$, but the fact that they are inconsistent with each other does not reflect back on the original sentence. So to assess consistency we need to think of formulae as producing a *set* of next approximations. The rule is that if $T!A$ is present in a set, there must be *a* next set in which A is present, although it is not to be in all. This means that we shall have to consider sets of next approximations to the ideal and sets of final idealizations. Intuitively, what is to matter is whether each such set is consistent.

It may be that modifications of Iiv would be desirable. What is obtained by realizing a toleration might not automatically feed through to subsequent approximations. The intuitive idea would be that something may be tolerated now, whereas were some ideal to become realized, it would no longer be tolerable: in that cast Iiv would need qualification.[16]

We want to iterate the procedure of generating a next ideal. This can be done by repeated use of these rules. If L^* is already a next approximation to the ideal and contains a sentence A, then except where A derives from realization of a toleration, it must transfer to further approximations to the ideal L^{**}. .... This is not so in general if A belongs to an original set L (for it may be a pity that A: A & $H!$ $\sim A$ is consistent). Here the idea is that once we are following out what is so in the progressive approximations to a perfect world, any realized ideal remains realized. The denizens of paradise do not move.

To get a feel for such a semantics consider the formula $H!p{\rightarrow}p$. This is not valid: $\{H!p, \sim p\}$ is satisfiable. The next approximation is $\{H!p, p\}^*$, and this is a final ideal and is consistent. (As the gloss of Iiv showed, p does *not* transfer through to L^* – as far as the original set goes, p may be a pity, and this is reflected in its absence from the final ideal.) Now however consider $H!$ $(H!p{\rightarrow}p)$. This is valid, for $T!$ $(H!p$ & $\sim p)$ is not satisfiable. By Iv $(H!p, \sim p)^*$ must be added as a next ideal. But the ideal under that is $\{H!p, p, \sim p\}^{**}$ which is inconsistent. Here is the operation of Iiii: it was already in this working out of the ideal that $\sim p$, so it stays there when we further consider the ideal obtained by realizing $H!p$ and generates inconsistency.

Transferred to these terms Hintikka's main worked example is this. Prior once took it as a "quite plain truth" of logic that

$$H!p \text{ \& } (p{\rightarrow}H!q){\rightarrow}H!q.$$

But $\{H!p, p{\rightarrow}H!q, T!$ $\sim q\}$ is perfectly satisfiable. In tree form and using the notion $= 0\Rightarrow$ to signify adding the next approximation to the ideal, we get:

$$H!p$$
$$T!\sim q$$
$$p \rightarrow H!q$$

$$\sim p$$
$$= 0 \Rightarrow \{H!p, p, \sim q\}^* \qquad\qquad\qquad\qquad \begin{array}{c} H!q \\ = 0 \Rightarrow \{H!q, q, \sim q\}^* \end{array}$$

The right-hand route is bound to contain the inconsistent set, but the left yields none – reflecting the fact that if something which ought to be so is not, obligations or norms or goals consequential on its being so need not be held either. As in the first example, something here is a pity, and this is reflected by the fact that $H!$ [$H!p$ & ($p \rightarrow H!q$)$\rightarrow H!q$] is indeed valid.

The possibility of valid formulae with wide scope $H!$ suggests a notion of "deontic validity" (Hintikka's term): in other words, although A may be consistent, $H!A$ need not be. In turn this gives us a needed notion: a person may be something worse than "immoral," or possessing contingently defective attitudes, but not be "inconsistent" in the sense of believing anything logically false. He may simply have ideals or goals which admit of no consistent realization.

This logic yields one reduction principle immediately: $H!H!p$ yields $H!p$. What about $T!T! \rightarrow T!p$? {$T!T!p$ & $H!\sim p$} = 0$\Rightarrow${$T!p$ & $H!\sim p$} and this too is inconsistent. This reflects the "one-dimensional" way in which realizations of goals are treated: we look through $H!$ and $T!$ to see what happens when they are realized, and this transparency extends to iterations of them. Many complexities could be introduced at this point and in connection with iterations generally.

The semantics also generates interesting sidelights on the original proposal for treating *modus ponens*. Suppose we took as an example "X is good, if X is good Y is good, so Y is good." Then a treatment like my original might render it:

$H!p$; $H!$ ($H!p \rightarrow H!q$) so $H!q$.

And this is indeed valid. But the satisfaction is short lived, for if we turn instead to "Giving makes happiness; if giving makes happiness then Christmas is a good thing, so Christmas is a good thing" a parallel treatment renders it:

p; $H!$ ($p \rightarrow H!q$) so $H!q$.

This argument is invalid. There is no way of reimporting the original p into the set of final ideals. Clearly a treatment which makes a big asymmetry between these two arguments is suspicious. However, my old proposal did not quite have this form – it involved no propositional calculus embedding of $H!p$. Now that such a form is available, obviously we shortcircuit these proposals simply to get $H!p$, $H!p{\to}H!q$, so $H!q$, and similarly for the second version. Each of these is valid.

So is Schueler right that my original proposal fails to show any inconsistency in the set containing the premises of a *modus ponens* inference, but a denial of the conclusion? As I mentioned, the original proposal for conditionals took seriously the idea that they create an indirect context – one where the propositions or attitudes normally expressed become, in some sense, the reference or topic of the utterance. In the present development conditionals are treated as disjunctions and broken open for example by tableau methods. Is there essential opposition here? Not necessarily. The issue is whether we can interpret endorsement of $(\backslash A\backslash{\Rightarrow}\backslash C\backslash)$ – the original interpretation – as equivalent in strength to $(\sim A \vee C)$ – the place conditionals now have in the logic. Only a little leeway with "endorsement" and "involves" ("$\Rightarrow$") is needed; as much in fact as gives the material implication its usual right to be thought of as rendering a conditional. Say: endorsing the involvement is tying oneself to the tree. In other words tying oneself to restricting admissible alternatives to those in which $\sim A$, and those in which C. You have one or the other. And the effect of this on the theory of inference, when A or C or both are evaluative, is brought out in the model theory.

CONCLUSION

Slow-track quasi-realism will want to say that these proposals analyze or give us the logical form of the arguments we are considering. Fast-track quasi-realism need not say this. It can say: "all this is very interesting." It shows how *little* is involved if we imagine us jumping ship – changing from an expressivist language to our normal forms. But it is unnecessary to claim that we make no jump at all. That would involve, for instance, defending the claim that negation is absolutely univocal as it occurs in $\sim H!p$ and in $\sim p$, and similarly for the other constants. But this need not be claimed. All we have is sufficient similarity of logical role to make the temptation to exploit *ordinary* propositional logic quite irresistible – and that is what we naturally do. The expressivist language serves as a model showing us why what we do is legitimate – but that may be all. This is what I meant by saying that fast-track quasi-realism can benefit from the security provided by the slow. I like this methodology. We bootstrap our way into appreciating how propositional expression, the arrival of indirect contexts, and the arrival of the truth predicate meet our needs, without in any way betraying the original, economical, metaphysical vision. At times we may have taken steps, benefiting from what are only analogies between these kinds of commitments and beliefs in order to treat the former as we treat the latter. But if so these steps are little and natural.

NOTES

1 G. F. Schueler, "Moral *Modus Ponens* and Moral Realism" (Chapter 18 in this volume).

2 B. J. Copeland, "What Is a Semantics for Classical Negation?" *Mind*, vol. 95 (1986).

3 Hartry Field, "Logic, Meaning and Conceptual Role," *Journal of Philosophy*, vol. 74 (1977).

4 Stig Kanger, "New Foundations for Ethical Theory," in *Deontic Logic: Introductory and Systematic Readings*, ed. R. Hilpinen (Dordrecht: Reidel, 1971), pp. 55–6.

5 M. Dummett, "The Justification of Deduction," in *Truth and Other Enigmas* (London: Duckworth, 1978), p. 293; A. Plantinga, *The Nature of Necessity* (London: Oxford University Press, 1974), pp. 126 ff.

6 H. Weyl, "The Ghost of Modality," in *Philosophical Essays in Memory of Edmund Husserl* (Cambridge, MA: Harvard University Press, 1940).

7 D. Prawitz, "Meaning and Proofs: On the Conflict between Classical and Intuitionistic Logic," *Theoria*, vol. 43 (1977).

8 A recent statement is my "Morals and Modals," in *Fact, Science and Value*, ed. G. MacDonald and C. Wright (London: Blackwell, 1986).

9 Simon Blackburn, *Spreading the Word* (London: Oxford University Press, 1984).

10 I. Kant, *The Critique of Judgement*, trans. J. C. Meredith (London: Oxford University Press). Although Kant believes that the judgment of taste is not a cognitive judgment (p. 41) and is determined by subjective sensation, he also thinks that since we wish to demand similarity of feeling from others, we "speak of beauty as if it were a property of things" (p. 52); Nietzsche, *The Genealogy of Morals*, first essay, II; L. Wittgenstein, *Remarks on the Foundations of Mathematics* (Oxford: Blackwell, 1956), p. 163, contains a particularly clear statement of the view that statements of mathematics mislead philosophers by their descriptive form.

11 M. Pendlebury, "Against the Power of Farce: Reflections on the Meaning of Mood," *Mind* 95 (1986): 361–73.

12 Bob Hale, "The Compleat Projectivist," *Philosophical Quarterly* 36 (1986): 65–85, anticipates the difficulties with validity.

13 H-N. Castañeda, *Thinking and Doing* (Dordrecht: Reidel, 1975), esp. chap. 2.

14 Michael Smith, "The Humean Theory of Motivation," *Mind* 96 (1987): 36–61.

15 J. Hintikka, "Deontic Logic and Its Philosophical Morals," in *Models for Modalities* (Dordrecht: Reidel), 1969.

16 In "Moral Quasi-Realism" (Proceedings of 1987 *Realism and Reason* Conference at St Andrews) Hale shows that Iiv is too strong as it stands and may better be replaced with a closer version of Hintikka's original rule. [A version of this paper appears as Chapter 20, this volume.]

20

CAN THERE BE A LOGIC OF ATTITUDES?

Bob Hale

1 EXPRESSIVE THEORIES, GEACH'S PROBLEM AND QUASI-REALISM

Can we be non-revisionist about morals without embracing moral realism? Can we see our moral talk and thought as philosophically quite in order, but devoid of commitment to any realm of distinctively moral facts or states of affairs? One way to pursue that goal is to argue that moral utterances are not, as their surface form invites us to suppose, genuine assertions, in the market for truth, but have some other role or function, such as to express attitudes of approval and disapproval and to encourage their formation in others. The epistemological and ontological attractions[1] of an expressive theory – no distinctively moral facts, and so no problem of explaining our epistemic access to such facts – are too obvious to require elaboration. Its advantage over naturalism – the reductionist option here – and crude subjectivism (construing moral utterances as self-ascriptions of pro- or con-attitudes) may seem scarcely less so; where each of these positions has trouble making room for moral disagreement, the expressive theorist locates it in clashes of attitude. The general approach is familiar enough, but has never won widespread acceptance. Lately, however, it has received a fresh lease of life as one component in the programme Simon Blackburn has labelled *quasi-realism*.[2] Briefly and somewhat provisionally, the *q*-realist sees us, when we moralize, as engaged in a *projection* of natural features of ourselves on to the world. We talk *as if* there were moral facts and falsehoods – we make free use of evaluative predicates, we embed sentences formed with them in contexts which seem to call for completion by items capable of truth-value, etc. Q-realism seeks to rehabilitate an expressive theory of such talk, whilst at the same time, and in contrast with error theories, aiming to make out that our continued employment of truth-idioms is perfectly respectable, and need not be seen as in any sort of tension with its projective origin.

Any sort of expressive theory, and so the q-realist programme, must confront and surmount some serious obstacles. Prominent among them is a difficulty rightly emphasized by Professor Geach, centred on what he labels the 'Frege point'.[3] Sentences of the kind which, when affirmed on their own, the expressive theorist wishes to construe as serving in an essentially expressive, non-fact-stating role, may occur, without change of meaning, in non-assertive contexts such as conditionals and disjunctions,[4] where they can scarcely be taken to express the attitudes they allegedly express when affirmed on their own. We happily affirm that if lying is wrong, getting others to lie is also wrong, without thereby expressing or endorsing the attitude of disapproval towards lying, or getting others to lie, which we should, according to the expressive theorist, be taken to express or endorse when we affirm the components in isolation. Crucially, compounds in which evaluative predications occur unasserted can combine with others to furnish premisses for intuitively valid inferences, such as:

(1) If lying is wrong, so is getting little brother to lie
(2) Lying is wrong
_____
(3) It is wrong to get little brother to lie

This constitutes an obstacle, but not, I think, a decisive refutation of any kind of expressive theory. It is an indisputable fact that we use sentences like 'lying is wrong' not only on their own but as 'unasserted' components of, for example, conditionals and disjunctions. And the capacity of sentences of both sorts to figure together in valid inferential transitions such as that on display imposes an important constraint on any attempt the expressive theorist may make to accommodate that fact; negatively, and minimally, it debars him from offering wholly disconnected accounts of the semantic role of asserted and unasserted components. If it were true that the expressive theorist is obliged to give wholly disconnected accounts of the semantic roles of asserted and unasserted components, or again, if it were true, not just that inferences like that just cited are valid, but that the sense in which they are so is the usual one (that is, that it is impossible for their premisses to be true without their conclusion being so as well), then – but, it seems to me, only then – Geach's point would be decisive. But it is not clear that either condition is satisfied.

To take the first point first: the expressive theorist holds that when I affirm that lying is wrong, I do no more than express disapproval of lying. Since, when I assert the conditional (1), I am *not* expressing that attitude, it might seem to follow that he must admit that, on his account, the semantic roles of the sentence are wholly distinct. But it does not follow. What does follow is that the expressive theorist must discern some complexity in the speech act of expressing an attitude, paralleling the complexity we can discern in ordinary assertive utterances. There we can say that the speaker both expresses a certain proposition and registers a commitment to its truth. When he asserts

387

a conditional with the same sentence as antecedent, he expresses the same proposition, but registers no such commitment to its truth. As I have been using the words, expressing an attitude is a speech act co-ordinate with assertion, rather than with the neutral act of expressing a proposition. So 'expressing disapproval of lying' is ill-suited to hit off what is common to normal utterances of (1) and (2). Rather than risk confusion by employing that phrase in different senses, I shall say that when a man (sincerely) affirms 'Lying is wrong', he both *presents* a certain attitude (disapproval of lying) and registers commitment to it. Someone affirming (1) presents the same attitude, but registers no commitment to it, and so does not, in our sense, express disapproval of lying.[5]

As for the second point: it is just not obvious that the *only* sense in which we can hold it to be inconsistent to endorse the premisses of our inference but reject its conclusion is one which requires us to think of them as bearers of truth-value, because inconsistency consists in the impossibility of joint truth. There may be available some decent notion of attitudinal inconsistency in terms of which the validity of moral *modus ponens* can be understood.

What Geach's points do incontrovertibly reveal is that the expressive theorist has some serious explaining to do. Given that one who sincerely affirms (1) is not thereby expressing the attitudes which he could, supposedly, be expressing, were he to affirm its components separately, what is the semantic role of those components? How *are* they to be understood, if not as conveying truths or falsehoods about matters evaluative? That is the first thing he must explain. And unless he is, quite implausibly, to reject as misleading the strong appearance of validity attaching to inferences such as (1), (2)/(3), he must explain it in a way that leaves room for – or, better, paves the way for – a further explanation, of what makes for the validity of such inferences, if not the impossibility of joint truth of premisses and falsehood of conclusion. At the very least, he must accomplish the first explanatory task without convicting such inferences of simple equivocation.

Blackburn has done much to persuade us that Geach's problem may not be insurmountable and, more generally, that the *q*-realist programme is a good one. I remain, however, unpersuaded. In what follows I try to make clear why. I shall find it convenient to organize my misgivings around a dilemma that seems to confront the *q*-realist. This concerns the interpretation of what are, in surface form anyway, conditionals with evaluative components – both purely evaluative conditions like (1), and 'mixed' conditionals like 'If Bill stole the money, he should be punished'. Roughly, the proposed dilemma is this: either such compounds are to be construed, as surface form suggests, as involving a dominant conditional operator, or they are, rather, to be understood as expressive of some attitude towards the truth of an appropriately specified proposition. The first construal promises to ease the problem of doing justice to the intuitive validity of moral *modus ponens* and the like, but (arguably) fails to provide for the kind of expressive interpretation q-realism calls for. Taking evaluative conditionals the other way accords well enough, with the expressivist thesis, but it is then far from clear that we can get a satisfactory account of intuitively valid inferences involving them.

That is, I ought to stress, no more than a preliminary and tentative formulation of the suggested dilemma. My main aim in the body of this essay will be to elaborate and sharpen a line of objection corresponding to it, and to explore the prospects for an effective q-realist rejoinder. To this end I shall consider in some detail two treatments of these issues by Blackburn – in his book *Spreading the Word*, and in a later paper 'Attitudes and Contents'[6] – principally because some of the difficulties they severally confront may be seen as illustrating the envisaged dilemma's two halves. But I shall not seek to confine my discussion of Blackburn's defence(s) of q-realism to what is strictly required by my main argumentative strategy. For whilst his earlier defence has already received some critical attention, there are, I believe, some further difficulties attending his more recent approach which deserve notice. Even if it should prove that the q-realist can either blunt one of the horns of my proposed dilemma, or steer a course between them, there is, I shall argue, an issue about how much of our seemingly realist moral talk and thought he can hope to rehabilitate (that is, under some suitably disinfected (re-)interpretation). Here it will be important to distinguish two versions of the q-realist programme. The q-realist whose aims were briefly sketched a few paragraphs back could be of a relatively modest sort: he will have accomplished all he set out to do, if he manages to explain how we can respectably and intelligibly talk and think as if there were moral truths and falsehoods – presenting our attitudinal commitments in propositional style, with all that that entails, by way of propositional embeddings – although there are in reality (as he conceives it) no such things. There is, on his account, no notion of truth applicable to moral judgements – or better, since he will surely wish to make room for our practice of endorsing moral judgements by the use of truth-idioms – there is no substantial notion of truth for those judgements, nothing that goes beyond a thin, merely disquotational use of phrases like 'That's true'.

Blackburn remarks, somewhat prophetically to my mind, that there is room for argument concerning 'the extent to which [expressive theories] can explain the appearance that we are making judgements with genuine truth-conditions. Ultimately it is the attempt to explain this which introduces the need for a wider theory of truth. ... We should realize that expressive theories, like reductive theories, may be uncertain about how much they need to explain.'[7] For Blackburn, as I read him, defence of the modest position is but the first stage of an altogether more ambitious programme. In part, this more ambitious programme is so because its scope goes well beyond morals – encompasses, for example, treatment along projectivist lines of causality, counter-factuals and modalities in general. But even in the field of morals, this more ambitious q-realist looks for more – most importantly, he looks to construct a substantial (but non-realist) notion of truth which really is applicable to moral judgements. I am sceptical, for reasons some of which I have sketched elsewhere and others which will occupy us in the sequel,[8] about this more ambitious project, but even if that scepticism is well-founded, it leaves wide open the question whether modest q-realism about morals is a defensible option.

So the plan of this essay is as follows: I shall first sketch Blackburn's earlier defence in sufficient detail to make plausible the contention that it runs foul of the second half of my proposed dilemma. I shall then turn to consideration of his more recent defence. This I shall discuss in rather more detail. The first part of my discussion will be directed towards disentangling a modest from a more ambitious q-realist enterprise, and arguing that the q-realist had better be modest in his aims. I shall then turn to further difficulties which seem to me to indicate that, if he adheres to this more recent approach, even the modest q-realist will be impaled on the first horn of the dilemma. By this stage it will, if all goes well, be clear that if the (modest) q-realist is to remain in play, he must do something to blunt the second horn. In my closing sections, I shall expound a line of thought directed to that end, and consider whether it can accomplish what the q-realist requires.

2 *SPREADING THE WORD*, CONDITIONALS AND HIGHER-ORDER ATTITUDES

The fact that one who affirms (1) above does not thereby express either disapproval of lying or disapproval of getting others to lie does not, of course, mean that it would be a mistake to regard (1) as a whole as serving to express an attitude, rather than as stating some sort of fact. It is clear enough that we may disapprove, for moral, aesthetic or other reasons, of combinations of things of which we do not separately disapprove, and it is plausible to view certain conditionals as voicing this sort of disapproval – for example 'If you're going to drink, you'd better not drive' (I don't mind you drinking, nor do I mind you driving, but I do mind you doing both). A simple suggestion would construe (1) along these lines, as expressing disapproval for combining refraining from lying yourself with getting little brother to do it for you. This suggestion captures something wanted – endorsement of (1) will be consistent with refusal to endorse (2) – but it is too simple. If argument is needed, consider the following – admittedly some-what bizarre, but clearly conceivable – case. You think there's nothing wrong with lying, nor with getting others to lie. But you also think that, other people's attitudes to these things being as they mostly are, it is generally prudent to get others to do your lying for you. So you refrain from lying, but not from getting others to lie. Suppose now that I'm well aware of your position. Does my endorsement of (1) commit me, *by itself*, to disapproval of your actions? Surely not – though of course, if I also endorse (2) I shall, or at least should, disapprove. But what I find objectionable, just insofar as I endorse (1), is not refraining from lying but getting others to do so, but thinking that while lying is wrong, getting others to lie is (morally) acceptable. There is, in the case as described, no reason to suppose that you merit disapproval on that score.

If that is right, we might do better to see (1) as serving to express a higher-order attitude – disapproval for a certain combination of attitudes (disapproval of lying and tolerance (= lack of disapproval) of getting others to lie). Combining that higher-order attitude with disapproval of lying (that is, endorsement of (2)) and tolerance of getting others to lie (that is, refusal to endorse (3)) lands you in some sort of attitudinal inconsistency – you both disapprove of a certain combination of attitudes and yourself combine those very attitudes.

That is not quite Blackburn's proposal in *Spreading the Word*, though not much separates the two. The theory there sketched[9] has two parts – an informal account, consonant with the general expressivist stance, of 'what we are up to when we use the conditional form with evaluative components', supplemented by a 'semantic theory'. The basic idea in the former is that it can be important to us, in thinking out and expressing our commitments, not just to voice our attitudes towards (types of) actions, but also to criticize or endorse dispositions to couple together different such (first-order) attitudes. The evaluative conditional comes into play as the natural device for endorsing certain combinations of attitude rather than others. In particular, the suggestion goes, someone who affirms (1) endorses (voices approval for) coupling disapproval for lying with the same attitude towards getting little brother to lie.

The accompanying semantic theory may strike purists as somewhat oddly so described, since it provides none of the model-theoretic apparatus underpinning a definition of truth – or, in the present case, some surrogate for truth – characteristic of what usually goes by the name. What we get instead is a sketch of a language – E_{ex} – in which evaluative commitments are conveyed, not, as in ordinary English, by sentences which give the appearance of propounding truths or falsehoods, but by sentences whose expressive character is fully explicit. The point, in part at least, is, as I understand it, this. To the extent that our use of declarative sentences, deploying, for example, evaluative predicates such as 'is wrong', in voicing our evaluative commitments, along with our readiness to embed them in, for example, conditionals, tempts us to think that those commitments are in the market for truth, it is philosophically misleading. So it ought to be possible to describe what it would be like for speakers to do transparently what, on the *q*-realist's view of the matter, they do in potentially misleading fashion when they employ truth-like idioms to voice their commitments. We could then view the sentences of E_{ex} as displaying the deep structure, or underlying logical form, of simple and compound evaluative sentences of ordinary English.

Transparently expressive English has a couple of operators – H! and B! – which are applied to gerundival phrases descriptive of actions to form sentences. Thus simple sentences expressive of approval and disapproval, such as 'Giving money to WoW is good', 'Lying is wrong' go over into 'H!(giving money to WoW)', 'B!(lying)'. They might be informally read as 'Hooray for giving etc.', 'Boo to lying'. To provide for the expression of complex, higher-order attitudes, two further devices are introduced. If, speaking E_{ex}, I wish to express disapproval of, for example, mixed race marriage, I can't just iterate B!; 'B!B! (mixed marrying)' is just ill-formed, since B! is not a sentential operator, but operates upon gerundives, as remarked. B! needs to be applied, not to a sentence expressing disapproval of mixed marrying, but to an expression which denotes the attitude which such a sentence expresses. To get an expression of this sort, Blackburn puts the sentence expressive of the attitude in question inside bars, thus: / B!(mixed marrying)/. I can now express my higher-order attitude by: B!(/B!(mixed marrying)/). The other new device is a binary operator on attitude descriptions; Blackburn writes the semi-colon between such descriptions to stand for the coupling of the attitudes described, or the involvement of one by/with the other.

With both devices in play, the premisses and conclusion of our instance of moral *modus ponens* look like this:

(4)   H!(/B!lying/;/B!getting little brother to lie/)

(5)   B!(lying)
———————————————————————————————————
(6)   B!(getting little brother to lie)

Glossing the premisses as expressing, respectively, 'approval of making (disapproval of getting little brother to lie) follow upon (disapproval of lying)' and 'disapproval of lying', Blackburn contends:

> Anyone holding this pair must hold the consequential disapproval: he is committed to disapproving of getting little brother to lie, for if he does not, his attitudes clash.[10]

The distinctive *q*-realist thought is then that, since anyone endorsing the attitudes expressed by the premisses but refusing to endorse that expressed by the conclusion is involved in inconsistency, it will be entirely natural for us to avail ourselves of a more familiar way of signalling that fact – we

> invent a predicate answering to the attitude, and treat commitments as if they were judgements, and then use all the natural devices for debating truth. If this is right, then our use of indirect contexts does not prove that an expressive theory of morality is wrong; it merely proves us to have adopted a form of expression adequate to our needs. *This is what is meant by 'projecting' attitudes onto the world.*[11]

Two minor worries about the theory on offer are as follows. First, it is just not clear that approval of making one attitude 'follow upon' another excludes toleration of holding the second attitude without subscribing to the first. The gap is, perhaps, most easily perceived if we consider simple attitudes: I may surely approve of giving money to WoW without thinking it intolerable not to do so. Because of this, it does not appear that approval of x-ing and intolerance of not-x-ing are related, as Blackburn's claim seems to require them to be, in the same way as the modalities 'L' and '-M-'. But if not, there does not have to be any clash of attitudes in one who endorses (4) and (5) but not (6).

There may, second, be some question concerning the q-realist's right to avail himself of Blackburn's gloss on /x/; /y/ as 'making y follow upon x'. This doubtless smooths the way to the thought that endorsing (4) and (5) but not (6) involves some sort of inconsistency. But the object of (this part of) the exercise is – is it not? – to *explain* what we are 'up to' employing conditionals with (non-truth-bearing) evaluative components, and the obvious worry is that this informal reading of ';', redolent as it is of the notion of conditionality, may smuggle in by the back door just what is to be explained. What does 'making disapproval of y-ing follow upon disapproval of x-ing' mean, if not something like 'ensuring that *if* you disapprove of x-ing, *then* you also disapprove of y-ing'?

Neither worry need detain us long. I see no reason why the q-realist should not simply concede that the ordinary notion of approval is not quite what's wanted – that he needs a somewhat stronger notion, which stands to toleration as necessity stands to possibility – but get what he wants, either directly, by stipulating that H!x is to be understood as expressing an attitude of insistence upon x, or indirectly, by taking toleration (T!x) as primitive, and defining H!x as expressing refusal to tolerate failure to x (that is, H!x = $_{df}$ ¬T! ¬x). B!x might then also be defined, in the obvious way, as refusal to tolerate x (that is B!x = $_{df}$ ¬T!x). There is more than one way to allay the second worry. We might stick to an austere reading of 'x; y' as simply 'combining x with y', and get what we want by representing (1), by obvious analogy with the truth-functional conditional, as

    (4a) B!(/B!lying/;/¬B!getting little brother to lie/)

– that is as expressing disapproval for combining disapproval for lying with lack of disapproval for getting little brother to do it. Coupling this with (5) and rejection of (6) would give a clash that involves combining attitudes ((5), (6)) of whose combination you expressly disapprove ((4a)). Alternatively, the richer reading of ';' might be defended, on the ground that while the conditional form is essentially involved, the components of the conditional are descriptive, not evaluative, so that its employment here is unproblematic.[12]

There is, however, a more fundamental ground for dissatisfaction. This emerges if we ask: just what is wrong, on the present account, with endorsing the premises of an instance of moral *modus ponens*, but refusing to endorse the conclusion? The answer we get, briefly, is that doing so involves you in a 'clash of attitudes'. In a little more detail: asserting (1) amounts to expressing approval for (or maybe better, insistence upon) ensuring that if you disapprove of lying, you also disapprove of getting little brother to lie. So if you also assert (2) and reject (3), your combined attitudes (disapproval of lying and toleration of getting little brother to lie) are in conflict with that insistence. Or on the variant account suggested, we would see (1) as voicing disapproval for combining disapproval of lying with lack of disapproval of getting little brother to lie. The fault, in endorsing (1) and (2), but rejecting (3), would then consist in holding a combination of attitudes of which you expressly disapprove. Faults these doubtless are, and no doubt we might naturally describe one who commits them as involved in some sort of inconsistency; but they seem to be *moral* faults, not logical ones. But as Wright has urged[13] the failing of one who endorses the premises of our sample inference but refuses to endorse its conclusion is not, or at least not merely, a moral failing, but a *logical* one. The kind of account on offer fails to do justice to this point, and thereby impales itself on the second horn of my dilemma.

Can the *q*-realist do better? I want now to consider Blackburn's more recent treatment of these issues.

3 ATTITUDES AND CONTENTS

In matters of syntax, at least, the theory of AC diverges sharply from that of StW. In E_{ex}, the operators H! and B! are applied to *descriptions* – gerundival phrases like 'lying', 'getting others to lie', etc. – and so are not, properly speaking, iterable. In the new theory, H! is retained, and the toleration operator T! is added. But now they behave as regular sentence-forming operators on *sentences*. Compounds so formed, such as H!p, T! (p & q), and the like, are allowed all the sentential embeddings that plain p can undergo. The syntax thus provides for iteration and for sentences expressing higher-order attitudes, such as H!(B!$p \to$ B!q) corresponding, roughly, to the earlier form H!(/ B!x/; /B!y/); though, as we shall see, Blackburn now prefers, with conditionals with attitudinal components to hand, to construe evaluative conditionals like Geach's as involving no higher than first-degree attitudes.

We have, then, in place of E_{ex}, something that looks very much like the formal languages of familiar intensional extensions of the language of standard first-order logic, with attitude operators supplanting the more familiar intensional operators. The thought is that we can adapt techniques already to hand for, for example, deontic logic to produce a generalized logic of attitudes which does justice, *inter alia*, to our sense that one who refuses to accept inferences such as (1), (2)/(3) is illogical, not just depraved. The particular approach to deontic logic Blackburn favours is Hintikka's method of model sets.[14] In essence, this formalizes the intuitive idea that a set of obligations is consistent if there is a possible situation in which all obligations in the set are fulfilled. Bringing in permissions complicates things a little. Roughly, the idea is that a set of obligations and permissions is consistent if there is a system of 'deontically perfect' possible worlds (connected by an accessibility relation) such that each permission is enacted at some world and each obligation is fulfilled at every world. (Hintikka prefers, of course, to put all this in terms of sets of sentences, and systems of such; talk of possible worlds is just convenient shorthand.)

The basic idea underlying Hintikka's way of defining deontic consistency is not, Blackburn observes, peculiarly applicable to statements of obligation and permission; rather, it has application to any kind of statement whose role is, in a quite broad sense, action-guiding, and so, he proposes, to statements expressive of attitude such as H!p, T!q, etc. are now being understood to represent. We can – the thought is – get a formal logic of attitudes by adapting deontic logic (Hintikka style). But Blackburn grants that it is not enough to provide a logic that is formally workable – it needs to be shown that it admits of a coherent interpretation when H!A and T!A are understood as fundamentally expressive in character, rather than descriptive. So he offers, also, an informal interpretation which tells us how to make sense of formulae like ¬T!p, $p \vee$ H!q, etc., when T!p and H!q are construed as expressive.

The system AC   Let L be a set of sentences, possibly containing some of the forms
H!A, T!A.

Then Blackburn defines[15] a *next approximation to the ideal*, L* of L as a set of sentences constructed by following these rules:

(1) If H!$A \in$ L, then H!$A \in$ L*
(2) If H!$A \in$ L, then $A \in$ L*
(3) If T!$A \in$ L, then a set L* containing A is to be added to the set of next approximations for L
(4) If L* is a next approximation to the ideal relative to some set of sentences L, then, if $A \in$ L*, $A \in$ subsequent approximations to the ideal L**, L***, ...

Rules (1) and (2) stipulate, in effect, that whilst a goal may go unrealized in the actual world (that is we may have H!A but ¬A), it must be fulfilled in all approximations to the ideal (relative to our initial attitude set), and must remain in force as a goal in those approximations. Rule (3) sees realization of a toleration as compatible with perfection, but not required for it. If the point of these rules is thus reasonably clear and straightforward, that of the fourth is rather less so. The following remark explains the general idea behind the rule, but hints also that a further restriction on reiteration from one ideal to another might be needed:

> If L* is already a next approximation to the ideal and contains a sentence A, then except where A derived from realization of a toleration, it must transfer to further approximations to the ideal L**. . . . Here the idea is that once we are following out what is so in the progressive approximations to a perfect world, any realized ideal remains realized. The denizens of paradise do not move.[16]

The intention is that when these rules, together with semantic tableau rules for ordinary sentential operators, are applied to an initial set of sentences L, they will generate a partially ordered set of sets of sentences (next ideals). An ideal is said to be *final* when further applications of the rules produces no new sentences. If L, or any next ideal, contains ordinary branching compounds, then there will be more than one *route* to a set of final ideals. What matters for the consistency of L is that there should be at least one set of final ideals providing for the realization, separately, of each of the T!A in or implied by L, compatibly with realization of all the H!B in or implied by L. Thus Blackburn defines:

> A set of sentences L is *unsatisfiable* iff each route to a set of final ideals from L terminates in at least one set of sentences containing both A and ¬A, for some A.[17]

So much for the logic. Can it be given an expressive interpretation? If H! and T! are taken as forming compounds expressive of attitude towards the (possible) states of affairs represented by the sentences they embed, there is an obvious worry about the legitimacy or intelligibility of more complex sentences in which such compounds figure as proper subformulae: how, given that H!A functions expressively, not descriptively, are we to interpret embeddings under ordinary sentential operators, like ¬H!p, $p \rightarrow$ H!q, . . . and iterations like T!H!p?

As far as negation goes, Blackburn's proposal[18] is that we can assign intelligible content to compounds in which negation dominates attitude operators by construing them as equivalent to other compounds, expressive of opposed attitudes, in which negation has its scope reduced to some proper subformula whose interpretation raises no problem, since what's negated is a genuine proposition, in the market for truth. Thus ¬T!p is taken as expressing the same attitude as H!¬p and ¬H!p, similarly, as equivalent to T!¬p. The prospects for generalizing this strategy to yield interpretations of other problematic compounds do not, however, look good. At least some conditionals, such as the Geach conditional 'if lying is wrong, so is getting others to lie', appear to have irreducibly evaluative constituents, and so to require formalization involving attitudinal compounds within the scope of a conditional operator. And it is anything but clear how the strategy could help with iterations.[19] Blackburn follows a quite different course, seeking to exploit the way binary compounds are standardly treated in tableaux methods. One who affirms p & H!q registers non-branching or conjunctive commitment – he commits himself both to accepting that p and to approving of, or endorsing, its being the case that q. One who affirms $p \lor$ H!q registers a branching or disjunctive commitment – it is the commitment, as Blackburn puts it,

> of one who is ... *tied to a tree*. That is, tied to (*either* accepting that p, or endorsing q), where the brackets show that this is not the same as (being tied to accepting that p) or (being tied to endorsing q). Rather, the commitment is to accepting the one branch should the other prove untenable.[20]

The proposal, as I understand it, is that we can characterize the sense of compounds whose components may be evaluative, not in terms of their truth conditions, but in terms of the inferential commitment involved in endorsing them. This makes, Blackburn now thinks, for a simpler and improved treatment of conditionals like (1). Discarding the higher-order attitude construal, he now sees someone asserting this as voicing an essentially disjunctive commitment – that of being 'tied to the tree of (either assenting to "lying yourself is not wrong" or to "getting your little brother to lie is wrong")'. If Geach's conditional can be construed as of the form H!$p \to$ H!q then we have, it seems, an agreeably simple resolution of our central problem – the failings of one who endorses (1) and (2) but rejects (3) is indeed a *logical* failing, for moral *modus ponens* is just what it appears to be, viz., a special case of *modus ponens*.

4 IDEALS

That is, I hope, a fair summary of the distinctive features of Blackburn's latest defence of the q-realist programme for morals. My principal misgivings about it concern the interpretation of the proposed logic of attitudes. These I shall come to shortly. I begin with some comments upon the logic itself and upon what strikes me as a fairly clearly undesirable feature of it.

Brief reflection on rules (1)–(3) reveals that they confer S4-like properties upon AC. Thus let L = {H!p, T! ¬H!p}. Then by rules (1) and (3) we have L* = {H!p, ¬H!p}. Since there are no alternative routes to the ideal from L, $\vdash_{AC}$H!$p \to$ H!H!p. It is easily verified that rules (1)–(3) suffice[21] to establish T!T!$p \to$ T!p, the analogue of the alternative characteristic S4 thesis. We have also analogues of the principle L$p \to$ (L($p \to q) \to$ Lq) of L-distribution and of the Rule of Necessitation. What we do not get – and of course do not want, since our ideals may go unrealized – is an analogue of the Law of

Necessity; the accessibility relation for AC-structures, as characterized by Blackburn's rules, is not reflexive. Nor is it symmetric. Just as well, for if it were, we should have the S5-like thesis T!p → H!T!p. Some sort of intuitive case might be made for it – if you tolerate p, should you not applaud toleration of p? – but given our rules are stated, its presence would be disastrous. For we would then have: {T!p, T! ¬p} ⇒ {H!T!p, T! ¬p} = 0 ⇒ {T!p, ¬p} = 0 ⇒ {p, ¬p}. That is, indifference – not minding whether p or not – would be inconsistent, and we would have the clearly unacceptable thesis T!p → H!p.

Well, we don't get this unwanted result, but we do get something which is, to my way of thinking, very nearly as bad, and the like of which is not a thesis even in S5, namely: $\vdash_{AC}$H!T!p → H!p, that is, {H!T!p, T!¬p} is demonstrably inconsistent by AC rules. For {H!T!p, T!¬p} gives {T!p, ¬p} (by rules (2) and (3)), from which we have {p, ¬p} (by rules (3), (4)). This seems to say that we should approve of/insist upon toleration of p only if we approve of/insist upon p itself. But consider: might I not think it desirable that I should not mind you not laughing at my feeble jokes (H!T!¬p), yet not mind if you do (T!p). Or again, you might want to insist upon toleration of National Front rallies, without insisting that they take place. These seem to be consistent positions, but AC says they are not.

The obvious ploy at this juncture, since the final step requires use of the unrestricted reiteration rule (4), would be to restrict that rule along the lines Blackburn suggested might, in any case, be desirable – that is to allow reiteration of A from L*···* to L*···** only when A does not derive from a T!-formula. But whilst that would certainly block unwanted derivations of inconsistency like this one, it will also block some that are wanted. Thus Blackburn wants H!(H!p → p) as a theorem, and is surely right to do so; but {T! ¬(H!p → p)} cannot be reduced to inconsistency with only the restricted version of (4) to hand.

The difficulty just disclosed seems to have its source in an important divergence which we have already remarked between the strong attitude operator H! and the usual necessity operator. What is necessarily true is true *simpliciter*, but what should be true in an ideal world may very well fail to be so in the actual world, and, at least on Blackburn's approach, may also fail to be true in worlds 'closer' to the ideal than ours, but still falling short of it. In his account, it is only in final ideals that all relevant formulae of the type H!A are realized. Under AC rules, H!A at L*···* only ever gets realized at the next ideal L*···**. Formally, this means that getting closure in certain cases where, intuitively, we should get it requires reiterating A into subsequent ideals, once it has got into a next ideal. Thus the need for (unrestricted) rule (4).

Since the usual strong deontic operator is like H! rather than the necessity operator in the relevant respect, and since AC is explicitly modelled upon Hintikka's system of deontic logic, we might expect to find a parallel difficulty there. Interestingly, we do not. AC diverges from Hintikka's system at this very point. Hintikka has no rule analogous to AC's rule (4); what he has is a quite different rule which says, in effect, that in any alternative to the actual world which is a candidate for deontic perfection, all relevant obligations are fulfilled.[22] The strict analogue of his rule for AC would be:

(4′) For any L* from L, if H!A ∈ L* then A ∈ L*

With (4′) replacing the troublesome rule (4), we no longer get {H!T!p, T!¬p} coming out inconsistent, but the amended rules are strong enough to validate H!(H!p → p). Indeed, so far as I have been able to see, the switch will give us everything we might want without giving us anything we definitely would not want. In short, it appears that the way to resolve this particular difficulty is to drop (4) in favour of (4′).

If the ill is thus so easily cured, why labour the point? Well, the real importance of the difficulty lies not so much in getting the rules right, as in getting clear about the philosophy behind them. Reflection on the intuitive justification for (4′) as opposed to (4) should lead us to make a distinction that is very much to our present purpose. The thought behind Hintikka's rule, I take it, is that whilst we can have Op holding but p false in L (some set of sentences representing a deontically flawed world, such as ours), we should not have this situation in (any) L*, since L* is supposed to be/represent a deontically 'perfect' alternative to L. There is, in Hintikka's system, no gradual approximation to deontic 'perfection'; rather, if reachable from L at all, it is reachable in a single step. By contrast, the idea of gradual approximation to the ideal is very much part of the philosophical picture underlying AC, as is clear from some of the informal explanations quoted above. It is true that Hintikka's system provides for *sequences* of deontic alternatives, but this should not be allowed to obscure the difference just pointed out: the need to bring in sequences of deontic alternatives arises, in his system, not because some alternative, L* say, may be less than deontically perfect, but simply because it may include unexercised permissions – consideration of further alternatives is then required to check for consistency, that is to verify that any such permissions could be exercised without violating any of the relevant obligations. But a world L** that differs from L* only in that some permission is exercised in the former but not in the latter is not thereby closer to perfection; we do not, in the interests of making the world a better place, have to do everything that is permitted. It remains the case that each L*···* in the system is deontically 'perfect', in the purely technical sense that it contains no relevant unfulfilled obligations ('full' or 'complete' might be less misleading than the rather irrelevantly suggestive 'perfect').

There are at least three reasons why it matters cleanly to separate the two notions of ideal in play here. One is that talk of successively closer approximation to the ideal is misleadingly suggestive of the project, adumbrated in StW, of constructing a q-realist notion of truth applicable to evaluations. The idea, it may be recalled, is that a notion of truth for evaluative statements can be built up in terms of the notion of belonging to the limiting set of attitudes which results from 'taking all possible opportunities for improvement'.[23] One obvious difficulty with this conception concerns the – clearly very substantial – presupposition that there is a unique best set of attitudes on which any series of improvements on any imperfect set converges. I can see little to encourage belief that this presupposition is fulfilled; but even if the prospects for this more ambitious q-realist project are better than I think, it is important to observe that there neither is nor need be any involvement with it, insofar as our aim is simply to work out a logic of attitudes. Then we are concerned just with how to check sets of attitudes (or sentences expressing them) for consistency; there is absolutely no reason to think that the process of doing that will generate sets of attitudes that are ideal in the sense of resulting from making all possible improvements. Certainly any set of attitudes constituting an ideal in that sense must be consistent, but there is no reason to think that there cannot be consistent sets of attitudes that are, in that sense, less than ideal. Getting to the ideal, in that sense, from our present set of attitudes may involve both discarding altogether attitudes we now have and acquiring new attitudes.

Reflection on the last point discloses a further reason. Let L be a consistent set of sentences (including some of the form H!A, and perhaps also of the form T!A). Let us say that L* is an ideal^A wrt L if L* results from making all possible improvements on L (so ideals^A are limit ideals in the sense of StW); and say that L* is an ideal^R wrt L if all relevant H!A are realized in L* (that is roughly, all H!A in or implied by L – so ideals^R correspond to Hintikka's deontically perfect worlds, but are perfect only in the special sense explained). Now consider AC's rule (1), which says we are to reiterate any H!$A \in$ L into any L* from L. This rule would be surely indefensible, if the L*···* were taken to be ideals^A – for it surely can be the case that, as things are in some less than perfect world, H!A is a good or at least acceptable goal to have, but that in some ideal^A wrt that world, it is not. Taking the L*···* to be ideals^R, however, the rule is quite sensible – a set of attitudes may turn out to be consistent, even if it could be improved by eliminating some attitudes and adding others.

A third reason why it matters to distinguish the two sorts of ideal, and to appreciate the independence of the task of circumscribing an appropriate notion of consistency for attitudes from the project of constructing a notion of moral truth, is afforded by a nasty looking dilemma posed by Wright. In the course of arguing that irrealist efforts to make good an expressive, or any other kind of non-assertoric, account of seemingly fact-stating moral and other (for example modal) types of utterances are misdirected, he says this:

> The goal of the quasi-realist is to explain how *all* the features of some problematic region of discourse which might inspire a realist construal of it can be harmonised with projectivism. But if this programme goes through, providing *inter alia* – as Blackburn himself anticipates – an account of what appear to be ascriptions of

truth and falsity to statements in the region, then we shall wind up – running the connection between truth and assertion in the opposite direction – with a rehabilitation of the notion that such statements rank as genuine assertions, with truth-conditions, after all. Blackburn's quasi-realist thus confronts a rather obvious dilemma. Either his programme fails – in which case he does not after all explain how the projectivism which inspires it can satisfactorily account for all the linguistic practices in question – or it succeeds, in which case it makes good all the things which the projectivist started out wanting to deny: that the discourse in question is genuinely assertoric, aimed at truth, and so on.[24]

The dilemma, Wright claims, is fatal unless the projectivist can make out that the notion of truth so rehabilitated is suitably irrealist. But if he can, then the route that proceeds through the idea – eventually scrapped – that the problematic statements are not genuinely assertoric but expressive must surely constitute at best an unnecessary detour. The proper focus of disputes between the realist with respect to a given class of statements is not, Wright contends, on whether those statements are genuinely assertoric or have rather some other, for example expressive, role, but on *what* notion of truth has application to them – the thought being that the tight connection between assertion and truth need not involve a distinctively *realist* notion of truth.

Whether or not that is the best direction for the irrealist to take, it might be thought that Wright's dilemma at least reveals that projectivism, and hence *q*-realism, is a blind alley. But that thought may, it seems to me, pay insufficient heed to the distinction I drew between modest and more ambitious sorts of *q*-realism. The former indeed seeks to 'rehabilitate' the notion of truth – to construct, as Blackburn has it, a conception of truth applicable to moral judgements – and so must confront the dilemma head on. But must a *q*-realist reinstate the notion of truth at all? The central thought of the last few pages – that we can effect a clean break between the task of making out a decent notion of logical inconsistency for sets of attitudes, and so a notion of validity for inferences involving evaluative components, and the project of constructing a notion of truth applicable to evaluative judgements – suggests not. The modest *q*-realist, if he is to be described as rehabilitating the notion of truth at all, will surely want to insist that this means nothing more than explaining how we can defensibly speak *as if* moral judgements were true or false, when in fact they are not. By his lights, moral statements are expressive and retain that character right through his explanation of those of our linguistic practices – including our inferential practices – that might suggest otherwise; the expressive theory is, for him, a permanent fixture, and not the throw-away ladder it appears to have to be for his more ambitious counterpart. In consequence, he need not engage Wright's dilemma, and his position may yet be playable.[25]

5 PROBLEMS OF INTERPRETATION

There may, then, still be room for a theory which sees our evaluative talk as expressive of attitude, syntactic appearances to the contrary notwithstanding. This modest q-realist theory will claim that by casting our expressions of attitude in propositional style, we secure the advantages of thinking and arguing about our commitments as we think and argue about matters of fact. And once presented in that style, it is only to be expected that we should be found endorsing the attitudes expressed using truth-idioms and ascribing attitudes to others using propositional attitude constructions – that is, that we should speak as if there are evaluative truths and falsehoods, fit objects of knowledge and belief, etc., when in reality there are not. And this theory could, it seems, avail itself of the characterization of consistency and validity embodied in (our revised version of) Blackburn's logic of attitudes. Or at least, it could do so, if that admits of satisfactory interpretation in expressive terms. There is, as I shall now try to show, a serious difficulty here.

It is clear enough how an expressive interpretation is to be secured for formulae like ¬H!p. They are to be understood as notational variants on equivalent formulae with dominant attitude operators. The difficulty concerns rather those formulae in which things like H!p lie within the scope of binary connectives, such as $p \rightarrow$ H!q, which Blackburn now wishes to regard as an appropriate formalization of mixed conditionals like 'if Bill stole the money, he should be punished'. If '$\rightarrow$' is understood as the ordinary truth-functional conditional, then the formula simply makes no sense, unless the components are interpreted as items capable of truth-value.

Doubtless it would be possible to supply a descriptive reading for H!q, analogous to the sort of descriptive reading deontic logicians usually have in mind for formulae such as Op and Pq, wherein these are construed as reports of which norms are in force within a certain community of agents. But the possibility of securing sense for $p \rightarrow$ H!q in this way can be of no interest here, since it would entirely fail to provide for an *expressive* interpretation of the formula. In other words, so long as the binary connectives of AC are read as the familiar truth-functions, this latest approach must fail to do justice to the idea that evaluative statements are expressive, not descriptive, and so must get stuck on the first horn of my original dilemma.

One way to avoid this problem would be to generalize the treatment proposed for negations of attitude formulae, that is: construe formulae like $p \rightarrow$ H!q as elliptical for others in which some attitude operator is principal.[26] Provided inner occurrences of attitude formulae are always read descriptively, we could then retain a truth-functional interpretation of the connectives. Indeed, I think this is, in effect, the only option. If I am right about this, then the q-realist will have to accept that inferences such as (1), (2)/(3), and that from (7) and

(8)   Bill stole the money

to

(9)   He should be punished

cannot, after all, be properly regarded as proceeding *modo ponente*.

It might be thought that Blackburn's interpretation of conditionals and disjunctions by way of the notion of being 'tied to a tree' provides the way past the difficulty that now threatens. For isn't the effect of that precisely to secure an expressive meaning for, for example, $p \to$ H!q which still allows us to see the conditional as the dominant operator, and so allows us to see these inferences as proceeding by *modus ponens*? Well, perhaps it appears to – but the appearance is deceptive. The essential point, as I see it, is this. Let it be agreed that by interpreting $p \to$ H!q in the tree-tying way, we get an expressive interpretation – what is expressed is a commitment to either denying p or insisting on q. The crucial question is whether the commitment distributes across the disjunction. Blackburn, as we have already seen, insists that it does not. We have a single disjunctive commitment, not a disjunction of commitments. Someone who affirms $p \vee$ H!q, he says, need not be committed to affirming p or committed to endorsing q; he is committed to (either affirming p or endorsing q). I think it is clear that that is the answer Blackburn has to give, if his expressive interpretation is to be credible. But it is fatal to the claim that $p \to$ H!q can figure as the major premiss for a step of *modus ponens*, or – what comes to the same thing – that the usual tableau rule for conditionals can be applied to it. For to pass from ..., $p \to$ H!q, ... to a pair of alternatives ..., $\neg p$, ... and ..., H!q, ... is precisely to treat the commitment as distributive. For it is tantamount to saying that if – in the actual world, say – you are committed to (either denying p or endorsing q) then – in the actual world – either you are committed to denying p or you are committed to endorsing q. To put the point slightly differently, if $p \to$ H!q registers a *non*-distributive commitment to (either denying p or endorsing q), then it has to be reckoned a possibility that this commitment goes unrealized in the actual (morally imperfect) world, just as any other evaluative commitment may go unrealized. The upshot is that, so far from facilitating the treatment of the evaluative inferences which concern us as straightforward instances of *modus ponens*, the proposed interpretation of conditionals and disjunctions in terms of being tree-tied actually debars us from so treating them.[27] In short, Blackburn's latest defence looks set to impale itself on one or other horn of my original dilemma: if formulae like $p \to$ H!q are read as ordinary (for example truth-functional) conditionals, their evaluative components demand a descriptive reading, and we lose our grip on the expressivist thesis; if the tree-tying interpretation is invoked to secure the construal as expressive of an essentially disjunctive commitment, a fatal gap opens up between the proposed logic and the preferred interpretation – in effect, when that interpretation is in play, it is no longer justifiable to treat such formulae as the logic treats them (that is as truth-functional conditionals).

6 CONSISTENCY, NORMS, AND BELIEFS

The q-realist's prospects ought by now to seem bleak. But it would be premature to conclude that his position is hopeless. For there remains at least one possibility to be investigated. He should accept that, if he is to sustain a thoroughgoing expressive interpretation of moral discourse, he must be able to locate, for each moral statement, a non-cognitive attitude which it primarily serves to express. If the notational apparatus deployed in our discussion thus far is retained, and the connectives are interpreted truth-functionally, that will mean finding, for each such statement, a representation of its logical form in which some attitude operator is principal. And that in turn will mean finally abandoning any hope of exhibiting inferences such as those we have been discussing as straightforward instances of *modus ponens*; but if I am right, that hope is vain in any case. But it is not yet clear that it must mean giving up all hope of exhibiting them as (corresponding to) formally valid inferences of some sort. One pitfall, we know, has to be avoided: failure to accept their conclusions must constitute a *logical* and not merely a moral shortcoming. But AC embodies a clear, and clearly logical, conception of consistency which does not require us to think of statements of the forms H!A and T!A as themselves true or false. The possibility still to be explored is that we may, whilst observing the constraint upon formalization of moral statements adumbrated above, be able to exhibit intuitively valid moral inferences as valid in a sense directly definable in terms of that notion of consistency, or perhaps some well-motivated adaptation of it.

If compounds with evaluative constituents are to be represented as involving dominant attitude operators, pure evaluative conditionals like (1) should be seen, as on the StW approach, as expressive of higher-order attitude. In contrast with that earlier approach, however, we are now construing evaluative attitudes as *propositional* attitudes. This suggests taking (1) to exemplify the form H!(B!$p \rightarrow$ B!q) or, equivalently, B!(B!p & T!$\neg q$). Under either formulation of its major premiss, the inference (1), (2)/ (3), though no longer, of course, an instance of *modus ponens*, is easily seen to be AC-valid: that is, we get a closing tree-structure for the set {H!(B!$p \rightarrow$ B!q), B!p, ¬B!q}. AC has no rules for B!, but we could easily add some; alternatively, we can handle B!-formulae by treating B!A as abbreviating H!¬A. Taking the latter course, ¬B!q boils down to T!q, so that our next ideal includes {q, H!¬$p \rightarrow$ H!¬q, H!¬p} (by rules (3), (2), and (1)). This splits into {q, T!p, H!¬p} and {q, H!¬q, H!¬p}. The first alternative generates the closed ideal $\{p, \neg p\}$ (by rules (3) and (2)), while the second gives the closed ideal $\{q, \neg q, \neg p\}$ (by rule (4')).

So far, so good. But we have yet to consider how to handle mixed conditionals, such as (7). On the present approach, we are to replace Blackburn's preferred representation of its form (that is $p \rightarrow H!q$) by one in which an attitude operator dominates. The obvious candidates are $H!(p \rightarrow H!q)$ (equivalently $B!(p \& \neg H!q)$) and $H!(p \rightarrow q)$ (or $B!(p \& \neg q)$). The former sees (7) as expressive of a higher-order attitude of sorts (approval for approving Bill's punishment, if he stole), while the latter construes it more simply, as expressive of approval for the truth of the conditional 'if Bill stole ..., he is punished'. I see no grounds for insisting upon the former – the present approach does not specifically enjoin *higher-order* treatment in every case; what it requires is a dominant attitude operator, and so higher-order construal in those cases where representation of the components themselves has to involve attitude operators. The real question concerns not the choice between these two ways of representing (7), but the adequacy of either. For it is easy to verify that neither $\{H!(p \rightarrow q), p, T!\neg q\}$ nor $\{H!(p \rightarrow H!q), p, T!\neg q\}$ comes out inconsistent in AC (whether amended along the lines suggested above, or not). That is, the immediate effect of representing (7) with dominant H! is that we can no longer disclose any inconsistency in the set representing the premises and negation of the conclusion of the intuitively valid inference (7), (8)/(9). No such problem arises on Blackburn's preferred representation of (7); the set $\{p \rightarrow H!q, p, T!\neg q\}$ is easily seen to be AC-inconsistent. The initial set splits into $\{\neg p, p, T!\neg q\}$ and $\{H!q, T!\neg q\}$; the first alternative closes immediately, and the second at the next ideal $\{\neg q, q\}$ (by rules (2) and (3)). The crucial difference, of course, is that the $\neg p$ branch from $p \rightarrow H!q$ is generated before the T!-rule is applied, so we get closure on that branch in virtue of the presence of p in the initial set. When $p \rightarrow H!q$ is replaced by $H!(p \rightarrow q)$ (or by $H!(p \rightarrow H!q)$), however, the $\neg p$ branch does not get generated until the next ideal, but the p of the initial set can not be reiterated into that set, so one alternative fails to close. Since the difficulty seems certain to recur on any dominant attitude operator formulation of (7), it is tempting to conclude that the present approach must fail to deliver the goods.

Tempting perhaps, but the point merits closer scrutiny. If it seems obvious that we *ought* to be able to locate an inconsistency in the conjunction of (7), (8), and ¬(9), *when these are construed expressively*, that is surely because we are supposing these sentences to be affirmed by a single subject, who may be presumed to have not only the normative attitudes, expressed by (7) and ¬(9), but also the *belief* expressible by (8). Certainly if a man believes (whether truly or not) that Bill did *not* take the money, his endorsement (7) and ¬(9) does not suffice to convict him of *inconsistency*. The worst that could be said of him is that he is guilty of a false belief, and that, were he brought to recognize its falsehood, he would be required to revise his normative attitudes – that is cease to endorse at least one of (7) and ¬(9). It might then be said that his normative attitudes are unstable, because co-tenable only so long as he retains his false belief. But that is, plainly, not to say that his total set of attitudes is inconsistent. Of course, it could be said (where he believes falsely that ¬(8)) that his normative attitudes are inconsistent with the *facts*, but that failing is equally present in one who simply holds (consistent) beliefs some of which are false; in neither case is the failing a specifically *logical* one.

This suggests that, if we are to interpret AC as a logic of attitudes, we ought to think of the initial sets of sentences to which its rules are applied, not as purporting to depict a collection of normative/evaluative attitudes held in certain circumstances but as characterizing the combined moral attitudes *and beliefs* of some single (possible) subject. The consistency-question we are concerned with, in other words, is not whether, *given that the facts are thus and so*, it is consistent to adopt such and such a collection of normative attitudes: but whether, *given that the subject has such and such beliefs about how things are*, he can consistently hold those normative attitudes. That is, when we start off considering some such set as $\{p \to \text{H}!q, p, \text{T}!\neg q\}$, it has to be understood that the sentences devoid of attitude operators represent the (germane) factual beliefs of some possible subject who also subscribes to the normative attitudes expressible by the remaining sentences. In short, and first appearances to the contrary notwithstanding, it is not just the member sentences with explicit attitude operators that are representative of attitudes: all are, the only difference being that those representing the subject's beliefs, or other cognitive attitudes, are not expressly marked as such.

This bears upon the significance of the tree-structures generated by the AC rules, and particularly that of open trees. Consider, for example, the tree we get for $\{\text{H}!(p \to q), p, \text{T}!\neg q\}$ – the premises and negated conclusion of (7), (8)/(9) on the simpler of my suggested renderings of the major premiss:

$$\{\text{H}!(p \to q), p, \text{T}!\neg q\}$$
$$\|$$
$$\{\neg q, p \to q\}$$
$$\{\neg q, \neg p\} \qquad \{\neg q, q\}$$
$$\times$$

The failure of the formal inference $\text{H}!(p \to q)$, $p/\text{H}!q$ will be totally unsurprising, since it exactly matches the failure, in standard deontic logics, of $O(p \to q)$, p/Oq (as contrasted with $p \to Oq$, p/Oq, which is of course straightforwardly valid, and which matches Blackburn's preferred formalization of our English inference). But, unless I am badly mistaken, the thought of the preceding paragraph calls into question the significance of that parallel. In a normal tableau in this style, a terminal open set of sentences establishes the consistency of the initial set, by depicting a possible situation in which all the members of the latter would be true together. And it is easy to suppose that that is precisely what the open set that terminates the left path in our tree does. Or rather (since we are no longer viewing the initial sentences as candidates for truth) that it establishes the consistency of the combination of attitudes represented by the initial set, by disclosing a situation in which they would all be realized. But that is not quite right. For whilst the left path remains open, one of its terminal set of sentences is the contradictory of a (non-evaluative) sentence in the initial set. What it shows, strictly, is that the *normative* attitudes of the initial set are consistent (= realizable) *provided that the subject's belief that* p *is false* – or, perhaps, *provided that the subject believes that* ¬p. Whichever of these provisos we might finally decide is the right one, we cannot, or so it seems to me, avoid this conclusion: that a sufficiently reflective subject who endorses (7) and (8) but rejects (9) will be able to see that his normative attitudes are jointly realizable only at the cost of his factual belief. He should recognize – should he not? – that something is amiss, and that he is logically obliged either to revise his belief or jettison one of his normative attitudes.

That suggests that it may yet be possible to construe (7) with dominant H!, as I have argued we should, and still do justice to our sense of logical impropriety attaching to the joint affirmation of (7) and (8) coupled with rejection of (9); the *q*-realist may, that is, still have the resources to blunt the first horn of my original dilemma. But what we have is no more than a suggestion; whether what it envisages is a real way forward, and not merely another blind alley, is another question, and one that is, I fear, too large and difficult to tackle here. There is, however, one problem that will certainly have to be faced; by way of a (somewhat inconclusive) conclusion, I shall venture a few thoughts about it.

It is clear that if anything worthwhile is to be made of this latest suggestion, we shall need to circumscribe an extended notion of consistency; we need a notion which takes seriously the thought that combinations of norms and beliefs can be inconsistent in a way that essentially involves both the norms and the beliefs figuring in the combination. Putting together a consistent set of normative attitudes with a consistent set of beliefs may – so the suggestion has it – result in a mixed set which is, as a whole, inconsistent. But in what sense? How exactly is the notion to be defined? We know what it is for a set of beliefs to be consistent – that is so just when it is possible for all the beliefs in the set to be true together. And we have a notion of consistency applicable to sets of normative attitudes – the notion which underlies AC, according to which, roughly, a set of normative attitudes is consistent if there is a system of possible worlds (meeting certain constraints) which realizes it. And now it might seem natural to define the extended notion we require by simply amalgamating these two notions: to say, roughly, that a mixed set of normative attitudes and beliefs is consistent iff there is a system of possible worlds which realizes all the normative attitudes and is such that every belief in the set is true at each world.

But, however natural that extension of the notion of consistency might seem, it has to be recognized that it has, pretty immediately, what appear to be totally unacceptable consequences. To pick out the worst of many, it becomes inconsistent both to believe that ¬p but hold that it ought to be otherwise (the tree for {¬p, H!p} is open, but its only terminal set contains p), and to believe that p but not hold that it ought to be so (the tree for {p, ¬H!p} is open, but its only terminal set contains ¬p). For entirely parallel reasons, it becomes inconsistent to find it tolerable that p whilst believing that ¬p, and to believe that p but find that intolerable. If the suggestion is not to be scrapped, we must, it seems, accomplish one of two things: we must either pin down an appropriately weaker notion of consistency for mixtures of belief and normative attitude, or we must somehow argue that the consequences of adopting this one are, contrary to first appearances, ones that we can live with. The former course requires, in effect, some non-arbitrary restriction on the range of a subject's beliefs which need to be held true conjointly with satisfaction of his normative attitudes, if his total norm-belief set is to be deemed consistent. The latter calls, essentially, for an explanation. For one who tries this route must, surely, emphasize that it need not be irrational or illogical to retain a combination of belief and normative attitude which is inconsistent in this sense – that is, which is such that not all his normative attitudes can be realized so long as all his beliefs are true. That is, he will want to hold that inconsistency, in this sense, does not always enjoin revision of one's beliefs or norms. But he will also want to hold that it sometimes does so. So he will need to explain what makes the difference – what makes it irrational for me to refuse to endorse Bill's punishment, when I believe that he stole and contend that if he stole, he should be punished, but not irrational for me to condemn lying, while recognizing that people tell lies.

It is important not to mislocate the problem just disclosed. It would be a relatively straightforward matter to put things formally right, as it were, by adding to AC what might be termed a 'fixity' operator, to be prefixed to precisely those non-evaluative sentences representing beliefs which are to be held constant – treated as fixedly true – through the search for a consistent realization of the subject's total attitude set. The obvious extra rule would then stipulate that each formula governed by this operator is to be reiterated into all next ideals. Equally obviously, this makes no advance on the real problem, which is to specify which non-evaluative sentences, among those expressing the subject's beliefs, are to be formalized as fixed. No question but that this will be a highly context-dependent matter – that is beliefs that are to be held fixed in some evaluative contexts will be 'movable' in others. It ought, nevertheless, to be possible, if the proposed logic of attitudes is to have significant application, to provide a general account of the criteria by which it is to be determined, in context, which beliefs are to be held fixed and which not.[28]

Neither course is transparently hopeless. Indeed, since it plainly is irrational to believe that Bill stole and that if he did so, he should be punished, and yet refuse to endorse punishing him, and is, equally plainly, not irrational to condemn lying, whilst acknowledging that people tell lies, there has, surely, to be an explanation for this difference. And assuming that explanation of the required sort is generally available, it is not implausible to suppose, further, that it will supply materials in terms of which a non-arbitrary restriction of the kind envisaged by the first course might be framed. That is, of course, no more than a promissory note. There is no reason to suppose that redeeming it will prove an easy or straightforward task. It is finally worth stressing, however, that – so far anyway – no clear reason has emerged for thinking either that the problem just aired distinctively afflicts the *q*-realist, or that it is one which he is especially ill-placed to address.[29]

NOTES

1 For a fuller statement, see Simon Blackburn, *Spreading the Word*, ch. 5 and especially pp. 167–71 [pp. 305–8, this volume].

2 See Blackburn, *Spreading the Word*, ch. 6.

3 P. T. Geach, 'Assertion', *Philosophical Review* 74.

4 Conditionals and disjunctions are not, of course, the only contexts in which evaluative or normative sentences can figure in positions where we expect to find candidates for truth, and which must, therefore, be viewed as problematic by the expressive theorist. There is no sense of impropriety attaching to the description of someone as knowing, or believing, that lying is wrong, that one ought to keep one's promises, etc., or in the embedding of such sentences in such contexts as 'It is true that … '. But I doubt that these other problematic contexts raise any essentially new problems for the expressivist. Once we have taken the step of expressing our attitudes in propositional style, it is only to be expected that the sentences thus employed should – in sharp contrast with, e.g., imperatives – enjoy the full range of propositional embeddings, and that we should thus ascribe to someone the attitude of disapproval for lying by saying that he believes that lying is wrong, use the form 'He knows that lying is wrong' to both ascribe that attitude and register our agreement in attitude, and use devices of truth-ascription to endorse attitudes.

5 That is, *expressing* an attitude is presenting it committedly. Presenting an attitude is to be thought of as an *abstraction* from the total speech act of expressing that attitude, much as expressing a proposition may be viewed as an abstraction from the total act of assertion. There need, of course, be no additional (overt or covert) performance that transforms presentation of an attitude into its expression – committed presentation can be just presentation accompanied by no indications of non-commitment.

6 Chapter 19, this volume.

7 Blackburn, *Spreading the Word*, p. 170.

8 For some of the reasons, see Bob Hale, 'The Compleat Projectivist', *Philosophical Quarterly* 36, pp. 75–6. For others, see the discussion of Wright's dilemma in § 4 of this paper.

9 See Blackburn, *Spreading the Word*, pp. 189–96.

10 Ibid., p. 195.

11 Ibid.

12 As Simon Blackburn was quick to point out, in correspondence on an earlier version of this essay.

13 See Crispin Wright, 'Realism, Anti-Realism, Irrealism and Quasi-Realism', in P. French, T. Uehling Jr. and H. Wettstein (eds), *Midwest Studies in Philosophy* 12, p. 33.

14 See, e.g., Jaakko Hintikka, 'Some Main Problems of Deontic Logic', in Risto Hilpinen (ed.), *Deontic Logic: Introductory and Systematic Readings*, pp. 59–104, or 'Deontic Logic and its Philosophical Morals', in J. Hintikka (ed.), *Models for Modalities*, pp. 184–214.

15 This comes more or less verbatim from Blackburn, *Spreading the Word*. For a number of reasons, I do not think (1)–(4) constitute an acceptable definiens for the open sentence 'L* is a next approximation to the ideal of L'. In particular, the bound occurrences of 'L*' in (3) and (4) prevent these clauses from imposing conditions upon L* in the definiendum. But it is sufficiently clear what is intended. I ought to point out that Blackburn's definition assumes (as he makes clear) that L and the various L*⋯* meet certain further, fairly obvious and standard, conditions in regard to formulae with standard logical operators dominant (e.g. A & B ∈ L*⋯* only if A, B ∈ L*⋯*, etc.).

16 Blackburn, 'Attitudes and Contents' [Chapter 19, this volume].

17 Ibid.

18 Ibid. G. H. von Wright makes a strikingly similar proposal, in the course of arguing for the possibility of a *prescriptive* interpretation of deontic formulae; see his 'Norms, Truth and Logic' in his *Practical Reason: Philosophical Papers, Vol. I*, pp. 130–209. Of particular interest, in view of its obvious parallel with the main claim I defend in section 5, is von Wright's contention that to secure a prescriptive interpretation for mixed norm-formulae, such as $p \rightarrow Oq$, it is necessary to construe them as elliptical for formulae with dominant deontic operators, such as $O(p \rightarrow Oq)$, in which any inner norm-formulae are accorded a descriptive reading (see esp. pp. 151–2). More generally, von Wright argues that norm-formulae of higher order, including iterations like POp, can be given a prescriptive interpretation; but that this requires interpreting embedded norm-formulae descriptively (cf. p. 135).

19 It might be supposed that iterations could be handled by appeal to appropriate reductive equivalences, such as H!H!p ↔ H!p, T!T!p ↔ T!p, etc. This will not do, for several reasons. For one thing, whilst AC sanctions some of the required reductions, such as those cited above, it would need to validate the full range of reduction principles, including the S5-like H!T!p ↔ T!p and T!H!p ↔ H!p, if iterations are to be generally interpreted in this way. It does not do so. More importantly, it is quite unclear how AC could be strengthened to get all the required reduction principles as theorems, whilst retaining any sort of fidelity to its intended interpretation. Getting the S5-like principles will require a symmetric, as well as transitive, accessibility relation among ideals, but then we shall also get the unwanted analogue of the Law of Necessitation, i.e. H!$p \rightarrow p$, which is quite unacceptable if H!p expresses a normative attitude. I ought to stress that Blackburn himself shows no tendency to follow the line criticized here. Nor, however, does he offer any alternative treatment of iteration; there is thus an important gap in his proposed expressive interpretation of AC at this very point.

20 Blackburn, 'Attitudes and Contents' [Chapter 19, this volume].

21 Assuming interchange of ¬H! and T! –, etc. is allowed.

22 See Hintikka, 'Some Main Problems', p. 71, the rule in question is (C. O)$_{rest}$.

23 Blackburn, *Spreading the Word*, p. 198 [p. 335, this volume].

24 Wright, 'Realism, Anti-Realism', p. 35.

25 Blackburn has indicated (in correspondence) that he is happy to see expressivism as a 'throw-away ladder', and so sees no particular threat to his (more ambitious variety of) *q*-realism in

the second half of Wright's dilemma. I continue to find this puzzling, for what I take to be essentially the same reason as Wright. If the thought is that, from some more enlightened (*q*-realist) vantage point, we can somehow see that the expressive theory is actually incorrect (as distinct, perhaps, from only incompletely capturing the truth about moral thought and talk), then I cannot see how any more can be claimed for the play with expressivism than that, by disclosing some essential features that the expressive theory ignores or mishandles, we can get into position to form a better account. It might be a useful expository device, but how could it be any more than that – how could flirtation with the expressive theory form an essential stage in the route to the *q*-realist truth about morals? – unless we are being offered, as I take it we are not, some sort of *genetic* theory of the evolution of the notion of moral truth. Quite apart from this general worry, it seems to me that Blackburn ought not to be content to discard quite so much of the expressivist starting point. For the notion of moral truth he wants is something along these lines:

> a moral statement is true if the attitude it expresses belongs to the limiting set of attitudes that results from taking all possible opportunities for improvement, etc.

and that involves retaining the idea that moral statements are expressive of attitude.

If that is right, then however precisely Blackburn's ambitious *q*-realism differs from the more modest position I have sketched, it ought not to be by ditching the idea that moral utterances are expressive, not descriptive. It may now seem that the better line (i.e. for the ambitious *q*-realist) would be that what is to be thrown out is not that idea, but the further notion standardly harnessed to it, that moral utterances are not, precisely because of their expressive character, in the running for truth. I have two worries about this suggestion.

First, if we take this line, then the contrast between *expressive* and *descriptive* needs to be retained, but that between *expressive* and *apt for truth-value* must go. So some sort of distinction needs to be made between a statement's being descriptive and its being apt for truth-value. But since any sort of descriptive statement is, *eo ipso*, a candidate for truth, we shall need to distinguish, it seems, some different notions of truth here – descriptive statements will be apt for truth of a kind to which expressive statements, though also in the running for truth (of some other kind), cannot attain. But now it looks – doesn't it? – as though the appropriate distinction here would be just between realist and non-realist truth. But if, as now seems on the cards, proper understanding of the expressivist claim involves *prior* appreciation of some such distinction, doesn't that mean that Wright was right after all in claiming that the proper focus of disputes between realists and their opponents is on what notion of truth has application to e.g. moral statements?

Second, the proposed *q*-realist treatment of the Geach problem (StW or AC version) must now seem needlessly roundabout. For if he needs in any case to make room (right from the outset) for a good sense in which moral utterances can be true or false, why shouldn't he dispose of the problem directly: we have a problem if we suppose that expressives are not true or false, but want to acknowledge the possibility of their figuring in unasserted contexts where, so it appears, only items apt for truth-value can go; but now we are in a position to just reject the presupposition about the incapacity of expressives to be true or false, so the problem doesn't get going. That is, the kind of response to Geach's problem which Blackburn advocates best subserves a modest, rather than ambitious, *q*-realism.

26 See note 18.

27 The argument given here met with considerable resistance in the conference discussion. In particular, Christopher Peacocke argued that there is no reason why Blackburn shouldn't be seen, in offering his 'tree-tying' account, as fixing a special, expressive, sense of e.g. '$p \to \text{H}!q$' by laying down inference rules for it. Blackburn himself sought to resist my argument by claiming that '$p \to \text{H}!q$' could be expressive in virtue of there being a *background* commitment on the part of one who asserts it, but still be properly treated by the ordinary tableau rule for conditionals. Probably these should be seen as alternative ways of elucidating and defending Blackburn's position, for the following reason, among others. It is agreed on all sides that if '$p \to \text{H}!q$' is an ordinary truth-functional conditional, it is well-formed only if '$\text{H}!q$' is read descriptively. Peacocke's proposal is that an alternative, appropriately expressive, type of conditional can be (completely) characterized by specifying its logical powers – by giving the inference rules governing it. Blackburn's proposal can, and may well have been intended to, retain the ordinary truth-functional conditional (and so have '$\text{H}!q$' read descriptively), whilst securing an expressive interpretation by reference to the commitment which its assertor has but does not make explicit.

To take Peacocke's proposal first: there is nothing necessarily amiss with the idea that we can specify the sense of a type of statement (or logical connective) by giving the inference rules for it (at least, so I shall grant for the sake of argument – there are, of course, well-known problems here (Tonk, etc.)). But if it is granted, as it is, that for the expressive interpretation, the conditional cannot be truth-functional, then specifying the inference rules in this case ought to *distinguish* the special, expressive form of conditional allegedly introduced from the ordinary truth-functional variety. Yet that the proposal manifestly fails to do, since the only inference rule proposed is just the usual tableau rule for the truth-functional conditional. Hence if a special expressive sense of conditionals is to be introduced in this way, it has to be conceded that it has not been completely specified. The crucial question is then: how is the meaning specification to be completed? And the trouble is that Blackburn wants '$p \to \text{H}!q$', etc., to have just the inferential liaisons of the ordinary truth-functional conditional. But then the proposal collapses.

A crucial question for Blackburn's proposals is: of what character is the background commitment in the presence of which '$p \to \text{H}!q$' functions expressively? If no specially expressive sense of $\to$ is being invoked (which we may assume, since the proposal is otherwise redundant), the background commitment *must* be evaluative, if the proposal is to capture the idea that a *moral* attitude is expressed in this oblique fashion. But now, granting that a sentence may be expressive, in a certain range of uses/circumstances, without being *explicitly* so, I have two objections:

(a) The object of the exercise was – wasn't it? – at least in part, to provide a formalism in which the (allegedly) expressive character of ordinary evaluative remarks is rendered *fully explicit*. The present proposal just gives up on that aim.

(b) (more importantly) Granted that a sentence may function expressively without there being any indication in its vocabulary or syntax that it is doing so, should it not be at least possible to produce an *equivalent* sentence which fully explicitly does the same thing? Compare the case of non-explicitly performative sentences like 'I'll do it'. On occasion, saying this constitutes the making of a promise. Though it is, quite properly, often left to be understood from context that a promise is being given, it must be at least possible to make explicit the character of the speech act – i.e. to give an explicitly performative

412

version of it. But an explicitly expressive version of '$p \rightarrow H!q$' (i.e. a version which does not rely upon the audience's knowledge of the speaker's background commitment for its recognition as expressive) is going to be either '$H!(p \rightarrow H!q)$' or something not relevantly different, having a dominant attitude operator. For this there will be no allowable distribution move, i.e. no allowable move from ... $H!(p \rightarrow H!q)$ ... to the alternatives ... $\neg p$ ... and ... $H!q$. ... Since $H!(p \rightarrow H!q)$ just gives full-dress expression to the same commitment as, in context, $p \rightarrow H!q$ expresses, the move is no more legitimate for the latter.

I am indebted to Harold Noonan for helpful discussion of these matters.

28 The idea of introducing a fixity operator was put to me in correspondence by Blackburn. I had independently begun to think along somewhat similar lines, but could see no generally adequate way to explain when, in his terms, a belief should count as fixed. I need hardly say that the paragraph to which this note is appended is not meant to suggest that he is in any danger of failing to appreciate the need for such an explanation. His proposal was that we should 'call a belief *fixed* if, *for some evaluative purpose in hand* it is immovable'. I think I have some feeling for the idea this is getting at, but would like to see it spelled out more fully, preferably without reliance on the equally problematic notion of a belief's being (im)movable. It is, of course, a familiar enough thought that moral judgements are typically made against a background of factual beliefs. If I thought that foxes would die of boredom if they weren't chased, that they derived great pleasure from giving the hounds a good run around, and that there was anyway a negligible chance of their being caught, I might well take a different view about the morality of foxhunting. The opposed beliefs, those which I actually have, are presumably fixed (for me) – immovable for the evaluative purpose of reaching a view on the morality of foxhunting. But another of my beliefs is that people do actually hunt foxes: does that count as fixed here? If unwanted inconsistency is to be avoided, it had better not. But now what makes the difference? It is tempting to think one could explain it in terms of the potential role of fixed beliefs as reasons for the moral judgement made: the belief that being pursued by a pack of bloodthirsty hounds is, to put it mildly, no fun for the fox is, maybe, one reason I have for disapproving; but the belief that people hunt foxes could scarcely figure as a reason for disapproving of their doing so. The snag is that someone who, irrationally, accepts that Bill stole the money, and that if he stole, he should be punished, but refuses to agree that he should be punished, precisely does not treat the belief that Bill stole as a reason for thinking that he should be punished. That is, tying the notion of fixity to the beliefs which the relevant moral subject would recognize as affording reasons for particular moral judgements looks as though it won't justify treating as fixed the beliefs that have to be so treated, if the subject is to be convicted of illogicality.

29 I am grateful to John Haldane and Crispin Wright for inviting me to contribute a paper to the conference. Special thanks are due to Simon Blackburn and Crispin Wright for a three-cornered discussion which provided much of the stimulus for writing this paper. I thank them, and my colleague John Benson, for helpful comments on earlier drafts.

Part 7

EXPRESSIVISM AND MINIMALISM ABOUT TRUTH

From what you have read thus far, how might you characterize expressivism? Perhaps you would start by saying something about moral judgements being expressions of attitude rather than assertions of belief? Or perhaps you would start by focusing on the fact that moral judgements are not truth-apt? It seems that there are two features central to any characterization of expressivism: *expression* and *truth*. The problem that concerns the philosophers in this Part is whether a minimalist theory of truth-aptness precludes expressivism because it makes such a characterization impossible. (It is important to keep in mind throughout this Part that there is distinction between minimalism about truth-aptness and minimalism about truth.)

How might you go about deciding whether something is assessable in terms of truth and falsity? Or, in other words, what criterion, or criteria, does a sentence have to fulfil in order to be truth-apt and, indeed, true? One traditionally very popular theory of truth has been the correspondence theory of truth. This says, in effect, that there is a property of truth that some suitably structured utterances have and that such things get to be true because they correspond with the world. Other utterances have the right sort of grammatical structure, but it just turns out that the world is not how they describe it as being, and such utterances are said to be false. Still more utterances just don't have the right grammatical structures that allows us to compare them with the world. For example, "Throw blue and wildly chairs drink up in off red" is meaningless; "Do this" is a command, not a truth-apt utterance.

Without going into the details here (see the pieces by David (2005), Engel (2002) and Kirkham (1992) in Further Reading below), some people don't like the correspondence theory of truth. Various theories of truth are possible and, indeed, some people deny that utterances can be truth and truth-apt at all. One group agrees with correspondence theorists that there are truth-apt sentences, but takes issue with an idea seemingly entailed by the correspondence theory, namely that the property of truth is a metaphysically 'meaty' type of property whose essential nature will be revealed by detailed philosophical reflection. (After all, in order for there to be correspondence, it seems as if both the utterance and the world have to be structured in certain ways and that such abstract structures have to be the same in order for the utterance to be true.) The people who oppose the correspondence theory adopt 'minimalism'. (Note, though, that sometimes this is used to name a specific position rather than used as a general term. Another general term often used in this capacity is 'deflationism'. See the piece by Stoljar (1997) listed in Further Reading below.) Minimalists hope that simply from thinking about the surface features of an utterance, we can conclude whether it is truth-apt. We need to ask two questions. First, does the sentence figure in an area of discourse that is *disciplined*? An area of discourse is disciplined if there are acknowledged standards of appropriate and inappropriate use for those sentences. Second, what *syntactic features* does the sentence have? Is it capable of being negated, being embedded in propositional attitudes, being conditionalized and so on? If the sentence under consideration has both these features then it is truth-apt.

Moral sentences have both these features. They certainly can be used appropriately and inappropriately and, as the last two Parts have made patently obvious, moral sentences certainly have syntactic features. So, given the minimalist conception of truth-aptness, moral judgements *are* truth-apt. But now there is a problem for the expressivist. For, as we stated, one of the key characteristics of expressivism is that moral judgements *are not* truth-apt. So, it seems, the expressivist better revise or reject minimalism about truth-aptitude.

In Chapter 21 Michael Smith argues the expressivist should *love* minimalism. (Notice that neither of the chapters in this Part defend expressivism or minimalism; the issue they discuss is their potential compatibility.) Smith argues that the expressivist can accept the minimalist criteria for a sentence being truth-apt, but deny that this causes her a problem. His reason depends on the other theme in our characterization of expressivism: *expression*. Essentially, his claim is that this allows the minimalist to distinguish apparent and genuine truth-aptitude.

In the first place, Smith discusses why expressivists are expressivists. It seems trivially true that if someone makes a moral judgement they will be motivated to act in a certain way. (See Part 11 for a detailed discussion of the relationship between moral judgement and motivation.) Arguably though, motivation requires belief *and* desire – belief alone can't motivate. (See Part 10 for a detailed discussion of this account of motivation.) And, as such, the expressivist claims that making a moral judgement such as 'Giving to charity is right' cannot be an expression of a belief. It is not an assertion at all.

With this point in place Smith has everything he needs to show that expressivism can be articulated even within the minimalist framework. If moral judgements can't express beliefs, and beliefs alone are truth-apt, then, although moral judgements have some of the *trappings* of truth-aptitude – the syntactic features of moral sentences and the discipline of moral discourse – they are not *genuinely* truth-apt because they are not assertions of belief. Thus minimalism doesn't preclude expressivism. If Smith is right, then minimalism is not so minimal as minimalists think it is, as it turns out that you *can't* just 'read off' from the surface features of a sentence whether that sentence is truth-apt; you need some further folk psychological considerations. (By this is meant a certain psychological theory concerning how belief and desire constrain which judgements are truth-apt.) So, according to Smith, the key to reconciling expressivism and minimalism boils down to adopting the right account of what expressivism is.

But you may worry that this looks out of place. How did all this discussion of belief and assertion get into the picture anyway? We started out with a question about what are the necessary and sufficient conditions for a sentence being *truth-apt* and there is no apparent mention of psychology here. As an answer we suggested two: discipline and syntactic features. Now it seems that Smith is trying to sneak a further consideration in. He wants to say that because the theory seems incompatible with expressivism, then we better revise the theory. If this is so, this sounds like prejudice towards the truth of expressivism. Indeed, it is along these lines that John Divers and Alex Miller argue in Chapter 22.

Divers and Miller are unimpressed by Smith's approach and argue that minimalism *is* as minimal as it first appears as it doesn't presuppose a specific folk psychological theory. Expressivism about value they claim shouldn't love minimalism about truth. Essentially Divers and Miller's thesis is that there are no good independent reasons for characterizing expressivism primarily in terms of the expression of noncognitive attitude rather than truth. They suggest that it is perfectly reasonable to start with the minimalist theory of truth-aptitude and then let *this* be our guide to the psychological theory. So, accepting Smith's 'platitude' that if someone utters an assertion (that is, utters a truth-apt judgement) then they are expressing a belief, we can claim that moral judgements *are* expressions of beliefs because they *are* truth-apt. There is then no presupposed psychological theory about belief and desire constraining which judgements can and cannot count as truth-apt. Truth-aptitude is a way to ascertain which judgements express beliefs and which don't. The view – letting minimalism guide our conclusions about assertion and belief – is what Divers and Miller label 'quietism about assertion'. The expressivist needs to argue against this position.

Divers and Miller suggest that a further discussion of assertion, expression and truth is not going to help Smith demonstrate that quietism about assertion is false. As it stands, there is then a stalemate between them. Divers and Miller suggest that to resolve this there needs to be a discussion concerning the justification of the Humean theory of motivation. Why? Well, if beliefs alone don't motivate as the Humean thinks (see Part 11) then Divers and Miller are going to struggle to argue that the minimalist account of truth-aptness should determine whether a sincere utterance expresses a belief or not. This is because if moral judgements express beliefs as minimalism commits us to, then Divers and Miller are going to find it hard to explain the connection between moral judgement and motivation. However, on the other hand, if beliefs alone can motivate and the Humean theory is mistaken, then there is no problem for Divers and Miller to drive the point home against Smith. Moral judgements express beliefs, but that is okay, because beliefs alone can account for motivation. Unsurprisingly then Divers and Miller end their article by stressing that Smith can't just help himself to the Humean account under the guise of it being a platitude.

Smith, Divers and Miller continue their debate in another pair of articles, which we list below in Further Reading. We leave you to see how Smith responds. (See also the article by Paul Horwich (1994) and Smith's (1994) response to it.) You should also think about how this part relates to Parts 10 and 11, both of which concern judgement and motivation. It might be worth coming back to this Part after reading these other two. In all of this, you should realize that this Part is about more than just what type of theory of truth is compatible with expressivism. You should pause to consider which theories of truth are compatible with all of the theories we have considered in this book and what metaethicists want from a theory of truth in the first place. Some guidance on theories of truth is also given below.

QUESTIONS TO CONSIDER AND TASKS TO COMPLETE

1   What is the relationship between minimalism about truth-aptitude and minimalism about truth?
2   Are there any good independent reasons for accepting minimalism about truth-aptitude?
3   Smith (Chapter 21) talks about 'platitudes'. What are they? How would you decide whether a claim is platitudinous? Try to give some of your own examples.
4   Apart from the Humean account of motivation, how else could you resolve the stalemate between our protagonists?
5   How would you characterize expressivism?
6   If the expressivist is forced to reject minimalism about truth-aptness, what other option is available for her?
7   Why should the expressivist care about this debate?

FURTHER READING

David, Marian (2005) 'The Correspondence Theory of Truth', *The Stanford Encyclopedia of Philosophy*, Edward N. Zalta (ed.), http://plato.stanford.edu/archives/fall2005/entries/truth-correspondence/

Divers, John and Miller, Alexander (1995) 'Platitudes and Attitudes: A Minimalist Conception of Belief', *Analysis,* vol. 55, no. 1, pp. 37–44.

Engel, Pascal (2002) *Truth* (Chesham, Bucks: Acumen).

Horwich, Paul (1994) 'The Essence of Expressivism', *Analysis*, vol. 54, pp. 19–20.

Kirkham, Richard (1992) *Theories of Truth* (Cambridge, MA: MIT Press).

Smith, Michael (1994) 'Minimalism, Truth-aptness and Belief', *Analysis,* vol. 54, no. 1, pp. 21–6.

Stoljar, Daniel (1997) 'Deflationary Theory of Truth', *The Stanford Encyclopedia of Philosophy* (Fall 1997 Edition), Edward N. Zalta (ed.), http://plato.stanford.edu/archives/fall1997/entries/truth-deflationary/

Wright, Crispin (1992) *Truth and Objectivity* (Cambridge, MA: Harvard University Press).

——(1996) 'Truth in Ethics', in Brad Hooker (ed.) *Truth in Ethics* (Oxford: Blackwell), pp. 1–18.

21

WHY EXPRESSIVISTS ABOUT VALUE SHOULD LOVE MINIMALISM ABOUT TRUTH

Michael Smith

Does expressivism about value depend on views about the nature of truth and truth-assessability beyond those that we glean from a minimalist account of truth and truth-assessability? More precisely, if minimalism tells us all there is to know about truth and truth-assessability, does it follow that there is no room left for the expressivist's distinctive claim that evaluations are not truth-assessable?

So two minimalists, Crispin Wright (1992) and Paul Horwich (1993), have recently argued. But it seems to me that they are very much mistaken. Expressivists who make this distinctive claim should *love* minimalism about truth, because minimalism shows us just how few assumptions about the nature of truth and truth-assessability are required to get going the problem with evaluations to which this distinctive claim is, according to the expressivists, the solution.

Don't misunderstand me. I am not a fan of the expressivist's solution. But I do think that expressivism is one of several solutions we might give to a problem with evaluations that expressivists, among others, rightly bring to our attention. I have elsewhere called this the 'moral problem' (Smith 1989, 1994). Unfortunately for minimalists, however, though that problem does indeed require certain assumptions about the nature of truth and truth-assessability, the assumptions required are just those that the minimalist makes as well.

The paper is in four main sections. In the first I explain why Crispin Wright thinks that minimalism excludes expressivism. In the second I explain why expressivists are expressivists, and why Wright's argument therefore fails. In the third I use the discussion of Wright outlined in the first and second sections to throw light on Paul Horwich's recent account of the relationship between minimalism and expressivism. And in the fourth section I explain the role minimalism has to play in our attempt to understand, and ultimately to solve, the moral problem. I hope, thereby, to explain why Wright and Horwich have been so misled.

1 WRIGHT ON MINIMALISM AND EXPRESSIVISM

According to Crispin Wright, a sentence is truth-assessable just in case it figures in an area of discourse which is *disciplined*, and just in case it possesses certain *syntactic features*. That is, a sentence *s* is truth-assessable just in case, first, it figures in an area of discourse for which 'there are firmly acknowledged standards of proper and improper uses of its ingredient sentences' (Wright 1992, p. 29). We regularly say things such as 'I said *s* before, but now I see that I was wrong', so subsequently withdrawing assertions that met the standards for assertion when they were first made. And just in case, second, the sentence is capable of 'conditionalisation, negation, embedding in propositional attitudes, and so on' (ibid.). We can say things such as 'If *s* then *s**', 'Not-*s*', 'I wonder whether or not *s*', 'I think that *s*, but I'm not sure', 'I believe that *s*', 'I desire that *s*' and the like. If these conditions are met, then, according to Wright, that is what it is for *s* to be truth-assessable.

Why is Wright's a *minimalist* theory of truth-assessability? Because the truth-assessability of a sentence can simply be read off from its surface features; from the fact that it figures in an area of discourse with all of the marks of truth-assessability. As Wright puts it:

> ... there is no notion of genuine – deep – assertoric content, such that a discourse which exhibits whatever degree of discipline ... and which has all the overt syntactic trappings of assertoric content ... may nevertheless fail to be in the business of expressing genuine assertions. Rather, if things are in all these surface respects as if assertions are being made, then so they are.
>
> (1992, p. 29)

This minimalist theory of truth-assessability then naturally gives rise to a minimalist theory of truth.

According to the minimalist, a truth-assessable sentence, *s*, is true if and only if the conditions on *s*'s proper use are met: that is, if and only if things are as *s* says they are. And to be prepared to say that things are as *s* says they are we, as theorists, need simply be prepared to utter *s* itself. No heavy-duty theory of truth there.

We can set this minimalist theory of truth to one side. For the expressivist's distinctive claim is that evaluative sentences, like 'It is right to give to charity', are not even truth-assessable; this is why they claim that utterances of such evaluative sentences are not assertions. Accordingly, in Wright's view, we only need the minimalist's theory of truth-assessability to exclude this distinctive expressivist claim. How does it do that?

As Wright points out, expressivists must agree that evaluative discourse exhibits discipline. For we just do ordinarily say things like 'I said that giving to charity is right, but now I see that I was wrong', and, when we do so, we do so under pressure from the acknowledged standards for the proper and improper use of sentences like 'Giving to charity is right', standards beyond those of correct assertion. Moreover, expressivists must also agree that the sentences we use in evaluative discourse have the syntactic features he identifies: they figure in conditional contexts – we say 'If giving to charity is right, then I will give to the Red Cross Appeal next time it is on', – they figure in negation contexts – we say 'It is not the case that it is right to give to charity' – and they figure in propositional attitude contexts – we say 'I wonder whether or not it is right to give to charity', 'I think that it is right to give to charity but I am not sure', 'I believe that it is right to give to charity', 'I desire that it is right to give to charity' and so on.

But if they agree with all of this then, according to Wright, given that there is no notion of deep assertoric content to be had, it follows that, contrary to the expressivist, evaluative sentences like 'Giving to charity is right' are truth-assessable. Or, better, to think that they are not must be to make assumptions about the nature of truth-assessability *beyond* the minimalist's assumptions. Minimalism excludes expressivism.

Wright's argument is potentially very powerful indeed. In the next section I will show that the argument needn't worry an expressivist, however. For it is simply unsound.

2 WHY EXPRESSIVISTS ARE EXPRESSIVISTS

Expressivists think that if someone utters the sentences 'Giving to charity maximizes happiness' and 'Giving to charity is right', then though it may appear that two assertions have been made, really only one has been made: 'Giving to charity maximizes happiness' is truth-assessable, and this the utterer does assert, but 'Giving to charity is right' is not truth-assessable, and, accordingly, this the utterer does not assert. But why do they say this?

Everyone agrees that a sentence that is truth-assessable, if uttered sincerely, is an assertion. And everyone agrees that the function of an assertion is to convey the fact that the utterer believes that what the sentence uttered says is so is so. Wright himself puts the latter point this way.

> ... assertion has the following analytical tie to belief: if someone makes an assertion, and is supposed sincere, it follows that she has a belief whose content can be captured by means of the sentence used.
>
> (1992, p. 14)

Thus, when someone says 'Giving to charity maximizes happiness', we take her to be expressing her belief that giving to charity has, as a consequence, the fact that happiness is maximized.

Belief is just the right kind of psychological state to be expressed in an assertion, because it is in the nature of beliefs that they purport to represent the way things are. That is, roughly speaking, beliefs can have as their contents all and only those contents apt for expression in truth-assessable sentences.[1] And this is in turn important, for it shows that our ideas of assertion and truth-assessability are tied to the idea of a folk psychology that recognizes a category of belief.

In fact however, though Wright does not acknowledge the point, our ideas of assertion and truth-assessability are tied to a folk psychology that recognizes even more kinds of psychological state. For an assertion is an action, and a psychology rich enough to explain actions must also recognize a category of desire, alongside the category of belief (Smith 1987).

Desires differ from beliefs in being, not representations of how things are, but representations of how things are to be. If we think of this difference between belief and desire as a functional difference – if we think, again very roughly, that the belief that p is a psychological state produced by the fact that p under appropriate circumstances, whereas the desire that p is a psychological state that makes it the case that p under appropriate circumstances – then we can see why beliefs and desires can together combine to produce actions, even though neither beliefs nor desires can manage to do that all by themselves.

Desires cannot produce actions all by themselves because, though they tell us how the world is to be, they do not tell us the way the world is, and thus don't tell us whether the world has to be changed at all in order to make it that way, let alone how it has to be changed. Thus, even if desires do typically cause things, they cannot cause anything all by themselves. And neither can beliefs produce actions all by themselves because, though they tell us how the world is, and thus tell us all manner of ways in which it could be changed to make it different, they do not tell us how it is to be changed. Beliefs and desires can together produce action, however, because then our beliefs have the role of telling us how the world is, and thus how it has to be changed if it has to be changed at all, in order to make it the way – now focusing on the role of desires – our desires tell us it is to be.

We have already noted that our ideas of assertion and truth-assessability are tied to the idea of a folk psychology that recognizes a category of belief – for assertions typically express beliefs. And what we have just seen is that, since an assertion is an action, those ideas are in turn tied to the idea of a folk psychology that recognizes a category of desire as well. These ideas therefore stand or fall together: truth-assessability, assertion, desire and belief.

What we want to know is why expressivists deny that sentences like 'Giving to charity is right' are truth-assessable. The answer is now easy to state. Expressivists deny this because they deny that, strictly speaking, such sentences are apt to give the content of the utterer's beliefs. The reason why goes back, of course, to Hume (1968, pp. 413–17). As he reminded us, when someone sincerely utters an evaluative sentence we are typically able to conclude something about what that person is disposed to do, given suitable means–ends beliefs, and thus we are able to conclude something about the state of her desires. If we know that someone has sincerely uttered the sentence 'Giving to charity is right' then we know that, other things being equal, *she desires to give to charity*. But how is it that knowledge of a person's sincere utterance puts us in a position to draw this conclusion? After all, if the utterance is an assertion, then it is an expression of that person's beliefs. So how can it be that a sentence which, when uttered, tells us about the content of the utterer's beliefs, also tells us about the state of her desires? If, according to our folk theory, no belief *is* a desire, that is problematic.

One answer – perhaps Hume's own (ibid., pp. 468–9) – requires a subjectivist account of the meaning of the sentence 'Giving to charity is right'. What that sentence literally means, according to the subjectivist, is 'I desire to give to charity'. This allows us to hold on to the idea that an utterance of the sentence is an assertion, because the sentence 'I desire to give to charity' is straightforwardly truth-assessable, apt to give the content of a belief, and so apt to be asserted. It therefore should come as no surprise, if this is what evaluative sentences like 'Giving to charity is right' mean, that we typically find out what an utterer desires when we know what evaluative sentences she asserts, even conceding that no belief is a desire.

But expressivists famously reject subjectivism. Under the influence of Moore they claim that, since the sentence 'I desire to give to charity, but it is not right to do so' is not self-contradictory, so it follows that the sentence 'It is right to give to charity' does not mean the same as 'I desire to give to charity' (Ayer 1936, Ch. 6; Smith 1986). And since they can think of no alternative content for the sentence 'Giving to charity is right', which would both allow it to express a belief and yet explain why an utterance of it, when sincere, tells us about the state of the utterer's desires, they go on to give what they think is the only plausible explanation of this fact. An utterance of the sentence 'Giving to charity is right' is not, strictly speaking, the expression of a belief at all; it is rather, typically, the expression of a desire.

This, then, is why expressivists deny that evaluative sentences are truth-assessable; this is the relevant contrast between the sentences 'Giving to charity maximizes happiness' and 'Giving to charity is right'. Expressivists agree with minimalists that truth-assessable sentences give the contents of beliefs, not desires. And they agree with minimalists that assertions express beliefs, not desires. But what they also think is that, as Hume reminded us, evaluative sentences, like 'Giving to charity is right', when uttered sincerely, typically tell us about the state of the utterer's desires. And they can see no way of squaring this with the fact that the utterance of an evaluative sentence is an assertion; no way of squaring it with the fact that the uttered sentence expresses the content of the utterer's beliefs. This is the relevant point of contrast with non-evaluative sentences like 'Giving to charity maximizes happiness'. For, according to expressivists, there is no corresponding problem in thinking of such non-evaluative sentences as giving the content of the utterer's beliefs.

Does expressivism make any assumptions about the nature of truth-assessability beyond those minimal assumptions made by Wright himself? It would seem that it does not. For in giving his minimalist account of truth-assessability Wright himself acknowledges that assertion has an analytical tie to belief: a sentence with assertoric content is, when asserted sincerely, apt to give the content of one of the utterer's beliefs. This is, in part, why he rightly insists that a necessary condition for a sentence's being truth-assessable is that it has, among its various syntactic features, the potential for being embedded in belief contexts. But what expressivists deny is precisely that evaluative sentences, even when uttered sincerely, are, strictly speaking, apt to give the contents of the utterer's beliefs.

The 'strictly speaking' is important. For expressivists need not deny that we ordinarily *say* such things as 'Y believes that it is right that p', and nor need they deny that we are entitled to do so, a fact to which we will return at the end. The point that expressivists insist upon is simply that, since the concepts of belief and desire are defined by their role in folk psychology, a theory that tells us, *inter alia*, the differential contribution of belief and desire to action, so the mere fact that we say such things as 'Y believes that it is right that p', and get away with it, is therefore insufficient to show that utterances of 'It is right that p' do express beliefs.

What we have to be able to do, in order to show that this is the case, is tell a story about the meaning of 'It is right that p', and a story about the meanings of 'belief' and 'desire' as those terms are used in folk psychology according to which, when someone utters the sentence 'It is right that p', we can take her to be expressing her belief that it is right that p, despite the fact that, typically, we thereby come to discover something about the state of her desires: that she desires that p. In essence, expressivism is the view that this cannot be done, and that we must therefore suppose that such sentences express desires instead.

3 HORWICH ON MINIMALISM AND EXPRESSIVISM

In *Wise Choices, Apt Feelings* (1990) Allan Gibbard argues that, for roughly the Humean reasons given above, we cannot think of an utterance of 'x is rational' as the expression of a belief. According to Gibbard, 'x is rational' is therefore not truth-assessable; it is rather a sentence whose utterance is best thought of as an expression of the utterer's desires concerning x (Gibbard 1990, pp. 6–10).

In 'Gibbard's Theory of Norms' Paul Horwich takes Gibbard to task for making this distinctive expressivist claim (1993). The reason for the complaint is that, according to Horwich, the minimal or deflationary theory of truth he defends elsewhere shows the claim to be false (1990). Horwich's main argument is much the same as Wright's. The interesting difference is that, according to Horwich, expressivists need not make this distinctive claim. Rather, in his view, expressivism's central insight is in fact consistent with minimalism. This is because, according to Horwich, the central expressivist insight is that we can analyse or define 'Y believes that x is rational' as 'Y has certain desires concerning x' (1993, pp. 76–7). And someone who accepts such an analysis simply has no reason to deny that 'x is rational' is truth-assessable; for, given the analysis, though that sentence does indeed express a desire, it expresses an appropriate belief *as well*.

I will have more to say about this sort of analysis in the next section. For now the important point is simply that the insight that for Horwich lies at the core of expressivism is something that, on my understanding, expressivists who go on to claim that moral sentences are not truth-assessable crucially think is false. Rather, adapting the points made about morals in the last section to the case of rationality, they think that someone who sincerely utters the sentence 'x is rational' typically has certain desires concerning x. And they think that, since there is no way that this could be so if the utterance were the expression of the utterer's beliefs, so it follows that, strictly speaking, an utterance of 'x is rational' must just be the expression of a desire; not the expression of a belief *at all*.

And again, the idea that the terms 'belief' and 'desire' are to be interpreted strictly is important. For, to repeat, Horwich's claim is precisely that expressivists

> ... should not, strictly speaking, deny that one can believe something to be rational; for what they really provide is an account of what any such belief consists in (that is, the possession of a certain pro-attitude).
>
> (1993, p. 77)

And my reply has been that this is exactly what expressivists who think that moral sentences are not truth-assessable should and do deny. For they think that the claim that a belief may be constituted by a desire is a claim we should make only if it is entailed by folk psychology, the theory we all use to explain the differential contribution of belief and desire to action. Given that they do not think that our folk theory entails any such claim, they insist that utterances of 'x is rational' are not, strictly speaking, expressions of beliefs.

The point is worth underscoring. For it suggests that minimalism about truth isn't really so minimal as the minimalists think. For, in essence, what we have seen in our discussions of both Wright and Horwich is that minimalism about truth in fact *presupposes* an understanding of folk psychology, an understanding of a theory whose concepts of belief and desire will in turn constrain which sentences can and cannot count as truth-assessable. But if minimalism presupposes an understanding of folk psychology in this way then, given that that theory is a substantive theory about the way human beings work, it follows that minimalism itself requires substantive assumptions in giving accounts of truth and truth-assessability after all. We will return to this point briefly below.

4 MINIMALISM AND THE MORAL PROBLEM

I said at the outset that expressivism is one of several solutions we might give to the moral problem. This problem can be stated in the form of three plausible, but apparently inconsistent, propositions:

1   Moral judgements express beliefs.
2   Moral judgements have a necessary connection of sorts with the will: that is, with being motivated.
3   Motivation is a matter of having, *inter alia*, suitable desires.

In this final section I want briefly to say what role minimalism has to play in our attempt to understand, and ultimately to solve, this problem. I hope, thereby, to diagnose the mistake made by Wright and Horwich.

To begin, note that there would seem to be just four sorts of response that we might give to the moral problem. One denies the alleged inconsistency by trying to find an analysis of evaluative sentences that makes it plain why (1) is true and yet consistent with (2) and (3). As we saw, this is the subjectivist's line. I have more recently attempted a variation on such a solution myself under the banner of the dispositional, or response-dependent, theory of value (Smith 1989, 1992, 1994). The remaining three responses all accept the inconsistency.

The first holds that, since (2) and (3) are true, so we must deny (1), and claim instead that moral judgements express the very desires that constitute our moral motivations. As we have already seen, this is the expressivist's line, taken by the likes of Ayer (1936), Hare (1952), Blackburn (1984) and Gibbard (1990). The second holds that, since both (1) and (3) are true, so we must deny (2), and claim instead that moral judgements have no special connection with motivation; that we can make moral judgements and yet, quite rationally, remain entirely unmoved by them. This is the externalises line, taken by the likes of Frankena (1958), Foot (1978), Scanlon (1982), Railton (1986) and Brink (1986). And the third holds that, since (2) is true, and since both (1) and (3) buy into an implausible Humean conception of belief and desire inconsistent with (2), so we should revise our understanding of folk psychology wholesale. We should do away with the

Humean idea that reality is motivationally neutral, an assumption the other solutions all make, and claim, instead, that whether or not there are any beliefs and desires, there are most certainly 'besires', to use J. E. J. Altham's (1986) wonderful term: states which are belief-like with respect to one content, and desire-like with respect to another. Another way of putting the same point would be this: whether or not there are beliefs and desires that are *distinct existences*, there are most certainly beliefs which *are* desires (Smith 1988). When a subject is in such a state, she is in a state apt to be expressed in an assertion – this is the belief-like part – and she is also therefore in a certain motivational state – this is the desire-like part. Evaluative sentences, according to this view, are apt to express besires. This is the line taken by anti-Humean theorists of motivation like McDowell (1978), Platts (1981) and Price (1989), and perhaps also by Nagel (1970).

Does minimalism about truth favour any particular solution to the moral problem? No it does not. Minimalism is a theory about the nature of truth and truth-assessability, not a meta-ethical theory, and so it has no bearing on the truth or falsity of (2). Nor, as we have seen, though it presupposes a folk psychological theory rich enough to explain actions like assertions, is minimalism itself an interpretation of folk psychology, and so it does not bear on whether or not folk psychology should be framed in terms of the concepts of belief and desire or, instead, besire – something that is, presumably, to be decided by arguments in the philosophy of mind. (Incidentally, Horwich's view that certain beliefs are constituted by desires may now be seen as an implicit endorsement of an interpretation of folk psychology according to which there are besires; and here, accordingly, lies the substantive psychological assumption that informs Horwich's minimalist account of truth and truth-assessability.) And finally, since minimalism is not itself a theory concerned with the analysis of evaluative sentences, so it has no bearing on whether or not there is available a plausible analysis of evaluative sentences that shows why (1), (2) and (3) are not really inconsistent. But in that case, what role does minimalism have to play in our attempt to understand, and ultimately to solve, the moral problem?

In my view, minimalism tells us something about what an expressivist solution to the moral problem would have to look like. For what minimalism reminds us is that evaluative sentences do in fact have many of the features of sentences that are truth-assessable. In Wright's terms, they figure in a disciplined area of discourse, and they have many of the syntactic features he mentions. We just do say things like 'If giving to charity is right then I will give to the Red Cross Appeal next time it is on', 'It is not the case that giving to charity is right', 'I wonder whether giving to charity is right', 'I think that giving to charity is right, but I am not sure', 'I believe that giving to charity is right', 'I desire that giving to charity is right' and so on.

Of course, in conjunction with (2) and (3), minimalism also tells us that (1) may yet not be true because, given that the concepts of belief and desire are defined, in part, by their role in folk psychology, a theory that tells us, *inter alia*, the differential contribution of belief and desire in the production of action, so we may be unable to account for the fact that evaluative sentences are apt to give the content of beliefs. But never mind that. At this stage the important point is that minimalism reminds us that the expressivist who *merely* denies (1) is in deep trouble.

What does minimalism tell us expressivists must do in addition? It tells us that expressivists must explain how it is that a sentence that is typically used to express a desire can yet have so many of the features of an assertion: that is, they must explain why utterances of evaluative sentences comprise a disciplined area of discourse, and why such sentences have so many of the syntactic features Wright mentions; why we are able to say all of the things he points out that we do say, including things like 'I believe that giving to charity is right'. Minimalism is not itself an explanation of this fact, of course. What is needed is a theory like Simon Blackburn's quasi-realism (1984, especially pp. 189–202). But it is minimalism that forces the expressivist to be in the business of giving a theory like quasi-realism.

It seems to me that this is where Wright and Horwich were misled. For quasi-realism, if successful, will explain how a set of sentences that are not truth-assessable can yet have so many of the features that minimalists fix on in giving an account of truth-assessability itself. It will even explain why we are entitled to say such things as 'I believe that it is right to give to charity', despite the fact that an utterance of 'Giving to charity is right' does not express a belief, strictly speaking. But so long as expressivists can make out the claim that utterances of evaluative sentences not just *are not*, but *cannot be*, expressions of beliefs, strictly speaking – that they are rather expressions of desires, as the terms 'belief' and 'desire' are used in a properly interpreted folk psychology – then it seems to me they will have a theory whose coherence minimalists will have to happily, even if in some cases reluctantly, concede.[2]

NOTES

1 'Roughly speaking' because of complications to do with sentences like 'The belief that p is false', which is truth-assessable but which I may not be able to believe if, for example, I believe that p; sentences that are too long to be entertained; and so on.
2 I am very grateful to Richard Holton, Frank Jackson, Philip Pettit and, especially, Peter Smith for their very helpful comments on an earlier version of this paper. Thanks also to Paul Horwich for saving me from a bad misunderstanding of his views.

REFERENCES

Altham, J. E. J. (1986) 'The Legacy of Emotivism', in *Fact, Science and Morality: Essays on A. J. Ayer's Language, Truth and Logic*, edited by Graham Macdonald and Crispin Wright (Oxford: Blackwell), 275–88.

Ayer, A. J. (1936) *Language, Truth and Logic* (London: Gollanz).

Blackburn, Simon (1984) *Spreading the Word* (Oxford: Oxford University Press).

Brink, David O. (1986) 'Externalist Moral Realism', *Southern Journal of Philosophy*, Supplement, 23–42.

Foot, Philippa (1978) 'Morality as a System of Hypothetical Imperatives', reprinted in her *Virtues and Vices* (Berkeley, CA: University of California Press), 157–73.

Frankena, William (1958) 'Obligation and Motivation in Recent Moral Philosophy', in *Essays on Moral Philosophy*, edited by A. I. Melden (Seattle, WA: University of Washington Press), 40–81.

Gibbard, Allan (1990) *Wise Choices, Apt Feelings* (Oxford: Clarendon Press).

Hare, R. M. (1952) *The Language of Morals* (Oxford: Oxford University Press).

Horwich, Paul (1990) *Truth* (Oxford: Blackwell).

——(1993) 'Gibbard's Theory of Norms', *Philosophy and Public Affairs* 22, 67–78.

Hume, David (1968) *A Treatise of Human Nature* (Oxford: Clarendon Press).

McDowell, John (1978) 'Are Moral Requirements Hypothetical Imperatives?', *Proc. Aristotelian Society*, Supp. Vol. 52, 13–29.

Nagel, Thomas (1970) *The Possibility of Altruism* (Princeton, NJ: Princeton University Press).

Platts, Mark (1981) 'Moral Reality and the End of Desire', in *Reference, Truth and Reality*, edited by M. Platts (London: Routledge), 69–82.

Price, Huw (1989) *Facts and the Function of Truth* (Oxford: Blackwell).

Railton, Peter (1986) 'Moral Realism', *Philosophical Review* 95, 163–207 [Chapter 9, this volume].

Scanlon, Thomas (1982) 'Contractualism and Utilitarianism', in *Utilitarianism and Beyond*, edited by Amartya Sen and Bernard Williams (Cambridge: Cambridge University Press), 103–28.

Smith, Michael (1986) 'Should We Believe in Emotivism?', in *Fact, Science and Morality: Essays on A. J. Ayer's Language, Truth and Logic*, edited by Graham Macdonald and Crispin Wright (Oxford: Blackwell), 289–310.

——(1987) 'The Humean Theory of Motivation', *Mind* 96, 36–61 [Chapter 31, this volume].

——(1988) 'On Humeans, Anti-Humeans and Motivation: A Reply to Pettit', *Mind* 97, 589–95 [Chapter 33, this volume].

——(1989) 'Dispositional Theories of Value', *Proc. Aristotelian Society*, Supp. Vol. 63, 89–111.

——(1992) 'Valuing: Desiring or Believing?', in *Reduction, Explanation and Realism*, edited by David Charles and Kathleen Lennon (Oxford: Oxford University Press), 323–60.

——(1994) *The Moral Problem* (Oxford: Blackwell).

Wright, Crispin (1992) *Truth and Objectivity* (Cambridge, MA: Harvard University Press).

22

WHY EXPRESSIVISTS ABOUT VALUE SHOULD NOT LOVE MINIMALISM ABOUT TRUTH

John Divers and Alex Miller

If we sympathize with the pressures I have described, we come to appreciate why it should be natural to treat expressions of attitude as if they were similar to ordinary judgements. We come to need a predicate whose behaviour is like that of others. Why not regard ourselves as having *constructed* a notion of moral truth? If we have done so then we can happily say that moral judgements are true or false, only not think that we have sold out to realism when we do so.

Simon Blackburn (1984, p. 196 [p. 354, this volume])

To the extent that generally acknowledged standards of appropriateness inform our appraisal of, for example moral judgement and argument, the claim that moral discourse is not genuinely assertoric will seem unmotivated in contradistinction to the idea that the truth predicate which applies within it is some sort of construct from the relevant notion of appropriateness.

Crispin Wright (1992, p. 10)

1

Taken together, these passages would appear to convict the advocate of minimal truth (i.e. Wright)[1] of a blatant misunderstanding of the proponent of (quasi-realistic) expressivism about value (i.e. Blackburn). For it would appear that Wright is attempting to undermine expressivism by arguing that moral discourse has certain features which render unmotivated the claim that the discourse is not assertoric, while Blackburn has already claimed that even though moral discourse has those very features we need not – indeed, must not – regard it as assertoric.

Michael Smith (Chapter 21, this volume) offers a straight-forward diagnosis of the source of this 'misunderstanding'.[2] He claims that Wright has not taken the expressivist's point which is that a predicate which has all of the formal characteristics of a truth-predicate may be deployed in moral discourse without satisfying all of the platitudes which are distinctive of (genuine) truth-aptitude in a discourse. In particular, the expressivist will claim, such a predicate may be deployed even though the sentences of the discourse are not fit genuinely to represent states of affairs, or to express genuine beliefs. And once that point is taken, Smith claims, it is evident that – far from it being the case that minimalism about truth precludes expressivism about value – the expressivist can actually exploit the platitudinous connection between belief and truth-aptitude (assertoric content) which is explicitly postulated by the minimalist in order to *sustain* the characteristic expressivist claim that (declarative) sentences expressing moral commitments are not truth-apt. In brief, the expressivist can mount an effective two-stage argument. The first stage proceeds thus: (1) The sincere utterance of a sentence expressing a moral commitment tells us something about how the utterer is motivated to act; (2) no belief can of itself motivate an agent to act in a particular way, so, since beliefs and desires are 'distinct existences', between which there can be no necessary connection, it follows that (3) moral commitments are not apt for the expression of the utterer's beliefs (rather they express desires). The second stage proceeds thus: by the truth platitudes which are the minimalist's stock in trade we have (4) if the (sincere) utterance of a sentence is the utterance of an assertoric (or truth-apt) sentence, then it is apt to express a belief whose content is captured by that sentence, and from (4) and (3) we may conclude finally that sentences expressing moral commitments are not assertoric (truth-apt).[3] Thus, Smith contends, minimalism about truth facilitates expressivism about value. But there is more.

Smith takes the foregoing argument, and in particular the (platitudinous) connections between assertion and belief which it exploits, to reveal that minimalism about truth is not so minimal as minimalists think that it is – he writes:

> (M)inimalism about truth in fact *presupposes* a psychological theory, a theory whose concepts of belief and desire will in turn constrain which sentences can and cannot count as truth-assessable. But if minimalism presupposes a psychological theory then, given that a psychological theory is a substantive theory about the way human beings work, it follows that minimalism itself requires substantive assumptions in giving accounts of truth and truth-assessability after all.
>
> (Chapter 21, this volume, pp. 429–30)

So it is alleged, Wright has failed to draw two important conclusions from the relationship which he endorses between the notions of (minimal) truth-aptitude and assertoric content on one hand, and the notion of belief on the other. Hence Smith's two central claims:

(A)   Minimalism about truth (is consistent with, and) can be used to support of expressivism about value.

(B)   Minimalism about truth is not so minimal as minimalists think that it is.

Our aim is to argue that Smith is wrong about the relationship between minimalism about truth and expressivism about value. We shall proceed by showing that minimalism about truth is as minimal as the minimalists think that it is (so that (B) is false) and by using that conclusion to show further that minimalism about truth indeed precludes expressivism about value (so that (A) is false).

2

Smith claims that minimalism about truth presupposes a psychological theory. But it is one thing to be committed to, or to presuppose, a psychological theory of some kind, and quite another for there to be one such theory to which one is committed. Smith intends the former sort of commitment and we agree that so much is entailed by the considerations which he adduces on behalf of expressivism. But once this point is clarified, the corollary is that the minimalist will be committed to *some substantive assumptions or other* about how humans work – not that there are particular substantive assumptions about how humans work to which the minimalist is committed. So the minimalist is not committed to any specific psychological-theoretical assumptions.

The form of our response to Smith's claim (B) is thus as follows: insofar as the minimalist has psychological-theoretical commitments, they are not of a (harmful) metaphysically substantial kind; and insofar as psychological theories involve pre-suppositions of a (harmful) metaphysically substantial kind, the minimalist is not committed to such theories.

Assume for the sake of argument that to be committed (*de dicto*) to some psychological theory which tells us *inter alia* the differential contribution of belief and desire in the production of action, is to be subject to some commitment which is incompatible with genuine minimalism about truth. The obvious strategy for the minimalist is to resist the claim that he is so committed, and we aim to vindicate such a line of minimalist resistance by arguing that it need not be *ad hoc*.

The natural position for the minimalist about truth to adopt is that he is committed *only* to as much psychology as is generated by those of his truth-platitudes which have psychological relevance. He certainly cannot be less committed than this, for there is no question that he is already committed to a proto-theory of belief which emerges from the platitudes linking belief, on one hand, with the notions of assertoric content and truth-aptitude on the other. Moreover, it is eminently reasonable to hold the minimalist about truth to account for the platitudinous extensions of the notion of belief to which minimalism about truth already commits him. So the minimalist about truth is committed to at least as much psychology as is implicated in platitudinous extensions of that conception of belief which is introduced by the truth (and assertion) platitudes, and the minimalist, we claim, is entitled to resist any further psychological commitments. But the question remains: to precisely how much psychology is the minimalist committed on the basis of the foregoing response? And the answer to that question depends on how far we take *platitudes* about belief to range. Is it a platitude that any creature with beliefs has desires?; is it a platitude that at least creatures who are capable of action (creatures such as ourselves) must be capable of desires as well as beliefs?; and crucially, how are we to decide these questions?

Following an interesting suggestion of Jackson (1992), let us think of minimalism as a *common ground* approach to circumscribing the platitudes which constrain a given concept: the platitudes are those assumptions which all theorists irrespective of their particular metaphysical commitments are prepared to make.[4] But then it does not emerge, or at least it does not emerge clearly as a platitude, that creatures who are capable of actions must be capable of both beliefs and desires, for it is not common ground (in the relevant sense) that both beliefs and desires must be implicated in the rational explanation of actions. Smith himself notes the position of those (e.g. McDowell, Platts and Price) who claim that certain actions may rationally be explained while no reference is required to any psychological states other than the beliefs of the agent.[5] But thereby the point emerges clearly that it is no platitude that the rational explanation of actions always implicates both beliefs and desires, and therefore – we argue – that such a theoretical commitment is no part of the presuppositions of minimalism about truth. A commitment to such a substantial psychological thesis marks the harbouring of a conception of belief which is metaphysically more portentous than that which is constrained by the platitudinous extensions of the platitudes linking belief with assertion. Consequently, the minimalist notion of truth does not carry hidden metaphysical weight and, we maintain, (B) is false – minimalism about truth *is* as minimal as the minimalists think that it is.

3

Given the case against (B) we are now in a position to make relatively short work of claim (A). The expressivist was supposed to be able to gain leverage on the alleged minimal truth-aptitude of moral sentences by exploiting the platitudes which relate truth-aptitude and assertion, on one hand, to belief on the other. But on reflection we can now see that what this expressivist tactic depends upon in practice is an appeal to a notion of belief which is far more robust than that which is constrained by the minimalist's platitudes about truth. And so, as Wright suggested, the expressivist argument against the minimal truth-aptitude of moral discourse is stopped in its tracks.

To see this more clearly, let us distinguish explicitly the minimal notions of truth and belief from a robust notion of truth and belief.[6] It follows from the links between truth-aptitude and belief that if the (declarative) sentences of moral discourse are robustly truth-apt then their sincere uses are expressions of correspondingly robust beliefs. Let us abbreviate this conditional relationship thus: $T_r \rightarrow B_r$. Now Smith's expressivist shows that since moral commitments (essentially) have motivational implications, and robust beliefs don't, moral sentences are not fit for the expression of robust beliefs – i.e. the expressivists shows: $\neg B_r$. And so, it is available to the expressivist to argue quite properly thus:

(E1) $T_r \rightarrow B_r, \neg B_r \models \neg T_r$

to the conclusion that the (declarative) sentences of moral discourse are not robustly truth-apt. However, Smith appears to think that his expressivist is entitled to the stronger claim that the (declarative) sentences of moral discourse are not minimally truth-apt, a claim that could be reached by the parallel argument (E2):

(E2) $T_m \rightarrow B_m, \neg B_m \models \neg T_m$.

But the expressivist is not entitled to the second premiss of this argument (i.e. $\neg B_m$) which has it that moral sentences are not fit for the expression of minimal beliefs. For, we have argued, it is no part of the minimal notion of belief that beliefs are implicated in the psychological explanation of actions in the way that the expressivist supposes that they must be. To put the point otherwise, if this is how Smith's expressivist is arguing he has, in effect, advanced the fallacious (E3):

(E3) $T_m \rightarrow B_m, \neg B_r \models \neg T_m$.

So how are we to read Smith's expressivist in such a way as to avoid the charge of fallaciousness? Perhaps what he is trying to establish is the conjunction $T_m \& \neg T_r$: that is, sentences which express moral commitments are indeed minimally truth-apt, but are not truth-apt in any strict or substantial sense. If so, how then is $T_m \& \neg T_r$ to be understood? It certainly *looks* indistinguishable from the sort of anti-realist position which Wright describes in his minimalist framework (1992). Such an anti-realist admits that the sentences of the relevant discourse are minimally truth apt – and hence assertoric – but goes on to deny that the truth-predicate for the discourse is substantial in a sense defined by the familiar realist/anti-realist cruxes which Wright develops (viz., the Euthyphro contrast, cognitive command, width of cosmological role, and evidence transcendence). So how can Smith avoid the collapse of the expressivist's conclusion, thus construed, into a position which is easily locatable *within* Wright's framework of options – and thereby simply *concede* the game to Wright's anti-realist?

He can do so, obviously, by providing an argument against the claim that minimally truth apt sentences are assertoric. Let *quietism about assertion* be the view that a set of sentences which are minimally truth apt – sustain all the characteristic appearances of assertion – just are assertoric. Then, what Smith has to do in order to avoid the collapse of his expressivist's conclusion into Wright's minimalism, is to provide an argument *against* quietism about assertion. Let us be absolutely clear about where the onus of proof lies here. Quietism about assertion, construed as above, is not so much a philosophical theory or thesis, but rather just the reflection of the fact that we have no pre-theoretical inclination to deny that sentences which properly sustain all the appearances of assertion are indeed assertoric. It is the default position and as such it does not need to be argued for, but if it is to be dislodged it does need to be argued against. And dislodge it Smith must, if he is to avoid the unwanted collapse we spoke of. But what form could a dislodging argument take here? We can think of just one possibility: *Quietism about assertion is false, because sentences which express moral commitments are minimally truth apt, or sustain all the appearances of assertion. But such sentences cannot be assertoric. For moral commitments are intrinsically motivational, whereas assertions express beliefs, psychological states which are not intrinsically motivational.* But construed as an argument against quietism about assertion, this argument begs the question. For it simply *assumes* that assertions must express substantial beliefs – beliefs as characterised in the expressivist's substantial psychological theory about the differential contribution of belief and desire to the production of human action. If, as with our minimalist, we fix on assertion as requiring only the expression of minimal belief, belief as characterised by the platitudinous extensions of the platitudes that have psychological relevance, this argument simply fails to get a grip: for there is nothing whatsoever in that characterisation of belief which prevents beliefs from indeed being intrinsically motivational in character, and so nothing which prevents us from viewing merely minimally truth apt moral sentences as assertoric.[7] Perhaps Smith will reply that there is something in the pre-theoretical notion of belief which eventually does force us to view even minimal belief as incapable of intrinsic motivational import, but it should be clear that the onus is now on Smith to say from where the pressure in this direction stems.

Thus, either Smith's expressivist's conclusion simply collapses into that of Wright's anti-realist, or the argument for that conclusion simply begs the question against the minimalist conception of truth which underlies that anti-realist position. So there appears to be no escape route from the charge of fallaciousness that we advanced above: for all Smith has shown us, expressivists about value should not love minimalism about truth.[8]

NOTES

1   The notion of minimal truth with which we operate throughout is that developed in Wright (1992). Note that Wright is concerned to distinguish his lightweight *minimal* conception of truth from the traditional, weightless, *deflationary* conception of truth (like that advocated by Frank Ramsey), which he takes to be inherently unstable. Unlike the traditional deflationist, Wright's minimalist does not deny that truth 'is a genuine property' or that it marks a norm which is not even potentially extensionally divergent from warranted assertibility. For a full account, see chs. 1 and 2 of Wright (1992).

2   For a similar diagnosis see Jackson (1992).

3   Such an argument is offered by Smith (Chapter 21, this volume).

4   It may seem initially extremely implausible that there are any such assumptions. Which assumptions, it is natural to ponder, might an eliminative materialist share with an out and out Cartesian? The answer is that such theorists can find common ground in endorsing a variety of conditional and biconditional claims which mark conceptual links without (metaphysical) commitment to the world being as it would have to be if the antecedents or consequents of such conditionals were true. It is entirely natural then that the platitudes which Wright suggests as constitutive of the concept of minimal truth should easily be rendered in conditional form; e.g., if the content of a sentence P is truth-apt then it is apt to state the content of the belief that P.

5   You might prefer to say that for McDowell, Platts and Price, such beliefs just *are* desires – so that what they deny is that an *independently intelligible* desire must always have a role to play in the production of action. If so, just read the references to desires in this paragraph as references to independently intelligible desires. (We are indebted here to Michael Smith.) In any event, our basic point here is untouched. And see also Jackson (1992) who highlights the point that the matters of how information is encoded in belief states and of how beliefs are causally related to linguistic and non-linguistic behaviour are philosophically controversial issues.

6   There are, of course, many dimensions along which the robustness of a notion of truth (belief) can be built and correspondingly many 'robust' notions of truth. (This is of course a central theme of Wright's (1992).) For neatness of exposition we proceed as though we are dealing with a simple dichotomy between a minimal notion of truth (and belief) and a robust notion of truth (and belief).

7   Note that we have now made room within a minimalist framework for the expressivist to say *almost* everything that he wants to say. For while conceding that moral sentences are often true he can deny that we track moral properties. He can do so either by arguing that they fall on the Euthyphronic side of Wright's order of determination contrast, or by arguing that they fail of wide cosmological role. Moreover the expressivist can maintain the positive thesis that declarative moral sentences express attitudes. What he cannot say consistently with his acceptance of minimal truth for moral sentences, is that such sentences express attitudes *rather than beliefs*, i.e., that they lack assertoric content. But it is precisely that thesis which demands the gruesome, and thus far unsuccessful, syntactic reconstructive manoeuvres which are distinctive of quasi-realism. For an account of these matters see Hale (1993).

8   We are very grateful to Michael Smith for allowing us to see a copy of his paper in advance of publication, and for helpful remarks on an earlier draft of our own paper. Thanks are also due to Peter Smith and Crispin Wright for useful comments and discussion.

REFERENCES

Blackburn, Simon (1984) *Spreading The Word* (Oxford: Oxford University Press).

Hale, Bob (1993) 'Can There Be a Logic of Attitudes?', in *Reality, Representation and Projection*, edited by J. Haldane and C. Wright (Oxford: Oxford University Press), 337–63 [Chapter 20, this volume].

Jackson, Frank (1992) Review of Crispin Wright, *Truth and Objectivity. Philosophical Books*.

Wright, Crispin (1992) *Truth and Objectivity* (Cambridge, MA: Harvard University Press).

Part 8

EXPRESSIVISM AND NONNATURAL MORAL REALISM

Imagine that you think that, in some fashion, moral value is dependent on humans. Perhaps you have read the previous papers and do not like the idea of making moral values mind-independent, nonnatural enitites, nor do you like the idea that moral value is somehow transformed into, or reduced to, something purely nonmoral and natural. And perhaps you reject error theory because you want to keep to the idea of moral value existing. This leaves two main approaches: a mind-dependent account of moral value, the leading contender of which is a modern form of nonnaturalism, and expressivism. What might advocates of these two positions say to each other?

As it happens, a lot. In our view, this is no historic accident and consideration of the debate had by leading exponents of the two positions tells us much about their rival positions, as well as other positions in metaethics and the purpose of metaethics themselves. The following three papers constitute part of the classic debate between John McDowell and Simon Blackburn concerning whether expressivism (or 'noncognitivism' or 'projectivism') can adequately characterize moral attitudes such that they do the work that is required of them and, correspondingly, whether sensibility theorists (or 'cognitivists', or 'realists') can make good on their claims that moral value is mind-dependent. These papers are three of the hardest in this book, but essentially the debate can be explained rather simply, even if the issues and questions it raises quickly become messy and complex. (Although we should also mention that what the debate really is about and what issues are essential to it might also be controversial issues!)

The debate is best framed in terms of a challenge issued to expressivists. We make conceptual distinctions all the time. We distinguish tables from chairs and further decide that all of *those* types of thing are to be labelled 'tree'. Similarly, we make conceptual divisions when we judge and reason morally. *These* things are the kind things, *these* other things are the selfish things, and so on. For argument's sake, let us assume that our divisions are correct (or 'true', or 'acceptable', or whatever such term sits best with the metaethical theory under consideration). Beyond that issue, another issue raises its head. It is taken as a given that any metaethical theory worth its salt has to account adequately for the rational nature of such conceptual divisions. By 'rational nature' is meant simply that when we make such divisions we do so for a reason. So when someone (correctly or acceptably) describes two things as kind, say, we assume that she thinks that there must be something in common such that she is justified in labelling them in the right sort of way. The alternative is simply to make judgements involving conceptual divisions on a whim, for no reason at all. In other words, there must be something that connects all of the things judged to be kind beyond the bare fact that they have been judged to be so. The challenge to expressivists is that they cannot explain what is going on if we assume moral judgement to be rational and non-capricious.

Why can't they? Expressivists are said to have two pieces of kit with which to work. When people say, "Charity-giving is kind", for example, expressivists claim that the judgement can be disentangled into two parts. There is the descriptive, nonevaluative aspect, such as a description of charity-giving (or, alternatively, a belief about what charity-giving is) and then the noncognitive, attitudinative element that is expressed towards the action type, in this case some approval. Now it is true that in our everyday lives we do not disentangle our judgements in such an explicit way. But the claim is only that expressivists are committed to this being possible in theory. The challenge is whether either element on its own can deliver the sort of rationality and consistency of judgement that is needed.

Imagine we deal with the descriptive element first of all. Think of all the actions that one might deem kind (or selfish, or just, or brave, or mean-spirited, or whatever). Is there one particular nonmoral feature that they all share (aside from 'Is judged to be kind') such that one is justified in grouping them under the heading 'kind'? And, with this question we can assume that an answer can be delivered in terms of any level of description; perhaps the connecting thing is something concerned with the movement of human limbs, or perhaps it is concerned with the movement of atoms. Many people think that there is no such connecting natural thing. After all, just think about the wide variety of things that are deemed 'kind': opening doors for people, giving to charity, refraining from telling someone that their new dress is hideous, indulging a child's sweet tooth in certain circumstances (and not in others), and so on. Perhaps there is a small set of such features that they all have in common? Again, this seems unlikely. Perhaps, further, there is what we might describe as a 'disjunctive' pattern of such features: a list of natural features that not all kind things have, but which indicate all the various criteria by which naturally different kind things get to be kind. So, perhaps something is deemed kind if and only if it has feature x, or feature y, or feature z? Aside from the (very large) worry that such a disjunctive description does not constitute the right sort of unified description that will lead us to justify putting all the things together under the heading 'kind' – after all, we might suspect that it's a bit *ad hoc* – we might worry that any such list need not stop there, at our z. Evaluative concepts such as 'kind', and 'just' and 'selfish' are complex things. Instead of a list with only three such elements we might have a list with many such elements. For example, we might say that something is kind if and only if has feature x, or feature y, or feature z, or features a and b, or features c and d but not a, or ... and so on. And that ' ... and so on' is thought to be crucial, because we might worry that evaluative concepts are so complex that they are irreducibly so. Perhaps there is no way of capturing at the natural level what is involved in a moral concept; perhaps our list could continue to infinity. Or, in yet further words, our moral concepts might *outrun* any nonmoral way of capturing them. If this is right, then there is no way in which we can point to a natural description of something and say, "We are justified in calling this thing 'kind' because it fulfils this natural description". We cannot do this because it has yet to be shown (and is suspected of being impossible to show) that one can justify the moral description purely on the basis of the natural description. Perhaps this thing has all of the natural characteristics of other things deemed kind but, because it has some extra natural feature, this neutralizes the kindness or even switches things so that another label – such as 'selfish' – is more appropriate. Let us give an example. It is normally said that lying is wrong. But, as we all know, sometimes it is permissible, even right, to lie. For example, perhaps it is right to lie when someone shows you her new hideous dress and asks you what you think of it. In which case, even though the action is a lie, there is an extra feature 'lying to stop someone from feeling hurt' that justifies the action. But, the situation might become more complicated. Perhaps the person has bought the dress to go to her birthday party, at which there will be (as you well know) your friend's mortal enemy who will surely mock her if she goes wearing the dress and try to turn other friends against her. So, even though it will hurt your friend's feelings – which previously justified your lie – we now have a longer description (such as 'lying is wrong unless one is doing so to save someone's feelings, but is still wrong even accepting that previous feature's presence just in case she would be exposed to ridicule despite her feelings being hurt when told the truth'). Again, the suspicion is we could go on like this all day and never reach an adequate natural characterization of what the right or kind thing to do would be that would capture *all* possible situations. In a slogan, the claim is that the 'moral is shapeless with respect to the natural'; there is no nonmoral shape that the moral has, as it has only a moral shape.

This might be hard to grasp, so here's one further way of saying what's happening. Imagine you might have an algorithm that takes you from a wholly natural description to the correct moral description. That is, you have 'wrongness' specified in wholly nonmoral terms so you know when to apply it. You simply look at what natural features of the situation are present, and apply the algorithm. However, presumably the algorithm will have only a finite number of elements to it. Perhaps you look at the situation – all the features involved in the situation when you are deciding whether to lie to your friend – and then compare with the algorithm. But if we can keep on altering the natural features, then your algorithm will be useless – you'll end up calling something 'wrong' that should be labelled 'right'. On the other hand, could one really come up with an algorithm that had an infinite number of elements to it prior to any full understanding of the moral concept (which is what expressivists supposedly have to do)? Probably not, and if one did get it right, it would be a sheer fluke!

What of the other element, the attitude? Perhaps we can use this to home in on what it is for something to be kind. But, the worry here is that attitudes, or desires, or whatever one calls the noncognitive element that is expressed, are not fine-grained enough to do the work. For example, imagine we say that things are kind if people approve of them. Yet, such a blunt, broad attitude won't do our work because we need to be able to distinguish kind things from brave things and just things, let alone distinguish these from the beautiful and the charming. Remember that we are trying to construct a nonevaluative way, a way that does not depend on our evaluative concepts, of mapping our existing conceptual divisions. What about something more fine-grained, such as 'elicits approval of a warm, contented type' as that which picks out the kind things? Well, this also does not seem to do the trick.

We might well judge something to be kind and not feel any such warmth inside, and we might get such a feeling when we are making other judgements, such as those judging the childlike and the innocent. Other such examples come to mind here. McDowell (Chapter 12) says that being able to distinguish the funny or amusing as that which makes us laugh won't do since we laugh at many things, such as the embarrassing. It seems that, very quickly, the only option left is to say that the kind things are those that elicit in us an approval that is normally associated with kindness. But this is hopelessly and viciously circular. It uses the evaluative notion that we – that is, expressivists – are supposed to be constructing in the first place.

The quick conclusion to our quick summary is that expressivists cannot account for the rationality and consistency of the conceptual divisions we use when making moral judge-ments. But, we have assumed that there is something that justifies all of those judgements being judgements of kind things, say, there is some reason to making them. It looks as if we should conclude that moral concepts such as kindness and selfishness cannot be disentangled in the way expressivists are committed to and, hence, it makes sense to think of kindness as a genuine concept, a concept that cannot be split into descriptive and attitudinative parts. Further to this, then, we might argue that the things that the situations and actions in the world have in common is a genuine property of kindness that our concept allows us to pick out. When we are thinking about how best to explain humans' interaction with the world, it seems best to assume that, at least for humans, kindness is a real thing that cannot be reduced to or separated into two nonevaluative elements.

There was an awful lot going on there. Here is a series of points about the quick summary of this argument. First of all, you should note that although McDowell makes the two charges in both pieces, he emphasizes the worry against using the descriptive content of the concept to rescue expressivism in Chapter 23, 'Noncognitivism and Rule-following', and emphasizes the point about attitudes in Chapter 25, 'Projection and Truth in Ethics'. Second, as previously mentioned, there is a question concerning what the debate is about. Is it concerned with showing simply that concepts are 'genuine'? Or, does it go beyond that and is the argument designed to show that it is best to assume that moral properties exist? In explaining the argument, we made this slide and presented it as natural to do so. But some might wonder whether an argument and discussion about conceptual practice being non-capricious can have as its output a metaphysical conclusion. It raises a whole host of questions as to what we might then mean by 'reality'. (Note that the final sentence of the previous paragraph has the crucial caveat of '. . . at least for humans . . .'. How much work is that doing? How innocent is it? It might be 'real' for humans to say that moral properties exist, but what about Martians? For more on the notion of 'real' see McDowell (1983) in Further Reading below.) Third, recall that we began by saying that we make conceptual divisions all the time and gave nonmoral examples of chairs and tables. This raises a question: What, if anything, is special about the ethical here? Ordinarily it seems as if we could not make the same sorts of move for the concept 'chair' as we did for 'kind'. But, on closer inspection, there might be a difference not in kind but only degree, especially if one starts to think about design galleries that have exhibitions of futuristic furniture. Could we come up with a concept with 'non-furniture' content that we could guarantee would map onto all legitimate uses of concepts such as 'chair' and 'table'? If you take on board some of McDowell's thoughts about Wittgensteinian rule-following, you might have reason to pause here. If the moral isn't so special here, then what does this mean for expressivism? We might say that it shows that moral properties are as real as objects and properties associated with furniture. Or, we might think differently (and return to our second comment about concepts and properties). We can't specify necessary and sufficient criteria for something being a chair in non-furniture language, but we still retain some scepticism about chairs being real features of the universe, particularly if we are attracted to some of the claims made by physicalist scientists. Similarly, just because we can't reduce the moral to the nonmoral, why should this be impressive enough for us to think that we have to think of the moral as real?

Aside from these thoughts, we might wonder whether the argument succeeds on its own terms. Briefly, the proponent of this argument is trying to reach the conclusion that the moral can outrun the nonmoral and this lead us to be committed to the genuineness of moral concepts in some way. But, it seems as if they have to assume this very thing, or something very much like it, in order to make their examples attractive in the first place. In the example of the birthday dress lie above, we casually mentioned that one could imagine that new features could be added seemingly to infinity and this mean that the natural information outrun the moral concepts that should be correctly applied to the situation. But many people might not be persuaded that such an infinite continuation would occur that would justify the claim about the moral being irreducibly complex. And, further, they might think that at bottom these ideas are the same thought. Whether or not one is inclined to believe this, using the conclusion as part of one's argument ('begging the question') – if this *is* what is happening – is a bad thing to do anyway.

There are many more issues that these papers – and this introduction – have raised, but we have introduced the main ones. Aside from the specifics of the debate, you should be thinking about the wider implications for metaethics. We have talked about expressivism throughout, but if our presentation is correct, McDowell's argument regarding the natural content of a moral concept works equally well against naturalistic reductionists. (See the 1993 exchange by Peter Railton and David Wiggins on this in Further Reading.) All of this should return you to the question we asked earlier: What is it to say that moral properties are real? Are they real in the same sense that tables or the smaller elements of atoms are real?

QUESTIONS TO CONSIDER AND TASKS TO COMPLETE

1   Try to explain in your own words McDowell's arguments in both of the readings (Chapters 23 and 25).
2   What is so important about using moral concepts non-capriciously?
3   What is Blackburn's (Chapter 24) reply to McDowell and how successful is it? Is the test set for the expressivist by McDowell a fair one? Can expressivists maintain the plausibility of their position whilst admitting that the moral is irreducibly complex?
4   Is it possible for expressivists to specify the moral attitude in a way that avoids McDowell's problem?
5   Does the argument against expressivists beg the question? If it does not, why not? Even if it does, does that matter so much? (It might be that expressivists (and reductionists) are forced to say that the moral is not irreducibly complex. But, when thinking about what it is for something to be a moral concept, and how we use such things in our everyday lives, we might say that the central idea employed against expressivists is so over-whelmingly plausible that people who don't agree with it show their position to be fundamentally flawed.)
6   In what way are moral and evaluative concepts different from concepts such as 'table' and 'chair'? What about concepts such as 'swift' and 'surprising'?

FURTHER READING

The debate between Blackburn and McDowell takes place against a backdrop of the rule-following considerations found in the later work of Ludwig Wittgenstein. A great deal has been written on this, but for more on it, see Wittgenstein (1953), Kripke (1982), Lang (2001) and Miller and Wright (2002).

Blackburn, Simon (1998) *Ruling Passions* (Oxford: Clarendon Press), sections 4.4, 4.3 and 4.4.

Crisp, Roger (1996) 'Naturalism and Non-naturalism in Ethics', in S. Lovibond and S. Williams (eds) *Essays for David Wiggins: Identity, Truth, and Value* (Oxford: Oxford University Press), pp. 113–29.

Dancy, Jonathan (1993) *Moral Reasons* (Oxford: Blackwell).

Gibbard, Allan (1992) *Wise Choice, Apt Feelings* (Oxford: Clarendon Press), part II.

Hurley, Susan (1989) *Natural Reasons* (Oxford: Oxford University Press), sections 1, 2 and 3.

Jackson, Frank (1998) *From Metaphysics to Ethics* (Oxford: Oxford University Press), especially chapter 4.

Kripke, Saul (1982) *Wittgenstein on Rules and Private Language* (Cambridge, MA: Harvard University Press).

Lang, Gerald (2001) 'The Rule-Following Considerations and Metaethics: Some False Moves', *European Journal of Philosophy,* vol. 9, pp. 190–209.

McDowell, John (1983) 'Aesthetic Value, Objectivity, and the Fabric of the World', in E. Schaper (ed.) *Pleasure, Preference and Value* (Cambridge: Cambridge University Press), pp. 1–16.

McNaughton, David (1988) *Moral Vision* (Oxford: Blackwell).

Miller, Alexander (1998) 'Rule-Following, Response-Dependence, and McDowell's Debate with Anti-Realism', *European Review of Philosophy*, vol. 3, pp. 175–97.

——(2003) *An Introduction to Contemporary Metaethics* (Cambridge: Polity Press), sections 3.6, 4.9 and 4.10, 5.4(d), and 10.1 to 10.3.

Miller, Alexander and Wright, Crispin (eds) (2002) *Rule-Following and Meaning* (London: Acumen).

Railton, Peter (1993a) 'What the Non-cognitivist Helps us to See the Naturalist Helps us to Explain', in John Haldane and Crispin Wright (eds) *Reality, Representation and Projection* (Oxford: Oxford University Press), pp. 279–300.

——(1993b) 'Reply to David Wiggins', in John Haldane and Crispin Wright (eds) *Reality, Representation and Projection* (Oxford: Oxford University Press), pp. 315–28.

Wiggins, David (1993a) 'Cognitivism, Naturalism and Normativity', in John Haldane and Crispin Wright (eds) *Reality, Representation and Projection* (Oxford: Oxford University Press), pp. 301–14.

——(1993b) 'A Neglected Position', in John Haldane and Crispin Wright (eds) *Reality, Representation and Projection* (Oxford: Oxford University Press), pp. 329–38.

——(1998) *Needs, Values, Truth*, 3rd edn (Oxford: Oxford University Press), chapter 3.

Wittgenstein, Ludwig (1953) *Philosophical Investigations*, trans. G. E. M. Anscombe (Oxford: Blackwell).

23

NONCOGNITIVISM AND RULE-FOLLOWING*

John McDowell

1

Noncognitivists hold that ascriptions of value should not be conceived as propositions of the sort whose correctness, or acceptability, consists in their being true descriptions of the world; and, correlatively, that values are not found in the world, as genuine properties of things are. Such a position should embody a reasoned restriction on the sort of proposition that does count as a description (or at worst misdescription) of reality: not merely to justify the exclusion of value-ascriptions, but also to give content to the exclusion – to explain what it is that value judgements are being said not to be. In fact presentations of non-cognitivist positions tend to take some suitable conception of the descriptive, and of the world, simply for granted. In this paper, if only to provoke non-cognitivists to explain how I have missed their point, I want to bring out into the open the nature of a conception that might seem to serve their purpose, and to suggest that there is room for doubt about its serviceability in this context.

According to the conception I have in mind, how things really are is how things are in themselves – that is, independently of how they strike the occupants of this or that particular point of view. With a literal interpretation of the notion of a point of view, this idea underpins our correcting for perspective when we determine the true shapes of observed objects. But the idea lends itself naturally to various extensions.

One such extension figures in the thought, familiar in philosophy, that secondary qualities as we experience them are not genuine features of reality. If, for instance, someone with normal human colour vision accepts that the world is as his visual experience (perhaps corrected for the effects of poor light and so forth) presents it to him, then the familiar thought has it that he is falling into error. This is not merely because the appropriate sensory equipment is not universally shared. That would leave open the possibility that the sensory equipment enables us to detect something that is really there anyway, independently of how things appear to us. But the familiar thought aims to exclude this possibility with the claim that the appearances can be satisfyingly explained away. If, that is, we suppose that how things really are can be exhaustively characterized in primary-quality terms, then we can explain why our colour experience is as it is without representing it as strictly veridical: the explanation reveals the extent to which the world as colour experience presents it to us is mere appearance – the extent to which colour vision fails to be a transparent mode of access to something that is there anyway.[1]

Now an analogy between colour experience and (so to speak) value experience seems natural. We can learn to make colour classifications only because our sensory equipment happens to be such as to give us the right sort of visual experience. Somewhat similarly, we can learn to see the world in terms of some specific set of evaluative classifications, aesthetic or moral, only because our affective and attitudinative propensities are such that we can be brought to care in appropriate ways about the things we learn to see as collected together by the classifications. And this might constitute the starting-point of a parallel argument against a naive realism about the values we find ourselves impelled to attribute to things.[2]

There is an extra ingredient that threatens to enter the argument about values and spoil the parallel. In the argument about colours, we are led to appeal to the explanatory power of a description of the world in primary-quality terms, in order to exclude the suggestion that colour vision is a mode of awareness of something that is there anyway. The parallel suggestion, in the case of values, would be that the members of some specific set of values are genuine features of the world, which we are enabled to detect by virtue of our special affective and attitudinative propensities. And it might be thought that this suggestion can be dismissed out of hand by an appeal to something with no analogue in the argument about secondary qualities; namely, a philosophy of mind which insists on a strict separation between cognitive capacities and their exercise, on the one hand, and what eighteenth-century writers would classify as passions or sentiments, on the other.[3] The suggestion involves thinking of exercises of our affective or conative natures either as themselves in some way percipient, or at least as expanding our sensitivity to how things are; and the eighteenth-century philosophy of mind would purport to exclude this a priori.

But perhaps this gets things the wrong way round. Do we actually have any reason to accept the eighteenth-century philosophy of mind, apart from a prior conviction of the truth of non-cognitivism?[4] The question is at least awkward enough to confer some attractions on the idea of a route to non-cognitivism that bypasses appeal to the eighteenth-century philosophy of mind, and proceeds on a parallel with the argument about secondary qualities, claiming that the character of our value experience can be satisfyingly explained on the basis of the assumption that the world – that is, the world as it is anyway (independently of value experience, at any rate[5]) – does not contain values. (I shall return to a version of the eighteenth-century philosophy of mind later: § 4 below.)

How is the explanatory claim made out? Typically, non-cognitivists hold that when we feel impelled to ascribe value to something, what is actually happening can be disentangled into two components. Competence with an evaluative concept involves, first, a sensitivity to an aspect of the world as it really is (as it is independently of value experience), and, second, a propensity to a certain attitude – a non-cognitive state which constitutes the special perspective from which items in the world seem to be endowed with the value in question. Given the disentangling, we could construct explanations of the character of value experience on the same general lines as the explanations of colour experience that we have in mind when we are tempted by the argument about secondary qualities: occupants of the special perspective, in making value judgements, register the presence in objects of some property they authentically have, but enrich their conception of this property with the reflection of an attitude.[6]

2

Now it seems reasonable to be sceptical about whether the disentangling manoeuvre here envisaged can always be effected: specifically, about whether, corresponding to any value concept, one can always isolate a genuine feature of the world – by the appropriate standard of genuineness: that is, a feature that is there anyway, independently of anyone's value experience being as it is – to be that to which competent users of the concept are to be regarded as responding when they use it; that which is left in the world when one peels off the reflection of the appropriate attitude.

Consider, for instance, a specific conception of some moral virtue: the conception current in a reasonably cohesive moral community. If the disentangling manoeuvre is always possible, that implies that the extension of the associated term, as it would be used by someone who belonged to the community, could be mastered independently of the special concerns which, in the community, would show themselves in admiration or emulation of actions seen as falling under the concept. That is: one could know which actions the term would be applied to, so that one would be able to predict applications and withholdings of it in new cases – not merely without oneself sharing the community's admiration (there need be no difficulty about that), but without even embarking on an attempt to make sense of their admiration. That would be an attempt to comprehend their special perspective; whereas, according to the position I am considering, the genuine feature to which the term is applied should be graspable without benefit of understanding the special perspective, since sensitivity to it is singled out as an independent ingredient in a purported explanation of why occupants of the perspective see things as they do. But is it at all plausible that this singling out can always be brought off?

Notice that the thesis I am sceptical about cannot be established by appealing to the plausible idea that evaluative classifications are supervenient on non-evaluative classifications. Supervenience requires only that one be able to find differences expressible in terms of the level supervened upon whenever one wants to make different judgements in terms of the supervening level.[7] It does not follow from the satisfaction of this requirement that the set of items to which a supervening term is correctly applied need contitute a kind recognizable as such at the level supervened upon. In fact supervenience leaves open this possibility, which is just the possibility my scepticism envisages: however long a list we give of items to which a supervening term applies, described in terms of the level supervened upon, there may be no way, expressible at the level supervened upon, of grouping just such items together. Hence there need be no possibility of mastering, in a way that would enable one to go on to new cases, a term which is to function at the level supervened upon, but which is to group together exactly the items to which competent users would apply the supervening term.[8] Under-standing why just those things belong together may essentially require understanding the supervening term.

I shall reserve until later (§ 5) the question whether there may be a kind of non-cognitivist who can happily concede this possibility. Meanwhile it is clear that the concession would at any rate preclude explaining the relation between value experience and the world as it is independently of value experience in the manner I described above (§ 1). And actual non-cognitivists typically assume that they must disallow the possibility I have envisaged.[9] They may admit that it is often difficult to characterize the authentic property (according to their standards of authenticity) that corresponds to an evaluative concept; but they tend to suppose that there must be such a thing, even if it cannot be easily pinned down in words. Now there is a profoundly tempting complex of ideas about the relation between thought and reality which would make this 'must' seem obvious; but one strand in Wittgenstein's thought about 'following a rule' is that the source of the temptation is the desire for a security which is actually quite illusory.

3

A succession of judgements or utterances, to be intelligible as applications of a single concept to different objects, must belong to a practice of going on doing the same thing. We tend to be tempted by a picture of what that amounts to, on the following lines. What counts as doing the same thing, within the practice in question, is fixed by its rules. The rules mark out rails along which correct activity within the practice must run. These rails are there anyway, independently of the responses and reactions, a propensity to which one acquires when one learns the practice itself; or, to put the idea less meta-phorically, it is in principle discernible, from a standpoint independent of the responses that characterize a participant in the practice, that a series of correct moves in the practice is really a case of going on doing the same thing. Acquiring mastery of the practice is pictured as something like engaging mental wheels with these objectively existing rails.

The picture comes in two versions. In one, the rules can be formulated, as a codification of the practice in independently accessible terms. Mastery of the practice is conceived as knowledge, perhaps implicit, of what is expressed by these formulations; and running along the rails is a matter of having one's actions dictated by proofs of their correctness within the practice, with these formulations as major premises. Sometimes, however, a practice of concept-application resists codification other than trivially (as in 'It is correct to call all and only red things "red"'), and in such cases we tend to resort to the other version of the picture. Here we appeal to grasp of a universal, conceiving this as a mechanism of an analogous sort: one which, like knowledge of an explicitly stateable rule, constitutes a capacity to run along a rail that is independently there.

The extending of a number series is an example of going on doing the same thing which should constitute an ideal case for the application of this picture. Each correct move in a series of responses to the order 'Add 2' is provably correct, as in what seems the clearest version of the picture. But in fact the idea that the rules of a practice mark out rails traceable independently of the reactions of participants is suspect even in this apparently ideal case; and insistence that wherever there is going on in the same way there must be rules that can be conceived as marking out such independently traceable rails involves a misconception of the sort of case in which correctness within a practice can be given the kind of demonstration we count as proof.

We can begin working up to this conclusion by coming to appreciate the emptiness, even in what should be the ideal case, of the psychological component of the picture: that is, the idea that grasp of a rule is a matter of having one's mental wheels engaged with an independently traceable rail. The picture represents understanding of, for instance, the instruction 'Add 2' – command of the rule for extending the series 2, 4, 6, 8, ... – as a psychological mechanism which, apart from mistakes, churns out the appropriate behaviour with the sort of reliability which, say, a clockwork mechanism might have. If someone is extending the series correctly, and one takes this to be because he has understood the instruction and is complying with it, then, according to the picture, one has hypothesized that the appropriate psychological mechanism, the engagement with the rails, underlies his behaviour. (This would be an inference analogous to that whereby one might postulate a physical mechanism underlying the behaviour of an inanimate object.)

But what manifests understanding of the instruction, so pictured? Suppose we ask the person what he is doing, and he says 'Look, I'm adding 2 each time'. This apparent manifestation of understanding will have been accompanied, whenever it occurs, by at most a finite fragment of the potentially infinite range of behaviour which we want to say the rule dictates. The same goes for any other apparent manifestation of understanding. Thus the evidence we have at any point for the presence of the pictured state is compatible with the supposition that, on some future occasion for its exercise, the behaviour elicited by the occasion will diverge from what we would count as correct, and not simply because of a mistake. Wittgenstein dramatizes this 'possibility' with the example of the person who continues the series, after 1000, with 1004, 1008, ... (§ 185). Suppose a divergence of the 1004, 1008, ... type turned up, and we could not get the person to admit that he was simply making a mistake; that would show that his behaviour hitherto was not guided by the psychological conformation we were picturing as guiding it. The pictured state, then, always transcends any grounds there may be for postulating it.

There may be a temptation to protest as follows: 'This is nothing but a familiar inductive scepticism about other minds. After all, one knows in one's own case that one's behaviour will not come adrift like that.' But this objection is mistaken in itself, and it misses the point of the argument.

First, if what it is for one's behaviour to come adrift is for it suddenly to seem that everyone else is out of step, then any sceptical conclusion the argument were to recommend would apply in one's own case just as much as in the case of others. (Imagine the person who goes on with 1004, 1008, ... saying in advance 'I know in my own case that my behaviour will not come adrift'.) If there is any scepticism involved, it is not especially about *other* minds.

Second, it is anyway a mistake to construe the argument as making a sceptical point: that one does not know that others' behaviour (or one's own, once we have made the first correction) will not come adrift. The aim is not to suggest that we should be in trepidation lest 'possibilities' of the 1004, 1008, ... type be realized.[10] We are in fact confident that they will not, and the argument aims, not to undermine this confidence, but to change our conception of its ground and nature. Our picture represents the confident expectation as based on whatever grounds we have *via* the mediation of the postulated psychological mechanism. But we can no more find the putatively mediating state manifested in the grounds for our expectation (say about what someone else will do) than we can find manifested there the very future occurrences we expect. Postulation of the mediating state is an idle intervening step; it does nothing to underwrite the confidence of our expectation.

(Postulation of a mediating brain state might indeed figure in a scientifically respectable argument, vulnerable only to ordinary inductive scepticism, that some specifically envisaged train of behaviour of the 1004, 1008, ... type will not occur; and our picture tends to trade on assimilating the postulation of the psychological mechanism to this. But the assimilation is misleading. Consider this variant of Wittgenstein's case: on reaching 1000, the person goes on as we expect, with 1002, 1004, ..., but with a sense of dissociation from what he finds himself doing; it feels as if something like blind habit has usurped his reason in controlling his behaviour. Here the behaviour is kept in line, no doubt, by a brain state; but the person's sense of how to extend the series correctly shows a divergence from ours, of the 1004, 1008, ... type. Of course we confidently expect this sort of thing not to happen, just as in the simpler kind of case. But a physically described mechanism cannot underwrite confidence in the future operations of someone's sense of what is called for; and once again postulation of a psychological mechanism would be an idle intervening step.[11])

What, then, is the ground and nature of our confidence? Stanley Cavell has described the view Wittgenstein wants to recommend as follows:

> We learn and teach words in certain contexts, and then we are expected, and expect others, to be able to project them into further contexts. Nothing insures that this projection will take place (in particular, not the grasping of universals nor the grasping of books of rules), just as nothing insures that we will make, and understand, the same projections. That on the whole we do is a matter of our sharing routes of interest and feeling, senses of humour and of significance and of fulfilment, of what is outrageous, of what is similar to what else, what a rebuke, what forgiveness, of when an utterance is an assertion, when an appeal, when an explanation – all the whirl of organism Wittgenstein calls 'forms of life'. Human speech and activity, sanity and community, rest upon nothing more, but nothing less, than this. It is a vision as simple as it is difficult, and as difficult as it is (and because it is) terrifying.[12]

The terror of which Cavell writes at the end of this marvellous passage is a sort of vertigo, induced by the thought that there is nothing that keeps our practices in line except the reactions and responses we learn in learning them. The ground seems to have been removed from under our feet. In this mood, we are inclined to feel that the sort of thing Cavell describes is insufficient foundation for a conviction that some practice really is a case of going on in the same way. What Cavell offers looks, rather, like a congruence of subjectivities, not grounded as it would need to be to amount to the sort of objectivity we want if we are to be convinced that we are *really* going on in the same way.

It is natural to recoil from this vertigo into the picture of rules as rails. But the picture is only a consoling myth elicited from us by our inability to endure the vertigo. It consoles by seeming to put the ground back under our feet; but we see that it is a myth by seeing, as we did above, that the pictured psychological mechanism gives only an illusory security. (Escaping from the vertigo would require seeing that this does not matter; I shall return to this.)

The picture has two interlocking components: the idea of the psychological mechanism correlates with the idea that the tracks we follow are objectively there to be followed, in a way that transcends the reactions and responses of participants in our practices. If the first component is suspect, the second component should be suspect too. And it is.

In the numerical case, the second component is a kind of Platonism. The idea is that the relation of our arithmetical thought and language to the reality it characterizes can be contemplated, not only from the midst of our mathematical practices, but also, so to speak, from sideways on – from a standpoint independent of all the human activities and reactions that locate those practices in our 'whirl of organism'; and that it would be recognizable from the sideways perspective that a given move is the correct move at a given point in the practice: that, say, 1002 really does come after 1000 in the series determined by the instruction 'Add 2'. It is clear how this Platonistic picture might promise to reassure us if we suffered from the vertigo, fearing that the Wittgensteinian vision threatens to dissolve the independent truth of arithmetic into a collection of mere contingencies about the natural history of man. But the picture has no real content.

We tend, confusedly, to suppose that we occupy the external standpoint envisaged by Platonism, when we say things we need to say in order to reject the reduction of mathematical truth to human natural history. For instance, we deny that what it is for the square of 13 to be 169 is for it to be possible to train human beings so that they find such and such calculations compelling. Rather, it is because the square of 13 really *is* 169 that we can be brought to find the calculations compelling. Moved by the vertigo, we are liable to think of remarks like this as expressions of Platonism. But this is an illusion. To suppose that such a remark is an expression of Platonism is to suppose that when we utter the words 'the square of 13 is 169', in the context 'It is because ... that we can be brought to find the calculations compelling', we are speaking not from the midst of our merely human mathematical competence but from the envisaged independent perspective instead. (As if, by a special emphasis, one could somehow manage to speak otherwise than out of one's own mouth.) We cannot occupy the independent perspective that Platonism envisages; and it is only because we confusedly think we can that we think we can make any sense of it.

If one is wedded to the picture of rules as rails, one will be inclined to think that to reject it is to suggest that, say, in mathematics, anything goes: that we are free to make it up as we go along.[13] But none of what I have said casts any doubt on the idea that the correctness of a move, in a mathematical case of going on doing the same thing, can be proved – so that it is compulsory to go on like that. The point is just that we should not misidentify the perspective from which this necessity is discernible. What is wrong is to suppose that when we describe someone as following a rule in extending a series, we characterize the output of his mathematical competence as the inexorable workings of a machine: something that could be seen to be operating from the platonist's standpoint, the standpoint independent of the activities and responses that make up our mathematical practice. The fact is that it is only because of our own involvement in our 'whirl of organism' that we can understand a form of words as conferring, on the judgement that some move is the correct one at a given point, the special compellingness possessed by the conclusion of a proof. So if dependence on the 'whirl of organism' induces vertigo, then we should feel vertigo about the mathematical cases as much as any other. No security is gained by trying to assimilate other sorts of case to the sort of case in which a hard-edged proof of correctness is available.

Consider, for instance, concepts whose application gives rise to hard cases, in this sense: there are disagreements, which resist resolution by argument, as to whether or not a concept applies.[14] If one is convinced that one is in the right on a hard case, one will find oneself saying, as one's arguments tail off without securing acceptance, 'You simply aren't seeing it', or 'But don't you see?' (cf. § 231). One will then be liable to think oneself confronted by a dilemma.

On the first horn, the inconclusiveness of the arguments results merely from a failure to get something across. This idea has two versions, which correspond to the two versions of the picture; of rules as rails. According to the first version, it is possible, in principle, to spell out a universal formula that specifies, in unproblematic terms, the conditions under which the concept one intends is correctly applied. If one could only find the words, one could turn one's arguments into hard-edged proofs. (If the opponent refused to accept the major premiss, that would show that he had not mastered the concept one intended; in that case his inclination not to accept one's words would reveal no substantive disagreement.) According to the second version, the concept is not codifiable (except trivially), and one's problem is to use words as hints and pointers, in order to get one's opponent to divine the right universal. (This is really only a variant of the first version. The idea is that if one could only convey which universal was at issue, the opponent would have a sort of non-discursive counterpart to the formulable proof envisaged in the first version; and as before, if he grasped what one was trying to get across and still refused to accept one's conclusion, that would show that there was no substantive disagreement.)

If neither of these alternatives seems acceptable, then one is pushed on to the second horn of the dilemma by this thought: if there is nothing such that to get it across would either secure agreement or show that there was no substantive disagreement in the first place, then one's conviction that one is genuinely making an application of a concept (genuinely going on in some same way) is a mere illusion. The case is one which calls, not for finding the right answer to some genuine question, but rather for a freely creative decision as to what to say.

In a hard case, the issue seems to turn on that appreciation of the particular instance whose absence is deplored, in 'You simply aren't seeing it', or which is (possibly without success) appealed to, in 'But don't you see?' The dilemma reflects a refusal to accept that a genuine issue can really turn on no more than that; it reflects the view that a putative judgement that is grounded in nothing firmer than that cannot really be a case of going on as before. This is a manifestation of our vertigo: the idea is that there is not enough there to constitute the rails on which a genuine series of applications of a concept must run. But it is an illusion to suppose one is safe from vertigo on the first horn. The illusion is the misconception of the mathematical case: the idea that provable correctness characterizes exercises of reason in which it is, as it were, automatically compelling, without dependence on our partially shared 'whirl of organism'. The dilemma reflects a refusal to accept that when the dependence that induces vertigo is out in the open, in the appeal to appreciation, we can genuinely be going on in the same way; but the paradigm with which the rejected case is unfavourably compared has the same dependence, only less obviously. Once we see this, we should see that we make no headway, in face of the discouraging effects of the vertigo, by trying to assimilate all cases to the sort of case where proofs are available. We should accept that sometimes there may be nothing better to do than explicitly to appeal to a hoped-for community of human response. This is what we do when we say 'Don't you see?' (though there is a constant temptation to misconceive this as a nudge towards grasp of the universal).

Once we have felt the vertigo, then, the picture of rules as rails is only an illusory comfort. What is needed is not so much reassurance – the thought that after all there is solid ground under us – as not to have felt the vertigo in the first place. Now if we are simply and normally immersed in our practices, we do not wonder how their relation to the world would look from outside them, and feel the need for a solid foundation discernible from an external point of view. So we would be protected against the vertigo if we could stop supposing that the relation to reality of some area of our thought and language needs to be contemplated from a standpoint independent of that anchoring in our human life that makes the thoughts what they are for us.[15]

At any rate, it is a bad move to allow oneself to conceive some area of thought from the extraneous perspective at which vertigo threatens, but then suppose one can make oneself safe from vertigo with the idea that rules mark out rails discernible from that external point of view. Just such a move – seeing the anthropocentricity or ethnocentricity of an evaluative outlook as generating a threat of vertigo, but seeking to escape the threat by finding a solid, externally recognizable foundation – would account for insistence (cf. § 2 above) that any respectable evaluative concept must correspond to a classification intelligible from outside the evaluative outlook within which the concept functions.[16]

The idea that consideration of the relation between thought and reality requires the notion of an external standpoint is characteristic of a philosophical realism often considered in a different, more epistemologically oriented context, and in areas where we are not inclined to question whether there are facts of the matter at all. This realism chafes at the fallibility and inconclusiveness of all our ways of finding out how things are, and purports to confer a sense on 'But is it *really* so?' in which the question does not call for a maximally careful assessment by our lights, but is asked from a perspective transcending the limitations of our cognitive powers. Thus this realism purports to conceive our understanding of what it is for things to be thus and so as independent of our limited abilities to find out whether they are. An adherent of this sort of realism will tend to be impressed by the line of thought sketched in § 1 above, and hence to fail to find room for values in his conception of the world; whereas opposition to this kind of realism about the relation, in general, between thought and reality, makes a space for realism, in a different sense, about values.[17]

4

I want now to revert to the eighteenth-century philosophy of mind, mentioned and shelved in § 1 above, and consider one way in which it connects with the line of thought I have been discussing.

What I have in mind is an argument for non-cognitivism that goes back at least to Hume (though I shall formulate it in rather un-Humean terms).[18] It has two premises. The first is to the effect that ascriptions of moral value are action-guiding, in something like this sense: someone who accepts such an ascription may (depending on his opportunities for action) *eo ipso* have a reason for acting in a certain way, independently of anything else being true about him. The second premiss is this: to cite a cognitive propositional attitude – an attitude whose content is expressed by the sort of proposition for which acceptability consists in truth – is to give at most a partial specification of a reason for acting; to be fully explicit, one would need to add a mention of something non-cognitive, a state of the will or a volitional event. Clearly, it would follow that ascriptions of value, however acceptable, can be at most in part descriptive of the world.

The key premiss, for my purposes, is the second. Notice that if this premiss is suspect, that casts doubt not only on the noncognitivism to which one would be committed if one accepted both premises, but also on a different position which rejects the non-cognitivist conclusion, and, keeping the second premiss as a fulcrum, dislodges the first. This different position might merit Hare's label 'descriptivism', meant as he means it something that is not true of the anti-non-cognitivism I would defend, which retains the first premiss.[19] (A version of descriptivism, without general insistence on the second premiss – exceptions are allowed in the case of reasons that relate to the agent's interest – but with a restricted form of it used to overturn the first premiss, is found in some of the writings of Philippa Foot.[20])

I suspect that one reason why people find the second premiss of the Humean argument obvious lies in their inexplicit adherence to a quasi-hydraulic conception of how reason explanations account for action. The will is pictured as the source of the forces that issue in the behaviour such explanations explain. This idea seems to me a radical misconception of the sort of explanation a reason explanation is; but it is not my present concern.

A different justification for the second premiss might seem to be afforded by a line of thought obviously akin to what I have been considering; one might put it as follows. The rationality that a reason explanation reveals in the action it explains ought, if the explanation is a good one, to be genuinely there: that is, recognizable from an objective standpoint, conceived (cf. § 3) in terms of the notion of the view from sideways on – from outside any practices or forms of life partly constituted by local or parochial modes of response to the world. This putative requirement is not met if we conceive value judgements in the way I would recommend: the ascription of value that one cites in giving an agent's reason for an action, so far from revealing the rationality in the action to an imagined occupier of the external standpoint, need not even be intelligible from there. By contrast, insistence on the second premiss might seem to ensure that the requirement can be met. For on this view an explanation of an action in terms of a value judgement operates by revealing the action as the outcome of an unproblematically cognitive state plus a non-cognitive state – a desire, in some suitably broad sense;[21] and if we think someone's possession of the desires in question could be recognized from a standpoint external to the agent's moral outlook, then it might seem that those desires would confer an obvious rationality, recognizable from that objective standpoint, on actions undertaken with a view to gratifying them.

I shall make two remarks about this line of thought.

First, I expressed scepticism (in § 2) about the possibility of mastering the extension of a value concept from the external standpoint (so that one could move to understanding the value concept by tacking on an evaluative extra). The scepticism obviously recurs here, about the possibility of grasping, from the external standpoint, the content of the envisaged desires. On this view there is a set of desires, a propensity to which constitutes the embracing of a particular moral outlook; if the content of this set can be grasped from the external standpoint then the actions required by that moral stance are in theory classifiable as such by a sheer outsider. This amounts to the assumption that a moral stance can be captured in a set of externally formulable principles – principles such that there could in principle be a mechanical (non-comprehending) application of them which would duplicate the actions of someone who puts the moral stance into practice. This assumption strikes me as merely fantastic.[22]

Second, the underlying line of thought inherits whatever dubiousness is possessed by its relatives in, say, the philosophy of mathematics. (See § 3, but I shall add a little here.)

Consider the hardness of the logical 'must'. One is apt to suppose that the only options are, on the one hand, to conceive the hardness platonistically (as something to be found in the world as it is anyway: that is, the world as characterized from a standpoint external to our mathematical practices); or, on the other (if one recoils from Platonism), to confine oneself to a catalogue of how human beings act and feel when they engage in deductive reasoning. (Taking this second option, one might encourage oneself with the thought: at least all of this is objectively there.) On the second option, the hardness of the logical 'must' has no place in one's account of how things really are; and there must be a problem about making room for genuine rationality in deductive practice, since we conceive that as a matter of conforming our thought and action to the dictates of the logical 'must'. If one recoils from Platonism into this second position, one has passed over a fully satisfying intermediate position, according to which the logical 'must' is indeed hard (in the only sense we can give to that idea), and the ordinary conception of deductive rationality is perfectly acceptable; it is simply that we must avoid a mistake about the perspective from which the demands of the logical 'must' are perceptible. (As long as the mistake is definitely avoided, there is something to be said for calling the intermediate position a species of Platonism.)[23]

Now it is an analogue to this intermediate position that seems to me to be most satisfying in the case of ethics. The analogue involves insisting that moral values are there in the world, and make demands on our reason. This is not a Platonism about values (except in a sense analogous to that in which the intermediate position about the logical 'must' might be called a species of Platonism); the world in which moral values are said to be is not the externally characterizable world that a moral Platonism would envisage.[24] Non-cognitivism and descriptivism appear, from this point of view, as different ways of succumbing to a quite dubious demand for a more objective conception of rationality. If we accept the demand, then they will indeed seem the only alternatives to a full-blown moral Platonism. But in the logical case, we should not suppose that recoiling from Platonism commits us to some kind of reduction of the felt hardness of the logical 'must' to the urging of our own desires.[25] In the ethical case too, we should not allow the different option that the intermediate position affords to disappear.[26]

5

Non-cognitivism, as I see it, invites us to be exercised over the question how value experience relates to the world, with the world conceived as how things are anyway – independently, at least, of our value experience being as it is. The non-cognitivism I have been concerned with assumes that evaluative classifications correspond to kinds into which things can in principle be seen to fall independently of an evaluative outlook, and thereby permits itself to return an answer to the question which clearly does not undermine the appearance that evaluative thinking is a matter of the genuine application of concepts. As one's use of an evaluative term unfolds through time, one is genuinely (by the non-cognitivist's lights) going on in the same way. Admittedly, the non-cognitive ingredient in what happens makes the case more complex than our usual paradigms of concept-application. But the non-cognitive extra, repeated as the practice unfolds, is seen as a repeated response to some genuinely same thing (something capturable in a paradigmatic concept-application): namely, membership in some genuine kind. To put it picturesquely, the non-cognitive ingredient (an attitude, say) can, without illusion by the non-cognitivist's lights, see itself as going on in the same way. Given that, the whole picture looks sufficiently close to the usual paradigms of concept-application to count as a complex variant of them. But I have suggested that the assumption on which the possibility of this partial assimilation depends is a prejudice, without intrinsic plausibility.

Might non-cognitivism simply disown the assumption?[27] If what I have just written is on the right track, it can do so only at a price: that of making it problematic whether evaluative language is close enough to the usual paradigms of concept-application to count as expressive of judgements at all (as opposed to a kind of sounding off). Failing the assumption, there need be no genuine same thing (by the non-cognitivist's lights) to which the successive occurrences of the non-cognitive extra are responses. Of course the items to which the term in question is applied have, as something genuinely in common, the fact that they elicit the non-cognitive extra (the attitude, if that is what it is). But that is not a property to which the attitude can coherently be seen as a response. The attitude can see itself as going on in the same way, then, only by falling into a peculiarly grotesque form of the alleged illusion: projecting itself on to the objects, and their mistaking the projection for something it finds and responds to in them. So it seems that, if it disowns the assumption, non-cognitivism must regard the attitude as something which is simply felt (causally, perhaps, but not rationally explicable); and uses of evaluative language seem appropriately assimilated to certain sorts of exclamation, rather than to the paradigm cases of concept-application.

Of course there are some who will not find this conclusion awkward.[28] But anyone who finds it unacceptable, and is sympathetic to the suggestion that the disputed assumption is only a prejudice, has reason to suspect that the non-cognitivist is not asking the right question. It is not that we cannot make sense of the non-cognitivist's conception of a value-free world; nor that we cannot find plausible some account of how value experience relates to it (causally, no doubt). But if we resist both the disputed assumption and the irrationalistic upshot of trying to read an account of the relation between value experience and the world so conceived, not based on the disputed assumption, as an account of the real truth about the conceptual content of the experience, then we must wonder about the credentials of the non-cognitivist's question. If we continue to find it plausible that asking how value experience relates to the world should yield a palatable account of the content of value experience, we must wonder whether the world that figures in the right construal of the question should not be differently conceived, without the non-cognitivist's insistence on independence from evaluative outlooks.[29] In that case the non-cognitivist's anxiety to maintain that value judgements are not descriptive of *his* world will seem, not wrong indeed, but curiously beside the point.

NOTES

* Much of § 3 of this paper is adapted from my 'Virtue and reason', the *Monist*, 62, no. 3 (July 1979); I am grateful to the Editor and Publisher of the *Monist* for permission to use the material here. In revising the paper I read at the conference, I have been unable to resist trying to benefit from some of Simon Blackburn's thoughtful comments; but most of the changes are merely cosmetic.

1 There is an excellent discussion of this line of thought (though more sympathetic to it than I should want to be myself) in Bernard Williams, *Descartes: The Project of Pure Enquiry*, Penguin, Harmondsworth, 1978, Chapter 8. (I shall not pause to criticize the application to secondary qualities.)

2 The parallel is suggested by Williams, ibid., when (p. 245) he writes of 'concepts ... which reflect merely a local interest, taste or sensory peculiarity'.

3 Cf. J. L. Mackie, *Ethics: Inventing Right and Wrong*, Penguin, Harmondsworth, 1977, p. 22.

4 Cf. Mackie, ibid., pp. 40–1 [pp. 78–9, this volume].

5 The non-cognitivist's conception of the world is not exhausted by primary-quality characterizations. (See David Wiggins, 'Truth, invention, and the meaning of life', *Proceedings of the British Academy*, 62 (1976), pp. 361–3.) So his notion of the world as it is anyway is not the one that figures in the argument about secondary qualities. What is wanted, and what my parenthesis is intended to suggest, is an analogy, rather than an addition, to the secondary-quality argument.

6 This formulation fits Mackie's error theory, rather than the different sort of non-cognitivism exemplified by R. M. Hare's prescriptivism (see, e.g., *Freedom and Reason*, Clarendon Press, Oxford, 1963), in which ordinary evaluative thinking has enough philosophical sophistication not to be enticed into the projective error of which Mackie accuses it. But the idea could easily be reformulated to suit Hare's position; this difference between Hare and Mackie is not relevant to my concerns in this paper.

7 Cf. Hare, ibid., p. 33 (on the thesis of universalizability): 'What the thesis does forbid us to do is to make different moral judgements about actions which we admit to be exactly or relevantly similar'. In Chapter 2, Hare claims that this thesis of universalizability just is the thesis that evaluative concepts have 'descriptive' meaning (which is Hare's version of the thesis I am sceptical about): see p. 15. The identification is undermined by my remarks about supervenience.

8 The point is not merely that the language may lack such a term: a gap that might perhaps be filled by coining one. (See Hare, 'Descriptivism', *Proceedings of the British Academy*, 49 (1963).) What I am suggesting is that such a coinage might not be learnable except parasitically upon a mastery of the full-blown evaluative expression.

9 See Hare, op. cit., Chapter 2. Mackie (op. cit., p. 86) objects to the idea that a corresponding value-neutral classification is (as in Hare's position) part of the meaning of an evaluative term, but evidently in the context of an assumption that there must be such a corresponding classification.

10 Nor even that we really understand the supposition that such a thing might happen; see Barry Stroud, 'Wittgenstein and logical necessity', *Philosophical Review*, 74 (1965), pp. 504–18.

11 In the context of a physicalistic conception of mind, this paragraph will be quite unconvincing; this is one of the points at which a great deal more argument is necessary.

12 *Must We Mean What We Say?*, Charles Scribner's Sons, New York, 1969, p. 52.

13 See Michael Dummett, 'Wittgenstein's philosophy of mathematics', *Philosophical Review*, 68 (1959), pp. 324–48. (For a corrective, see Stroud, op. cit.)

14 Simon Blackburn objected that the central 'rule-following' passages in Wittgenstein discuss cases where following the rule is a matter of course. (There are no hard cases in mathematics.) In the end I do not mind if my remarks about hard cases correspond to nothing in Wittgenstein; they indicate (at least) a natural way to extend some of Wittgenstein's thoughts. (Where hard cases occur, the agreement that constitutes the background against which we can see what happens as, e.g., disputes about genuine questions cannot be agreement in judgements as to the application of the concepts themselves: cf. § 242. What matters is, for instance, agreement about what counts as a reasonable argument; consider how lawyers recognize competence in their fellows, in spite of disagreement over hard cases.)

15 This is not an easy recipe. Perhaps finding out how to stop being tempted by the picture of the external standpoint would be the discovery that enables one to stop doing philosophy when one wants to (cf. § 133).

16 The idea of rules as rails seems to pervade Chapter 2 of Hare's *Freedom and Reason* (cf. notes 7 and 9 above). Hare argues there that evaluative words, if used with 'that consistency of practice in the use of an expression which is the condition of its intelligibility' (p. 7), must be governed by principles connecting their correct application to features of value-independent reality (that which can be 'descriptively' characterized, in Hare's sense of 'descriptively'). Hare mentions Wittgenstein, but only as having introduced '"family resemblance" and "open texture" and all that' (p. 26) into 'the patter of the up-to-date philosophical conjurer' (p. 7). It is hard to resist the impression that Hare thinks we can respect everything useful that Wittgenstein said, even while retaining the essentials of the picture of rules as rails, simply by thinking of the mechanism as incompletely rigid and difficult to characterize in precise terms.

17 I distinguish opposition to the realism that involves the idea of the external standpoint from anti-realism in the sense of Michael Dummett (see, e.g., *Truth and Other Enigmas*, Duckworth, London, 1978, *passim*), which is the positive doctrine that linguistic competence consists in dispositions to respond to circumstances recognizable whenever they obtain. (See my 'Anti-realism and the epistemology of understanding', in Jacques Bouveresse and Herman Parret (eds), *Meaning and Understanding*, De Gruyter, Berlin and New York, 1981.)

18 See *A Teatise of Human Nature*, III. I. I, in the edition of L. A. Selby-Bigge, Clarendon Press, Oxford, 1896, p. 457.

19 As Hare uses the word 'descriptive', a descriptive judgement is, by definition, not action-guiding. Hare does not consider a resistance to non-cognitivism that accepts the first premiss of the Humean argument.

20 See especially *Virtues and Vices*, Blackwell, Oxford, 1978, p. 156. From the point of view of a resistance to non-cognitivism that accepts the first premiss of the Humean argument, the difference between non-cognitivism and descriptivism tends to pale into insignificance, by comparison with the striking fact that they share the disputable conception of the world as such that knowing how things are in it cannot by itself move us to moral action.

21 Either, as in non-cognitivism, acceptance of a moral judgement really is a composite state including a desire; or, as in descriptivism, the moral judgement is itself strictly cognitive, but it makes the behaviour intelligible only in conjunction with a desire.

22 See my 'Virtue and reason' (cited in the note to the title of this chapter).

23 The following passage seems to be an expression of the intermediate position:

What you say seems to amount to this, that logic belongs to the natural history of man. And that is not combinable with the hardness of the logical 'must'.

But the logical 'must' is a component part of the propositions of logic, and these are not propositions of human natural history.

(RFM VI, 49)

24 Hence Mackie's error is not committed. (It is a fascinating question whether Plato himself was a moral Platonist in the sense here envisaged: I am myself inclined to think he was not.)
25 On these lines: to 'perceive' that a proposition is, say, a conclusion by *modus ponens* from premises one has already accepted, since it constitutes having a reason to accept the proposition, is really an amalgam of a neutral perception and a desire (cf. non-cognitivism); or the perception constitutes having a reason only in conjunction with a desire (cf. descriptivism). I am indebted to Susan Hurley here.
26 For the suggestion that Wittgenstein's philosophy of mathematics yields a model for a satisfactory conception of the metaphysics of value, see Wiggins, op. cit., pp. 369–71.
27 Simon Blackburn pressed this question, and what follows corresponds to nothing in the paper I read at the conference.
28 I mean those who are content with a view of values on the lines of, e.g., A. J. Ayer, *Language, Truth and Logic*, chap. 6.
29 The pressure towards conceiving reality as objective, transcending how things appear to particular points of view, is not something to which it is clearly compulsory to succumb in all contexts, for all its necessity in the natural sciences. See Thomas Nagel, 'Subjective and objective'.

24

REPLY: RULE-FOLLOWING AND MORAL REALISM

Simon Blackburn

Hume wrote, of reason and taste:

> The one discovers objects as they really stand in nature, without addition or
> diminution: the other has a productive faculty, and gilding or staining all natural
> objects with the colours, borrowed from internal sentiment, raises in a manner a
> new creation.
>
> (Appendix 1 of the *Enquiry Concerning the Principles of Morals*)

The focus of our problem is the way in which his theory of the productive or projective
power of the mind should be defined and debated. His idea is that the world proper, the
sum totality of facts, impinges upon us. In straightforward judgement we describe the
facts that do so. But in addition to judging the states of affairs the world contains, we
may react to them. We form habits; we become committed to patterns of inference; we
become affected, and form desires, attitudes and sentiments. Such a reaction is 'spread
on' the world, as Hume puts it in the *Treatise*, by talking and thinking as though the
world contains states of affairs answering to such reactions. The important thing about
a part of discourse to which this theory is appropriate is that it serves primarily as an
expression of the habits and sentiments of the people using it.

There seem to be three possible reactions to a projective picture about some area of
discourse. One might say that it is not really assessable, marking no genuine alternative
to a straightforward acceptance of the judgements in question as descriptions of a larger
reality. The world, on this view, could not be partitioned so as to contain some states of
affairs (e.g. physical ones) but not others (e.g. moral, or counter-factual, or causal
ones). Or, one might say that there is a debate and that a realist (as I shall call one who
opposes Hume's picture) wins it; finally one might hold, as I do, that there is a debate,
and the Humean wins it. In denying the existence of a perspective from which one
could, as it were, take an entirely neutral peek at the contents of reality, and find that

values are or are not among them, John McDowell (Chapter 23, this volume) seems to embrace the first view. Perhaps it is only from this mythical perspective that we can accept any explanation of our evaluations: to philosophize at all is to step to a place that does not exist. Myself I see the boot on the other foot: we will be able to give sense to the perspective if we can see how to conduct the debate. By so doing we construct our right to talk of the God's-eye view. But McDowell seems to veer towards the second view, that realism wins, both in his belief that there are specific arguments against projective theories, and in his embrace of the idea that our affective natures expand our sensitivity to how things are, on the lines of any mode of perception. Perhaps he feels he is allowed to sympathize with both because he thinks the burden of defining the debate falls entirely upon the projectivist: it is he who has 'to explain what it is that value judgements are being said not to be'. But the questions about the existence of the debate affect both the parties to it. A projectivist must focus sharply enough on notions like description, truth, the world, to explain what he thinks moral judgements are *not*; a realist must focus sharply enough to explain what he thinks they *are*. My own view is that this is very hard for him. When, in part 3 of this paper, I describe the programme which I have called 'quasi-realism', which shows how far a projectivist may adopt the intellectual practices supposedly definitive of realism, it becomes hard to see what else a realist can want – what point *he* can be making in opposition to projectivism.

But surely we do have a serviceable way of describing the debate, at least as far as it concerns evaluations and morals. It is about explanation. The projectivist holds that our nature as moralists is well explained by regarding us as reacting to a reality which contains nothing in the way of values, duties, rights and so forth; a realist thinks it is well explained only by seeing us as able to perceive, cognize, intuit, an independent moral reality. He holds that the moral features of things are the parents of our sentiments, whereas the Humean holds that they are their children. Each side will then attempt to belittle the other's explanation, and remove whatever obstacles are presented to his own, and this is exactly what McDowell does, both by alleging various difficulties for the projectivist, and by trying to rebut the association with Platonism, which is naturally (and I think rightly) worrying to anyone who believes that it is a causal, or at least explanatory, process, starting with the goodness of a thing, which ends with our approving of it.

Since we have this way of placing projectivism, I find it hard to sympathize with McDowell's propensity to hint that it is pointless. It has as much point as any attempt to understand ourselves. But of course it is true that we will need some way of evaluating the competing explanations, and it is theoretically possible that we come to regard their difference as illusory. But I see little danger of that. It is quite different if we generalize projective theory. It is undoubtedly tempting to apply Hume's mechanism not only to such things as gods and values but also, as he did, to causes, and (once we are in the swing of it) to conditionals, generalizations, other minds or even our spatial and temporal descriptions of the world. To stem the tide we might indeed become sceptical about whether in some of these applications we have a distinct theory, or only a notational difference from simple realism.[1] But the main reason why projectivism might turn out to be no real rival to realism about, say, our description of the world as containing causally interacting particulars in space and time, is that we may lack a conception of the reality upon which this creation is raised; hence we could have no explanation of how this thin reality works on an imaginative mind to give us our thoughts. This difficulty does not afflict the evaluative case, and whatever view we take about a global theory of truth, the question of whether we are to see values as things to which we respond or as things which we spread on the world will remain. And as McDowell's own paper shows, people will certainly believe that they have arguments for one side or the other.

In the next section I turn to McDowell's specific argument against a projective theory. In the subsequent section I turn to the positive theory of objectivity in moral judgement, derived from his interpretation of Wittgenstein, and argue that it is badly mistaken, both giving us no conception of moral truth in many places when we need it, and giving an entirely spurious authority to majority consensus. I then try to earn, on behalf of the projectivist, a right to use the concepts of truth and objectivity, which delude people into realism.

1

McDowell's main argument against the projectivist raises the problem of disentangling the objective (by the non-cognitivist's standards) from the appetitive or projected:

> Now it seems reasonable to be sceptical about whether ... corresponding to any value concept, one can always isolate a genuine feature of the world ... to be that to which competent users of the concept are to be regarded as responding when they use it. ... If the disentangling manoeuvre is always possible, that implies that the extension of the associated term, as it would be used by someone who belonged to the community, could be mastered [by an outsider].
>
> (p. 455, this volume)

The outsider is someone who has no tendency to share the community's reaction, nor has he even embarked on an attempt to make sense of it. The point is that to him the class of things eliciting the admiration, or whatever other reaction is in question, may have no shape. He cannot see why one thing or another belongs to it, and cannot reliably go on to classify new cases. But the projectivist is supposed to be claiming that in principle he could still lack any understanding of the reaction, yet come to understand the *kind* of thing eliciting it. He could come to see the things which the community reacts to as genuinely forming a kind.

At the symposium from which these papers grew I expressed scepticism about whether a projectivist is committed to this, and McDowell now admits the possibility that he need not be. (He takes it up in his § 5.) However, I think it is still worth going through the argument I used, since the point has some intrinsic interest, and since the option McDowell considers in § 5 is one against which he finds objection (I come to that later).

Let us suppose for a moment that some group of human beings does share a genuine tendency to some reaction in the face of some perceived properties or kinds of thing. Surely it need not surprise us *at all* that they should know of no description of what unifies the class of objects eliciting the reaction, except of course the fact that it does so. We are complicated beings, and understand our own reactions only poorly. Now suppose the outsider, who fails either to share or to understand the reactive tendency, cannot perceive any such unifying feature either. Then he will be at a loss to extend the associated term to new cases, and there will be no method of teaching him how to do so. To take a very plausible candidate, it is notoriously difficult or impossible to circumscribe exactly all those things which a member of our culture finds comic. Any description is likely to have a partial and disjunctive air which would make it a poor guide to someone who does not share our sense of humour, if he is trying to predict those things which we will and will not find funny. This may not be a merely practical matter: there is no a priori reason to expect there to really *be* a unifying feature. Let us describe this by saying that the grouping of things which is made by projecting our reactive tendency onto the world is *shapeless* with respect to other features. The puzzle then is why McDowell sees shapelessness as a problem for a projective theory. The necessary premise must be that a reactive tendency cannot be shapeless with respect to those other features which trigger it off, whereas a further cognitive ability can pick up features which are shapeless with respect to others. But why? Do we really support a realist theory of the comic by pointing out the complexity and shapeless nature of the class of things we laugh at? On the contrary, there is no reason to expect our reactions to the world simply to fall into patterns which we or anyone else can describe. So the plight of the outsider affords no argument against a Humean theory.

Now even if our sense of humour is in my sense shapeless, this does not entail the lack, on any particular occasion of humour, of an objective feature to which we are reacting. We might want to regard it as true that on any occasion the comic reaction is a reaction to some perceived set of features. It is just that all these sets form a class which independently of our tendency to find them funny, has no shape. It may on occasion be hard to say quite which features were the funny ones (the twitch of the eyebrow, the timing of the remark), and of course there is no presumption that the humorist or his audience knows which features they are. But on occasion we might do: for instance

I tell a joke just by enumerating certain features of a situation. I don't in addition tell you that the feature of being really comic was also present. But in this case the implication said to hold in the passage I have quoted does not hold. For we may know to which features a person reacts on particular occasions yet still have a disjunctive and partial class which could not enable the outsider to predict the comic effect of new occasions.

Of course, it *is* hard to tell just what was so funny about some occasion for humour. But McDowell admits some form of supervenience (pp. 455–6, this volume), and supervenience is only a requirement because things are funny (or admirable, or whatever) in virtue of their other properties. But once this is said the difficulty of coming to understand just what it is in virtue of which something is funny or good is a universal difficulty for anyone interested in humour or value. It is no harder for the projectivist, seeking to detect what shape he can in our reactions than it is for the realist, seeking what shape he can in the world we describe as funny and good.

So I conclude that the belief that we had here an especial difficulty for the projective theory was erroneous.

It is not clear to me that anything in the attack on projectivism which, I hope, I have just deflected, connects with the use of Wittgenstein in McDowell's paper. The connection he alleges is that projectivists refuse to take my way out – that of being unconcerned by the shapeless nature of our attitudes – because, in a pre-Wittgensteinian muddle about 'following a rule', they think that there *must* be an 'authentic' property (at the objective level) corresponding to the extension of the projected property – a real 'kind' to which all and only comic or good things belong (p. 456, this volume). I think I can see two different thoughts here, but I am not sure that either of them would arise only from a pre-Wittgensteinian muddle, or desire for an illusory security. The first thought a projectivist might have is this. Since we are after all only animals in a natural world, whose reactions, however complex, are elicited by the things we come across, surely there must be some explanation possible of why we react as we do. This explanation must proceed by trying to find common elements in the things eliciting the reactions. I cannot see that Wittgenstein has shown this thought to be mistaken. It certainly expresses no desire for an illusory *security*. It expresses the desire for further understanding of ourselves, and on the whole I think we ought to approve of it, whether it is in principle satisfiable or not.

The other thought which might lead a projectivist to suppose that there has to be an 'authentic' property shared by all and only the things to which he reacts in some way is this. He worries: 'Unless the things to which I react alike fall into "kinds", then when I approve of some new thing I cannot regard myself as "going on in the same way"; and if someone fails to approve of it, I cannot criticize him on the grounds that his reaction is inconsistent with his previous practice. But we need this concept of consistency in moral practice. Hence the things to which we react must fall into kinds.'

I don't think this is a very impressive argument (see § 3, part 5). But in any case on p. 456 (this volume) McDowell looks set to rescue the non-cognitivist from it. It afflicts him only if he forgets how all cases of going on in the same way are founded on nothing but shared human responses. Once he realizes this he will demand no further classification into kinds, to reassure him about the consistency of his tendency to respond to things in the same or different ways. This kind of tendency is all that you could ever have anyway, so even if things did divide into kinds at the natural, pre-evaluative level, so that we could see ourselves as having only shapely reactions, this offers no superior account of consistency – no underpinning for it, leaving it untainted by our bare natures.

But this cannot be McDowell's point! He cannot believe that Wittgenstein delivers one from the threat which shapelessness poses to a respectable notion of consistency. For in § 5 he presses exactly the same attack: he urges that a projective theory which tolerates shapelessness cannot regard evaluative assertions as making genuine judgement, because new evaluations could only be seen as 'going on in the same way' by a 'grotesque' error (this volume, p. 466). So although on p. 456 he writes as though it is pre-Wittgensteinian illusion which leads the unwary projectivist into thinking that attitudes must be shapely, throughout § 5 he himself endorses this thought. I suppose that he must have had some other problem for the projectivist in mind, but I do not know what it is. It would need to claim a projectivist cannot accept the Wittgensteinian. thoughts about the sources of consistency lying in our own natures, whereas a realist can accept those thoughts. But there is no reason to believe this.

Myself, I believe that we do require a conception of 'going on in the same way' in ethics, not in the sense that we demand that all the things to which we have a given attitude form one kind, but in the sense that it worries us if we cannot draw distinctions when we react differently. I later give my own explanation of why this thought is proper to a Humean. But in any case I doubt whether the 'whirl of organism' explanation is at all adequate, because, as I argue in the next section, we can well fear that although we all naturally and unhesitatingly react alike to case A and case B, still we might be wrong to do so. This brings us to the positive theory which McDowell builds upon Wittgenstein's work.

2

When I was asked to reply in this symposium, I was aware of the colonial ambitions of the rule-following considerations, but I had thought that the territory of ethics was safe from annexation, for two important reasons. One is that the passages in Wittgenstein explicitly concern only cases where 'everything is a matter of course'; where 'disputes do not break out' (§ 240); where there is no element of inspiration or any 'hearkening' or special sensitivity. By contrast ethical evaluations or descriptions, and in particular 'hard cases', are often not at all a matter of course, do provoke disputes, and do involve questions of special sensitivity; indeed the hard cases in question could be defined as ones in which this is especially so. The whole stress in Wittgenstein is on the automatic and compelling nature of rule-following. The mental life of one who refuses to compute as we do after a standard training in arithmetic may be indescribable, and it may be quite literally unimaginable. But the mental life of one who parts company on a hard ethical case is usually all too imaginable, or at least we fail to imagine it only if we have had part of our natures amputated.

McDowell concedes that his application marks an extension of Wittgenstein's cases (note 14) – an extension from cases where we cannot really understand the hypothesis of a divergent practice to cases where we can. But this marks an extremely important divide. For it could be that we have some title to regard ourselves as thinking the truth when (as when we accept a proof) we can form no conception of what it would be to think differently. But it would not follow at all that we have the same title when we are all too aware of the possibility of thinking differently. I believe that some of John McDowell's views on virtue suggest that with increasing virtue comes an increasing approximation to the mathematical case, so that the virtuous man is eventually distinguished by a certain inability to see how reasonable men can differ. This, I must say, represents a value over which I find it hard to enthuse (Edward Heath is not every-one's cup of tea); but in any case, however it is with the virtuous man, with us who are less exalted there exists a lively sense of the objectivity of ethics alongside a lively awareness of alternative points of view. And this is not the case in Wittgenstein's examples.

Second, one of the essential possibilities for a moral thinker is that of self-criticism, and of the thought that our own culture and way of life leads us to corrupted judge-ment. We can think that evaluations which to us are routine and matter-of-course might be in principle capable of improvement. And it is not easy to see how this thought is to be construed if objectivity is somehow 'based on' consonance in a form of life. Wittgenstein's work has often been charged with leading to a kind of relativism (if it's your game then it's right for you), and especially if we extend his work to cases where we actually know of different systems of thought, it will be important to avoid the trap. I do not think this has been done: it seems to me that in McDowell's development there is no room for a concept of moral truth which allows that a man who dissents from the herd may yet be right.

We can come to see the difficulty by following McDowell's treatment of our thoughts about 'hard cases', where we have a conviction that we are right, and they are wrong, about some fine or disputed evaluation. I believe that it is fair to represent his views like this. There is a dilemma which is apt to grip us when we think about such cases. The dilemma is that either there must be a hard proof, forcing everyone to concede the correctness of one side and incorrectness of the other, or there can only be 'free creative decision'. However, this dilemma should only grip us if we fail to profit from Wittgenstein's rule-following considerations. These show us the way in which any rule-following has a consensual origin: they wean us from the idea that there are Platonic rails in the mind, laying down the way in which new cases must be described, and show us how simple consensus in new applications of terms amounts to the only or the fundamental reality underlying any process of judgement. Once this is appreciated we can see how to retain the conviction that, in a disputed case, just one side is right and the other wrong. In this way Wittgenstein can be used to give a foundation to a notion of ethical objectivity.

This is highly mysterious. Let us imagine a 'hard case': two groups (them and us) apparently use an expression with some evaluative component in fair agreement. But a case arises in which we are adamant that the word applies, and they are equally adamant that it does not. All efforts to find a hard proof, making them see that they must agree with us, or vice versa, fail. The problem is to avoid the conclusion that the matter is one of free creative decision. To put the same problem equivalently, it is to license the thought, which each group is likely to have, that there is a real truth of the matter – that they are wrong and we are right. I quite agree that this problem is fundamental to the metaphysics of ethics. I give my own solution of it below. But far from helping us towards a solution Wittgenstein's considerations point quite the other way. In so far as they are relevant, they provide reason for quite dismissing talk of one side being right and the other wrong; they force us to impale ourselves on McDowell's dilemma.

For Wittgenstein is taken to teach us that the judgement of inconsistency or blindness, which we each want to make of the other group, is really, somehow, consensual. Coming adrift, that is going wrong in a new application of an old term, is not a matter of jumping pre-existent Platonic rails determining which way one ought to go, for there can be no such things. It is a matter of getting out of step, of having an organism that whirls differently from the others. Suppose this is true. If that is the kind of way to see judgements of inconsistency and blindness, then it follows that they cannot be made when, as in the hard cases, there is no consensus to serve as a background upon which they are based. To take an analogy, being 'in step' in a marching body without an instructor is a matter of consensus: somebody can be judged out of step only in relation to a consensus stepping the other way. For just this reason it follows that there could be no sense to a dispute between two divergent halves of a body as to which one is really in step. Similarly an anthropocentric consensus founds judgements of consistency only if it exists, and *ex hypothesi* in the hard cases it does not: there are simply organisms which whirl one way and ones which whirl the other.

To put the point another way, suppose we grant that judgement grounded on the success of the appeal 'But don't you see?' is genuine judgement. Nothing *more grand* than this ever exists as a foundation for a notion of correctness in judgement. McDowell wishes to infer that something *less grand* does just as well – for in the hard cases the appeal is, *ex hypothesi*, not successful. But unfortunately it is wrong to infer, from the proposition that routine consensus is sufficient to justify the notion of correctness in new application of a term, the startling conclusion that correctness may exist even when consensus does not. Instead, as the anti-private-language use of his ideas shows, Wittgenstein regarded consensus as a necessary as well as perhaps sufficient foundation for the notion of correctness. So the only proper use of his teaching would conclude that it is an illusion that there is a real right or wrong answer when groups of organisms whirl differently. He drives us on to the first horn of the dilemma, since finding a hard proof would exactly be finding something which precludes anyone from whirling the other way, and only then does objective correctness make sense. If Wittgenstein leads us this way, however, he fails to allow for the possibility that goose-stepping along with everyone else can yet lead to moral error.

I can think of only two replies to this. One could be to deny the possibility of persistently hard cases. McDowell talks of us appealing to 'a hoped-for community of human response'. Now the open-ended nature of moral argument means that this hope is never entirely extinguished. But it can become quite unrealistic. The moral half-nelson forcing convergence on some issue may always be just around the corner, but experience teaches us that there are people who will just never see moral or aesthetic questions the way we do. Yet still we may properly retain the conviction that we are right and they are wrong. A related idea would be that the consensus on the *previous* judgements made with the disputed term is all that is needed for the generation of the idea of correctness. The lack of consensus on the new case does not undermine the notion of the objective correctness of just one side, because that notion is somehow extended on to it from our agreement in preceding or central cases. I get a vague sense that McDowell is manoeuvring towards this position from the end of his note 14. In any case, it will not do, for it amounts to saying that where there is correctness there is really a proof: there is no way of reconciling the divergence at this case with the practice exhibited in previous cases. If there is no such proof either way, then to see the previous practice as yet determining correctness for just one side, would be like seeing the practice of golf as determining the rules of tennis. In a hard case we come up against the fact that our form of life, our practices or whirls of organism, are flexible enough to be extended in either of two directions. Reference to their preceding shape is not enough for human beings to see only one way to extend them. It is precisely here that it is difficult, and essential, to give some sense to the thought that nevertheless one judgement may be right and the other wrong. But it is precisely this that Wittgenstein's discussion, taken in McDowell's way, forbids us to do.

3

I should now like to say how I think we should approach the issue of assessing a projective picture of morality. We should say: let us suppose that the picture is correct. Then how far can it go to capture the elements in our thinking about morality which at first sight seem explicable only on a realist metaphysic? The same question, it should be noticed, can be put for anti-realism about many other kinds of discourse, and the results achieved in one area (e.g. morality) can often be applied to others (e.g. the use of counterfactuals, or judgements of chance or cause). I now list a number of problems often alleged for the projective picture, and show how the 'quasi-realist' copes with them. I shall start with the problem which has loomed so large in the preceding section.

1   Moral judgements are not based on consensus in such a way that they cannot be turned on that consensus, and find it lacking. In this they differ from judgements of secondary properties, with which they are sometimes compared. If most of us come to taste phenol-thio-urea as bitter, then that is *what it is* for the stuff to become bitter.[2] If most of us come to find wanton violence admirable, that is not what it is for wanton violence to become admirable: it is what it is for most of us to deteriorate, in a familiar and fearful way. How can we account for this notion of fallibility, on a projective picture?

On that picture a moral disposition or sensibility is a tendency to seek, wish for, admire, emulate, desire, things according to some other features which one believes them to possess. Such dispositions vary. Some, one admires. Some, one does not. One's own may well contain elements which seen in the open one would not admire. We don't *have* to be smug. We could learn that we come to admire things too often because of propensities which we regard as inferior: insensitivities, fears, blind traditions, failures of knowledge, imagination, sympathy. In this way we can turn our judgements on our own appetitive construction, and may find it lacking. The projection of this possibility is simply the expression of fallibility: I think that X is good, but I may be wrong. Thus a projectivist can go beyond saying of our moral sensibility that it might change, to saying that it might improve, and not only because of improving knowledge, but also because of improving reactions to whatever information we have.

The solution of McDowell's dilemma is then immediate. A decision in a hard case need never present itself as a free creative decision. For one may feel, and often should feel, that in letting a verdict fall some way one might be falling victim to an inferior determination of attitude – giving rein to tendencies which one would disavow, could one see them for what they are. Equally, even if the consensus of opinion agrees, we may all be treating alike the very cases which we should not: the herd may fail to mark the very divisions which it should.

This only comes as a surprise if people feel: surely the projectivist denies that there is a right and wrong way to 'spread' attitudes on the world – no ('real') truth or falsity to generate a standard of correctness. But the fallacy is clear. The projective theory indeed denies that the standard of correctness derives from conformity to an antecedent reality. It does not follow that there is no other source for it. And there is: to moralize at all involves commitment to some way of using an input of information to determine an output of reaction. And we are extremely sensitive (and surprisingly unanimous: the general character of the wise man is usually painted in the same way) to the features in such dispositions which we count as flaws and excellences. But we often do not know how much our own sensibilities betray such weaknesses, and how much our age and culture encourages dispositions which, could we see them, or could we improve upon them, we would be unable to endorse.

Of course, these evaluations of dispositions are themselves 'subjective': they are ours. But there is no circularity in using our own evaluations to enable us to assess, refine, improve upon, our own evaluations, any more than there is in rebuilding Neurath's boat at sea. Nor is anything given an axiomatic status (although, as I have remarked, our beliefs about what makes a good sensibility are often very firm): relying upon other planks we can criticize each plank in turn. A critic might say: 'But can you really say that someone who is satisfied with a differently shaped sensibility, giving him different evaluations, is *wrong*, on this theory?' The answer, of course, is that indeed I can. If his system is inferior, I will call it wrong, but not, of course, mean that it fails to conform to a cognized reality. But it ought to be changed, for the better.

Notice, too, how simply this theory explains the way in which other projections become objectified. We can say 'I fear that some of the things I (or we) find funny, are not really all that funny'. This need mark no error, no involvement with a prehistoric metaphysic of a world containing one real distribution of comedy.[3] It expresses a worry whether our reaction is a function of things we could endorse if we knew them, and we are often right to be so disturbed.

2   The next problem which threatens is indeterminacy. We have just seen the projectivist able to give sense to notions of improvement, refinement, and progress towards correct opinion. He can rule out some moral opinion as just wrong. But there is no particular reason for him to think that the core of attitudes which any admirable human being must share is sufficient to force improvement to tend towards just one limit. So aren't we really denying that there is a moral truth after all?

The problem was to give an account of those of our operations with a concept of moral truth which we cannot do without. But the idea that in the end of progress there should be just one package of attitudes and dispositions possible for the virtuous man is one which we can well do without. When there arise cases in which, in Hume's phrase, there is such divergence of opinion as is *'blameless on both sides'* we have indeterminacy. As we have seen, it is not inevitable that I immediately classify the man who diverges from me as victim of an inferior sensibility. For I may doubt my own, and I may be impressed by other evidence that his is as good as mine; experience may teach me that his is better, since as I improve I may find my judgement tending towards the ones he made all along. Such occasions give us opportunities for learning, whereas the existence of coarse or horrendous moral dispositions (the Nazi of endless examination papers) is philosophically quite uninteresting. This is also independent of the question which Williams takes to be important when we consider our reaction to a rival sensibility, namely whether it is a live option for *us* to actually come to share *their* views.[4] But I learn about, say, aesthetic truth when I learn that someone whose ear I cannot despise, whose discriminations are as fine as mine in other cases, whose acquaintance with music is as large or larger, actually likes Wagner, even if experience shows that it is not a live option for me to come to share his passion.

The image, then, is of a tree where the trunk represents a core of attitude which we regard as beyond discussion. To lack it is to be beyond the moral pale. The branching represents such divergence of opinion as is blameless on both sides. But in the actual practice of moral dispute, there is no decision procedure for telling whether one is at a node. In practice we must proceed as though there is a right answer (this is why 'relativism' is so grotesque), and often there will be one, for it will turn out that branching one way was inferior after all.

3   We now need to consider whether the theory of meaning to be associated with projections is adequate to the ways we actually use sentences expressing our opinions. In particular, we use them in indirect contexts, where they do not function to commit us to any attitude. When I say 'If kicking dogs is wrong, so is kicking cats' I do not express an attitude towards kicking dogs. So what is the sentence 'kicking dogs is wrong' doing in this context?

This popular problem has in fact an easy answer. Let us call sentences used as a projective theory claims ones which express *commitments*, as opposed to ones for which a simple realist theory of truth is appropriate, which we say express *judgements*. Now in using a conditional form we work out the implications of a certain supposition: we imagine a supposition added to our other stock of judgements and commitments (with minimum appropriate change) and express ourselves on the other changes it implies. So the question is whether the relevant notion of making a supposition is capacious enough to embrace both judgements and commitments. The idea that it is not arises from thinking of us as hypostatizing a state of affairs – the one making the antecedent true – and since the projectivist is supposed to be denying the existence of such a thing, he cannot cope. But there is no need for this picture. When we are committed to a notion of moralizing well or badly, as I have shown us to be, we need to work out the implications of commitments just as much as of judgements. In other words, we want to express ourselves on what else is involved if we make a certain commitment – we want to say things like 'You cannot commit yourself to that (have that attitude) without committing yourself to this other, or making this other judgement'. The hypothetical form shows us doing this. Often, but not always, it will itself

481

show another moral commitment, because only from some moral perspective is it accepted that one attitude or commitment involves another. I agree that if kicking dogs is wrong, then so is kicking cats, because my attitude is that cats deserve as well as dogs. This means that we can smoothly explain how one conditional may embed in another, since in exactly the same way we might want to explore the implications of *that* commitment: 'If that's right', you might argumentatively challenge, 'stamping on ants must be wrong too'.[5]

Because I believe that quasi-realism is perfectly able to cope with indirect contexts, I don't wholly approve of the label 'noncognitivism' for the metaphysics of the projectivist. Among the contexts which are explicable are 'I don't just believe that kicking dogs is wrong, I know it', or 'I believe that . . . but it would be presumptuous to claim to know it', or 'The trouble with moralists like them is that they treat all their opinions as knowledge'. We do not have to link the concept of knowledge with only those judgements which are read off from the world. We can quite well separate out, among our commitments, those of which we hold that no improved perspective yielding a revision is possible, from others. The former are those which we regard as being in the trunk of the tree: that kicking dogs is wrong is there, but that the government ought to spend more on philosophy is more marginal, while the trouble with lots of moralists is that they do indeed see all their opinions as immune to any possibility of improvement.

4   Delicacy in treating indirect contexts is also essential to handling the issue of the 'mind-dependence' of commitments on a projective picture. Thus, suppose a projective theory must involve us in believing things like 'If we had different attitudes it would not be wrong to kick dogs', or 'If we did not have the habits and expectations we do, trees would not cause shade'. Then clearly it is refuted, because these things are absurd. Fortunately, however, the projective account of indirect contexts shows quite clearly how to avoid them. The counterfactual 'If we had different attitudes it would not be wrong to kick dogs' expresses the moral view that the feature which makes it wrong to kick dogs is our reaction. But this is an absurd moral view, and not one to which a projectivist has the least inclination. Like anyone else he thinks that what makes it wrong to kick dogs is that it causes them pain. To put it another way: he approves of a moral disposition which, given this belief as an input, yields the reaction of disapproval as an output; he does not approve of one which needs belief about our attitudes as an input in order to yield the same output, and this is all that gets expression in the counterfactual.

A projectivist is only tangled in these unlovely counterfactuals if he makes the mistake of thinking that after all there is a state of affairs making the projected commitment true, only one about *us*. He must not think this, nor is there any reason for him to do so, provided he has a proper appreciation of the theory of meaning which must be attached to his metaphysic. To make an evaluative remark is to commit yourself, not to describe yourself, and to use an indirect context to describe the commitment is often to reveal further beliefs and commitments – such as the one about kicking dogs.

For semantics, it is going to be important to use the notions of truth and falsity in assessing commitments. Otherwise such things as a conjunction of which one part is moral and the other descriptive will not be understood as using the normal truth-functional conjunction, and this would be disastrous. But if we are wedded to the idea that interpretations should be specified for sentences, in a recursive theory of meaning, by describing situations in which the sentence is true, then quasi-realism offers no obstacle. The sentence '*a* is good' is indeed true, in English, if and only if *a* is good. That is, if and only if we are committed to the goodness of *a* will we allow that the English sentence is true. That is its rule of use. But saying this tells us nothing about the kind of commitment it is: it is quite irrelevant to the metaphysics.[6] The important task for the projectivist is to license the operations with the concept of truth which we go in for, and this I have tried to show him doing. He must also show how his conception of what is done by the sentences in question explains what is done when they are embedded, and this I have tried to start upon. The main problem recedes when we see that new sentences, resulting from putting evaluative sentences in conditionals, counterfactuals and so on, themselves express new commitments of the same sort (or of familiar sorts – they might be logically true or factually true) so that multiple embeddings will provide no problem.[7]

5　A final remark about consistency and shapelessness might help, if only to show how far we are from regarding uses of evaluative language as 'sorts of exclamation' or 'sounding off'. Why should a projective theory expect us to be worried if, for all we can show, we are reacting to like cases very differently? Shouldn't it be perfectly happy if our responses are not only rich and complicated, but also, for all we can tell, fickle? The answer to this takes us back to the first part of this section. I there pointed out our ability to step back from our moral sensibilities, to see whether we can endorse them or not and to worry about the kinds of function from belief to reaction that describes us. Now it is not at all surprising that a fickle function – one which has an apparently random element through time, or across similar cases – is one which we cannot readily endorse or identify with. Partly this is a question of the purpose of moralizing, which must at least partly be social. A fickle sensibility is going to be difficult to teach, and since it matters to me that others can come to share and endorse my moral outlook, I shall seek to render it consistent. But partly it arises simply from the value of justice. When I react to like cases differently I risk doing an injustice to the one which is admired the least, and one of our common values is that we should be able to defend ourselves against such a charge. This requires an ability to mark the divisions. On the other hand, when we are rightly regarded as just 'sounding off' I take it that we don't much care about getting social agreement, and we might not much care about doing injustice ('I know I am being frightfully unjust but ... '). We can do this, but we do not have to, and in serious evaluative practice we do not.

Of course, it is true that our reactions are 'simply felt' and, in a sense, not rationally explicable. But we should not be too worried about reason here. In general, reason follows where truth leads. Once we happily categorize certain moral judgements as true, we will conform to our general usage of the word 'reason' if we classify dispositions which tend to their acceptance as reasonable. A quasi-realist need not be frightened of the concept. He might, like Hume, prefer to reserve the term for dispositions to genuine, non-projected, judgement, and there would be a point in doing this, since we have quite enough invective at our disposal for people with horrid or queer desires. The areas where we are certain of our ways of achieving the truth are ones where we want to condemn variations as unreasonable and we are not often so certain in our evaluations. But I do not think there is any good way of defining a projectivist-descriptivist debate by calling on the concept of rationality or reason. The difficult concept for the projectivist to master is that of truth, and once that is done reason looks after itself.

4

The successes of quasi-realism leave us with an acute problem of deciding whether there is a debate between realist and projective theories in an area, or whether we have no debate, but only pictures and metaphors, from which we can profit as we please. The most depressing conclusion (for surely it would be depressing to find that such a great and persistent debate has no method of conducting itself; that the philosophies of, say, Hume, or Kant, or Peirce, are not real philosophies at all) would be to see the debate as entirely empty. Someone with realist sentiments makes the world rich, and the interpreting mind lazy; someone with the opposite instincts makes the world poor, and the interpreting mind busy. The only sure way to decide would be to discover that our conception of a fact or state of affairs puts constraints upon judgement. If we could be sure that there could be no such thing as a moral, or conditional, or causal, or whatever, fact, then projectivism wins. Thus, I have argued elsewhere that it is difficult to give a satisfactory conception of a moral state of affairs, enabling it to relate in the right way to those natural facts upon which it is logically supervenient.[8] If such a kind of argument is possible, then one side may win. It is however here that the later Wittgenstein provides an obstacle, and I shall end by saying a little about how I regard the problem he seems to raise.

The debate between a realist and his opponent must arm itself with a conception of a fact or state of affairs which makes it significant to ask whether such things could exist, to make true the statements from some part of our discourse. But the later Wittgenstein must surely counsel us *not* to come to issues in philosophy with a preconception of some kind of thing which a fact must be, then to debate whether there are any of a certain sort. Rather, you look at the discourse first, and tailor the concept of truth to fit it afterwards. The mistake of the *Tractatus* is to insist a priori that the only states of affairs are arrangements of objects in a space – leaving no room for facts about agency, or the self, or morality, and so on. Seen in this spirit, the later Wittgenstein must lead us to conclude that there is no debate (and there may be other themes in his thought which tend to this conclusion too).[9]

But I was very struck, on reading McDowell's persuasive exposition of the 'rule-following considerations', by the extent to which they illustrate precisely the kind of argument which, on the above account, Wittgenstein would have us avoid. In fact, they conform very closely to a paradigm of that kind of argument, namely Hume's treatment of the concept of cause.[10] Causal powers were supposed to be items which relieve the vertigo we feel when we contemplate the continued order of the physical world. They are items which existing at one time yet cast their straightjacket over other times, guaranteeing continuation and order. According to Hume we cannot conceive of a state of affairs with this potency. This is not primarily an epistemological point, although he can add that the 'ground and nature' of confidence in powers is nothing else than confidence in the continued order of nature anyhow. But the primary worry is metaphysical, about the kind of fact we can conceive there to be, and the projective theory is a metaphysical solution to it. In Wittgenstein there can be no fact, such as the fact that a man has understood a term, or is obeying a rule, which relieves the vertigo we feel when we contemplate the continued order of his classifications. There is no fact which exists to make true any description of his past understanding or intentions, and which provides a logical standard of correctness for his future sayings. The only fact there turns out to be is one of a consensus in behaviour, and this is not quite what we expected. We wanted an 'act of meaning' which can anticipate reality (§ 188) just as before Hume we might have wanted a power to do so. But 'you have no model of this superlative fact' (§ 192). Furthermore the consequence is exceedingly close to Hume: 'it is not possible that there should have been only one occasion on which someone obeyed a rule' (§ 199). We were seduced into thinking that there was a 'superlative fact' of some sort, and there is none.

Now I do not primarily want to discuss whether Wittgenstein is right about this. But I do want to make two points. The first is that *if* he is right about it then he faces the paradox that language itself becomes impossible. In other words, we can become gripped by what I call a *wooden* picture of the use of language, according to which the only fact of the matter is that in certain situations people use words, perhaps with various feeling like 'that fits', and so on. This wooden picture makes no room for the further fact that in applying or withholding a word people may be conforming to a pre-existent rule. But just because of this, it seems to make no room for the idea that in using their words they are expressing judgements. Wittgenstein must have felt that publicity, the fact that others do just the same, was the magic ingredient turning the wooden picture into the full one. It is most obscure to me that it fills this role: a lot of wooden persons with propensities to make noises is just more of whatever one of them is. (Notice that Hume would have been quite happy with the parallel point about causes.)

Be that as it may, the more immediate point is that Wittgenstein is here quite blatantly doing what the official picture has him avoiding. He is attacking a certain conception of a fact: the fact that lies behind our use of words and directs it; the one which makes true the proposition that a man understands a word; the one which points beyond the present and constrains future applications; the essential thing which is only indicated by success with a word, and only 'guessed at' when we teach someone to understand a word (§ 210). So Wittgenstein cannot be hostile to a certain kind of anti-realism, or, at any rate, he cannot be hostile to a certain way of conducting the debate, for it is that which he himself is using. The anti-realist, too, charges his opponent with inventing a 'superlative fact' with various extravagant powers. He alleges that the realist conception of a moral fact, or causal fact, or whatever, is false, for the world could contain no such thing, just as Wittgenstein is arguing that the world could contain no such thing as a piece of understanding, on a traditional interpretation of it.

Still, it may be replied, Wittgenstein is not so much attacking the existence of certain facts – for otherwise he would be stuck with the consequence of the wooden picture, that judgement is impossible – but he is teaching us to see them rightly. Of course people follow rules, have flashes of understanding, and so on, and of course a man can go wrong in his applications of a term. It is just that the kind of fact which makes these things true is not what we thought it was, but is something to do with his agreement with social practice. So Wittgenstein must allow one kind of metaphysics – that which reinterprets the kind of state of affairs making certain judgements true or false – but it does not follow that he is ever sympathetic to a realist/anti-realist debate.

This is right, so far as it goes. But it means that Wittgenstein is a poor ally. For the kind of critique that he mounts, in favour of a reinterpretation of the kind of fact making a judgement true, might easily be powerful enough to make us think that no such reinterpretation could be successful: there will be nothing deserving the name of a fact or state of affairs which could do the job (if I am right that a lot of wooden people is just more of whatever one of them rule-following will be a case in point). In that case anti-realism will offer the only salvation. In fact, I am not sure that Wittgenstein would have denied this. For example, when he discusses the first-person he urges the view that sentences which certainly seem to be used to describe states of affairs are not to be regarded as doing so, but are really expressive in function. Thus 'I am in pain' should be seen as an utterance which expresses pain, rather than describes myself (I do not think this is plausible, actually). Again, he remarks 'My attitude towards him is an attitude towards a soul. I am not of the *opinion* that he has a soul' (p. 178). In such cases the fact that we have no 'model' for the truth conditions of some remark is a sufficient motive for an expressive or projective theory of it. So it is hard to see Wittgenstein as consistently hostile to the kind of debate we want.

If quasi-realism is successful, a projectivist has the right to think of moral judgements as true or false, as reasonable or unreasonable, and so on. He can use the same evaluations of them that we use of ordinary judgement, even saying that some of them correspond to the facts, represent how things are, accord with the world – for all these are ways of endorsing such judgements. His achievement was to derive our right to think of moral judgements in this way, by showing how, in 'objectifying' our sentiments, we commit no mistake but merely adopt a needed intellectual orientation towards them. By expressing them in the same way that we express ordinary beliefs we can reflect on our judgements and conduct our debates, and there is no question in doing this of succumbing to any illusion. I think this, too, is a conclusion broadly consonant with Wittgenstein's later thought. At least some of his efforts seem to have been aimed at rescuing our right to think of such things as truth, certainty and proof, whilst facing up to the anthropocentric sources of our thought; the trouble is that he never seems to have really dispelled the relativistic and sceptical implications of this thought. But a more sympathetic reading might well identify him as a protagonist of quasi-realism.

If there is no illusion in kidnapping 'cognitivist' terminology for projected qualities, how should we think of the old debate? It needs a shared conception of genuine judgement, genuine truth, accessible to proof and understanding, so that intuitionists or realists can say that evaluations fall within that area, and sentimentalists or projectivists can deny it. But if, without error, we can see the notions as capacious enough to cover projections of sentiment, then to whom should we award victory? It seems that we could, after all, say that evaluations are judgements, are true and false and rational, so that intuitionists won – yet it seems hard to use the very successes of projectivists against it.

But this is too hasty. Although we have given the projectivist the riches of ordinary evaluations of judgement, it does not follow that all the attributes of traditional truths or states of affairs are given to moral facts. Moral 'states of affairs', above all, play no role in causing or explaining our attitudes, their convergences, their importance to us. They are constructs from our procedures, not their originators, their children, not their parents. The objectivist illusion was (and I fear still is) to think that mentioning a moral reality, and flattering our understandings of it, affords some explanation of our practices in evaluation and judgement. The realist has no explanation of our evaluations, and he has no explanation of the structure of moral truth – such things as supervenience simply become brute mysteries. His illusion was to think that he had a theory, that by citing moral reality he could do away with the need to earn the concepts associated with objectivity.

Morally I think we profit from the sentimentalist tradition by realizing that a training of the feelings rather than a cultivation of a mysterious ability to spot the immutable fittingnesses of things is the foundation of knowing how to live. Metaphysically we profit by seeing how much of the apparatus of objectivity can be acquired on slender means, by earning what is otherwise just handed out. There is virtue in this; one appreciates it more. One is less easily deluded about its relation to other things, such as consensuses of opinion. And one is less inclined to the guilt about possessing it, which issues in scepticism.

NOTES

1 I have tried to come at the theme in two other papers: 'Opinions and chances', in D. H. Mellor (ed.) *Prospects for Pragmatism: Essays in Honour of F. P. Ramsey*, Cambridge University Press, 1980; and 'Truth, realism and the regulation of theory', in *Midwest Studies in Philosophy, vol. V (Epistemology)*, Morris, MN: Minnesota University Press, 1980.

2 The example is Jonathan Bennett's: 'Substance, reality and primary qualities', in C. B. Martin and D. M. Armstrong (eds) *Locke and Berkeley*, London: Macmillan, 1966.

3 I here dissent from John Mackie, who takes this kind of fact to indicate a mistaken metaphysics in ordinary thought. Cf. his *Ethics: Inventing Right and Wrong*, Harmondsworth: Penguin, 1977, pp. 30–5.

4 Bernard Williams, 'The truth in relativism', *Proceedings of the Aristotelian Society* (1974–5), p. 221 ff.

5 I first gave this answer in 'Moral realism', in John Casey (ed.) *Morality and Moral Reasoning*, London: Methuen, 1971.

6 I have the impression that the opposite view is held by some of the followers of Tarski, but I do not know why.

7 In the background for this section is the theory of conditionals in general put forward by Ernest Adams and Stalnaker. The strictures of David Lewis ('Probabilities of conditionals and conditional probabilities', *Philosophical Review* (1976)) can be met by prohibiting needless embeddings, I think. See Bas van Fraassen, 'Probabilities of conditionals', *Foundations of Probability Theory etc.*, 1 (1976). Stalnaker's theory is in 'Probability and conditionals', *Philosophy of Science* (1970); Adams's is in *The Logic of Conditionals*, Dordrecht: Reidel, 1975.

8 'Moral realism', op. cit., part II.

9 Derek Bolton, *An Approach to Wittgenstein's Philosophy*, London: Macmillan, 1979, brings out this aspect of the difference between the early and late philosophies.

10 After I had noticed this and talked about it at the symposium, it was brought to my attention that Saul Kripke had drawn exactly the same parallel, in a lecture given in Ontario (1976) and Cambridge (1978). Rogert Fogelin also notices the parallel, in *Wittgenstein*, Arguments of the Philosophers, London: Routledge & Kegan Paul, 1976.

25

PROJECTION AND TRUTH
IN ETHICS

John McDowell

1

Projection is what the mind engages in when, as Hume puts the idea, it "spreads itself" on to the external world.[1] This image certainly seems to fit some ways of thinking and talking that we can be tempted into: consider for instance the confused notion that disgustingness is a property that some things have intrinsically or absolutely, independently of their relations to us – a property of which our feelings of disgust constitute a kind of perception. That this notion is confused is of course no reason to suppose it cannot be true that something is disgusting. But the image of projection, figuring as it does in an explanation of how the confused notion comes about, might be useful in correcting a possible misconception of what such truth would amount to. My question in this lecture is whether the image is well suited to a similar employment in the field of ethics.

In connection with the prospects for crediting ethical statements or judgments with truth, David Wiggins has pressed a distinction between what he calls "valuations," on the one hand, and "directives or deliberative (or practical) judgments," on the other.[2] It is in relation to the former category that the attribution of truth is most immediately attractive: valuations are not easily assimilated to, for instance, decisions what to do, but naturally strike us as correct or incorrect according to whether or not they accurately delineate the values that are to be found in their subject matter. This feature of valuations makes them also the most immediately tempting field for an application of the idea of projection: the phenomenology that makes the attribution of truth attractive can seem well explained as the upshot of a projection of what Hume would call "sentiments" on to their objects. Without prejudice to the possibility of extending the discussion to Wiggins's other category, for the purposes of this lecture I shall generally have valuations in mind.

In the case of the supposedly absolute or intrinsic property of disgustingness, what projection leads to is error: one takes what one in fact spreads on to the external world to be something one finds in the world on to which one spreads it, something that is there anyway – that is, there independently of human or sentient responses to things. It may seem that any projective thinking must be metaphysically erroneous in this way: the associated "error theory" in ethics was embraced, as is well known, by J. L. Mackie.[3] But we have to take note of a different use of the image of projection, which has been elaborated in a number of writings by Simon Blackburn. The position Blackburn describes and recommends for ethics in particular, is what he calls "quasi-realism." This aims to demonstrate that, starting from the claim that a mode of thinking (valuation in our particular case) is projective, we can see how it can, without confusion, exemplify nevertheless all the twists of thought and speech that might seem to signal a fully realist metaphysic, although – since they are now provided for within a projectivist framework – it must be a mistake to suppose they signal any such thing.[4] According to Hume, when our "taste" is projected on to the world, it "raises in a manner a new creation."[5] Blackburn's proposal, in effect, is that this "new creation" can be sufficiently robust to underwrite the presence of the trappings of realism, so to speak, in thought and speech which is correctly understood as projective; and that participants in such thought and speech need not be led by those elements of it into missing its projective nature. We can be clear, even as we suppose that our judgments accurately delineate the contours of reality, that it is only the "new creation," a product of projection, that is in question.

2

A tension arises in Blackburn's separation of projectivism from an error theory. (I mention this not to make it a problem for him, but to bring out a point that will be important in what follows.) To begin with at least, it is natural to put the projectivist thought, and Blackburn characteristically does put it, by saying that ethical commitments should not be understood as having truth-conditions. That would represent ethical remarks as statements about how things are, and according to projectivism they should be taken rather to express attitudes or sentiments.[6] But quasi-realism is supposed to make room for *all* the trappings of realism, including the idea that the notion of truth applies after all to ethical remarks. In that case, the original sharp contrast between putting forward a candidate for being true and expressing an attitude or sentiment cannot be right: a remark that expresses an attitude can also affirm a truth. Does this mean that projectivist quasi-realism is self-defeating?[7]

Not if we can distinguish what the projectivist starting-point rejects from what the quasi-realist conclusion establishes as acceptable. It may be tempting to suppose that this can be done only if we discern two different *notions* of truth, one to figure in the projectivist denial that ethical statements can be true, and the other to figure in the quasi-realist reinstatement of ethical truth.[8] However, this is not how Blackburn resolves the tension.[9] What Blackburn does – and this is centrally important to the point I want to make – is to contrast an *unearned* appeal to the notion of truth, which is what the projectivist rejects, with an *earned* right to the use of the notion, which is what the quasi-realist reinstates. The point about the application of the notion of truth that quasi-realism is supposed to make available is that we do not merely help ourselves to it, but work for it.

The contrast – the unearned employment of the notion of truth that projectivism rejects – is a position that expands reality by mere postulation, beyond what the projectivist is comfortable with, to include an extra population of distinctively value-involving states of affairs or facts. Corresponding to this, it purports to equip us with special cognitive faculties by whose exercise we become aware of this special field of knowable fact. These special cognitive faculties are vaguely assimilated to the senses, but no detailed account can be given of how they operate, such as might make it clear to us – as clear as it is in the case of the senses – how their exercise affords us access to the relevant range of circumstances. The assimilation to the senses gives this intuitionistic position the superficial appearance of offering an epistemology of our access to valuational truth but there is no substance behind this appearance.

How does projectivism improve on this rather clearly disreputable position?

The basic projectivist idea is that ethical remarks express not mysterious "cognizings" of valuational facts, but attitudes. Now if that were the whole story, there would not be much prospect of a substantial notion of truth; think of the practice of expressing one's attitudes to various flavors of ice cream. But there is an extra ingredient to the story, which quasi-realism exploits. The attitudes are the upshot of sensibilities: that is, propensities to form various attitudes in response to various features of situations. Ethical sensibilities are themselves subject to attitudes of approbation or disapprobation; and – that is the crucial thing – these attitudes to sensibilities are a matter for argument and criticism.[10] We are not content simply to go along with the flow of our sensibilities as they stand, regardless of how they fare under critical scrutiny; and we are not at liberty to rank sensibilities at random and still be taken seriously as participants in ethical discussion. Truth, in a remark that has to be understood in the first instance as expressive of an attitude can now be explained in terms of the fact that the sensibility from which the attitude issues stands up to the appropriate kind of criticism.

To complete the picture, we should need an account of the nature of the criticism to which ethical sensibilities are subject. In part the critical assessment in question is formal, involving requirements like consistency. But there are also substantive constraints on whether a sensibility is acceptable: these derive – so Blackburn seems to suggest – from the function of ethical thought and speech in helping to secure such goods as social order and co-operation.[11] This sketch will serve for the present: as we shall see, a crucial issue opens up when one sets out to be less schematic.

3

It is hard to imagine that anyone would explicitly deny that if truth in ethics is available, it needs to be earned. It seems clear moreover, that one would be deceiving oneself if one thought that those vague analogies with perception amounted to earning it. If the idea that truth must be earned is located as, precisely, a corrective to the unhelpful intuitionistic realism that Blackburn is primarily concerned to reject, it can seem to establish a conclusion about a metaphysical basis on which ethical truth must be worked for: realism shirks the obligation and the clear alternative is projectivism. But it is questionable whether that is the right setting in which to place the idea that truth must be earned.

Consider a view of the current predicament of ethics on the lines of Alasdair MacIntyre's in *After Virtue*.[12] According to MacIntyre, the description of ethical language given by C. L. Stevenson – although it is not, as Stevenson claimed, a correct description of ethical language as such – has come to be true of the ethical language that is actually at our disposal. One crucial ingredient of Stevenson's picture is the implication that no substantial distinction can be drawn among methods of inducing people to change their minds on ethical matters, between making reasons available to them on the one hand and manipulating them in ways that have nothing in particular to do with rationality on the other. I do not want to go into the question whether MacIntyre is right in contending that we now lack the means to draw such distinctions; the point is that if he is right, then clearly there is no prospect of achieving, in ethical thought with its present conceptual resources, anything that we could count as truth in any serious sense. No doubt it is always possible for anyone to use "It is true that . . ." as an indication of willingness on his own part to affirm whatever follows "that." But if MacIntyre's Stevensonian picture is correct, we lack what a more substantial notion of truth seems plainly to require, a conception of better and worse ways to think about ethical questions which connects with the idea that there are reasons for being of a certain mind on a question, in contrast with the idea that there is nothing to ethical thinking but rationally arbitrary subjective stances and whatever power relations might be exploited to shift people's ethical allegiances.[13]

Earning the notion of truth, in the face of this sort of suggestion, would thus be a matter of arguing that we do after all have at our disposal a conception of reasons for ethical thinking which is sufficiently rich and substantial to mark off rationally induced improvements in ethical stances from alterations induced by merely manipulative persuasion.

Positions like MacIntyre's suggest a quite different context for the thought that the availability of truth in ethics is something that it would take work to establish. The problem about truth in ethics, viewed in this context, is not that it fails to be as the intuitionist realist supposes, so that establishing its availability requires a different metaphysical basis. The problem is that a question is raised whether our equipment for thinking ethically is suited only for mere attitudinizing – whether our ethical concepts are too sparse and crude for ethical thought to seem an exercise of reason, as it must if there is to be room in it for a substantial notion of truth.[14] It is really not clear why addressing a problem of this sort should seem to require a metaphysical move at all.

4

It may still seem that, even if earning truth in the face of this sort of challenge to its availability requires something other than an explicitly metaphysical move, namely vindicating the richness and robustness of the conception of reasons for ethical judgments that our conceptual resources equip us with, nevertheless, as soon as we concede that attaining truth is not simply a matter of "cognizing" valuational facts, we must have implicitly adopted a projectivist metaphysic. This appearance reflects an assumption that, at the metaphysical level, there are just two options: projectivism and the unattractive intuitionistic realism that populates reality with mysterious extra features and merely goes through the motions of supplying an epistemology for our supposed access to them. But the assumption is questionable.

The point of the image of projection is to explain certain seeming features of reality as reflections of our subjective responses to a world that really contains no such features. Now this explanatory direction seems to require a corresponding priority, in the order of understanding, between the projected response and the apparent feature: we ought to be able to focus our thought on the response without needing to exploit the concept of the apparent feature that is supposed to result from projecting the response. In the sort of case I cited at the beginning, it is plausible that this requirement is met: disgust, or nausea, we can plausibly suppose, are self-contained psychological items, conceptualizable without any need to appeal to any projected properties of disgusting-ness or nauseatingness. (No doubt a full explanation of the psychological phenomena would group things together in terms of their tendency to produce those responses, but those tendencies are not properties that need to be explained as projections of the responses.) The question, now, is this: if, in connection with some range of concepts whose application engages distinctive aspects of our subjective make-up in the sort of way that seems characteristic of evaluative concepts, we reject the kind of realism that construes subjective responses as perceptions of associated features of reality and does no work towards earning truth, are we entitled to assume that the responses enjoy this kind of explanatory priority, as projectivism seems to require?

It may help to consider a non-ethical case in which an intuitionistic realism is obviously unattractive, and in which Blackburn proceeds as if projectivism is obviously correct: the case of the comic or funny. To begin with at least, this looks like a good field for a projective account. But what exactly is it that we are to conceive as projected on to the world so as to give rise to our idea that things are funny? "An inclination to laugh" is not a satisfactory answer:[15] projecting an inclination to laugh would not necessarily yield an apparent instance of the comic, since laughter can signal, for instance, embarrassment just as well as amusement. Perhaps the right response cannot be identified except as amusement; and perhaps amusement cannot be understood except as finding something comic. I need not take a view on whether this is correct. But if it is correct, there is a serious question whether we can really *explain* the idea of something's being comic as a *projection* of that response. The suggestion is that there is no self-contained prior fact of our subjective lives that could enter into a projective account of the relevant way of thinking: in the only relevant response, the conceptual apparatus that figures in the relevant way of thinking is already in play. No doubt the propensity to laugh is in some sense a self-contained prior psychological fact. But differentiating some exercises of that unspecific propensity as cases of *amusement* is something we have to learn, and if the suggestion is correct, this learning is indistinguishable from coming to find some things comic. Surely it undermines a projective account of a concept if we cannot home in on the subjective state whose projection is supposed to result in the seeming feature of reality in question without the aid of the concept of that feature, the concept that was to be projectively explained. And surely this scepticism cannot tend in the direction of a relapse into the intuitionistic sort of realism.

Blackburn himself is remarkably casual about this. I know only one place where he discusses the question whether this kind of consideration poses a problem for projectivism; and in that place he simply asserts that there is no problem for projectivism if the only way to describe a supposedly projected subjective response is in terms of seeming to find the supposed upshot of projecting it in something one confronts.[16] I think this reflects the assumption I mentioned earlier, that if we are not realists of the unsatisfactorily intuitionistic sort then we cannot but be projectivists.

Blackburn's view of the available options is well summed up in these words of his (they apply to morality in particular, but the structure is quite general):

> The projectivist holds that our nature as moralists is well explained by regarding us as reacting to a reality which contains nothing in the way of values, duties, rights and so forth; a realist thinks it is well explained only by seeing us as able to perceive, cognize, intuit, an independent moral reality. He holds that the moral features of things are the parents of our sentiments, whereas the Humean holds that they are their children.[17]

Realism here is the unsatisfactory position that helps itself to an unearned notion of truth. So if the choice is the one Blackburn offers in this passage, it seems compulsory to opt for regarding the "features of things" that are in question as children of our sentiments rather than their parents. There is no room to raise a problem about whether the sentiments have the requisite explanatory independence. But why do we have to limit ourselves to those two options? What about a position which says that the extra features are neither parents nor children of our sentiments, but – if we must find an apt metaphor from the field of kinship relations – siblings?[18] Such a view would be appropriate for amusement and the comic, if that case is as I have suggested it might be. Denying that the extra features are prior to the relevant sentiments, such a view distances itself from the idea that they belong, mysteriously, in a reality that is wholly independent of our subjectivity and set over against it. It does not follow that the sentiments have a priority. If there is no comprehending the right sentiments independently of the concepts of the relevant extra features, a no-priority view is surely indicated. There are two possible ways of not being an intuitionistic realist, and the image of projection really fits only one of them.

In the case of the comic, the threat in face of which it would be necessary to earn truth – if one wanted to – would not be that any persuasion seems indistinguishable from manipulation; argument is not an important ingredient in that part of our lives. (The attempt to persuade someone that something is funny is typically self-defeating.) But there is a sameness underlying this difference. In both cases, the threat to a substantial notion of truth lies in the idea that there is nothing really to choose between different sensibilities, and that any convergence is best thought of as a mere coincidence of subjectivities rather than agreement on a range of truths – the sort of view that would be natural if everyone came to prefer one flavor of ice cream to any other. And in both cases, the threatening thought can be put like this: different sensibilities cannot be ranked according to whether there are better *reasons* for one sensibility's response than another's. Whether or not the sensibilities are conceived as typically altered by argument, so that the issue can be whether persuading someone counts as giving him reasons to change his mind, the challenge can be put as a query whether a mode of thought that engages subjective responses allows for a sufficiently substantial conception of reasons for exercises of it to be capable of truth.

The interest of the no-priority view, now, is that it opens up the possibility that it might be respectable to use the apparently world-describing conceptual resources with which we articulate our responses, in earning truth in one of the relevant areas. Blackburn's simpler structure of options suggests that we must deny ourselves those resources, on pain of lapsing back into a bald intuitionism. A serious projective quasi-realism about the comic would construct a conception of what it is for things to be really funny on the basis of principles for ranking senses of humor which would have to be established from outside the propensity to find things funny. The contrasting idea would be that we might regard our conception of greater and less refinement and discrimination in senses of humor as derivative from an understanding of what it is for things to be really funny: something we can acceptably aim to elaborate from within the propensity to find things funny. The concept of the comic is not a device for a rationally isolated grouping of items, things whose satisfaction of it we take to be simply a matter of their eliciting the appropriate reaction from us; having the concept involves at least inklings of a place it occupies in a rationally interconnected scheme of concepts, and we should aim to exploit such inklings in working out an aesthetic, so to speak, of humor. A ranking of sensibilities would flow from that, rather than being independently constructed ("from what materials?"[19]) and used to deliver verdicts on when things are really comic. Of course we might not be able to squeeze much in the way of rankings of senses of humor out of our understanding of the funny. And anything on these lines that we did come up with would be liable, as such constructions always are, to accusations of fraud, on behalf of people whose senses of humor we represented as blunter than they might be. We would need to take great care to be sure that we were not merely projectively conferring a bogus objectivity on the deliverances of a sensibility that was in fact rationally on a par with any other. But, although we must of course acknowledge the risks and do our best to guard against them, we would not be guaranteed to fall into self-deception of this sort, simply by virtue of working from within.

The no-priority view allows, then, that it might be possible to do something recognizable as earning truth by focusing on the funny itself. The idea of what is really funny need not be explained in terms of an independently established conception of what makes a sense of humor more discriminating. This contrasts with a constraint that seems to be implicit in a serious projectivism, according to which the idea of a superior discernment has to be made clear without exploiting exercises of the way of thinking which is to be explained as projective, so that it is available for use in certifying some such exercises as (quasi-realistically) true.

Analogously in the ethical case; here again, the possibility of the no-priority view brings out that we do not need to choose between, on the one hand, lapsing into intuitionism – simply helping ourselves to truth – and, on the other, disallowing ourselves, in earning truth, the conceptual equipment that projectivism sees as the product of projection. Earning truth is a matter of supplying something that does satisfactorily what is merely pretended by the bogus epistemology of intuitionism. Instead of a vague attempt to borrow the epistemological credentials of the idea of perception, the position I am describing aims, quite differently, at an epistemology that centers on the notion of susceptibility to reasons. The threat to truth is from the thought that there is not enough substance to our conception of reasons for ethical stances. When we try to meet this threat, there is no reason not to appeal to all the resources at our disposal, including all the ethical concepts that we can lay our hands on, so long as they survive critical scrutiny; and there need be no basis for critical scrutiny of one ethical concept except others, so the necessary scrutiny does not involve stepping outside the point of view constituted by an ethical sensibility.

Notice that this does not make it a foregone conclusion that the threat will be satisfactorily met: MacIntyre's picture of our present predicament, for instance, cannot be ruled out without actually looking into the resources we still have. Aiming to meet the threat from within is not helping ourselves to ethical truth in the manner of an intuitionistic realism; and it would be quite wrong to suppose that it is helping ourselves to ethical truth in the different sense that the issue is prejudged in favor of truth being attainable.

5

Blackburn has purported to respond to the suggestion that truth in ethics might be earned from within ethical thinking; and similarly in other areas where an issue about projection arises. His claim is that such a suggestion merely shirks a plainly necessary explanatory task: one in which

> we try to place the activity of moralizing, or the reaction of finding things funny ... In particular we try to fit our commitments in these areas into a metaphysical understanding of the kinds of fact the world contains: a metaphysical view which can properly be hostile to an unanalysed and *sui generis* area of moral or humorous ... facts. And relative to this interest, answers which merely cite the truth of various such verdicts are quite beside the point. This ... is because there is no theory connecting these truths to devices whereby we know about them – in other words no way of protecting our right to [conditionals of the form "If it hadn't been the case that *p* I would not be committed to *p*"].[20]

This passage raises several questions. I shall end this lecture by making three points about it.

First, note how the passage still strikes the note of theft as against honest toil, as if the target were still the kind of intuitionism that merely helps itself to a novel range of facts. This looks quite unwarranted once it is clear that there are three positions and not just two. The suggestion is not that we "merely cite the truth" – presumably alleged to be detected by some mysterious quasi-sensory capacities – of specific ethical verdicts, or judgments to the effect that something is funny. The aim is to give an account of how such verdicts and judgments are located in the appropriate region of the space of reasons. No particular verdict or judgment would be a sacrosanct starting-point, supposedly immune to critical scrutiny, in our earning the right to claim that some such verdicts or judgments stand a chance of being true. That is not at all to say that we must earn that right from an initial position in which *all* such verdicts or judgments are suspended at once, as in the projectivist picture of a range of responses to a world that does not contain values or instances of the comic.

The second point relates to the "metaphysical understanding" that Blackburn mentions. This fixes an inventory of "the kinds of fact the world contains." It fixes also, in parallel, a conception of the kinds of cognitive occurrence that can constitute access to facts: nothing will serve except what can be conceived in terms of the impact on us of the world as the "metaphysical understanding" understands it. That is why one is not allowed to count as protecting one's right to a conditional of the form "If it had not been the case that *p*, I would not have become committed to the belief that *p*" if one establishes that one would not have arrived at the belief that *p* had it not been for good reasons for it, with the excellence of the reasons vindicated from within the relevant way of thinking.

But how good are the credentials of a "metaphysical understanding" that blankly excludes values and instances of the comic from the world in advance of any philosophical enquiry into truth?[21] Surely if the history of philosophical reflection on the correspondence theory of truth has taught us anything, it is that there is ground for suspicion of the idea that we have some way of telling what can count as a fact, prior to and independent of asking what forms of words might count as expressing truths, so that a conception of facts could exert some leverage in the investigation of truth. We have no point of vantage on the question what can be the case, that is, what can be a fact, external to the modes of thought and speech we know our way around in, with whatever understanding of what counts as better and worse execution of them our mastery of them can give us. If there is enough substance to that understanding to enable us to rule out positions like MacIntyre's with a clear conscience, that is what it is for truth to be attainable in such thought and speech, and so much the worse for any prior "metaphysical understanding" which holds that there cannot be facts of that kind.[22] It is a matter for diagnosis and exorcism, not something that can be allowed without further ado to be a good starting-point for a philosophy of ethics or humor. To reiterate the first point, we need not be frightened out of this line by the bogey of "an unanalysed and *sui generis* area of moral or humorous … facts." That is what one gets if one accepts a familiar "metaphysical understanding" – one which is in fact quite dubious even in the areas where it is most tempting – with its picture of facts and our access to them, and then tries to accommodate exercises of ethical sensibilities or senses of humor within its framework; but that was never the proposal.

The third point is about "placing" ethics or humor. I have been suggesting that an undefended "metaphysical understanding" cannot impose binding intellectual obligations on anyone. But that is not to say there are no good questions in this general vicinity. Consider the world as natural science describes it. It is plausible (although not beyond dispute) that that "world" would not contain moral values or instances of the comic. (This is no concession to the "metaphysical understanding": what is missing is a reason to suppose that natural science has a foundational status in philosophical reflection about truth – that there can be no facts other than those that would figure in a scientific understanding of the world.) Now there is no reason not to raise the question as to how ethics or humor relate to the scientifically useful truth about the world and our dealings with it. There is no reason to dispute that a good answer to such questions can contribute to our making ourselves intelligible to ourselves in a way that we ought to find desirable. Finding things funny, for instance, can seem, from a certain fully intelligible perspective, a peculiar and even mysterious aspect of our lives, quite unlike, say, being able to tell what shapes things have, or even what colors things have. Anything that alleviated this sense of mystery would be welcome, and it would be anti-intellectual or obscurantist to deny that. What is unclear, however, is why it seems so obvious to Blackburn that this kind of consideration supports projectivism. No doubt reflections about the benefits of co-operation and social order go some distance towards "placing" ethics – making it intelligible that we inculcate ethical sensibilities in our young, trying to give ethics the importance to them that we believe is proper. (It is not at all obvious what might play an analogous role with senses of humor.) But we do not need to suppose that such "placing" functions by allowing us to make sense of a range of subjective responses to a world that contains nothing valuable, or funny- responses that we can then see as projected on to that world so as to generate the familiar appearances. What we "place" need not be the sort of sentiments that can be regarded as parents of apparent features: it may be pairs of sentiments and features reciprocally related – siblings rather than parents and children.

There is surely something right about the Humean idea of a "new creation" – the idea of a range of seeming states of affairs which would not be as they are if it were not for the distinctive affective coloration of our subjectivity. What does not follow is that the seeming states of affairs can be understood as creatures of independently intelligible operations of our affective nature. These seeming objectivities need not be a shadow or reflection of a self-contained subjectivity: understanding the genesis of the "new creation" may be understanding an interlocking complex of subjective and objective, of response and feature responded to. And in that case it is a mistake to think we can illuminate the metaphysics of these matters by appealing to the image of projection.

NOTES

1 See *A Treatise of Human Nature* I, iii. 14.

2 See his "Truth, Invention, and the Meaning of Life," *Proceedings of the British Academy* 62 (1976): 332–78, at pp. 338–9.

3 See chap. 1 of his *Ethics: Inventing Right and Wrong* (Harmondsworth: Penguin Books, 1977).

4 Among many other writings, see chap. 5 and 6 of Blackburn's *Spreading the Word* (Oxford: Clarendon Press, 1984).

5 *An Enquiry Concerning the Principles of Morals*, App. I.

6 See, e.g., *Spreading the Word*, pp. 167–71 [pp. 305–8, this volume].

7 Blackburn raises the question whether "a projective approach is too good to be true" at p. 219.

8 See Crispin Wright, "Realism, Anti-Realism, Irrealism, Quasirealism," *Midwest Studies in Philosophy*.

9 See p. 257: "Does this make moral commitments true in the same sense as others, or only in a different sense? I do not greatly commend the question."

10 See *Spreading the Word*, p. 194.

11 See, e.g., pp. 192, 197 [pp. 351 and 354–5, this volume]. I think Blackburn would regard Hume's treatment of the artificial virtues as a model of the kind of thing that would be required in a full version of the quasi-realist project, constructing truth out of an account of how projective thinking can allow for a substantial notion of better and worse ways of doing it.

12 London: Duckworth, 1981.

13 I am not suggesting that any ethical thought and language of which an account which is in some sense emotivist is true must dissolve such distinctions: cf. *Spreading the Word*, p. 197. (I have not questioned that ethical thought and speech engages our affective nature, and I suppose that is an emotivist insight.) But Stevenson's account does dissolve such distinctions: so it affords a good picture of a kind of threat in face of which earning truth should seem a good thing to attempt. (If MacIntyre is right, earning truth would involve a conceptual reform.)

14 This requires me to take issue with Blackburn when he says things like the following: "Of course, it is true that our reactions are 'simply felt' and, in a sense, not rationally explicable. But we should not be too worried about reason here. In general, reason follows where truth leads" [pp. 483–4, this volume]. By my lights this is the wrong way round. If we could not convince ourselves that our rankings of sensibilities were capable of being grounded in reason (as Blackburn's appeals, when it suits, to argument and criticism suggest they are), there would not be any reason to suppose that we had regained an application for the notion of truth.

15 Compare Blackburn's "Errors and the Phenomenology of Value," in Ted Honderich (ed.), *Morality and Objectivity* (London: Routledge & Kegan Paul, 1985), pp. 1–22, at p. 9.

16 This is at pp. 180–1 of "Opinions and Chances," in D. H. Mellor (ed.), *Prospects for Pragmatism* (Cambridge: Cambridge University Press, 1980), pp. 175–96. Blackburn makes the point that it would not be surprising, given a projectivist view, that "our best vocabulary for identifying the reaction should be the familiar one using the predicates we apply to the world we have spread." This seems right: once we have done the spreading, the resulting way

of talking will no doubt seem more natural to us than any other. But that is not the same as saying that there is no alternative way of identifying the response; if there is *no* alternative way, then there is no way of saying what has happened, in detail, in terms of the image of projection, and it is obscure why we should allow *that* to be consistent with projectivism.

17 [P. 471, this volume]. It may be worth mentioning in passing that the idea of rights as children of our sentiments seems an over-simplification of Hume's view.

18 See David Wiggins, "Truth, Invention, and the Meaning of Life," at p. 348; and for an elaboration of the thought there expressed that "an adequate account of these matters will have to treat psychological states and their objects as equal and reciprocal partners," see now "A Sensible Subjectivism?" in his *Needs, Values, Deliberation and Truth* (Oxford: Blackwell, 1987).

19 This is a serious question for anyone who is sympathetic to a quasi-realist projectivism about the comic. Much of what is ordinarily appealed to in ranking objects for amusement is suitably external but just for that reason not obviously relevant to *this* issue: for instance much humor that one may deplore as being "in bad taste" (usually on moralistic grounds) is not thereby shown not to be extremely *funny*. It seems highly implausible that we could extract out of the function of the sense of humor (if we knew it) something that would even seem to do the sort of work in a quasi-realist ranking of sensibilities that Blackburn seems to suggest is done in the ethical case by the function of ethical thinking.

20 "Errors and the Phenomenology of Value," pp. 17–18: the material in square brackets is supplied from p. 16.

21 Blackburn is extraordinarily unconcerned with this question. See *Spreading the Word*, p. 39, where "the best philosophical problems" are said to arise when "we get a sense of what the world is like, what it must be like," and cannot find room in it for this or that which we are loath to give up: for instance, "consciousness, agency, causation, or value." The question where we get this sense, and what its credentials might be, is not raised. Similarly at p. 146: "Once such doubts are felt – motivated in whatever way – a number of attitudes are possible." Again there is the striking lack of concern with the origin of the doubts, and this leaves no room for addressing the question of their merits. It is as if any bit of philosophy that comes naturally to us must be all right, ahead of any inquiry into why it comes naturally to us. (In my "Values and Secondary Qualities," in Honderich (ed.), op. cit., pp. 110–29 [Chapter 12, this volume], I consider and reject the suggestion that the favoritism of the "metaphysical understanding" might be defended on the basis of a conception of the real as what is explanatorily indispensable. Blackburn's purported response, in "Errors and the Phenomenology of Value," pp. 17–18, still takes the "metaphysical understanding" not to need defending: the response does not make contact with its purported target.)

22 Blackburn considers (see *Spreading the Word*, p. 236) the thesis that "there is no way in which any mind can step back from its own system of belief, survey without its benefit a reality the system aims to depict, and discover whether it is doing well or badly." I am not sure I understand his attitude to this thesis. In the chapter from which I have quoted those words, he considers (as in the passage under discussion in my text) only "correspondence conditionals" with directly causal underpinnings – cases where we can take quite literally the idea of reality making an impact on us. It would surely be a mistake to suppose that when we cite such causal underpinnings for the idea that we are capable of attaining the truth in some area, we are somehow managing after all to step outside reliance on the best we can do, from within our "system of belief," to afford reasons for bits of it. And one might think this

thought ought to neutralize "correspondence conditionals" in particular: that is just one shape that rationally underwritten "correspondence conditionals" can take. Blackburn, however, writes (pp. 247–8) as if such a thought involves a "gestalt-switch" akin to Idealism, and in competition with ascribing to objects and facts "their independence of us and our believings." It seems to me quite clear that there is no competition here. I am accordingly led to wonder if Blackburn is, in some submerged way, conceiving the causal impact on us of some facts as a way in which after all the World itself – what we would like to get a glimpse of head on, if we could only "step back" – penetrates the veil of our "system of belief" and gets through to us.

Part 9
THICK CONCEPTS

Thick *what*? Although it is a slightly odd term, we all use 'thick concepts' every day.

Imagine you are told that Jill is morally good. Given typical linguistic conventions, you probably get a strong sense that the person describing Jill is approving of her, or asking you to approve of her, or somesuch. Yet, people can be morally good in many, many ways, so you probably have little impression of the actions she typically performs and a concrete idea of her typical character. Now imagine that you are told that Jill is compassionate and kind. Again given typical linguistic conventions, you now probably have a slightly more detailed sense of Jill's character and her typical actions, more so than previously. After all, though he is also morally good, if we describe Jack as upright and honourable you start to form a different picture of him compared with that you might form of Jill. It's true that we still haven't pinpointed exactly Jill's typical character in this second case – people can be compassionate in many ways – but we get more of a sense of what she is like. However, the interesting thing, given our typical language, is that when Jill is described as compassionate we still get a strong, positive sense about her, that is she is still seemingly being approved of in some way.

Thick evaluative concepts – normally just 'thick concepts' – are those concepts and associated terms that in some fashion combine both some evaluative, attitudinative aspect with a descriptive, nonevaluative aspect in some fashion. Compassion and kindness might be thought to be two moral examples. But there are a whole host more: selfishness, just, mean-spiritedness, courage, slyness, loyalty, and so on. And thick concepts occur all over the place. In aesthetic discourse, let's imagine, we might describe paintings, novels and the rest as naïve, exhilarating, dark, static, playful, limp, strained and bubbly. Similarly, we might describe someone as reliable, or imaginative, or moody. These are not straightforward moral terms (or needn't be), but seem to have both descriptive and evaluative elements. Thick concepts are normally contrasted with thin concepts. Examples of the latter in the moral case include the aforementioned goodness, but also badness, rightness, wrongness and associated ideas such as obligation and duty. It might be harder in the aesthetic case to give uncontroversial examples of thin concepts, although beauty and ugliness might be good candidates, but the general idea might hold. In cases that are not straightforwardly moral or aesthetic, perhaps 'fine', 'okay', 'acceptable' and the like often function as thin terms. The general idea, then, behind an evaluative concept being thin is that it has only evaluative, attitudinative content, whereas thick concepts have this and descriptive content as well.

At this point many questions raise their heads, all of which metaethicists should think about. First, is there a sharp divide between the thin and the thick? Probably not. Working out why there is no sharp divide and thinking about the landscape of evaluation that emerges is interesting ('thinnish' and 'thicker' concepts, say). Following on from this, second, is there a sharp divide between the supposedly evaluative, on the one hand, and the descriptive or nonevaluative on the other? This is a tricky question both to formulate and to answer. Part of the philosophical interest and appeal of the thick is that it supposedly undermines the thought that there is always a sharp divide between the two. But, in that case, how exactly can we formally define the thick if not in terms of such concepts being combinations of descriptive and evaluative aspects, as this formulation presupposes the possibility of theoretical division in the first place. (Is there a real problem here? What do we mean by 'aspect' and 'element' in the first place?) A third question continues the general theme. Is there such a sharp division between, say, the moral and the aesthetic? Are there some concepts and associated terms that have aspects of both and have legitimate application to some objects and situations only because they are an interesting mixture of the moral and the aesthetic? A fourth issue has obvious repercussions for the first. Can a concept change its thickness across contexts? It seems that many can. For example, even though duty is often rightly thought to be fairly thin, in the mouth of an Italian Mafioso when talking about his family, or when used in a philosophy seminar about Kant's ethics, this term has all sorts of rich connotations that might justify thinking of it as being slightly thicker than normal. Similarly, terms might change their meaning over time. And additionally, the use of sarcasm and other linguistic devices might subvert typical conventions in all sorts of ways. Not only might a term change from being thin to being thick, but it might change from being positive to negative, say. For example, people might describe Jill as being good, but say it with a sarcastic tone, implying that she is a goody-goody two-shoes who's no fun and who unjustifiably sticks to the rules too often. There seems to be as much variety and fluidity regarding the thin and thick as there is in our typical language use. One final issue that then emerges is how important thick concepts are to understanding the evaluative viewpoints of cultures different from one's own. Because of the interesting mix of description and evaluation, some people think that it is very important to focus and understand the thick concepts first. And this leads some to think of the thick concepts as being central, with the thin concepts of approval and disapproval being somehow secondary.

As we've said, it is important for metaethicists to think about all of these issues. In this short Part we focus on an issue that carries on from Part 8. (So, the reader might wish to familiarize themselves with the papers in that Part first of all.) As we saw previously, expressivists are charged with the claim that they cannot explain our rational use of evaluative concepts as they must think them separable into two logically distinct elements of description and attitudinative evaluation. Debate about the thick supposedly brings this issue into sharp focus. (Note that quite a few thick concepts were employed in Part 8 as examples.) In the first paper in this Part, Stephan Burton (Chapter 26) mounts a defence of expressivism ('non-cognitivism'). He wishes to accommodate the insight from John McDowell and others that we looked at previously. We can put the argument against expressivism slightly differently. Seemingly, one can understand the use and meaning of thick terms only if one is in some way part of the practice oneself, either as an active participant or an imaginative onlooker who has tried to engage with how the people think. And it is certainly true that people can understand others' evaluative practices. Is it possible to achieve such understanding if one focuses only on the descriptive, nonevaluative features of situations and actions that are grouped together using the same evaluative term? No, because the moral is shapeless with respect to the natural. Therefore, any understanding must be a cognitive process that focuses on moral features and uses genuine moral concepts. We cannot separate the evaluative and descriptive aspects of thick concepts. In opposition to this, Burton claims that one can think this and still say that for many concepts and (possibly all) such concepts can be logically separated into two distinct parts, hence keeping one of the central ideas of expressivism alive. You will have to read his paper for the details, but the general idea is that the evaluatory part of the thick concept is the basic part, to which particular descriptive features are added, that is particular to an individual object or situation. In effect he wishes to undermine the McDowellian argument. Just because we cannot map wholly descriptive concepts onto our evaluative ones, this does not mean that we cannot separate evaluatory attitudinative elements from descriptive ones in many or all cases.

Are Burton's claims and argument successful? Eve Garrard and David McNaughton (Chapter 27) believe not. They start from cases where a term's typical evaluative aspect (sometimes referred to as its 'evaluative valency') is changed. For example, Jill's being thought sarcastically to be good, or delicacy being out of place in a triumphal arch. They note that Burton has to think that there is a nonevaluative version of the concept that is legitimately applied (so Jill is still good in a way since she follows the rules, and the arch really is delicate) with the difference coming from the reversal of the attitude. Garrard and McNaughton wonder how it is this nonevaluative, descriptive concept can be generated and this not run counter to Burton's main thesis. They suggest two ways in which this might happen, and reject both. Burton argues in Chapter 28 that neither way provides evidence that his position is wrong.

We leave the reader to think through the various ideas and counter-arguments offered by the authors. The main issue between them is what an expressivist has to be committed to in order to maintain her expressivism and, correspondingly, what realists (at least irreducible-realists) have to be committed to. How should we best characterize what we are doing when we pick out objects and situations in the same evaluative fashion? Can we pick out the delicate things nonevaluatively from outside an evaluative practice, but only understand and make finer-grained judgements from within the practice as Burton suggests?

As you read through the papers you should have concern for the questions we raised above. In particular, how should we characterize the work of anthropologists? How is it that they are able to understand the evaluative practices of peoples that they are investigating? And, what implications does this have for our ideas about the thick and for metaethics generally? Indeed, this raises one final question, which by now we hope you are used to. For much of the time we have talked about thick *concepts*. But what about thick *features* and *properties*? What implications does this have for moral metaphysics?

QUESTIONS TO CONSIDER AND TASKS TO COMPLETE

1   Try to explain the difference between the thin and the thick in your own words.
2   What is Burton's (Chapter 26) main argument in his paper? Why is his position expressivistic?
3   Try to think of some examples different from those you read about where the concept has an evaluative aspect different from its normal one. What is the reason for this change? Does it make sense to speak of 'normal' evaluative aspects for all thick concepts?
4   Explain in your own words Garrard and McNaughton's (Chapter 27) two ways in which Burton might construct the nonevaluative concept that maps onto the evaluative one. Why do they think neither will do?
5   Do the papers in Part 8 have particular relevance for thick evaluative concepts? In what way, if any, does the debate between expressivists and irreducible-realists become pronounced when we consider the thick rather than the thin? Which do you think is the logically prior type of concept, if either?

FURTHER READING

Blackburn, Simon (1992) 'Morality and Thick Concepts', *Proceedings of the Aristotelian Society*, suppl. vol. 66, pp. 285–99.

——(1998) *Ruling Passions* (Oxford: Oxford University Press), sections 4.2, 4.3 and 4.4.

Dancy, Jonathan (1995) 'In Defense of Thick Concepts', in Peter A. French, Theodore E. Uehling Jr., and Howard K. Wettstein (eds) *Midwest Studies in Philosophy, XX: Moral Concepts* (Minneapolis, MN: University of Minnesota Press), pp. 263–79.

Geertz, Clifford (1973) *The Interpretation of Cultures* (London: Fontana, pub. 1993), chapter 1, 'Thick Description: Toward an Interpretive Theory of Culture', pp. 3–32.

Gibbard, Allan (1992) 'Morality and Thick Concepts', *Proceedings of the Aristotelian Society*, suppl. vol. 66, pp. 267–83.

Moore, A. W. (2003) 'Williams on Ethics, Knowledge and Reflection', *Philosophy,* vol. 78, pp. 337–54.

Scanlon, T. M. (2003) 'Thickness and Theory', *Journal of Philosophy,* vol. 100, no. 6, pp. 275–87.

Scheffler, Samuel (1987) 'Morality through Thick and Thin: A Critical Notice of *Ethics and the Limits of Philosophy*', *The Philosophical Review,* vol. 96, no. 3, pp. 411–34.

Sreenivasan, Gopal (2001) 'Understanding Alien Morals', *Philosophy and Phenomenological Research,* vol. 62, no. 1, pp. 1–32.

Williams, Bernard (1985) *Ethics and the Limits of Philosophy* (London: Fontana), chapters 8 and 9.

26

'THICK' CONCEPTS REVISED

Stephan Burton

The sort of analysis of so-called 'thick' ethical concepts usually proposed by non-cognitivists has given rise to a problem for their account of ethical evaluation, since it is by no means clear that such an analysis can always be carried out. This problem can be overcome by a simple revision of the usual sort of analysis.

1

Ethical non-cognitivists seek to maintain a strict distinction between description and evaluation. To the extent terms have evaluative force, they seek to construe them as merely expressing approval, commendation, or endorsement, as opposed to conveying cognitive content. Thick ethical concepts like 'courage' have thus seemed to some to pose a challenge for non-cognitivists due to their obvious element of descriptive content.

The challenge has usually been met by analysing such terms into strictly separate descriptive and evaluative components. Thus courage involves, perhaps, sticking to one's guns (literally or figuratively) despite great personal risk, among other possible purely descriptive elements of the concept. To such elements those cultures that share our concept of courage attach an additional note of approval, which constitutes the separate evaluative element.

In general, on the usual view, thick concepts are basically descriptions to which evaluative force has been tacked on for good measure. As Bernard Williams puts it, '[a]ny such concept, on that account, can be analysed into a descriptive and a prescriptive element: it is guided round the world by its descriptive content, but has a prescriptive flag attached to it'.[1] He goes on to add that non-cognitivism holds that 'what governs the application of the concept to the world is the descriptive element and the evaluative interest of the concept plays no part in this'. He concludes: 'It follows that, for any concept of this sort, you could produce another that picked out just the same features of the world but worked simply as a descriptive concept, lacking any prescriptive or evaluative force.'

The trouble is, according to Williams, that there is no reason to believe that this will always be possible. How we 'go on' from one application of a concept to another is a function of the kind of interest that the concept represents, and we should not assume that we could see how people 'go on' if we did not share the evaluative perspective in which this kind of concept has its point. In this opinion Williams is at one with John McDowell, who has argued at length that participation in an evaluative practice may play an essential role in ability to use the associated evaluative concepts.[2] Thus perhaps one who did not participate in the evaluative practice of our and related cultures might not so much as be able to identify the courageous acts – to tell them apart from the merely foolhardy ones, for example.

This problem becomes particular acute in the case of aesthetic evaluation. Indeed it is in precisely those cases where thick ethical concepts have a certain 'aesthetic' feel to them – where their application seems to be a matter of taste – that Williams's and McDowell's challenge seems most plausible. While many ethical theories come well supplied with purely descriptive rules for evaluation, in aesthetics they are notoriously hard to come by; it has often been argued that there just *aren't* any useful general principles of aesthetic evaluation based on descriptive properties alone.[3] This point applies not only to the most general aesthetic evaluations, but to thick aesthetic concepts like *delicate* as well.[4]

Thus, in particular, it might plausibly be argued that one cannot so much as correctly apply a term like 'delicate' (in its evaluative sense), by means of any set of purely descriptive criteria – that one cannot tell a delicate watercolour from a merely bland one, for example, without fully engaging in the practice of aesthetic evaluation.

Now there are, of course, certain characteristic marks of delicacy of a purely descriptive character. It may involve small size, pale colours, fragility, and so on. But not just *any* small size, pale colours, and fragility will do the trick. Only some small, pale, fragile things are delicate; the vast majority are merely bland. So use of such marks alone will not enable one to identify objects as at all likely to be *good* in virtue thereof, if at all. To accomplish that, one must enter fully into the evaluative practice.

But if this is right, and in certain cases one could not even pick out what falls under some thick evaluative concept without oneself engaging in the relevant evaluative practice, then in such cases it might seem as if evaluation were playing an ineliminable cognitive role. This would endanger the non-cognitivist's distinction between description and evaluation. If that distinction is to be maintained, no such apparently cognitive role can be allowed for the purely evaluative component of thick evaluative concepts. If one claims that 'courage' means something like 'sticking to one's guns despite great personal risk ... and therefore (*pro tanto*) good', where 'good' is to be construed as merely expressing approval, commendation, or endorsement, then one had better be able to pick out the courageous actions simply by applying the first part of the analysis without resorting to evaluation one way or the other, or it will look as if one's analysis has failed successfully to separate out the purely descriptive from the purely evaluative components in the concept. The same goes for any comparable attempt to analyse 'delicate', *mutatis mutandis*.

In general, so long as the (positively valenced) thick concept 'C' is to be analysed as 'X, Y, Z, etc. ... and therefore (*pro tanto*) good', where 'X, Y, Z, etc.' are purely descriptive and 'good' is purely prescriptive, one must be able to apply 'C' by means of 'X, Y, Z, etc.' alone. But it seems that this is something one cannot always count on being able to do.

2

Note that the whole problem rests on the usual non-cognitivist account of thick evaluative concepts, which interprets them as basically descriptions to which evaluative force has been tacked on for good measure. But that is only one way of attempting to separate the evaluative from the descriptive in such concepts. Why not try going the other way round, interpreting thick aesthetic concepts as basically *evaluations* with added descriptive *qualifications*?

If a concept picks out some purely descriptive kind, then one might reasonably expect what falls under it to be susceptive of purely descriptive identification. But if a concept is basically expressive of evaluation, there is no reason to expect it to pick out some independently identifiable descriptive kind. Why should the psychological states associated with approval, commendation, or endorsement be geared to properties neatly assessable in terms of the categories of physical science?

So instead of analysing (positively valenced) thick concept 'C' as 'X, Y, Z, etc. ... and therefore (*pro tanto*) good' one might define it as '(*pro tanto*) good ... in virtue of some particular instance of X, Y, Z, etc.', where again 'good' is purely prescriptive and 'X, Y, Z, etc.' are purely descriptive. The purpose of applying such a concept is basically to express an evaluation, but an evaluation that zeros in on certain particular aspects of what one values. Thus 'delicate' means not 'small, pale, fragile, etc. ... and therefore (*pro tanto*) good', but, rather, '(*pro tanto*) good ... in virtue of some particular instance of small size, pale colours, fragility, etc.'. Similarly, 'courage' means not 'sticking to one's guns despite great personal risk ... and therefore (*pro tanto*) good', but, rather, '(*pro tanto*) good ... in virtue of some particular instance of sticking to one's guns despite great personal risk'.

The phrase 'some particular instance of' is crucial, since it avoids the implication that the specified descriptive elements constitute a purely descriptive reduction of the 'thick' concept in question, or even that any such reduction is possible. In each unique case, a C thing is (*pro tanto*) good in virtue of something much more specific than just X, Y, Z, etc. It's not as if merely being X, Y, Z, etc. is sufficient to make something C: most X, Y, Z, etc. things are *not* C. Still, there are any number of cases in which something will be good in virtue of *particular instances* of X, Y, Z, etc. One groups all such cases together under the thick evaluative concept 'C', simply ignoring the fact that one's evaluation in each such case depends on the various different characteristics and contexts of the various particular instances of X, Y, Z, etc.

In sum, this analysis of thick evaluative concepts maintains a strict distinction between description and evaluation while allowing for the fact that one may not be able correctly to apply such concepts by means of purely descriptive criteria alone.

On the other hand, the goodness (or badness) of other evaluative qualities may be clearly governed by principles. Perhaps a definitive descriptive reduction of 'courageous' is available that always differentiates it from 'foolhardy', for example. I don't know. If it is, then anything fitting that descriptive reduction *will* be (*pro tanto*) good in virtue thereof, in which case '(*pro tanto*) good ... in virtue of some particular instance of X, Y, Z, etc.' will simply collapse into 'X, Y, Z, etc. ... and therefore (*pro tanto*) good'. But that's all right, since these will just be the cases where the usual analysis didn't lead to any problems anyway.

3

Nothing restricts the account of thick evaluative concepts proposed above to the exclusive use of non-cognitivists; indeed quite apart from its application to the dispute between cognitivists and non-cognitivists, I think the revision provides a perspicuous and true-to-the-facts picture of the operation of such concepts, and particularly of their relation to their non-evaluative counterparts. After all, 'delicate' is not always a term of praise: in a battle hymn or a triumphal arch delicacy is probably not even *pro tanto* good; one can sensibly criticize someone's brushwork as being too delicate, by which one may well not mean that it is too '*pro tanto* good etc.'. Evidently there must be a purely descriptive use of the term. But how is that possible, if, as I claim, thick concepts are basically evaluations?

I think it's easy to see how each thick evaluative concept will automatically generate a corresponding non-evaluative concept. Everything that satisfies the purely descriptive part of the analysis of the former will satisfy the latter, whether or not it is any good in virtue thereof. So anything that is small, pale, fragile, etc., will count as 'delicate' in a purely descriptive sense, whether or not it is *good* in virtue of small size, pale colours, fragility, etc. Now obviously there is no paradox in complaining of such a quality in a battle hymn or triumphal arch, or in criticizing an excess of it in someone's brushwork.

Thus even though the particular constellations of qualities picked out by such concepts may have special relevance to our evaluative interests, they turn out to be independently useful for purely descriptive tasks.[5]

NOTES

1 This and the following quotations from Bernard Williams are all from page 141 of his *Ethics and the Limits of Philosophy* (Cambridge, MA: Harvard University Press, 1985).
2 Williams cites McDowell's 'Are Moral Requirements Hypothetical Imperatives?', *Proceedings of the Aristotelian Society*, suppl. vol. 52 (1978), pp. 13–30, and 'Virtue and Reason', *Monist* 62 (1979), pp. 331–50; see also 'Non-cognitivism and Rule Following' [Chapter 23, this volume].
3 The *locus classicus* of this position is Arnold Isenberg's 'Critical Communication', in *Aesthetics and the Theory of Criticism: Selected Essays of Arnold Isenberg* (Chicago, IL: University of Chicago Press, 1973), pp. 156–71.
4 See, e.g., Frank Sibley's 'Aesthetic Concepts', in *Art and Philosophy Readings in Aesthetics*, 2nd edn, edited by W. E. Kennick (New York: St Martin's Press, 1979), pp. 687–706.
5 I wish to thank Kendall Walton, Peter Railton, the editor of this journal, and an anonymous referee for their helpful comments on an earlier draft of this essay.

27

THICK CONCEPTS REVISITED: A REPLY TO BURTON

Eve Garrard and David McNaughton

In Chapter 26 of this volume, '"Thick" concepts revised', Stephan Burton offers an interesting defence of the non-cognitivist analysis of 'thick' ethical (and aesthetic) concepts against an objection raised both by Bernard Williams and John McDowell. The non-cognitivist claim is that such concepts can always be analysed into independent descriptive and evaluative components; the evaluative dress can always be peeled off to reveal the descriptive underwear beneath. The objection to this view is that correct application of 'thick' concepts requires, in at least some of the cases, participation in the evaluative practice itself, without which we may not be able to identify the relevant non-evaluative properties from case to case. These properties may form a group which is quite shapeless at the non-evaluative level. In such cases, participation in the relevant evaluative stance seems to be *cognitively* necessary for the correct application of the concept, in contradiction to the non-cognitivist analysis.

Burton's proposal is that 'thick' evaluative concepts (such as 'delicate') should not be analysed as a set of descriptive properties (such as paleness, smallness, and fragility) plus an evaluation, but rather as a basic evaluation with descriptive qualifications at the token level (so 'delicate' is analysed as (*pro tanto*) good, in virtue of some *particular* instantiations of paleness, smallness and fragility etc.). This analysis maintains a sharp distinction between cognitive and evaluative elements, while allowing that a grasp of the descriptive properties is insufficient for the correct application of the concept – there are times when things are small, pale and fragile, but are bland rather than delicate. What we have here is a particularist form of non-cognitivism: the evaluation is attached to a cluster of property-tokens rather than property-types. Discerning just which cases of smallness, paleness and fragility are delicate (and hence aesthetically good) will require participation in the aesthetic evaluative practice, thus meeting the objection at issue.

A crucial problem for this analysis arises in cases where the 'thick' concept seems to be correctly applied, but with a neutral or reversed evaluative valency. (Delicacy may not be aesthetically desirable in a triumphal arch or battle hymn.) Here Burton suggests that 'each thick concept will automatically generate a corresponding non-evaluative concept' [p. 514, this volume] which can be correctly applied in cases where the evaluation is absent or reversed. But now we must ask how this non-evaluative concept of delicacy is to be constructed.

Is it the case that *anything* 'that is small, pale and fragile etc., will count as "delicate" in a purely descriptive sense', as Burton claims [p. 514, this volume] (Burton has reaffirmed this claim in private correspondence.) If this were the case, then we would have access to the non-evaluative concept of delicacy through purely descriptive criteria, but knowledge of which of these cases were also evaluatively delicate would be acquired only through extensive familiarity with the evaluative practice, thus preserving Williams's and McDowell's insight. This move will not work, however, since we have it from Burton himself [p. 512, this volume] that many cases of smallness, paleness and fragility etc. are not delicate at all, but merely bland. So this way of generating the non-evaluative concept of delicacy leaves us unable to discriminate between cases where something is small, pale and fragile etc. and is non-evaluatively delicate, but isn't even *pro tanto* good, and cases where something is small, pale and fragile etc., but isn't delicate at all.

The alternative possibility is that the construction of the non-evaluative concept of delicacy starts from just those instantiations of smallness, paleness and fragility etc. which are evaluatively delicate. This move will not work either. We already have it from McDowell and Williams (whose arguments Burton is trying to accommodate) that these instantiations are shapeless at the non-evaluative level. In any case, a construction starting with these instantiations would not, of course, be available independently of the evaluative practice, as Burton requires for the concept of non-evaluative delicacy (see the final sentence of Chapter 26, this volume).

So either way of constructing the non-evaluative concept which corresponds to some 'thick' evaluative concept turns out to run counter to central features of Burton's argument. The route from subvenient base properties to non-evaluative concept leaves us unable to distinguish the delicate from the bland (the very distinction which motivates his particularist version of non-cognitivism). The route from the evaluative to the non-evaluative concept ignores the epistemological and metaphysical claims which his account of thick concepts purports to accommodate.[1]

NOTE

1   We are grateful to Stephan Burton, Jonathan Dancy and Brad Hooker for comments on an earlier version of this paper.

28

REPLY TO GARRARD AND McNAUGHTON

Stephan Burton

Eve Garrard and David McNaughton (Chapter 27, this volume) sketch two ways of 'constructing the non-evaluative concept which corresponds to a "thick" evaluative concept' and object that 'either way ... turns out to run counter to central features of Burton's argument'. My reply is that neither does.

The first way I described as follows in '"Thick" Concepts Revised' (Chapter 26, this volume):

> each 'thick' evaluative concept will automatically generate a corresponding non-evaluative concept. Everything that satisfies the purely descriptive part of the analysis of the former will satisfy the latter, whether or not it is any good in virtue thereof. So anything that is small, pale, fragile, etc., will count as 'delicate' in a purely descriptive sense, whether or not it is *good* in virtue of small size, pale colours, fragility, etc.
>
> (p. 514, this volume)

These non-evaluative counterparts are, in fact, available independently of participation in any particular evaluative practice. But it doesn't follow that the evaluative versions are as well, since the non-evaluative counterparts mark out much broader extensions: all the (evaluatively) delicate things are (non-evaluatively) delicate, but not vice versa. Anything that is small, pale, fragile, etc., is delicate in a purely descriptive sense, whether or not it is any good in virtue thereof. So anyone who can pick out smallness, paleness, fragility, etc., can pick out the non-evaluatively delicate things – but it takes a lot more than that to pick out the evaluatively delicate things, i.e. participation in the relevant evaluative practice. You have to be able to tell which things 'work' in virtue of their small size, pale colours, fragility, etc., and which things don't.

I think this matches ordinary usage: there are all sorts of things I would call delicate in a non-evaluative sense that I wouldn't call delicate in an evaluative sense. For example, if someone were to draw two lines on a blackboard, one jagged, the other gently curved, and then ask which one was delicate, anyone could see that it was the gently curved one (albeit not in virtue of small size, paleness, or fragility – there must be something in the 'etc.' about gently curved lines). But obviously one would not intend to praise such a line by calling it delicate: this is the broad, non-evaluative usage, mastery of which would in no way enable one to recognize evaluative delicacy – for example, to distinguish the exquisite delicacy of much of Fauré's chamber music from the mere blandness of much of Saint-Saëns'.

In short, on my account certain non-evaluative counterparts of thick evaluative concepts are available independent of any particular evaluative practice, but I don't think this is a problem, since McDowell's and Williams's point only applies to the evaluative versions of such concepts, which remain, on my account, much less easily accessible.

To this McNaughton and Garrard object that 'this way of generating the non-evaluative concept of delicacy leaves us unable to discriminate between cases where something is small, pale and fragile etc. and is nonevaluatively delicate, but isn't even (*pro tanto*) good, and cases where something is small, pale and fragile etc., but isn't delicate at all', observing that I myself claim 'that many cases of smallness, paleness and fragility etc. are not delicate at all, but merely bland'. But throughout the earlier part of '"Thick" Concepts Revised' I consistently use 'delicate' only in its evaluative sense – so my claim (p. 512, this volume) that 'only some small, pale, fragile things are delicate; the vast majority are merely bland' is entirely consistent with my later claim (p. 514, this volume) that anything that is small, pale, fragile, etc., will count as "delicate" in a purely descriptive sense'. In other words, in this descriptive sense there just *aren't* any 'cases where something is small, pale and fragile etc., but isn't delicate'.

McNaughton and Garrard's second way is not described in '"Thick" Concepts Revised'; they characterize it like this: 'construction of the non-evaluative concept of delicacy starts from just those instantiations of smallness, paleness and fragility etc. which are evaluatively delicate'. To this they object that 'these instantiations are shapeless at the non-evaluative level' and that 'construction starting with these instantiations would not, of course, be available independently of the evaluative practice, as Burton requires'.

Now I do require such independent availability for the non-evaluative usage described above, but not for this second non-evaluation usage, which is another matter entirely. There probably is some such non-evaluative usage of thick concepts that might share the same extension as their evaluative usage – i.e., the familiar 'inverted commas' usage, which I would gloss along the lines of 'what is thought (but not by me!) good in virtue of some particular instance of x, y, z etc'. This extension might be shapeless apart from the evaluative practice of those other than oneself who use the expression sincerely, in which case its correct use would require at least extensive familiarity with that evaluative practice. For example, one might be so *over*-familiar with French chamber music that one has bred in oneself contempt for *all* of it, in which case one might reliably distinguish Fauré's delicacy from Saint-Saëns' blandness without valuing either. So far as I can tell, such cases contradict neither McDowell's and Williams's point nor my account in '"Thick" Concepts Revised'.

Part 10

JUDGEMENT AND MOTIVATION

You are talking with someone about the beauty of Autumn, the rusty browns and the fire bright oranges. However, to your amazement you discover that she has been blind from birth and that she can only talk about colours by 'reading them off' from the light frequency emitted by things. After learning this you test her and find out that she can use all colour terms very well. But now, knowing what you do, you worry whether she really grasps the colour concepts.

This may seem a strange – if not a contrived! – starting point for Part 10. After all, what has this got to do with moral judgement and motivation? Well, it highlights the apparent intractability of debates concerning whether or not someone has grasped a concept. If, for instance, you insisted that the blind person did understand the colour concepts and someone insisted that they didn't, then what would you do to resolve the debate? It seems that on the face of it you'd have to agree to disagree.

As it stands, this looks similar to discussions in metaethics concerning the relationship between judgement and motivation, and in particular it looks similar to the debate between *internalists* and *externalists* about motivation. The internalist claims that there is a necessary conceptual connection between making a moral judgement and being motivated to act. Thus, if I judge that it is right to poke cats with sticks then, as matter of necessity, I'll be motivated to do so (if internalism is right). There are two things to note right away about this claim. First, the debate is only about the relationship between the judgement someone makes and their being motivated. We are not concerned with whether their judgement is true or false. Second, the idea is only that there is some degree of motivation. It could be that I judge that I should poke a particular cat, but also judge that I should leave the scene before the angry, cat-owning, animal rights activist catches me and punishes me for all the previous occasions I've poked their cat. Perhaps the motivation to run away is stronger than the motivation to poke their cat. But even if there were motivation of *some* strength to poke the cat, then the internalist claim can be upheld.

We can put the internalist claim another way. If a cat wanders by, and I judge it is right to poke this cat, and I have a stick in my hand (and there is no other physical impediment to my doing so), and I don't make other judgements that would bring with them motivations to run away or otherwise fail to poke the cat, then it looks as if I haven't really understood what I say. If internalism is right, then I have somehow failed to grasp the concepts involved. Either that, or there is something strange about my general motivational state. (There will be more on this last caveat in the final paragraph.)

Externalists, in contrast, are not committed to there being some conceptual confusion. They hold that if I judge that it is right to poke the cat with a stick, then I will be motivated only if I *also* have a desire to do so. So if I have a stick in my hand and a cat wanders by and I don't poke it, then this is not because I've failed to understand what I mean when I make the moral judgement. I simply lack the relevant desire. In other words, externalists think of the connection between judgement and motivation as contingent, not necessary.

The debate between the internalist and externalist then seems to boil down to the same sort of issues as the debate about the blind colour judge. How do we ascertain whether or not someone has grasped a concept? Have we really understood what it is for something to be right if we fail to be motivated? Without some further consideration it seems like the internalist and externalist are going to have to agree to disagree – certainly an unsatisfactory state of affairs.

In the first article in this Part, Michael Smith (Chapter 29) argues that there is no need to be downhearted, because there is a fact that both internalists and externalists should agree on, but only the internalist can adequately explain. There is a *striking fact* that people's motivations reliably track their judgements. If we judge that it is right to trip people over and are so motivated, we would expect that if we came to believe that it was wrong to do so, our motivation would change accordingly.

Drawing our attention to this striking fact helps because it is easy for the internalist to explain: if there is a conceptual connection between moral judgement and motivation then, necessarily, if judgement changes motivation will also change. The externalist, Smith claims, will struggle to explain it. Here's why.

The externalist has two options in accounting for the striking fact. This is evident once we notice that it is ambiguous to claim, simply, that a particular person desires to do what is right. It could mean that for each thing that is in fact right that person desires to do that thing. (Smith calls this the *de re* reading.) Or it could mean that that person has a desire with the content 'to do whatever is right' and ends up doing the things that fall under such a description. (Smith calls this the *de dicto* reading.) In other words, two agents, both of whom wish to do right things, might end acting in the same way but for different reasons. One agent, acting according to the *de re* reading, will be focused on the right things themselves, whilst the other agent, who acts according to the *de dicto* reading, will be focused on the rightness of the things. According to Smith, the problem is that neither interpretation can do the job for externalists in explaining the striking fact.

According to the *de re* reading, an agent must be motivated by what in fact makes an action right. But say we desire to trip people up. This desire is not apt to change *merely because* we change our belief, at least on an externalist reading. If the link between judging that it is right to trip people up and being motivated to do so is contingent in the first place (as it is according to externalists), then changing the belief needn't bring with it any change in motivation at all. To think otherwise throws suspicion on the idea that the link is contingent. To think that there is always a change, but that each and every time such a change happens we have only a pure coincidence, might strike us as too far-fetched.

More likely the externalist would take the second *de dicto* route, where the agent is said to have a standing desire to do what ever in fact turns out to be right. If we change our belief concerning what is right, then this new belief will, as it were, 'plug into' the standing desire to do what is right and as such the motivation tracks changes in moral judgement.

However, Smith claims that this *de dicto* externalist model is also problematic as it misinterprets the psychology of moral agents. In particular, it turns the moral agent into a *moral fetishist*. If we judge that it is right to give money to charity, what motivates us to do so ought to be, say, that we will help starving children. If our motivation for giving money to charity is that this is what we are morally required to do, then this doesn't seem to fit with what we expect from the psychology of a morally good agent. We don't think that the good agent would desire to help starving children instrumentally. That is see such an action as instrumental towards satisfying the thing that she really cares about, namely pursuing moral rightness. If someone has this extra desire to do what is right (*de dicto*) then this seems to be simply one thought too many. (We can put this another way, both to help with the readings and to anticipate a thought below. It is as if the agent fails, what we can call, the *basic tracking condition*. We want people, in their desires, to track what it is right to do. But it seems that agency, according to the *de dicto* reading, isn't meeting the basic tracking condition in the right sort of way. An agent is doing all of the right things, but for the wrong reasons. They are doing them only because they are on the list of the right things to do, not because they care about people and the like.)

If Smith is correct, then the externalist has a problem. On the one hand she accepts the striking fact, on the other she cannot accommodate it. The debate has ceased to be intractable and the internalist emerges triumphant.

James Dreier in Chapter 30 defends externalism. He claims that Smith's discussion is incomplete as it misses out two externalist options.

The first option centres on the *suggestible* person. She has a disposition to desire to perform a certain kind of action upon coming to believe that that kind of action is morally right. So, she doesn't have a standing belief that poking cats with sticks is right. But, as she comes to believe that such an action falls under the description 'is right', she sees – by some strange process – that it is right to poke cats with sticks. This accounts for the striking fact because *whatever* you come to believe you will have the appropriate desire. Importantly, the desire will be original and noninstrumental, and hence not fetishistic.

You might worry though that this isn't going to avoid the problems Smith raised. If, as with the morally suggestible person, the desire *depends* on the belief, then it *is* instrumental, and if the desire is instrumental then isn't the morally suggestible agent also guilty of fetishism? Well, Dreier thinks not. Sure the desire depends on the belief, but only in the same way that your desire to poke cats with sticks depends on your belief that there are such things as cats. If you believed that there were no such things as cats then your desire would cease to exist. It is to this type of dependency that this externalist model is committed and this type of dependency isn't problematic. As such, Dreier argues, we can't accuse the morally suggestible person of moral fetishism.

So the morally suggestible person is a genuine candidate for the externalist model of motivation. However, Dreier thinks that it is not the only one and, in fact, that it is not even the best.

Dreier's second suggestion is an agent who has a desire to acquire noninstrumental desires to perform acts with right-making features. He calls this a *second order desires* model because it ascribes desires about desires to the agent. What is important to notice is that this isn't the same as the suggestible agent just discussed. Dreier makes this clear with examples.

Ursula is a morally suggestible agent who is a utilitarian and as such desires that the net happiness of sentient beings be maximized. She is aware that she is suggestible and also aware that it is possible, though not likely, that some individual rights should properly act as side constraints against utility maximization. This troubles her because she thinks that she might someday *correctly* become convinced that rights theory is correct, and no longer pursue utilitarianism. But then this means much of the suffering that she could relieve would remain in the world. It is no good for her to think (now) that she would think (in the future) that respecting people's rights is good because, at this moment, she doesn't care about people's rights. This, Dreier claims, is the entirely wrong attitude for a good moral agent. A good moral agent who believes in utilitarianism but thinks that there is a chance that a rights-based theory is correct would surely want to investigate this possibility.

This contrasts with David who has a second order desire that he desires to do whatever is right. If he thought that it possible that moral side constraints were a fundamental feature of true morality, his second order desire would motivate him to investigate. For he desires to have desires of a certain sort, and he knows that probably the only way he can have desires of that sort is through investigation. Ursula doesn't desire to have desires of a certain sort; she has the desires that she is disposed to have.

So, the morally suggestible model is not the same as the second order desire model, because the former can't respect this *sophisticated tracking constraint*, where motivations follow not simply beliefs, but also one's uncertainty as to whether one is correct in one's beliefs. On the other hand, an agent understood according to the second order desire does meet this new condition. So it seems then that if Dreier is right the externalist should adopt the second order desire model which can accommodate both the basic and sophisticated tracking condition. There is only one hurdle left. Dreier ends his paper by showing that the second order desire model is not another form of fetishism. So, if Dreier is right, it seems that we need not adopt internalism. There is no need to deny the possibility of an agent who is psychologically normal but who judges that something is right but fails to be motivated. But of course, the question remains whether Dreier is right. You might, for instance, worry that he is inventing rather than discovering the moral psychology he discusses. Or you might find that when you read and think about his work the two positions that he outlines are not distinct. Or that it is now not as clear what the argument between the internalist and externalist is.

One last thought to take us back to Smith's position. Recall earlier the caveat to the effect that internalism is right for every case unless we are dealing with a person who has some odd psychology. Such psychologies might be 'odd' and 'abnormal', but might be far from rare. The sorts of case Smith has in mind are cases of weakness of will where we judge that we shouldn't eat the chocolate cake because we're on a diet, but end up gorging ourselves nonetheless; and various cases of mental illness such as depression, where we might judge that our job and family are important to us but nevertheless feel little motivation to go to work or nurture our relationships. Many other types of case might abound. Smith has to excuse these types of case because, if they are genuine phenomena, they threaten internalism before we even begin to discuss what we've been discussing. Clearly, in these cases, judgement and motivation are not necessarily linked: we 'judge' that it is bad to eat the cake but do so nevertheless. We then have to provide a reason – either general or for every particular example – as to why someone has seemingly employed the right concepts in their thinking, but haven't really done so. Whether Smith can successfully do this is another question you should ask yourself. (See also Miller (1996, 2003) and Smith (1996) in Further Reading below.)

QUESTIONS TO CONSIDER AND TASKS TO COMPLETE

1   What does it mean to say that it is fetishistic to desire to do whatever is right (*de dicto*)?
2   Illustrate the distinction between a contingent and a conditioned desire.
3   Dreier (Chapter 30) criticizes the morally suggestible person because her motivations do not 'seem to track her general doxastic state in quite the right way'. What does this mean? Is he correct?
4   What would Smith (Chapter 29) disagree with in Dreier's two externalist models?
5   Why does Dreier think that talking about second order desires allows him to respond to the fetishistic challenge?
6   Read the discussion about Humeanism in Part 11. Is Dreier a Humean?
7   Is there a possible position that is neither internalist nor externalist?
8   What role should empirical research have in this debate?

FURTHER READING

Joyce, Richard (2002) 'Expressivism and Motivation Internalism', *Analysis*, vol. 62, no. 4, pp. 336–44.

Lillehammer, Hallvard (1997) 'Smith on Moral Fetishism', *Analysis*, vol. 57, no. 3, pp. 187–95.

Miller, Alexander (1996) 'An Objection to Smith's Argument from Externalism', *Analysis*, vol. 56, no. 3, pp. 169–74.

——(2003) *An Introduction to Contemporary Metaethics* (Cambridge: Polity Press), pp. 217–27.

Simpson, Evan (1999) 'Between Internalism and Externalism in Ethics', *Philosophical Quarterly*, vol. 49, no. 195, pp. 201–14.

Smith, Michael (1996) 'The Argument for Internalism: Reply to Miller', *Analysis*, vol. 56, no. 3, pp. 175–83.

Stratton-Lake, Philip (1998) 'Internalism and the Explanation of Belief/Motivation Changes', *Analysis*, vol. 56, pp. 311–15.

Van Roojen, Mark (2000) 'Motivational Internalism: A Somewhat Less Idealized Account', *Philosophical Quarterly*, vol. 50, no. 199, pp. 233–41.

——(2002) 'Humean and Anti-Humean Internalism about Moral Judgements', *Philosophy and Phenomenological Research*, vol. 65, no. 1, pp. 26–49.

Zangwill, Nick (2003) 'Externalist Moral Motivation', *American Philosophical Quarterly*, vol. 40, no. 2, pp. 143–54.

29

THE EXTERNALIST CHALLENGE

Michael Smith

1 INTERNALISM VS. EXTERNALISM

Suppose we debate the pros and cons of giving to famine relief and you convince me that I should give. However when the occasion arises for me to hand over my money I say 'But wait! I know I *should* give to famine relief. But you haven't convinced me that I have any *reason* to do so!' And so I don't.

I suggested earlier that such an outburst would occasion serious puzzlement. Having convinced me that I should give to famine relief you seem to have done everything you need to do to convince me that I have a reason to do so. And having convinced me that I have a reason to give to famine relief – absent weakness of will or some other such psychological failure – you seem to have done everything you need to do to motivate me to do so. Puzzlement would thus naturally arise because, having convinced me that I should donate, you would quite rightly expect me to hand over my money. *Believing I should* seems to bring with it *my being motivated to* – at least absent weakness of will and the like.

This idea that moral judgement has a practical upshot, is generally referred to as 'internalism' (Falk, 1948; Frankena, 1958; Davidson, 1970; Williams, 1980; Brink, 1986; Korsgaard, 1986; Railton, 1986; Wallace, 1990; Darwall *et al.*, 1992). Unfortunately, however, 'internalism' is a vague label in the philosophical literature, used to refer to several quite different claims about the connection between moral facts or judgements on the one hand, and having reasons or being motivated on the other (as noted by both Brink and Wallace). Let me begin by spelling out some of these rather different claims.

Sometimes the idea behind internalism is that there is the following conceptual connection between moral judgement and the will (Nagel, 1970; McDowell, 1978, 1979, 1985; Platts, 1979, 1981).

> If an agent judges that it is right for her to φ in circumstances C, then she is motivated to φ in C.

In other words, moral judgement brings motivation with it *simpliciter*. This is a very strong claim. It commits us to denying that, for example, weakness of the will and the like may defeat an agent's moral motivations while leaving her appreciation of her moral reasons intact. And for this very reason it is, I think, a manifestly implausible claim as well. However I will not have anything more to say about it here; rather I defer discussion of this version of internalism until the next chapter, when it re-emerges as a consequence of one sort of anti-Humean theory of motivation.

More plausibly, then, the idea behind internalism is sometimes that though there is a conceptual connection between moral judgement and the will, the connection involved is the following *defeasible* one (Blackburn, 1984: 187–9, 1995; Johnston, 1989; Pettit and Smith, 1993a).

> If an agent judges that it is right for her to φ in circumstances C, then either she is motivated to φ in C or she is practically irrational.

In other words, agents who judge it right to act in various ways are so motivated, and necessarily so, absent the distorting influences of weakness of the will and other similar forms of practical unreason on their motivations. I will have more to say about this idea in what follows.

And sometimes the idea behind the internalism requirement is not, or at least is not primarily, that there is a conceptual connection of some sort between moral judgement and motivation, but that there is the following conceptual connection between the content of a moral judgement – the amoral facts – and our reasons for action (Nagel, 1970; Korsgaard, 1986).

> If it is right for agents to φ in circumstances C, then there is a reason for those agents to φ in C.

In other words, moral facts are facts about our reasons for action; they are themselves simply requirements of rationality or reason.

This last internalist claim might be offered as an explanation of the previous one, for it plausibly entails the previous claim. The proof of this will be spelled out in some detail elsewhere, but in general terms the idea can be put like this. It is a platitude that an agent has a reason to act in a certain way just in case she would be motivated to act in that way if she were rational (Korsgaard, 1986). And it is a consequence of this platitude that an agent who judges herself to have a reason to act in a certain way – who judges that she would be so motivated if she were rational – is practically irrational if she is not motivated to act accordingly. For if she is not motivated accordingly then she fails to be rational by her own lights (Smith, 1992). But if this is right then it is clear that the third form of internalism entails the second. For, according to the third form, the judgement that it is right to act in a certain way is simply equivalent to the judgement that there is a reason to act in that way.

The reverse does not hold, however. The second internalist claim does not entail the third. Expressivists, for example, agree that someone who judges it right to act in a certain way is either motivated accordingly or practically irrational in some way, but deny that moral requirements are requirements of rationality or reason. They thus accept the second internalist claim because they think that a moral judgement is the expression of a preference, or perhaps the expression of a disposition to have a prefer-ence; but they reject the third because they think that fully rational creatures may yet differ in the preferences that they have, or are disposed to have.

Let me give the second and third internalist claims names. I will call the second, the one that may be accepted even by those who deny the third internalist claim, 'the practicality requirement on moral judgement'. And, for obvious reasons, I will call the third internalist claim 'rationalism'. These two forms of internalism allow us to distin-guish corresponding forms of externalism.

One form of externalism amounts to a denial of rationalism. This kind of external-ism is consistent with the practicality requirement. Expressivists are typically both externalists and internalists in this sense (Ayer, 1936; Hare, 1952; Blackburn, 1984). They are externalists in so far as they are anti-rationalists, and yet they are also internalists in so far as they accept the practicality requirement on moral judgement. But the other kind of externalism, the stronger form, amounts to a denial of the practicality requirement. Since rationalism entails the practicality requirement, this form of externalism therefore excludes rationalism as well. Many of those who think, against the expressivists, that moral judgements purport to be descriptive are externalists in this stronger sense (Foot, 1972; Sturgeon, 1985; Railton, 1986; Brink, 1986, 1989).

My task in the present chapter is to defend both these forms of internalism – both rationalism and the practicality requirement – against two externalist challenges. The first comes from David Brink (1986). Brink's challenge is directed primarily against the weaker internalist claim: that is, against the practicality requirement. The second comes from Philippa Foot (1972). Her challenge is directed primarily against the stronger internalist claim: that is, against rationalism.

In what follows I will begin by clarifying the kind of rationalism to which we are committed by the stronger internalist claim. I then consider Brink's and Foot's challenges in turn. As a matter of fact both Brink and Foot accept the stronger form of externalism, the form that excludes both rationalism and the practicality requirement. However, as we will see, being an externalist of either kind involves far more contro-versial and counter-intuitive commitments than either Brink or Foot seem to realize.

2 RATIONALISM AS A CONCEPTUAL CLAIM VS. RATIONALISM AS A SUBSTANTIVE CLAIM

John Mackie draws a distinction between two quite different claims a rationalist might make (Mackie, 1977: 27–30). As I see it, it is Mackie's appreciation of this distinction that allows him to argue for his 'error theory': the view that all moral thought and talk is infected with an error of presupposition; the presupposition that the world contains objectively prescriptive features (Smith, 1993a).

We can best introduce this distinction by way of an analogy. Suppose we are interested in whether or not there are any witches. How are we to go about answering our question? First we must ask a *conceptual question*. What is our concept of a witch? Let's suppose we answer this conceptual question as follows. Our concept of a witch is the concept of a person who exploits his or her relationship with a supernatural agency in order to cause events to happen in the natural world. Then, second, we must ask a *substantive question*. That is, having now fixed on what our concept of a witch is, we must ask whether there is anything in the world instantiating our concept of a witch. If we do not think that there are any supernatural agencies for anyone to have a relationship with, then we will answer this substantive question in the negative. We will say that there are no witches.

Mackie's idea is that, when we ask whether there are any moral facts, we have to follow exactly the same procedure. We must first of all ask a conceptual question. What is our concept of a moral fact? Mackie answers that our concept of a moral fact is the concept of an 'objectively prescriptive' feature of the world. And then, according to Mackie, we must go on to ask a substantive question. Is there anything in the world answering to our concept of a moral fact? Mackie's answer to this question is, famously, that once we are clear about what it is that we are looking for, we see that there are no moral facts. For we see that our concept of an objectively prescriptive feature is not instantiated anywhere in the world.

I said that Mackie draws our attention to two different claims a rationalist might make. This is because, in light of his distinction between conceptual claims and substantive claims, rationalism might now be taken to be a conceptual claim: the claim that our concept of a moral requirement is the concept of a reason for action; a requirement of rationality or reason. Or alternatively, rationalism might be taken to be a substantive claim. That is, rationalists might be telling us that there are requirements of rationality or reason corresponding to the various moral requirements. Taken in the first way, rationalism is a claim about the best analysis of moral terms. Taken in the second way, rationalism is a claim about the deliverances of the theory of rational action.

As I see it, when Mackie tells us that our concept of a moral fact is the concept of an objectively prescriptive feature of the world, he is telling us that the rationalists' conceptual claim is true. And when he tells us that there are no objectively prescriptive features in the world, he is telling us that the rationalists' substantive claim is false. That is, as I see it, Mackie's argument for the error theory may be reconstructed as follows.

Conceptual truth: If agents are morally required to φ in circumstances C then there is a requirement of rationality or reason for all agents to φ in circumstances C

Substantive claim: There is no requirement of rationality or reason for all agents who find themselves in circumstances C to φ

Conclusion: Agents are not morally required to φ in circumstances C

That we are able to reconstruct Mackie's argument in this way is important, for it shows that in defending the rationalists' conceptual claim we do not thereby beg any questions. Even if we accept the rationalists' conceptual claim, we must still go on to defend the rationalists' substantive claim. And conversely, even if we deny the rationalists' substantive claim, we must still engage with the rationalists' conceptual claim.

This distinction between rationalism as a conceptual claim and rationalism as a substantive claim is to be central in what follows. For note that the stronger internalist claim – what I have called 'rationalism' – is simply a claim about our concept of rightness: it is a claim about the content of an agent's judgement that her action is right, not a claim to effect that judgements with such contents are *true*. Moreover, note that it is this conceptual claim that entails the practicality requirement. The *truth* of the substantive claim is simply not required for that entailment to hold.

It is thus rationalism as a conceptual claim that is to be at issue in the present chapter, not rationalism as a substantive claim. Rationalism as a substantive claim will come up for discussion in later chapters, but for now the focus is to be purely conceptual.

3 BRINK'S 'AMORALIST' CHALLENGE

In 'Externalist Moral Realism' David Brink argues that we must reject the practicality requirement. Since the rationalists' conceptual claim entails the practicality require-ment, his argument thus threatens to refute rationalism as well. Here is Brink.

Much moral skepticism is skepticism about the objectivity of morality, that is, skepticism about the existence of moral facts. But another traditional kind of skepticism accepts the existence of moral facts and asks why we should care about these facts. Amoralists are the traditional way of representing this second kind of skepticism; the amoralist is someone who recognizes the existence of moral considerations and remains unmoved.

The ... [defender of the practicality requirement] ... must dismiss the amoralist challenge as incoherent ... We may think that the amoralist challenge is coherent, but this can only be because we confuse moral senses of terms and 'inverted commas' senses of those same terms ... Thus ... apparent amoralists ... remain unmoved, not by what they regard as moral considerations, but only by what others regard as moral considerations.

The problem ... is that ... [this] ... does not take the amoralist's challenge seriously enough ... We can imagine someone who regards certain demands as moral demands – and not simply as conventional moral demands – and yet remains unmoved ... [If] ... we are to take the amoralist challenge seriously, we must attempt to explain why the amoralist should care about morality.

(1986: 30)

Brink's argument is simple enough.

According to defenders of the practicality requirement, it is supposed to be a concep-tual truth that agents who make moral judgements are motivated accordingly, at least absent weakness of will and the like. But far from this being a conceptual truth, it isn't any sort of truth at all. For amoralists use moral terms to pick out the very same proper-ties we pick out when we use moral terms. Their use of moral terms may therefore be reliably guided by the moral facts in the same way as our uses of those terms. But amoralists differ from us in that they see no reason at all to do what they thus take to be morally required. In other words, amoralists make moral judgements without being motivated accordingly, and without suffering from any sort of practical irrationality either. The practicality requirement is thus false.

As Brink notes, defenders of the requirement have generally not responded to this challenge by boldly denying that amoralists exist. And nor could they with any credi-bility, for amoralists are among the more popular heroes of both philosophical fantasy and non-philosophical fiction. Brink mentions Plato's Thrasymachus and Dickens's Uriah Heep. But nor are amoralists confined to the world of make-believe. There are, after all, real-life sociopaths like Robert Harris, the thrill-killer whose story is faithfully retold and analysed by Gary Watson (1987). Harris claims that he knew that what he was doing was wrong and that he simply chose to do it anyway; that he felt no conflict. It therefore seems quite wrong to suppose that he suffered from weakness of will, or, perhaps, from any other kind of practical irrationality either.

What defenders of the requirement have tended to insist is therefore rather that, properly described, the existence of amoralists is not inconsistent with the practicality requirement. For, they claim, amoralists do not *really* make moral judgements at all. Even if they do use moral words to pick out the same properties that we pick out when we use moral words, they do not really judge acts to be right and wrong; rather they judge acts to be 'right' and 'wrong'. That is to say they use moral words in a different sense; in the inverted commas sense Brink mentions.

According to Hare, for example, the sentence 'φ-ing is right' as used by an amoralist does not mean 'φ-ing is right'; but rather means 'φ-ing is in accordance with what other people judge to be right' (Hare, 1952: 124–6, 163–5). And, as such, the fact that an amoralist may judge it 'right' to φ without being either motivated to φ or suffering from weakness of will is no counter-example to the requirement. For the requirement tells us that those who judge it right to φ are motivated accordingly, absent weakness of will, not that those who judge is 'right' to φ are motivated accordingly, absent weakness of will.

Now Brink thinks that this inverted commas response doesn't take the amoralist challenge 'seriously' enough. And I must confess that I share his misgivings, at least as regards the details of Hare's version of the response. For, as Brink points out, there seems to be nothing incoherent about the idea of an amoralist who claims to have special insight into what is *really* right and wrong; an amoralist whose judgements about what it is right and wrong to do are therefore, even by her own lights, out of line with the judgements of others. But if this is right, then the judgements of amoralists can hardly be thought of as judgements about what other people judge to be right and wrong.

Despite these misgivings, however, I think that the inverted commas response to the amoralist challenge is along exactly the right lines. In what follows I want therefore to give a two part reply to Brink. First I will say what the inverted commas response really amounts to; how it differs from what Hare says. And second I will say why defenders of the requirement are right to think that the requirement is a conceptual truth.

4 REPLY TO BRINK'S CLAIM THAT AMORALISTS REALLY MAKE MORAL JUDGEMENTS

As I see it, defenders of the practicality requirement are right to say that amoralists do not really make moral judgements, they simply go wrong in trying to say more than this. The point is not that amoralists really make judgements of some other kind: about what other people judge to be right and wrong, for example. The point is rather that the *very best* we can say about amoralists is that they try to make moral judgements but fail. In order to see why this is not *ad hoc*, consider an analogy.

There is a familiar problem about the conditions under which we should say of someone that she really makes colour judgements (Peacocke, 1985: chapter 2; Tawil, 1987). The problem can be brought out by reflecting on the case of someone, blind from birth, who has a reliable method of using colour terms. We might imagine that she has been hooked up to a machine from birth that allows her to feel, through her skin, when an object has the appropriate surface reflectance properties.

Now such a person certainly has a facility with colour terms, a facility that allows her to engage in many aspects of the ordinary practice of colour ascription. For she uses terms with the same extension as our colour terms, and the properties of objects that explain her uses of those terms are the very same properties as those that explain our uses of colour terms. (This is similar to what we said earlier about the amoralist's use of moral language.) And we can even imagine, if we like, that her colour judgements are far more accurate and reliable than those made by sighted folk. When she makes colour judgements, she is therefore not appropriately thought of as making judgements about what other people judge to be red, green and the like. (This is again similar to what we have said about the amoralist.)

However, despite the facility such a blind person has with colour language, many theorists have thought that we should still deny that she possesses colour concepts or mastery of colour terms. For, they say, the ability to have the appropriate visual experiences under suitable conditions is partially constitutive of possession of colour concepts and mastery of colour terms (Peacocke, 1985: 29–30, 37–8). And what such theorists thereby commit themselves to saying is that, despite her facility with colour terms, such a blind person does not *really* make colour judgements at all. They do not have to say that she is really making judgements of some other kind, of course. Rather they can insist that though she is trying to make colour judgements, because she doesn't count as a possessor of colour concepts, she fails. When she says 'Fire-engines are red', 'Grass is green' and the like, she is therefore best interpreted as using colour terms in an inverted commas sense: she is saying that fire-engines are 'red', grass is 'green' and so on.

It is, I hope, clear that the structure of this debate over the conditions for mastery of colour terms is in crucial respects identical to the structure of the debate we are engaged in with Brink. One side says that a subject has mastery of colour terms (moral terms), and thus really makes colour judgements (moral judgements), only if, under certain conditions, being in the psychological state that we express when we make colour judgements (moral judgements) entails having an appropriate visual experience (motivation). The other side denies this holding instead that the ability to use a term whose use is reliably explained by the relevant properties of objects is enough to credit her with mastery of colour terms (moral terms) and the ability really to make colour judgements (moral judgements). Having the appropriate visual experience (motivation) under appropriate conditions is an entirely contingent, and optional, extra. The debate is a real one, so how are we to decide who wins?

Imagine someone objecting that those who say that the capacity to have certain visual experiences is partially constitutive of mastery of colour terms do not take 'seriously' enough the challenge posed by people who can reliably say 'Grass is green', 'Fire-engines are red', and so on, while yet being completely blind. Suppose the objector insists that since blind people can reliably use colour terms in this way, it just follows that they have full mastery of colour terms. Would the objection be a good one? I do not think so. For the objection simply assumes the conclusion it is supposed to be arguing for. It assumes that blind people have mastery of colour terms, something that those who think that mastery requires the capacity to have the appropriate visual experiences under the appropriate conditions deny.

It seems to me that Brink's amoralist challenge is flawed in just this way. He puts a prejudicial interpretation on the amoralist's reliable use of moral terms. He assumes that the amoralist's reliable use is evidence of her mastery of those terms; assumes that being suitably motivated under the appropriate conditions is not a condition of mastery of moral terms. But those who accept the practicality requirement do not accept the account of what it is to have mastery of moral terms that makes this prejudicial interpretation of the amoralist's use of moral terms appropriate.

What this suggests is that, in order to adjudicate the debate with Brink, what we really need is an independent reason for accepting one or the other account of mastery. In what follows I want therefore to provide such an independent reason. The argument is to be that the account of mastery offered by those who defend the practicality requirement is to be preferred because it alone is able to provide a plausible explanation of the reliable connection between moral judgement and motivation in the good and strong-willed person.

5 AN ARGUMENT FOR THE PRACTICALITY REQUIREMENT

All we have said so far about the strong externalists' account of moral motivation is that, by their lights, it is a contingent and rationally optional matter whether an agent who believes that it is right to act in a certain way is motivated to act accordingly. But more quite evidently needs to be said.

By all accounts, it is a striking fact about moral motivation that a *change in motivation* follows reliably in the wake of a *change in moral judgement*, at least in the good and strong-willed person. A plausible theory of moral judgement must therefore explain this striking fact. As I see it, those who accept the practicality requirement can, whereas strong externalists cannot, explain this striking fact in a plausible way.

Suppose I am engaged in an argument with you about a fundamental moral question; a question about, say, whether we should vote for the libertarian party at some election as opposed to the social democrats. In order to make matters vivid, we will suppose that I come to the argument already judging that we should vote for the libertarians, and already motivated to do so as well. During the course of the argument, let's suppose you convince me that I am fundamentally wrong. I should vote for the social democrats, and not just because the social democrats will better promote the values that I thought would be promoted by the libertarians, but rather because the values I thought should and would be promoted by libertarians are themselves fundamentally mistaken. You get me to change my most fundamental values. In this sort of situation, what happens to my motives?

Though the precise answer to this question will of course depend, *inter alia*, on the very point at issue, this much at least can be accepted by defenders of the practicality requirement and strong externalists alike. If I am a good and strong-willed person then a new motivation will follow in the wake of my new judgement. So let's add in the assumption that I am a good and strong-willed person. Then, since I no longer judge it right to vote for the libertarians, I will no longer be motivated to do so. And since I have come to judge it right to vote for the social democrats, I will now be motivated to do that instead. The question is: how are we to explain the *reliability* of this connection between judgement and motivation in the good and strong-willed person? How are we to explain why, under a range of counterfactual circumstances, the good and strong-willed person's moral motivations will always fall in line behind her newly arrived at moral judgements?

As I see it, there are only two possible answers. On the one hand we can say that the reliable connection between judgement and motivation is to be explained *internally*: it follows directly from the content of moral judgement itself. The idea will then be either that the belief that an act is right *produces* a corresponding motivation (this is the rationalists' alternative), or perhaps that the attitude of accepting that an act is right is itself *identical* with the state of being motivated (this is the expressivists'). Or, on the other hand, we can say that the reliable connection between judgement and motivation is to be explained *externally*: it follows from the content of the motivational dispositions possessed by the good and strong-willed person. Those who defend the practicality requirement opt for the first answer, strong externalists opt for the second.

Consider the first answer. Since those who defend the practicality requirement think that it is in the nature of moral judgement that an agent who judges it right to ϕ in circumstances C is motivated to ϕ in C, at least absent weakness of will or some other such psychological failure, they will insist that it comes as no surprise that in a strong-willed person a *change* of moral motivation follows in the wake of a *change* in moral judgement. For that is just a direct consequence of the practicality requirement.

Moreover, and importantly, note that defenders of the requirement are in a position to insist that what an agent is thus motivated to do when she changes her moral judgement is precisely what she judges it right to do, where this is read *de re* and not *de dicto*. Thus, if an agent judges it right to ϕ in C, and if she has not derived this judgement from some more fundamental judgement about what it is right to do in C, then, absent weakness of will and the like, defenders of the practicality requirement can insist that she will be motivated non-derivatively to ϕ in C. This is because, on the rationalist alternative, a non-derivative desire to ϕ in C is what her judgement that it is right to φ in C causes in her, or because, on the expressivist alternative, the judgement that it is right to φ in C is itself just the expression of such a non-derivative desire. In the example under discussion, then, in deciding that it is right to vote for the social democrats, defenders of the practicality requirement can insist that I acquire a non-derivative concern for social democratic values.

But now consider the second answer, the answer favoured by the strong externalist. She will say that the defender of the practicality requirement has conveniently over-looked a crucial part of the story: namely, the stipulation that I am a *good* and strong-willed person. She will therefore insist that what explains the reliable connection between judgement and motivation is a motivational disposition I have in virtue of which I count as a good person. In other words, what explains the reliability of the connection is the *content of my moral motivation*. But what exactly *is* the content of my moral motivation, according to the strong externalist?

Before the argument began I was motivated to vote for the libertarians. Could it be that it was my having a non-derivative concern for libertarian values that made me count as a good person, when I judged it right to vote for the libertarians? Evidently not. After all, as a result of the ensuing argument I have come to reject my earlier judgement that it is right to vote for the libertarians in favour of the judgement that it is right to vote for the social democrats. But since, on this way of seeing things, my initial motivation was not itself rationally mandated by my earlier judgement – since it was just a wholly contingent and rationally optional extra – so the mere fact that I have found reason to change my judgement gives me no reason to change this motive. I may therefore quite rationally continue to have a desire to vote for the libertarians; though of course I would have to judge that in so doing I am motivated to do something that I now judge wrong. Having a non-derivative concern for liberatarian values while judging it right to vote for the libertarians is thus not what makes me a good person. For it cannot explain why I change my motivation when I change my judgement.

What this forces the strong externalist to admit is that, on their way of seeing things, the motive in virtue of which I am to count as a good person must have a content capable of explaining not just why I am motivated to vote for the libertarians when I judge it right to vote for the libertarians, but also why I stop being motivated to vote for the libertarians when I give up judging that it is right to do so. And the only motivational content capable of playing this role, it seems to me, is a motivation to do the right thing, where this is now read *de dicto* and not *de re*. At bottom, the strong externalist will have to say, having this self-consciously *moral* motive is what makes me a good person.[1]

Note that if this were the content of the good person's motivations, then the strong externalist would indeed be able to explain the reliability of the connection between moral judgement and motivation. A change in the good person's motivations would follow a change in her moral judgements because her motivations would be derived from her judgements together with her self-consciously moral motive. Thus, according to this story, when I no longer believe that it is right to vote for the libertarians, I lose a *derived* desire to vote for them, and when I come to believe that it is right to vote for the social democrats, I acquire a *derived* desire to vote for them. But my motivations are in each case derivative because they are derived from my current judgement about what the right thing to do is together with my basic moral motive: a non-derivative concern to do what is right.

However, if this is the best explanation the strong externalist can give of the reliable connection between moral judgement and motivation in the good and strong-willed person then it seems to me that we have a straightforward *reductio*. For the explanation is only as plausible as the claim that the good person is, at bottom, motivated to do what is right, where this is read *de dicto* and not *de re*, and that is surely a quite implausible claim. For commonsense tells us that if good people judge it right to be honest, or right to care for their children and friends and fellows, or right for people to get what they deserve, then they care non-derivatively about these things. Good people care non-derivatively about honesty, the weal and woe of their children and friends, the well-being of their fellows, people getting what they deserve, justice, equality, and the like, not just one thing: doing what they believe to be right, where this is read *de dicto* and not *de re*. Indeed, commonsense tells us that being so motivated is a fetish or moral vice, not the one and only moral virtue.

It is worthwhile underscoring the present objection by comparing it to a related objection of Bernard Williams's to the kind of moral philosophy that emphasizes impartiality (1976). Williams asks us to consider a man who, when faced with a choice between saving his wife or a stranger, chooses to save his wife. Many moral philosophers think that, even in such a case, a morally good person would be moved by impartial concern; that this man's motivating thought would therefore have to be, at best, 'that it was his wife, and that in situations of this kind it is permissible to save one's wife'. But, Williams objects, this is surely wrong. It provides the husband with 'one thought too many'. And in order to see that this is so he asks us to consider matters from the wife's perspective. She would quite rightly hope that her husband's 'motivating thought, fully spelled out' is that the person he saved was *his wife*. If any further motivation were required then that would simply indicate that he doesn't have the feelings of direct love and concern for her that she rightly wants and expects. He would be alienated from her, treating her as in relevant respects just like a stranger; though, of course, a stranger that he is especially well placed to benefit (Williams, 1976: 18).

The present objection to externalism is like Williams's objection to the kind of moral philosophy that emphasizes impartiality, only more powerful still; for it does not require the assumption, controversial by the lights of some, that morality itself embraces partial values like love and friendship. For the objection in this case is simply that, in taking it that a good person is motivated to do what she believes right, where this is read *de dicto* and not *de re*, externalists too provide the morally good person with 'one thought too many'. They alienate her from the ends at which morality properly aims. Just as it is constitutive of being a good lover that you have direct concern for the person you love, so it is constitutive of being a morally good person that you have direct concern for what you think is right, where this is read *de re* and not *de dicto*. This is something that must be conceded even by those moral philosophers who think that the only right course of action is one of impartiality. They too must agree that a morally good person will have a direct and non-derivative impartial concern; her concern for impartiality must not itself be derived from a more basic non-derivative concern *de dicto* to do the right thing.

We have therefore found a decisive reason to reject the strong externalists' explanation of the reliable connection between moral judgement and motivation in the good and strong-willed person. For, in short, the strong externalists' explanation commits us to false views about the content of a good person's motivations; it elevates a moral fetish into the one and only moral virtue. And the remedy, of course, is to retreat to the alternative, internalist, explanation of the reliability of the connection between moral judgement and motivation. But if we do that then, of course, we have to accept that the practicality requirement is a constraint on the content of a moral judgement after all.

The conclusion is important. For it means that we now have the independent reason we needed for giving an account of mastery of moral terms according to which the practicality requirement is itself a condition of having mastery. Only so can we explain the reliable connection between moral judgement and motivation in the good and strong-willed person. Brink's 'amoralist' challenge thus collapses. For despite the facility they have with moral language, amoralists do not have mastery of moral terms, and they therefore do not really make moral judgements. The fact that they make 'moral' judgements without being motivated or suffering from practical irrationality thus provides us with no challenge to the practicality requirement.

NOTE

1   To my knowledge this point is never admitted by the externalists themselves, largely because the problem to which admitting this point is the solution is never explicitly addressed: that is, the problem of explaining the reliability of the connection between moral judgement and motivation in the good and strong-willed person. Indeed, both Brink and Foot seem to think that externalism offers a *better* explanation of the connection between moral judgement and motivation than that offered by defenders of the practicality requirement (Brink, 1989: 49; Foot, 1972: 165–7). Whether they would still think so if they were to think about the point currently under discussion I do not know.

REFERENCES AND BIBLIOGRAPHY

Altham, J. E. J. (1986) 'The Legacy of Emotivism', in Graham Macdonald and Crispin Wright, eds, *Fact, Science and Morality: Essays on A. J. Ayer's Language, Truth and Logic*. Blackwell, pp. 275–88.

Anscombe, G. E. M. (1957) *Intention*. Blackwell.

Ayer, A. J. (1936) *Language, Truth and Logic*. Gollancz. second edn, 1946.

——(1954) 'Freedom and Necessity', reprinted in Gary Watson, ed., *Free Will*. Oxford University Press, 1982, pp. 15–23.

Blackburn, Simon (1971) 'Moral Realism', in John Casey, ed., *Morality and Moral Reasoning*. Methuen, PP. 101–24.

——(1984) *Spreading the Word*. Oxford University Press.

——(1985a) 'Errors and the Phenomenology of Value', in Ted Honderich, ed., *Morality and Objectivity*. Roudedge & Kegan Paul, pp. 1–22.

——(1985b) 'Supervenience Revisited', in Ian Hacking, ed., *Exercises in Analysis: Essays by Students of Casimir Levy*. Cambridge University Press.

——(1986) 'Morals and Modals', in Graham Macdonald and Crispin Wright, eds, *Fact, Science and Morality: Essays on A. J. Ayer's Language, Truth and Logic*. Blackwell, pp. 119–42.

——(1987) 'How to Be an Ethical Antirealist', in Peter A. French, Theodore E. Uehling, Jr. and Howard K. Wettstein, eds, *Midwest Studies in Philosophy Volume XII: Realism and Anti-Realism*. University of Notre Dame Press, pp. 361–75.

——(1994) 'Circles, Finks, Smells, and Biconditionals', in James Tomberlin, ed., *Philosophical Perspectives: Volume VII, Language and Logic*. Ridgeview Press, 259–81.

——(1995) 'Flight from Reality', in Rosalind Hursthouse, Gavin Lawrence and Warren Quinn, eds, *Virtues and Reasons, a Festschrift for Philippa Foot*. Oxford University Press.

Boyd, Richard (1988) 'How to be a Moral Realist', in Geoffrey Sayre-McCord, ed., *Essays on Moral Realism*. Cornell University Press, pp. 181–228.

Brink, David O. (1984) 'Moral Realism and the Skeptical Arguments from Disagreement and Queerness', *Australasian Journal of Philosophy*, 111–25 [Chapter 6, this volume].

——(1986) 'Externalist Moral Realism', *Southern Journal of Philosophy* Supplement, 23–42.

——(1989) *Moral Realism and the Foundations of Ethics*. Cambridge University Press.

Campbell, John (1993) 'A Simple View of Colour', in John Haldane and Crispin Wright, eds, *Reality, Representation and Projection*. Oxford University Press, pp. 257–68.

Carnap, Rudolf (1963) 'Replies and Systematic Expositions', in P. A. Schilpp, ed., *The Philosophy of Rudolf Carnap*. Open Court.

Collins, John (1988) 'Belief, Desire and Revision', *Mind*, 333–42.

Dancy, Jonathan (1993) *Moral Reasons*. Blackwell.

Daniels, Norman (1979) 'Wide Reflective Equilibrium and Theory Acceptance in Ethics', *Journal of Philosophy*, 256–82.

Darwall, Stephen (1983) *Impartial Reason*. Cornell University Press.

Darwall, Stephen, Gibbard, Allan and Railton, Peter (1992) 'Toward *Fin de siècle* Ethics: Some Trends', *Philosophical Review*, 115–89.

Davidson, Donald (1963) 'Actions, Reasons and Causes', reprinted in Davidson (1980), pp. 3–20.

——(1970) 'How is Weakness of the Will Possible?', reprinted in Davidson (1980), pp. 21–42.

——(1978) 'Intending', reprinted in Davidson (1980), pp. 83–102.

——(1980) *Essays on Actions and Events*. Oxford University Press.

Davies, Martin and Humberstone, Lloyd (1980) 'Two Notions of Necessity', *Philosophical Studies*, 1–30.

Divers, John and Miller, Alex (1994) 'Why Expressivists about Value Should Not Love Minimalism about Truth', *Analysis* [Chapter 22, this volume].

Dreier, James (1990) 'Internalism and Speaker Relativism', *Ethics*, 6–26.

Dworkin, Ronald (1977) *Taking Rights Seriously*. Duckworth.

Evans, Gareth (1980) 'Things Without the Mind – A Commentary on Chapter Two of Strawson's *Individuals*', in Zak van Straaten, ed., *Philosophical Subjects: Essays Presented to P. F. Strawson*. Clarendon Press, pp. 76–116.

Falk, W. D. (1948) '"Ought" and Motivation', *Proceedings of the Aristotelian Society*, 111–38.

Foot, Philippa (1958) 'Moral Arguments', reprinted in Foot (1978), pp. 96–109.

——(1972) 'Morality as a System of Hypothetical Imperatives', reprinted in Foot (1978), pp. 157–73.

——(1977) 'Approval and Disapproval', reprinted in Foot (1978), pp. 189–207.

——(1978) *Virtues and Vices*. University of California Press.

Frankena, William (1958) 'Obligation and Motivation in Recent Moral Philosophy', in A. I. Melden, ed., *Essays on Moral Philosophy*. University of Washington Press.

Frankfurt, Harry (1971) 'Freedom of the Will and the Concept of a Person', reprinted in Gary Watson, ed. (1982) *Free Will*. Oxford University Press, pp. 81–95.

Gauthier, David (1975) 'Reason and Maximization', *Canadian Journal of Philosophy*, 411–34.

——(1986) *Morals by Agreement*. Clarendon Press.

Gibbard, Allan (1990) *Wise Choices, Apt Feelings*. Clarendon Press.

Hale, Bob (1986) 'The Compleat Projectivist', *Philosophical Quarterly*, 65–84.

——(1993) 'Can There Be a Logic of Attitudes?' [Chapter 20, this volume], in John Haldane and Crispin Wright, eds, *Reality, Representation and Projection*. Oxford University Press, pp. 337–63.

Hare, R. M. (1952) *The Language of Morals*. Oxford University Press.

——(1981) *Moral Thinking*. Oxford University Press.

Harman, Gilbert (1973) *Thought*. Princeton University Press.

——(1975) 'Moral Relativism Defended', *Philosophical Review*, 3–22.

——(1977) *The Nature of Morality*. Oxford University Press.

——(1985) 'Is There a Single True Morality?', in David Copp and David Zimmerman, eds, *Morality, Reason and Truth*. Rowman and Allanheld.

——(1986) 'Moral Explanations of Natural Facts – Can Moral Claims Be Tested Against Moral Reality?', *Southern Journal of Philosophy* Supplement, 69–78.

Hart, H. L. A. (1961) *The Concept of Law*. Clarendon Press.

Horwich, Paul (1992) 'Gibbard's Theory of Norms', *Philosophy and Public Affairs*, 67–78.

——(1994) 'The Essence of Expressivism', *Analysis*.

Humberstone, I. L. (1992) 'Direction of Fit', *Mind*, 59–83.

Hume, David (1888) *A Treatise of Human Nature*. Clarendon Press, 1968.

Hurley, S. L. (1985) 'Objectivity and Disagreement', in Ted Honderich, ed., *Morality and Objectivity*. Routledge & Kegan Paul.

Jackson, Frank (1992) 'Critical Notice of Susan Hurley's *Natural Reasons: Personality and Polity*', *Australasian Journal of Philosophy*. [Chapter 11, this volume.]

——(1994) 'Armchair Metaphysics', in Michaelis Michael and John O'Leary Hawthorne, eds, *Philosophy in Mind*. Kluwer Press.

Jackson, Frank and Pargetter, Robert (1987) 'An Objectivist's Guide to Subjectivism about Colour', in *Review Internationale de Philosophie*, 127–41.

Jackson, Frank and Pettit, Philip (1988) 'Functionalism and Broad Content', *Mind*, 381–400.

Jackson, Frank, Oppy, Graham and Smith, Michael (1994) 'Minimalism and Truth-Aptness', *Mind*.

Johnston, Mark (1989) 'Dispositional Theories of Value', *Proceedings of the Aristotelian Society* Supplementary Volume, 139–74.

Kant, Immanuel (1786) *Foundations of the Metaphysics of Morals*. Library of Liberal Arts, 1959.

Kennett, Jeanette (1993) 'Mixed Motives', *Australasian Journal of Philosophy*, 71: 256–69.

Kennett, Jeanette and Smith, Michael (1994) 'Philosophy and Commonsense: The Case of Weakness of Will', in Michaelis Michael and John O'Leary Hawthorne, eds, *Philosophy in Mind*. Kluwer Press.

Korsgaard, Christine (1986) 'Skepticism about Practical Reason', *Journal of Philosophy*, 5–25.

Kripke, Saul (1980) *Naming and Necessity*. Blackwell.

Kymlicka, Will (1989) *Liberalism, Community and Culture*. Clarendon Press.

—— (1990) *Contemporary Political Philosophy*. Oxford University Press.

Lewis, David (1970) 'How to Define Theoretical Terms', *Journal of Philosophy*, 427–46.

—— (1972) 'Psychophysical and Theoretical Identifications', *Australasian Journal of Philosophy*, 249–58.

—— (1988) 'Desire as Belief', *Mind*, 323–32.

—— (1989) 'Dispositional Theories of Value', *Proceedings of the Aristotelian Society* Supplementary Volume, 113–37.

Loar, Brian (1981) *Mind and Meaning*. Cambridge University Press.

McDowell, John (1978) 'Are Moral Requirements Hypothetical Imperatives?', *Proceedings of the Aristotelian Society* Supplementary Volume, 13–29.

—— (1979) 'Virtue and Reason', *The Monist*, 331–50.

—— (1981) 'Non-Cognitivism and Rule-Following', in Steven Holtzman and Christopher Leich, eds, *Wittgenstein: To Follow a Rule*. Routledge, pp. 141–62 [Chapter 23, this volume].

—— (1985) 'Values and Secondary Qualities', in Honderich (1985), pp. 110–29 [Chapter 12, this volume].

McGinn, Colin (1982) *The Character of Mind*. Oxford University Press.

—— (1983) *The Subjective View*. Oxford University Press.

Mackie, J. L. (1976) *Problems from Locke*. Clarendon Press.

—— (1977) *Ethics: Inventing Right and Wrong*. Penguin.

McNaughton, David (1988) *Moral Vision*. Blackwell.

Monro, D. H. (1967) *Empiricism and Ethics*. Cambridge University Press.

Moore, G. E. (1903) *Principia Ethica*. Cambridge University Press.

Nagel, Thomas (1970) *The Possibility of Altruism*. Princeton University Press.

—— (1986) *The View from Nowhere*. Oxford University Press.

Nozick, Robert (1981) *Philosophical Explanations*. Harvard University Press.

Parfit, Derek (1984) *Reasons and Persons*. Oxford University Press.

Peacocke, Christopher (1979) *Holistic Explanation*. Oxford University Press.

—— (1985) *Sense and Content*. Oxford University Press.

Pettit, Philip (1987) 'Humeans, Anti-Humeans and Motivation', *Mind*, 530–3 [Chapter 32, this volume].

—— (1993) *The Common Mind*. Oxford University Press.

Pettit, Philip and Smith, Michael (1990) 'Backgrounding Desire', *Philosophical Review*, 565–92.

—— (1993a) 'Practical Unreason', *Mind*, 53–79.

—— (1993b) 'Brandt on Self-Control', in Brad Hooker, ed., *Rationality, Rules and Utility*. Westview Press, pp. 33–50.

—— (1997) 'Parfit's P', in Jonathan Dancy, ed., *Reading Parfit*. Blackwell.

Platts, Mark (1979) *Ways of Meaning*. Routledge & Kegan Paul.

—— (1981) 'Moral Reality and the End of Desire', in Mark Platts, ed., *Reference, Truth and Reality*. Routledge & Kegan Paul, pp. 69–82.

Price, Huw (1988) *Facts and the Function of Truth*. Blackwell.

—— (1989) 'Defending Desire-as-Belief', *Mind*, 119–27.

Prior, Elizabeth W., Pargetter, Robert and Jackson, Frank (1982) 'Three Theses About Dispositions', *American Philosophical Quarterly*, 251–7.

Putnam, Hilary (1981) *Reason, Truth and History*. Cambridge University Press.

Rachels, James (1971) 'God and Human Attitudes', reprinted in Tom L. Beauchamp, Joel Feinberg and James M. Smith, eds, *Philosophy and the Human Condition*. Prentice Hall, 1989, pp. 509–16.

Railton, Peter (1986) 'Moral Realism', *Philosophical Review*, 163–207 [Chapter 9, this volume].

—— (1993a) 'What the Noncognitivist Helps Us to See the Naturalist Must Help us to Explain', in John Haldane and Crispin Wright, eds, *Reality, Representation and Projection*. Oxford University Press, pp. 279–300.

—— (1993b) 'Reply to David Wiggins', in John Haldane and Crispin Wright, eds, *Reality, Representation and Projection*. Oxford University Press, pp. 315–28.

Ramsey, Frank P. (1931) 'Theories', in his *The Foundations of Mathematics*. Routledge & Kegan Paul.

Rawls, John (1951) 'Outline of a Decision Procedure for Ethics', *Philosophical Review*, 177–97.

Sayre-McCord, Geoffrey (1988) 'Moral Theory and Explanatory Impotence', reprinted in Geoffrey Sayre-McCord, ed., *Essays on Moral Realism*. Cornell University Press, pp. 256–81.

Scanlon, Thomas (1982) 'Contractualism and Utilitarianism', in Amartya Sen and Bernard Williams, eds, *Utilitarianism and Beyond*. Cambridge University Press, pp. 103–28.

Schueler, G. F. (1991) 'Pro-Attitudes and Directions of Fit', *Mind*, 277–81.

Sidgwick, Henry (1907) *The Methods of Ethics*. Hackett, 1981.

Singer, Peter (1973) 'The Triviality of the Debate over "Is-Ought" and the Definition of "Moral"', *American Philosophical Quarterly*, 51–6.

Smart, J. J. C. (1975) 'On Some Criticisms of a Physicalist Theory of Colour', reprinted in his *Essays Metaphysical and Moral*. Blackwell, 1987.

Smith, Michael (1986a) 'Peacocke on Red and Red', *Synthese*, 559–76.

——(1986b) 'Should We Believe in Emotivism?', in Graham Macdonald and Crispin Wright, eds, *Fact, Science and Morality: Essays on A. J. Ayer's Language, Truth and Logic*. Blackwell, pp. 289–310.

——(1987) 'The Humean Theory of Motivation', *Mind*, 36–61, [Chapter 31, this volume].

——(1988a) 'On Humeans, Anti-Humeans and Motivation: A Reply to Pettit', *Mind*, 589–95, [Chapter 33, this volume].

——(1988b) 'Reason and Desire', *Proceedings of the Aristotelian Society*, 243–56.

——(1989) 'Dispositional Theories of Value', *Proceedings of the Aristotelian Society* Supplementary Volume, 89–111.

——(1991) 'Realism', in Peter Singer, ed., *A Companion to Ethics*. Blackwell, pp. 399–410.

——(1992) 'Valuing: Desiring or Believing?', in David Charles and Kathleen Lennon, eds, *Reduction, Explanation, and Realism*. Oxford University Press, pp. 323–60.

——(1993a) 'Objectivity and Moral Realism: On the Significance of the Phenomenology of Moral Experience', in John Haldane and Crispin Wright, eds, *Reality, Representation and Projection*. Oxford University Press, pp. 235–6.

——(1993b) 'Colour, Transparency, Mind-Independence', in John Haldane and Crispin Wright, eds, *Reality, Representation and Projection*. Oxford University Press, pp. 269–78.

——(1994a) 'Why Expressivists about Value Should Love Minimalism about Truth', *Analysis*, 1–12, [Chapter 21, this volume].

——(1994b) 'Minimalism, Truth-Aptitude and Belief', *Analysis*, 21–6.

Stocker, Michael (1979) 'Desiring the Bad: An Essay in Moral Psychology', *Journal of Philosophy*, 738–53.

Stroud, Barry (1977) *Hume*. Routledge & Kegan Paul.

Sturgeon, Nicholas (1985) 'Moral Explanations', in David Copp and David Zimmerman, eds, *Morality, Reason and Truth*. Rowman and Allanheld, pp. 49–78, [Chapter 8, this volume].

——(1986) 'What Difference Does It Make Whether Moral Realism Is True?', *Southern Journal of Philosophy* Supplement, 115–41.

Tawil, Nathan (1987) *Reference and Intentionality*. Ph.D. Dissertation, Princeton University.

Velleman, J. David (1992) 'The Guise of the Good', *Noûs*, 3–26.

Wallace, Jay (1983) *Motivation and Moral Reality*. Bachelor of Philosophy thesis. Oxford University.

——(1990) 'How to Argue about Practical Reason', in *Mind*, 267–97.

Watson, Gary (1975) 'Free Agency', reprinted in Gary Watson, ed., *Free Will*. Oxford University Press, 1982, pp. 96–110.

——(1987) 'Responsibility and the Limits of Evil', in Ferdinand Schoeman, ed., *Responsibility, Character and the Emotions: New Essays in Moral Psychology*. Cambridge University Press, pp. 256–86.

Wiggins, David (1987) 'A Sensible Subjectivism', in his *Needs, Values, Truth*. Basil Blackwell, pp. 185–214.

——(1993a) 'Cognitivism, Naturalism, and Normativity: A Reply to Peter Railton', in John Haldane and Crispin Wright, eds, *Reality, Representation and Projection*. Oxford University Press, pp. 301–14.

——(1993b) 'A Neglected Position?', in John Haldane and Crispin Wright, eds, *Reality, Representation and Projection*. Oxford University Press, pp. 329–36.

Williams, Bernard (1976) 'Persons, Character and Morality', reprinted in Williams (1981), pp. 1–19.

——(1980) 'Internal and External Reasons', reprinted in Williams (1981), pp. 101–13.

——(1981) *Moral Luck*. Cambridge University Press.

——(1985) *Ethics and the Limits of Philosophy*. Harvard University Press.

Wilson, George (1985) 'Davidson on Intentional Action', in Ernest LePore and Brian McLaughlin, eds, *Actions and Events: Perspectives on the Philosophy of Donald Davidson*. Blackwell, pp. 29–43.

Wolf, Susan (1982) 'Moral Saints', *Journal of Philosophy*, 419–39.

Woods, Michael (1972) 'Reasons for Action and Desire', *Proceedings of the Aristotelian Society* Supplementary Volume, 189–201.

Wright, Crispin (1988) 'Moral Values, Projection and Secondary Qualities', *Proceedings of the Aristotelian Society* Supplementary Volume, 1–26.

——(1992) *Truth and Objectivity*. Harvard University Press.

30

DISPOSITIONS AND FETISHES

EXTERNALIST MODELS OF MORAL MOTIVATION*

James Dreier

1 INTRODUCTION

Here is a well known thesis about the relation between moral judgment and motivation:

(Internalism) If an agent judges that it is right for her to φ, then she is motivated to φ.[1]

Internalism is presented as a conceptual truth about moral judgment, not as a substantive moral thesis. It is at issue in *meta*ethics, rather than in normative theory proper. Not a metaethical theory itself, Internalism is an alleged fact about ordinary moral thought, a datum for which a metaethical theory must account. If it is a fact, then a theory gains an advantage insofar as it explains Internalism, and loses ground if it is inconsistent with Internalism. But metaethicists do not agree about Internalism. Those who take it to be a fact about ordinary moral thinking are Internalists. Others are Externalists. Externalists, it appears, simply don't share the intuitions that seem so powerful to Internalists.[2]

The disagreement between Internalists and Externalists runs deep, and it lingers even in the face of clever intuition pumps.[3] This debate in metaethics might be at a standoff, each side standing fast on its intuitions. Standoffs of this sort in philosophy are depressing.

In "Persons, Character, and Morality" Bernard Williams told an influential story whose point was intended to be a point inside of normative theory proper.[4] Williams considers a discussion of Charles Fried's[5] in which a man could "save one of two persons in equal peril, and one of those in peril was, say, his wife." Fried remarks that

547

"surely it would be absurd to insist that … he must treat both equally, perhaps by flipping a coin." Williams adds, "surely *this* is a justification on behalf of the rescuer, that the person he chose to rescue was his wife?" And he says that by this something "ambitious" might be intended,

> essentially involving the idea that moral principle can legitimise his preference, yielding the conclusion that in situations of this kind it is at least all right (morally permissible) to save one's wife. … But this construction provides the agent with one thought too many: it might have been hoped by some (for instance, by his wife) that his motivating thought, fully spelled out, would be the thought that it was his wife, not that it was his wife and that in situations of this kind it is permissible to save one's wife.[6]

I will take it that the lesson to draw from the example is that there is something objectionable about a person who is motivated by the thought that saving his wife is the right (or permissible) thing to do, rather than by the thought that he can only save one and that woman is his wife. What "might have been hoped" was that the man would be motivated by a desire to save his wife, and not by a desire to do the right thing.

Intuitions about Williams' example are strong, and they appear to be independent of metaethical theory. In *The Moral Problem*, though, Michael Smith pressed Williams' point into service on behalf of Internalism, against Externalism, in what I will call (following Hallvard Lillehammer[7]) the Fetishism argument. Smith presents this argument as a kind of dilemma, but Lillehammer focuses on one horn of the dilemma, the "fetishism horn." Here is Smith's argument.[8]

A good and strong-willed person will be reliably motivated to do what he believes to be right. Each metaethical theory must explain this fact. Internalist metaethical theories will already have an explanation, for any Internalist theory has already explained a conceptual connection between moral judgment and motivation. Externalists have no explanation of any such conceptual connection, because they do not believe that there is one. But they too must clearly agree that there is a conceptual connection between being a *good*[9] *moral agent* and being reliably motivated to do what is right. Externalists will explain this connection by saying what it is to be a good moral agent. Smith thinks that they have to say that a good moral agent is one with good moral motivations, and that in one or another way this characterization will be cashed out by saying that a good moral agent is one who is motivated to do what is right. Now consider the following sentence attributing moral motivation to Kalista:

(K) Kalista desires to do what is right.

(K) is ambiguous. It could mean that for each thing that is in fact right, Kalista desires to do that thing. Or it could mean that Kalista has a desire whose content is: to do whatever is right. Smith calls the first reading the *de re* reading, and the second the *de dicto* reading. The argument against Externalism is a dilemma. If the Externalist chooses the *de dicto* reading he is impaled on one horn, and if he chooses the *de re* reading then he is impaled on the other.

Suppose (K) is given the *de re* reading. Kalista is a good moral agent in virtue of her desiring to do what is, as a matter of fact, right. Now clearly she won't be a good moral agent if her motivation is, say, to get a promotion by pleasing her fine upstanding boss. Rather she must be motivated *non-derivatively* as Smith says, or as I shall say, *originally*, by whatever features of actions make them right. But now suppose that Kalista is at first a libertarian, but comes to be convinced that libertarianism is incorrect and that a more utilitarian moral theory is correct. Then good moral agent that she is, she will stop voting for Libertarian political candidates and start voting for, say, Social Democrats. A good moral agent's motivations track her moral beliefs. Call this the *tracking condition*. The *de re* interpretation of (K) cannot explain the tracking condition. For original concern for certain values is not apt to change in the wake of changing belief. The *de re* reading is impaled on the tracking horn.

Suppose (K) is instead given the *de dicto* reading. Kalista is a good moral agent in virtue of her desiring to do whatever turns out to be the right thing to do. This desire is one she could have even if she has no idea of what the right thing to do is, or if she is uncertain. On the *de dicto* reading, (K) does explain tracking. But if the *de dicto* reading of (K) does characterize Kalista, then she appears to be the sort of agent that Williams found unattractive. She is motivated to vote for Social Democrats, or to give money to famine relief, not by the thought that in so doing she will benefit the starving and the needy, but by the thought that in so doing she will do what she is morally required to do. And this motivation is *not* what characterizes a good moral agent. It is *fetishistic*, focusing on an aspect of the action removed from the aspect that motivates good moral agents.[10] So the *de dicto* reading is impaled on the fetishism horn.

If Smith's argument is successful, then the standoff in metaethics might be broken. It would, at least, draw support for Internalism from some more squarely normative intuitions, and that would be very welcome help. Unlike Lillehammer, I do think that the Fetishism argument is at least largely successful against the *desire de dicto* Externalist explanation of moral motivation.[11] But this is far from the end of the story. For there are Externalist alternatives.

In § 2, I present one of the alternatives: what I call the model of Suggestible People. I consider two objections to this model and answer them. A fuller answer to the second objection occupies § 3, where I explain two different ways in which a desire can be conditional. In § 4, I present a different alternative Externalist model: the model of a person with the second order desire to desire to do whatever is in fact right. I also argue (a) that this model is distinct from the model of Suggestible People, and (b) that it is superior to the model of Suggestible People. In § 5, I reply to an objection to the second order desire model, namely, that it suffers from its own sort of fetishism. I conclude that there is no sound argument from Williams' point to Internalism.

2 A THIRD EXTERNALIST MODEL: SUGGESTIBLE PEOPLE

An analogy will help to clarify Smith's argument, and also to suggest the third path for Externalists.

2.1 My list of foods

Suppose that I kept a list of foods, changing my list from time to time and giving you hints about what was on the list, occasionally showing it to you. And suppose that you had a desire to eat whatever was listed. There are two ways you could want to eat what was on my list. First, it might just so happen that I have listed exactly those foods that you like to eat. Or maybe it isn't a coincidence, maybe I have been keeping tabs on you, and my list is called "Things you like to eat." Then your desire would be *de re*: it is true of each item on my list that you desire to eat it. Admittedly this would be an odd thing for me to do. But second, you might be the odd one. You might have a peculiar desire *de dicto*, whose content was: to eat whatever is on the list. Then you would ask me what was listed today and try to sneak a peek every now and then. If you saw me writing "avocado," you would want to eat some avocados, even though at the moment you can't stand them.

Now clearly in the first case you would not meet the tracking condition. As my list changed, your culinary desires would not change in step with it (unless by amazing coincidence, or if I were trying to list your favorite foods and kept good track). The *de re* desire (or really, desires, since it would be at best very unnatural to say that you had a single desire: to eat those things which are, as a matter of fact, on my list; we would surely say that you had a bunch of desires, one desire to eat avocados, one desire to eat banana chips, one to eat cucumbers, and so on) does not meet the tracking condition.

The problem with the *de re* desire to do what is right is precisely that it does not meet the tracking condition. A good moral agent will meet the tracking condition; her motivations will change to keep in step with her moral beliefs.

In the second case, you would clearly meet the tracking condition. Insofar as your beliefs about my list were correct, your motivations would change with my list, you would continue over time to desire (*de dicto*) to eat what was listed. And even when your beliefs were false, you would still desire to eat what you believed to be on my list, and your motivations would track your beliefs. In this respect, you would be like the second Externalist model of the good moral agent, whose motivations track what she believes to be good, even as those beliefs change.

But when you came to desire to eat avocados, a true avocadophile would frown, for you would not want to eat avocados for the right reason. You would want to eat them only because they are listed. The avocadophile thinks this is a disgusting attitude, a kind of list fetish. And the second Externalist model of the good and strong-willed moral agent is subject to a fetishism objection, too. A good moral agent wants to relieve the suffering of others, not because relieving suffering is right, not because it is in the extension of "right," not because it is on the List of Right Actions, but because she cares directly for those who suffer. She likes avocados.

Can we imagine a person who meets the tracking condition and also avoids fetishism?

2.2 Suggestibility explained

Suppose you have no particular desire (*de dicto*) to eat what is listed, but you do have an equally odd disposition: you are disposed to desire all and only those foods you come to believe are on my list. Maybe you wear a patch on your arm that delivers a slow but steady drip of medication that maintains this disposition by exploiting your endocrine system. To you it feels like this: you can't stand oysters, but as you watch me inscribe "oysters" on my list, you suddenly warm to the idea, and you develop a craving for them. Call a person with such a disposition, *suggestible*.

A suggestible person wants to eat whatever she believes is on my list. She does not have any desire *de dicto* with the content: to eat what is on my list. And when she comes to desire avocados, she does so in a way that an avocadophile admires, for she just loves them. The suggestible person wants avocados (when she sees them named on my list) in as thoroughly non-instrumental a way as can be. So she is no fetishist. But obviously she does meet the tracking condition.

The *morally suggestible* person has a (structurally) similar disposition. It is a disposition to want to perform a certain kind of action upon coming to believe that that kind of action is morally right. The morally suggestible person has no standing *de dicto* desire to do what is right, or what she believes is right, and when she does desire to do certain actions which she believes right, she doesn't desire them in a fetishistic way. She really does love avocados. And she meets the tracking condition. Because of her suggestibility, she predictably and regularly wants to do whatever she believes to be right.

David Copp has proposed something very like this model as an alternative to the two Externalist models suggested and rejected by Smith. Copp writes,

[C]onsider the idea of a disposition to desire straightaway to do what one believes to be right. A good and strong-willed person might have this disposition. If so, and if she comes to believe it is right to vote, she desires straightaway to vote without deriving this desire from an underlying desire.[12]

It is this sort of person that I have in mind. I am calling such a person, a morally suggestible person. A morally suggestible person meets both challenges: she meets the tracking condition, and she is no fetishist. Can an Externalist use moral suggestibility as a model of good moral agency? Or is there something wrong with the model?

2.3 Two objections

First Objection

The description of suggestible people is a sham, because it attributes to such people certain dispositions while denying that they have certain *de dicto* desires. The dispositions attributed simply *are* the *de dicto* desires in question. So it's as though you have attempted to stipulate that a certain polygon has three sides but not three angles.

I think this objection may be one that Michael Smith used in *The Moral Problem*, though not as an objection so much as a hasty way to conclude that on an Externalist model, a good moral person *must* be one who desires to do what is right. He attributes to the Externalist the claim "that what explains the reliable connection between judgement and motivation is a motivational disposition I have in virtue of which I count as a good person."[13] Smith adds, "In other words, what explains the reliability of the connection is the *content of my moral motivation*." And then he canvasses the two possible motivational contents: the content given by the *de re* reading of (K) and the one given by the *de dicto* reading of (K). Later, Smith puts what I take to be the same point like this.

[Externalists could say] that moralists change their motivations in this way because what makes someone a moralist is the fact that they are simply so disposed that they change their desires given that they change their moral beliefs. ... In other words, the moralist is someone who simply desires, contingently, to do what is right.[14]

I think Smith is essentially making my First Objection.

Here is a simple reply to the First Objection. When the suggestible person discovers that I have listed avocados, she comes to desire avocados in an *original* way, directly, not instrumentally as a way to satisfy her general desire to eat what is on my list. Someone with the *de dicto* desire to eat what is on my list comes to desire avocados only instrumentally, when she learns that I have listed them. So that is an obvious difference. But it suggests the Second Objection.

Second Objection

The reply just given, saying that the desires that the morally suggestible person is disposed to have are not instrumental desires, contradicts the definition or essence of an instrumental desire. For an instrumental desire is one that is contingent upon a certain belief. That is the only grasp we have on the notion of an instrumental desire.

I don't think Smith has ever made this objection, but it is suggested by the first. The idea is an essentially functionalist one. It is that what makes a desire to φ instrumental is that, for some ψ, it is contingent on a belief that by φ-ing one will ψ. What identifies my desire to be wealthy as an instrumental desire is that it is contingent on my beliefs about what wealth can get me, whereas by contrast someone who has fetishized wealth wants to be wealthy independent of what he thinks money can buy. Since a suggestible person's desire to eat avocados is contingent on her belief that I have listed avocados, that desire is instrumental, and similarly, the morally suggestible person's desire to help the poor is contingent on his belief that helping the poor is right, and so it is an instrumental desire.

But the thought behind this Second Objection seems to be false. For if you are suggestible, and come to believe that I have listed avocados, what happens to you is that you suddenly find yourself wanting to eat avocados. You would find the very thought of eating avocados to drive you wild with desire. Your mouth waters as you contemplate guacamole. Imagine instead a person who would, upon learning that I had listed avocados, feel a very grudging desire to eat some. Her lips would pucker up with disgust, but she would think, "Oh well, I guess I'd better." It seems exactly apt to ascribe to her the *de dicto* desire to eat what is on my list. But it seems particularly *inapt* to ascribe that desire to the suggestible person.

While this reply seems compelling, it rests heavily on the phenomenology of desire. That is not a good resting place. For the Second Objector might plausibly deny that desires are mainly characterized by their phenomenology, and especially that such a deep and structural feature of a desire as whether it is instrumental could depend on how it feels. I have some sympathy with this claim, myself. Fortunately, I have a more satisfactory, though more complicated reply.

3 TWO WAYS A DESIRE CAN BE CONDITIONAL

I said above that a suggestible person's desire to eat avocados is contingent on her belief that by eating them she will eat what is on my list (that is to say, on her belief that avocados are on the list). But there are two ways in which a desire can be contingent. A desire's instrumentality is related to only one of those ways, and not to the way in which the suggestible person's desire is contingent.

So first, a desire can be contingent on some proposition, p (for example, the proposition that Martha believes I have listed avocados) in the sense that its existence depends on p. If tomorrow p is no longer the case, then the desire will no longer exist; if p had not been the case, the desire would not have existed. A suggestible person's desire for avocados is contingent in this way on the proposition that she believes avocados are listed. But second, a desire can be contingent on p in the sense that its content, or its satisfaction condition, is itself conditioned on p. For example, your desire to fly a kite in the park tomorrow is conditional on there not being a hurricane. The desire is not satisfied if you fly a kite in the park tomorrow in a hurricane. It is common to have desires whose existence is contingent on a certain proposition, but whose content is not conditioned on the proposition. For example, Derek Parfit's desire that Venice not sink into the sea[15] is obviously contingent on the proposition that Parfit is alive, for it would not exist if he were not alive and it will not exist when he dies. But its content is not conditional on Parfit's being alive, for its satisfaction conditions in no way entail that he lives. I will say that a desire is *contingent* on p if its existence depends on p, and *conditioned* on p if its content or satisfaction depends on p.

Now a desire to ϕ that is conditioned on the proposition that by ϕ-ing one will ψ is, plausibly at least, an instrumental desire; one desires to ϕ only as a means to ψ-ing.[16] But a desire to ϕ that is contingent on one's believing that by ϕ-ing one will ψ is not, at least not necessarily, an instrumental desire. To see this, consider Julius.

Julius has an unpleasant and irrational antipathy to Romans. This antipathy is caused, in some extrarational way, by his belief that one of his ancestors is Roman. Julius does not know which ancestor it is, nor does he have any other feelings or beliefs about this ancestor. It's not that he dislikes the ancestor, is ashamed of him, or anything like that. But if Julius came to believe that he does not after all have a Roman ancestor, he would immediately lose his prejudice against Romans. So Julius desires to avoid Romans, and this desire is contingent on his belief that by avoiding Romans he will avoid people from the birthplace of one of his ancestors. But it is clearly wrong to say that he desires to avoid Romans *in order* to avoid people from the birthplace of one of his ancestors. If this is not clear enough, think of what would happen if Julius came to believe that none of his ancestors was Roman after all. He would lose his prejudice. And then he would certainly not desire to avoid anyone from the birthplace of one of his ancestors. By losing the belief, he would lose not only the contingent desire, but the only plausible candidate for the end toward which the contingent desire might be a means. But instrumental desires don't work that way. If I want to swallow this pill as a means to reducing my fever, and then come to believe that swallowing the pill will *not* reduce my fever, I do not lose the desire to reduce my fever.

So desires that are contingent on one's believing a conditional proposition are not thereby shown to be instrumental desires. The sort of contingency that demonstrates instrumentality is the other kind, the conditionality of a desire. A suggestible person's desire for avocados is not conditioned on the person's belief that avocados are listed, nor is it conditioned on avocados actually being listed. But that is exactly the sort of contingency that is relevant to instrumentality. So the suggestible person's desire for avocados is not instrumental. By contrast, a person who desires *de dicto* to eat what is on my list *does* have a merely instrumental desire to eat what is on my list, for that desire is conditioned on avocados being listed. Similarly, a morally suggestible person's desire to help the needy is contingent on her belief that by helping the needy she will be doing the right thing, but it is not conditioned on the proposition that by helping the needy she will be doing the right thing. Her desire to help the needy is conditioned on nothing at all. So the morally suggestible person desires originally, not instrumentally, to help the needy.

The Second Objection is thus refuted. I don't think it should be surprising that it fails. For remember Williams' point. It was that the man who is motivated by the thought that helping his wife is morally right seems somehow defective in his motivations. An agent is a moral fetishist, in our sense, just in case what appeals to the agent about the moral actions that she wants to perform, is that they are moral actions. The good moral agent, by contrast, finds attractive the properties that *ground* the rightness, the right-making properties, or what she takes to be the right-making properties. But then it seems very plain that the morally suggestible person is no fetishist. For her disposition is a disposition to desire to φ when she comes to believe that φ-ing is right. For instance, when she comes to believe that helping the needy is right, she develops a desire to help the needy. And then it is the thought, "By giving money to the Red Cross I will help the needy" that motivates her to give money to the Red Cross. There is no thought of rightness as such in her motivating thought.

I am going to argue that moral suggestibility is not a good Externalist model of moral motivation. First, though, I will introduce another alternative. The problem with the moral suggestibility model will emerge more clearly by comparison with this alternative.

4 ANOTHER EXTERNALIST MODEL: SECOND ORDER DESIRES

In reply to the suggestion of Copp's I mentioned above, Smith writes, "Instead of saying, as I suggest, that moralists possess a desire to do the right thing, they [Copp and

David Brink] both suggest what makes someone a moralist is the fact that they have a desire to acquire noninstrumental desires to perform acts with right-making features."[17] I don't think that was Copp's suggestion. It may have been Brink's suggestion.[18] But as a matter of fact, whether it was anyone's suggestion at all, it matches nicely an idea introduced by David Schmidtz in another context.

4.1 Second order desires and maieutic ends

Schmidtz argues[19] that even according to a generally instrumental conception of practical reasoning, a person might still be able to choose final ends. A final end is one that is pursued for its own sake and not merely for the sake of something else. Traditionally it has been supposed that an instrumentalist about practical reason cannot accept that final ends might be chosen, or at least not chosen for a reason, since the only practical reasons we can have are instrumental ones. But Schmidtz introduces the idea of a *maieutic* end: "an end achieved through the process of coming to have other ends."[20] As an example, he offers the goal of having a career. You might choose a career in medicine instrumentally, perhaps because you want to have a large income and believe that by having a career in medicine you would have a large income. Or you might just think that careers come with certain goals of their own, goals which are satisfying to pursue. You choose medicine for this reason, an instrumental one. But once you have chosen medicine as a career, the goals you have – of relieving suffering, being a respected member of the medical community, and so forth – are goals you pursue for their own sakes. Having adopted these goals for one reason, you then pursue them not for that reason but for reasons internal to the outlook of your profession.

Notice that some maieutic ends can only be satisfied by the adoption of some fairly specific sort of final end. For instance, you might want to have a career that feels intrinsically rewarding, that "fills your life with meaning," that gives you a sense of purpose. It is plausible that only a career anchored by final ends like the end of relieving the suffering of the sick can achieve this maieutic end. Becoming the sort of doctor who cares for his patients only instrumentally just won't do the trick.[21]

A maieutic end is much like a second order desire. To have a maieutic end is to desire to have certain ends, or ends of a certain type. If your end is to have a career, and part of having a career is having certain other ends, then one of your ends is to have ends of a certain kind. Your desire would be to have the desires constitutive of a rewarding career (and also, of course, to have the other things that constitute a rewarding career). You would want to desire to cure the sick, you would want to desire to have the respect of the medical community, and so forth. This want is a second order desire. Now not all second order desires are effective. I might want to stop desiring junk food, but my wanting it doesn't make it so. But suppose that a particular second order desire, the desire to value for their own sake those things that are (or that one believes to be) morally right, is an effective one. Then someone who had such a desire would be the sort of person Smith thinks that Brink and Copp are describing. And such a person would, I think, be a plausible model for an Externalist of a good moral agent. Let's call him David. According to this model, "what makes someone a moralist is the fact that they have a desire to acquire noninstrumental desires to perform acts with right-making features" (as Smith puts it in the quotation cited above).

The model passes both tests. David's motivations will track his changes in moral view, for once he comes to believe that, say, voting for Social Democrats is right, David's second order desire will kick in and he will actually desire to vote for Social Democrats. And David is no fetishist. For his end of having moral ends is maieutic, and the ends to which it gives rise are, once arisen, free standing, final ends rather than instrumental ones. He desires to vote for Social Democrats because (a genuinely causal "because") he believes that it is right to do so, but once the desire is generated it is not conditioned on the belief that voting for Social Democrats is right, any more than our doctor's desire to cure the sick is conditioned on his belief that medicine would be a satisfying career. The doctor chose medicine *because* he expected it to be satisfying (and lucrative) but once chosen and its constitutive ends adopted, the career is no longer pursued for (merely) instrumental reasons.

4.2 Moral suggestibility is not a second order desire

Smith is wrong to say that Copp's model, which is a model of a morally suggestible person, is a model of someone with a second order desire to do what is right. To show that he is wrong, I will provide a new test, a more sophisticated version of the tracking condition. We will see that the moral suggestibility model fails this test, while the second order desire model passes it. The argument will show both that the two models are distinct, and that the second order desire model is superior.

A morally suggestible person meets the tracking condition: her motivations change in step with her moral beliefs. But her motivations do not seem to track her general doxastic state in quite the right way. The example of Ursula shows why not.[22]

Suppose Ursula is a utilitarian. She believes that utilitarian moral theory is true. And suppose that she is morally suggestible. So Ursula desires that the net happiness of sentient beings be maximized. Like many utilitarians, and contrary to unflattering portrayals of utilitarianism, Ursula cares about people (and other animals) and their happiness and suffering; she is not concerned originally with abstract quantities or measures. But although she does believe that utilitarian theory is correct, Ursula has a healthy sense of her own fallibility. She has found herself unable to give answers to challenges raised recently in her moral philosophy class by adherents to rights-based theories. She thinks it is possible, though not likely, that some individual rights should properly act as side constraints against utility maximization.

Ursula is sufficiently self-aware that she knows she is morally suggestible. So she knows that if she ever does come to believe in genuine moral side constraints, she will desire to abide by them. This troubles her, but not in the way such uncertainty might trouble you or me. You or I would, presumably, be troubled by the thought that in our juggernautic pursuit of utilitarianism we might be doing something terribly wrong. What troubles Ursula is that she might someday *correctly* become convinced that a rights theory is correct, and then she would no longer pursue utilitarianism whole-heartedly. Naturally this bothers her a great deal, because it means much of the suffering that she could relieve would remain in the world. For her, there is no compensation in the fact that she would be respecting people's rights, because Ursula doesn't care at all about anyone's rights. This attitude seems strange, but it is the attitude of a morally suggestible person.

It is not the attitude of a person with a second order desire that she desire to do whatever is right – of David, say. David wants to desire to do whatever is in fact the right thing to do. If David thought it possible that moral side constraints were a fundamental feature of true morality, his second order desire would motivate him to investigate. For he wants to have desires of a certain sort (namely, ones whose objects are morally right actions) and he knows that there is a significant chance that the only way he can have desires of that sort is by thorough moral reflection and investigation. So he will be motivated to investigate. But the attitude of a morally suggestible person like Ursula will be more like a fear that she might come to change her mind.

To see that this must be the attitude of the morally suggestible, note that in considering the possibility that there are genuine and important moral rights, Ursula acquires no motivation whatsoever. She does not now care about any such rights, and she has no conditional desire to respect them if they really are well grounded theoretically. Her moral suggestibility provides her with no such concern. The connection between her moral beliefs and her motivations is a pure disposition, a rational connection. Some analogous examples may help to make Ursula's situation more plain.

Recall Julius, who has the unpleasant and irrational antipathy to Romans, caused by his belief that one of his ancestors is a Roman. But suppose we have caught Julius before he has found out anything about his ancestors. So far, he has no prejudice against Romans, but if he were to discover that one of his ancestors is a Roman, he would come to have that prejudice. Suppose that Julius is keenly self-aware, so that he knows he has this disposition to develop prejudices. Since Julius, like you and me, does not want to be saddled with irrational prejudice, he is glad that he doesn't believe that any of his ancestors is Roman. But he is worried, because he thinks he might just possibly have a Roman ancestor, and he is afraid that if he learns more about his family tree, there is a small chance that he will find some Roman ancestor lurking in his past.

Julius's reaction, quite sensibly it seems, is to avoid finding out any more than he already knows about his ancestry. For he does not want to develop a desire to avoid Romans. Of course, he thinks it is unlikely that any of his ancestors are Roman, but there is a chance, and it is not one he wants to take. Ursula's epistemic situation is analogous to Julius's. That is why she wants to avoid engaging in any more moral theorizing. She is afraid she might possibly learn that individual rights are morally important, and that her suggestibility would be triggered and she would no longer do everything she could to relieve suffering and promote happiness. Unlikely, but not a chance she is willing to take.

Here is a different example. This example will confuse the issue, but only, I hope, temporarily. Mark does not like snails. Mark is suggestible; he is disposed to desire to eat things upon discovering that they are on my list. And he knows that he is suggestible. Though Mark does not believe that I have listed snails, he thinks that I just might do a disgusting, sneaky thing like that, and of course he knows that if he ever does discover that I have listed snails, he will desire to eat them. What should Mark's attitude be toward acquiring further information about my list? An old joke: I don't like snails, and I'm glad I don't, because if I liked them I would eat them, and I can't stand the creepy things. But Mark, no doubt, will at least have no aversion to finding out that I've added snails to my list. He knows he would then desire to eat snails, and he does not now desire to eat snails, but this ought not to *bother* him. Why is Mark's attitude not analogous to Ursula's or Julius's? Is one of the stories wrong?

Even beyond their preferences for foods, most people have a desire to eat things they like. This desire is not a mere "desire by courtesy," like the general desire that one's desires be satisfied, or the general belief that one's beliefs are true. The desire to eat things you like has independent force and import. For it means that you now desire that you will eat snails five years hence if you will like snails five years hence, even if you do not like them now. And it means that you prefer that *if you did* like snails, you would eat them even if you do not as a matter of fact like them. The desire to eat things you like is, as far as I can tell, just an instance or instrument of the more general desire for pleasurable experiences. Eating things you like is a pleasurable experience. This is why Mark's case is unlike Julius's or Ursula's. For most people, eating snails has no independent importance above and beyond the provision of pleasurable (or unpleasant) experience. It might be different if snails were particularly wholesome or particularly unwholesome. If they were, or if Mark had some other special reason to want to avoid snails, his case would be different.

Ursula and Julius do not expect to gain any particularly pleasurable experience by acquiring and acting on the desires they might acquire if they learned more. Or perhaps they would, but the importance to them of these experiences pales in comparison to other aspects of the desires and their targets. For Julius, the problem is that if he were to discover that one of his ancestors were Roman, and thus acquire a desire to avoid

Romans, he would frustrate a desire (or better, a value) that he now has. The prejudice would interfere with the ordinary important running of his life, and furthermore it is a trait of character which he now finds disturbing. For Ursula, the problem is that if she were to learn that rights really are morally important, and thus acquire a desire to respect them, her present desire to contribute to the welfare of sentient beings would be at least partly frustrated. And this desire, unlike a desire to avoid eating snails, is not conditioned on its own persistence.

Now surely Ursula's is entirely the wrong attitude for a good moral agent. A good moral agent who believes utilitarianism but thinks that there is a chance that a rights-based theory is correct would surely want to investigate the possibility. So while a morally suggestible person does meet the simple tracking condition, in that her motivations follow around her moral beliefs, she does not meet a more sophisticated tracking condition, because her motivations do not respond properly to her moral uncertainty.

I conclude that the moral suggestibility model is distinct from the second order desire model of moral motivation, and that moral suggestibility is not a good model because it fails the sophisticated tracking condition. The second order desire model, on the other hand, looks so far to be an acceptable Externalist alternative.

In the final section, I will consider a challenge to the second order desire model. I will argue that the challenge is not successful, and that the second order desire model is indeed an acceptable Externalist alternative.

5 FETISHISM AT THE SECOND ORDER OF DESIRE

As I said, Smith attributes the second order desire model to Brink and Copp. And he objects to this view, he says, for exactly the same reason that he objects to the *de dicto* model of the morally good person, namely, that it is a model of a fetishist, not of a good moral agent. I find his reasoning somewhat difficult to follow, but here is what he says.

> It thus is not the case that they [Brink and Copp, as defenders of the second order desire model] are committed to the false view that morally virtuous people are ultimately motivated by the fact that their acts have right-making features, rather, when they act, they are motivated by the features that they believe to be right-making features themselves.
>
> Sure enough, when they act, they are appropriately motivated. But what ultimately moves them, as moralists? All Brink and Copp have managed to do is to reorient the fetish that their so-called morally virtuous people possess. It isn't now about their actions. Rather it is about themselves and their own desires. As I described them they were ultimately motivated by a desire that their acts have

right-making features, not be the features that they believed to be right-making features themselves. This seems to me perverse, and Brink and Copp apparently agree. But as Brink and Copp describe morally virtuous people they are ultimately motivated by the fact that they have noninstrumental desires to perform acts with right-making features, not by the fact that they have noninstrumental desires to perform acts with the features that they believe to be the right-making features themselves. ... They should therefore agree that the morally virtuous person they describe sounds equally precious, equally self-absorbed, equally fixated on something that isn't of any moral significance: the moral standing of the contents of his first-order desires, rather than the features in virtue of which his first-order desires have the moral standing they have.[23]

As I understand it, Smith's complaint is that a second order desire with the content, that whatever is right I desire to do, is fetishistic. To clarify, we might again distinguish senses of a desire attribution by disambiguating scope. (Or to put it as Smith did originally, there are two desires, the second order one and its first order object, that might be *de re*.)

(D)   D. desires that he desire to do what is right.

This time we have three possibilities.

(i)   Desiree desires that (Desiree desires that (x) (if x is right then Desiree does x)).
(ii)   David desires that (x) (if x is right then (David desires that David does x)).
(iii) (x) [If x is right, then (Dana desires that (Dana desires that Dana does x))].

The first attributes to Desiree the desire to be a fetishist.

The third is what Smith thinks must be true for Dana to be a good moral agent. But (iii) could not explain tracking.

The second is the claim that Smith attributes to Brink and Copp, and he thinks it means that David is a fetishist. It's not that David's desire to *act* has been misplaced. It's that his desire to desire things is misplaced. For example, suppose David comes to believe that it is right to end the practice of using chimps in medical research. So he desires that he desire to prevent such use. But David has this second order desire only instrumentally, only as a way of achieving his real goal, which is to desire to do those things which are, in fact, morally right. A good agent would care *originally*, not instrumentally, about desiring to save chimps.

Smith also appears to be suggesting that David's first order motivations are infected with the fetishism of his second order motivations, for he says: "as Brink and Copp describe morally virtuous people they are ultimately motivated by the fact that they have noninstrumental desires to perform acts with right-making features." Whether or not Smith means to say so, it does not appear to be true. There is a sense in which the second order desire is David's "ultimate" motivation, but the ultimacy is only causal. His first order motivations are caused by his second order motivations, but once in place they no longer depend, in any rational way, on the existence or content of the second order motive. In Schmidtz's terminology, the end of having moral ends is maieutic; once it gives birth to the moral ends themselves, those new ends have their own lives, and might be sustained by other new concerns or merely by their own inertia.

Still, there is a challenge to be met. Even if David is not convicted of *acting* for the wrong reasons, out of the wrong motives, he might be guilty of *desiring* for the wrong reasons.

Does (ii) mean that David is a fetishist? To be moved by the thought of righteousness is to have one's motivations removed from their proper target, which is the characteristics of the action that *make* it right.[24] But now we are wondering whether a similar point holds when you are thinking about what to desire. You are sitting in your office, thinking about Williams' example, and you wonder what would motivate you in such a situation. You hope, let's suppose, that you would be motivated by the thought that it is your wife (or your husband). Why do you hope so? If (ii) is true, David hopes so because he thinks that is the morally best motivation to have. Smith thinks that David's hope ought to be motivated, not by the thought this is the morally right motivation to have, but by the thought that, after all, it would be his wife. That is Smith's complaint against the second order desire model. But Smith is wrong.

First, notice that nobody can complain about the desire itself, the second order desire that (ii) attributes. It is common ground that a person ought to want to be moved by right-making characteristics of actions, and that she ought to want this even if she is not sure what the right-making features of actions are. If she were told that some day in the future she will see clearly what features of actions are the right-making ones, and asked whether she hopes that when that day comes she will be motivated by those features, she surely must say that she does hope so. Otherwise she could hardly be called a good moral agent. So it is not (ii) itself that provides any ground for complaint, not its truth. The ground for complaint would have to be that the second order desire attributed by (ii) is playing the role in the model that really ought to be played by something else.

But second, it would be a mistake to think that the second order desire plays too much of a role. While the second order desire does play an original causal role in generating the admirable first order motivations, it needn't play any maintenance role once the first order motivation is formed. Think of what happens once David has appreciated the rightness of working to end chimp experimentation. He now cares originally, not instrumentally about ending the experiments. And because he cares about ending the experiments, he cares about those means that are instrumental toward ending them, and in particular, he desires, hopes, to continue to be motivated by the thought of chimpanzee suffering (since he won't act unless he cares, and he wants to act). So now he has another second order desire: he wants to continue to want to end chimp experimentation. This new second order desire is thoroughly *de re*. No thought of rightness enters into it. It is an important desire, I think. A first order desire to end chimp experimentation that was maintained *only* by the general second order desire to want what is right, would seem rather too tenuous, too much like Mark's desire to avoid eating snails.

Third, David's first order desire to end chimp experimentation is not at all conditioned on its being right to do so. This last point may not be obvious. It is an open question, not settled by anything said about David so far, whether his desire to end chimp experimentation is *contingent* on his continuing to believe that it is right to do so. I am not sure, myself, whether a good moral agent's desires would all be contingent in this way. I suspect not. I suspect that if you were persuaded that contributing money to aid the suffering was morally right, that you would continue to care about it even if you were later convinced that rugged individualism was a sounder basis for moral prescription. But in any case, whether contingent or not, the first order desire is not conditioned on the rightness of the action. The simplest way to show this is to examine the formula (ii). The consequent of its quantified conditional is just the formula,

David desires that David does *x*

and not, in particular,

David desires that David does *x* so long as *x* is right

The content of the first order desire that is generated by the second order desire is not conditioned on the rightness of doing *x*.

Let me sum up.

It would be important, and gratifying, and interesting if the Internalist/Externalist impasse in metaethics could be broken by appeal to Bernard Williams' "one thought too many" point from normative theory. Michael Smith argues that any Externalist model of moral motivation is subject to the fetishism objection derived from Williams' point, or else it fails (what I called) the tracking condition. Smith originally considered only two Externalist models: the *de dicto* desire to do what is right, and the *de re* desire to do what is right. The first is fetishistic. The second fails the tracking condition.

I explained two alternative models that an Externalist might employ: the model of a Morally Suggestible person, and the model of someone with a second order desire that for every right action *x*, he desire to do *x*. I showed that these models are genuinely distinct, both from the first order *de dicto* desire model and from each other. And both new models meet Smith's original criteria: neither is a model of a fetishist, both meet the tracking condition. The Moral Suggestibility model, however, fails a more sophisticated tracking condition, since a Morally Suggestible person will not respond in the intuitively right way to her own moral uncertainty. The second model, on the other hand, is an adequate model for an Externalist. It meets even the more sophisticated tracking condition. And, contrary to Smith's complaint, an agent with a second order desire to desire to do what is right is not a fetishist, even at the second order of desire.

Internalists will have to rejoin the dispute with Externalists back at the metaethical level.

NOTES

* Thanks to David Schmidtz for some comments on a draft; to an anonymous referee for two useful suggestions; and to Sarah Wright for some insightful remarks about the general subject that she made in a seminar. Sarah's comments got me thinking along the lines presented in this paper.

1 This is one version of Internalism, a simplified derivative of the one Michael Smith uses (Smith 1994); see pp. 60–1 [pp. 533–4, this volume], and for other versions see the works cited on those pages.

2 For example, in Brink (1986; 1989, esp. chapter 3; and more recently, 1997).

3 As Dennett (1980) calls them. The pumps I'm thinking of are Hare's Missionaries, in Hare (1952), 9.4, pp. 148–50, and also Horgan and Timmons' Moral Twin Earth, in Horgan and Timmon (1992). Hare imagines a missionary captured by cannibals who intend to eat him. The missionary attempts to persuade the cannibals that it would be wrong to eat him. At first they do not understand what he means by "wrong"; the missionary explains by telling them what sorts of things are called "wrong." The cannibals come to understand the descriptive content, but wonder why the wrongness of eating a missionary should count *against* it.

Horgan and Timmons' Moral Twin Earth is populated by English speakers who subscribe to a broadly utilitarian moral system in reflective equilibrium, so that although they agree with earthling Anglophones in many moral judgments, they disagree in some significant ways. Horgan and Timmons claim that the disagreement does not show that the twin-English word "wrong" merely has a somewhat different meaning from the English word; we are still inclined to think that we and the Twin Earthlings *disagree* about something, that our dispute isn't merely semantic.

4 Williams (1981).

5 Fried (1970), p. 227.

6 Williams (1981), p. 18.

7 Lillehammer (1997).

8 Smith (1994), pp. 71–6 [pp. 537–41, this volume]. In what follows I ignore some technical difficulties in sorting out distinctions between desires to do what is right and desires to do what one believes to be right. Some of these are discussed by Lillehammer. I don't think it is important to the argument to spell out the different sorts explicitly, and to do so would encumber the exposition to follow.

9 Good and strong-willed, that is. Hereafter I omit the "strong-willed." Smith (1997) uses

"moralist" instead of "good and strong-willed person," and at p. 111, n. 27, he explains that he regrets using the earlier terminology which he now thinks is misleading.

10 What Smith calls "fetishism" may be what J. J. C. Smart has in mind when he says that deontological theories are infected with "rule worship." See Smart and Williams (1973), p. 6.

11 I say "largely" because while I think that a concern with rightness *per se* does look morally unattractive when the object of moral concern is a particular person and her well-being, and especially so when the person bears some special morally significant relationship to the deliberator, the unattractiveness seems to me to dissipate somewhat when the object of moral concern is something more abstract like equality, or fairness, or fidelity to promises. Is it so ugly for a promissor to use the rightness of promise-keeping as his reason for honoring a promise, rather than having an original concern for keeping promises? I suppose I do think it is more admirable to be motivated by a direct concern for promise-keeping, or perhaps for whatever it is that is important about promise-keeping, rather than for promise-keeping's rightness. But it's harder to get excited about it than it is to scorn the man who is motivated by the thought that it is morally right to save one's wife. Felicia Ackerman pointed this out to me in conversation.

12 Copp (1997), p. 50.

13 Smith (1994), p. 73 [p. 539, this volume].

14 Smith (1997), p. 112.

15 See Parfit (1984), p. 151.

16 Only "plausibly," because there are various complications. For one thing, one might be desiring to φ as a *way* of ψ-ing, for example, if I desire to run as a way of getting exercise. Furthermore, one might be desiring to φ, not as a way or means to φ-ing, but as a way or means to doing something that has φ-ing as a byproduct, for example, my desire to take an aspirin only if by taking an aspirin I will lower the column of mercury in the thermometer sticking out of my ear. I do not desire to take the aspirin as a means of lowering the column of mercury, but as a means to something that has lowering the column of mercury as a byproduct. I will ignore these complications.

17 Smith (1997), p. 115.

18 In Brink (1997). Brink notes, "It is quite plausible that morality itself enjoins intrinsic concern for oneself and one's intimates" (p. 27), and later, "It is not that these forms of special concern causally bring about dutiful action; it is, rather, that they are part of one's duty" (p. 29).

19 Schmidtz (1994).

20 Schmidtz (1994), p. 228.

21 Thanks to an anonymous referee for suggesting that I spell out explicitly the point in this paragraph.

22 Sarah Wright used an example like my Ursula example, as an objection to the Moral Suggestibility model of moral motivation, in some comments delivered in a seminar at Brown. I thank her for it.

23 Smith (1997), pp. 115–16.

24 As Korsgaard puts it, the reason for acting is not that the action is right; rather, "the reasons why an action is right and the reasons why you do it, are the same" (1986, p. 10).

REFERENCES

Brink, David O. (1986) "Externalist Moral Realism," *Southern Journal of Philosophy* supplement, pp. 23–42.

——(1989) *Moral Realism and the Foundations of Ethics*, Cambridge University Press, New York.

——(1997) "Moral Motivation," *Ethics*, vol. 108(1), pp. 4–32.

Copp, David (1997) "Belief, Reason, and Motivation: Michael Smith's *The Moral Problem*," *Ethics*, vol. 108(1), pp. 33–54.

Dennett, Daniel (1980) "The Milk of Human Intentionality," *Behavioral and Brain Sciences*, vol. 3, pp. 428–30.

Fried, Charles (1970) *An Anatomy of Values*, Harvard University Press, Cambridge, MA.

Hare, R. M. (1952) *The Language of Morals*, Clarendon Press, Oxford.

Horgan, T. and Timmons, M. (1992) "Troubles for New Wave Moral Semantics: The 'Open Question Argument' Revived," *Philosophical Papers*, vol. 21, pp. 151–73 [Chapter 10, this volume].

Korsgaard, C. (1986) "Skepticism about Practical Reason," *Journal of Philosophy*, vol. 83, pp. 5–25.

Lillehammer, Hallvard (1997) "Smith on Moral Fetishism," *Analysis*, vol. 57(3), pp. 187–95.

Parfit, Derek (1984) *Reasons and Persons*, Clarendon Press, Oxford.

Schmidtz, David (1994) "Choosing Ends," *Ethics*, vol. 104(2), pp. 226–51.

Smart, J.C.C. and Bernard Williams (1973) *Utilitarianism: For and Against*, Cambridge University Press, New York.

Smith, Michael A. (1994) *The Moral Problem*, Blackwell, Oxford.

——(1997) "In Defense of *The Moral Problem*: A Reply to Brink, Copp, and Sayre-McCord," *Ethics*, vol. 108(1), pp. 84–119.

Williams, Bernard (1981) "Persons, Character, and Morality," in B. Williams (ed.) *Moral Luck*, Cambridge University Press, New York, pp. 1–19.

Part 11

THE HUMEAN THEORY OF MOTIVATION

You will have read about motivation elsewhere in this collection (especially in the previous Part), but what is it to be motivated to do something? We say things such as, "He lacked any motivation to stop smoking", or "It was his love for her that motivated him to travel that far". Or, more relevant to us, "It was his judgement that it was right that motivated him to turn in the gun he found". What are we saying in such cases? What psychology are we ascribing to the agent?

It is clear that in such cases we are not committed to any claims about what in fact people do. Recall the point about 'having a motivation of some strength' from the previous Part. So, you might be motivated to turn in a gun you've found but things conspire against you and you keep it. In such a case we don't conclude that we weren't really motivated.

What then does being motivated amount to? Consider an example. Suppose that you've done your exams and the results are due soon. Imagine you have a belief that the letter has arrived with your results. (You hear the doorbell ring, let's imagine.) This, on its own, might not motivate you to do anything. It seems that you need an accompanying desire, such as a desire to know your results. Once you have both elements, then you will be directed to go to the door. In contrast, imagine you have no belief at all about where your results are and when they will arrive. You might still have a desire – a gnawing, irritating desire – to know your results. Now it's odd to imagine how this desire might show itself if you have no belief at all about how you might get to know the results. (After all, we might say that you would ask people if your results have arrived. But why ask them unless you have a belief of some sort that they will be able to help you.) Perhaps your desire shows itself in odd, nervous behaviour, such as your prowling the house and being irritated by people and snapping at them before your results come. We *might* talk of you being motivated here, but you certainly do not have any *directed* motivation. That will come only if you have beliefs about when and where to find out your results.

As this example highlights, we think that in any instance you can have a belief without a desire and vice versa. They seem 'modally distinct' things. Importantly, it seems that the desire is the 'senior partner' when it comes to motivation. There seems to be some sort of motivation in the case when one has a desire but no belief, even if it isn't directed well at all. Indeed, this is a slightly odd characterization. We might go so far as to say that desire *simply is* a state of being motivated. (It's not as if there are *three* distinct things – a belief, a desire, and some motivation in addition.) This whole view – that beliefs and desires are separate and distinct types of mental state, and that desiring (and not believing) simply is the state of being motivated – is precisely the view put forward by holders of the Humean Theory of Motivation (HTM). (Whether or not this was in fact David Hume's view will not concern us, but we will retain the name for continuity and simplicity.)

There is considerable interest in the HTM, primarily because it appears incompatible to hold it whilst also holding two other views at the same time, two views already discussed in other Parts: that moral judgements express beliefs and that moral judgements necessarily motivate. If moral judgements express beliefs, then moral judgements must have some necessary connection to desires if they are to entail motivation, or beliefs must motivate alone. However, to take this line of thought is to give up on the HTM. Thus, if you find cognitivism and internalism plausible then it appears you have either to reject the Humean account of motivation or to tell a story about why, despite appearances, the three claims are not in internal conflict.

Michael Smith takes the latter approach. In his article in this Part he defends the HTM against a number of recent criticisms and gives independent reasons for accepting it. We will briefly consider one problem and one main way he supports his position.

First, on the face of it, there seem to be a whole host of examples showing that the Humean account is false. You may believe that the bubbling springs at Yellowstone Park are great for a midnight swim and desire to go for a midnight swim, but in fact they reach 150–210 degrees Fahrenheit and you'd probably be scalded to death. An outsider might point out that, although you have a belief and an appropriately related desire to go swimming, you surely don't have a reason to go. So here is a case that seems to undermine the Humean account. But Smith (Chapter 31) claims it doesn't and he introduces a crucial distinction to show why: the distinction between *motivating* and *normative reasons*. Sure, it is true that you have a motivating reason to go for a swim, as the Humean would suggest. However, there is no normative reason for you to go for a swim. And it is confusion over this that flatters the example with more force than it deserves. Smith's claim then is that such counter examples to the HTM aren't really counter examples, because the HTM concerns motivating reasons not normative ones.

Second, you might not understand the power and attraction of the HTM unless you have the right account of what a desire is. You might reason as follows. Often there is a certain psychological feeling associated with desires. Perhaps, then, what it is to have a desire is to have a certain psychological feeling. But, Smith claims, if you reasoned like this you'd be mistaken. After all, as popular 'self-help culture' often highlights, we are sometimes not the best judge of the desires we have. Just think back to the example of the exam results. Perhaps you deny that you desire to know your exam results when asked, and speak sincerely. But observers might look at your odd, irritated behaviour and think otherwise. It might then make sense to say, "So-and-so wants to know what they got in their exams", even though you deny it. To this thought Smith adds, crucially, that desires have propositional content. We desire *that* the letter comes, say, or we desire *that* a chocolate bar finds its way into our mouths. In contrast, feelings don't have propositional content. (We don't pain *that* such-and-such; we don't joy *that* such-and-such.) As such, it is important, Smith claims, to distance the HTM from this phenomenological conception of desires.

Once we see this, we can see why the HTM – and its conception of beliefs and desires – is attractive. A metaphorical way of characterizing the difference between beliefs and desires is in terms of 'direction of fit'. Beliefs are those things that try to fit with the world and desires are those things that 'reach out' and try to change the world. Taking this metaphor as a starting point, Smith develops a functionalist account of beliefs and desires in terms of them being states that ground certain dispositions. A desire is the state that grounds dispositions to act in certain ways in certain situations at certain times.

This approach improves on the phenomenological account. It allows us to say that a desire may be associated with a certain psychological feeling without being a psychological feeling. This is because desires may or may not ground the disposition to feel a certain way and whether they do is not essential to them being characterized as desires. Furthermore, we are not the best judge of the dispositions we have and the way we are disposed to act in various situations is, arguably, what it is for a desire to have propositional content.

If Smith is right and beliefs and desires are both states that ground dispositions and both lack a characteristic phenomenology and both have propositional content, why say there are two states at all? Smith claims that the difference lies in their functional role. Consider a perception not-p and a desire that p, in such an instance the desire tends to endure and dispose the agent to bring it about that p. This contrasts with a perception of not-p and the belief that p; in such an instance the belief will go out of existence.

At this point you may wonder why Smith thinks this will help him defend the HTM. For nothing said so far seems to tell us anything about what is needed for motivation. Smith introduces what he calls the 'direction of fit' argument to make the link between his characterization of beliefs and desires and justifying the HTM.

Imagine you are motivated to win the world Sudoku championships. Smith claims that another way of writing this is that winning the world Sudoku championship is a *goal* you have. This, Smith claims, can be thought of as you trying to change the world to fit your desire. (Presently, no one has won the championship, and there is some probability that people other than you can win it. You want to change the world so that you have won the championship.) Having a goal is, in other words, having the disposition to change the world. But, as Smith has said, the desire to do something is the state that grounds the disposition to bring about that something. This must mean that – given there is no good reason to think that any other state is such a disposition – only desires can constitute an agent having certain goals. So, motivating reasons are partially constituted by a state that embodies a goal, to have a goal is to have a desire, therefore motivating reasons are partially constituted by a desire. So Smith has defended the HTM via his functionalist account of beliefs and desires.

Is Smith's thesis convincing? Philip Pettit in Chapter 32 thinks not. One of Pettit's reasons is that he believes Smith has misrepresented the debate between the Humean and the non-Humean. Pettit holds that non-Humeans could grant Smith's conclusion – that motivating reasons are partially constituted by a desire – but reject the claim that such a desire is modally distinct from belief. But, Pettit continues, this is precisely what the HTM, and therefore Smith, wants to hold. Whether Pettit is right and what, in fact, the debate amounts to we leave for the reader to decide. In the final article of this Part, Smith (Chapter 33) responds to this and other worries that Pettit raises.

QUESTIONS TO CONSIDER AND TASKS TO COMPLETE

1   Has Smith (Chapter 31) done enough to distinguish beliefs from desires?
2   Explain in your own words what the difference is between motivating and normative reasons. Is this distinction a good one?
3   What is the real argument between the Humean and non-Humean?
4   Explain in your own words Smith's dispositional account of desire. Does it work? What is a disposition anyway?
5   Does Smith's 'direction of fit' argument work?
6   Can we, or should we, give a monolithic account of motivation?
7   Could there be a psychological state that is neither a belief nor a desire? How could you show that it existed?
8   Once it is accepted, is the Humean hypothesis falsifiable?

FURTHER READING

Clark, Philip (2000) 'What Goes without Saying in Metaethics', *Philosophy and Phenomenological Research*, vol. 60, no. 2, pp. 357–79.

Cuneo, Terence (2002) 'Reconciling Realism with Humeanism', *Australasian Journal of Philosophy*, vol. 80, no. 4, pp. 465–86.

Dancy, Jonathan (2003) 'Replies', *Philosophy and Phenomenological Research*, vol. 67, no. 2, pp. 468–90.

Humberstone, I. L. (1992) 'Direction of Fit', *Mind*, vol. 101, no. 401, pp. 59–83.

McDowell, John (1981) 'Non-cognitivism and Rule-Following', in Steven Holtzman and Christopher Leich (eds), *Wittgenstein: To Follow a Rule* (London: Routledge & Kegan Paul), pp. 141–62 [Chapter 23, this volume].

Nagel, Thomas (1970) *The Possibility of Altruism* (Princeton, NJ: Princeton University Press).

Platts, Mark (1981) 'Moral Reality and the End of Desire', in Mark Platts (ed.) *Reference, Truth and Reality* (London: Routledge & Kegan Paul), pp. 69–82.

Smith, Michael (2003) 'Humeanism, Psychologism, and the Normative', *Philosophy and Phenomenological Research*, vol. 67, no. 2, pp. 460–7.

Zangwill, Nick (1998) 'Direction of Fit and Normative Functionalism', *Philosophical Studies: An International Journal for Philosophy in the Analytic Tradition*, vol. 91, no. 2, pp. 173–203.

31

THE HUMEAN THEORY OF MOTIVATION

Michael Smith

1 TWO PRINCIPLES

It has recently been argued that the Humean Theory of Motivation is a dogma in philosophical psychology, that the dogma is fundamentally incorrect, and that the Humean theory should therefore be replaced in philosophical psychology with a more plausible theory of motivation. I am thinking in particular of recent work by Tom Nagel, John McDowell, and Mark Platts.[1]

In fact the Humean seems committed to two claims about motivating reasons, a weaker and a stronger. However, there is no agreement amongst non-Humeans as to whether the weaker and the stronger are both equally unacceptable, or whether it is only the stronger that we have reason to reject. The stronger – the claim that is, as I understand it, constitutive of the Humean theory – is the claim that motivation has its *source* in the presence of a relevant desire and means-end belief. This claim finds more formal expression in the following principle:

P$_1$.   R at t constitutes a motivating reason of agent A to ϕ iff there is some ψ such that R at t consists of a desire of A to ψ and a belief that were he to ϕ he would ψ.[2]

Non-Humeans are united in their rejection of P$_1$. However, P$_1$ entails the following weaker principle:

P$_2$.   Agent A at t has a motivating reason to ϕ only if there is some ψ such that, at t, A desires to ψ and believes that were he to ϕ he would ψ.

– the principle that motivation requires the *presence* of a relevant desire and means-end belief – and non-Humeans are not at all united in their rejection of P$_2$. Thus, for instance, while Tom Nagel, and John McDowell following him, have argued that P$_2$ is acceptable because consistent with the claim that the desires and means-end beliefs that must be present whenever there is motivation are not themselves the *source* of such motivation[3] – other nonHumeans, such as Mark Platts, have argued that P_2 is also unacceptable because either 'phenomenologically false ... or utterly vacuous'.[4]

I am inclined to agree with the non-Humeans that the Humean theory is a dogma in philosophical psychology, a 'dogma' in the sense that both P_1 and P_2 seem to find a fair degree of uncritical acceptance. However, unlike the non-Humeans, I do not believe that the Humean theory, as characterized by P_1, is fundamentally incorrect (and thus I do not think that P_2 is either phenomenologically false or utterly vacuous). My task in the present paper is thus to offer an explicit argument for the Humean theory, and to defend it against the objections offered by the likes of Nagel, McDowell, and Platts. If the argument offered here is correct, then the Humean theory is the expression of a simple but important truth about the nature of motivating reasons, a truth that non-Humeans have failed to appreciate either because they have failed to distinguish motivating reasons from other sorts of reasons, or because they have an inadequate conception of desire, or because they have overlooked the implications of the fact that reason explanations are teleological.

2 MOTIVATING REASONS AND NORMATIVE REASONS

P_1 is a principle connecting *motivating* reasons with the presence of desires and beliefs. We must begin by emphasizing this fact, otherwise it will seem simply implausible to suppose that P_1 provides individually necessary or jointly sufficient conditions for a state's constituting a motivating reason.

In order to see this, consider the following counterexamples to the claim that P_1 provides necessary conditions:

(i) Suppose I now desire to purchase an original Picasso, but I do not now believe that were I to purchase the painting before me I would do so – suppose I don't believe that it is a Picasso. Surely it would be appropriate for an outsider to say that I have a reason to purchase the painting before me. But I lack the relevant belief.

(ii) Suppose that I am standing on someone's foot so causing him pain, and that I know that this is what I am doing. Surely we can imagine its being appropriate for an outsider to say that I have a reason to get off his foot even though I lacked the relevant desire, and, indeed, even if I desired to cause him pain.

Consider now the following counterexample to the claim that P_1 provides a sufficient condition:

(iii) Suppose I now desire to drink a gin and tonic and believe that I can do so by mixing the stuff before me with tonic and drinking it.[5] Suppose further that this belief is false – the stuff before me is not gin, it is petrol. Surely it would be appropriate for an outsider to say that I had no reason to mix this stuff with tonic and drink it. Yet I have both the relevant belief and desire.

Do we have, in examples the like of these, the makings of an objection to P_1, and hence to the Humean theory? We do not. The reason why was perhaps evident from the start. The outsider's perspective is not irrelevant to the examples.

It has been noticed before that the claim that A has a reason to φ is ambiguous. It may be a claim about a *motivating* reason that A has or a claim about a *normative* reason that A has.[6] The crucial feature these reasons have in common is that each purports to justify certain behaviour on A's behalf; for there is an a priori connection between citing an agent's reasons for acting in a certain way and giving a partial justification for his acting in that way, that is, a specification of what was to be said for acting in the way in question. This is not to say that the existence of a reason for acting in a certain way, be it motivating or normative, entails that, all things considered, acting in that way is justified. But it is to say that, abstracting away from other considerations, the action is justified from the perspective of the reason (more on this below). However, in virtue of their differences, motivating and normative reasons forge the connection between justification and action differently.

The distinctive feature of a motivating reason to φ is that in virtue of having such a reason an agent is in a state that is *potentially explanatory* of his φ-ing.[7] (Note the 'potentially'. An agent may therefore have a motivating reason to φ without that reason's being overriding.) It is thus natural to suppose that an agent's motivating reasons are, as we might put it, *psychologically real*, for it would seem to be part of our concept of what it is for an agent's reasons to have the potential to explain his behaviour that his having those reasons is a fact about *him*; that is, that the goals that such reasons embody are *his* goals.[8] And it is also natural, therefore, to assign to an agent's motivating reasons the minimal justificatory role possible: the role of justifying from the perspective of the value that that very reason embodies. For a motivating reason, even when it does explain an agent's behaviour, may reveal little of value in what the agent did even from his own point of view. Consider Davidson's example of the man who has always had a yen to drink a can of paint, and who ultimately yields, but not because he thinks that doing so is really worthwhile.[9] None the less, knowing that he has always had a yen to drink a can of paint does provide us, and him, with a partial justification for his action, albeit a justification that justifies only from a perspective that assigns value to the drinking of a can of paint, a perspective that he himself may occupy only to the extent that he has a yen to drink a can of paint, and that we none of us may actually share.

However, to say that someone has a normative reason to ϕ is to say something different. It is to say that there is some normative requirement that he ϕ's. It is therefore to justify his ϕ-ing from the perspective of the normative system that generates that requirement. For present purposes there is no need to be precise about the kinds of normative requirement, and hence the kinds of normative reasons, that there may be. For all that has been said here there may therefore be as many kinds of normative reason as there are normative systems for generating reasons: normative reasons of rationality, of prudence, of morality, and perhaps normative reasons of other kinds. Nor is there any need to be precise about the relation between the normative reasons an agent has, at a time, and the motivating reasons he has at that time. Rather, the important point to note is that, on any plausible conception of what it is for there to be a normative requirement and the relation that therefore exists between this normative requirement and an agent's motivating reasons, he may well be motivated to do what he is required to do (that is, he may have a motivating reason to do what he has a normative reason to do), he may be motivated to do something that there is no normative requirement for him to do (that is, he may have a motivating reason to do what he has no normative reason to do), and there may be a normative requirement that he do what he has no motivation to do (that is, he may have a normative reason to do what he has no motivating reason to do).[10] Given that motivating and normative reasons may come apart, we must therefore emphasize that P_1 purports to give necessary and sufficient conditions for the existence of *motivating* reasons. P_1 is silent concerning the conditions under which an agent has some *normative* reason.

Consider now the examples. I said that the outsider's perspective is not irrelevant. The reason is that the outsider's perspective draws our attention to the normative requirement in each case. Thus, note that in (i) the reason that I have to buy the painting in front of me is a normative reason. For it suffices for the truth of the claim that I have such a reason, that there is a requirement – in this case, in the broad sense, a requirement of rationality[11] – that I buy the painting in front of me. For I want to buy a Picasso and the painting in front of me is a Picasso. But the existence of such a normative reason does not suffice for my having a motivating reason to buy the painting in front of me. For, since I do not believe that that painting is a Picasso, I am not in a state that is potentially explanatory of my buying it. (I am, of course, in a psychological state that is potentially explanatory of my buying a Picasso, for I desire to buy a Picasso and believe that were I to buy a Picasso I would buy a Picasso. But the Humean will say that this is not to have a motivating reason to buy the painting in front of me. It is rather to have a motivating reason to buy a Picasso. He will thus regard an agent's desire to ϕ together with the trivial belief that were he to ϕ he would ϕ as the limiting case of having a motivating reason to ϕ.) Thus the example in no way undermines the necessity of having a means-end belief for having a motivating reason.

A similar point applies in (ii), the case in which I have a reason to get off someone's foot when I am causing him pain. For it suffices for the truth of the claim that I have a reason to get off his foot that there exists a requirement – in this case moral – that I do not cause him pain, and that, in the present circumstances, in order to comply with that requirement I have to get off his foot. But, once again, the mere existence of this normative reason is consistent with the claim that I am not in a state that is potentially explanatory of my behaviour. (Indeed, note that this ought to be conceded even by those who think that moral reasons are rational requirements on action. For, as we have seen, rational requirements are in turn simply further normative reasons, and may thus exist in the absence of motivating reasons.) Thus this kind of example does not by itself show that having a desire is not a necessary condition for having a motivating reason.

Consider now (iii), the counterexample to the sufficiency of the condition. In what sense do I not have a reason to mix the stuff before me with tonic and drink it? Clearly, one thing we can say is that *prudence* would not require that I mix the stuff before me with tonic and drink it, for the stuff before me is petrol, and drinking petrol mixed with tonic would not be in my interests. However, I am in a state that is potentially explanatory of my mixing the stuff before me with tonic and drinking it, for I desire to drink a gin and tonic and believe that the stuff before me is gin. Moreover, if that state did explain my doing so, we would certainly know what was to be said for doing so, from my point of view. Though prudence does not require my mixing the stuff before me with tonic and drinking it, and hence there is a sense in which I do not have a reason to do so, yet it seems entirely correct to suppose that I now have a motivating reason to do just this. So this is no counterexample to the claim that P_1 provides a sufficient condition for a state's constituting a motivating reason.

Let me emphasize what little I take myself to have shown here. In the light of the distinction between motivating and normative reasons, I have emphasized the fact that the Humean's is a theory about the nature of *motivating* reasons. His theory may yet be false. But it is not shown to be false simply by showing that P_1 fails to give necessary and sufficient conditions for the existence of normative reasons. Though I take this to be a fairly trivial point, it suffices to undermine one of Tom Nagel's principal arguments against the Humean theory in *The Possibility of Altruism*; an objection based largely on consideration of the conditions under which we would ordinarily say of someone that he has a reason. Nagel's objection centres on the Humean's explanation of prudential motivation.

3 A PRELIMINARY OBJECTION: NAGEL

Prudential motivation is possible only if an agent's recognition of the fact that he will have a desire to φ in the future somehow gives him a reason now to take steps to promote his ɸ-ing then. The task of explaining this possibility takes on a particular form for a Humean. For, as we have seen, he holds that now having a motivating reason to ɸ requires *presently* desiring to ɸ. He must therefore explain how an agent's recognition that he *will* desire to ɸ in the future gives rise to a *present* desire to promote his ɸ-ing then. The Humean's answer is fairly predictable. He says that agents who are motivated by prudential considerations each have a quite general present desire to further their future interests.

However Nagel offers the following objection to the Humean's giving this answer:

> The two features of the system to which I object are (a) that it does not allow the expectation of a future reason to provide by itself any reason for present action, and (b) that it does allow the present desire for a future object to provide by itself a reason for present action in pursuit of that object.[12]

Thus, as he points out, the following constitute possibilities under the Humean theory:

> First, given that any desire with a future object provides a basis for reasons to do what will promote that object, it may happen that I now desire for the future something which I shall not and do not expect to desire then, and which I believe there will then be no reason to bring about. Consequently I may have a reason now to prepare to do what I know I will have no reason to do when the time comes.
>
> Second, suppose that I expect to be assailed by a desire in the future: then I must acknowledge that in the future I will have a prima facie reason to do what the desire indicates. But this reason does not obtain now, and cannot by itself apply derivatively to any presently available means to the satisfaction of the future desire. Thus in the absence of any further relevant desire in the present, I may have no reason to prepare for what I know I shall have reason to do tomorrow.[13]

The response that Nagel wants to elicit from us, faced by these examples, is that, in the first case, I have no reason to promote the future object despite my present desire, and that, in the second, I do have a reason to promote the object of my future desire despite my lacking a relevant present desire.

Myself I think that we do have this response and that we are right to. But I do not think that this fact counts against the Humean theory. In order to see that this is so, consider Nagel's own summary objection to the Humean theory's licensing such possibilities:

> A system with consequences such as this not only fails to require the most elementary consistency in conduct over time, but in fact sharpens the possibilities of conflict by grounding an individual's plottings against his future self in the apparatus

of rationality. These are formal and extremely general difficulties about the system, since they concern the relation of what is rational to what will be rational; no matter what source of reasons is operative.[14]

Thus if we accept Nagel's own diagnosis of our response to these examples – and I think we should – it emerges that examples like these fail even to touch the Humean. For, to take just the first (the second follows suit), Nagel's objection to the Humean's claim that an agent may have a *motivating* reason now to promote his ϕ-ing in the future, despite the fact that he believes that he will have no motivating reason to ϕ then, is that it would not be *irrational* to do so; that is, that he now has no reason from the perspective of rationality to do so. But this is to conflate the claim that an agent has a motivating reason to ϕ with the claim that he has a normative reason from the perspective of rationality to ϕ. The Humean is making only the first claim, not the second.

Moreover, if Nagel is right that it is irrational to promote ϕ-ing in the future believing that one will then have no motivating reason to ϕ, then the Humean can accept this on his own terms; by claiming that a theory of rationality requires that agents have the desire to promote their future interests.[15] For, importantly, the tasks of constructing a theory of motivating reasons and a theory of the normative reasons of rationality are just different tasks. I therefore do not see that the rationality of prudence makes for an especial difficulty with the Humean's theory of motivation. (It may indeed provide a problem for Hume's own theory of rationality.)[16]

4 WHY BELIEVE THE HUMEAN THEORY?

We have seen that we will find no easy refutation of P_1 – the claim that motivating reasons are constituted by the presence of desires and means-end beliefs – by reflecting on those cases in which we would ordinarily say of someone that he has a reason to ϕ. But can we find some reason actually to believe this claim?

John McDowell has attempted to diagnose commitment to the Humean theory in the following terms. He begins by isolating what he takes to be the distinctive feature of the Humean's theory; namely, that 'to cite a cognitive propositional attitude', that is, a belief, 'is to give at most a partial specification of a reason for acting; to be fully explicit, one would need to add a mention of something non-cognitive, a state of the will or a volitional event' or, in the terms in which we have put it, a desire.[17] He then goes on:

I suspect that one reason people find ... [this claim] obvious lies in their inexplicit adherence to a quasi-hydraulic conception of how reason explanations account for action. The will is pictured as the source of forces that issue in the behaviour such explanations explain. This idea seems to me a radical misconception of the sort of explanation a reason explanation is, but it is not my present concern.[18]

I am not sure that I understand McDowell's diagnosis here. But, in so far as I do, it seems to me to get things entirely wrong.[19]

According to McDowell, one reason people believe the Humean theory is that they have a 'quasi-hydraulic' conception of how reason explanations account for action; that is, in less prolix terms, because they have a *causal* conception of reason explanations. Moreover, in McDowell's view, this lays the Humean theory so supported open to an objection; for, he says, a causal conception of reason explanations is a 'radical misconception'. Let me begin with the second point first.

Those of us who do not agree that causal conceptions are radically misconceived may well think that McDowell has here provided *us* with good reasons for believing the Humean theory; for McDowell suggests that the Humean theory is supported by something that we believe to be true. However, it seems to me that we would be conceding too much to McDowell if we were to argue in this way. For, now taking up his first point, I doubt that there is any support to be found for the Humean theory in a causal conception of reason explanations.

In order to see this we only need ask why a causal conception should be thought to support especially the Humean theory. To be sure, one who holds that reason explanations are causal must conceive of some psychological states as possessed of *causal force*. But why, as McDowell seems to assume, must he think that *desires* are the only psychological state possessed of causal force? Why mightn't he think instead that only certain *beliefs* are possessed of causal force? McDowell offers no argument on this point.

Indeed, when we consider the reason causal theorists actually give for holding a causal conception, it emerges that no such argument is forthcoming. For they reason roughly as follows: 'We ordinarily say of agents that they ϕ *because* they have reason to ϕ. The "because" here may uncontroversially be regarded as the "because" of rationalization; or, better, the "because" of teleological explanation. But now observe that an agent may have reason to ϕ and ϕ, and yet not ϕ because he has reason to ϕ. What then is the feature that makes the difference between this case and the case in which the agent ϕs *because* he has reason to ϕ? The only illuminating answer available is that the reasons in the second case *cause* the agent to ϕ.'[20] It thus emerges that the argument causal theorists give for a causal conception of reason explanations makes no substantial assumption about the nature of the reasons we have. So, it seems, we should be able to accept or reject this argument quite inde-pendently of our views concerning the nature of reasons. The upshot is that if Humeans and non-Humeans alike may have a causal conception of reason explanations then it cannot be that holding a causal conception supports especially the Humean theory.

I think this shows that the Humean is engaged in a debate that is both independent of and more fundamental than the debate over whether reason explanations are causal. In short the difference is this. The causal and non-causal theorist can both accept that reason explanations are teleological explanations without enquiring further into what it is about the nature of reasons that makes it possible for reason explanations to be teleological explanations – that is, explanations that explain by making what they explain intelligible in terms of the pursuit of a goal. For their disagreement concerns the further question whether such explanations are themselves in turn a species of causal explanation; a disagreement which may, as I have suggested, cut across disagreements concerning the nature of reasons. But, as I see it, the Humean and non-Humean are precisely engaged in a dispute concerning what it is about the nature of reasons that makes it possible for reason explanations to be teleological explanations. If this is right, then it would seem that there will be only one reason to believe the Humean's theory, if indeed we should believe his theory at all, and that is that the Humean's theory is alone able to make sense of motivation as the pursuit of a goal.

I want to argue that this is indeed the case in the remainder of this paper. My reason for believing this is relatively simple – it seems to me to follow from a proper conception of desire. I therefore proceed by focussing on two different conceptions of desire. One of these gives no support to the Humean theory. I argue that this conception is anyway implausible. Perhaps unsurprisingly, this seems to be the conception of desire held by many opponents of the Humean theory. There is, however, an alternative and more plausible conception. This conception enables us to see that desires must be constituents of reasons given that reasons must themselves be constituted by goals.

5 DESIRES AND PHENOMENOLOGY

According to Hume, desires are a species of the passions, and passions are, in turn, a certain kind of *feeling*. Hume seems to hold that this is so not just in the trivial sense that passions are a species of perception and perceptions are a kind of feeling.[21] Rather he seems to be suggesting that when we desire something 'we feel an ... emotion of aversion or propensity';[22] as though, as Stroud puts it when discussing Hume's conception of desire, his view is that we are '*directly aware*' of the presence of the desires that we have.[23]

Hume's suggestion is not entirely misguided. For there is such a thing as the phenomenology of desire; as, for instance, to use one of Hume's own examples, 'when I am angry I am possest with the passion'.[24] That is, we may agree with Hume that, on occasion, when I have a desire, I am possessed with a psychological feeling; an analogue of a bodily sensation. This may suggest an elaboration of Hume's view. For if we take quite seriously his suggestion that all desires are known by the way they make us feel, then, in an attempt to explain why this is so, we may be led to identify desires with such psychological feelings. And this may in turn lead us to endorse what I shall call the 'strong phenomenological conception' of desires; the view that desires are, like sensations, simply and essentially states that have a certain phenomenological content.

Perhaps unsurprisingly, I think that the strong phenomenological conception of desires ought to be rejected. For it seems to me that there is no way such a conception can be married with a plausible epistemology of desire.[25]

Now I suspect that there will be some who think that this objection doesn't even get off the ground. For they will say: 'Surely the strong phenomenological conception of desire makes the epistemology of desire unproblematic. For the epistemology of desire becomes like the epistemology of sensation. Thus, just as it is plausible to hold that a subject is in pain if and only if he believes that he is in pain – for we take it that a subject is in a state with a certain phenomenological content if and only if he believes himself to be in a state with that content – so, if we think of desires on the model of sensations, it is plausible to hold that a subject desires to ϕ if and only if he believes that he desires to ϕ.' What exactly is wrong with this? There are two things wrong with it. I begin with an objection that concedes more to the strong phenomenological conception than strictly ought to be conceded. Doing so teaches us a valuable lesson.

As I understand it, the principle that a subject desires to ϕ if and only if he believes that he desires to ϕ is supposed to express a necessary truth; the putative truth that we are infallible about what we desire. But, intuitively at any rate, this principle is simply false. Thus, conceding for the moment that the strong phenomenological conception does entail that a subject desires to ϕ if and only if he believes that he desires to ϕ, it ought to be rejected. I argue by counterexample.

Suppose each day on his way to work John buys a newspaper at a certain newspaper stand. However, he has to go out of his way to do so, and for no apparently good reason. The newspaper he buys is on sale at other newspaper stands on his direct route to work; there is no difference in the price or condition of the newspapers bought at the two stands; and so on. There is, however, this difference between the stands. There are mirrors behind the counter of the stand where John buys his newspaper. Given their placement, one who buys a newspaper there cannot help but look at himself. Let's suppose, however, that if it were suggested to John that the reason he buys his newspaper at that stand is that he wants to look at his own reflection, he would vehemently deny it. And it wouldn't seem to John as if he were concealing anything in doing so. However, finally, let's suppose that if the mirrors were removed from the stand, his preference for that stand would disappear. If all this were the case, wouldn't it be plausible to suppose that John in fact desires to buy his newspaper at a stand where he can look at his own reflection; that, perhaps, he has a narcissistic tendency and that buying his newspaper at that stand enables him to indulge it on the way to work? And wouldn't it also be plausible to suppose that he does not believe that this is so, given his, from his point of view, sincere denials? If this is agreed, then we have reason to reject the principle left to right.[26]

Consider another example. Suppose John professes that one of his fundamental desires is to be a great musician. However, his mother has always drummed into him the value of music. She is a fanatic with great hopes for her son's career as a musician; hopes so great that she would be extremely disappointed if he were even less than an excellent musician, let alone if he were to give up music altogether. Moreover, John admits that he has a very great desire not to upset her, though he denies that this in any way explains his efforts at pursuing excellence in music. However, suppose now that John's mother dies, and that, upon her death, he finds that all of his interest in music vanishes. He gives up his career as a musician and pursues a career in film as an actor. In such circumstances, wouldn't it be plausible to suppose that John was just mistaken about what he originally wanted to do and that, despite the fact that he believed that achieving excellence in music was a fundamental desire of his, it never was? If so, then we have reason to believe that the principle is false right to left as well.

If this is agreed, then any conception of desires that entails that a subject desires to φ if and only if he believes that he desires to φ is a conception that is to be rejected, rejected for the simple reason that the epistemology it provides is implausible. Thus, if the phenomenological conception entails such a principle, it ought to be rejected. This teaches us the following lesson. It is an adequacy constraint on any conception of desire that the epistemology of desire it recommends allows that subjects may be fallible about the desires they have.

I said that the first objection concedes more to the strong phenomenological conception than strictly ought to be conceded. What it concedes is that the strong phenomenological conception does entail that a subject desires to φ if and only if he believes that he desires to φ. But this it most certainly does not do. Here, then, is a second objection.

Let's grant for the moment that desires are like sensations in that they essentially have phenomenological content. It must be noted that they differ from sensations in that they have in addition *propositional* content. For ascriptions of desires, unlike ascriptions of sensations, may be given in the form 'A desires that p', where 'p' is a sentence. Thus, whereas A's desire to φ may be ascribed to A in the form *A desires that he φs*, A's pain cannot be ascribed to A in the form *A pains that p*.[27]

It is therefore ambiguous to claim that the epistemology of desire is 'like the epistemology of sensation'. To be sure, if desires are essentially phenomenological states, then the epistemology of the phenomenological content of a desire may be based on the epistemology of sensation. But what about the epistemology of the propositional content of desire? This cannot be based on the epistemology of sensation at all, for sensations have no propositional content. It therefore turns out that we have an even stronger reason to reject the strong phenomenological conception of desire. For, according to this conception, there is simply no difference between desires and sensations. Each is a state which simply and essentially has phenomenological content. The strong phenomenological conception of desires is thus unable to account for the fact that desires *have* propositional content *at all*. Little wonder that it cannot provide a plausible epistemology of the propositional content of desires.

I suspect that, for this very reason, some will have thought that the strong phenomenological conception of desire was a straw man all along. But note that, with our objections to the strong phenomenological conception firmly in place, we are now in a position to argue against all versions of the phenomenological conception, even the more plausible weaker conceptions according to which desires are *like* sensations in that they have phenomenological content essentially, but *differ* from sensations in that they have propositional content as well. For we can now say this about all such conceptions: they in no way contribute to our understanding of what a desire as a state with propositional content is, for they cannot explain how it is that desires have propositional content; they therefore in no way explain the epistemology of the propositional content of desire; and they thus require supplementing by some independent and self-standing account of what a desire is which explains how it is that desires have propositional content and which explains how it is that we have fallible knowledge of what it is that we desire.

The question that immediately arises with regard to weaker phenomenological conceptions is then why we should believe that any such conception is true. The only answer available is that a phenomenological conception is alone true to the phenomenology of desire. But is this answer plausible? Do we really believe that desires are states that have phenomenological content essentially? That is, do we believe that if there is nothing that it is like to have a desire, at a time, then it is not being had at that time?

I should say that, at least as far as common sense opinion goes – and what else do we have to go by in formulating a philosophical conception of folk psychological states? – we evidently have no such belief. Consider, for instance, what we should ordinarily think of as a long term desire; say, a father's desire that his children do well. A father may actually feel the prick of this desire from time to time; in moments of reflection on their vulnerability, say. But such occasions are not the norm. Yet we certainly wouldn't ordinarily think that he loses this desire during those periods when he lacks such feelings. Or consider more mundane cases like those that Stroud mentions in his discussion of Hume, cases in which, as we should ordinarily say, I desire to cross the road and do so, or in which I desire to write something down and so write it down. As Stroud points out, in such cases 'it is difficult to believe that I am overcome with emotion ... I am certainly not aware of any emotion or passion impelling me to act'; rather 'they seem the very model of cool, dispassionate action'.[28] However, it would be grossly counter to our common sense opinion to conclude that simply because I do not introspect the presence of desires in such cases so I incorrectly attribute desires to myself – that I cross the road and write things down even though I do not want to!

Of course, if we thought that there was nothing for a desire to be, in the absence of its being felt, then we might, in our role of philosophical theorist, feel ourselves forced into concluding that some of our common sense attributions are mistaken, and hence feel ourselves forced into revising our common sense opinions in favour of a phenomenological conception. But given that a phenomenological conception is unable to deliver an account of desire as a state with propositional content, we should feel no such pressure in our role of philosophical theorist. Rather we should concede that a desire may be had in the absence of its being felt.

This is significant. For many non-Humeans seem to work with a phenomenological conception of desire, and then use the fact that we do not introspect the presence of desires whenever there is motivation against the Humean theory.

Consider, for instance, the following argument of Mark Platts's:

> The crucial premiss ... is the claim that any full specification of a reason for an action, if it is to be a reason for the potential agent for action, must make reference to that agent's desires. At first sight, it seems a painful feature of the moral life that this premiss is false. We perform many intentional actions in that life that we apparently do not desire to perform. A better description of such cases appears to be that we perform them because we think them desirable. The difficulty of much of moral life then emerges as a consequence of the apparent fact that desiring something and thinking it desirable are both distinct and independent.
>
> The premiss can, of course, be held true by simply claiming that, when acting because we think something desirable, we do indeed desire it. But this is either phenomenologically false, there being nothing in our inner life corresponding to the posited desire, or utterly vacuous, neither content nor motivation being given to the positing of the desire. Nothing but muddle (and boredom) comes from treating desire as a mental catch-all.[29]

Thus, according to Platts, the Humean may hold that when we believe that something is desirable we do desire it. However, if he does, then Platts claims that he is impaled on the horns of a dilemma. But consider the horns of Platts's dilemma.

If there is no reason why *any* theorist should accept a phenomenological conception of desire, as we have seen that there is not, then it can hardly be an objection to the Humean's theory that we are unable to introspect the presence of each and every desire that he says we have. Thus we should not force the Humean onto the phenomenological falsehood of the first horn. Platts might agree. But, he would say, this merely forces the Humean onto the second horn of his dilemma. Here Platts seems to claim that if we do not accept a phenomenological conception of desire, then the positing of a desire must be 'utterly vacuous', or without 'content'.[30] But, as we have seen, given just the assumption that desires are states with propositional content, an assumption that must be accepted even by one who does wish to endorse a phenomenological conception, the *only* way that we can give content to the concept of such a state, and hence to the positing of a desire, is precisely via some independent and self-standing non-phenomenological conception. So, far from non-phenomenological conceptions making ascriptions of desire 'utterly vacuous', non-phenomenological conceptions alone make the ascription of desires with propositional contents possible.

Indeed, even John McDowell, who himself rejects a phenomenological conception, covertly ascribes such a conception to the Humean when arguing against him.[31] This emerges in McDowell's defence of his own view that the virtuous agent may be motivated by his conception of the situation in which he finds himself, something that, according to McDowell, may properly be thought of as a cognitive state. McDowell rightly supposes that the Humean would respond that, if someone who has such a conception is indeed motivated, then getting him to have such a conception must involve getting him to have a certain desire. But he then interprets this as the suggestion that:

> 'See it like this' is really a covert invitation to feel, quite over and above one's view of the facts, a desire which will combine with one's belief to recommend acting in the appropriate way.[32]

And he rightly rejects this suggestion. But, unless it is compulsory to accept a phenomenological conception of desire, why give the Humean's response that interpretation? To be sure, getting someone to have a certain view of the facts may not involve getting him to *feel* a certain desire, but it may involve getting him to *have* a certain desire none the less.[33]

6 DESIRES, DIRECTIONS OF FIT, AND DISPOSITIONS

We have seen that there must be an alternative to phenomenological conceptions of desire, an alternative that allows us to make sense of desires as states with propositional contents and that thus allows us to make sense of our common sense desire attributions. But what is the alternative to be? Surprisingly enough, Platts himself outlines the alternative I favour; a suggestion about the difference between beliefs and desires that he attributes to Anscombe. Platts's own summary is so succinct and makes the idea sound so plausible that I shall merely quote it. (I consider below why Platts is himself subsequently so unsympathetic towards the idea.)

Miss Anscombe, in her work on intention, has drawn a broad distinction between two *kinds* of mental states, factual belief being the prime exemplar of one kind and desire a prime exemplar of the other ... The distinction is in terms of the *direction of fit* of mental states with the world. Beliefs aim at the true, and their being true is their fitting the world; falsity is a decisive failing in a belief, and false beliefs should be discarded; beliefs should be changed to fit with the world, not vice versa. Desires aim at realisation, and their realisation is the world fitting with them; the fact that the indicative content of a desire is not realised in the world is not yet a failing *in the desire*, and not yet any reason to discard the desire; the world, crudely, should be changed to fit with our desires, not vice versa.[34]

Myself I think that this characterization of the difference between beliefs and desires captures something quite deep in our thought about their nature. Moreover, I want eventually to argue that the idea that desires are states with which the world must fit allows us to bring out an important connection between our concepts of desire and motivation.

However, as Platts notices, talk of the direction of fit of a state is highly metaphorical. This is problematic. For it seems that we would be unjustified in appealing to the concept in characterizing desires, and in illuminating the connection between desires and motivation, if we had no way of understanding it in non-metaphorical terms. Moreover, as once again Platts notices, if we take the characterization quite strictly, it is unclear whether it allows us to characterize desires at all. For, he claims, since 'all desires appear to involve elements of belief', desires are not states whose direction of fit is entirely of the second kind: the question arises whether there are any such states.[35]

It seems to me that Platts is right to highlight these problems with the metaphor, but that we would be wrong to think that the problems he raises are insurmountable. For I want to suggest that the metaphorical characterization of desires as states which are such that the world must fit with them meshes with another, and more plausible, suggestion about the epistemology of desires; a suggestion inspired, ironically enough, by certain other remarks of Hume's.

Hume realized all too well that alongside the 'violent passions' that affect the subject who has them, there are 'calm passions', passions that lack phenomenological content altogether. Hume was therefore cognizant of the fact that his official line on the epistemology of desires – that they are known by their phenomenology – was totally inadequate as an account of the epistemology of the calm passions, and that he therefore needed an alternative account of the epistemology appropriate for them. As a result, Hume suggested that, by contrast with the violent passions, the calm passions 'are more known by their effects than by their immediate sensation'.[36]

When Stroud considers this suggestion, he points out that it commits Hume to the view that desires are to be conceived of as *the causes of actions*.[37] It might therefore be thought that Hume's suggestion should be of little interest to us. For I have argued that the only argument for the Humean theory, if there is to be one at all, will be that it alone is able to make sense of reason explanation as a species of teleological explanation, and that one may accept that reason explanations are teleological without accepting that reason explanations are causal (see § 4). Yet if we accept this conception of desire we immediately lock ourselves into a causal conception.[38]

However, though this makes acceptance of Hume's suggestion as it stands inappropriate, it seems to me that we would be wrong to abandon Hume's suggestion altogether. For if we are less interested in *Hume*'s view than in a *Humean* view then it seems to me that we can find in Hume's suggestion about the epistemology appropriate for the calm passions, the inspiration for a somewhat different conception of desires; a conception that allows us to remain neutral about whether desires are causes.

According to this alternative conception, desires are states that have a certain *functional role*. That is, according to this conception, we should think of the desire to φ as that state of a subject that grounds all sorts of his dispositions: like the disposition to φ in conditions C, the disposition to φ in conditions C′, and so on (where, in order for conditions C and C′ to obtain, the subject must have, *inter alia*, certain beliefs). For Hume's suggestion about how the calm passions are known may then be translated into the thought that the epistemology of desire is simply the epistemology of dispositional states – that is, the epistemology of such counterfactuals. This does not commit us, *as Humeans*, to the thesis that desires are to be conceived of as the causes of actions. For it is a substantial philosophical thesis to move from the claim that desires are dispositions to the claim that desires are causes.

A dispositional conception of desires enables us to solve many of the problems that we have confronted so far. For instance, a dispositional conception is precisely an account of what a desire is that explains how it can be that desires have propositional content, for the propositional content of a desire may then simply be determined by its functional role. (I say that it may 'simply' be determined by its functional role. But of course, there need be nothing simple about the functional theory that determines content.) A dispositional conception of desires also meets the constraint on the epistemology of desire argued for earlier; that the epistemology of desire allows that subjects may be fallible about the desires that they have.[39] For, given just the assumption that desires are dispositions to act in certain ways under certain conditions, it is implausible to suggest quite generally that if the counterfactuals that are thus true of a subject who desires to φ are true of him then he believes that they are, and it is likewise implausible to suggest quite generally that if a subject believes that such counterfactuals are true of him, then such counterfactuals are true of him.[40] Furthermore, a dispositional conception of desires is consistent both with the claim that certain desires have phenomenological content essentially and with the claim that certain desires lack phenomenological content altogether. For, according to this conception, desires have phenomenological content just to the extent that the having of certain feelings is *one* of the things that they are dispositions to produce under certain conditions. Some desires may be dispositions to have certain feelings under all conditions: these have phenomenological content essentially. Other desires, though they are dispositions to behave in certain ways, may not be dispositions to have certain feelings at all: these lack phenomenological content altogether.

We are also able, given a dispositional conception of desires, to see why Platts is right that, in myriad ways, desires 'involve elements of belief'. For if the desire to ϕ is a certain sort of complex dispositional state of the kind described then desiring to ϕ may 'involve' elements of belief in each of the following ways: the obtaining of the conditions in which the subject ϕs may require that he has certain beliefs; the truth of the counterfactual 'Were the subject in conditions C he would ϕ' may require that the subject has certain other beliefs due to holistic constraints on desire attribution; and so on. Indeed, if we take Platts's own claims about the phenomenology of desire quite seriously, then we might suggest that desires involve beliefs in other more direct ways. For, if we agree with Platts that oftentimes when we act our only awareness of the desires we have comes via our beliefs concerning the desirability of various options then we might think that this too ought to be reflected in the kind of disposition a desire is. Thus, we might say, the desire to ϕ is also, *inter alia*, a disposition to believe, under certain conditions, that ϕ-ing is *prima facie* desirable (= 'is desired by me'); or that there is a reason to ϕ; and so on.

Finally, a dispositional conception enables us to see why, despite the fact that in these many ways desires may involve elements of belief, we may properly say of one who has a desire that he is in a state *with which the world must fit*. Moreover, and for the Humean's particular purposes perhaps more importantly, a dispositional conception of desires enables us to cash the metaphor characterizing beliefs and desires in terms of their direction of fit, and therefore draws support from it. For the difference between beliefs and desires in terms of direction of fit comes down to a difference between the counterfactual dependence of a belief and a desire that *p*, on a perception that *not p*: roughly, a belief that *p* is a state that tends to go of existence in the presence of a perception that *not p*, whereas a desire that *p* is a state that tends to endure, disposing the subject in that state to bring it about that *p*. Thus, we may say, attributions of beliefs and desires require that different *kinds* of counterfactuals are true of the subject to whom they are attributed. We may say that this is what a difference in their directions of fit *is*.

These are important results. For they serve to make a dispositional conception of desire attractive *period*, quite independent of the theory of motivation that one happens to favour. Moreover, they license us to talk unashamedly of desires as states with which the world must fit, for such talk, though metaphorical, captures the feature that distinguishes desires from beliefs; that is, such talk, though metaphorical, aptly describes the kind of dispositional state that a desire is.

The Humean's reasons for believing P_1 – the principle that a motivating reason is constituted by the presence of a desire and a means-end belief – may now be stated rather simply. Given that, as we have seen, all theorists should accept a dispositional conception of desires, and given that this conception licenses us to talk of desires as states with which the world must fit, the Humean's reasons are also, I think, both intuitive and compelling.

7 DESIRES, DIRECTIONS OF FIT, GOALS AND MOTIVATING REASONS

What is it for someone to have a motivating reason? The Humean replies as follows. We understand what it is for someone to have a motivating reason at a time by thinking of him as, *inter alia*, having a goal at that time; the '*alia*' here includes having a conception of the means to attain that goal. That is, having a motivating reason just *is*, *inter alia*, having a goal. But what kind of state is the having of a goal? It is a state with which *direction of fit*? Clearly, the having of a goal is a state *with which the world must fit*, rather than *vice versa*. Thus having a goal is being in a state with the direction of fit of a desire. But since all that there is to being a desire is being a state with the appropriate direction of fit, it follows that having a goal just *is* desiring. In short, then, the Humean believes P_1 because P_1 is entailed by the following three premises:

(1)   Having a motivating reason *is*, *inter alia*, having a goal
(2)   Having a goal *is* being in a state with which the world must fit

and

(3)   Being in a state with which the world must fit *is* desiring.

Simple though it is, this argument is, I think, really quite powerful. After all, which premise in the argument could plausibly be denied? Let's consider them in turn.

Given just the assumption that reason explanations are teleological explanations (see § 4), (1) seems unassailable; indeed it has the status of a conceptual truth. For we understand what it is for someone to have a motivating reason in part precisely by thinking of him as having some goal.[41] (2) is likewise unassailable. For learning that the world is not as the content of your goal specifies is not enough for giving up that goal, but rather puts pressure on you to change the world. The most vulnerable premise is perhaps (3), the claim that being in a state with which the world must fit is desiring. I can imagine two sorts of objection to this premise. But neither objection goes very far.

First, according to Platts, Anscombe claims only that desire is 'a prime exemplar' of those states with which the world must fit. But, he might say, there are other states that have this direction of fit as well: hopes, wishes, and the like. Therefore, given (1) and (2), we should surely say that such states may constitute the having of goals as well. But, *ex hypothesi*, hopes and wishes are not desires.

However, an attack of this kind on the Humean's argument is clearly not an attack on the *spirit* of his argument, it is rather an attack on the *details* of his argument. The Humean may therefore concede the details to the objector. That is, if *desire* is not a suitably broad category of mental state to encompass all of those states with the appropriate direction of fit, then the Humean may simply define the term 'pro-attitude' to mean 'psychological state with which the world must fit', and then claim that motivating reasons are constituted, *inter alia*, by pro-attitudes.[42]

A second objection to (3) tackles the assumption that there are only states with one or the other direction of fit. Thus, it might be asked, why couldn't there be a state with *both* directions of fit; a state which is both such that the world must fit with it, and such that it must fit the world? If such a state were possible then, it might be said, it could constitute the having of a goal. But it would not be a desire, nor even a pro-attitude; for desires and pro-attitudes have only one direction of fit.[43]

However, though it may sound like a coherent possibility that there should be such a state, it really isn't. For, as we have understood the concept of direction of fit, the direction of fit of a state with the content that p is determined, *inter alia*, by its counterfactual dependence on a perception with the content that *not p*. A state with both directions of fit would therefore have to be such that *both*, in the presence of such a perception it tends to go out of existence, *and*, in the presence of such a perception, it tends to endure, disposing the subject that has it to bring it about that p. Taken quite literally, then, the idea that there may be a state with both directions of fit is just plain incoherent.

Of course, a more subtle objector might find fault with this reply. He might say that the reply works only if we take the suggestion that there is a state with both directions of fit quite literally. But, he might well ask, why take it so literally?

Indeed, he might go on the offensive. For he might suggest that our resistance to the suggestion shows the extent to which we are in the grip of what might be called an 'austere' psychological theory; a theory which, as far as the explanation of action goes, both makes use of and makes do with the concepts of belief and desire: states having the one or the other direction of fit, as that has been defined here. The objector may well admit that an austere theory can explain some of the phenomena. But he might insist that we recognize that it cannot explain all of the phenomena; that there are certain goings on that we can explain only if we enrich our psychological theory with the concept of a state that has, in a more relaxed sense, *both* directions of fit. He might cite the example of a moral 'quasi-belief' that x is good ('quasi-belief' because, as we shall see, it is no ordinary belief). For, he might point out, since a subject who has such a quasi-belief tends to go out of this state when presented with a perception that x is not good, this makes it appropriate to describe a moral quasi-belief as being such that it must fit the world. But since a subject's having the moral quasi-belief that x is good disposes him to promote x, this makes it appropriate to describe such a quasi-belief as being, in a more relaxed sense, such that the world must fit with it. Indeed, he might go on to insist that since the factor that determines the kinds of concept our psychological theories can make use of is the evidence that needs to be explained by our theories, so the example just given shows that we positively have reason to enrich our austere psychological theory with the concept of a quasi-belief: a state that is both belief-like and desire-like though identical with neither. For the evidence – our moral practices – can only be explained by the richer theory.

This more subtle objection needs careful handling. I do not know whether the richer theory is really coherent – no surprise, since to my knowledge no-one has actually attempted to formulate such a theory. But I do not think that we need to follow the objection that far down the line in order to find fault with it. For, as I see it, the problem with the objection is that it requires that we *revise* our psychological theories without proper warrant. If I have correctly described the objection, its success depends entirely on the claim that there is evidence that cannot be explained by an austere psychological theory. But the evidence the objector cites can be easily accommodated by the resources of an austere theory; that is, within the accepted framework of beliefs and desires.

In order to see that this is so, consider the following parody of the argument just given: 'There is evidence for the existence of state that is belief-like and desire-like but identical with neither. Consider, for instance, the "quasi-belief" that ϕ-ing is *prima facie* desirable ("quasi-belief" because, as we shall see, it is no ordinary belief). This state is appropriately described as having both directions of fit because, first, a subject tends to go out of this state if he is presented with a perception with the content that ϕ-ing is not *prima facie* desirable, and, second, because a subject's being in such a state disposes him to ϕ.' But this argument is hopeless. For, within the confines of our austere psychological theory, we may say that there are beliefs that a subject can have only if he has certain desires. Thus, we may say, a subject's quasi-belief that ϕ-ing is *prima facie* desirable is best thought of as being such a state. It is a genuine belief because it is a state that must fit the world; that is (since 'is *prima facie* desirable' = 'is desired by me') because its truth requires that ϕ-ing has the property of being desired by him. But it is also a belief the condition for having which is that a subject desires to ϕ (*modulo* fallibility about one's desires). We can thus explain why one who believes that ϕ-ing is *prima facie* desirable is generally disposed to ϕ by noting that the normal condition for having such a belief is desiring to ϕ, and desiring to ϕ is, *inter alia*, a disposition to ϕ.[44]

We therefore do not need to introduce a state of some further, mysterious, hybrid kind, over and above beliefs and desires, in order to explain why beliefs about the desirability of certain courses of action are, in a certain respect, practical. Nor, if this is right, do I see why we need to introduce a state of some further, mysterious, hybrid kind in order to explain why moral beliefs are, in a certain respect, practical. Rather, we should think of moral properties on the model of the property of being *prima facie* desirable. For we may then think of moral quasi-beliefs as being genuine *beliefs* about the properties that persons, actions, states of affairs, and the like have. But, since they have these properties in virtue of standing in certain relations to the desires that the subject has, they are beliefs that the subject can have only if he has certain *desires*.[45]

8 NAGEL, McDOWELL AND PLATTS AGAIN

If some version of the argument given in the last section is correct then we should be able to diagnose the flaws in the as yet unconsidered objections of Nagel, McDowell and Platts to the Humean theory; and, indeed, we should be able to diagnose the flaws in the theories of motivation with which they would replace the Humean theory. I want to close with some necessarily brief remarks aimed at showing that this is indeed the case.

(i)   Early on in *The Possibility of Altruism* Tom Nagel puts forward an objection to the Humean theory that seems aimed not so much at *refuting* the theory, as at *deflating* it, thereby opening up room for his own non-Humean view:

> The assumption that a motivating desire underlies every intentional action depends, I believe, on a confusion between two sorts of desires, motivated and unmotivated ... The claim that a desire underlies every act is true only if desires are taken to include motivated and unmotivated desires, and it is true only in the sense that *whatever* may be the motivation for someone's intentional pursuit of a goal, it becomes in virtue of his pursuit *ipso facto* appropriate to ascribe to him a desire for that goal. But if the desire is a motivated one, the explanation of it will be the same as the explanation of his pursuit, and it is by no means obvious that a desire must enter into this further explanation. Although it will no doubt be generally admitted that some desires are motivated, the issue is whether another desire always lies behind the motivated one, or whether sometimes the motivation of the initial desire involves no reference to another, unmotivated desire.[46]

But there is confusion here only if the idea of a desire motivated by a state that is not a desire is itself plausible. Is it plausible? The Humean thinks not. He argues as follows.

A motivated desire is a desire had for a reason; that is, a desire the having of which furthers some goal that the agent has. The agent's having this goal *is*, in turn, *inter alia*, the state that constitutes the motivating reason that he has for having the desire (from (1)). But if the state that motivates the desire is itself a reason, and the having of this reason is itself constituted by his having a goal, then, given that the having of a goal is a state with which the world must fit rather than *vice versa* (from (2)), so it follows (from (3)) that the state that motivates the desire must itself be a desire. Thus, the Humean will say, the idea that there may be a state that motivates a desire, but which is not itself a desire, is simply implausible.[47]

The same point can be made in another way, by considering how, according to Nagel's own preferred theory of motivation, a state that is not a desire may yet motivate a desire. Suppose a subject now accepts the judgement 'At t I have (tenselessly: i.e. have or will have) reason to speak Italian'. This judgement may properly be thought of as the expression of a *belief* that the subject presently has. In Nagel's view, this belief may motivate a subject to promote his speaking Italian at t quite independently of the relation he believes *t* stands in to *now*.[48] Here, then, we have an example of a belief that, according to Nagel's theory, may suffice to explain a subject's action. And since whenever there is something sufficient to explain motivation there is enough to warrant the ascription of a desire, so, *a fortiori*, according to Nagel, that belief may also explain his having a desire; the desire to promote his speaking Italian at t. But, as is perhaps already evident, the Humean has a principled objection to Nagel's theory of motivation. For consider Nagel's theory in the light of (1) – the claim that having a motivating reason *is*, *inter alia*, having a goal. Does the subject who now believes that he has at t (tenselessly) reason to speak Italian necessarily now have a goal that he speaks Italian at t? Evidently not. The subject may indeed now believe that at t he has (tenselessly) a goal that he speaks Italian. But this belief cannot constitute his having a goal *now* that at t he speaks Italian, for it is a state with the wrong direction of fit (from (2)). Nor does the truth of this belief require that he has as a goal *now* that he speaks Italian at t. Rather, its truth requires that *at t* he has a goal that he speaks Italian.

The Humean will therefore say this about Nagel's theory of motivation, and hence about the theory according to which it is possible for a desire to be motivated by a state that is not itself a desire. Either this theory requires a conception of motivating reasons that is inconsistent with (1) – a claim we should have thought to be a conceptual truth about the connection between having a motivating reason and having a goal – or it requires a conception of belief that permits tenseless beliefs to be such that the world must fit with them, that is, a conception inconsistent with (3) – a claim we should have thought to be a conceptual truth about the nature of desire.

This is a pleasant result. For it is on the basis of the distinction between motivated and unmotivated desires, and the alleged possibility that a desire may be motivated though not by another desire that Nagel, and McDowell following him, think that they can concede P_2 to the Humean – the claim that motivation requires the *presence* of a desire and means-end belief – without thereby accepting P_1 – the claim that motivating reasons are *constituted* by desires and means-end beliefs. But, if the argument given here has been correct, it emerges that P_2 is not a principle that we have any reason to believe in its own right. Rather, properly understood, our only reason for believing P_2 is that it is entailed by P_1.

(ii)   As I said earlier, Mark Platts in fact considers, and rejects, a defence of the Humean theory based on a conception of desires as states with which the world must fit (see § 5). But why does he reject it? Platts rightly points out that we should demand of the Humean an 'argument for the claim that any full specification of a reason for action must make reference to a mental state of the second, non-cognitive kind *vis-à-vis* direction of fit with the world'.[49] But he fails even to put a response to this demand in the Humean's mouth. Rather, he asks rhetorically, 'Why should it not just be a brute fact about moral facts that, without any such further element entering, their clear perception does provide sufficient grounding for action?'[50] But the answer to this can now be seen to be relatively simple.

Given that reason explanations are teleological, a subject's clear perception of some moral fact could provide sufficient grounding for action only if (from (1)) it constituted his having some goal. But that would require in turn (from (2)) that the perception be a state with which the world must fit. However, a perception is not a state with which the world must fit. Thus we have reason to reject Platts's suggestion. This is not, of course, to deny that the 'clear perception' of some moral fact may be something that a subject can have only if he has certain desires. This is parallel to the way in which the clear perception of the desirability of some state of affairs is something that a subject can have, in normal circumstances, only if he has certain desires. But then, though a subject who has such a clear perception may be disposed to act in certain ways, the state that grounds this disposition will be a desire, not a clear moral perception. I am therefore unimpressed by Platts's own reasons for rejecting a defence of the Humean theory based on direction of fit considerations.

(iii)   In short, this is my objection to John McDowell's view that the virtuous agent may be motivated by his conception of a situation in which he perceives some moral requirement – something that McDowell claims is properly thought of as a cognitive state.[51] McDowell simply overlooks the possibility that, though the virtuous agent's conceptions are cognitive states, and though his having those conceptions suffices for his being in a state that motivates him, none the less the state that motivates him is a desire. This possibility is opened up once we realize that the Humean may admit that there are cognitive states that a subject can be in only if he is in some non-cognitive state.

(Nor need this be interpreted as the simple-minded idea that for each virtue an agent has, he has a corresponding desire, and that the condition for his having the conceptions associated with having that virtue is his having that desire.[52] Rather, we may think that having a virtue requires being disposed to have different sorts of desires in different sorts of situations. Taking this view allows us to hold that, though having certain desires is the condition for having the conceptions that a particular virtue makes possible, there is no straightforward mapping of desires onto virtues.)

9 CONCLUSION

It is, I hope, beginning to look as though the Humean theory is more plausible than many people have thought. The argument I have given for the theory has been really quite simple. However, it seems to have been overlooked by non-Humean theorists of motivation. Some have done so because they fail to distinguish motivating reasons from normative reasons. Others have done so because they hold a weak phenomenological, and hence inadequate, conception of desire. Most have done so because they have overlooked the implications of the fact that having a motivating reason is, *inter alia*, having a goal. However, once we keep it firmly before our minds that the Humean's is a theory of motivating reasons and equip ourselves with an adequate conception of desire, we see that only the Humean's claim that motivating reasons are constituted, *inter alia*, by desires is able to make proper sense of reason explanations as teleological explanations. For only an agent's desires may constitute his having certain goals. So, at any rate, I have argued.[53]

NOTES

1 See Nagel, *The Possibility of Altruism*, Princeton, NJ, Princeton University Press, 1970, Part 2; McDowell, 'Are Moral Requirements Hypothetical Imperatives?', in *Proceedings of the Aristotelian Society Supplementary Volume*, 1978, 'Virtue and Reason', in *The Monist*, 1979, and 'Non-cognitivism and Rule Following', in *Wittgenstein: To Follow a Rule*, London, Routledge & Kegan Paul, 1981, edited by Holtzman and Leich [Chapter 23, this volume]; Platts, *Ways of Meaning*, London, Routledge & Kegan Paul, 1979, Chapter 10, and 'Moral Reality and the End of Desire', in *Reference, Truth and Reality*, London, Routledge & Kegan Paul, 1980, edited by Mark Platts. I shall hereafter refer to the Humean Theory of Motivation as the 'Humean theory'.

2 Compare Davidson's 'Actions, Reasons and Causes', in his *Essays on Actions and Events*, Oxford, Clarendon Press, 1980, p. 5.

3 *The Possibility of Altruism*, p. 29; 'Are Moral Requirements Hypothetical Imperatives?', p. 15.

4 *Ways of Meaning*, p. 256.

5 The example comes from Williams, 'Internal and External Reasons', in his *Moral Luck*, Cambridge University Press, 1981, p. 102.

6 I borrow these terms from *The Possibility of Altruism*, p. 4 and p. 18. In his 'Reasons for

Action and Desire', in *Proceedings of the Aristotelian Society Supplementary Volume*, 1972, Michael Woods makes room for a somewhat similar distinction when he notes that 'the concept of a reason for an action stands at the point of intersection, so to speak, between the theory of the explanation of actions and the theory of their justification' (p. 189).

7 It will emerge in § 4 that, in the sense in which we need to think of motivating reasons as being explanatory, we need only think of them as being teleologically explanatory; we do not need to think of them as being causally explanatory.

8 Compare Christopher Peacocke's objections to instrumentalism in Chapter 8 of his *Sense and Content*, Oxford, Clarendon Press, 1983.

9 'Actions, Reasons and Causes', p. 4.

10 Here I assume that the mere existence of the materials with which to construct a partial justification for acting in a certain way from the agent's point of view – that is, the mere existence of a motivating reason to act in that way – does not suffice for the existence of a normative reason to act in that way. If that assumption is wrong, then there will be at least one kind of normative reason for which these claims are false. That will not affect the argument that follows. For the argument requires only that there are some kinds of normative reasons for which these claims are true.

11 In suggesting that the requirement is 'in the broad sense' a requirement of rationality I am following Williams, in 'Internal and External Reasons', pp. 102–3 and Parfit, in *Reasons and Persons*, Oxford, Clarendon Press, 1984, especially note 2a to Part I and pp. 117–20. For both Williams and Parfit think that a theory of rationality would tell us what an agent has reason to do, and both think that what an agent has reason to do from the perspective of rationality will depend on what an agent desires together with the *truth*. It will thus not depend on what he believes given that he may have false beliefs. (What I am calling a 'normative reason of rationality' seems to be what Williams calls an 'internal reason'.)

12 *The Possibility of Altruism*, p. 39.

13 *The Possibility of Altruism*, pp. 39–40.

14 Ibid., pp. 40–1.

15 Compare *Reasons and Persons*, pp. 131–6.

16 This seems to be Nagel's real objection to the Humean on pp. 64–5 of *The Possibility of Altruism*.

17 'Noncognitivism and Rule Following', p. 154 [p. 463, this volume].

18 Ibid., p. 155 [p. 463, this volume].

19 Though, in fairness to McDowell, see my comments on Hume's own view in § 6, and footnote 38 below.

20 This is a summary of the argument in 'Actions, Reasons and Causes', pp. 8–11, the *locus classicus* of arguments for a causal conception of reason explanations.

21 See *Treatise of Human Nature*, Oxford, Clarendon Press, 1958, p. 190.

22 *Treatise*, p. 414.

23 See Barry Stroud, *Hume*, London, Routledge & Kegan Paul, 1977, p. 163.

24 *Treatise*, p. 415.

25 I suspect that there will be some who think that this is all too obvious. They will think that the strong phenomenological conception is a strawman and thus not worth considering. However, I disagree. I think that it is worth working through our objections to strong phenomenological conceptions in order better to understand our objections to phenomenological conceptions quite generally. Those who disagree may prefer to skip the next six paragraphs.

26 Indeed, it seems to me that there are more mundane counterexamples to the principle left to right. Consider cases in which you go to the refrigerator convinced that there is something in particular that you want, though you aren't quite sure what it is. Then, while looking at the contents you suddenly, as we should put it, 'realise what it was that you wanted all along'. If we wish to respect this common sense description of such occurrences then we should reject the principle left to right.

27 Compare 'Moral Reality and the End of Desire', pp. 74–7.

28 *Hume*, p. 163.

29 *Ways of Meaning*, p. 256.

30 I say 'seems', for Platts does in fact consider an alternative characterization of desires. I discuss the alternative characterization in § 6. I discuss Platts's assessment of the support that the alternative characterization gives to the Humean theory in § 8 (ii).

31 I say McDowell rejects a phenomenological conception. He nowhere says that he rejects such a conception. But given that he thinks that 'consequentially ascribed desires are indeed desires' ('Are Moral Requirements Hypothetical Imperatives?', p. 25), he must. For the point of consequentially ascribed desires is that there may be no phenomenological ground for their ascription. The idea of 'consequentially ascribed desires' derives from the work of Tom Nagel. For a discussion of the idea that some desires are merely consequentially ascribed see § 8 (i).

32 'Are Moral Requirements Hypothetical Imperatives?', p. 22.

33 I briefly discuss McDowell's view further in § 8 (iii).

34 *Ways of Meaning*, pp. 256–7.

35 Ibid., p. 257.

36 *Treatise*, p. 457.

37 *Hume*, p. 165.

38 Perhaps this link between Hume's own conception of desire and a causal conception of reason explanations explains why McDowell thinks that the Humean theory finds support from a causal conception (see § 4).

39 Here I am grateful to Frank Jackson.

40 Thus, I contend that a subject's false belief that he desires to φ is not a state that is potentially explanatory of his behaviour. Everyday experience supports this contention. Reflect on occasions when you stand at the edge of a cold swimming pool thinking that you desire to jump in. On some such occasions your body is totally unresponsive to the desires that you profess to have. As you stand there motionless you sometimes come to the conclusion that, contrary to what you thought, you didn't really want to go swimming after all. Thus, just as we would expect if this contention were true, there are cases in which a subject believes that he desires to φ right up until the time that he is supposed to act only to discover that he in fact has no such desire when his body fails to respond to his desire. Of course, we can construct cases in which it might *appear* that an agent's false beliefs about what he wants motivate him. The example of John the musician may perhaps be such a case. But I should claim that in such cases, as in John's, we will find that the appearance is misleading, and that there is in fact some other desire that does the motivating.

41 See § 8 (i) for a discussion of (1) in relation to Nagel's views.

42 Compare Davidson on the difference between desires and pro-attitudes in 'Actions, Reasons and Causes', p. 4.

43 David McNaughton put this objection to me.

44 Does the 'normal' provide a problem here? I think not. The argument succeeds just in case it shows that there is a necessary connection of a certain kind between having the belief that φ-ing is *prima facie* desirable and being disposed to φ, a connection of much the same kind as that which exists between the belief that φ-ing is good and the disposition to φ. The 'normal' merely allows that it is a remote possibility that beliefs about desirability and desire come apart; a possibility that must be admitted because we must admit that subjects have only fallible access to their desires. But in order for this to provide a problem the objector would have to insist that there is no remote possibility that a subject who believes that φ-ing is good, be not disposed to φ. Yet what could the evidence for this claim be? Indeed, as far as evidence one way or the other is concerned, the evidence seems to point in just the opposite direction: see, for instance, Michael Stocker, 'Desiring the Bad' in *The Journal of Philosophy*, 1979, in which he reminds us that, in certain fits of depression, or self-deception, or in certain conditions of physical tiredness, one may believe that a certain course of action is good and yet be totally indifferent to it. I would myself resist the externalist conclusions that some would have us draw by consideration of such examples; that is, I resist the idea that the connection between moral judgement and motivation is wholly contingent, requiring some wholly added on desire to be moral. By all means, I say, let's give the internalist in ethics his due. But his due does not require any more than that we admit that there is a necessary connection of sorts between making a moral judgement and being disposed to act; his due requires only that we admit that, under certain conditions, moral judgement entails a disposition to act. But that we have admitted.

45 I have defended this view in my 'Should We Believe in Emotivism?', in *Fact, Science and Morality: Essays on A. J. Ayer's Language, Truth and Logic*, ed. Crispin Wright and Graham Macdonald, Blackwell, Oxford, 1986. See also my comments on McDowell in § 8 (iii).

46 *The Possibility of Altruism*, p. 29.

47 The objection here is that the idea that there is such a state is implausible. If we had some argument to the effect that the very concept of a state having 'both directions of fit' (see § 7) is incoherent, then we would be able to make a correspondingly stronger objection to Nagel's argument.

48 *The Possibility of Altruism*, pp. 68–9.

49 *Ways of Meaning*, p. 258.

50 Ibid.

51 'Are Moral Requirements Hypothetical Imperatives?', p. 18; 'Virtue and Reason', pp. 335–6, 345–7.

52 'Non-cognitivism and Rule Following', pp. 144–5 [pp. 455–6, this volume].

53 I am grateful to the following people for comments on an earlier version of this paper: Simon Blackburn, Jonathan Dancy, Gilbert Harman, Frank Jackson, Mark Johnston, Lloyd Humberstone, David McNaughton, Michaelis Michael, Nathan Tawil, and Jay Wallace.

32

HUMEANS, ANTI-HUMEANS, AND MOTIVATION

Philip Pettit

In 'The Humean Theory of Motivation' Michael Smith (Chapter 31, this volume) attempts two tasks: he offers an account of the debate about motivation between Humeans and anti-Humeans and he provides arguments that are designed to show that the Humeans win.[1] While the paper is of great virtue in clarifying the debate, I believe that it falls short of both its goals. It does not highlight the really central issue between Humeans and anti-Humeans and it does not provide arguments which would settle that issue in favour of the Humean side.

Smith makes three points in setting up the debate between Humeans and anti-Humeans.

1   The primary issue has to do with whether the constituent elements of a motivating reason always include a desire.

2   A motivating reason to φ is one such that in virtue of having a reason of that kind an agent is not only justified to some extent in φ-ing: he 'is in a state that is potentially explanatory of his φ-ing' (p. 38 [p. 577, this volume]). A motivating reason contrasts with a merely normative reason to φ: that is, a reason the having of which may justify φ-ing but can hardly serve, because of the agent's acknowledged lack of awareness or sensitivity, to explain it.

3   Desires, like beliefs, are dispositions to enact or undergo certain changes in appropriate circumstances. Thus the desire that p certainly involves the disposition to bring it about that p and may or may not involve the disposition to have certain feelings (p. 53 [pp. 590–1, this volume]). The desire that p differs from the belief that p by being generally insensitive to the perception that not-p: 'a belief that p is a state that tends to go [out] of existence in the presence of a perception that not p, whereas a desire that p is a state that tends to endure, disposing the subject in that state to bring it about that p' (p. 54 [p. 591, this volume]).

I believe that these points define a more or less unambiguous debate. The only extra qualification that needs to be entered is probably this. The fact that a desire is held to go into the constitution of a motivating reason does not mean that the existence of the desire is one of the considerations which the agent explicitly takes into account. It may only mean that he would not take account of certain of those considerations unless he was moved by corresponding desires.[2] Unless this point is made, it will seem immediately obvious that desires are unnecessary for motivation.

Once the debate is defined in this way then I agree with Michael Smith that a very simple argument establishes the necessity of desires. The argument, with some paraphrase and schematic illustration, is that having a motivating reason to ϕ is having a goal: say, the goal that p; that having such a goal is being disposed to bring it about that p, where that disposition is naturally capable of surviving the perception that not p; and that being so disposed is desiring that p (p. 55 [p. 592, this volume]).

But although I think that victory in this debate goes the Humean way, I do not believe that the debate focuses on the core issue between the two sides. What divides Humeans and anti-Humeans, by all accounts, is a difference of view about the potency of reason in motivating behaviour. The issue between them is not whether motivating reasons always involve desires but whether they always involve the presence of non-cognitive states, states which reason on its own is incapable of producing. If the thesis about desires is relevant to that issue, that is only because it is assumed that desires are non-cognitive states of this kind.

This cannot be assumed, however, since there are two extant ways of denying it. The first, a minority preference, is to hold that desires or, more precisely degrees of desire, are an agent's estimates of objective goodness or utility.[3] This line is not generally favoured, because it runs against the common assumption that it is only beliefs which are capable of having cognitive status. That assumption probably comes of the thought that if propositional attitudes are cognitive, that must mean that they are discursive: that they lend themselves to the argumentative resolution of differences. Beliefs are more obviously amenable to discursive process than desires and so it is natural to think that only beliefs can have cognitive status.[4]

I intend to go along with this assumption and so I come to the second way in which desires may be vested with cognitive status. Suppose that some of the desires which figure in motivating reasons are such that their presence is entailed by the presence of certain beliefs.[5] In particular, suppose that an agent's desire that p is entailed in this way by a belief – a desiderative belief, we might call it – that it is good or appropriate or useful that p. We must regard the desire in that case as inheriting the cognitive or discursive status of the desiderative belief. The desire that p may be insensitive to the perception that not p but it will be sensitive to the perception that it is not good or not appropriate or not useful that p. It will be a state, or so it appears, which reason alone is capable of producing in the agent.

In order for the Humean to establish his point of view he needs to be able to resist at least the possibility that desires can inherit cognitive status in this way. Smith implicitly recognizes the fact when he poses an objection which maintains precisely that desires enjoy such an inheritance (pp. 56–8, 60–1 [pp. 593–5, 596–8, this volume]). But what he says in response to the objection does not display an appreciation of the depth of the challenge which the Humean faces.[6]

Smith argues that the Humean need not be concerned about the objection, because he is in a position to accommodate any evidence which may be produced in support of it. His idea is that for any example of a desiderative belief that the anti-Humean mentions – say, the belief that it is prima facie desirable that p – the Humean can construe it as a belief on the agent's part about his own desires: say, as the belief that he desires that p, 'since "is *prima facie* desirable" = "is desired by me"' (p. 57 [p. 594, this volume]). He goes on: 'We can thus explain why one who believes that ϕ-ing is *prima facie* desirable is generally disposed to ϕ by noting that the normal condition for having such a belief is desiring to ϕ, and desiring to is, *inter alia*, a disposition to ϕ' (p. 57 [p. 594, this volume]). Although the line is illustrated with a desiderative belief involving prima facie desirability, he thinks that it can be extended to cover even desiderative beliefs of a moral kind (p. 58 [p. 595, this volume]).

But it is not enough for Smith to show that this accommodation is possible. What he has to demonstrate is, not that it is an available account, but that it is the best account on offer: in particular, that it is a better account of desiderative beliefs than that which the anti-Humean provides.

Smith may think he has ground for ignoring this demonstrative task. He casts the Humean theory as 'an "austere" psychological theory' and he may think that its austerity makes it preferable to any anti-Humean story, just so long as it can account, however awkwardly, for the data cited by the anti-Humean (pp. 56–7 [pp. 593–4, this volume]). This thought ought not to move him, however, for he acknowledges elsewhere that the enterprise about which Humean and anti-Humean quarrel is one of 'formulating a philosophical conception of folk psychological states' (p. 48 [p. 586, this volume]); it is not one of constructing a psycho-logical theory from scratch but of analysing the theory with which we all already operate.

The debate between Humeans and anti-Humeans remains open. Smith has made a considerable advance in enabling us to focus the issue between them but he has not established that the issue ought to be resolved in the Humeans' favour. In conclusion, I would like to identify three ways in which a Humean might reasonably seek to press his case. They turn around three claims which would individually undermine the possibility of desiderative beliefs to which the anti-Humean clings.

The first claim that the Humean might try to defend is a psychological one: the proposition that there are no such states as desiderative beliefs.[7] The argument, familiar from subjective theories of decision, will be that the only evidence for the existence of desiderative beliefs is the occurrence of desiderative assertions and that the occurrence of such assertions is better explained as the expression of desires.

The second claim that the Humean might seek to support is a metaphysical one: the thesis that even if there are belief-like states of a desiderative kind, there are no desiderative facts, and therefore no desiderative perceptions, for them to be sensitive to. That will mean that contrary to appearances the desiderative beliefs, and the desires associated with them, will not be cognitive or discursive.

Finally, the Humean might try to defend a common analytical thesis to the effect that whatever of the psychological and metaphysical matters involved, the only sort of belief which could get close to entailing the presence of desires is a belief which bears on the existence of precisely those appetitive states. The accommodation of desiderative beliefs for which Smith looks would be supported on the grounds of being the only satisfactory account available.

We may look forward, I believe, to a continuing debate between Humeans and anti-Humeans. There will be plenty of material for the two sides to contest, for there is no shortage of arguments for and against the three propositions mentioned. Let battle be rejoined.

NOTES

1 *Mind*, 1987, pp. 36–61 [Chapter 31, this volume].
2 See my 'Universalizability without Utilitarianism', *Mind*, 1987, on the difference between reason-supposed and reason-supplying considerations. In particular, see n. 9, p. 79.
3 See D. H. Mellor 'Objective Decision-Making', *Social Theory and Practice*, 1983.
4 This assumption is not so natural if beliefs are thought of as subjective probabilities and that is probably why Mellor rejects it.
5 In such a case it would seem to be natural to say that the desires are constituted by the beliefs, that the beliefs are themselves desires. Smith would seem to have reason for going along with this, for he says at one point that desires are states that 'ground' the dispositions by which they are distinguished (p. 52 [p. 590, this volume]). But elsewhere he takes a different line, requiring that desires are insensitive to all perceptions: as he puts it, 'desires and pro-attitudes have only one direction of fit' (p. 56 [p. 593, this volume]).
6 Sometimes it seems that Smith fails to see how significant the possibility of inheritance is. He suggests that the possibility is not contrary to the Humean spirit when he considers the claim that clear moral perception, or the perception of the virtuous agent, may be sufficient to provide a motivating reason (pp. 60–1 [pp. 597–8, this volume]). He quotes the fact that an agent has such a perception 'only if he has certain desires' and he says that this observation is enough to establish the Humean point of view: 'though a subject who has such a clear perception will be disposed to act in certain ways, the state that grounds this disposition will be a desire' (p. 60 [p. 597, this volume]). In making these remarks, however, he may only be meaning to recall the response described in the text.
7 It will be sufficient for the Humean to defend this only if he makes the assumption, which we noted earlier, that desires are not directly cognitive states.

33

ON HUMEANS, ANTI-HUMEANS, AND MOTIVATION: A REPLY TO PETTIT

Michael Smith

1

In 'The Humean Theory of Motivation' (Chapter 31, this volume) I argued for the thesis that R at t is a motivating reason of an agent A to ϕ if and only if there is some ψ such that R at t consists of a desire of A to ψ and a belief that were he to ϕ he would ψ.[1] I called this 'P$_1$'. I claimed, further, that P$_1$ is definitive of the Humean theory of motivation.

The argument I gave for P$_1$ was relatively simple (this volume, pp. 588–95). It is a commonplace that when an agent has a motivating reason to ϕ his reason is partially constituted by a state that embodies his having ϕ-ing a goal. But how does this map on to talk of beliefs and desires? Well, what belief and desire are may uncontroversially be characterized using the metaphor of directions of fit.[2] Beliefs are states that aim to fit the world, whereas desires are states that aim to have the world fit them. This metaphor can be rendered non-metaphorical in terms of a functional analysis. Thus, very roughly, the belief that p is a state that tends to go out of existence in the presence of a perception that not-p, whereas the desire that p is a state that tends to endure in the presence of a perception that not-p, disposing the subject to bring it about that p. Now having ϕ-ing as a goal is also a state that aims to have the world fit it. It too must therefore be a disposition to realize ϕ-ing. But in that case we can say that, since the desire to ϕ is a disposition to realize ϕ-ing, and since we have no good reason to think that any other state is such a disposition (in particular, since we have good reason to believe that no belief is a disposition to ϕ), so only desires (and certainly no belief) can constitute an agent's having ϕ-ing as a goal. Thus P$_1$. Call this the 'direction of fit' argument.

In 'Humeans, Anti-Humeans, and Motivation' Philip Pettit (Chapter 32, this volume) makes two claims against me.[3] He insists that, first, I do not 'highlight the really central issue between Humeans and anti-Humeans', and that, second, I do not 'provide arguments which would settle that issue in the Humean's favour' (this volume, p. 602). I will consider these claims in turn.

2

In Chapter 31 of this volume I say that the issue dividing Humeans from non-Humeans is P_1. Pettit says he disagrees. His reason for disagreeing is that, in his view, the non-Humeans can accept P_1, the claim that motivating reasons are constituted, *inter alia*, by desires, for what they disagree with is rather the Humean's claim that the desires that constitute motivating reasons are themselves non-cognitive states, 'states which reason on its own is incapable of producing' (this volume, p. 603). In Pettit's view P_1 is relevant to that issue 'only because it is assumed that desires are non-cognitive states of this kind' (this volume, p. 603). But this cannot be assumed (he continues) as there is at least one plausible way of denying it.[4]

> Suppose that some of the desires which figure in motivating reasons are such that their presence is entailed by the presence of certain beliefs. In particular, suppose that an agent's desire that p is entailed in this way by a belief – a desiderative belief, we might call it – that it is good or appropriate or useful that p … It will be a state, or so it appears, which reason alone is capable of producing. In order for the Humean to establish his point of view he needs to be able to resist at least the possibility that desires can inherit cognitive status in this way.
>
> (pp. 603–4, this volume)

In Pettit's view we therefore need to distinguish between two kinds of desire in order to state clearly the Humean's view: desires whose presence is entailed by the presence of beliefs (call these 'desires = beliefs') and desires whose presence is not entailed by the presence of beliefs (call these 'desires ≠ beliefs').[5] The Humean's view is then that R at t is a motivating reason of agent A to ϕ, if and only if there is some ψ such that R at t consists of a desire ≠ belief of A to ψ and a belief that were he to ϕ he would ψ. Call this 'P-Pettit'. In Pettit's view, non-Humeans deny P-Pettit, not P_1. Indeed the most plausible form of non-Humean theory denies P-Pettit by arguing for the existence of desires = beliefs, and hence by accepting P_1.

Does this suffice to show that I do not highlight the really central issue between Humeans and non-Humeans? I do not think so. Pettit's way of characterizing that issue differs from my own only if P_1 and P-Pettit are different principles. But they are not. P_1 and P-Pettit are the same principle.

P_1 and P-Pettit are the same principle just in case 'desire' in P_1 means the same as 'desire ≠ belief' in P-Pettit. Of course, I did not use the word 'desire ≠ belief' in P_1. But I would have thought that in Chapter 31 I said enough about the relationship between beliefs and desires to indicate that, in the terminology of Chapter 31, what Pettit calls a 'desire = belief' would not deserve the name 'desire' or 'belief', but ought rather to be called a 'quasi-belief', and hence that what Pettit calls a 'desire ≠ belief' would rather be called a 'desire' pure and simple. Here is what I said:

> The [non-Humean] might insist that we recognize that [belief-desire psychology] cannot explain all the phenomena; that there are certain goings on that we can explain only if we enrich our psychological theory with the concept of a state that has, in a more relaxed sense, both directions of fit. He might cite the example of a moral 'quasi-belief' that x is good ('quasi-belief' because, as we shall see, it is no ordinary belief). For, he might point out, since a subject who has such a quasi-belief tends to go out of this state when presented with a perception that x is not good, this makes it appropriate to describe a moral quasi-belief as being such that it must fit the world. But since a subject's having the moral quasi-belief that x is good disposes him to promote x, this makes it appropriate to describe such a quasi-belief as being, in a more relaxed sense, such that the world must fit with it. Indeed, he might go on to insist that since the factor that determines the kinds of concept our psychological theories can make use of is the evidence that needs to be explained by our theories, so the example just given shows that we positively have reason to enrich our austere [belief-desire] psychological theories with the concept of a quasi-belief: *a state that is both belief-like and desire-like though identical with neither.* For the evidence – our moral practices – can only be explained by the richer theory.
>
> (pp. 593–4, this volume, emphasis added)

The crucial feature of a quasi-belief is thus that it has, in the loose sense I define, both directions of fit. That is, it has the functional properties of a belief with respect to one content ('x is good') and a desire with respect to another ('I promote x'). I resisted calling this state both a 'belief' and a 'desire' because, as I said in Chapter 31, I supposed an objector might insist that desires (and beliefs) have only one direction of fit (p. 593). Indeed, I said that that was an assumption of the original argument (p. 593). But, of course, if we relax this assumption, then what in the jargon of Chapter 31 is a quasi-belief will be a desire = belief, and then what in the jargon of Chapter 31 is a desire, will be a desire ≠ belief. But then, since P_1 is written within the set of assumptions about how to use the terms 'belief', 'desire', and 'quasi-belief' I proposed in Chapter 31, it turns out that P_1 is P-Pettit.

Pettit and I therefore agree about the issue dividing Humean from non-Humean theorists of motivation. Pettit chooses to describe final resistance to the Humean's view in terms of a commitment to the existence of desires = beliefs, I choose to describe such resistance in terms of a commitment to the existence of quasi-beliefs. But this does not signal a disagreement about what the issue *is*, it merely signals a disagreement about how to use the terms 'desire' and 'belief' in *describing* that issue.

3

Though Pettit and I agree about what the issue is that divides Humean from non-Humean theorists of motivation, I think that confusion would result if we were to take too literally his initial quite general formulation of that issue (I am not saying that Pettit is himself confused about this). He tells us that, 'by all accounts', what divides Humeans from non-Humeans is 'a difference of view about the potency of reason in motivating behaviour', and that they therefore disagree about whether motivating reasons 'always involve the presence of non-cognitive states, states which reason on its own is incapable of producing' (this volume, p. 603). But what exactly does it mean to say that reason can (or cannot) produce a motive? Does it mean the same as saying that having certain beliefs entails (or does not entail) having certain desires?

The claim that reason can produce a motive is generally made in the course of describing the disagreement between Hume and Kant over whether reason 'is, and ought only to be the slave of the passions'.[6] In context, this is a disagreement about whether the norms of morality reduce to the norms of reason. The rationalists (following Kant) insist that they do, and the anti-rationalists (following Hume) insist that they do not. The disagreement thus very quickly becomes a disagreement about the precise content of the norms of reason. Rationalists and anti-rationalists can of course agree about quite a lot. They can agree that there are norms of theoretical reason telling us that, for example, if a subject believes both that p and that $p \rightarrow q$, then he prima facie ought to believe that q. But rationalists think, in addition, that there are norms of practical reason, in particular, that there are norms telling us that if an agent has certain beliefs – for example, the belief that someone is in pain and that he (the believer) can relieve his pain by ϕ-ing – then he (the believer) prima facie ought to have certain motives – for example, the motive to ϕ.[7] The rationalist's view is then that, just as in the theoretical case fully rational creatures will believe that q when they believe that p and that $p \rightarrow q$, for the beliefs that p and that $p \rightarrow q$ will produce the belief that q in such creatures (something with which anti-rationalists will presumably agree), so in the practical case fully rational creatures will be motivated to ϕ when they believe that someone is in pain and that they can relieve his pain by ϕ-ing, for the relevant beliefs will produce this motive. For his part, the anti-rationalist denies that there are such principles of practical reason.

It should now be clear that this issue is quite different from the issue that Pettit and I agree divides Humean from non-Humean theorists of motivation. After all, do the rationalists think that the presence of the relevant beliefs entails the presence of these motives? No. They think that the relevant beliefs only entail the presence of these motives in fully rational creatures. Creatures who are less than fully rational may well have the beliefs without the motives, much as (the suggestion goes) creatures who are less than fully rational may fail to believe that q when they believe that p and that $p \rightarrow q$.[8]

Moreover, and more importantly, it should also be evident that even if reason does produce a motive in this sense, that will be neither here nor there as regards the debate in the theory of motivation. For to say that beliefs may produce motivating reasons in this sense is not to tell us about the nature of motives, it is rather to tell us about their rational genesis. True, if the rationalists win this debate then certain motives are, in a sense of that term, cognitive states: they will be fit subjects of a certain kind of rational criticism. But, in another perfectly good sense of that term, their cognitive status will be left indeterminate. For you could think that the rationalists win this debate and yet still be baffled about what motives are, or consist in. That is, the question 'Are motives desires or beliefs or states of some other kind?' might still remain open, a real question. And answering this question seems the proper task of a theory of motivation. Indeed, it was precisely because I wanted to keep these different sorts of issue separate that I insisted, in Chapter 31, that 'the tasks of constructing a theory of motivating reasons and a theory of the normative reasons of rationality are just different tasks' (this volume, p. 581). So though I think that Humean and non-Humean theorists of rationality disagree about whether reason can produce a motive in this sense, and thus whether motives are in this sense cognitive, I think that we would be wrong to suppose that this is the issue that divides Humean from non-Humean theorists of motivation.[9]

4

Let me now return to Pettit's second criticism of Chapter 31. The criticism is that we do not find there 'arguments that would settle [the] issue in favour of the Humean side' (this volume, p. 602). But why does Pettit find the argument I gave so unconvincing?

Pettit and I agree that the direction of fit argument provides a compelling argument against the view that motivating reasons might be constituted by a belief whose presence does not entail the presence of a desire, what in Chapter 31 I called a 'belief'. What we disagree about is whether the direction of fit argument provides an argument against the view that motivating reasons might be constituted by desires = beliefs, what in Chapter 31 I called a 'quasi-belief' (from now on I will omit the translations and simply adopt Pettit's terminology).[10] As I understand it, this turns on whether the non-Humean can provide us with good reason to believe that there are any desires = beliefs.

And, as the extended quotation from Chapter 31 above indicates, it seems to me that his best shot at convincing us that there are desires = beliefs is to focus on examples of what appear to be practical beliefs. He should therefore focus our attention on moral practice. For in moral practice it may certainly appear that having a belief about what is of value entails being motivated to promote what we believe to be of value. But does moral practice provide the kind of evidence we would need to believe that there are desires = beliefs? In Chapter 31 the suggestion is that it does not. For, I argued, if we think of values as (roughly) properties that elicit certain desires in us under certain conditions, then we can explain both why agents do have beliefs about what is of value, and why agents tend to desire to promote what they believe to be valuable, without supposing that their having beliefs about what is of value entails their having desires to promote what they believe valuable; that is, without postulating the existence of desires = beliefs.[11] This is what Pettit finds unconvincing:

> But it is not enough for Smith to show that this accommodation is possible. What he has to show is not that it is an available account, but that it is the best account on offer: in particular, that it is a better account of desiderative beliefs than that which the anti-Humean provides. Smith may think that he has ground for ignoring this demonstrative task. He casts the Humean theory as 'an "austere" psychological theory' and he may think that its austerity makes it preferable to any anti-Humean story, just so long as it can account, however awkwardly, for the data cited by the anti-Humean (this volume, pp. 593–4). This thought ought not to move him however, for he acknowledges ... that the enterprise about which Humean and anti-Humean quarrel is one of 'formulating a philosophical conception of folk psychological states' (this volume, p. 586); it is not one of constructing a psycho-logical theory from scratch but of analysing the theory with which we all already operate. The debate between the Humeans and anti-Humeans remains open.
>
> (p. 604, this volume)

I take Pettit's point. But it seems to me that he ignores an important part of what I said in Chapter 31. To be sure, this strategy will be successful only if moral practice seems better explained by a theory that thus weakens the connection between evaluative beliefs and motivation – a tendency is not the necessary connection postulated by the non-Humean. No mere 'awkward' accommodation of the data will do. But in Chapter 31 I do in fact cite some examples of Michael Stocker's that count against the stronger connection but not the weaker (this volume, p. 601, n. 44). For, as I point out, Stocker reminds us that in certain fits of depression, or self-deception, or in certain conditions of physical tiredness, we sometimes believe that a certain course of action is good and yet seem totally indifferent to it; not motivated at all to do what we believe good.[12] Such examples are an embarrassment to the non-Humean who thinks that the evidence provided by moral practice supports the view that there are desires = beliefs. But they are no embarrassment to the Humean who follows the strategy I offer him. For he will think that such examples merely help to give content to the 'certain conditions' in which alone values that we recognize in fact elicit desires in us. If this argument is successful – and Pettit says nothing to make us think that it is not – then, far from the issue between the Humean and the non-Humean remaining open, in Chapter 31 that issue was adjudicated in the Humean's favour.

5

Unimpressed by my own efforts, Pettit closes Chapter 32 by outlining three ways in which the Humean might try to argue for his view. He tells us that these 'turn around three claims which would individually undermine the possibility of desiderative beliefs to which the anti-Humean clings' (this volume, p. 604). Pettit does not himself comment on the relative merits of these three argumentative strategies. But it seems to me fairly plain that only two are really worth considering, and that only one shows any sensi-tivity to the strength of the non-Humean's case. Let's consider them in turn.

> The first claim that the Humean might try to defend is a psychological one: the proposition that there are no such states as desiderative beliefs. The argument, familiar from subjective theories of decision, will be that the only evidence for the existence of desiderative beliefs is the occurrence of desiderative assertions and that the occurrence of such assertions is better explained as the expression of desires.
>
> (p. 604, this volume)

But this is unconvincing. It is as if the Humean has to be blind to part of the evidence provided by moral practice; as if all he can see in need of explanation is why we make moral assertions. For many urge that an important part of what needs explaining about moral practice is its distinctive phenomenology.[13] The experience of moral value, they say (supposedly platitudinously), presents itself to us as the experience of a property possessed by the thing that is of value, not as the experience of your own inner state – a desire or whatever – and the best explanation of this is that moral experience is the experience of moral value. Of course, the evidence is merely prima facie. But it does suggest that there is no knock-down argument against the existence of desiderative beliefs; that there is no alternative to considering head-on what it would be for there to be desiderative facts.

> The second claim that the Humean might seek to support is a metaphysical one: the thesis that even if there are belief-like states of a desiderative kind, there are no

desiderative facts, and therefore no desiderative perceptions for them to be sensitive to. That will mean that contrary to appearances the desiderative beliefs, and the desires associated with them, will not be cognitive or discursive.

(p. 605, this volume)

But this seems to me plainly wrong. After all, in the spirit of certain recent discussions along these lines, it might be said that if there are no desiderative facts then that means just that all of our desiderative beliefs are false.[14] That would certainly undermine the claim that we have any veridical experience of desiderative facts. But it does not seem to undermine the claim that we have such experience and such beliefs now, prior to the discovery of the metaphysical truth, at all. Indeed, it seems to presuppose that. Thus, for all that the Humean who defends this claim tells us, motivating reasons may actually be constituted by desires = beliefs now, though these are none of them true. This brings us to Pettit's final suggestion.

Finally, the Humean might try to defend a common analytical thesis to the effect that whatever of the psychological and metaphysical matters involved, the only sort of belief which could get close to entailing the presence of desires is a belief which bears on the existence of precisely those appetitive states. The accommodation of desiderative beliefs for which Smith looks would be supported on the grounds of being the only satisfactory account available.

(p. 605, this volume)

And so I have been trying to argue.[15]

NOTES

1 See my 'The Humean Theory of Motivation', Chapter 31, this volume, pp. 575–601.

2 See G. E. M. Anscombe's *Intention*, Oxford, Blackwell, 1957, section 2.

3 See his 'Humeans, Anti-Humeans, and Motivation', Chapter 32, this volume, pp. 602–05.

4 Pettit actually mentions two, but he only thinks that one is plausible. I omit discussion of the conception of desire that Pettit thinks is implausible, though it seems to me that what I go on to say in the text is relevant by way of a response there as well.

5 If having certain beliefs entails having certain desires then, as Pettit puts it, 'it would seem natural to say that the desires are constituted by the beliefs, that the beliefs are themselves desires' (Chapter 32, this volume, p. 605, n. 5). This is why I refer to them as 'desires = beliefs'.

6 See David Hume's *Treatise of Human Nature*, ed. Selby-Bigge, Oxford, Clarendon Press, 1958, p. 415.

7 As the example indicates, I am taking Tom Nagel as my candidate rationalist (see his *The Possibility of Altruism*, Princeton, NJ, Princeton University Press, 1970).

8 Tom Nagel is quite explicit about this in *The Possibility of Altruism*, pp. 63–7, as is Christine Korsgaard in her 'Skepticism About Practical Reason', *Journal of Philosophy*, 1986, pp. 13–15.

9 I further discuss the issue dividing rationalists from anti-rationalists in my 'Reason and Desire', *Proceedings of the Aristotelian Society*, 1987–8.

10 Pettit's terminology may indeed be preferable. For, as Pettit has pointed out to me, the choice of the term 'quasi-belief' to describe the states in question may carry the undesired implication that these states have a content that is not really truth-assessable. That is certainly not what I had in mind, as the quotation from Chapter 31 above indicates. Perhaps James Altham's term 'besire' would be even better (see his 'The Legacy of Emotivism', in *Fact, Science and Morality: Essays on A. J. Ayer's Language, Truth and Logic*, ed. Graham Macdonald and Crispin Wright, Oxford, Blackwell, 1986).

11 Actually, in Chapter 31 the argument is more guarded still. For, as I said there, I am not sure that the concept of a desire = belief is really coherent (this volume, pp. 593–4). I argued rather that, even if the concept of a desire = belief is coherent, the non-Humean offers us no good reason to believe that there are any desires = beliefs. Note, however, that David Lewis and John Collins have made the somewhat stronger logical objection that the non-Humean's claim that there are desires = beliefs collides with decision theory (see Lewis's 'Desire as Belief' and Collins's 'Belief, Desire and Revision', both in *Mind*, 1988).

12 See Michael Stocker's 'Desiring the Bad: An Essay in Moral Psychology', *Journal of Philosophy*, 1979.

13 This seems to be a common theme running through the writings of David Wiggins and John McDowell (see, for example, Wiggins's 'Truth, Invention and the Meaning of Life' and 'A Sensible Subjectivism?', both in his *Needs, Values, Truth*, Oxford, Blackwell, 1987, and McDowell's 'Values and Secondary Qualities', in *Morality and Objectivity*, ed. Ted Honderich, London, Routledge & Kegan Paul, 1985 [Chapter 12, this volume]). But, perhaps more importantly in the present connection, many of those who reject the conception of value Wiggins and McDowell argue for actually accept the point about phenomenology (see, for example, John Mackie's *Ethics: Inventing Right and Wrong*, Harmondsworth, Penguin, 1977, Ch. 1, and Colin McGinn's *The Subjective View*, Oxford, Clarendon Press, 1983, pp. 145–58). I discuss the phenomenological issues further in my 'Objectivity and Moral Realism: On the Significance of the Phenomenology of Moral Experience', in *Realism and Reason*, ed. Crispin Wright and John Haldane, Oxford, Oxford University Press.

14 I have in mind John Mackie's discussion in Ch. 1 of his *Ethics: Inventing Right and Wrong*.

15 I have had the benefit of useful comments from and conversations with Simon Blackburn, James Dreier, Gideon Rosen, Jay Wallace, and, especially, Philip Pettit. The final version of this paper was written while I was a Visiting Fellow at the Department of Philosophy, Research School of Social Sciences, Australian National University.

GLOSSARY

As we have said elsewhere, there is a lot of terminology in metaethics, and some of the common terms are used in a variety of ways. We hope this provides you with a helpful guide, however.

Amoralist An agent who is psychologically normal but who is unmotivated by her moral judgements. The externalist about motivation thinks amoralists are common. The internalist about motivation typically thinks that the amoralist is a *conceptual* impossibility.

Cognitivism/noncognitivism Cognitivists think that one can cognize, that is represent, (supposed) moral properties, and that such properties can be known about. Noncognitivists deny this.

Cornell Realism The view that moral properties exist and are irreducible (*sui generis*), but are natural properties.

Correspondence theory of truth The view that there is a property of truth that some suitably structured utterances have and that such things get to be true because they correspond with the world.

Deflationary theories of truth The view that the concept of truth is of only technical use and can be dispensed with in most cases. This is sometimes referred to as 'minimalism about truth', although some commentators offer finer-grained definitions that distinguish between these two labels.

Error theory Error theorists are cognitivists but not realists. They agree that we are trying to represent moral properties, but just think there is nothing in the world that fits this representation. The idea then is that moral judgements are systematically and uniformly false.

Ethical scepticism The denial that there are any such ethical properties and, in addition, that the whole idea of things having value in any sense is nonsense. (Note: strictly some people use 'ethical scepticism' to refer to the idea that we cannot know either way whether there are any moral properties.)

Expressivism A form of noncognitivism that holds that moral judgements are expressions of the speaker's noncognitive attitude rather than a description of anything. This is not to be confused with subjectivism. Earlier versions of expressivism were called 'emotivism'.

Externalism about motivation The view that the link between moral judgement and motivation is contingent. An agent is motivated to do what they judge to be right if they have the right desire – normally described as the desire to do what is right. (You won't have met this idea much in this collection, but it is nicely contrasted with 'Externalism about reasons'.)

Externalism about reasons   The view (roughly) that if agent A has moral reason to act, then the grounding for such a reason can be based on things other than the desires, commitments, beliefs and general projects that are important to A.

The Frege–Geach problem   This is thought to be the main problem for noncognitivists since it supposedly shows that noncognitivists cannot accommodate our everyday understanding of logic and reasoning.

Full-information analysis   The view that there is some intimate connection between what is good for us (both morally and nonmorally) and ourselves conceived of as fully informed and rational.

Humean theory of psychology   The view (possibly not Hume's) that motivation only arises when a belief combines with an appropriately related desire – where desire takes the lead role. For this account to be Humean, belief and desire must be modally distinct (that is, one cannot entail the other).

Internalism about motivation   The view that there is a *conceptual and necessary* connection between moral judgement and motivation. (You won't have met this idea much in this collection, but it is nicely contrasted with 'Internalism about reasons'.) Notice that there is no entailment from internalism about motivation to internalism about reasons, nor from internalism about reasons to internalism about motivation.

Internalism about reasons   The view (roughly) that if agent A has moral reason to act, then the grounding for such a reason is based on the desires, commitments, beliefs and general projects that are important to A.

Intuitionism   A view in moral epistemology that holds that there is at least one moral claim, and possibly many, that are self-evidently justifiable. This does not rule out other ways of justifying moral claims, nor does this mean that intuitionists believe judges to be infallible.

Methodological naturalism   The view that philosophy should proceed via a posteriori investigation, using the empirical sciences as a guide. It is a general scepticism about the use of a priori conceptual investigation as a way of doing philosophy.

Minimalism about truth-aptitude   The view that a sentence is truth-apt (up for being true or false) if it figures in an area of discourse where there are appropriate and inappropriate uses for it and if the sentence has certain syntactic features.

Moral irrealism   Used interchangeably with 'anti-realism'. Normally signifies a more general scepticism about the realist/anti-realist debate.

Moral realism and anti-realism   Realists think that moral properties exist, anti-realists do not. 'Realism', particularly, is used in a bewildering variety of ways.

Motivating reason   The reasons that motivate us to act. How these reasons are accounted for depends on your account of motivation. If, for example, you are a Humean then if you desire to do x, and have the appropriate belief, then you have a motivating reason to do x.

Normative reason   Reasons we have to act in certain ways that do not seem obviously linked to psychological states of an agent. You have a reason to stop jumping on my foot, even though you quite enjoy it, or want to, or believe I deserve it, and the like. It is a reason that *ought* to become a motivating reason for us.

Quasi-realism   An account that attempts to incorporate the realist-seeming grammar of our moral language without accepting cognitivism. Normally associated with forms of expressivism.

Reductionism Refers to either *ontological* or *semantic* reduction. Semantic reductionism is the conceptual analysis of evaluative terms in nonevaluative ones. Ontological reductionism is the claim that moral properties are nonmoral, natural properties.

Relativism The view that moral standards depend on the norms of an individual or society or culture (etc.) and that there is no standard independent of these in virtue of which we can judge them.

Scientism The view that science is the only standard in virtue of which a discipline can be gauged as true or worthwhile; the view that science has a monopoly on truth.

Sensibility theory A realist theory. There are moral properties that we can cognize. Moral judgements are representations or descriptions, and moral properties are mind-dependent.

Subjectivism The view that moral language is descriptive and definable in terms that refer to the individual. (For example, 'good' means 'what makes me [the speaker] happy'). This is sometimes used as a synonym for 'relativism', although you should try not to use it in this way. It is certainly not to be confused with expressivism.

Substantive naturalism The view that we can define central moral terms as nonmoral, natural ones. This may or may not be done via conceptual analysis.

Supervenience This comes in a variety of forms, but (roughly) A-properties (or A-features, or whatever) are said to supervene on B-properties (or B-features, or whatever) if and only if: two situations that have exactly the same B-properties have exactly the same A-properties, and (for some commentators) there is some interesting link between the two types of property. (That is, it is not utterly mysterious why A- and B-properties have this relation, nor is it some sort of logical truth that they are connected.) A corollary of this relation is that there is a change in A-properties only if the B-properties change.

Thick concepts Concepts that seem to have both an evaluative and descriptive role. For example, kindness, loyalty and trustworthiness. These contrast with thin concepts, such as goodness and rightness.

INDEX

Related titles from Routledge

What is this thing called knowledge?

Duncan Pritchard

**What is Knowledge? Where does it come from?
Can we know anything at all?**

This lucid and engaging introduction grapples with these central questions in the theory of knowledge, offering a clear, non-partisan view of the main themes of epistemology including recent developments such as virtue epistemology and contextualism.

Duncan Pritchard discusses both traditional issues and contemporary ideas in thirteen easily digestible sections which include:

- the value of knowledge
- the structure of knowledge
- virtues and faculties
- perception
- testimony and memory
- induction
- scepticism.

What is this thing called knowledge? contains many helpful student-friendly features. Each chapter concludes with a useful summary of the main ideas discussed, study questions, annotated further reading, and a guide to web resources. Text-boxes provide bite-sized summaries of key concepts and major philosophers, and clear and interesting examples are used throughout, whilst a helpful glossary explains important terms. This is an ideal first textbook in the theory of knowledge for undergraduates taking a first course in philosophy.

ISBN 10: 0–415–38797–3 (hbk)
ISBN 10: 0–415–38798–1 (pbk)

ISBN 13: 978–0–415–38797–2 (hbk)
ISBN 13: 978–0–415–38798–9 (pbk)

**Available at all good bookshops
For ordering and further information please visit:
www.routledge.com**

Related titles from Routledge

Epistemology
2nd edition

Robert Audi

'No less than one would expect from a first-rate epistemologist who is also a master expositor: lucid, comprehensive, well-structured, and excellently informed both by the tradition and by recent developments. A superb introduction.' Ernest Sosa, *Brown University*

'A state-of-the-art introduction to epistemology by one of the leading figures in the field.' William Alston, *Syracuse University*

'Impressively up-to-date.' Dr T.J. Diffey, *University of Sussex*

'An excellent book. It is comprehensive in scope and very systematically organised. Its most impressive quality is the balance it achieves between argumentative complexity and simplicity of exposition.' *Philosophical Books*

'A good introduction to how we know what we know.' *New Scientist*

Epistemology, or the theory of knowledge, is concerned with how we know what we do, what justifies us in believing what we do, and what standards of evidence we should use in seeking truths about the world and human experience. This comprehensive book introduces the concepts and theories central for understanding knowledge. It aims to reach students who have already done an introductory philosophy course.

This revised edition builds on the topics covered by the hugely successful and widely read first edition. It includes new material on subjects such as virtue epistemology, feminist epistemology and social epistemology. The chapter on moral, scientific and religious knowledge has also been expanded and revised. Robert Audi's style is exceptionally clear and highly accessible for anyone coming to the subject for the first time.

ISBN10: 0–415–28108–3 (hbk)
ISBN10: 0–415–28109–1 (pbk)

Available at all good bookshops
For ordering and further information please visit:
www.routledge.com